"Although entitled a handbook, this volume is far more than simply a reference book. Consisting of original essays by distinguished scholars, it offers creative approaches to understanding the relationship between institutional norms and pragmatic action, showing through theoretical insights and significant examples how planning can be both effective and legitimate."
Susan S. Fainstein, Senior Research Fellow, Harvard Graduate School of Design, USA

"The defining feature of planning scholarship has been its unwavering interest in theorizing action. By centering decision-making within institutions, the authors in this brilliant edited volume chart pathways to reconcile structure with agency in the study of planning practice. Of interest to both planning theorists and those conducting comparative research, the chapters explain both the persistent variations as well as the profound consistencies in urban form across places."
Rachel N. Weber, Professor and Director of Graduate Studies, Urban Planning and Policy Department, University of Illinois at Chicago, USA

"Written by leading planning theory and related scholars, this book is an astute exploration of institutional action and innovation. Its pragmatically orientated chapters draw on both theory and empirical evidence to deliver insightful understandings across the wide range of planning and public policy orientated institutions that shape our contemporary world."
Michael Gunder, School of Architecture and Planning, University of Auckland, New Zealand

THE ROUTLEDGE HANDBOOK OF INSTITUTIONS AND PLANNING IN ACTION

The Routledge Handbook of Institutions and Planning in Action contains a selection of 25 chapters prepared by specialized international scholars of urban planning and urban studies focusing on the question of how institutional innovation occurs in practices of action. The contributors share expertise on institutional innovation and philosophical pragmatism. They discuss the different facets of these two conceptual frameworks and explore the alternative combinations through which they can be approached. The relevance of these conceptual lines of thought will be exemplified in exploring the contemporary practices of sustainable (climate-proof) urban transition. The aim of the handbook is to give a boost to the turn of institutional analysis in the context of action in changing cities.

Both philosophical pragmatism and institutional innovation rest on wide international uses in social sciences and planning studies, and may be considered as complementary for many reasons. However, the combination of these different approaches is all but evident and creates a number of dilemmas. After an encompassing introductory section entitled Institutions in Action, the handbook is further divided into the following sections:

- Institutional Innovation
- Pragmatism: The Dimension of Action
- On Justification
- Cultural and Political Institutions in Action
- Institutions and Urban Transition

Willem Salet is professor emeritus of urban and regional planning at the Faculty of Social and Behavioural Sciences, University of Amsterdam, the Netherlands. He chaired the group Urban Planning until 2017. He was the scientific director of the Amsterdam Study Centre for the Metropolitan Environment (AME) 2008–2013. He was the president of the Association of European Schools of Planning (AESOP) 2008–2010 and was awarded an honorary membership of AESOP in 2016.

THE ROUTLEDGE HANDBOOK OF INSTITUTIONS AND PLANNING IN ACTION

Edited by Willem Salet

NEW YORK AND LONDON

First published 2018
by Routledge
711 Third Avenue, New York, NY 10017

and by Routledge
2 Park Square, Milton Park, Abingdon, Oxon, OX14 4RN

Routledge is an imprint of the Taylor & Francis Group, an informa business

© 2018 Taylor & Francis

The right of Willem Salet to be identified as the author of the editorial material, and of the authors for their individual chapters, has been asserted in accordance with sections 77 and 78 of the Copyright, Designs and Patents Act 1988.

All rights reserved. No part of this book may be reprinted or reproduced or utilised in any form or by any electronic, mechanical, or other means, now known or hereafter invented, including photocopying and recording, or in any information storage or retrieval system, without permission in writing from the publishers.

Trademark notice: Product or corporate names may be trademarks or registered trademarks, and are used only for identification and explanation without intent to infringe.

Library of Congress Cataloging-in-Publication Data
Names: Salet, W. G. M., editor.
Title: The Routledge handbook of institutions and planning in action / edited by Willem Salet.
Description: New York, NY : Routledge, 2018.
Identifiers: LCCN 2017050147 | ISBN 9781138085732 (hardback)
Subjects: LCSH: Urban policy. | Social planning. | City planning. | New institutionalism (Social sciences)
Classification: LCC HT153 .R735 2018 | DDC 307.1/216–dc23
LC record available at https://lccn.loc.gov/2017050147

ISBN: 978-1-138-08573-2 (hbk)
ISBN: 978-1-315-11123-0 (ebk)

Typeset in Bembo
by Out of House Publishing

Printed and bound by CPI Group (UK) Ltd, Croydon, CR0 4YY

*To my children
Ceciel, Ernst and Tijmen*

CONTENTS

List of Figures / Tables	xiii
Contributors	xv
Preface	xxi
Willem Salet (Ed.)	
Foreword	xxii
Richard Bolan	

PART 1
Institutions in Action   1

1   Institutions in Action   3
    Willem Salet

2   Developing a 'Sociological Institutionalist' Approach to Analysing
    Institutional Change in Place Governance   24
    Patsy Healey

3   Political Articulation and Hegemonic Practices in the Institutionalization
    of the Urban Order   43
    Enrico Gualini

PART 2
Institutional Innovation   59

4   Discursive Institutionalism and Planning Ideas   61
    Simin Davoudi

5 Institutions in Urban Space: Land, Infrastructure, and Governance in the Production of Urban Property   74
   André Sorensen

6 Moving Towards a Flat Ontology of Institutional Innovation: Actor-Relational Lessons Learned from Early Water Management Perspectives   92
   Luuk Boelens

7 Planning and the Politics of Hope: A Critical Inquiry   108
   Jonathan Metzger

PART 3
Pragmatism: The Dimension of Action   123

8 Adapting Different Planning Theories for Practical Judgement   125
   Charles Hoch

9 From Garbage in the Streets to Organizers' Opportunities: Navigating the Institutional Pragmatics of Democratic Inter-Subjectivity   139
   John Forester

10 What Can We Learn from Evolutionary Theory When Confronting the Deep Challenges of Our Times?   151
    Luca Bertolini

11 Learning and Governance Culture in Planning Practice: The Case of Otaniemi   165
    Raine Mäntysalo, Kaisa Schmidt-Thomé & Simo Syrman

PART 4
On Justification   183

12 Constitutions, Laws and Practices: Ethics of Planning and Ethics of Planners   185
    Stefano Moroni

13 How to Contextualize Legal Norms in Practices of Sustainable Development? Distinguishing Principles, Rules and Procedural Norms   196
    Anoeska Buijze, Willem Salet & Marleen van Rijswick

14 Interpreting Planning as Actions 'in Plural': From Democratic Claim to Diverse Institutional Change   212
    Monika De Frantz

15 Provenance, Ideology and the Public Interest in Planning   228
    Leonie Janssen-Jansen & Greg Lloyd

PART 5
Cultural and Political Institutions in Action   243

16 Contextualizing Institutional Meaning through Aesthetic
    Relations: A Pragmatist Understanding of Local Action   245
    Julie-Anne Boudreau

17 'London's Vatican': The Role of the City's New Architectural Icons
    as Institutional Imaginaries   257
    Maria Kaika

18 The Political Nature of Symbols: Explaining Institutional Inertia
    and Change   274
    Federico Savini & Sebastian Dembski

19 The Urban Commons and Cultural Industries: An Exploration of the
    Institutional Embeddedness of Architectural Design in the Netherlands   289
    Robert C. Kloosterman

PART 6
Institutions and Urban Transition   301

20 Pragmatism and Institutional Actions in Planning the Metropolitan
    Area of Milan   303
    Alessandro Balducci

21 Paradoxes of the Intervention Policy in Favelas in São Paulo: How
    the Practice Turned Out the Policy   315
    Suzana Pasternak & Camila D'Ottaviano

22 Ambiguity as an Opportunity: Coping With Change in Urban
    Megaprojects   331
    Stan Majoor

23 Instituting Resilience in the Making of the Istanbul Metropolis   347
    Ayda Eraydin & Tuna Taşan-Kok

24 Urban Transformation in the Northern Randstad: How Institutions
    Structure Planning Practice   364
    Jochem de Vries & Wil Zonneveld

Reflection 379

25　Weaving the Threads of Institutions and Planning in Action 381
　　Mickey Lauria

Index 390

LIST OF FIGURES/TABLES

Figures

Photograph Cover: Ueno (Tokyo). Author: Robert C. Kloosterman

1.1	Co-evolution of pragmatic and institutional approaches	13
2.1	Transformation initiatives in governance dynamics	34
5.1	The urban property triangle: Relationships between categories of urban institutions	85
6.1	Ontological scheme	96
6.2	Overview of water management in West-Flanders from the tenth until the thirteenth century AD	98
6.3	Map of the Brugse Vrije	102
10.1	Dynamics of biological evolution (left) and translation to the social domain (right)	156
10.2	Dynamics of stability and change in the social domain	157
11.1	Argyris and Schön's cybernetic model of single-loop and double-loop learning	167
11.2	The student union representative presenting the locations of student housing and private housing in the Otakaari area in their alternative scheme, in the second Otaniemi OK meeting	170
16.1	Élisabeth's online post, mapCollab project, October 2014	249
16.2	Contextualizing institutional meaning through aesthetic	255
17.1	St Paul's Heights views protection	267
18.1	Visual representation of the relation between political coalitions (circle), social and electoral communities (square) and the complex system of norms (dashed circle)	280
22.1	Zuidas's emerging urban programme around het Gustav Mahlerlaan	335
22.2	Ørestad's post-crisis housing row development complementing its pre-crisis apartment blocks	337

22.3 Dockland's Victoria Harbour development and underused
Harbour Esplanade   339
23.1 Instituting resilience within the urban planning system   351
24.1 Conceptual framework of how environmental norms as institutions
structure communicative planning practices   370

Tables

2.1 Analysing initiatives in governance change   33
2.2 Analysing transformative change with a relational 'sociological
institutionalist' approach   35
8.1 Differences between Hopkins and Beauregard   130
21.1 Households and population residing in favelas, per capital city, 2010   318
22.1 Summary of tactics to adapt Zuidas, Ørestad and Docklands in the
face of turbulence   341

CONTRIBUTORS

Alessandro Balducci has an MS in architecture and a PhD in urban and regional planning. He is full professor of planning and urban policies at Politecnico di Milano, Italy. He has been deputy mayor for urban planning in the city of Milan, vice rector of Politecnico di Milano, director of the PhD program in spatial planning and urban development, president of AESOP, founding member of the European Urban Research Association (EURA), and chair of the Italian Society of Urbanists (SIU). His most recent publication, *Situated Practices of Strategic Planning: An International Perspective*, co-edited with Louis Albrechts and Jean Hillier, was published by Routledge in 2017.

Luca Bertolini is professor of urban and regional planning at the University of Amsterdam, the Netherlands. His research and teaching focus on the integration of transport and land-use planning, on methods for supporting the option-generation phase of the planning process, on concepts for coping with uncertainty in planning, and on ways of enhancing theory–practice interaction. Main publication topics include planning for sustainable accessibility in urban regions, conceptualizing urbanism in the network society and the application of evolutionary theories to planning.

Luuk Boelens is full professor of spatial planning at Ghent University, Belgium. He is director of the Centre of Mobility and Spatial Planning (AMRP), chairs the Flemish think tank on climate adaptation, the MORO-trust and the BECP of ESPON and URBACT, and is vice chair of the Research Centre for Sustainable Mobility.

Richard Bolan has a 60-year career in urban planning. Graduating from Yale, MIT and New York University, USA, he was a practitioner for ten years before joining the faculty at Boston College, USA. Since 1985 he has been a faculty member in the Humphrey School of Public Affairs at the University of Minnesota, USA. His focus has been teaching and research in planning theory. His most recent work, *Urban Planning's Philosophical Entanglements: The Rugged, Dialectical Path from Knowledge to Action*, was published by Routledge in 2017.

Julie-Anne Boudreau is Doctor of Urban Planning from the School of Public Policy and Social Research of the University of California at Los Angeles, USA. She is Researcher at the

Instituto de Geografia of the Universidad Nacional Autonoma de Mexico and at the Institut National de la Recherche Scientifique. Her most recent book is entitled *Global Urban Politics: Informalization of the State* (2017).

Anoeska Buijze is an assistant professor of administrative law at Utrecht University, the Netherlands. Buijze's research focuses on the interplay between law and various fields of science. Her current research at the Utrecht Centre for Water, Oceans and Sustainability Law (UCWOSL) focuses on the barriers in administrative law to making effective use of the knowledge produced by climate models.

Camila D'Ottaviano is an architect and urban planner. She holds an undergraduate degree (1994), a master's degree in urban environmental structures (2002) and a PhD in architecture and urbanism (2008) from the Faculty of Architecture and Urbanism at the University of São Paulo (FAUUSP), Brazil. She has practical experience in architecture and urban planning, with an emphasis on the areas of housing, urban design, city history, habitat and demographics. She is a faculty member of the Architecture and Urbanism's Methodology Group at the University of São Paulo.

Simin Davoudi, FRTPI, FAcSS, FRSA, is director of the Global Urban Research Unit (GURU) at Newcastle University, UK. She is past president of the Association of European Schools of Planning (AESOP). Her latest books include *The Resilience Machine* (Routledge, in press), *Justice and Fairness in the City* (2016) and *Reconsidering Localism* (Routledge, 2015).

Monika De Frantz is author of *Capital City Cultures* on culture-led urban transformation in Vienna and Berlin (P.I.E.-Peter Lang, 2014) and of *Urban Politics*, a theoretical monograph on institutions and agency in globalisation (forthcoming). She has a PhD in political and social sciences from the European University Institute, Florence, Italy. She has held academic positions at the University of Chicago, USA, the University of New Orleans, USA, London School of Economics, UK, Bauhaus University Weimar, Germany, the University of Vienna, Austria, the University of Innsbruck, Austria, and the European University Institute, Florence, Italy.

Sebastian Dembski is a lecturer in planning in the Department of Geography and Planning at the University of Liverpool, UK. His research focuses on the transformation of city regions from an institutional perspective, including the relationship between symbolic markers and patterns of social norms as well as administrative and legal conditions.

Ayda Eraydin is a professor in the Department of Urban and Regional Planning at Middle East Technical University, Turkey. She has been coordinating the Regional Planning programme since 2005. Her research interests and publications focus on local economic development, the socio-spatial dynamics of cities and regions and planning theory and practice. She has been involved in several international projects supported by COST, URBAN-NET and the Seventh Framework Programme (FP7).

John Forester is professor of city and regional planning at Cornell University, USA. He received his BS (1970) and MS (1971) in mechanical engineering and his MCP (1974) and PhD (1977) in city and regional planning from the University of California, Berkeley, USA. Forester's research on the micro-politics of planning has explored issues of power and conflict, negotiation and mediation and practices of organizing, deliberation and improvisation. Forester's best known books are *Planning in the Face of Power* (1989), *The Deliberative Practitioner* (1999), and *Dealing with Differences: Dramas of Mediating Public Disputes* (2009). His recent publications include *Planning in the Face of Conflict* (2013), *Conflict, Improvisation, Governance* (with David Laws, Routledge, 2015), and *Rebuilding Community after Katrina* (with Ken Reardon, 2016). A senior editor of the research journal *Planning Theory and Practice*, his *Changing Cities, Reimagining Cities* (with Daniela DeLeo, 2017) is forthcoming.

Enrico Gualini is professor of planning theory and urban-regional policy analysis at the Berlin University of Technology, Germany. His research interest is in the social construction of spatiality and the political dimension of socio-spatial practices, with a focus on their contested nature and on resulting challenges for urban democratic politics.

Patsy Healey is professor emeritus at the Global Urban Research Unit, in the School of Architecture, Planning & Landscape, at Newcastle University, UK. She is a specialist in planning theory and practice. In 2004, she was recognized as an honorary member by the Association of European Schools of Planning (AESOP). In 2009, she was awarded an ordinary fellowship from the British Academy for distinction in urban planning theory and practice. In October 2006, she received the Royal Town Planning Institute's (RTPI) Gold Medal Award for outstanding achievement in the field of town and country planning.

Charles Hoch has taught at the University of Illinois at Chicago, USA, in the Department of Urban Planning & Policy since 1981. He studies how people and organizations make urban plans and the kind of work plans do. Hoch teaches planning theory, spatial planning and a variety of workshop/studio classes.

Leonie Janssen-Jansen regrettably passed away on April 11, 2018. She was professor of land-use planning at Wageningen University and Research Centre, the Netherlands. From 2010–2012, she was president of the International Academic Association on Planning, Law and Property Rights (PLPR), an academic association to promote interdisciplinary and cross-national exchange between academics in planning, law and real estate studies. Her recent research focused on metropolitan solutions, land management, property development, urban transformation, smart growth, regional governance and planning and planning and law.

Maria Kaika is professor of urban, regional and environmental planning at the University of Amsterdam, the Netherlands. She holds an MA in architecture and planning (from NTU, Athens, Greece) and a PhD from Oxford University, UK. She has taught at the University of Oxford, UK (tenured), Vienna University of Technology, Austria, the University of Leuven, Belgium, and the University of Paris-Est, France. She is author of *City of Flows* (Routledge, 2005) and co-editor (with N. Heynen and E. Swyngedouw) of *In the Nature of Cities* (Routledge, 2006).

Robert C. Kloosterman is professor of economic geography and planning at the University of Amsterdam, the Netherlands. His research focuses on how social, economic and cultural transitions have affected cities and why different outcomes have emerged. He has published on labour market developments in urban areas, migrant entrepreneurship and on cultural industries, especially music and architectural design, and planning issues related to cultural amenities.

Contributors

Mickey Lauria, PhD, is professor of city and regional planning and director of the transdisciplinary PhD program in planning, design and the built environment at Clemson University, USA. He currently serves as a co-editor of the *Town Planning Review*. He has published articles on urban regimes and regulation theory, community-based development organizations, urban redevelopment, patterns and impacts of housing foreclosures, and the politics of planning in planning, geography and urban studies journals. His recent research interests include planning ethics, neighbourhood change and planning issues involving race and class; and conservation easements and affordable housing.

Greg Lloyd is professor emeritus in urban planning at Ulster University, UK, and a visiting professor at Wageningen University, the Netherlands. He is a fellow of the Academy of Social Sciences. He was Ministerial Independent Adviser to the Northern Ireland Assembly Government on its reform of land-use planning; served on the Best Commission into a Sustainable Future for Housing in Northern Ireland; and is a trustee of the Planning Exchange Foundation.

Stan Majoor is professor of the coordination of urban issues at the Amsterdam University of Applied Sciences, the Netherlands, and the coordinating professor of the university's interdisciplinary research programme, Urban Management. His research interests include new approaches to coordinated area development, the crossover between planning theory and organizational studies and policy innovation in urban laboratories in which public, private, civic and knowledge partners cooperate.

Raine Mäntysalo (DSc, architect) is professor of strategic urban planning in the Department of Built Environment at Aalto University, Finland. He is also an adjunct professor at the University of Oulu, Finland. He has recently published articles on strategies, trading zones, democracy and power in spatial and land-use planning. He is currently leading an international research consortium developing integrative approaches to strategic spatial planning in Finnish urban regions.

Jonathan Metzger is an associate professor of urban and regional studies at the KTH Royal Institute of Technology in Stockholm, Sweden. Most of his work concerns decision-making processes relating to complex environmental issues – often with a focus on urban and regional planning, policy and politics.

Stefano Moroni is professor of planning at Milan Polytechnic University, Italy. He works on planning theory and on ethical and legal issues. Recent publications include, *Contractual Communities in the Self-Organizing City* (with G. Brunetta, 2013); *Ethics, Design and Planning of the Built Environment* (with C. Basta, 2014); *Cities and Private Planning: Property Rights, Entrepreneurship and Transaction Costs* (with D. Andersson, 2014); *Space and Pluralism: Can Our Cities Be Places of Toleration?* (with D. Weberman, 2016).

Suzana Pasternak is an architect and urban planner, with an undergraduate degree in public health from the University of São Paulo (1970), Brazil. She specialized in urban planning at the Panthéon-Sorbonne University, France (1968), and earned both a master's degree (1975) and a PhD in public health (1983) from the University of São Paulo. She has retired from her post as full professor at the Faculty of Architecture and Urbanism at the University of São Paulo (FAUUSP). She is currently the local coordinator of São Paulo Metropolis Observatory.

Contributors

Willem Salet is professor emeritus of urban and regional planning at the Department of Geography, Planning and International Development Studies, at the University of Amsterdam, the Netherlands. He graduated in spatial planning and sociology. He was a researcher at the Scientific Council for Government Policy (1980–1995). He chaired the program group Urban Planning from 1998–2016. From 1998–2003, he chaired the Amsterdam Research Institute for the Metropolitan Environment. He was the president of AESOP (2007–2009). In 2016, he was awarded an AESOP Honorary Membership.

Federico Savini is an assistant professor in the Department of Geography, Planning and International Development Studies at the University of Amsterdam, the Netherlands. He specializes in the political and institutional analysis of planning policies and land development. He has conducted extensive research on the legal, financial and electoral dynamics of urban policymaking.

Kaisa Schmidt-Thomé works as senior researcher at Demos Helsinki, an independent Nordic think tank. She has a background in planning geography (Lic.Phil. University of Helsinki) and obtained her PhD in land-use planning and urban studies from Aalto University, Finland, in 2015. Her research interests have covered a wide range of topics from European spatial development, urban-rural interaction and climate change adaptation to everyday urbanity and geographies of life-course. Her current projects deal with urban development strategies and the possible future paths of urbanization.

André Sorensen is professor of urban geography at the University of Toronto, Canada. His current research examines planning, urban property and temporal processes in urbanization and urban governance from an institutionalist perspective. His paper 'Taking Path Dependence Seriously' (2015), published in *Planning Perspectives*, won the Association of European Schools of Planning Best Paper Award in 2016.

Simo Syrman works as a doctoral candidate in the Department of Built Environment at Aalto University, Finland. He has a master's in sociology (MSocSc) and an undergraduate degree in urban geography (BSc), both from the University of Helsinki, Finland. His research interests include accessibility, lifestyle and travel behaviour. His forthcoming doctoral thesis concentrates on mobilities in different travel modes.

Tuna Taşan-Kok is associate professor of urban planning at the University of Amsterdam, the Netherlands. She has initiated, coordinated and been involved in some large-scale international research projects since 1996. Currently, she is co-coordinating the EU (FP7-funded) DIVERCITIES (a research project studying urban diversity, with particular focus on social cohesion, social mobility and economic performance in today's hyper-diversified cities). She is also leading the FAPESP-ESRC-NWO-funded PARCOUR (*Public Accountability to Residents in Contractual Urban Redevelopment*) Project.

Marleen van Rijswick is professor of European and Dutch water law and is director of the Utrecht University Centre for Water, Oceans and Sustainability Law, the Netherlands. She researches how law can contribute to a sustainable and equitable use of water, land and natural resources based on shared responsibilities. She participates in the OECD Water Governance Initiative and is a visiting professor at both the Université Panthéon-Assas in Paris, France, and the University of Malta. She was also a visiting professor at Wuhan University in China in 2015.

Jochem de Vries is an associate professor at the Department of Human Geography, Planning and International Development Studies at the University of Amsterdam, the Netherlands. His teaching and research interests include the institutional and cultural conditions of planning and urban development, cross-border cooperation and negotiations and sustainable urban development, in particular the nexus between water management and spatial planning.

Wil Zonneveld is a full professor of urban and regional planning at the Faculty of Architecture and the Built Environment at Delft University of Technology, the Netherlands. He received his master's degree as well as his PhD in spatial planning from the University of Amsterdam, the Netherlands. His research focuses on strategic planning at the regional and national level, the role of concepts and visions, the interplay between visioning and project decision-making and the Europeanization of territorial governance.

PREFACE

The Routledge Handbook of Institutions and Planning in Action explores the avenues of a new orientation in planning studies that addresses the 'dialectic between institutional and pragmatic approaches in processes of social action'. Institutions are conceived as the patterning of public norms that condition purposive systems. Pragmatism focuses on social aspirations and aims to find solutions to the problems of the public. Institutional approaches look for the patterning sets of normative conditions and serve as conditions to action providing a critical normative feedback mechanism for the actions performed in response to problems. Both are validated in ongoing processes of action. Public norms and public objectives are not the same. They fulfil complementary roles as two sides of the same coin: the one cannot function well without the other. Their underlying rationality and logic, however, are so fundamentally different that a productive co-habitation thus far has proven difficult in theories of public action and planning. Both streams of thought may rest on a wide and long tradition in the social sciences but attempts of a productive co-evolution are still scarce. This handbook explicitly aims to explore relevant strategies that enable a productive dialectic between the two streams of thought.

The handbook is not just a collection of papers. It has been written by a selective group of planning experts from several countries with the joined mission to explore conceptual ways of understanding the confrontation and close connection between institutional and pragmatic orientations in planning studies. The authors were chosen because they share this mission and they were prepared to write new chapters on behalf of this itinerary. The book aims in the first place to upgrade the institutional perspectives in planning studies to a level of maturity, and, secondly, to combine the normative power of institutional knowledge with the experimental action of the philosophy of pragmatism.

Concepts and draft papers have been intensively exchanged at a two-day seminar in Amsterdam, kindly sponsored by the Van Eesteren-Fluck & Van Lohuizen Foundation, the Centre of Urban Studies and the Thematic Group of Urban and Regional Planning at the University of Amsterdam. My thanks go to Anouk van der Horst for her careful preparation of the layout of the handbook.

Willem Salet (editor)
University of Amsterdam
June 2017

FOREWORD

Richard Bolan

We live in a world where language is often confusing. I, for instance, am not entirely sure of the word 'handbook' – the first word in the title of this volume. The Merriam-Webster dictionary offers this: "a book capable of being conveniently carried as a ready reference" – in effect a technical pocketbook. However, an online dictionary (Dictionary.com) goes further: "a scholarly book on a specific subject, often consisting of separate essays or articles", and this volume you are holding is clearly that. Moreover, this handbook deals profoundly with the words 'institution' and 'action', and these two terms also have many meanings in the foundational linguistic philosophy of the English language (Wittgenstein, 1953; Hayakawa, 1941). The two words are explored in detail in this handbook providing a variety of very positive and helpful approaches for those of us in the urban planning profession.

The word 'institution' indeed has perhaps too many meanings. It has bothered me for many years, starting with a visit a long time ago to a Bahamian island where I rented a car and was told to drive on the left hand side of the road. Doing that was psychologically very unsettling and somewhat frightening. Doing that in my home country is a very serious violation of institutional behaviour – drive on the right-hand side of the road or you are in serious trouble!

A most fundamental definition of institution suggests the word applies to established laws, practices or customs. This has been described in detail by David Elder-Vass, of Loughborough University (UK), who argues that the creation of institutions begin with what he terms 'norm circles'. The individual people involved (either immediately or successively) in such circles have the causal power to produce a tendency in individuals subsequently to follow standardized practices (Elder-Vass, 2012, p. 23).

With the invention and widespread use of the automobile, driving on the right-hand side of the road quickly became a custom that evolved into a law for much of the world. John Searle, a social philosopher at the University of California, Berkeley, identifies what he calls "deep-seated structural institutions": money, private property, marriage, government (Searle, 2010, p. 91). When I was very young, I saw these all as definitely constant unchanging laws, customs and practices – that is, until my parents decided to divorce. In today's terms, private property has some deep changes going on – particularly with the rise of condominium and cooperative residences and a seriously declining market in shopping malls. Money is becoming an increasingly digitized custom – pieces of paper and round metal coins are being used less and less. In the United States, the current divorce rate ranges from 41% to 50%, so marriage as a deep-seated structural institution is actually undergoing meaningful change (including the new legality of same-sex marriage).

The term institution also applies to organizations. Drawing again from Searle, we urban planners constantly encounter governmental organizations that are typically defined as institutions. These not only include government legislatures, executive agencies, judiciary organizations but also military organizations and police forces. We also define special-purpose organizations as institutions, such as religious organizations, hospitals, schools, universities, museums, trade unions. Also important for urban planners are economic institutions: corporations, banks, real estate agencies, brokers and venture capital firms. The real sources of persistent racial and class segregation can be found in the customary behaviours underlying one set of economic institutions – the real estate housing market (Bolan, 2000).

The word 'action' is also important in this volume. While there is stress on pragmatic action, the meaning of action has been a source of philosophical investigation for many years from many different points of view. Pragmatists have explored it, analytical philosophers have explored it, and phenomenologists and those in hermeneutics have explored it. In my most recent publication, I have reviewed all of these perspectives from the point of view of the practising planner (Bolan, 2017).

Deciding on a form of action is clearly a complex relationship of mind and body for an individual decision-maker. Nevertheless, planners are typically in situations where many people are collectively deciding what to do. Often these are people having different titles within differing agencies and differing levels of power. Deciding on what to do in the context of an urban plan today generally means reaching agreement on what to do by a very complicated array of decision-makers involving a complex hierarchy of social norms. Pragmatists, following John Dewey, often view action decisions as 'experiments'. Nevertheless, more fundamentally, action decisions are normative. Social and physical science can reasonably portray present circumstances and past history. This provides help in deciding what to do, but deciding what to do involves not what a situation is but rather what it ought to be. Thus deciding what to do simultaneously involves behavioural norms, morality and aesthetics – all within a reality in which forecasting is always problematic. This is complex for us as individuals but it is even more difficult for urban planners as they attempt to gain the assent of multiple decision-makers in complex institutional and power circumstances.

The chapters that comprise this handbook all tackle the variety of complications involved in institutional norms and pragmatic decision-making. In so doing, they begin to constructively formulate a more fundamental understanding of planning theory and practice. They include theoretical and philosophical discussions, and there are also chapters with illustrative case studies – case studies taking place in different nations and consequently in circumstances with differing institutional frameworks and foundational behavioural norms.

This book is important because of many serious challenges facing urban planning at the present time. First and foremost, of course, is the current trend of the world population moving towards increasing urban rather than rural living. This has important implications for future urban spatial demand and potential challenges for urban density (Angel, 2012). An increasing world urban population also poses many challenges in terms of economic development, especially in today's world where international corporatism dominates over local free market enterprise (Lynn, 2010). Finally, the challenge of climate change and global warming distinctly impacts urban areas over the entire world. Consequently, the need for enriched advanced urban planning theories and practices is more important today than it has ever been. This book is a very meaningful and especially important contribution to these challenges.

References

Angel, S. (2012). *Planet of Cities*. Cambridge, MA: Lincoln Institute of Land Policy.
Bolan, R. (2000). Social Interaction and Institutional Design: The Case of Housing in the USA. In W. G. M. Salet & A. Faludi (Eds.), *The Revival of Strategic Spatial Planning* (pp. 25–39). Amsterdam: Royal Dutch Academy of Sciences.
Bolan, R. (2017). *Urban Planning's Philosophical Entanglements: The Rugged, Dialectical Path from Knowledge to Action*. New York: Routledge.
Elder-Vass, D. (2012). *The Reality of Social Construction*. Cambridge, UK: Cambridge University Press.
Hayakawa, S. I. (1941). *Language in Action*. New York: Harcourt Brace & Co.
Lynn, B. C. (2010). *Cornered: The New Monopoly Capitalism and The Economics of Destruction*. Hoboken, NJ: John Wiley & Sons.
Searle, J. R. (2010). *Making the Social World: The Structure of Human Civilization*. Oxford: Oxford University Press.
Wittgenstein, L. (1953). *Philosophical Investigations*. G. E. M. Anscombe (Trans.). Oxford: Blackwell.

PART 1

Institutions in Action

1
INSTITUTIONS IN ACTION

Willem Salet[1]

Relational Analysis of Planning: A Common Denominator

Since Melvin Webber produced the first studies on non-place urban realms (in the early 1960s), the territorial concepts of city and place have been progressively deprived of their static, place-bounded substance matter (Webber, 1964). Numerous trans-scalar relationships of urban activities have been empirically demonstrated in the relational geographies of the last decades (LeGalès, 2002). Nowadays, urban place might be characterized dynamically as the "diversity of the complex co-location of multiple webs of relations that transect and intersect across an urban area, each with their own driving dynamics, history and geography, and each with highly diverse concerns about, and attachments to, the places and connectivities of an urban area" (Healey, 2007, p. 3; see also Healey, 2004). As a consequence, the planning and public guidance of places has to be understood as an active arrangement of focus within frameworks of multi-actor and multi-level governance. Healey wrote: "Places are created by socio-political processes through which places and their qualities are drawn into attention, to become a nodal force among multiple, dynamic, co-existing but not necessarily spatially contiguous webs of relations" (Healey, 2016, referring in particular to Healey, 2010). The new trans-local reality urges urban planning to define itself in this dynamic and multileveled context.

A genuine relational analysis of planning goes deeper than just adapting the focus of study to a more complex reality. Relational analysis requires a radical contextualization of the planning subject. The crux of relational planning analysis is that it does not accept the explicit or implicit assumption of an autonomous planning subject (Salet, 2014, 2016; Savini et al., 2014). If the post-war gulf of planning modernism and its recent failure have demonstrated anything, it is the vulnerability of the alleged planning subject. The problem of planning subjectivism is that it explicitly or implicitly postulates the planner as the 'agent of change' who is moving the 'object of change' into a desired state. Obviously, planning is intentional and it has the function to guide, but the real world does not turn around a planner's lever. The world is not an object, it consists of social subjects and structures with its own conflictive order and conditions for planning (Gualini, 2001). Public guidance or planning may catalyse or constrain ongoing social processes but planners cannot create a social order of their own. The real challenge of public guidance and planning is not to invent a new desired state of the world but to discover and reflect on its normative direction in deep interconnectivity with this complex and contentious social order: both in terms of acquiring legitimacy and effectiveness. This is why relational planning research does not start its analysis by outlining the desires and resources of planning subjects but first examines the actual intercourse of the social subjects, the problems and the normative patterns in society. The crucial premise of relational planning analysis is that the role of public guidance and planning originates in this social intercourse and that its legitimacy and its ultimate effectiveness are to be analysed through the complex fabric of social interaction in society. The use of this analytical framework facilitates the exploration of a wide array of issues concerning public guidance and planning, ranging from civic public initiatives to interventions by the state. It does not exclude hierarchical forms of planning or legislation but it rests in all empirical cases, the hierarchical included, on the analysis of processes of legitimation and effectuation reasoned from the social intercourse instead of an autonomous planning authority.

Investigating planning from a relational perspective is not new, but it is in need of a renaissance, especially following the epoch of expansive modernist planning which has taken place since the 1960s. This study has two fundamental orientations: institutional thought and philosophical pragmatism, both of which adhere to the premises of relational analysis.

In institutional studies, it is almost self-evident that institutional patterns of social norms depend on underlying processes of social interaction. The analysis of institutional norms cannot be framed in a 'subject–object' scheme because these norms are produced and reproduced in interaction between subjects (Moroni, 2010b; Salet, 2002). Without recognition and acceptance in the relevant constituting social intercourses, institutional norms would simply not come into existence nor continue to be sustained. Having said this, however, that does not mean that all subjects are equal or that all social norms are fair and just. Processes of social normalization reflect the dominant social characteristics of societies, including inequalities and asymmetries of power (Bolan, 2000). For instance, the institution of private property in Western societies is not known for its fairness or social equality. However, this institution has been 'normalized' through time and it is widely recognized and accepted, not just by those in power but – even more important for the underpinning of the premise of inter-subjectivity – also by social subjects. Without the latter, this particular norm would not have survived as an instituted norm. Citizens do not necessarily agree with social norms (consensus is not a premise) but they should at least recognize and accept these norms as being appropriate (March & Olsen, 1989). Processes of normalization, socialization and internalization may take generations and are continuously refined by passing through different situations and social conditions. A fascinating example of this is the mainstreaming of language during the nation-building processes of national states. Bourdieu analysed the processes of power behind the institutionalization of a particular dialect as the official and general language of France (Bourdieu, 1991). Another example is Thompson's deep analysis of the "making of the English working class" (Thompson, 1963). Or, see Habermas's examination of the institutionalization of the rule of law tracing back to the 'Declaration of the Rights of Man' by Thomas Paine in 1791 (Habermas, 1996). The setting of institutions is an active and continuous process of institutionalization, reproduction and adaptation in new situations. The processes of normalization are undergoing all sorts of social influences (political and economic, educational, incidental occurrences, etc.) but the framework of subject–subject relationships is key in all stages of genesis.

Pragmatism is also explicit – if not radical – in its relational focus (Dewey, 1920/1964; James, 1909/1963; Mead, 1934). Philosophical pragmatism is rooted in pre-war communitarian America. It is fascinating to see how this pre-modernist thought of public action survived planning modernism (Harper & Stein, 2006; Healey, 2009; Hoch, 2007, 2016) and has now widely been rediscovered as a source of inspiration in mainstream planning approaches, and even in recent 'post-political' theories (Marres, 2007), precisely because of its radical premises of relational analysis. The pragmatist forerunners Dewey and James declined abstract sources of knowledge and instead made real, empirically observable problems related to social interaction central to their theory of knowledge and consequentially directed action (Dewey, 1929/1960, 1991/1927; James, 1909/1963). Dewey explained the need of all public action out of the need to solve the uncontrolled consequences of social intercourse (Dewey, 1991/1927, p. 15). His starting point for analysing public action is definitively not in the considerations of the policymakers but it is in social interaction itself. If the consequences of social interaction must be responded to but are beyond the control of the subjects involved (which would be the source for private action), a *public of the indirectly affected* arises and intends to find solutions for the problematic consequences (public action). The intentions and problem perceptions of 'the public' are crucial in this approach. The public may arrange the search for solutions via civic cooperation or via public sector agency but in all cases they should define and try to solve the problems that are felt as problems by those affected in the social intercourse. Dewey consequently refused to analyse problems which are autonomously defined as problems by politics, public agency or planning authorities. He does not investigate an independent or autonomous planning subject because it is too abstract and it does not know the real problems that come as a consequence of social interaction. Planning agency is instrumental to the intentions and the problem perception of the public, and not the other way around. Also technical expertise and law are positioned as means to be arranged by the public rather than serving the established powers. Dewey's concept of state as such was made changeable and dependent on the intentions and problem perceptions of the public. His concept of 'state' was never the same, it had to be rediscovered and rearranged time after time by the problem-shaped public instead of progressing autonomously (Dewey, 1991/1927, p. 34). It is a radical (and not uncontentious) position of relational analysis. Dewey explicitly considered planning, state and law as instruments of a public that intends to find effective solutions for their perceptions of problems. While thus mobilizing the government and other arrangements to solve problems, Dewey criticized the self-centredness of modernist planning and the administrative state before it was even invented! There is much more to say on the pragmatist premises, but for the present argument it is important to understand the crucial notion of inter-subjectivity in the relational framework of analysing public policy and planning. This basic premise has been sustained throughout the twentieth century. Pragmatism and institutional thought differ deeply in many regards but the fact that both orientations are rooted in a relational framework of analysis is a welcome common denominator in the search for the potential of dialectical co-evolution.

Fundamental Differences in Pragmatism and Institutional Thought

Before explaining the relevance of both classic orientations for the contemporary research of public action and planning and the exploration of options for mutual cross-pollination, we have to make explicit the different meanings and the different functions of the two conceptual streams in planning research. Pragmatism and institutional thought employ different rationalities of public action that are prone to clashes. In order to investigate this systematically, we make an analytical distinction between the two underlying rationalizations. The level of abstraction is different and thus public action is justified in different ways. Not infrequently are these two ideas opposed to one another. The two orientations employ two fundamentally different rationales:

a. Purposive and consequential relationships;
b. The patterning of public norms, imposing conditions.

Purposive and Consequential Relationships

Pragmatism is committed to purposive relationships: purposive in the sense of the intention to remove problematic obstacles. The pragmatist orientation is essentially intentional, problem-led and solution focused. And it is consequential, in the sense that its practical judgement in the pursuit of public purpose is informed by comparison of the consequences of different options (Hoch, Chapter 8, in this volume). It does not delve into historical causes, ideologies, underlying social structures of action, or other external appeals and possible causes of social problems but situates the problem of public action in concrete settings of social interaction and focuses the attention on the consequences of an action, linking purpose, context and expected outcome (Hoch, 2002; see also Hoch, Chapter 8, in this volume). These problems are not abstract: they are empirically observable in situated contexts as the uncontrolled consequences of social interactions between people in their environment. These consequences are perceived by the affected public as a concern which necessitates public action. As far as wider causes and normative backgrounds (including institutions) play a role, they have to be perceived in this concrete setting of social interaction. Politics and planning is a matter of practical inquiry, integrating all sorts of values and motives in a practical judgement about the meaning of a problem and specific purposes in a particular context. The public arranges strategies in order to search, imagine and compare the consequences of alternative solutions (see Hoch, Chapter 8, in this volume). The justification of the public action is in the deliberate intention to remove the obstacles under the instigation of the public. The ethics of public action is also instrumental to the consequences of action (consequentialism): many solutions may be attempted but ethically relevant and good ones are only those solutions that prove to be effective. So, within pragmatism, there is not a separate world for deliberating about objectives, planning knowledge and the means of planning, etc.; instead, the origin and ultimate meaning of public action and all its ingredients (ethics, knowledge, etc.) is in precisely situated practices and their consequences.

The Patterning of Public Norms: Imposing Conditions

Institutions also legitimate the behaviour of participants in processes of social interaction. Institutions may be made up of principles, normative rules, patterned values or patterned social norms. These institutional norms may be informal or formal; they may be economic, political or cultural. We define institutions categorically as 'patterning sets of public norms which impose conditions on social interaction'. The patterning of social norms condition processes of social interaction and initiatives of public action. Institutions may be procedural (outlining different positions, rights and duties, and responsibilities of participants, and defining the 'rules of the game') or they may be material (containing general substantive norms). Institutions are general codes of behaviour that indicate what is appropriate to do and what is not (March & Olsen, 1989). They do not tell you how to achieve your goals but define normative conditions that must be taken into account when you are pursuing your objectives. Thus, while being expressed in daily activities they serve as conditions to action rather than accomplishing the action itself. Because of the underlying inter-subjectivity of institutional conditions, people can have reliable expectations of each other about the conditions of action, which also hold in situations of complexity and uncertainty. Legitimation of institutional meaning is essentially based on inter-subjective relations although this may be very indirect in large groups.

These elementary indications already demonstrate that institutions appear in diverse forms, but in all forms there are apparent differences in abstraction and ways of legitimation and effectuation compared with the contextually situated, purposive and consequential orientation of pragmatism. Institutional norms are more abstract; they have a general rather than particular meaning. They are not bounded to problem solving in a particular situated context but – on the contrary – they are proved and refined through many different concrete situations. They are not targeted towards particular solutions and outcomes but serve as conditions for action. The different functions of pragmatism and institutional thought can be summed up as such: while pragmatism focuses on intentions and solving the situated problems of the public, institutions serve to give a critical normative feedback to the actions performed in response to such problems. Institutions have a critical function in keeping participants aware of playing their genuine role. Institutions critically question the position from which agents may act and the normative expectations that other upholders of the social norms may have from you: What might others expect from you in a certain position? What entitles you to act in a certain way? If you are expected to fulfil a certain role, what public norms do you take into consideration?

The distinction made above is an analytical distinction. Obviously, the two orientations overlap and meet (implicitly and explicitly) both in theory and in practice. However, in order to improve the search for the interrelationships between both orientations, we have to first distinguish the different analytical positions. For politics and planning, the tentative and experimental research of purposive relationships (contextual purposes, problems, alternative solutions, consequences) is needed in order to be responsive to the stream of social problems in dynamic societies. However, it is also necessary, not to say imperative, to invest in critical normative feedback (analysis of the role of institutions) on these instrumental itineraries via the use of institutional research. So, both pragmatic analysis and institutional thinking have their own rationality and are required in practices of planning. In their dialectical encounters, the different rationalities of the two orientations appear to have a mutual added value for the legitimation and effectuation of planning. Still, however, the conceptual challenge is great, as the two rationalities tend to define each other as irrational. It is not simply a matter of adding together the two rationalities because – at least in part – they appear to suppress one another. In the next two sections, I consider the revival of the each of the two orientations in contemporary debates on planning. In the final section, I define the challenge of their co-habitation and co-evolution and discuss the other avenues of co-evolution that are explored in the further contributions to this volume.

The Logic of Philosophical Pragmatism

How can we explain the recent rediscovery and resurgence of the classic roots of philosophical pragmatism in planning research, even a century after its birth? While some parts of this classic orientation did not stand the test of time, the fundamental propensity to make the research of public action directly responsive to practically situated problems and to search for legitimacy in action fits seemingly with the post-war aspirations of an open and responsive society (Kagan, 2001; Nonet & Selznick, 1978). Although, paradoxically, the over-socialization of post-war Western administrations created new national and local bureaucracies for some decades, the underlying appeal of making public action more directly responsive to solving the problems of the public never lost its appeal and has even acquired new relevance in the aftermath of modernist planning (Forester, 2013; Harper & Stein, 2006; Healey, 2009; Hoch, 2007; Innes & Booher, 1999; Mäntysalo & Jarenko, 2014; Salet et al., 2012). The next three epistemological dimensions, in particular, appear to contribute to pragmatism's vitality in current planning research:

a. The moral dimension;
b. The democratic and communicative dimension;
c. The experimental dimension.

The Moral Dimension

Public action is legitimated in situated practices of problems experienced as a consequence of social interaction. The concrete problem perception of the public and the practical pursuit of public purpose is the primary source of legitimation; there is no ethical abstraction but the experience of intentions and problems in an observable context. The factual observation and experience of problems is linked to justificatory practices (Bernstein, 2010). The identification of the problem and the intentional selection of ways to cope with it is an open and critical process of joint inquiry (instead of top-down selection by officials or experts) and it is in pursuit of community (instead of liberal partisans). Ideas are helpful to select possible responses. The intention to act is informed by comparing the imagined consequences of ideas, enabling the pragmatist to come to a practical judgement (see Hoch, Chapter 8, in this volume). The moral dimension of pragmatism is problem-driven in situated context, it is intentional on public purpose and it is consequential in its practical judgement about the way to act. Only those outcomes that eventually bring the solutions to the problems experienced are considered as ethically relevant. Pragmatic ethics is not just about good intentions; it is consequential (Dewey, 1929/1960; James, 1909/1963).

The Democratic and Communicative Dimension

The second dimension refers to the origins and sentiments of social interaction and communication in community development at the beginning of the previous century but has resurged frequently in planning research. This pragmatic source of inspiration has been seen most recently in the turn to argumentative and communicative planning research (Fischer & Forester, 1993; Hajer & Wagenaar, 2003) and in the post-crisis trends of social self-regulation (Hajer, 2009; Innes & Booher, 2010). These turns consider the meaning of democracy not as a formal and authoritative system but as a communicative and deliberative process of *dialogue* and *persuasion*. In line with Dewey, it is all about human dialogue and communication (Dewey, 1991/1927, p. 218). Dewey outlined the concept of democracy not as a matter of positivist knowledge and rationalization but as a committed and sincere process of discovering knowledge in action and communication, also relying on ethos, passionate commitment and emotion, as "ideas that are communicated, shared and reborn in expression" (Dewey, 1991/1927, p. 218). It comes close to what Habermas would later describe as "the public sphere" (Habermas, 1996; see also Calhoun, 1992; Durrant, 2016). Even in the communitarian America of his time, Dewey was not naïve in expecting consensus as the necessary outcome of communication but facing the increasing pluralism of society he considered "the improvement of the methods and conditions of debate, discussion and persuasion" as the essential need of democracy (Dewey, 1991/1927, p. 208).

The Experimental Dimension

The third dimension refers to the permanent experimentation of intentions and possible solutions. Public action cannot rely on perfect certainty *a priori* in a complex society (Dewey, 1929/1960). Knowledge acquires its meaning in action (Dewey, 1920/1964; Friedmann & Hudson, 1974). It appreciates "the role of chance and contingency in the universe, against mechanical determinism" (Bernstein, 2010, p. 8). This notion has inspired a lot of contemporary planning research (Bertolini, 2010; Harper & Stein, 2006; Healey, 2009; Hoch, 1984, 2007). According to pragmatism, it is in the processes of acting, experimenting and testing of possible solutions that knowledge and interpretation may grow. Dewey did not refer to the experiments in the laboratory; he used the experimental dimension as a logic of discovery:

> Such a logic involves the following factors: First, that those concepts, general principles, theories and dialectical developments which are indispensable to any systematic knowledge be shaped and tested as tools of inquiry. Secondly, that politics and proposals for social action be treated as working hypotheses, not as programs to be rigidly adhered to and executed.
>
> *(Dewey, 1991/1927, p. 202)*

Experimental in this sense implies the permanent observation of the consequences that are produced by proposals and the state of permanently being prepared to adapt if they don't work.

The moral, democratic and experimental dimensions provide pragmatism with its characteristic immediate responsiveness to real problems that are experienced in concrete situations in society. Its morality is critically opposed to the paternalism and opaque self-centredness of the post-war administrative state; it appeals to the communitarian identity of citizens and their genuine responsibility for social self-regulation and as underlying dimension of regulation; and it interchanges the quest for certainty in positivist planning knowledge for an elegant hypothetical and consequential logic of experimental discovery. Almost all present-day approaches to planning research find inspiration in these three dimensions of this classic philosophy for action. Its intentional instrumentalism and consequentialism are key to understanding the scientific premises of the pragmatist epistemology. However, it is also exactly here that the differences with institutional thinking are largest and that the two orientations of legitimating and effectuating public action reject each other's logic. I take inspiration from the three abovementioned dimensions of pragmatism but I would argue that the premises of immediacy and consequentialism have been driven too far and might impede the use of mediating forms of legitimizing public action. The logic of pragmatism has no antenna for institutional meaning (Bernstein, 2010, p. 87).

The lack of institutional thinking does not rest on an incidental mistake of the concept or on the historic circumstances of early pragmatist thought but it is a consequence of the radical and consequent use of the epistemological premises. Dewey and James feared the depersonalization of institutions (Dewey, 1929/1960; James, 1909/1963). Dewey, in particular, appeared to be very well aware of institutions but he refused to accept the mediation of 'abstract' institutional legitimation while he was pointing at the directedness and un-orderly logic of situated experience and legitimation of the public. He considered institutional mediation as a negative point of reference. The state was not to be considered as a patterning set of durable institutions that in their abstractness might legitimate the actual policies of the government. Dewey did not accept the distinction of the state as 'institution' and the government as 'organization' (Dewey, 1991/1927). Such a distinction might lead (in his eyes) to the absurd situation that a government could be criticized for its wrong policies while the state would keep its sacrosanct holiness of institutional authority. He did not accept the (by him imputed) reification of institutional norms nor the distinction between state and government; instead he radically aligned the concepts of state and government and derived its legitimacy from the need of the public to find solutions for the problems as the consequences of social interaction in situated practices. Rather than being guided by general institutional norms, Dewey's state became an instrument of a situated public. He fully accepted the dynamic consequence that the public is temporally and locally diversified and in its multiplicity creates a plethora of states. The pragmatist concept of the state is not solidified, it is in a permanent state of instrumental and consequential discovery, and it should not solidify beyond the direct experience of problems. He acknowledges the "brute compulsiveness of experience" (Bernstein, 2010, p. 52). In the words of Dewey:

> The same forces which have brought about the forms of democratic government, general suffrage, executives and legislators chosen by majority vote, have also brought about conditions which halt the social and humane ideals that demand the utilization of government as the genuine instrumentality of an inclusive and fraternally associated public. The democratic public is still largely inchoate and unorganized.
>
> *(Dewey, 1991/1927, p. 109)*

The radical founding and justification of the concepts of 'state', 'democracy', and 'public action', but also the meaning of 'planning' and 'law' in situated public, and the immediate instrumentality of finding solutions for problematic consequences of social interaction gives pragmatism its flavour of immediate responsiveness and legitimation in action but it is also its Achilles heel. It fails to meet the challenges of public action in crucial ways:

- First, it reduces public action to immediate response in a situational and ad hoc logic of experience. The wider meaning of history, social structure and society is reduced to the problems experienced by the public in immediate context. It is pulverized to instant and situational experience, which is useful in itself but neglects wider experience in an increasingly complex and plural society. It also struggles with the intelligence of the patterning public norms that have evolved in a wide number of situations in order to deal with social complexity;
- Second, it conceptualizes and reduces the meaning of responsiveness to instrumental strategies. By exclusively emphasizing the direct instrumentality of public action, it strips law and state, and all public action of their intrinsic normative qualities and thus from their function of giving normative feedback to agencies in processes of action. State and law are not just instrumental to situated problem experience and its search for solutions but also reproduce a set of public norms that define the positions of agencies and the codes of appropriateness in the legitimate relationship between citizens and state (Fuller, 1964; Habermas, 1996). In the debate on planning and law, the instrumentalist position of pragmatism is rather controversial (although widely applied in practice);
- Third, pragmatism tends to de-personalize institutions by qualifying these as forms of reification. The patterning of norms from the past (which continue to expand) are considered as a constraint and hindrance rather than a support in response to new situations. The meaning of institutional norms has allegedly become abstract because of its likeness to outdated experience. The enabling role of institutions is neglected and the innovation of institutions in practices of action is not considered. Rather, the response to new experiences of problems is expected to be 'extra-institutional' (Marres, 2007).

Considering the frictions between pragmatism and institutional thought, a co-evolution of the two orientations might easily turn into a marriage of convenience. However, the differences of position also keep both alert, providing mutual challenges. Institutional researchers may claim the underlying inter-subjectivity of institutional norms but the mirror of pragmatism challenges them to explain whether and how the real meaning of institutions is being validated in the situated problem experiences of the here and now. Institutional researchers may claim the added value of general – instead of situation specific – institutional norms that have been refined through a number of different situations but pragmatism challenges them to explain their actual relevance to the problem at hand. And how exactly would institutional theory address the issues of institutional change? It is time to discuss the logic of institutional thought.

The Logic of Institutional Thinking

Thus far, I have referred to institutional thought cautiously in a broad sense as a normative 'orientation'. Actually, it is a wide and very rich orientation with a large number of differentiated paradigms. While pragmatism maintained, in essence, the coherence and consistency of its paradigmatic premises, we have to recognize and respect a wider and deeper variety of institutional research. For this single reason, our exploration of a co-evolution and dialectic of pragmatism and institutional thought may never result in one all-encompassing approach. Different institutional paradigms emphasize different trajectories of normative research, and when we explore options for the co-evolution with pragmatism it will be a field with distinguished sets of encounters and multiple productive ways in which cross-pollination can occur rather than one fixed approach of recombination.

The different institutional approaches, however, do have a common denominator. The potential benefit of all institutional paradigms is in providing critical normative feedback on the purposive and problem-solving planning investigations and practices. Their premises do not start in the purposive framework of planners, who are in search of solutions to the problems at hand, but first reflect critically on the positions and patterns of material norms from which different actors relate to each other. Possible roles for planning agencies and other subjects are positioned within these frameworks. When planning is in search of 'reflection in action', institutional theories may provide deep insights into the different normative indicators that guide these processes of reflection. While pragmatism positions its analysis of problem solving in the *direct reciprocity* of affected agents in a situated context (inspiring in this way the contemporary interactive and communicative approaches of planning), institutional thought provides a critical reflection on these practices by referring to general patterns of public norms that do not originate in the direct interaction and communication of the involved agents in a concrete situation but in wider (spatially and temporally) processes of social normalization. These patterns of norms are more general and abstract because they are not derived from the specifics of a particular situated context (on the contrary they are being continuously refined in many different situations) and do not focus on targeting alternative solutions to the problems at hand but 'only' provide conditional norms to situated practices of planning and public guidance. In this sense institutional norms may be expected to mediate practices of 'direct reciprocity'. The crux of this *institutionally mediated reciprocity* is that their abstract and general meaning has to be reaffirmed time after time in specific practices of action. Institutions are not just external conditions to concrete contexts of planning (although their processes of formation are spatially and temporally wider than the ad hoc situation) but their conditional meaning has to be proved time after time in very specific contexts, in ongoing processes of action. It is a normative feedback in daily practices which also innovates in daily practices: we call this 'institutions in action'. Thus, it is in these same daily practices that purpose and norm meet (providing different background, different logic and enabling critical interaction).

Planning theory has a fascinating tradition of reflection in action, inspired by the pivotal work of Donald Schön who urges professionals to make planning practices more robust, in the first instance by explicitly referring to their personal experiences of life and their lessons of previous planning processes (Schön, 1983). The lessons of experience and prudency introduced a new order of deliberation in planning (abstracting from the ad hoc situation). The example of Donald Schön is followed widely and extended in contemporary communicative planning studies by John Forester who adds to this framework the 'personal stories' of participants in order to better understand the values and emotions of those involved in planning processes, and their 'conflicts of value' and the 'faces of power' (Forester, 1999, 2013; see also Hajer &

Wagenaar, 2003; Gualini, 2015a, 2015b;Verloo, 2015).This reflective communicative trajectory has introduced an important dimension of deliberation in planning theory; however, the institutional dimension is not always explicitly distinguished from the prevailing purposive considerations and purposive negotiation. Also at the level of organization, the reflective dimension of deliberation is explored in single, double, and even more 'loops of learning' following the pivotal work of Argyris and Schön (1996). It leads the attention of planners to organizational change, cultivating the norms of openness versus defensive attitudes to change and challenging policymakers and planners to face discomfort and to learn from confrontation (Giezen et al., 2014). In many cases, notions of institutional theory may be observed in this reflective tradition; however, a systematic search of institutional paradigms has not yet matured (see Mäntysalo et al., Chapter 11, in this volume). Institutional theory brings in a wider critical reflection on the patterns of social norms from beyond the situated problem setting and may – critically – reflect on the planner in its familiar role of purpose seeker, problem solver and negotiator in situation bounded settings. It might also enable reflection on collective action by casting out the planner first and (potentially) re-introducing her in a different role. Maturating the concept of reflective institutional thought in planning studies requires a wider – more interdisciplinary – scope in social sciences.

Exploring the wide and varied field of institutional thought, it is important to distinguish and respect the different paradigms and the different premises within which they are set. It is possible to combine (elements of) different paradigms but it is crucial to know first the differences and the potential of the separate paradigms. Assemblage of mixed paradigms is not always a productive exercise as their most important function is to make the discovery of research 'researchable' in a traceable way. Sometimes, it might prove better to use different paradigms for different and complementary research questions. In a forthcoming publication, I extensively analyse the particular premises and strengths for planning research of six institutional paradigms that have matured in social sciences, economics and the philosophy of law, and are progressively becoming used in planning studies (Salet, 2018, forthcoming). Although far from being complete (there are dozens of institutional paradigms), they delineate the relevant scope for our exploration of dialectic and cross-fertilization with the more familiar tradition of pragmatic approaches:

- Cultural and sociological institutions (Giddens, Bourdieu, Healey);
- Philosophy of state and law (Fuller, Hayek, Moroni);
- Path-dependence analysis (Pierson, Mahoney, Sorensen);
- Institutional actor theory (Elinor Ostrom);
- Urban regime analysis (Stone, Elkin, Fainstein, Kantor);
- Critical political analysis/regulation theory (Harvey, Brenner, Swyngedouw).

These approaches provide institutional reflection in action in divergent ways (see Figure 1.1). Even the definition of institutions differs in these paradigms (within a common general framework). Cultural and legal studies address institutional norms and their innovation in order to justify the decisions of development and planning. Path-dependence analysis enables one to reflect on structuring historic conditions in the making of actual choices. Institutional actor analysis searches for ways to institutionalize norms that enable efficiency of action and the conditions of self-regulation. Regime and regulation studies reveal the conditions of power underlying the institutional norms in planning processes.

I will briefly summarize these perspectives.

The perspective of *social and cultural institutions* is the most difficult to grasp because of its wide and highly varied set of particular approaches. Characteristic is the intrinsic embedding of

Institutions in Action

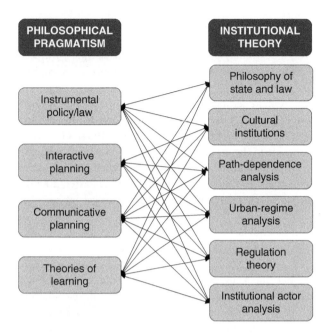

Figure 1.1 Co-evolution of pragmatic and institutional approaches
Source: Willem Salet (2018)

social and cultural context in social interaction, rather than relying on a rationalized perspective of the *homo economicus*. Social and cultural studies often focus on the interconnectivity of objective social structure and agency where subjects both reproduce certain objective conditions of structure or class (such as cultural, social or economic capital) and, in social interaction, further develop certain sets of social dispositions (Bourdieu, 1977; Giddens, 1984). Institutions do not appear here as external conditions to action but as socialized and internalized sets of norms. Characteristic of processes of normalization is that people enculturate certain interpretations of public norms and that they may be (socially) sanctioned by other upholders of the norm in case of non-compliance. In planning studies, this kind of interpretative institutional meaning and the changes of normative discourses are investigated because of their potential for social mobilization. Healey takes this cultural sociological position in institutional planning research (Healey, 2010; overview of Healey's contributions in Hillier & Metzger, 2015; see also Healey, Chapter 2, in this volume). The meaning of norms and social codes may be marked or symbolized and differences with other meanings may be profiled in order to enlarge their impact in social interaction. There is a wide tradition of social and cultural studies in anthropology and ethnography, but also in planning the potential of these paradigms is increasingly used (Boudreau, 2007, also Chapter 16 in this volume; Dembski, 2015; Dembski & Salet, 2010; Neuman, 2012; de Vries, 2015). A lot of attention is given here to the innovation of institutions: the active institution of new meaning by canonizing, inculcating, and repeating (Bell, 1992; Bourdieu, 1991).

Legal institutions of the philosophy of state and law deserve a lot of attention in our search of co-evolution because of the recurrent controversies between the positions of instrumentalism in philosophical pragmatism versus the conceptions of the rule of law in legal institutions (Habermas, 1996). Highly relevant for institutional thought on planning and law are the pivotal works of Hayek and Fuller (Fuller, 1964; Hayek, 1973–1979). Hayek is not a protagonist of planning; he turned against the aspirations of planning as such and relied instead on the spontaneous order of complex societies. Nevertheless, his notions about general rules (versus objectives and targets) are highly relevant for planning. In particular, his distinction between nomocracy (relating to a spontaneous complex order) and teleocracy (the made order) with the corresponding distinction of general rules versus outcome focused interventions has inspired new debates on planning and law (Hayek, 1973–1979; Moroni, 2007, 2010a, also Chapter 12 in this volume; Talen, 2004). In the same vein, Fuller made a fundamental distinction between a morality of aspirations and a morality of rights and duties, not as a contrast (like Hayek) but as a very delicate challenge to balance interventions in this field of tension (Fuller, 1964). This classic source is also actively used to breathe new life in the debates on planning and law and to oppose instrumentalist interpretations of law (Brunnée & Toope, 2010; Rijswick & Salet, 2012). See also in planning theory the debates on public interest (Campbell & Marshall, 2002; Porter, 2006).

Path-dependent analysis links actual occurrences with a sequence of historical processes. It may inform planners that actual development is not just an ad hoc occurrence but a structured process in a historical, almost determinist sequence. Historical trajectories may become self-reinforcing (with positive feedback), keeping a certain development on its trajectory even when a change of path might be considered as more productive (Mahoney, 2000; Pierson, 2000). This may turn into a lock-in situation, but under highly disruptive conditions, a critical juncture of the path-dependent trajectories may occur. The role of institutions in this paradigm is, in particular, to amplify the self-reinforcing processes of positive feedback (such as established cultures, routines and transaction costs that keep development on existing tracks). Innovation of these institutions is often (but not always convincingly) sought after by researchers (Buitelaar et al., 2007; Lambooy & Boschma, 2001; Thelen, 2004). Still, the most distinctive and explicatory value of path-dependence analysis appears to be in explaining self-reinforcing mechanisms. Path dependency is a robust claim because there is choice at any stage of a trajectory: claiming a recurring positive feedback at a trajectory, and thus requires a frequent and empirical demonstration that self-reinforcement is preferred above a change of pathway (Sorensen, 2015; also Chapter 5 in this volume). The interest in this paradigm is growing in planning studies (Low, 2013; Vermeulen, 2011). Sorensen, recently, proposed a detailed and very promising research agenda to use this historic paradigm in planning studies (Sorensen, 2015).

Institutional actor analysis builds on economic rational actor theories, where the efficiency of collective action is held to be dependent on hierarchical norms in order to prevent economically maximizing individuals from sub-optimizing collective benefits. Very relevant for planning studies is Elinor Ostrom's reconstruction of this economic framework in a social and political sense: she did not limit individual choices to economic rationalization (instead extending individual choice to social and political ratios of action). Furthermore, she was in search of institutional conditions that enable self-regulation rather than hierarchical norms because of the characteristic lack of information at central level. Rather than focusing on a better implementation of centralized policies, she searched for the conditional norms that might enable effective strategies of self-regulation (Ostrom, 1990). This particular approach has been used and refined a number of times, with applications since 2000 particularly in the field of ecological governance and environmental planning (for an overview of Ostrom's work, see https://worldcat.org/identities/lccn-n80-1519/). Very relevant for planning is that Ostrom investigated institutional norms as dependent variables in order to 'discover' and 'institute' conditions of self-regulation (via setting new rules but also informal trust building) rather than analysing these as independent variables (fixed constraints to action) (Ostrom, 1990; see also Folke et al., 2005; Janssen-Jansen, 2004; Scharpf, 1997).

Regime studies analyse the forces of political and economic power behind norms. They make a distinction between normative frameworks at system level and the action spaces of quotidian policies (Krasner, 1983). Regimes are widely investigated in international relations but also in urban studies. Urban regime studies focus in particular on the impact of informal norms of convergence on daily urban policies. Urban regimes are not hierarchical; instead they include convergent actor expectations around principles, norms, rules and decision procedures. The existence of these regimes is far from obvious; they are drawn from the informal collaboration of contrarian governmental and non-governmental interests that join their resources around an identifiable agenda (Stone, 1989, 2005; see also Mossberger & Stoker, 2001). In this model of analysis, daily planning is not completely free to choose and to deliberate, it is highly conditioned by the normative framework of the regime. The powers of this regime may be highly asymmetric (Fainstein, 2008). In a historical study of the American Republic, Elkin demonstrated how difficult it is to achieve a fair balance between the two underlying principles of political economic regimes: financial accountability (generating income) and electoral accountability (reflecting the electoral moods of the community) (Elkin, 1987). This model of explanation is widely used, criticized, refined and re-used at different scales, increasingly also in planning studies, for instance by exploring the margins of policymaking of cities in face of international markets (Kantor et al., 2013; Savini, 2012; Savini & Salet, 2016; Savitch & Kantor, 2002).

Regulation theory is rooted in the critical political economic tradition of historic materialism and situates both planning and its institutions in the restructuring of international markets, politics and social organization. Regulation – also at local level – is not an independent local invention of policymakers but fits in a macro-political economic setting with dialectical and highly contradictive forces of capitalist growth. The need for economic growth is endemic to the development of capitalist systems but this growth has an intrinsic propensity to self-destruction and crisis because of over-accumulation and its intrinsic conflict with labour (Harvey, 1990). Regulation theory makes a distinction between the 'regimes of accumulation' that pave the way for growth via coherent production and consumption but end up in new crisis, and the 'mode of regulation' consisting of the complete set of institutions, norms, habits and regulation that have to respond to crisis, to settle social stability and to normalize the proceeding development. Institutions and regulation are thus created to consolidate new responses to crisis. Harvey considers spatial displacement as one of the most overt strategies to open new avenues for growth, such as the fixing of new spaces; see, for instance, the new state spaces (urban regions) identified by Brenner or the suburban frontiers identified by Peck (Harvey, 1990, 2000; Brenner, 2004; Peck, 2013). The dialectical perspective of regulation theory is widely applied on relevant themes for planning, such as in studies on large urban projects (Swyngedouw et al., 2002), (sub) urban land and development (Peck, 2013), or the politicizing of ecological studies via 'political ecology' (Heynen et al., 2005; Swyngedouw & Kaika, 2014).

The array of institutional paradigms opens up a diverse number of tangible ways to critically investigate the underlying relations of power and the indicators that could be used for the justification of norms in the 'reflection in action' strategies of planning. The differences with the purposive strategies of justification in philosophical pragmatism are clear, but purpose and norm meet in the same processes of action. The crucial challenge is to organize productive encounters of reflection between these different ratios of justification and effectuation, both in planning studies and in practice.

Towards a Co-Evolution of Norm and Purpose

This volume suggests that spatial planning might be an appropriate case for the co-evolution and dialectic of the experimental methodology of philosophical pragmatism and the normative perspectives of institutional research. Experimental action is crucial for making planning responsive to urgent problems in society. However, too narrow an instrumental focus on targeting specified outcomes would neglect wider sources of social normalization and fail to meet the conditions of uncertainty and social complexity. Public planning also needs a critical institutional reflection on the past and still evolving patterns of norms in society. This volume brings together international scholars to discuss the different facets of these conceptual frameworks and the alternative combinations through which they can be approached. The conceptual combinations will then be used to explore whether and how these lines of thought might be used to examine the ongoing practices of sustainable urban transition.

Pragmatism is so appealing because it conceptualizes the study of planning as a study of deliberate public action. According to this philosophy, planning processes may be considered as intentional experiments in largely unknown worlds, where insights are gradually developing through the investigation of reactions to ideas and actions and the (expected) consequences of interventions. It utilizes the strategy of learning by acting and improving, via trial and error, in the knowledge of uncertainty. The pragmatism of John Dewey and William James is not in search of definitive causes and perfect knowledge. On the contrary, it is solution-oriented, with each solution considered as an option to be further examined as a hypothesis, rather than pretending to find definitive answers. Although pragmatism makes itself, at times, over-dependent on the consequences of action in practice (epistemic consequentialism) and considers legislation, in a rather instrumental way, as vehicle to try out solutions, it still offers elegant avenues for evolutionary contemporary planning research (Bertolini, 2007, also Chapter 10 in this volume; Innes & Booher, 2010). This is certainly the case in a period in which uncertainty and complexity are perpetually growing.

We search for ways to combine the experimental concept of pragmatism with a critical institutional approach that investigates the position from which subjects act and justify their action. This co-evolutionary potential and dialectic requires further consideration, with pragmatism usually associated with direct action, ready for instrumental experiments of problem solving, while institutional thought urges reflection in a critical way precisely regarding that immediacy. Also, the dilemmas of planning and law reflect the tension between instrumentalism and institutionalism. The critical element of institutional thought is also manifest in the assumption that subjects and agencies might act beyond their position. It is far from evident that planning agencies should take the lead in public action, it is usually socially instigated (Boelens, 2010; see also Chapter 6 in this volume). It should be justified first, considering the role of diverse social actors. When an intervening role of public sector agency appears to be convenient, it might be a conditioning role instead of performing the action. For planning research this critical deliberation is particularly relevant as a lot of empirical planning research takes place within practical settings and it is often conducted in collaboration with planning practitioners.

Planning and policymaking initiators run the risk of being captured in exclusive 'means–ends' relationships or in direct exchanges of interests with other stakeholders. This 'instrumentalism' is considered as a negative point of reference in institutional research. An institutional approach enables one to step back from the directness of these policy approaches. It does not criticize politicians and policymakers for searching for effective solutions, but it criticizes the 'immediacy' of these search processes. By critically investigating the evolution of social norms (rites, rules, internalized practices) and identifying those that are still being reproduced in current circumstances, institutional approaches examine the systematic expectations of the subjects and whether and how these are used to justify their action (Healey, 2004, 2007; Salet, 2002). Usually, this requires some examination because subjects tend to 'instantly' legitimate the problem or aspiration using a 'situational ad hoc logic', rather than reflect on their position, subject to formal and informal expectations. Considered from an institutional point of view, a researcher should not identify with the positioning of practising public officials as central agents of change (Boelens, 2010; Davoudi & Madanipour, 2015; Ostrom, 1990). Planners are not automatically doing 'good'; their interventions are also harmful, depending on the eyes of the upholders of the norms. Institutional eyes urge for a critical disassociation (Metzger, 2014). Even when governmental agencies are authorized to intervene, they are not justified to imbue and take over the spaces of social action. A planning authority cannot automatically act as the central mobilizer. The justification for governmental intervention is first of all in the consideration and weighing up of problems in social interactions and in the reflection on the set of norms of public interest and the rights and margins that these entail (Campbell & Marshall, 2002; Porter, 2006), including the rules of due process. It is not just a matter of immediate action or problem solving, there is also institutional justification. The justification of spatial intervention is an act of reconstruction in which both the purposes in social processes (*in situ*) and the evolved general rules and patterns of social norms must be weighed up (Campbell & Marshall, 2002; Moroni, 2014).

How do institutions innovate? Institutions (legal, cultural or political codes) are often critiqued for conserving public norms which are consolidated over time and for constraining new processes of collective action. The problem of institutional viscosity should be taken seriously, with institutions refined through circumstance and subject to patterns of path dependency, with change usually more gradual than changes in actual and conflicting policy situations (Gualini, 2015a). Sometimes, urban conflicts openly manifest against institutionalized patterns, creating new spaces for experimentation (Gualini, 2015a). Experimental strategies of action usually change faster than patterns of norms and may take different routes. However, experiments and normative patterns interact, as norms shape conditions and enable action. The mainstreaming of new experiments depends on its institutional embedding. Also institutions change in processes of action; they are not carved in stone. Institutions reflect the social norms that are carried forward and reproduced by actors, making them subject to continual adjustment. This is what makes the confrontation with actual policy situations so fascinating because it is in these encounters (including social conflicts) that the gradual shifts in institutional meaning manifest themselves. Our questions focus on the changing meaning of institutions in action. This is highly relevant when investigating the ongoing transitions of urbanization. While the nested normative patterns of citizens and their political representatives still largely reflect the city of the previous stage of urbanization, via consolidated social, cultural and political institutions, changes in social and economic behaviour are simultaneously taking place and gradually change institutional patterns (Kloosterman, 2010). Cultural and political articulation might imbue processes of institutional innovation (Boudreau, 2007; De Frantz, 2013; Kaika & Karaliotas, 2014; Savini & Dembski, Chapter 18, in this volume; deVries, 2015). This evolution is examined in the transformation of city patterns from monocentric into polycentric configurations and the gradual endorsement of institutional innovation. One might contemplate this institutional change, for instance, in the fragile symbolic elucidation of changing cities (Boudreau, 2007; Dembski, 2015) and in the search for new legitimacy of the political governance in the urban periphery (Salet & Savini, 2015; Savini, 2012).

The mutual cross-pollination of pragmatism and institutional thought will be explored and illustrated within the context of the actual transition of cities in the face of new challenges associated with climate-proof development and social coherence in their newly emergent polycentric configurations. Over the last two decades, many city-regions have seen a shift from the hierarchical centralized pattern of urban spaces towards decentralized and polycentric formations. The external connectivity's of social and economic activities have strongly increased in volume and intensity. Increasingly, urban activities are becoming functionally specialized and spatially sorted out over wider urban spaces. If the worldwide process of urbanization continues, however, this will no longer occur exclusively around the core of the city and no longer with the once so evident arrangement of centre and periphery. This transition of city and adjoining countryside has had a dramatic impact on the urban agenda and the priorities of research. The crucial problem is that the challenges of public action regarding the sustainability and resilience of a climate-proof urban system (economic, social and ecological) now have to be envisioned and experienced in a fragmentary, multi-layered and asymmetric fabric of relationships. The spatial decomposition of the urban phenomenon has significantly increased the uncertainty and complexity of the urban question at the beginning of the twenty-first century. The social and spatial contrasts have been polarized which makes a process of coherent and balanced governance more difficult (Balducci, 2012; Eraydin & Taşan-Kok, 2013; Majoor, 2009; Zonneveld, 2010). The combined insights of pragmatism and institutional innovation will be needed to analyse these processes of urban transition. The crucial question is how can spatial interventions be made legitimate and become effective in this complex and changeable order.

To Conclude: The Research Questions for this Volume

This volume aims to question and deepen the concepts surrounding the co-evolution of philosophical pragmatism and institutional innovation to urban transition and position it in the international planning literature. The authors are also challenged to use their conceptual explications on a number of predefined questions related to the sustainable transition of city-regions. The volume is broken down into six parts:

1. Institutions in Action;
2. Institutional Innovation;
3. Pragmatism: The Dimension of Action;
4. On Justification;
5. Cultural and Political Institutions in Action;
6. Institutions and Urban Transition.

The first four parts explain the quintessential concepts of pragmatism and institutional approaches and positions these in the planning literature. When exploring the links between institutionalism and pragmatism, the different logic of the two orientations is taken seriously: the institutional chapters take on the challenge to respond to (critical) comments from pragmatism.
Institutional theories are criticized by pragmatism for being 'reified' because they are abstracted from real occurrences in the here and now. Furthermore, institutions are alleged to be conservative in consolidating the normative patterns of the past and constraining the innovation of public action. This makes the crucial questions here:

How is institutional meaning validated in real ongoing practices?
How, exactly, do institutions innovate?

Vice versa, the pragmatist explanations deal with the allegations from the institutional side. Pragmatism is criticized in institutional approaches for its odium of instrumentalism. It appears to lack the normative feedback of institutionalized norms (for instance in legal justification) and its targeting of solutions also seems to lack attention to the wider structural and historical embedding of actual situations. This makes the crucial questions here:

What is the relevance of institutional norms in pragmatist approaches? How does institutional deliberation happen in a pragmatist setting?
How is this assessed in the dilemmas of planning and law, and how does it respond to issues of legitimation?

On both sides, the different options for the co-evolution of these different approaches will be explored.

These conceptual explorations are undertaken in the final chapters of this volume where these lines of thought are explored in the practical context of changing city-regions, in particular with regards to issues of public guidance of sustainable transition. Before that, attention will be directed to the cultural and political institutions in action of changing city-regions and to the governance aspects of sustainable urban transition. The relevant additional questions, here, are the following:

Do social and cultural institutional parameters constrain the actual changes of a city or can innovation of these institutional conditions make them supportive to transition processes? How might we achieve such a cultural institutional innovation in peripheral zones of urban transition?
How can political articulation in changing cities and peripheries escape the margins of hegemony and the power of settled political institutions? Are there innovative ways of legitimation in political governance in peripheral zones of urban transition?
How can sustainability and resilience be institutionalized in processes of sustainable urban transition?

Note

1 This chapter recapitulates the argument of the forthcoming monograph of Willem Salet, *Public Norms and Aspirations: The Turn to Institutions in Action*, which is due to be published by Routledge simultaneously with this volume. This chapter refers so frequently to this monograph (under construction) that no particular references are mentioned. The author thanks Patsy Healey, Charles Hoch and Sebastian Dembski for many wise comments, and Stephanie Richards for the critical editing.

References

Argyris, C., & Schön, D. A. (1996). *Organizational Learning II: Theory, Method and Practice*. Reading, MA: Addison-Wesley.
Balducci, A. (2012). Creative governance in dynamic city regions. *disP*, 40(158), 21–26.
Bell, C. (1992). *Ritual Theory, Ritual Practice*. Oxford: Oxford University Press.
Bernstein, R. J. (2010). *The Pragmatic Turn*. Malden, MA: Polity Press.
Bertolini, L. (2007). Evolutionary urban transportation planning? An exploration. *Environment & Planning A*, 39(8), 1998–2019.
Bertolini, L. (2010). Coping with the Irreducible Uncertainties of Planning: An Evolutionary Approach. In P. Healey & J. Hillier (Eds.), *Ashgate Research Companion to Planning Theory: Conceptual Challenges for Spatial Planning* (pp. 413–424). Aldershot: Ashgate.
Boelens, L. (2010). Theorizing practice and practising theory: Outlines for an actor-relational approach in planning. *Planning Theory*, 9(1), 28–62.
Bolan, R. (2000). Social Interaction and Institutional Design: The Case of Housing in the USA. In W. G. M. Salet & A. Faludi (Eds.), *The Revival of Strategic Spatial Planning* (pp. 25–39). Amsterdam: Royal Dutch Academy of Sciences.
Boudreau, J.-A. (2007). Making new political spaces: Mobilizing spatial imaginaries, instrumentalizing spatial practices, and strategically using spatial tools. *EPA*, 39(11), 2593–2611.

Bourdieu, P. (1977). *Outline of a Theory of Practice*. Cambridge, MA: Cambridge University Press.
Bourdieu, P. (1991). *Language and Symbolic Power*. Cambridge, MA: Harvard University Press.
Brenner, N. (2004). *New State Spaces: Urban Governance and the Rescaling of Statehood*. Oxford: Oxford University Press.
Brunnée, J., & Toope, S. T. (2010). *Legitimacy and Legality in International Law: An Interactional Account*. Cambridge: Cambridge University Press.
Buitelaar, E., Lagendijk, A., & Jacobs, W. (2007). A theory of institutional change. *Environment and Planning A*, 39(4), 891–908.
Calhoun, C. (1992). *Habermas and the Public Sphere*. Boston, MA: MIT Press.
Campbell, H., & Marshall, R. (2002). Utilitarianism's Bad Breadth? A Re-Evaluation of the Public Interest Justification for Planning. In R. Paddison (Ed.), *Urban Studies Society* (pp. 163–187). London: Sage.
Davoudi, S., & Madanipour, A. (2015). *Reconsidering Localism*. London: Routledge.
Dembski, S., & Salet, W. G. M. (2010). The transformative potential of institutions: How symbolic markers can institute new social meaning in changing cities. *Environment & Planning A*, 42(3), 611–625.
Dembski, S. (2015). Structure and imagination of changing cities: Manchester, Liverpool and the spatial in-between. *Urban Studies*, 52(9), 1647–1664. Retrieved from: http://dx.doi.org/10.1177/0042098014539021.
Dewey, J. (1929/1960). *The Quest for Certainty: A Study of the Relation of Knowledge and Action* (11th ed.). New York: Putnam's Sons.
Dewey, J. (1920/1964). *Reconstruction in Philosophy* (enlarged ed.). Boston, MA: The Beacon Press.
Dewey, J. (1991/1927). *The Public and Its Problems*. Athens, OH: Swallow Press/Ohio University Press.
De Frantz, M. (2013). Culture-Led Urban Regeneration: The Discursive Politics of Institutional Change. In M. E. Leary & J. McCarthy (Eds.), *Routledge Companion to Urban Regeneration: Global Constraints, Local Opportunities*. New York: Routledge.
Durrant, D. W. (2016). *The Role of Civil Society in Mega-Transport Project Decision-Making* (Thesis UCL). London: Bartlett School of Planning.
Elkin, S. L. (1987). *City and Regime in the American Republic*. Chicago, IL: Chicago University Press.
Eraydin, A., & Taşan-Kok, T. (2013). *Resilience Thinking in Urban Planning*. Berlin: Springer.
Fainstein, S. S. (2008). Mega-projects in New York, London and Amsterdam. *IJURR*, 32(4), 768–785.
Fischer, F., & Forester, J. (1993). *The Argumentative Turn in Policy Analysis and Planning*. Durham, NC: Duke University Press.
Folke, C., Hahn, T., Olsson, P., & Norberg, J. (2005). Adaptive governance of social-ecological systems. *Annual Review of Environment and Resources*, 30, 441–473. Retrieved from: http://dx.doi.org/10.1146/annurev.energy.30.050504.144511.
Forester, J. (1999). *The Deliberative Practitioner*. Cambridge, MA: MIT Press.
Forester, J. (2013). On the theory and practice of critical pragmatism: Deliberative practice and creative negotiations. *Planning Theory*, 12(1), 5–22. Retrieved from: http://dx.doi.org/10.1177/1473095212448750.
Friedmann, J., & Hudson, B. (1974). Knowledge and action: A guide to planning theory. *Journal of the American Institute of Planners*, 40(1), 2–16.
Fuller, L. L. (1964). *The Morality of Law*. New Haven and London: Yale University Press.
Giddens, A. (1984). *The Constitution of Society: Outline of the Theory of Structuration*. Cambridge: Polity Press.
Giezen, M., Bertolini, L., & Salet, W. (2014). Adaptive capacity within a mega project: A case study into planning and decision-making in the face of complexity. *European Planning Studies*, 23(5), 999–1018. Retrieved from: http://dx.doi.org/10.1080/09654313.2014.916254.
Gualini, E. (2001). *Planning and the Intelligence of Institutions*. Aldershot: Ashgate.
Gualini, E. (2015a). *Planning and Conflict*. New York: Routledge.
Gualini, E. (Ed.). (2015b). *Planning/Conflict: Critical Perspectives on Contentious Urban Developments*. New York: Routledge.
Habermas, J. (1996). *Between Facts and Norms*. Cambridge, MA: MIT Press.
Hajer, M. (2009). *Authoritative Governance: Policy Making in the Age of Mediatization*. Oxford: Oxford University Press.
Hajer, M., & Wagenaar, H. (2003). *Deliberative Policy Analysis: Understanding Governance in the Network Society*. Cambridge: Cambridge University Press.
Harper, T., & Stein, S. M. (2006). *Dialogical Planning in a Fragmented Society: Critically Liberal, Pragmatic and Incremental*. New Brunswick, NJ: Center for Urban Policy Research, Rutgers University.
Harvey, D. (1990). *The Condition of Postmodernity*. Oxford: Blackwell.
Harvey, D. (2000). *Spaces of Hope*. Edinburgh: Edinburgh University Press.

Hayek, F. A. (1973–1979). *Law, Legislation and Liberty* (Vols. 1–3). London: Routledge and Kegan Paul.
Healey, P. (2004). The treatment of space and place in the new strategic spatial planning in Europe. *IJURR*, 28(1), 45–67.
Healey, P. (2007). *Urban Complexity and Spatial Strategies: Towards a Relational Planning for Our Times*. London: Routledge.
Healey, P. (2009). The pragmatic tradition in planning thought. *Journal of Planning Education and Research*, 28(3), 277–292.
Healey, P. (2010). *Making Better Places*. Basingstoke, UK: Palgrave.
Healey, P. (2016). Making Better Places through Citizen-Centred Action. Talk for Waseda Machizukuri Symposium, 9/10 July 2016 (draft, not published).
Heynen, N., Kaika, M., & Swyngedouw, E. (Eds.). (2005). *In the Nature of Cities: Urban Political Ecology and the Politics of Urban Metabolism*. New York/London: Routledge.
Hillier, J., & Metzger, J. (2015). *Connections: Exploring Contemporary Planning Theory and Practice with Patsy Healey*. Farnham: Ashgate.
Hoch, C. J. (1984). Pragmatism, planning, and power. *Journal of Planning Education and Research*, 4(2), 86–95.
Hoch, C. J. (2002). Evaluating plans pragmatically. *Planning Theory*, 1(1), 53–76.
Hoch, C. J. (2007). Pragmatic communicative action theory. *Journal of Planning Education and Research*, 26(3), 272–283.
Hoch C. J. (2016). Utopia, scenario, plan: A pragmatic integration. *Planning Theory*, 15(1), 6–22.
Innes, J. E., & Booher, D. E. (1999). Consensus building as role playing and bricolage: Toward a theory of collaborative planning. *Journal of the American Planning Association*, 65(1), 9–26.
Innes, J. E., & Booher, D. E. (2010). *Planning with Complexity*. New York: Routledge.
James, W. (1909/1963). *Pragmatism and Other Essays*. New York: Washington Sq. Press.
Janssen-Jansen, L. B. (2004). *Regio's Uitgedaagd: 'Growth Management' ter inspiratie voor nieuwe paden van proactieve ruimtelijke planning*. Assen: Van Gorcum.
Kagan, R. A. (2001). On Responsive Law. In R. A. Kagan, M. Krygier & K. Winston (Eds.), *Legality and Community: On the Intellectual Legacy of Philip Selznick*. Lanham: Institute of Governmental Studies Press/Rowman & Littlefield.
Kaika, M., & Karaliotas, L. (2014). The spatialization of democratic politics: Insights from indignant squares. *European Urban and Regional Studies*, 23(4), 556–570. Retrieved from: http://dx.doi.org/10.1177/0969776414528928.
Kantor, P., Lefèvre, C., Saito, A., Savitch, H. V., & Thornley, A. (2013). *Struggling Giants*. Minneapolis, MN: University of Minnesota Press.
Kloosterman, R. (2010). This is not America: Embedding the cognitive-cultural urban economy. *Geografiska Annaler Series B Human Geography*, 92(2), 131–143.
Krasner, S. D. (Ed.). (1983). *International Regimes*. Ithaca, NY: Cornell University Press.
Lambooy, J. G., & Boschma, R. A. (2001). Evolutionary economics and regional policy. *Annals of Regional Science*, 35(1), 113–133.
LeGalès, P. (2002). *European Cities: Social Conflict and Governance*. New York: Oxford University Press.
Low, N. (2013). *Transforming Urban Transport*. New York: Routledge.
Mahoney, J. (2000). Path dependence in historical sociology. *Theory and Society*, 29(4), 507–548.
Majoor, S. (2009). The disconnected innovation of new urbanity in Zuidas Amsterdam, Ørestad Copenhagen and Forum Barcelona. *European Planning Studies*, 17(9), 1379–1403.
Mäntysalo, R., & Jarenko, K. (2014). Communicative planning theory following deliberative democracy theory. *IJEPR*, 3(1), 38–50.
March, J. G., & Olsen, J. P. (1989). *Rediscovering Institutions: The Organizational Basis of Politics*. New York: The Free Press.
Marres, N. (2007). The issues deserve more credit: Pragmatist contributions to the study of public involvement in controversy. *Social Studies of Science*, 37(5), 759–780. Retrieved from: http://dx.doi.org/10.1177/0306312706077367.
Mead, G. H. (1934). *Mind, Self, and Society: From the Standpoint of a Social Behaviorist*. Chicago, IL: University of Chicago Press.
Metzger, J. (2014). Commentary. *EPA*, 46, 1001–1011.
Moroni, S. (2007). Planning, liberty and the rule of law. *Planning Theory*, 6(2), 146–163.
Moroni, S. (2010a). Rethinking the theory and practice of land-use regulation: Towards nomocracy. *Planning Theory*, 9(2), 137–155.

Moroni, S. (2010b). An evolutionary theory of institutions and a dynamic approach to reform. *Planning Theory*, 9(4), 275–297.
Moroni, S. (2014). Two different theories of two distinct spontaneous phenomena: Orders of actions and evolution of institutions in Hayek. *Cosmos + Taxis*, 1(9), 9–23.
Mossberger, K., & Stoker, G. (2001). The evolution of urban regime theory: The challenge of conceptualization. *Urban Affairs Review*, 36(6), 810–835.
Neuman, M. (2012). The image of the institution: A cognitive theory of institutional change. *Journal of the American Planning Association*, 78(2), 139–156.
Nonet, P., & Selznick, P. (1978). *Law and Society in Transition: Towards a Responsive Law*. New York: Harper & Row.
Ostrom, E. (1990). *Governing the Commons: The Evolution of Institutions for Collective Action*. Cambridge: Cambridge University Press.
Peck, J. (2013). Neoliberal suburbanism: Frontier space. *Urban Geography*, 32(6), 884–919.
Pierson, P. (2000). Increasing returns, path dependence, and the study of politics. *American Political Science Review*, 94(2), 251–267.
Porter, L. (2006). Rights or containment? The politics of Aboriginal cultural heritage in Victoria. *Australian Geographer*, 37(3), 355–377.
Rijswick, M. van, & Salet, W. (2012). Enabling the contextualization of legal rules in responsive strategies to climate change. *Ecology and Society*, 17(2), 18. Retrieved from: http://dx.doi.org/10.5751/ES-04895-170218.
Salet, W. (2002). Evolving institutions: An international exploration into planning and law. *Journal of Planning Education and Research*, 22(1), 26–35.
Salet, W. (2014). The authenticity of spatial planning knowledge. *European Planning Studies*, 22(2), 293–305. Retrieved from: http://dx.doi.org/10.1080/09654313.2012.741567.
Salet, W. (2016). Reinventing Strategic Spatial Planning: A Critical Act of Reconstruction. In L. Albrechts, A. Balducci & J. Hillier (Eds.), *Situated Practices of Strategic Planning* (pp. 373–385). Oxon, UK: Routledge.
Salet, W. (2018, forthc.). *Public Norms and Aspirations: The Turn to Institutions in Action*. New York: Routledge.
Salet, W., Bertolini, L., & Giezen, M. (2012). Complexity and uncertainty: Problem or asset in decision making of mega infrastructure projects. *IJURR*, 37(6), 1984–2000.
Salet, W., & Savini, F. (Guest Editors) (2015). Theme issue environment & planning C: Urban periphery. *Environment & Planning C*, 33(3), 444–551.
Savini, F. (2012). Who makes the (new) metropolis? Cross-border coalition and urban development in Paris. *Environment and Planning A*, 44(8), 1875–1895. Retrieved from: http://dx.doi.org/10.1068/a44632.
Savini, F., Majoor, S., & Salet, W. (2014). Dilemmas of planning: Intervention, regulation and investment. *Planning Theory*, 44(8), 1875–1895. Retrieved from: http://dx.doi.org/10.1177/1473095214531430.
Savini, F., & Salet, W. (2016). *Planning Projects in Transition: Interventions, Regulations and Investments*. Hamburg: Jovis.
Savitch, H.V., & Kantor, P. (2002). *Cities in the International Marketplace*. Princeton, NJ: Princeton University Press.
Scharpf, F.W. (1997). *Games Real Actors Play*. Emeryville, CA: Avelon Publishing.
Schön, D. (1983). *The Reflective Practitioner: How Professionals Think in Action*. London: Temple Smith.
Sorensen, A. (2015). Taking path dependence seriously: An historical institutionalist research agenda in planning history. *Planning Perspectives*, 30(1), 17–38.
Stone, C. N. (1989). *Regime Politics: Governing Atlanta, 1946–1988*. Lawrence, KS: University of Kansas Press.
Stone, C. N. (2005). Looking back to look forward: Reflections on urban regime analysis. *Urban Affairs Review*, 40(3), 309–341.
Swyngedouw, E., Moulaert, F., & Rodriguez, A. (2002). Neoliberal urbanization in Europe: Large-scale urban development projects and the new urban policy. *Antipode*, 34(3), 542–577.
Swyngedouw, E., & Kaika, M. (2014). Urban political ecology: Great promises, deadlock… and new beginnings? *Documents d'Analisi Geogràfica*, 60(3), 459–481.
Talen, E. (2004). *City Rules: How Regulations Affect Urban Form*. Washington, DC: Island Press.
Thelen, K. (2004). *How Institutions Evolve: The Political Economy of Skills in Germany, Britain, The United States and Japan*. Cambridge: Cambridge University Press.
Thompson, E. P. (1963). *The Making of the English Working Class*. Harmondsworth: Penguin Books.
Verloo, N. (2015). Develop Stories, Develop Communities: Narrative Practice to Analyze and Engage in Urban Conflict. In E. Gualini (Ed.), *Planning/Conflict: Critical Perspectives on Contentious Urban Developments*. London: Routledge.

Vermeulen, R. (2011). Exhibition centre development in Europe: A multidimensional historical analysis. *Tijdschrift voor Economische en Sociale Geografie*, 102(4), 441–454.

Vries, J. de (2015). Planning and culture unfolded: The cases of Flanders and the Netherlands. *European Planning Studies*, 23(11), 2148–2164.

Webber, M. M. (1964). The Urban Place and the Non-place Urban Realm. In M. M. Webber, J. W. Dyckman, D. L. Foley, A. Z. Guttenberg, W. Wheaton & C. Bauer Wurster (Eds.), *Explorations into Urban Structure* (pp. 79–153). Harmondsworth: University of Pennsylvania Press.

Zonneveld, W. (2010). Governing a Complex Delta. In H. Meyer, I. Bobbink & S. Nijhuis (Eds.), *Delta Urbanism: The Netherlands* (pp. 100–113). Chicago, IL: American Planning Association.

2
DEVELOPING A 'SOCIOLOGICAL INSTITUTIONALIST' APPROACH TO ANALYSING INSTITUTIONAL CHANGE IN PLACE GOVERNANCE

Patsy Healey[1]

Introduction

It is difficult to conceive of the concepts and practices associated with planning and place governance without some attention to 'institutions' (Verma, 2007; see also Teitz, 2007). Even if broadly understood as some kind of governance activity, planning ideas have been concerned with how to introduce and institutionalise new governing policies and practices, in order to sustain and encourage particular place forms and qualities. My definition of 'planning' as a field of inquiry and practice centres on place governance (Healey, 2010). This leads me to be interested in both conceptions of place and place qualities and how these get mobilised into public attention, and in the principles and practices of place governance through which such attention gets translated into collective action programmes and produces material and symbolic effects. I have been particularly interested in how far it is possible, through intentional collective action, to transform places and their qualities. Normatively, I have searched for knowledge and understanding about what kind of interventions in what contexts might have the potential to improve the everyday living experience of the diverse many in our continually changing societies. Such a programme of inquiry requires some consideration of 'institutions', especially given the emerging twenty-first century context of multi-layered institution-building and selective sedimentation, and shifting interactions between the spheres of state, economy and civil society. Through such inquiries, I have evolved a version of a 'sociological institutionalist' approach.[2] In contrast to some characterisations of 'sociological institutionalism' (Hall & Taylor, 1996), I have used such an approach to explore how place governance practices shift and change, and how they offer the potential for transformative change.[3]

In the planning literature, as elsewhere in the social sciences, the terms 'institutions' and 'institutionalisation' are used in several ways. Firstly, there is the question of meaning. For some, institutions are the formal structures and procedures of public bodies. In this definition, they get treated sometimes as actors, at other times as firms or organisations,[4] linking the discussion to the field of organisational sociology. In a much broader understanding, however, they become the cultural norms and practices which pattern how we behave in social situations (Giddens, 1984; March & Olsen, 1989). My contributions have tended towards the latter end of the spectrum of meanings. Secondly, institutions can be treated as an object of inquiry. However, the intention of the 'new institutionalism' is, in diverse ways, to provide a conceptual lens and analytical vocabulary through which to view institutional structures and practices (Lowndes & Roberts, 2013; Peters, 1999; Pierre et al., 2008). In my own work, I have a conceptual lens through which institutions and institutionalised practices come into view, though I am not sure how far it helps to label this as 'institutionalist'.

The various contributions to the 'new institutionalism' as discussed in the political science literature derive from very different philosophical traditions about both social organisation and about research method (Hall & Taylor, 1996; Immergut, 1998; Lowndes & Roberts, 2013; Pierre et al., 2008; Sorensen, 2017). We are familiar with these traditions from the planning literature. I therefore need to position my own thinking in relation to them. I view the worlds of place governance through a conceptual lens which is relational and constructivist – that is, I am continually aware of the complex multi-layering and intersecting of the webs of relations through which social life is accomplished, the meanings and materialities brought to life and mobilised through these relations, and the nodal points where struggles over meanings and materialities are made manifest[5]. For me, place governance is an activity brought to life through its practices, understood in a social-cultural way (see Boudreau, Chapter 16, in this volume). I therefore find the 'interpretive' methodology in policy analysis much more sympathetic to my inquiries than the 'positivist' methodology to be found in much of the 'rational choice' tradition of the 'new institutionalism'.[6] A relational approach provides a dynamic orientation, emphasising the continual flux of social and environmental processes. Institutional *change* is not the puzzle in such a conception. Instead, it becomes important to understand whether and how stabilities are created through time, and to inform judgements about whether and how to create or disrupt institutional stabilities.[7]

I am also deeply embedded in the 'practice turn' that has been emphasised in the planning field for many years. This has both an action and an intellectual implication. In terms of action, the planning tradition encourages a focus on how to address specific issues in specific contexts, wider knowledge flowing into the particular. Intellectually, it emphasises that social practices are highly complex, in which ontologies and epistemologies (subjectivities and understandings) are being continually re-negotiated but are always unfinished. This leads towards a pragmatist realisation of human ambitions. Rather than reaching for a pre-defined ideal, and hoping for some 'hard science' to underpin our judgements, the pragmatist tradition emphasises the provisionality and contingency of our understanding and our acting in the world. In parallel with, and to an extent infusing the post-structuralist arguments, a pragmatist orientation encourages experimentation, learning and reaching towards continually re-imagined 'utopias' rather than marching forward in defined steps towards a specified end (Healey, 2009). This is similar to the position recently promoted as 'strategic navigation' by Jean Hillier (2011).

In summary, and drawing on a recent exchange with Willem Salet (Summer, 2016), I have come to a dynamic, relational view of institutional formation, stabilisation and destabilisation. In such a view, institutions are the patternings which shape the discourses and practices (ways of thinking and acting) of social life. These patternings express norms, concepts/frames and values, though often so embedded that they are not discerned by those involved even by critical reflection-in-practice.[8] This is why some effort in what Foucault refers to as genealogical excavation may be needed to reveal such deep structures of thought and behaviour (Rabinow,

1984/1991; Rose, 1999). Institutions operate on many scales. In what I have come to call a 'governance landscape', there may be many arenas of activity and potentially many different institutions which are brought into conjunction at particular nodes in a complexity of networks. Within a formal organisation also, several institutions may be intersecting, and sometimes clashing with each other (e.g. within a municipal administration). Within formal organisations, but also between them, and in other ways, 'communities of practice'[9] may build up which generate a micro-level of patterned discourses and practices which themselves constitute a form of institution. How any governance interventions directed at improving place qualities work out depends a great deal on how the different institutional patternings play out in the arenas and webs of relations touched (or intended to be touched) by the intervention. So institutions are 'patterns' not 'things'. They are more like 'threads' in the way meant (as I understand it) by Deleuze and Guattari.[10] These threads carry structuring power in the way imagined by Giddens (1984). In a relational view, there is no sharp boundary between exogenous and endogenous forces. Each constitutes the other. There may, of course, be all kinds of social practices attempting to create or break 'boundaries' and 'nodes/arenas' within relational webs. Place governance, in this conception, operates in an institutionalised governance landscape, but also may exert a force to mould it.

My approach to understanding institutions therefore comes from a particular direction, with a strongly socio-cultural and transformative agenda (Healey, 2007a). Following the orientation of the planning tradition,[11] I have an explicit normative agenda, by which I mean not just a focus on social norms in a meaning given by Peters (1999, 2008), but on opportunities to turn situations in better rather than more harmful directions, with concern for the ethical dilemmas embodied in such judgements.

To conclude this introduction, I provide three questions to organise the account of my search for a form of 'sociological institutionalism'.[12]

a. How to think about the structuring role of institutions?
b. How to think about innovation and transformative change in institutions?
c. What is the implication of a 'pragmatist philosophy' for evaluating and designing institutional innovations in governance practices?

The chapter is in two main parts. The first part is an account of my personal journey towards a transformative version of a 'sociological institutionalist' approach to the analysis of place governance experiences. I should acknowledge here that André Sorensen has already provided a careful and critical account of this journey (Sorensen, 2015b). Through such an account, my intention is not only to show how one's understanding grows through the challenges of practical work and empirical encounter, but to chart a journey through the evolution of 'planning theory' over the past half-century. Secondly, I provide an outline of the main dimensions of such an approach and its implications for research and practice activity. Here I am particularly thinking of how I might write an account of my recent experiences with civil society enterprises.

Understanding the Institutional Dimensions of Place Governance: A Personal Exploration

Planning as Practised versus Planning as a Decision Process

As many planning graduates do, my first serious encounter with the planning field was in a practice – a local government planning office in London in the 1960s. The world I found myself immersed in was completely unfamiliar to me, coming as I did from an academic family and having previously worked a few years as a school teacher (Healey, 2017). It was more like the factory floor of a textile company where I had worked as a student, full of formal rules and mysterious bypassing practices. As a newcomer, I could get good answers to my 'what' and 'how' questions (What am I to do and how should I do it?), but few to my 'why' questions (Why do we do this? Why do we think this? And why don't we do that?). Today, I would know that I had entered into a small community of practice (Wenger, 1998) (a part of the planning office), in an organisation which was filled with such practice communities, all negotiating their daily lives in interaction with the wider organisational and political processes of municipal government and, importantly, all kinds of relations and commitments with the other worlds in which each of us lived – family, friends, social and political commitments, etc. – the stuff of daily office chatting. Where, I wondered, was the promise of the 'planning project', which I vaguely understood at the time as "a process by which society discovers its future" (Friedmann, 1973, p. 4), with all the transformational meaning embodied in such an idea?

In seeking to address this puzzle, I embarked on doctoral studies, which took me to examine how the idea of planning was materialised in urban contexts in Venezuela and Colombia, both experiencing significant economic and political change (Healey, 1974, 2017). My intellectual foundations for this were a mixture of the emerging academic planning literature and the broad field then called 'development studies'. In the former, I found the canon which we now know in the planning field as the rationalist tradition. While in part inspired by the insights of some of the contributors to this tradition, I was also put off by its formalised proceduralism and lack of historical and sociological sensitivity. Many of the great texts of the time – Simon, Dahl and Lindblom, Churchman, Dyckman – deserve re-reading. They are deeply infused with American pragmatism and the promise of scientific inquiry as a way forward in managing public affairs. Institutions are central to their accounts. As an example, Simon's *Administrative Behavior* (1945) is full of a rich awareness of the socio-cultural practices of organisational life. But he lacks concepts and vocabulary with which to recognise these. In the end, this body of work focuses attention on decision-making processes and their formalisation into procedural steps. Institutions fade into the background in this conception, justified by the assumption of the 'end of ideology',[13] a unified public interest, and a belief that people going about political and administrative life make individual rational calculations of their best interests.

In this conception, scientifically informed rational calculation was the way to transform policy goals into practice. The challenge was to displace bureaucratic inertia, expressed in rule-following behaviour and/or clientelistic practices. Organisations were treated in this game primarily as individual actors, able to carry the banner of social change forward. The goal-oriented process was a way to relate political concerns to technical expertise, releasing expert creativity in searching for the best way to achieve policy objectives. This pragmatic, experimental idea lives on in the new public management movement. But the pragmatism was undermined by an increasing focus in the rationalist tradition on a narrow individualism, a positivist approach to science and to calculation, a displacement of social learning and experimentation with procedural rules about how to translate new policies into actions, and a displacement of politics by technical expertise (Rose, 1999).[14] A similar narrowing has produced the practices associated with new public management, and similar ideas underpin the 'rational choice' version of institutionalism developed in political science.

None of this seemed to relate to my London planning experience, or to the complex processes of transformative change I was discovering in my Latin American work. Just as Meyerson and Banfield (1955, chapter 11), in their study of Chicago's housing programme in the 1950s, discovered that public administrations were not autonomous entities but were cut across by political party networks, so I found in Latin America that complex social, political and economic relations cut across municipal government agencies, and that several different ways of producing and regulating urban development were being 'invented' and consolidated – what I would now call processes of institutional formation and consolidation. But these could not be seen by looking just at formalised decision processes. This encouraged me subsequently to search in phenomenology for ideas about socio-cultural practices and in Marxist political economy for a greater understanding of the driving forces of social and economic change.

Planning Ideas and Planning Practices

The result of this inquiry has shaped the subsequent trajectory of how I think about the planning project. It encouraged a much richer sociological understanding as well as a critique not only of the rationalist canon, but of the kind of Marxist political economy dominant at the time (1970s). I drew from phenomenology a constructivist appreciation of social patterning and a recognition of the significant power of active agency. My understanding of actors, as creative, fallible, aesthetically sensitive and emotionally entangled, was deeply pragmatic (as I have since come to realise) but also much richer than that of the rationalists. It was no longer possible to equate an organisation easily with an actor. Nor was it possible to conceive of actors as isolated individuals. Instead, these ideas reinforced my view of people as continually inventive, responding to the challenges of life, yet inherently shaped by the social worlds into which we are born and live our lives. A key force for change lies in this tension between creative learning and aspiring and socio-cultural shaping, the dilemma captured by Marx in his aphorism: we make history but not in circumstances of our own choosing.[15]

By this time, I had returned as a researching academic to assess the practices I had been involved in in municipal government in London (Healey & Underwood, 1978). John Forester, Judith Innes and others in the United States were also setting out to push for a 'practice turn' in planning thought, away from the focus on formalised decision procedures.[16] But European social science in the 1970s was awash with Marxist political economy, which I had also drawn on in my Latin American work. I could not ignore the discussion of the structural determinants of social dynamics. My inspiration for addressing the tension between a recognition of agency power and of structuring dynamics was found in the sociologist Anthony Giddens's structuration theory (1984), which drew on both phenomenology and Marxist political economy, and was positioned in a rich grasp of sociological thought. A few others in the planning and policy analysis fields also drew inspiration from Giddens, notably Richard Bolan (1996) and John Bryson (Bryson & Crosby, 1992).

For me, this work did not mature until the 1990s, when I was also able to weave into my thinking the development of ideas which came to be known as 'regulation theory' in regional economic development, as well as the inspiring development of a relational approach to understanding spatial dynamics by the great and sadly late geographer Doreen Massey (Massey, 1984, 2005). But during the 1980s, I stepped away from a focus on planners working in municipal planning offices, to a broader analysis of the structuring of these practices by the economic and political dynamics of their contexts. In the book I and my colleagues generated from government-sponsored work on how 'development plans' were 'implemented' in practice, we outlined the first signs of what came to be seen as some kind of 'institutionalist approach' (Healey et al., 1988). We identified key variables affecting the relationship between policies in such plans and actual planning practices as related to a mixture of conflicting interests, formal tools of the planning system, institutional arrangements for interest mediation and modes of policy-making.

By the 1990s, some methodological sophistication was developing in our work. Bryson and Crosby (1992) became interested in the way policy issues moved through different kinds of settings, which they referred to as 'forums, arenas and courts'. Innes began to look at the social, intellectual and political capital developed through 'group' or 'collaborative processes' of policy development (Innes & Booher, 1999), a concept I later used as knowledge, relational and mobilisation resources in institutional capacity-building (Healey, 1998; Healey et al., 2003). From Giddens, I drew out three strands of relations which connected structure and agency – allocative relations (addressing the flows of material resources), authoritative relations (addressing regulatory practices) and the realm of ideas or discourses,[17] applying this initially in analysis of the interaction between planning practices and land and property development processes (Healey & Barrett, 1990).

These conceptual developments brought the acting subject back into view as a rich human being rather than the rational calculator of the rationalist school or the structurally determined pawn of hegemonic forces. They also allowed recognition of organisational cultures as 'assumptive worlds' (Newton, 1976) and performative practices, which helped to shape habits and routines that could become part of the taken-for-granted patterning of the daily life of governance practices. And they emphasised the complex connections between this daily life and the surrounding worlds – not just within an organisation, but beyond it to scientific and professional cultures and the institutionally complex dynamics of economic and political relations.[18] These ideas echoed pragmatist thinking in the focus on people's lived experience rather than formal ideals, and in their emphasis on promoting creativity through collaborative working. This new thinking also encouraged a view of social processes as dynamic, always changing as individuals and groups learned to do things differently, but nevertheless highlighted how institutionalised norms and habits build strong resistances to interventions which, implicitly or explicitly, challenge them. It left open how far transformative change through collective intervention is possible in governance landscapes already populated by many agencies and multiple cross-cutting networks, each filled with particular norms and discursive traditions.

Analysing Attempts at Governance Change

By the 1990s, my empirical focus, with colleagues at Newcastle, was on the sequence of urban regeneration initiatives as they played out in our region. These were driven by policy intentions to improve place qualities and, in doing so, to 'reform' governance practices. In a situation where social changes, transformations in the local economy, political realignments and land and property development challenges were interwoven in complex ways, the tensions were very evident between such reform attempts and institutionalised political and professional traditions, as well as habits of practice.

Meanwhile, the intellectual resources for analysing such dynamics were rapidly expanding through multiple and overlapping strands of post-positivist social science. I cannot review them here, but they include work expanding Foucault's concepts of governmentality, and other uses of Foucault's thinking, notably Maarten Hajer's analysis of discourse structuration and institutionalisation (Hajer, 1995); Stone's work on urban regimes, which have inspired many accounts of urban 'growth machines' (Stone, 1989); Jessop's development of a strategic-relational approach to social formation (Jessop, 2002), and the insights of Moulaert and colleagues into processes of social innovation (Moulaert et al., 2016); the concepts of the transformative effects of ideas and technologies developed by what has come to be called actor-network theory; post-structuralist ideas about the complexity of social relations and the unpredictable emergence of social and environmental futures; the ideas of the radical pluralists, notably Connolly, Mouffe and

Rancière; the developing literature on network governance, and, from a different scientific direction, the work on complexity science and complex adaptive systems. These strands of work have greatly enriched the planning literature in the past two decades, although there have been only a few links to the expanding discussion of the 'new institutionalism' in political science which several chapters in this book now engage with.

This multistranded wave of intellectual development largely shares a relational view of social and environmental processes, in which the future unfolds in ways which are difficult to foresee but yet is shaped in part by human agency. Protagonists disagree over many things, including the nature and significance of structuring dynamics, but share a recognition of the way governance relations cut across and through formal government organisational structures. They also share a focus on the power relations of governance, recognising the emancipatory as well as disciplinary role of ideas, and the power carried by rules, material resources and technologies. This fosters a research interest in the ambiguous interaction of discourses and performative practices. Such ideas also encourage an interest in how governance practices shape political identities and the formation of publics. (Institutions appear in this work primarily as the taken-for-granted norms and values which are called up and clash in governance arenas and practices.) There is a strong emphasis in the more critical strands of this diffuse literature on how to disrupt established institutional stabilities.[19]

The various strands mobilise different theories of how change in institutional landscapes comes about. They emphasise that social and environmental processes are always dynamic, evolving through multiple dimensions and pressures, and hence are unpredictable. Pressures for change can arise from many different locations, and trajectories often emerge through processes of struggle between different pressures. A key force for change arises through 'frame reflection' (Rein & Schön, 1993) and 'aspect change' (Norval, 2007), as people come to see issues and relations in new ways, challenging old assumptions, providing the ideational fuel for social movements. Deliberate programmes involving policy change may arise from such challenging movements, but also from efforts by established groups to contain such pressures. Yet some argue that 'public innovation' is possible and desirable (Torfing, 2016). There are several ways in which these ideas parallel the thinking of the pragmatists, and in some cases directly draw on them. Examples include the emphasis on transformative learning, on policies as experiments, on initiating processes of social learning and experimentation, and on the treatment of utopias as imaginative resources to inspire action rather than as programmes to be achieved in a linear way.

Overall, such ideas highlight the complex challenges of efforts at deliberate institutional innovation and design, involving the changing of practice habits as well as formal structures and rules. Yet research in these strands, most notably on the impact of new public management and neo-liberal governance ideas more generally, shows that such deliberate interventions have significant effects. Their impact on my own thinking has been less fundamental than on some younger scholars, as I was already too 'institutionalised' into my own approach. Instead, these contributions have helped sharpen my thinking and forced me to engage in continual 'translation' efforts, to see what these different concepts and vocabularies imply for what I have been interested in. The next section outlines how I have consolidated these various inspirations into a version of 'sociological institutionalism'.[20]

Conceptualising Innovation and Transformative Change in Place Governance in a 'Sociological Institutionalist' Perspective

Grounded in a constructivist and relational perspective, I understand place dynamics in a relational way. From this viewpoint, the assemblages that get to be recognised as 'places' are seen as produced by the complex interplay of diverse webs of relations, each with a distinctive spatial reach and temporal range.[21] What have become recognised as 'place qualities' are socially produced from the mixture of material experiences and socio-cultural reflections which individuals and collectivities bring forward into attention. I understand governance as a broad term, encompassing the various ways human communities seek to manage their collective affairs. All societies and groups have some form of governance and some kind of governance landscape. Formalised government (comprising the systems and organisations of formal law, politics and administration and the practices associated with this activity) is only one element of this, though in our societies it has become a very dominant one. In terms of the 'object' of transformation, I am therefore interested in the social processes through which qualitatively different place qualities get produced and qualitatively different governance landscapes come to emerge.

This leads me to a concern with the interrelation between materialities and meanings, which is why I find the 'interpretive' literature in policy analysis very helpful.[22] This tends to focus on agency, and how people produce and mobilise meanings in the context of public action. Such a focus needs to be linked to how the mobilisation of meaning relates to the mobilisation of resources and regulatory power, and in turn produces broader configurations and patterned assemblages, the phenomena usually termed 'structural power'. There is substantial debate in the social sciences on the meaning and existence of 'structures', and how they are formed. I draw on Giddens's structuration theory as a way to combine a phenomenological understanding of how meanings are produced and have effects with a recognition of the power of structuring dynamics (Giddens, 1984). His approach builds on an interactive relation between the power of agency to create new practices and meanings, which may, in time, consolidate into patterns which then shape how agents think and act.[23] As Foucault also recognises, Giddens stresses that power is not just the ability to control but the ability to achieve outcomes.[24] Since the outcomes of such power struggles cannot be predicted, the contingencies and particularities of specific situations as they evolve in time and space cannot be ignored. As a result, "if all social life is contingent, all social change is conjunctural" (Giddens, 1984, p. 245). This suggests that an analysis of innovation and transformation in place governance needs to look at the situated struggles and moments of challenge to 'the way things are, and go on' (i.e. institutional patternings), the "configurations of the minor", as Rose (1999, p. 12) calls them, to see how far these exploit and create moments of opportunity which can lead to generating new place qualities and governance dynamics in particular places and to wider impacts across a political community.[25]

Giddens's structuration theory offers more than just a recognition of the power dynamics of agency initiative and structuring processes. As already mentioned, he argues that the key linkages are to be found in the way authoritative and allocative power are used. By authoritative power, he refers not just to rules and regulations, but to the less formal and culturally positioned norms and values that are brought to bear when actions are designed, performed, discussed and evaluated. By allocative power, he refers to the processes through which material resources – land, labour and capital – are deployed to produce particular distributions of assets and possibilities, and the creation of new products. Complementing these, I have always drawn out the significance of modes of thought and framing ideas, the kind of 'discursive power' which Foucault has emphasised. These both reflect and shape how authoritative and allocative power are exercised.[26] Giddens sees institutionalisation as a process through which the patterning of authoritative and allocative power of one period gets 'stored' into the norms, routines and habits of the next. In other words, institutionalisation processes generate 'path-dependent' resistances to the next round of transformation initiatives.

So analytically we may ask: does a particular intervention reflect or challenge established rules, resource flows and framing ideas, and has it the potential to change these to produce new place qualities and new governance landscapes? Although all these three dimensions combine in any situation through which agency power is converted into and shaped by structural patternings, analytically they provide a way of thinking about how particular interventions may or may not convert into transformations. This approach also urges caution about assumptions that a particular rhetoric and set of practices promoted at the national level of formal government will then wash across a whole governance landscape in a hegemonic way. It highlights the ever-present possibility of agency resistance and re-conceptualisation of governance tasks, and the multiplicity of arenas which need to be mobilised to achieve a hegemonic domination.[27]

The underlying 'theory of change' in this approach thus stresses the indeterminacy of social change, as do many more recent post-positivist and post-structuralist conceptions. Institutions, and the patterning of authoritative and allocative power (and their discursive supports), are pushed into new trajectories as people reflect not just on how to work within their immediate social worlds, but on the institutional constitution of their society. Through critical reflection, people may mobilise critique which acts as a 'provocation' leading to disruptions and disintegration of previous arrangements. These in turn feed conjunctures which may become moments of opportunity for major shifts in the way authoritative and allocative resources are deployed.

So within this perspective, I began to develop a 'theory of change' which expands Giddens's dimensions of structuration with recognition of the multiple layering of social dynamics in a political community and its governance landscape.[28] I conceptualised these in terms of three levels of social dynamics: governance episodes (sequences of focused activity), institutionalised processes and the broader cultural movements of thought through which the wider society judges governance activity.[29] At the level of episodes, there are a multiplicity of work groups 'doing governance business' of one kind or another. Their activities are always staged in some way, and performed with a range of communicative repertoires – tropes, referents, texts, rhetorics, and they are linked to other areas of life through multiple networks. Formalised in variable ways, they draw on wider norms and practices of the setting of which they are a part, and of the wider political community and social groups to which they feel they belong. Through time, such groups may create a 'community of practice' (Wenger, 1998) among themselves with its own habits of thought and practice, but, especially if they draw on diverse external referents, there may be too many differences among them for this to happen. I refer to this level as an 'episode'.

Work groups of any kind are located within an array of governance arrangements which collectively form a governance landscape. I suggest that this landscape forms a second level or layer of activity. In an earlier paper, I referred to this level as the governance processes through which bias is mobilised (Healey, 2004). This is the level along which institutions are consolidated and recognised both in formal structures, but more importantly in the norms (values and standards), practices (ways of doing and acting, staging and performing) and discourses (modes of thinking and presenting) which are displayed in both formal justifications and explanations, and in routine activity. These may include the agencies of formal government (political parties, public administrations, formal law), but an array of other organisations from lobby groups and NGOs to protest movements and private organisations involved in surveillance and security. Such governance landscapes are thus very diverse, with conflicts within and among them, all institutionalised into repeated practices and patterns in some way. This consolidation creates a firm 'lock' on authoritative and allocative power, informed and sustained by discursive power. Such phenomena are highlighted in Foucault's concepts of disciplinary power and governmentality, and in Rancière's idea of the 'policing' of social formations (2014). To achieve transformative effects is thus a bold ambition. Even political cabinets with electoral majorities and apparent command over formal law and public resources often have a hard job shaking up a governance landscape with its sedimented cultures of practice.[30] To have transformative effects, an initiative has to find ways to penetrate into these consolidated bastions.

But governance landscapes are never static. They continually evolve – through internal changes generated by conflicts and new challenges, the experience of innovative episodes showing different ways of doing things, and also through the shifting judgements of the wider civil sphere[31] of which they are a political expression. Through the various media, through voting, through consultation processes, through informal discussions in the flow of life, people are continually evaluating what goes on in a governance landscape, commenting and debating what institutions are doing. This civil sphere, in which people express their political subjectivity and sense of citizenship, is infused with diverse discourses, norms, performative practices and many conflicting positions and viewpoints, though never static and always potentially challenging. Yet it draws together into a 'common realm' all those who feel an allegiance to a political community and seek 'voice' within it. Such political communities may themselves be multi-scalar and overlapping with other political communities, in a complex fabric fraught with tensions between scales and domains. The power of this civil sphere lies in the legitimacy it gives to the governance institutions which operate in the name of a political community. This power (or force and/or energy) operates especially through meanings, conceptions and discourses and especially exploits gaps experienced between rhetoric and realities. Many governance institutions have developed sophisticated practices for manipulating what people think about them, but yet they have to respond if trust and legitimacy erodes. The critical pressure from the civil sphere may thus act as a trigger for episodes of innovation and add weight to their strength as a force changing aspects of governance landscapes. These three levels are summarised in Table 2.1.

In a Conference paper in 2003, I then combined the concepts of structuring relations with that of three levels of power to analyse the transformative potential of a series of interventions aimed to reform urban governance in the city of Newcastle, UK (Healey, 2006).

Figure 2.1 shows the general diagram used to analyse each initiative. This relates a conception of levels to the dynamics of authoritative, allocative and discursive power. Transformative change in a governance landscape shifts the discourses and practices of governance institutions, and the way these are evaluated and legitimated in the wider civil sphere. Such processes evolve through time, often at different speeds in different parts of a governance landscape, and involve frequent struggles, as particular agencies and groups of actors seek to innovate or resist in

Table 2.1 Analysing initiatives in governance change

Level	Dimension
Specific episodes	*Actors* – key players – positions, roles, strategies and interests
	Arenas – institutional sites
	Ambiences and interactive practices – communicative repertoires
Governance processes through which bias is mobilised (governance institutions)	*Networks and coalitions*
	Stakeholder selection processes
	Discourses – framing issues, problems, solutions, interests, etc.
	Practices – routines and repertoires for acting
	Specification of laws, formal competences and resource flow principles
Governance cultures	*Range of accepted modes of governance*
	Range of embedded cultural values
	Formal and informal structures for policing discourses and practices

Source: Healey (2006, p. 306)

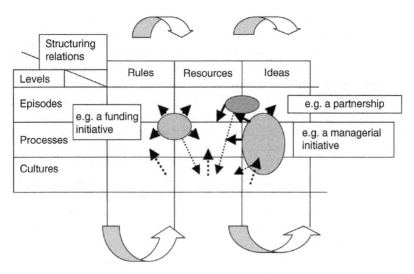

Figure 2.1 Transformation initiatives in governance dynamics
Source: Healey (2004, p. 3)

the face of pressures to change. Initiatives 'outside the state' are continually confronted with efforts from established governance agencies to shape the discourses of the civil sphere and generate their own innovations (Rose, 1999). 'Disciplining' effects and 'co-option' are ever-present possibilities.

Transformative change happens, in this approach, as the broad force for social change accumulates when innovative episodes and technologies combine with upwelling cultural sensibilities to undermine embedded institutional practices. Such transformative moments may arise in multiple institutional sites, and are highly variable in space and time (Gonzalez & Healey, 2005, p. 2065). So also are the trajectories of change. Unfolding the stories of pressures and possibilities for transformative change in governance landscapes therefore requires historically informed longitudinal research.

In summary, then, the 'sociological institutionalist' approach presented here develops from a constructivist and relational ontology and an epistemology which recognises the provisional and multiple ways of knowing and learning from experience which inform governance action. A relational view of the world emphasises the webs of relations or 'entangled meshwork' (Ingold, 2011) which constitute any set or system of governance relations, and the processes by which such sets develop and institutionalise (i.e. create patterns in) ways of thinking and acting. Such webs of relations, with their arenas/nodes and complex intersections, built from past patternings live on only if continually revived in ongoing discourses and performative practices, yet there is always a degree of re-interpretation in these revivals. In Table 2.2, I summarise the implications of such an approach into a set of focusing elements for the study of place governance practices and for those actively seeking to shift such practices to achieve better outcomes of some kind.

The various activities which make up place governance touch people along many dimensions in the flow of life experience. Place governance practices are an important arena of inquiry for understanding how the micro-politics of daily life-in-place generates an experience of living in wider worlds of complex multistranded struggles over values, resource flows and regulation.

Table 2.2 Analysing transformative change with a relational 'sociological institutionalist' approach

Intellectual challenges	Focus: The transformative possibilities and constraints
Problematisation – the object, subject and setting of attention	In that particular time and place, what is at issue, for whom and why? Why is intervention considered? What improvements are sought and could be sought? What values are or could be in play?
Contextualisation – mapping a dynamic governance landscape	What sets/systems of relations are in play? What is their spatial and temporal reach? What are their individual power dynamics and evolutionary trajectories? Who speaks 'for' them? How do the sets and systems intersect and produce key arenas/nodal points in a governance landscape? Where do formal organisations of government fit? Where do the sets and arenas which are the focus of research/practice attention fit in this evolving picture?
Unit of analysis	One or more key relations, with some kind of evolving morphology, and the deployment of rules, resources and ideas within them.
Analytical emphasis	The evolving patterning of these relations as reflected in rules, resources, discourses and practices; their power dynamics; their implications for 'what is at issue' and who is affected.
Transformative potential	The levers of change available – through authoritative, allocative and discursive power, and their potential in relation to the particular context and issue(s) at stake; and the scale of change which such levers are likely to achieve.
Evaluation/Design	How broad and deep are the impacts of the interventions likely to be, over what range of relations? What values are advanced and which neglected? Who gains and loses? What could be done to make a difference, at what scale and for whom, given the issue(s) at stake?

Source: Healey

It also provides a revealing window on how formal political and policy interventions aimed to 'reform' governance practices actually flow, in specific situations, in floods or trickles, into these practices and into people's lives. A researcher can never expect to grasp the whole of the dynamic complexity of any situation. Instead, the researcher arrives with a magnifying lens, focused initially by an initial problem/problem situation. A research inquiry then sets up a probe into the relational complexity (Lindblom, 1990), drawing particular relations and conjunctions out of the complexity for intense scrutiny. Then, placing them back into the complexity and completing the study, the lens can shift to another puzzle or problem, perhaps highlighted by the previous study. In my current work on civil society enterprises (CSEs), for example, I have a phenomenon and a problematisation: How do such enterprises sustain themselves through time? What does it take to manage the trick of institutionalising while maintaining creative flexibility? What are their wider impacts and transformative possibilities in the multi-scalar governance landscapes of which they are a part? But I will have to choose whether to focus on a single CSE, or take a comparative approach, and to select some episodes, perhaps because they may be 'critical junctures', and even narrow down to particular activities, such as the relations surrounding housing provision, energy supply or welfare services. The important thing, however, is never to cut off awareness of the wider sets of relations which are outside the magnifying lens, as they can never be completely 'isolated' from the specific matter of inquiry.

An actor in place governance practice, however, cannot afford such selectivity. The focusing framework becomes instead a resource for ongoing reflection as the challenges of practice unfold. It encourages continual revising and reframing of assumptions and understandings about what is going on, and about the art of the possible, honing that deeply pragmatist idea, the 'art of practical judgement'.

The Key Questions Reviewed
The Structuring Role of Institutions

The approach I have outlined recognises structuring forces, but also brings the acting subject into view.[32] Just as economic relations are not the only source of structuring dynamics (as cultural and political associations of many kinds are also significant), so acting subjects (agency) are motivated by more than their supposed or expressed interests and preferences. People generate agency power by adaptive creativity and moral judgement. Yet habits of thought and acting in the world which become institutionalised provide key channels through which the past shapes the future. Laid down in one period, they are powerful ways through which one generation shapes the next. These habits of thought and acting are multi-level phenomena, ranging from the practices of a particular work group to broad ways a political community comes to think about what its public life should be like. These habits then infuse particular interventions in governance change which create organisations, regulations and ways of using and distributing material resources which we associate with formal government. These may be absorbed into existing patterns of thinking and acting, but may also act as disruptive forces and in time settle into new patterns and habits. Individuals cannot escape from these shaping processes. But we can reflect on them critically, learning from systematised knowledge and from experience, and in doing so exercise emancipatory force.

It is this capacity for transformative learning, translated into collective mobilisation,[33] which generates disruptions and innovations to governance rhetorics, organisation and practices, though not necessarily in consistent ways. These processes of critical reflection and transformative learning may support but may also erode trust in established institutions, and erode the reverence (and hence legitimacy) we may have once felt for them, undermining their legitimacy. This can be deeply problematic if such erosion applies to formal law, which depends on being perceived as legitimate. Perhaps our present period in many Western countries such as the UK and the Netherlands can be characterised as a time of decay of reverence for our post-war welfare state settlements, but despite the inroads of neo-liberal ideology, new stabilities are slow in appearing. So, in summary, some institutions may be past expressions of normative patterns, but others may be innovations as a result of deliberate political reform programmes, and all are subject to the continual process of interpretation and re-interpretation as people translate broad frameworks into detailed habits of thought and practice.

Innovation and Transformative Change in Institutions

Despite many assumptions about 'sociological institutionalism' and about 'institutionalisms' in general, I have emphasised the inherent and non-linear flux of social processes, continually evolving and emergent. Attention to institutions enables exploration of the way past patternings shape emergent ones, and helps, in particular contexts, to identify dynamics which lead towards, on the one hand, increasing consolidation of particular ways of thinking and acting, and on the other, situations where old patterns are decaying, creating tensions and cracks which provide moments of opportunity, critical junctures and crises, through which new patterns ('aspect change' as Norval calls it) can emerge. For critical activists, an institutional understanding helps identify targets for disruptive strategies. For the designers of policy programmes, it helps to shape the design of interventions aimed to achieve particular ends, to make a specific difference to how things go on. Although it is possible to generalise in broad terms about shifts in economic relations, technological capabilities, cultural identifications, social formations and political allegiances, in any actual situation there are potentially multiple institutions in play, each with its own internal tensions while in tension with those around and intersecting with it. The approach I have outlined suggests that sources of institutional change can be found in how these tensions play out in specific instances and at specific scales, while change dynamics are carried forward through authoritative and allocative power and through discursive shifts.

Such a focus on the institutional patterning of processes of social change is particularly important in present times, when so many boundaries between spheres of activity are shifting. Economic relations have been pushed into formal government activity, and private sector agencies are called upon to deliver what were once considered public services. Civil society is under pressure to move into governance activity formerly provided by the state/public sector. As a result, all kinds of taken-for-granted practices and expectations are under challenge, only partially stabilised by the thin and decaying veil of neo-liberal rhetoric. It is as if the deep contradictions of our societies are being exposed to disturb our consciousness and disrupt the worlds we thought we lived in, rather than being concealed in the habits and routines of a settled order. Yet there is no general answer to how or what new institutional patternings may emerge in this era of uncertainties, and what of the past may be carried forward. Willem Salet (Chapter 1 in this volume) asks how we can escape the 'odium of conservatism'. The question might instead be: what needs to be struggled for in particular situations by those who care about inclusive and generous conditions for human flourishing in particular places?

A Pragmatic Approach to Governance Interventions

The social philosophy articulated by the early pragmatists does not flow directly into the contributions which help to fill out the kind of 'sociological institutional' approach I have articulated here, but yet a similar attitude underlies much of the thinking. Pragmatism is a method for going on in the world, where truths are never settled and laws are always provisional. Rather than deriving guidance on what should be done from some transcendent source, such as scientific knowledge or religious belief, upon which to build an idea of a specific Utopia to be achieved, a pragmatist orientation focuses on reaching for what we, as some kind of social collective, perceive to be better.[34] Utopias in this understanding help to suggest directions we could reach towards, rather than a blueprint we can specify (Levitas, 2007). This leaves it open to search for means to move in particular directions, rather than reifying particular means (such as 'nationalisation') into key goals. The pragmatist argument, these days re-worked in post-structuralist ways, emphasises the cultivation of experimental attitudes to place governance interventions, which values creative responses to particular problems and a capacity for collective learning from such experiences. It stresses that our grasp of present dynamics is always provisional, and our ideas about 'what should be done' always open to question, but yet it is reasonable to come to some agreed understanding, some 'temporary resting place' (Ploeger, 2015), on which our acting in the world can settle for a time. In the planning field, such an approach has been repeatedly asserted in the literature and, from time to time, in governance interventions. Experiences of the latter, however, underline that institutionalising such pragmatist habits of thought and practice across a governance landscape is a major undertaking. It cannot be pursued just as a professional project by experts. It involves the way political leaders think and act, and how civil society and economic actors engage with such ways of working and come to judge them as legitimate or not.

Concluding Comment

In our research on urban partnerships in the 1990s, it was evident that pressures for doing place governance differently were welling up not just from the episodes generated by policy-directed initiatives at reform, but by the demands of civil society arising from people's feelings that formal government no longer delivered to their expectations nor seemed aware of their needs and feelings. This 'disconnect' has been widely noted in the political science and policy literatures over the past two decades. It has multiple causes and is only partly the result of the so-called neo-liberal dismantling of the welfare state and the economic effects of globalisation on traditional working classes. There are also issues about the loss of identity and moral value generating feelings which are being actively exploited by narrow nationalist and 'identitarian' movements. In developing Figure 2.1, I imagined that a kind of 'cultural upwelling' could come to overwhelm the resistances of the embedded processes of formal government which had come to be seen as so distant from people's lives and needs.

Maybe such an upwelling is now underway, and maybe we are in the midst of a 'critical juncture'. If so, as academics and researchers we are all called upon to help shape what now emerges. For me, the project of 're-enchanting democracy',[35] grounded in an appreciation of people's daily life experiences of 'co-existing in shared space' (Healey, 1997/2006), which has been my normative concern for so many years, has become very urgent. The multiple challenges of coexistence in place, with all the multi-scalar relations which weave through what gets to be recognised collectively as a 'place', provides a micro-arena in which people get to learn what doing governance work could mean (Healey, 2018). It is a time now for vigorous experimentation with alternative ways of doing governance work, in ways through which people can come to recognise and learn about what is important for them about the public realm and the civic sphere. There is no quick fix here, and there are all kinds of alternative directions in which the future can unfold. Those privileged under old orders will struggle to re-group themselves, and frightening new movements may get traction. This is why I, for one, will continue working as a governance activist and trustee of a civil society enterprise in the 'place' where I live.

Notes

1 My thanks to Willem Salet, André Sorensen and other participants at the *Institutions in Action* seminar for their comments on this chapter, and for participants in the *Innovations in Spatial Planning* seminar (IRS Berlin-Erkner Feb, 2016), who contributed to a discussion that shaped the second part of this chapter.
2 I have been labelled as an 'institutionalist' (Verma, 2007) and have adopted this label myself, though until the mid-1990s I was unaware of the developing 'new institutionalism' in political science.
3 There are many similarities between the approach I have developed and Sorensen's work on 'historical institutionalism', particularly the interest in transformative change (Sorensen, 2015a, 2017). There are also parallels with several of the nine 'strands of institutionalism' identified by Lowndes and Roberts (2013, p. 31) (the normative, historical, sociological, network and discursive strands).
4 See Alexander (1995) and several chapters in Verma (2007).
5 I share many of the ideas associated with Jessop's 'strategic-relational' approach to the analysis of social formations (Jessop 2008a, 2008b), though I give less emphasis to macro structural forces and more space for micro initiatives. See Fuller (2010) who, in his work on urban partnerships, emphasises a greater role for agency within some understanding of structuring dynamics.

6 I notice this especially in the emphasis in the rational choice and related traditions on measurement and testing, versus narrative resonance (see Pierre et al., 2008).
7 See Metzger (2013) for an example of this, and Geels (2014) for a discussion in the context of the 'low carbon' or 'green' transitions literature.
8 This phenomenon limits the explanatory insights which can be gained from oral histories and autobiographical accounts on their own.
9 I understand this term in the micro-sociological way of Wenger's own work (Wenger, 1998).
10 My understanding of their work is based on discussions in Hillier (2007) and Rose (1999).
11 All academic 'disciplines' have some link to the normative concerns of the wider societies in which they exist, although often this is deeply implicit. In the case of the planning 'discipline', normative concerns are always kept explicit.
12 These are based on the questions Willem Salet set in the call for contributions to the *Institutions in Action* seminar and this book.
13 A claim made by the American sociologist Daniel Bell in 1960.
14 This experience provides a revealing instance of the selective institutionalisation of new policy ideas.
15 Marx wrote: "Men make their own history, but they do not make it as they please; they do not make it under self-selected circumstances, but under circumstances existing already, given and transmitted from the past. The tradition of all dead generations weighs like a nightmare on the brains of the living" (Marx, 1852/1978, chapter 1).
16 See Haselsberger (2017), for biographical accounts from Forester, Innes and myself.
17 Note that attention in particular to discourses is central to the Foucauldian tradition, and to interpretive policy analysis. It has been developed into a form of institutionalism by Schmidt (2012).
18 See Lowndes (2008) who notes how the field of 'urban politics' developed as a reaction to a focus on local government institutions in British political studies.
19 See Mouffe (1999) on agonism; and Rancière (2014) on politics versus the police.
20 I have used this label because I draw in particular on sociological literature and sensibilities.
21 See Healey (2004, 2006, 2007b).
22 Hajer & Wagenaar (2003); Wagenaar (2011); see also Bevir & Rhodes (2015).
23 Giddens's project at this time was partly to challenge prevailing structural Marxist theories of structural causation, and linear evolutionary theories of development.
24 Giddens in 1984 considered Foucault's work as giving too little emphasis to the power of agents to challenge and exploit opportunities to change institutionally embedded power, yet this was an important theme in Foucault's work (Tully, 2008).
25 The concept of 'moments of opportunity' comes from the social movement literature, but is very similar to Sorensen's concept of 'critical junctures' (Sorensen, 2017).
26 I used this first in an approach to analysing land and property dynamics (Healey & Barrett, 1990). But see also Healey (1997/2006).
27 The limits of the extent to which the so-called 'neo-liberal project' has achieved a hegemonic position provide a rich example of such tensions. See Fuller, (2010); Holden & Scierri, (2015); Sager (2012, 2015).
28 See especially Gonzalez & Healey (2005); see also Healey (2004, 2006).
29 My notion of the three levels was in part a re-working of Lukes (1974). There are some parallels with the levels used in the ideas about a multi-level perspective, developed in the 'sustainability transitions' literature (Geels, 2011).
30 Fuller (2010) provides a revealing account of these tensions in the urban regeneration initiatives of the 2000s UK Labour government.
31 I take this term from Alexander (2006).
32 Along with Jessop (2008a, 2008b), I also emphasise the importance of working with a structure/agency relationship, which seems to be neglected in many of the contributions to Pierre et al. (2008). But unlike Jessop, I do not think that capitalist economic relations are the only ones which shape social formations in contemporary societies.
33 This links to arguments about the role of critical reflection urged on individual actors by Schön (1983), and more generally converted into social movements disrupting the 'police' with 'active politics' as conceived by Rancière (2014), as well as into the ideological programmes which often inform policy innovations.
34 A direction sought for the planning field by Campbell et al. (2014).
35 Eva Sorensen and Jacob Torfing organised an insightful seminar originally with this name in 2009. See also Healey (2012).

References

Alexander, E. R. (1995). *How Organizations Act Together – Interorganizational Coordination in Theory and Practice*. Luxembourg: Gordon and Breach.
Alexander, J. C. (2006). *The Civil Sphere*. Oxford: Oxford University Press.
Bevir, M., & Rhodes, R. (2015). *The Routledge Handbook of Interpretive Political Science*. London: Routledge.
Bolan, R. (1996). Planning and Institutional Design. In S. Mandelbaum, R. Burchell & L. Mazza (Eds.), *Explorations in Planning Theory* (pp. 497–513). New Brunswick, NJ: Center for Urban Policy Research.
Bryson, J., & Crosby, B. (1992). *Leadership in the Common Good: Tackling Public Problems in a Shared Power World*. San Francisco, CA: Jossey Bass.
Campbell, H., Malcolm T., & Watkins, C. (2014). Is there space for better planning in a neoliberal world? Implications for planning practice and theory. *Journal of Planning Education and Research*, 34(11), 45–59.
Friedmann, J. (1973). *Re-Tracking America: A Theory of Transactive Planning*. New York: Anchor Press.
Fuller, C. (2010). Crisis and institutional change in urban government. *Environment and Planning A*, 42(5), 1121–1137.
Geels, F. W. (2011). The multi-level perspective on sustainability transitions. *Environtmental Innovation and Social Transitions*, 1, 24–40.
Geels, F. W. (2014). Regime resistance against low-carbon transitions: Introducing politics and power into the multi-level perspective. *Theory, Culture & Society*, 31(5), 21–40.
Giddens, A. (1984). *The Constitution of Society*. Cambridge: Polity Press.
Gonzalez, S., & Healey, P. (2005). A sociological institutionalist approach to the study of innovation in governance capacity. *Urban Studies*, 42(11), 2055–2070.
Hajer, M. (1995). *The Politics of Environmental Discourse*. Oxford: Oxford University Press.
Hajer, M., & Wagenaar, H. (Eds.). (2003). *Deliberative Policy Analysis: Understanding Governance in the Network Society*. Cambridge: Cambridge University Press.
Hall, P., & Taylor, R. (1996). Political science and the three institutionalisms. *Political Studies*, XLIV(5), 936–957.
Haselsberger, B. (Ed.). (2017). *Encounters in Planning Thought*. London: Routledge.
Healey, P. (1974). Plaweand change. *Progress in Planning*, 2(3), 143–237.
Healey, P., & Underwood, J. (1978). Professional ideals and planning practice. *Progress in Planning*, 9(2), 73–127.
Healey, P. (1997/2006). *Collaborative Planning: Shaping Places in Fragmented Societies*. London: Macmillan.
Healey, P. (1998). Building institutional capacity through collaborative approaches to urban planning. *Environment and Planning A*, 30(9), 1531–1456.
Healey, P. (2004). Creativity and urban governance. *Policy Studies*, 25(2), 87–102.
Healey, P. (2006). Transforming governance: Challenges of institutional adaptation and a new politics of space. *European Planning Studies*, 14(3), 299–319.
Healey, P. (2007a). The New Institutionalism and the Transformative Goals of Planning. In N. Verma (Ed.), *Planning and Institutions* (pp. 61–87). Oxford: Elsevier.
Healey, P. (2007b). *Urban Complexity and Spatial Strategies: Towards a Relational Planning for Our Times*. London: Routledge.
Healey, P. (2009). The pragmatist tradition in planning thought. *Journal of Planning Education and Research*, 28(3), 277–292.
Healey, P. (2010). *Making Better Places: The Planning Project in the Twenty-First Century*. London: Palgrave Macmillan.
Healey, P. (2012). Re-enchanting democracy as a way of life. *Critical Policy Studies*, 6(1), 19–39.
Healey, P. (2016). Transforming governance: Challenges of institutional adaptation and a new politics of space. *European Planning Studies*, 14(3), 299–319.
Healey, P. (2017). Finding my way: A life of inquiry into planning, urban development processes and place governance. In B. Haselsberger (Ed.), *Encounters in Planning Thought*. London: Routledge.
Healey, P. (2018). Creating public value through caring for place. *Policy and Politics*, 46(1), 65–79.
Healey, P., & Barrett, S. M. (1990). Structure and agency in land and property development processes. *Urban Studies*, 27(1), 89–104.
Healey, P., Magalhaes, C. de, Madanipour, A., & Pendlebury, J. (2003). Place, Identity and Local Politics: Analysing Partnership Initiatives. In M. Hajer & H. Wagenaar (Eds.), *Deliberative Policy Analysis: Understanding Governance in the Network Society* (pp. 60–87). Cambridge: Cambridge University Press.

Healey, P., McNamara, P., Elson, M., & Doak, J. (1988). *Land Use Planning and the Mediation of Urban Change*. Cambridge: Cambridge University Press.

Hillier, J. (2007). *Stretching Beyond the Horizon: A Multiplanar Theory of Spatial Planning and Governance*. Aldershot: Ashgate.

Hillier, J. (2011). Strategic navigation across multiple planes: Towards Deleuzian-inspired methodology for strategic spatial planning. *Town Planning Review*, 82(5), 503–528.

Holden, M., & Scierri, A. (2015). Justification, compromise and test: Developing a pragmatic sociology of critique to understand the outcomes of urban redevelopment. *Planning Theory*, 14(4), 360–383.

Immergut, E. M. (1998). The theoretical core of the new institutionalism. *Politics and Society*, 26(1), 5–34.

Ingold, T. (2011). *Being Alive: Essays in Movement, Knowledge and Description*. London: Routledge.

Innes, J., & Booher, D. (1999). Consensus-building as role-playing and bricolage. *Journal of the American Planning Association*, 65(1), 9–26.

Jessop, B. (2002). Institutional re(turns) and the strategic-relational approach. *Environment and Planning A*, 33(7), 1213–1235.

Jessop, B (2008a). Institutions and Institutionalism in Political Economy: A Strategic-Relational Approach. In J. Pierre, B. G. Peters & G. Stoker (Eds.), *Denating Institutionalism* (pp. 210–231). Manchester: Manchester University Press.

Jessop, B. (2008b). *State Power*. Cambridge: Polity Press.

Levitas, R. (2007). Looking for the blue: The necessity of utopia. *Journal of Political Ideology*, 12(3), 289–306.

Lindblom, C. E. (1990). *Inquiry and Change: The Troubled Attempt to Understand and Shape Society*. New Haven, CT: Yale University Press.

Lowndes, V. (2008). Urban Politics: Institutional Differentiation and Entanglement. In J. Pierre, G. Peters & G. Stoker, *Debating Institutionalism* (pp. 152–175). Manchester: Manchester University Press.

Lowndes, V., & Roberts, M. (2013). *Why Institutions Matter: The New Institutionalism in Political Science*. London: Palgrave Macmillan.

Lukes, S. (1974). *Power: A Radical View*. London: Macmillan.

March, J. G., & Olsen, P. (1989). *Rediscovering Institutions: The Organizational Basis of Politics*. New York: Free Press.

Marx, K. (1852/1978). *The Eighteenth Brumaire of Louis Bonaparte*. New York: W.W. Norton & Company.

Massey, D. (1984). *Spatial Divisions of Labour*. London: Macmillan.

Massey, D. (2005). *For Space*. London: Sage.

Metzger, J. (2013). Raising the regional leviathan: A relational-materialist conceptualization of regions-in-becoming as public-in-stabilization. *International Journal of Urban and Regional Research*, 37(4), 1368–1395.

Meyerson, M., & Banfield, E. (1955). *Politics, Planning and the Public Interest*. New York: Free Press.

Mouffe, C. (1999). Deliberative democracy or agonistic pluralism? *Social Research*, 66(3), 745–758.

Moulaert, F., Jessop, B., & Mehmood, A. (2016). Agency, structure, institutions, discourse (ASID) in urban and regional development. *International Journal of Urban Science*, 20(2), 167–187.

Newton, K. (1976). *Second City Politics: Democratic Processes and Descion-Making in Birmingham*. Oxford: Clarendon Press.

Norval, A. (2007). *Aversive Democracy: Inheritance and Originality in the Democratic Tradition*. Cambridge: Cambridge University Press.

Peters, G. (1999). *Institutional Theory in Political Science: The 'New Institutionalism'*. London: Continuum.

Peters, G. (2008). Institutional Theory: Problems and Prospects. In J. Pierre, G. Peters & G. Stoker (Eds.), *Debating Institutionalism* (pp. 1–21). Manchester: Manchester University Press.

Pierre, J., Peters, G., & Stoker, G. (2008). *Debating Institutionalism*. Manchester: Manchester University Press.

Ploeger, J. (2015). Impossible Common Ground: Planning and Reconciliation. In J. Metzger, P. Allmendinger & S. Oosterlynck (Eds.), *Planning Against the Political* (pp. 107–128). London: Routledge.

Rabinow, P. (Ed.). (1984/1991). *The Foucault Reader*. London: Penguin.

Rancière, J. (2014). *Hatred of Democracy*. London: Verso.

Rein, M., & Schön, D. (1993). Reframing Policy Discourse. In F. Fischer & J. Forester (Eds.), *The Argumentative Turn in Policy Analysis and Planning* (pp. 145–166). Durham, NC: Duke University Press.

Rose, N. (1999). *Powers of Freedom: Reframing Political Thought* Cambridge: Cambridge University Press.

Sager, T. (2012). *Reviving Critical Planning Theory: Dealing with Pressure, Neo-Liberalism and Responsibility in Communicative Planning*. London: Routledge.

Sager, T. (2015). Ideological traces in plans for compact cities: Is neo-liberalism hegemonic? *Planning Theory*, 14(3), 268–295.

Schmidt, V. (2012). Discursive Institutionalism: Scope, Dynamics and Philosophical Underpinnings. In F. Fischer & H. Gottweis (Eds.), *The Argumentative Turn Revisited* (pp. 85–113). Durham, NC: Duke University Press.

Schön, D. (1983). *The Reflective Practitioner*. New York: Basic Books.

Simon, H. (1945). *Administrative Behavior*. New York: Free Press.

Sorensen, A. (2015a). Taking path dependence seriously: An historical institutionalist research agenda in planning history. *Planning Perspectives*, 30(1), 17–38.

Sorensen, A. (2015b). Transforming Land and Property: Varieties of Institutionalism and the Production of Urban Space. In J. Hillier & J. Metzger (Eds.), *Connections: Exploring Contemporary Planning Theory and Practice with Patsy Healey* (pp. 423–436). Farnham: Ashgate.

Sorensen, A. (2017). New Institutionalism and Planning Theory. In M. Gunder, A. Madanipour & V. Watson (Eds.), *Routledge Handbook of Planning Theory*. London: Routledge.

Stone, C. N. (1989). *Regime Politics: Governing Atlanta, 1946–1988*. Lawrence, KS: University of Kansas Press.

Teitz, M. B. (2007). Planning and the New Institutionalism. In N. Verma (Ed.), *Planning and Institutions* (pp. 17–35). Oxford: Elsevier.

Torfing, J. (2016). *Collaborative Innovation in the Public Sector* (DSc Thesis). Roskilde: Roskilde University, Department of Society and Globalization.

Tully, J. (2008). *Public Philosophy in a New Key: Vol 1: Democracy and Freedom*. Cambridge: Cambridge University Press.

Verma, N. (Ed.). (2007). *Planning and Institutions*. Oxford: Elsevier.

Wagenaar, H. (2011). *Meaning in Action: Interpretation and Dialogue in Policy Analysis*. New York: M. E. Sharpe.

Wenger, E. (1998). *Communities of Practice: Learning, Meaning and Identity*. Cambridge: Cambridge University Press.

3
POLITICAL ARTICULATION AND HEGEMONIC PRACTICES IN THE INSTITUTIONALIZATION OF THE URBAN ORDER

Enrico Gualini

Introduction

This chapter addresses the topic of 'institutions in action' from two combined perspectives.

In the first place, it argues that the meaning of 'institutions in action' (and *a fortiori*, as I will argue, the *locus* of institutional thinking today) consists in the co-evolution of institutional orders and social practices. In so doing, it privileges an understanding of 'institutions' as knowledge-based processes and as a social construction, the contingent, processual and co-evolutive outcome of which is captured by the notion of institutions as constitutive elements of reality.

In the second place, this chapter aims at contributing to a renewed reflection on the political dimension of urban development and planning. It argues that the process by which institutions in action are constituted is 'political' in a way that is different from and challenging for traditional, classic 'institutionalist' accounts of politics. The chapter therefore explores how and in how far thinking about institutions in action can – against all apparent odds – contribute to a post-foundational and post-essentialist understanding of the political and, moreover, to a radical political-theoretical underpinning of planning theory.

The underlying thesis is that, against a wholesale critique of 'institutionalism', developments in thinking about institutions in action and about institutionalization, as key dimensions of the social construction of reality, contribute to addressing questions concerning the political dimension of planning in our times, and this not only in strictly theoretical but possibly also in pragmatic terms, in the sense of addressing the current dilemmas of planning practice. Accordingly, this contribution embraces the aim of bridging the paradigmatic divide between institutional analysis and pragmatism in current planning theory and practice. With one caveat, however: that of avoiding any normative rush – as understanding institutions in action is, above all, a critical accomplishment.

The chapter is divided in three parts. The first part is devoted to discussing the theoretical underpinnings for understanding institutions in action as defined above, and is largely based on my previous work (Gualini, 2001). The starting point resides in identifying a critical nexus between neo-institutionalist perspectives on institutions in action and key notions in use in analysing and interpreting contemporary political practices, such as governance-regulation governmentality. The second part develops from this nexus in an attempt at discussing the nature of the urban 'political' in 'post-political' times. The third part, in conclusion, remarks on the dilemmas planning faces in relation to the phenomena discussed, and warns against the pitfalls of unreflective normativism in dealing with them.

'Institutions in Action': Neo-Institutionalist Perspectives

Institutional Orders and the Institutionalization of Meaning

Focusing on institutions in action reflects the perception that institutional orders are constitutive elements of reality that are defined – and potentially contested – in ongoing dialectics of persistence and change. Such a perspective is premised on understanding institutions as processes and social constructions. This understanding puts emphasis on the symbolic-cognitive and discursive dimension of social orders, and lends ontological and epistemological primacy to these dimensions over formal or structural institutional properties – like their juridical or formal-prescriptive dimensions. It therefore emphasizes the social construction of institutional orders and the process of *institutionalization* as being defined by the interplay of a symbolic-cognitive dimension (frames, scripts, discourses, narratives, 'paradigms') and a processual-iterative dimension (prevailing strategies, routines, modes of interaction): through their degrees and articulations, their interplay defines the nature of institutional orders or regimes and their possible contingent degrees of formalization.

This sociologically informed neo-institutionalist perspective (see Gualini, 2001) is characterized by a prevailing attention to the *symbolic-cognitive dimension* of institutional phenomena, understood as collective, dynamic and co-evolutive constructs, as outcomes of experiential processes, defined at the same time by their belonging to a determined social reality and by their being constitutive of their own reality.

This bears some important implications. The first is a focus on the dynamics of institutional phenomena, that is, on aspects of institutionalization rather than on static-comparative definitions of institutions. This neo-institutionalist attitude stands in contrast with what has been defined as the 'metaphysical pathos' of classic institutionalism, characterized by the combination of a structuralist, prevailingly formalistic and static conception of institutional forms with a deterministic interpretation of institutional conduct.

The second implication is the crucial meaning attributed to the nexus between *institutions* and *action*. Attention to the dimension of agency emphasizes the micro-analytical foundations of institutional analysis. Accordingly, new institutionalism is characterized by an emphasis on the 'conditional' – constitutive and endogenously determined – rather than causal determination of agency. This implies attention to the links between the social construction of institutions and their macro-sociological effects. By this, neo-institutionalist analysis aims at bridging micro-macro divides by rejoining the interpretation of micro-sociological factors (procedures, rules, values) and macro-sociological factors (structures and organizations) of institutionalization processes. Attention to their diachronic co-determination and co-evolution highlights the nested and multidimensional character of levels of institutional analysis.

Consequently, new institutionalism tends to assume a dual 'phenomenological' and 'structuralist' connotation (cf. Jepperson, 1991; Powell & DiMaggio, 1991), in the sense – as put by Giddens (1984, p. 17) – that "social systems, as reproduced social practices, do not have 'structures' but rather exhibit 'structural properties' and that structure exists, as time-space presence, only in its instantiations in such practices and as memory traces orienting the conduct of knowledgeable human agents". Similarly, new institutionalism assumes a dialectic between their subjective foundation and their social objectivation, in as far as at the centre of the institutionalization process stands the creation of an *intersubjective* dimension of action, by which 'institutions' direct action – thus bearing a subjective dimension – while being perceived as 'external' and 'objective' (see Lanzalaco, 1995).

Institutional analysis, in this sense, is intended as a sociological inquiry into the determinations of a superior order of socially constructed realities: if institutions may be defined as social patterns or orders endowed with a certain status or property, institutionalization may thus be defined as the peculiar process of reaching this status.

Such an interpretation places emphasis on the role of symbolic-cognitive processes in the framework of a dynamic conception of institutionalization processes: on the everyday, process-like connotation of cognitive activity, driven by rules, frames, scripts and taken-for-granted procedures, which constitute the pre-analytical foundations of practical forms of action and of social conduct (Berger & Luckmann, 1966; Berger, Berger & Kellner, 1973; Meyer & Rowan, 1977; Zucker, 1977, 1987). Accordingly, institutions are seen as relatively stabilized patterns of repetitive sequences of activities, which owe their stabilization and survival to relatively self-activated and self-sustained processes. In the course of the process of institutionalization, institutions tend to assume a character of *taken-for-grantedness* (Berger & Luckmann, 1966; Zucker, 1977): the focus on institutionalization processes highlights the dimensions of *reification* and *externalization* of knowledge, which are key to the interpretation of the nexus between subjectivation and objectivation – that is, between, on the one hand, the subjective and interactive foundation of knowledge and, on the other hand, the empirically perceived stability of the social order. The social construction of meanings is defined by a movement from the knowledge of everyday life and from the prototypical intersubjective condition of face-to-face interactions – through ongoing and progressively anonymized typifications – towards the constitution of social structure as "the sum total of these typifications and of the recurrent patterns of interaction established by means of them" (Berger & Luckmann, 1966, p. 33). Institutionalization as progressive *taken-for-grantedness* develops as an outcome of forms of reciprocity, which tendentially nullify the reflexive dimension of knowledge: "[i]nstitutionalization occurs whenever there is a reciprocal typification of habitualized actions by types of actors. Put differently, any such typification is an institution" (ibid., p. 54).

As such, institutions and processes of institutionalization are understood primarily as endogenous constituents rather than as exogenous constraints of social conduct – an assumption which is key to March and Olsen's endogenist approach to new institutionalism in political science (March & Olsen, 1989) and to a new 'cultural approach' to institutionalist explanations of politics (Hall & Taylor, 1996).

Institutionalization, however, is at the same time understood as a *relative* property, which is dependent on context and contingency as well as on relationality and positionality within a specific field or domain of social practices. Exceptions and transgressions to the logic of these domains – be it in the form of a suspension of sense or of a crisis – are always potentially factors for a renewal of reflexivity.

Governance and Regulation as Emergent Institutional Orders

How does a perspective on institutions in action, as outlined above, tie into an analysis of current practices in the domain of urban politics and planning? It does so, in first instance, in as far as practices of governance and regulation represent exceptions and transgressions to a traditional, classic logic of institutions and institutional analysis.

Notwithstanding its polysemantic and ambiguous status – leading to critique to its nature as an 'empty signifier' (Offe, 2009) – there is scholarly convergence on an understanding of 'governance' and 'regulation' as notions which mark a significant difference in understanding the rationale of governing practices and of their institutional features (see Gualini, 2010). The notions of governance (plus meta-governance) and regulation have gained meaning, in particular, as they have started being used to refer to practices of 'governing' beyond 'political steering', and to specifically address forms of political agency beyond those defined in a classic, Eastonian state-centred model of the political system, mainly concerned with forms, means and processes of goal-oriented state intervention, in which the state takes an active and direct role in the production of public goods. Such an understanding of governance based on classic theory of political steering, as noted by Mayntz (1987), implied a systematic distinction between the subject and the object of steering – that is, between the 'steering capacity' of state actors, and the 'amenability to steering' of existing social subsystems. On the contrary, the emergence of a critical theory of governance marks a shift towards an understanding of 'governance' as 'regulation', intended as resulting from a mix of different forms of regulation (Mayntz & Scharpf, 1995) as well as from a combination of rationales of a variety of agents contributing to such forms of regulation in context-specific relational settings (Kooiman, 1993; Rhodes, 1996; Stoker, 1998).

The nature of 'governance' is hence neither adequately captured by looking at a simple 'extension' of traditional policymaking arenas nor by assuming it as 'other' than 'government': it is rather best defined as the situationally determined principle by which forms of regulation are re-articulated – and forms of institutional agency and policymaking redefined – in contexts that exceed formal-hierarchical arenas. Accordingly, the management of public issues is seen as being premised upon an extended but loose framework of interdependencies between governmental and non-governmental actors. In this sense, 'governance' can be defined as a public activity "concerned with the resolution of (para-)political problems (in the sense of problems of collective goal-attainment or the realisation of collective purposes)" (Jessop, 1995, p. 317) under new emergent configurations of actors, organizations and institutions that structurally involve decentralized non-state actions and initiatives stemming from the field of economic and social activities.

Governance research argues about the emergence of systems of governance as a process of re-articulation of different modes of regulation across different social sub-sectors, in which outcomes of governance/regulation are seen as emergent, that is, relatively stabilized systems of relations, and practices of governance/regulation as contingent, constitutively experimental and plural (cf. Le Galès, 1998).

Governance and regulation are intended as categories of (para-)political agency within the specific policy domains they co-constitutively contribute to define. Accordingly, governance research and regulation theory share a common historical-sociological neo-institutionalist matrix in their theoretical assumptions and analytical approach, as they refer, on the one hand, to "the complex totality of coexistent forms of collective regulation of societal relations" (Mayntz, 2004, p. 66) and as they focus, on the other hand, on the path-dependent, constitutive relationship between modes of governance/regulation and objects of governance regulation (Jessop, 1995, p. 326). In a neo-institutionalist perspective, the outcomes of governance regulation are seen as relatively stabilized patterns of relations. Practices of governance and regulation concur to modes of institutionalization of an essentially emergent, non-intentional, co-evolutive nature: in Jessop's terms, "[n]ew governance mechanisms, like new structural forms, emerge from a trial-and-error search process which operates through evolutionary variation, selection and retention. It is in this context that issues of strategic selectivity and strategic capacities are so crucial and that attention must be paid to the material and discursive appropriateness of proposed responses" (Jessop, 1995, p. 322).

It is also in this perspective, however, that critical research has as well highlighted the normative fallacy of governance practices and discourses marked by a 'problem-solving bias', that is, by a "functionalist misassumption that existing institutions have emerged in the interest of solving collective problems" (Mayntz, 2004, p. 18; see also Offe, 2009). Governance is a manifestation of a redefinition of politics and of relations of power in the changing domain of national-statehood. Understanding governance and regulation as pragmatist struggles and as emergent and contingent institutional orders premised on a legitimating framework of collective problem solving is integral to developments in critical state theory (Jessop, 2002a, 2008; see also Crouch, 2004), as it explores the way different manifestations of a 'crisis' of the national-state define a shift from a 'logic of sovereignty' to a 'logic of regulation' in the nature and forms of state agency and in their discursive legitimation.

Public policy is defined not solely or primarily by formal principles of authority, but by new forms of agency for which a Gramscian notion of the state 'in the integral sense', as well as a focus on the emergence of 'state effects', is more adequate than reference to formal state structures. This also affects the specific forms of spatiality and the spatial features of state agency: accordingly, it requires moving beyond an understanding of state space in the 'narrow' sense, as "the state's distinctive form of spatial organization as a discrete, territorially centralized, self-contained, and internally differentiated institutional apparatus", in favour of an understanding of state space in the 'integral' sense, as "the territory-, place-, and scale-specific ways in which state institutions are mobilized to regulate social relations and to influence their locational geographies" (Brenner, 2004, p. 78). In a perspective of the state in an 'integral' sense, practices of governance and regulation are an expression of processes of restructuring of the modes and rationales of state action that affect "the changing geographies of state intervention into socio-economic processes within a given territorial jurisdiction" but also encompass "the indirect socio-spatial effects that flow from apparently aspatial policies" (Brenner, 2004, pp. 78–79; see also Painter, 2010).

We can see therefore a convergence between new institutionalism and critical-interpretive policy analysis around the way the changing nature of the political is being thematized by critical governance and regulation research. Both the new institutionalism and critical-interpretive policy analysis pursue an understanding of 'meaning in action' and of the way meaningful knowledge is constituted in the domain of public policy (Fischer, 2003; Stone, 2002; Wagenaar, 2011; see also Voß & Freeman, 2015). Both contribute to directing attention to an extended range of factors which define and/or influence governance and policy practices in specific political-institutional environments: for example, the role of informal norms and codes of conduct, their symbolic-cognitive, cultural and discursive dimensions, their non-deterministic relationship to 'structure', as well as the importance of 'rules-in-use' and their mutual, non-hierarchical relationships. Moreover, both have developed new analytical and explanatory perspectives on the features taken by governance and public policy in specific political-institutional environments: the discursive framing and patterning of conduct, the role of institutional logics and routines of action, and the tension established between factors of path dependency and factors for change.

Most importantly, new institutionalism and critical-interpretive policy analysis share a move towards endogenist interpretations of political-institutional orders and of processes of policy and institutional change, re-directing attention from exogenous to endogenous factors and modes of policy and institutional change (or resistance to change). Rather than primarily being focused on the formal or structural aspects, their interest is on the emergence, contingent consolidation and change of practices and discourses which define the rationale of policymaking and institutional agency in concrete contexts of action.

This attitude is consistent with political theory assumptions which ground a post-foundational understanding of governance and policy. Against a reified conception of institutions as 'fixed' frameworks for agency, governance and policy are conceived as contingent orders emerging through the articulation of the various contingent meanings which inform actors' conducts. This conception requires an action-centred analysis of governance and policy practices as social constructions which emerge through the ability of actors to constitute meanings and to constitute alliances that sustain these meanings in response to perceived challenges and dilemmas (see Bevir, 2003; Bevir & Rhodes, 2003, 2006).

It is for this reason, moreover, that we should view emergent governance and regulation practices and their processes of institutionalization in a perspective of hegemony theory and governmentality (see Gualini, 2010). Governance practices redefine the sphere of the 'political' according to a new discursive space, made of discursive structures and of articulatory practices which tend to reconstitute and reorganize social relations according to representations that are no longer available or no longer possible within a classic state-centred institutionalist paradigm. Governance practices raise claims for new pragmatic sources of legitimation while, by the same token, produce legitimation by the performativity of a discursive formation which becomes increasingly hegemonic. Even as it deploys 'empty signifiers', discourse on governance articulates the field of historical contingency and related societal forces as historical necessities sustained by universal meanings (Laclau & Mouffe, 1985). It is at this point that my arguments on governance and institutions in action turn towards exploring some possible implications in a perspective of critical research on the urban *political*.

Urban 'Institutions in Action': Exploring the Dis-/Re-Articulation of Urban Political Orders

In what follows, my arguments on institutions in action turn towards an attempt at outlining a critical research perspective on the urban *political*. In this perspective, the notion of 'governance' as discussed above constitutes a key theoretical nexus. In fact, the following discussion is premised on an understanding of 'governance' as summary term that identifies emergent practices of governing, which develop under conditions of institutional uncertainty and change and which affect the rationales of state policy in terms of a need for jointly redefining sites, objects and modes of regulation (Bevir, 2003; Bevir & Rhodes, 2003, 2006; Gualini, 2010; Jessop, 2002a, 2002b).

In contrast to approaches that study urban governance and view its practices (in an analytical perspective) as an expression of a changing political-institutional order in cities, or (in a normative perspective) as an expression of a political, institutionally enabled practice of 'social innovation', I propose here to view urban governance (in a critical-interpretive perspective) as an expression of a hegemonic struggle for establishing an urban order (see Gualini, 2015). This perspective partly differs from an understanding of governance as a static, or institutionally established, expression of the 'post-political' (cf. Metzger, Allmendinger & Oosterlynk, 2015): it rather directs attention to governance as a series of co-evolutive practices, co-constitutively involved in hegemonic struggles for defining a political order.

Adopting such a view allows one to understand urban governance policy and planning as practices of *policing* and practices producing *policing effect*s. Urban policy and planning are part of regimes of practices which constitute the political sphere according general formal-institutional and legal principles of liberal democracy but, as such, they also partake in defining the partition between 'politics' as 'the political' (see Rancière, 1995, 1999; see also Mouffe, 2000, 2013). In Mouffe's terms, the sphere of politics is constituted by "the ensemble of practices, discourses and institutions that seek to establish a certain order and to organize human coexistence in conditions which are always potentially conflicting", as they pertain to the dimension of the political. This is, in turn, the dimension of antagonism that is ever-present and can never be fully suppressed in the sphere of social relations (Mouffe, 2013, pp. 2–3). In similar, if terminologically distinctive terms, Rancière defines the 'police' as "the set of procedures whereby the aggregation and consent of collectivities is achieved, the organization of powers, the distribution of places and roles, and the systems for legitimizing this distribution" (Rancière, 1999, p. 28). 'Police' is not the same as state apparatus, but rather the ensemble of *dispositifs* that define "the configuration of the perceptible in which one or the other is inscribed" (ibid., p. 29). Contestation and conflict, the expression of dissent, on the other hand, are expressions of 'the political' (Mouffe) and of 'politics' (Rancière), as premised on the insurgence and the radical ineluctability of pluralism, and on "the dimension of antagonism that the pluralism of values entails and its ineradicable character" (Mouffe, 2000, p. 99).

Urban policy and planning constitute practices which articulate the inherent antagonistic nature of social relations. In doing so, they constitutively partake in a field of hegemonic practices. I understand here hegemonic practices in line with Laclau and Mouffe's critical analysis (1985) of the role of discursive practices in constituting hegemony. Hegemonic practices are "practices of articulation through which a given order is created and the meaning of social institutions is fixed" (Mouffe, 2013, p. 2; see also Laclau & Mouffe, 1985, p. 103 ff.). According to this understanding, the order that confers a disciplining frame to urban policy and governance, that constitutes them as a policing effect, constitutes "the temporary and precarious articulation of contingent practices" (Mouffe, 2013, p. 2) which are always potentially subject to challenge by antagonistic practices.

Hegemonic practices are defined by a dialectic of articulation between recursive practices of *dis-articulation* and *re-articulation*. The capacity of political subjects to dis- and re-articulate a given situation, and to transform it into a new configuration, is crucial to hegemonic struggles. The articulation of the urban order expressed by hegemonic practices is always subject to the possibility of dis-articulation as the result of challenges by antagonistic and/or counter-hegemonic practices. Conversely, there is always the possibility of a re-articulation of an order as result of the re-appropriation of elements of social antagonism within hegemonic practices. This is the nature of hegemonic practices: that of a discursive struggle for meaning and for its social validation, for the establishment of "an order of the visible and the sayable" (Rancière, 1999, p. 29) in a field of differently constituted subject positions.

In this perspective, *antagonism* and *hegemony* are necessary and dialectically interrelated dimensions of the political in a struggle for establishing and for questioning a contingent political order. While practices of social antagonism develop forms of dis-articulation which challenge the urban order, urban policy and planning develop practices which attempt a re-articulation of this order.

'Governance Innovation' and Hegemonic Practices

The perspective sketched above allows one to view 'governance innovation' as a set of policy and planning practices by which the hegemonic articulation of an urban order is attempted and possibly contingently realized.

In a context where no 'fixed' or institutionalized framework for agency is given, governance is experimental and emergent. This conception is in line with an anti-foundational understanding of governance practices. Following Bevir and Rhodes (Bevir, 2003; Bevir & Rhodes, 2003, 2006), and leaning on Rancière's notion of 'police' (Rancière, 1999), I understand governance and planning as constituents of an *emergent policing order*. Against a reified conception of institutions as 'fixed' frameworks for agency, this implies adopting an agency-centred analysis of governance practices. In a context of 'decenteredness' and indeterminacy, governance and planning are constituted by assemblages of practices, narratives and beliefs by which actors attempt to constitute meanings, and alliances that sustain these meanings, in response to arising challenges and dilemmas.

These challenges and dilemmas include facing antagonistic and counter-hegemonic movements. Insurgent urban practices have gained much attention in critical urban studies. In particular, the appropriation of urban spaces is seen a key performative moment of political affirmation and of reconstitution of the *political*. In line with this interpretation, counter-hegemonic urban movements, as constitutive of 'spaces of resistance', highlight their conflicting relationship with the unidirectional model of urban development driven by neo-liberalization tendencies. Claims for urban space are an important part of counter-hegemonic mobilizations to address social problems and social inequalities through challenging hegemonic power (Laclau & Mouffe, 1985; Rancière, 1995, 1999), both from a historical perspective (Castells, 1983) and in the context of neo-liberal trends in urban policies (Brenner & Theodore, 2002; Leitner, Peck & Sheppard, 2006). As such, they are seen as contributing to a re-politicization of urban space (Dikeç, 2007; Holston, 2008; Swyngedouw, 2009, 2011).

However, little attention has been devoted yet to exploring the evolutionary nature of current urban governance in terms of its capacity to appropriate and transform these tensions within its practices. As critical contributions to the analysis of 'neo-liberal' urban policy practices highlight, this reading is consistent with an interpretation of neo-liberalism as a polyvalent emergent construct (Jessop, 2002b, p. 453) involving not only strategic-relational practices of restructuring market-state relations and establishing new patterns of economic, political and social organization, but also developing complex discursive formations in their support.

The features of advanced phases of neo-liberalization processes define it as a 'roll-out neo-liberalism' that addresses the reconstruction of new modes of regulation, by which "[r]egulatory landscapes are continually made and remade through this intense, politically contested interaction between *inherited* institutional forms and policy frameworks and *emergent* strategies of state spatial regulation" (Brenner & Theodore, 2002, p. 356).

According to such a reading, neo-liberal policies increasingly include moments of active co-optation and the incorporation of democratic rhetoric and practices in order to function, by the same token providing sources of legitimation (Purcell, 2009) and 'neutralizing' the subversive contents of counter-hegemonic movements (Mouffe, 2013). Neo-liberalism can be interpreted therefore as "a process of discursive re-articulation of existing discourses and practices" (Mouffe, 2013, p. 73), capable of realizing a 'transition' in terms of an outcome of hegemonic intervention (see Boltanski & Chiappello, 2005). In relation to practices of urban governance, following Mouffe, I refer to the Gramscian notion of 'hegemony through neutralization' to capture situations where claims which challenge an established hegemonic order are institutionally re-incorporated. In Gramscian terms, such practices of 'hegemony through neutralization' realize "a situation where demands which challenge the hegemonic order are appropriated by the existing system so as to satisfy them in a way that neutralizes their subversive potential" (Mouffe, 2013, p. 73).

This is, in a critical-interpretive perspective, the meaning I attach to the notion of 'innovative' practices of governance. Notwithstanding the possibility of assessing their prospects and outcomes – based on consensual sets of normative criteria and values – in terms of 'social innovation' (Moulaert et al., 2013), 'governance innovation' constitutes a re-articulation of a challenged order which may result in (contingently) realizing governing effects. It is a practice of governmentality which may (contingently) succeed in re-establishing, within a contested hegemonic field, an "order of the visible and the sayable" (Rancière, 1999, p. 29) and, by extension, of the feasible.

'Governance innovation' operates a re-articulation of the urban order by means of translation, that is, of assemblages of practices, narratives and beliefs by which meanings are constituted and alliances that sustain these meanings are realized. This argument can be developed along the three ensuing areas of reasoning.

Governance Practices as Moments of Institutionalization

This chapter moves from an understanding of policy objects and problems as argumentative and discursive constructs (Fischer, 2003; Hajer, 1993), and from an understanding of a policy as a claim resulting from processes of fact-object building that co-define and uphold this claim to the objectivation-reification and discursive institutionalization of such constructs (see Hajer, 1994; Gualini, 2001). A policy as a claim thus embodies both a set of interests and goals and the way they are argumentatively and discursively constructed as a fact-object. This definition has two implications: On the one hand, a policy thus defined is the outcome of performative acts, resulting from a contingent combination of different forms of agency, which institute a policy as an interpretive construct amenable to collective recognition and appropriation, as a fact-object, within an institutional environment. As such, the form a policy takes is not necessarily the expression of predefined rationales or preferences. On the contrary it is largely a matter of interpretation, translation, sense-making and rationalization by actors involved in struggles for constructing and upholding a claim. On the other hand, a policy thus defined potentially constitutes a moment of institutionalization. This is, in my view, in line with a constructivist understanding of policymaking and governance (Bevir & Rhodes, 2006; Kingdon, 1984) but also with a line of reasoning in governance studies which understands policies and their instrumentation, their tools and modes of operation, beyond purely 'instrumental' assumptions. On this view, public policy instruments reveal "a (fairly explicit) theorization of the relationships between the governing and the governed", and "constitute a condensed and finalized form of knowledge about social control and ways of exercising it". Far from being neutral devices, they create specific effects "which structure public policy according to their own logic". They are devices in both a technical and social sense, in that they organize specific social relations, have political effects and shape power relations, according to the representations and meanings they convey (Lascoumes & Le Galès, 2007, p. 3, p. 11).

In such an extended perspective, a policy can be seen as a moment of institutionalization, emerging as an outcome of the performative acts that define a policy as a fact-object.

This leads to two interim observations. First, both the structuring and organizing dimension and the symbolic-cognitive dimension appear as indivisible in defining a policy. Second, and similarly, the effects a policy may generate in relative autonomy and the power relations that define it can be distinguished only in an analytical sense. We need therefore to overcome determinism to understand structure/agency relationships, and to look at how these interact in co-evolutive and strategic-relational terms in defining a policy.

Governance Practices as Inscription Devices

The nature of a policy thus defined is the outcome of processes of fact-object building. Fact-object building is intended here with reference to the notion of fact-building or 'fact construction' developed by Latour (1987, 2005) and Callon (1986) in their analysis of technoscience. Accordingly, a policy can be understood – to use the term employed by Latour (1987, p. 67 ff.) – as an *inscription device*, as an interface which realizes a number of associations between resources and connections or alliances between actors mobilized in support of a claim.

As an inscription device, a policy thus embodies the complex assemblage of resources of different natures – cognitive and discursive as well as material – which are cumulated and bundled together in order to successfully sustain societal 'trials of strength' in upholding a claim against others.

A policy, as it is concretely conceived and performed, realizes effects of structuration in a field of societal forces defined by a set of interests. Such effects neither necessarily result from a clear-cut causal intentionality nor from a homogenization of interests: they are rather conceived by a selective and transformative alignment along a set of collective orientations. This is realized through practices of translation.

A key moment in the process of building a policy fact-object is *translation*, intended as a strategy "to enroll others so that they participate in the construction of the fact" and "to control their behaviours in order to make their actions predictable" (Latour, 1987, p. 108).

While, in principle, translation is of a symbolic-cognitive and argumentative nature, it entails different strategies which affect forms of interaction and the nature of network associations between actors and their interests. Translation, in its simplest form, involves defining the object or problem of a policy in such a way as to cater to actors stated ('explicit') interests, thus realizing an identification between a claim and a fact-object and associating actors to it; it may also involve realizing argumentative 'detours' as a new rendering of others' interests that recognizes their alignment to a claim by persuasively representing the detour as inevitable to others' interests (Latour, 1987, pp. 110–112). But it may also involve more distinctively transformative practices of reshuffling others' stated ('explicit') interests through tactics of displacement (Latour, 1987, pp. 114–116). Translation acts by re-articulating the forms of knowledge and interests relevant for fact-object building; by enrolling and binding actors through an articulation of their interests, and by building new associations through adaptations and shifts in their relationships and definitions (Latour, 2005).

Through practices of translation, articulation-proposition, and association-substitution, interests and the understandings and meanings attached to them by actors are tied to a policy, which comes to perform as a device that holds together new alliances and redefines inside/outside relationships.

A policy as an inscription device realizes associations – that is, it associates actors and their interests "in such a way that they make others do things" (Latour, 2005, p. 107), through chains of mediated transformations of their claims. A policy seen as an inscription device presents thus an analogy to the relationship Latour conceives between 'sociogram' and 'technogram'. To paraphrase Latour's terms, the internal-external division that defines the policy environment can be thus seen as the provisional outcome of a reverse relationship between the 'outside' recruitment of interests (sociogram) and the 'inside' recruitment of new allies (technogram). The policy environment thus defined is a system of alliances held together by a policy device. Similar to a black box, a policy, "when it is successful, concentrates in itself the largest number of hardest associations" (Latour, 1987, p. 139).

Through chains of translations, a fact-object construction is corroborated and, in a sociological neo-institutionalist perspective, 'institutionalized' – as far as possible – 'becoming indispensable', as it holds together a number of associations, enrols relevant actors and their interests, lets them be perceived as pursuable only within its framework, and thus makes such enrolment inescapable.

Governance Practices as Strategic-Relational Claims

Viewing policies as inscription devices directs attention to three relevant aspects of policy-making. First, a policy as an inscription device is premised on translation – that is, on the symbolic-cognitive enrolment of 'others' and other's strategies and the capacity to influence their behaviour in view of achieving their own strategy. This implies more or less explicit negotiations on meanings that require readiness to extend chains of agreement and consent and to adapt strategies according to this. Second, a policy as an inscription device is premised on the capacity of 'framing', of realizing effects of 'frame alignment' among actors and their interest definitions and understandings. Viewed from the perspective of its institutional embeddedness, it is premised on institutional practices of frame resonance which ultimately may produce (selective) effects of frame alignment within an institutionalized framework (Snow et al., 1986; Snow & Benford, 1988). Third, a policy as an inscription device is both a strategic and a relational construct, always contingent on the co-evolutive relationship between structural context and specific forms of agency, re-acting to and exerting structuration effects on it. Understanding policies as a moment of institutionalization requires moving beyond an understanding of institutions in dualistic terms, as either 'conditions of choice' (in an ontological, exogenist perspective) or 'objects of choice' (in a constructivist, endogenic perspective), to address the differential capacity of actors and the effects of power and hegemony in defining dynamics and trajectories of institutionalization.

The strategic-relational approach developed by Jessop (2001) and Hay (2002) moves beyond such structure-agency and context-conduct dualisms towards understanding their relation as a form of co-evolution. This means that, in the first place, duality is substituted by a focus on mutual strategic-relational effects, and that, in the second place, "structures [are analysed] in terms of their structurally inscribed strategic selectivities and actions in terms of (differentially reflexive) structurally oriented strategic calculation" (Jessop, 2001, p. 1223). In other words, "[s]tructures are thereby treated analytically as strategic in their form, content, and operation; and actions are thereby treated analytically as structured, more or less context sensitive, and structuring" (Jessop, 2001, p. 1223).

This 'methodological relationalism' implies treating social phenomena – including policies and governance forms – as social relations (Jessop, 2001, p. 1223) in specific spatio-temporal as well as broadly 'institutional' contexts.

In this perspective, 'agency' is not seen as equal to unconstrained strategic intentionality, but rather as the "possibility of reflection on the part of individual or collective actors about the strategic selectivities inscribed within structures so that they come to orient their strategies and tactics in the light of their understanding of the current conjuncture and their 'feel of the game'. This can (but need not) extend to self-reflection about the identities and interests that orient their strategies". Similarly, in viewing 'structure(s)', the focus is on the "tendency for specific structures and structural configurations to reinforce selectively specific forms of action, tactics, or strategies and to discourage others" (Jessop, 2001, p. 1224).

Policies intended as strategic-relational constructs are an outcome of the mutual interplay of selectivity-reflexivity, and their 'structured coherence' an outcome of their co-evolution over time. As such, their 'structured coherence' is always only tendential, since achieving it involves "a structurally inscribed strategic selectivity that rewards actions that are compatible with the recursive reproduction of the structure(s) in question" (Jessop, 2001, p. 1225).

Given that there is always scope for external as well as internal contradictions – deviant behaviour, strategic-cognitive uncertainty, ambiguity, instrumental inadequacy, as well as controversy, contestation and antagonism – the capacity of actors to reflexively (re-)constitute institutions or, in my terms, to constitute a policy as a moment of institutionalization, is constrained: it "depends both on the changing selectivities of given institutions and on their own changing opportunities to engage in strategic action" (Jessop, 2001, p. 1226). On the one hand, "the scope for the reflexive reorganization of structural configurations is subject to structurally inscribed strategic selectivity (and thus has path-dependent and path-shaping aspects)"; on the other hand, "the recursive selection of strategies and tactics depends on individual, collective or organizational learning capacities and on the 'experiences' resulting from the pursuit of different strategies and tactics in different conjunctures" (Jessop, 2001, p. 1224).

In the critical-interpretive perspective pursued in this chapter, this highlights two issues. On the one hand, the trajectories of evolution a policy may take depend on a capacity of strategic reflexivity, intended as the actors' capacity of effective response to strategic-relational 'trials of strength'. On the other hand, such strategic reflexivity may depend on capacities of reflexive framing – that is, on the actors' capacity of reframing and of realizing effects of frame alignment in response to strategic-relational challenges. In this sense, a policy can be seen as a strategic-relational claim, as an argumentative and discursive construct that is upheld and corroborated – in a hegemonic sense – through reflexive adaptation to strategic-relational challenges.

Provisional Conclusions and Critical Perspectives

This chapter has presented some arguments on 'institutions in action' based on, first, identifying a nexus between institutional theory and critical governance research and, second, on discussing their contribution to redefining the meaning of the 'political' in 'post-political' times. In this very tentative and preliminary exploration, urban governance and regulation have been viewed as part of processes that contribute to the institutionalization of an urban order: in other words, as practices of policing and producing policing effects. Urban policy and planning are practices which articulate the inherent antagonistic nature of social relations. In doing so, they constitutively partake in a field of hegemonic practices, intended as practices of articulation which create social orders and social meanings. The policing order that urban policy and planning constitute is a temporary and precarious articulation of practices always potentially subject to antagonistic challenges. As such, hegemonic practices stand in a dialectic of dis-articulation and re-articulation. The articulation of an urban order is always subject to possible dis-articulation as a result of antagonistic and/or counter-hegemonic practices. Conversely, re-articulation of an order is always possible as a result of the re-appropriation of antagonistic elements within hegemonic practices. This perspective allows one to view 'governance innovation' as a set of practices by which this articulation is attempted and possibly realized. In a context of indeterminacy and decenteredness, where no 'fixed' or institutionalized framework for agency is given, governance operates a strategic-relational re-articulation of the urban order by means of translation – that is, through assemblages of practices, narratives and beliefs by which meanings are constituted and alliances that sustain these meanings realized. Thus, 'governance innovation' may operate a translation of elements of antagonistic dis-articulation into elements of a new 'policing order'.

This conception also directs attention to the dimension of governmentality involved in developments of forms of governance and regulation and to the way it informs current understandings of the domain of democratic politics: a critical perspective on institutions in action – as they are instantiated in and by contemporary governance and policy practices – may well serve as a contribution to a critical engagement with the meaning of 'the political' in 'post-political' times. As long as we can conceive of governance and policy practices as constitutive of an emerging 'policing order', we are reminded of the fact that the domain of democratic politics is not exhausted by its formal structures, rules and guarantees – that is, by its 'formal constitution' – but is the more so defined by actual social practices – that is, by its 'material constitution' with its variegated symbolic-cognitive and discursive frames of reference. Institutions in action, according to this view, are an expression of the political intended as a field of 'hegemonic practices' – that is, of the practices of symbolic-cognitive and discursive articulation through which a given order is created and a meaning is conferred to social institutions and 'fixed'. Such a hegemonic order is constitutively temporary and precarious in as far as it results from the articulation of contingent practices: always facing the possibility of dis-articulation as result of challenge by antagonistic and/or counter-hegemonic practices, but also always facing the possibility of re-articulation as result of re-appropriation within hegemonic practices.

As far as openness is granted for articulating critique to a given order, and as far as no 'closure' of the 'political' is given, practices of dis-articulation/re-articulation within a field of 'hegemonic practices' are always possible and may inform strategies and tactics aimed at transforming a given institutional (hegemonic) order. Similarly, however, forms of resistance to change are also always possible, and result from forms of hegemonic intervention, by which emerging challenges to the hegemonic order are re-appropriated within an existing order – in a process of 'hegemony through neutralization' – in order to adapt and neutralize their counter-hegemonic potential.

This reminds us of the fact that institutions in action – as the expression of the contingent and co-evolutionary nature of institutional orders – are always the result of a struggle involving a significant meaning-making dimension. In this perspective, received notions from classic institutionalism such as 'institutional reforms', 'institutional design' or 'institutional innovation' – and their derivatives, such as 'policy design' and 'governance' or 'social innovation' – appear as nothing but contingent forms under which the ongoing struggle for hegemonic order is conducted. In these notions, the idea of acting on institutions as the 'structures' or as the 'context' (constraining/enabling) in which agency takes place, mistakes – or misrepresents – the fact that institutions in action define 'context' as the pattern of relations and meanings developed by actors through their interactions which may become relatively stabilized or de-stabilized according to the way hegemonic practices are played out in a contingent moment in space-time.

In a critical-reflective planning perspective that aims at reconciling institutional thinking and philosophical pragmatism, and at overcoming the divide between institutional determinants and pragmatic imperatives, thinking in terms of institutions in action offers significant theoretical clues as it unveils significant dilemmas. In essence, such dilemmas reside in the normative aspiration for planning – in its pursuit of 'progressive' goals – to be capable of intentionally, purposefully dealing with 'institutions in action' as an object of (meta-)intervention. The fallacy of this aspiration resides in the way planning practices, in pursuing such aspirations, are prone to adopt an action frame of 'institutional reform' or 'design' – thus either failing to recognize the dialectic of the hegemonic practices of which they are part, or failing to play a hegemonic role altogether. In other words, the fallacy resides in the fact that practices of 'institutional reform' or 'design' are prone to reproducing hegemonic practices instead of acting on their transformation – and ultimately of failing its own intents. As in the chess metaphor used, among others, by Umberto Eco, this is a case for a 'knight's move': for combining 'requisite irony' (Jessop, 2003), openness to contradiction and non-linear, abductive reasoning.

References

Berger, P. L., & Luckmann, T. (1966). *The Social Construction of Reality: A Treatise in the Sociology of Knowledge*. Garden City, NY: Doubleday.

Berger, P. L., Berger, B., & Kellner, H. (1973). *The Homeless Mind: Modernization and Consciousness*. New York: Random House.

Bevir, M. (2003). A Decentered Theory of Governance. In H. H. Bang (Ed.), *Governance as Social and Political Communication* (pp. 200–222). Manchester: Manchester University Press.
Bevir, M., & Rhodes, R. A. W. (2003). *Interpreting British Governance*. London/New York: Routledge.
Bevir, M., & Rhodes, R. A. W. (2006). *Governance Stories*. London/New York: Routledge.
Boltanski, L., & Chiappello, E. (2005). *The New Spirit of Capitalism*. London/New York: Verso.
Brenner, N. (2004). *New State Spaces: Urban Governance and the Rescaling of Statehood*. Oxford: Oxford University Press.
Brenner, N., & Theodore, N. (2002). Cities and the geographies of 'actually existing neoliberalism'. *Antipode*, 34(3), 349–379.
Callon, M. (1986). Some Elements of a Sociology of Translation: Domestication of the Scallops and the Fishermen of St Brieuc Bay. In J. Law (Ed.), *Power, Action and Belief: A New Sociology of Knowledge?* (pp. 196–223). London/New York: Routledge.
Castells, M. (1983). *The City and the Grassroots: A Cross-Cultural Theory of Urban Social Movements*. London: Arnold.
Crouch, C. (2004). *Post-Democracy*. Oxford: Blackwell.
Dikeç, M. (2007). *Badlands of the Republic: Space, Politics and Urban Policy*. Oxford: Blackwell.
Fischer, F. (2003). *Reframing Public Policy: Discursive Politics and Deliberative Practices*. Oxford: Oxford University Press.
Giddens, A. (1984). *The Constitution of Society: Outline of a Theory of Structuration*. Oxford: Polity Press.
Gualini, E. (2001). *Planning and the Intelligence of Institutions: Interactive Planning Approaches between Institutional Design and Institution-Building*. Aldershot: Ashgate.
Gualini, E. (2010). Governance, Space and Politics: Exploring the Governmentality of Planning. In J. Hillier & P. Healey (Eds.), *The Ashgate Research Companion to Planning Theory: Conceptual Challenges for Spatial Planning* (pp. 57–85). Aldershot: Ashgate.
Gualini, E. (2015). Conflict in the City: Democratic, Emancipatory – and Transformative? In Search of the Political in Planning Conflicts. In E. Gualini (Ed.), *Planning and Conflict: Critical Reflections on Contentious Urban Developments* (pp. 3–36). London/New York: Routledge.
Hajer, M. A. (1994). *The Politics of Environmental Discourse: Ecological Modernization and the Policy Process*. Oxford: Clarendon Press.
Hajer, M. A. (1993). Discourse Coalitions and the Institutionalization of Practice: The Case of Acid Rain in Britain. In F. Fischer & J. Forester (Eds.), *The Argumentative Turn in Policy Analysis and Planning* (pp. 43–76). London: Duke University Press.
Hall, P. A., & Taylor, R. C. R. (1996). Political science and the three new institutionalisms. *Political Studies*, 44(5), 936–957.
Hay, C. (2002). *Political Analysis: A Critical Introduction*. Basingstoke: Palgrave.
Holston, J. (2008). *Insurgent Citizenship: Disjunction of Democracy and Modernity in Brazil*. Princeton, NJ: Princeton University Press.
Jepperson, R. L. (1991). Institutions, Institutional Effects, and Institutionalism. In W. W. Powell & P. J. DiMaggio (Eds.), *The New Institutionalism in Organizational Analysis*. Chicago, IL: University of Chicago Press.
Jessop, B. (1995). The regulation approach, governance and post-Fordism: Alternative perspectives on economic and political change? *Economy and Society*, 24(3), 307–333.
Jessop, B. (2001). Institutional (re)turns and the strategic-relational approach. *Environment and Planning A*, 33(7), 1213–1235.
Jessop, B. (2002a). *The Future of the Capitalist State*. Cambridge: Polity Press.
Jessop, B. (2002b). Liberalism, neoliberalism, and urban governance: A state–theoretical perspective. *Antipode*, 34(3), 452–472.
Jessop, B. (2003). Governance and Metagovernance: On Reflexivity, Requisite Variety, and Requisite Irony. In H. Bang (Ed.), *Governance as Social and Political Communication* (pp. 101–116). Manchester: Manchester University Press.
Jessop, B. (2008). *State Power*. Cambridge: Polity Press.
Kingdon, J. W. (1984). *Agendas, Alternatives and Public Choices*. Boston, MA: Little Brown.
Kooiman, J. (Ed.). (1993). *Modern Governance*. London: Sage.
Laclau, E., & Mouffe, C. (1985). *Hegemony and Socialist Strategy: Towards a Radical Democratic Politics*. London: Verso.
Lanzalaco, L. (1995). *Istituzioni organizzazioni potere. Introduzione all'analisi istituzionale della politica*. Roma: La Nuova Italia Scientifica.

Lascoumes, P., & Le Galès, P. (2007). Introduction: Understanding public policy through its instruments – from the nature of instruments to the sociology of public policy instrumentation. *Governance*, 20(1), 1–21.

Latour, B. (1987). *Science in Action*. Cambridge, MA: Harvard University Press.

Latour, B. (2005). *Reassembling the Social: An Introduction to Actor-Network Theory*. Oxford: Oxford University Press.

Le Galès, P. (1998). Regulations and governance in European cities. *International Journal of Urban and Regional Research*, 22(3), 482–506.

Leitner, H., Peck, J., & Sheppard, E. S. (Eds.). (2006). *Contesting Neoliberalism: Urban Frontiers*. New York: The Guilford Press.

March, J. G., &. Olsen, J. P. (1989). *Rediscovering Institutions: The Organizational Basis of Politics*. New York: The Free Press.

Mayntz, R. (1987). Politische Steuerung und gesellschaftliche Steuerungsprobleme: Anmerkungen zu einem theoretischen Paradigma. *Jahrbuch zur Staats- und Verwaltungswissenschaft*, 1, 89–110.

Mayntz, R. (2004). Governance im modernen Staat. In A. Benz (Ed.), *Governance – Regieren in komplexen Regelsystemen* (pp. 65–76). Wiesbaden: VS Verlag für Sozialwissenschaften.

Mayntz, R., & Scharpf, F. W. (1995). *Gesellschaftliche Selbstregelung und politische Steuerung*. Frankfurt/New York: Campus.

Metzger, J., Allmendinger, P., & Oosterlynk, S. (Eds.). (2015). *Planning Against the Political: Democratic Deficits in European Territorial Governance*. London/New York: Routledge.

Meyer, J. W., & Rowan, B. (1977). Institutionalized organizations: Formal structure as myth and ceremony. *American Journal of Sociology*, 83(2), 340–63. Reprinted in W. W. Powell & P. J. DiMaggio (Eds.). (1991). *The New Institutionalism in Organizational Analysis*. Chicago, IL: University of Chicago Press.

Mouffe, C. (2000). *The Democratic Paradox*. London: Verso.

Mouffe, C. (2013). *Agonistics: Thinking the World Politically*. London/New York: Verso.

Moulaert, F., MacCallum, D., Mehmood, A., & Hamdouch, A. (Eds.). (2013). *The International Handbook On Social Innovation: Collective Action, Social Learning and Transdisciplinary Research*. London: Elgar.

Offe, C. (2009). Governance: An 'empty signifier'? *Constellations*, 16(4), 550–562.

Painter, J. (2010). Rethinking territory. *Antipode*, 42(4), 1090–1118.

Powell, W. W., & DiMaggio, P. J. (Eds.). (1991). *The New Institutionalism in Organizational Analysis*. Chicago, IL: University of Chicago Press.

Purcell, M. (2009). Resisting neoliberalization: Communicative planning or counter-hegemonic movements? *Planning Theory*, 8(2), 140–165.

Rancière, J. (1995). *On the Shores of Politics*. London/New York: Verso.

Rancière, J. (1999). *Disagreement: Politics and Philosophy*. Minneapolis, MN: Minnesota University Press.

Rhodes, R. A. W. (1996). The new governance: Governing without government. *Political Studies*, 44(4), 652–667.

Snow, D. A., & Benford, R. D. (1988). Ideology, frame resonance, and participant mobilization. *International Social Movement Research*, 1(1), 197–217.

Snow, D. A., Burke Rochford Jr., E., Worden, S. K., & Benford, R. D. (1986). Frame alignment processes, micromobilization, and movement participation. *American Sociological Review*, 51(3), 464–481.

Stoker, G. (1998). Governance as theory: Five propositions. *International Social Science Journal*, 50(155), 17–28.

Stone, D. (2002). *Policy Paradox: The Art of Political Decision Making*. New York: Norton.

Swyngedouw, E. (2009). The zero-ground of politics: Musings on the post-political city. *New-Geographies*, 1, 52–61.

Swyngedouw, E. (2011). *Designing the Post-Political City and the Insurgent Polis (Civic City Cahier 5)*. London: Bedford Press.

Voß, J.-P., & Freeman, R. (Eds.). (2015). *Knowing Governance: The Epistemic Construction of Political Order*. London: Palgrave Macmillan.

Wagenaar, H. (2011). *Meaning in Action: Interpretation and Dialogue in Policy Analysis*. Armonk/London: M. E. Sharpe.

Zucker, L. G. (1977). The role of institutionalization in cultural persistence. *American Sociological Review*, 42(5), 726–743. Reprinted in W. W. Powell & P. J. DiMaggio (Eds.). (1991). *The New Institutionalism in Organizational Analysis*. Chicago, IL: University of Chicago Press.

Zucker, L. G. (1987). Institutional theories of organizations. *Annual Review of Sociology*, 13, 443–464.

PART 2

Institutional Innovation

4
DISCURSIVE INSTITUTIONALISM AND PLANNING IDEAS

Simin Davoudi

Introduction

The ideas of economists and political philosophers, both when they are right and when they are wrong, are more powerful than is commonly understood. Indeed the world is ruled by little else. Practical men, who believe themselves to be quite exempt from any intellectual influences, are usually the slaves of some defunct economist. Madmen in authority, who hear voices in the air, are distilling their frenzy from some academic scribbler of a few years back. I am sure that the power of vested interest is vastly exaggerated compared with the gradual encroachment of ideas … the ideas that civil servants and politicians and even agitators apply to current events are not likely to be the newest. But, soon or late, it is ideas, not vested interests, which are dangerous for good or evil.

(Keynes, 1936, p. 241)

The above are the words of John Maynard Keynes whose own influential ideas contributed to the revisionist approaches to classical liberalism of the nineteenth century and led to the rise of the post-war welfare states. They suggest that ideas play a significant, and even determining, role in political behaviour and outcomes. Acknowledging the role of ideas in motivating political action has long been a feature of cultural studies of politics as is reflected in Webber's famous metaphor of 'switchman of history'. Students of social learning have also stressed the significance of ideas in policymaking. An early example is the work of Hugh Heclo on social policy in Britain and Sweden. He argued that "Governments not only 'power' … they also puzzle", because "Politics finds its sources not only in power but also in uncertainty" (Heclo, 1974, p. 305).

More recently, political scientists who adopt a constructivist approach to policy analysis stress the role of ideas and discourses in politics and policymaking (Dryzek, 2010; Fischer, 2003), in transnational policy transfer (Dolowitz & Marsh, 2000) and in international relations (Parsons, 2003). Another sign of these developments is the rising interest in discourse analyses where several studies have demonstrated that actors' interpretive frameworks and shared ideas are as important in determining political outcomes as the policy dilemmas they face. Indeed, for some scholars "ideas are a primary source of political behavior" (Béland & Cox, 2011, p. 3) because, if ideas did not matter why would Foucault (2000) talk about the impossibility of escaping from the ideational domination of the powerful?

The history of planning is full of stories about visionary ideas that have radically changed planning thoughts and practices. Consider the contributions of the pioneers (the so-called 'founding fathers') of the planning movement in the UK, or the great urban visionaries of the twentieth century elsewhere. Contemporary planning scholars have been centrally engaged in (re)producing, disseminating and using ideas but, surprisingly, they have seldom studied 'ideas' as the object of their inquiry. That is to say, they have paid little attention to the relative analytical *power* of ideas, compared with interests or institutions, in explaining change or continuity in planning theory, polity or policy.

This chapter provides the first step towards studying the role of planning ideas. It argues that ideas matter and should be taken seriously in the narratives about change and stability of planning polity and policy, and in understanding planning outcomes. It provides an overview of key debates in the field and highlights some critical issues to be attended to in future research. Given that the emergence of new institutionalism in the 1980s has been a key factor in the rising prominence of ideational analyses, the chapter first briefly outlines different types of new institutionalism. The aim is to position discursive institutionalism (discussed later) in the wider debate and unpick the relationship between ideas and institutions, and by doing so, to situate this chapter in the framework presented by Willem Salet in Chapter 1 in this volume. Following this, I focus on the significance of 'ideas', their multiple meanings and types, levels of operation in public policy, and their relationship with interests and with change. In the final part, I address a critical question in discursive institutionalism: why some ideas succeed while others fail; particularly focusing on the rhetorical appeal to ethos. To conclude I identify possible avenues for future research on planning ideas.

New Institutionalism

Studying the role of institutions in policymaking goes back to the 1930s when traditional political scientists (especially in the United States) analysed the formal structures and rules of Western governments' institutions as represented, for example, in the executive, legislative and judicial institutions. In the 1960s, attentions moved away from institutional influence towards the actions of political actors. By the 1980s this behaviouralist perspective and its focus on individual choices became the dominant analytical framework for explaining policy change. The emergence of new institutionalism at that time was a reaction to this pendulum swing, and a call for bringing institutions back to the analyses of policy change and stability. James March (an American political scientist) and Johan Olsen (a Norwegian political scientist), who are credited as the founders of new institutionalism, argued that without understanding institutional constraints, analysts are unable to understand the choices made by the individuals who operate in those institutions (March & Olsen, 1984, 1989).

Since then, there has been widespread agreement that institutions matter but the question of how much they matter has been subject to long and contested debates. At the centre of the dispute is the weight given to the role of ideas as compared with the role of individual choices and actions, and the wider social and cultural contexts. In a highly cited paper, Peter Hall and Rosemary Taylor (1996) identified three distinct analytical approaches to, or types of, new institutionalism which they called rational choice institutionalism, historical institutionalism and sociological institutionalism. In order to understand the differences between these, they examined how they respond to two fundamental questions of institutional analyses: a) how to interpret the relationship between institutions and individual behaviour? and b) how to explain the process by which institutions originate, are maintained and change? In other words, how do actors behave, what do institutions do and why do institutions persist or change? According to Hall and Taylor (1996, p. 939), new institutionalists' responses to these questions fall broadly into two categories: 'the calculus approach' and the 'the cultural approach'.

The Calculus Approach

The calculus approach puts the emphasis on actors' instrumentally strategic behaviour to achieve a set of goals driven from their preferences. In doing so, they undertake strategic calculation by canvassing all possible options and selecting the ones that maximize their benefits (Davoudi et al., 2014). According to this approach, the role of institutions is to provide certainty about the behaviour of other actors through mechanisms such as: information provision, enforcement, penalties and incentives. Thus, institutions shape individuals' actions by changing their expectations about other actors' likely actions. The calculus approach suggests that institutions persist because they embody equilibrium in such a way that individuals would be worse off if they do not adhere to institutional patterns of behaviour – in particular, the institutional resolution of collective action dilemmas.

The calculus approach is strongly associated with *rational choice institutionalism* which has its roots in economic organizational theory and considers institutions as systems of rules and incentives (carrots and sticks). Douglas North (2005), who won the Nobel Prize for economics in 1993, suggests that institutions are created through utility maximizing or optimizing behaviour of individuals but once institutions are established they structure the action of individuals. Agent-based modelling and Game Theory are used to explain actors' political decisions.

The Cultural Approach

The cultural approach suggests that an individual's behaviour is not fully strategic, rational or purposive but rather bounded by their worldview. So, their choice of a particular action is based on their interpretation of a situation and the meanings they give to their action, rather than purely instrumental calculation. According to this approach, institutions provide both cognitive and moral framework for such interpretation through symbols, texts, routines and rituals. This implies that institutions provide not only strategically useful information (suggested by the calculus approach), but also the lens through which actors' identities, self-images and preferences are shaped. "Institutions influence behavior not simply by specifying what one should do, but also by specifying what one can imagine oneself doing in a given context" (Hall & Taylor, 1996, p. 948). Here, institutions are defined broadly to mean not just the formal rules, procedures or norms, but also the wider social milieu in which both individuals and formal institutions are embedded. Thus, the very idea of self-interest and utility is determined by the social and cultural 'fields' or 'habitus' in which actors are embedded and against which they measure the appropriateness of their actions. According to the cultural approach, institutions persist because a) many of their conventions are taken for granted and are not visible for direct scrutiny, and b) they are collective constructs and hence not readily transformable by the action of individuals. They are resistant to change because they frame the likely reform choices of individuals. On the other hand, institutional practices may change not because the new practices provide better means-ends efficiency but because they advance institutional legitimacy and social appropriateness.

Change and stability are explained through 'logic of social appropriateness' rather than the 'logic of instrumentality' (Hall & Taylor, 1996).

The cultural approach is strongly associated with *sociological institutionalism* which is rooted in sociology, anthropology and cultural studies. Traditionally, it was concerned with the normative impact of institutions on individual behaviour in the sense that actors tend to normalize institutional rules that are attached to their roles. Contemporary sociological institutionalists emphasize the cognitive impact of institutions on individual behaviour through the provision of cognitive scripts, categories and models that are indispensable for action, because without them the behaviour of others cannot be interpreted. The relationship between individuals and institutions is considered to be interactive and mutually co-constitutive and constructed through practical reasoning rather than mere strategic calculation.

Hall and Taylor's (1996) third type of new institutionalism is *historical institutionalism* which, they argue, draws on both the calculus and cultural approaches. However, in relation to the latter, historical institutionalists put the emphasis on the historical legacy of institutional structures and conventions which, they argue, have been ossified over time into worldviews. Historical institutionalists assert that institutional rules and constraints and the reactions to them over a long period of time can explain the behaviour of political actors. For them, social change is path dependent and consists of a period of continuity punctuated by critical junctures or a process of punctured equilibrium, similar to the ecological perspective on resilience (Davoudi, 2012). They challenge the image of efficient and purposive institutions by demonstrating the unintended consequences of the functions of existing institutions. Asymmetry of power is seen as a critical factor in institutional development with the uneven access to decision-making processes creating losers and winners of political action. Historical institutionalists often associate institutions with organizations and define them as the formal and informal rules, procedures and conventions that are promulgated by them (such as constitution, bureaucracy, trade unions).

The above summary shows that 'new institutionalism' is a multifaceted phenomenon with diverging theories and methods, to the extent that it would be misleading to use the term in singular. Indeed, Peters (1998) identified no less than seven forms of new institutionalism. However, Hall and Taylor's 1996 classification has remained insightful and continues to be the touchstone of more recent work. Critics argue that although different types of new institutionalism offer valuable analyses of the structures that govern policymaking, they are less useful in explaining the content of policy choices. For example, Béland and Hacker (2004, p. 45) argue that "the institutional perspective is considerably more instructive as an explanation of the prospects for policy reform than as an explanation of the specific form that policy change takes". To understand the latter, they advocate that a focus on ideas is more fruitful.

Ideational Approaches and Discursive Institutionalism

As shown above, the rise of ideational approaches is in part due to the rise of new institutionalism and a reaction to its overemphasis on the role of institutions. It is argued that in its reaction to the dominant behaviouralist approaches of the 1980s, new institutionalism has swung too far towards institutions and away from actors; that agency is attended to but not taken seriously. The swing is reflected in a recent statement by March and Olsen (2008, p. 14) who suggest that "'new institutionalism' tries to avoid unfeasible assumptions that require too much of political actors, in terms of normative commitments (virtue), cognitive abilities (bounded rationality), and social control (capabilities). The rules, routines, norms, and identities of an 'institution', rather than micro-rational individuals or macro-social forces, are the basic units of analysis". It should be noted that, Willem Salet's position, outlined in Chapter 1 in this volume, takes a broader perspective on institutions and considers them as 'patterns of social norms'.

To bring the *agency* back into the analyses, they have turned to ideas. Various terms are used to define the ideational approaches including, for example, ideational institutionalism (Hay, 2001), constructivist institutionalism (Hay, 2006, 2011), and discursive institutionalism (Schmidt, 2008, 2011). The latter is used by Vivien Schmidt as an umbrella concept to refer to the work of those political scientists who "take account of the substantive content of ideas and the interactive processes of discourse that serve to generate those ideas and communicate them to the public" (Schmidt, 2011, p. 47).

Ideational approaches agree with other institutionalist approaches about the importance of institutions but they differ in their definition of institutions and in their logic of explaining change and continuity, as discussed below. According to ideational approaches, "ideas are embedded in the design of institutions" and are "the foundation of institutions" (Béland & Cox, 2011, p. 9). Similarly, Hay (2011, p. 69) argues that "Institutions are built on ideational foundations that exert an independent path-dependent effect on their subsequent development".

Discursive institutionalists challenge the basic premises of the three aforementioned types of new institutionalism and their overemphasis on fixed rationalist preferences (rational choice institutionalism), self-reinforcing historical paths (historical institutionalism), or all-defining cultural norms (sociological institutionalism). For them, institutions are not the external rule-following structures that primarily condition actors' choices and actions through rationalist incentives, historical path or cultural norms. Instead, they are both given and contingent, serving as structures that constrain actions and constructs that are created and changed by actors (Schmidt, 2008). In this account institutions are "simultaneously constraining structures and enabling constructs internal to 'sentient' (thinking and speaking) agents" (Schmidt, 2011, p. 48). Thus, the relationship between institutions and the individuals and groups out of whose practices institutions are made up and on whose experiences they impinge, are seen as dynamic and fluid (Hay, 2011).

This resembles sociological institutionalism and particularly Giddens's structuration theory which considers the relationship between structure and agency as co-constitutive. Wendt (1987, p. 395) moves closer and considers social structures as constituting "an inherently discursive dimension in the sense that they are inseparable from the reasons and self-understandings that agents bring to their actions". What discursive institutionalism adds to these and to the question of *what* (the nature of the relationship between structure and agency) is the question of *how*: how actors change or maintain institutional practices? I will return to these questions later when discussing the relationship between ideas and change.

Conceptualizing 'Ideas'

Ideas are ubiquitous in politics and everyday life. Consider the role of ideas in the spread of the Enlightenment, in the creation of the welfare states, in our understandings of the evolution of life on earth, in our appreciations of landscape, in our moral and ethical deliberations, and in our visions of a 'good' city and a 'good' life. In planning, as in other areas of public policy, ideas are central in setting agendas, motivating action, triggering social movements, creating conceptual categories, assigning meanings to action, defining values and preferences, producing interpretive frameworks and building institutions and political coalitions. Indeed, planning institutions can be seen as embodiments of ideas that are in turn inspired by interests, aspirations, ideologies or practices.

Significance of Ideas

To say that ideas matter is to state the obvious, but while few people question the role of ideas in political life, many define them instrumentally as a "means to ends that have been predetermined by other structural or self-interested reasons" (Mehta, 2011, p. 24). Marxists, for example, consider ideas as mere smokescreens which powerful players use to hide their material interests. Rational choice theorists talk about ideas but see them as indicators of self-interested, utility-maximizing actors (Bates et al., 1998). New institutionalists are often attentive to the role of ideas but focus on how institutions shape ideas, rather than how ideas influence institutions.

By contrast, those who take ideas seriously suggest that an idea matters when "it (a) shapes people's actions and (b) is not reducible to some other non-ideational force" (Mehta, 2011, p. 24). For them, the focus of analyses should be less on whether ideas matter, and more on *how* and *to what extent* they matter. In the context of planning, this means formulating research questions such as how do ideas influence change and stability, how do they shape political behaviour and outcomes, how can a focus on ideas enrich our understanding of politics, and crucially, to what extent does an idea about, for example, a particular urban form work independently of the perceived interests that advocate that form and lead to the reconfiguration of urban futures.

Meanings of Ideas

Like knowledge, ideas carry multiple meanings. Some people interpret them as triggers for interests, road maps or focal points (Goldstein & Keohane, 1993). Others consider them as strategic constructs (Jabko, 2006), event-shaping narratives (Roe, 1994), frames of reference or collective memories (Rothstein, 2005). In public policy literature, ideas often refer to "policy prescriptions, norms, principled beliefs, cause-effect beliefs, ideologies, shared belief systems, and broad worldviews. They can thus range from quite specific, concrete, programmatic ideas … to broader, more general ideas" (Tannenwald, 2005, p. 14). The latter refer to the core of ideologies, rationalities and mentalities such as neo-liberalism. Emmerij et al. (2005, p. 214) define ideas as "beliefs held by individuals or adopted by institutions that influence their attitudes and actions". As such, ideas are seen as products of cognition. For example, Béland and Cox (2011, p. 4) argue that ideas are produced in people's mind (with or without the help of our sensory perceptions) and are connected to the material world through their interpretations of the world. This implies that ideas postulate connections (causal or relational) between people and things and guide their action. Hence, all theories can be seen as ideas because they are a form of cognitive ordering of the world, and given the existence of multitudes of ideas (i.e. interpretations of the world), and the absence of a single and universal truth, there is always room for politics.

According to this perspective, politics is the "struggle for power and control among people who are motivated by myriad ideas" (Béland & Cox, 2011, p. 3). These in turn can include perceived interests as well as emotions (fear, hope and pride), ideals and aspirations. This considers history not as the contest of ideas versus material interests but as the contest of the multidirectional interactions between ideas, interests and, indeed, emotions, desires and practices. The latter is worth stressing because Béland and Cox's perspective on ideas implies a linear and unidirectional relation between ideas and actions with the former guiding the latter. However, a unified account of knowing and doing consider ideas as being embodied in the actions that people are engaged in (Davoudi, 2015). For discursive institutionalists, ideas are the *substantive* contents of discourse. By bringing discourse into analyses, they highlight the significance of social processes and power relations.

Ideas and Levels of Operation

Ideas operate at various levels. They can include highly visible public frames, discourses and ideologies as well as less visible background assumptions and paradigms (Campbell, 2004). Drawing on Kingdon (1984), Mehta (2011, p. 25) and Schmidt (2008, p. 306) divide ideas into distinct analytical categories. They suggest that in the context of public policy, ideas operate at three levels of generality: specific policies or policy solutions, general programs and public philosophies. At the second level, general programmatic ideas or paradigms underpin policy proposals and act as frames of reference. These define the policy problems to be solved and hence shape policy solutions as well as the particular mechanisms for implementing them. While policy and programmatic ideas (first and second levels) are in the foreground and hence are regularly revisited and changed, philosophical ideas are in the background and as such are often left unarticulated, taken for granted, and unamenable to scrutiny (Campbell, 2004). They are rarely contested except in times of upheaval and crisis.

Along a somewhat similar line of argument, Hall (1993, p. 278) suggests that policy change is a process that involves three variables: overarching goals or paradigms, policy instruments and the settings for these instruments. Paradigms define "not only the goals of policy ... but also the very nature of the problems they are meant to be addressing" (ibid). They "constitute the underlying principles, values, beliefs and worldviews about, for example, the purpose of government and its relationship with society and the market" (Hall, 1993, p. 279). Hall also concurs with Kingdon that instruments and settings can be reformulated frequently; but only when the overarching goals are also radically transformed, can we speak of a new "policy paradigm". He refers to the shift from Keynesian to monetarist forms of macroeconomic regulations in 1980s' Britain as an example of such a wholesale change. Consequently, inflation replaced unemployment as the primary goal of policymakers, and this led to a focus on achieving a balanced budget and a reduction in direct taxation and on using monetary instead of fiscal policy as the main policy instrument.

It is worth mentioning that from a governmentality perspective, both the 'core philosophical ideas' and 'overarching goals' are considered as government rationalities (the ends), while policy instruments, programs and settings are seen as government technologies (the means). Thus, from a governmentality perspective, the 1980s' 'paradigm shift' in macroeconomic policy in Britain can be seen as one – albeit significant – part of a broader shift in the mentality and technologies of government with far-reaching implications for not only economic policy, but also the ways in which the relationship between citizens and the state were reconfigured. It was a shift from one form of liberalism (known as welfarism) to another (known as neo-liberalism), and from one set of ideas about liberty, economy, society, and the role of the state and citizens to another (Davoudi & Madanipour, 2015).

Types of Ideas

At all three levels of generality (policy, programmes and philosophies) ideas can be primarily cognitive (i.e. what to do and how to do it – for example, producing roadmaps, recipes and guidelines) and primarily normative (i.e. what is bad or good and what ought to be done, producing values). They speak to "how policies can solve problems as well as attaching values to and legitimating political action" (Schmidt, 2008, p. 307). While cognitive ideas may be considered as constitutive of interests, and normative ideas as constitutive of values, they are not dichotomous. On the contrary, they are often mutually reinforcing and work together to not only "prescribe what is to be done", but also "codify what is to be known" (Davoudi,

2015, p. 10). They shape our sense of "what counts as self-evident, universal and necessary" (Foucault, 1991, p. 76). As Schön (1983, p. 348) suggests, "the struggle to define the situation, and thereby to determine the direction of public policy, is always both intellectual and political. Views of reality are both cognitive constructs … and instruments of political power". Ideas can be communicated through multiple forms, such as narratives, myths, frames, stories, texts, images and symbols. They are dynamic, iterative, and continuously (re)produced and (re)defined through interactive processes among actors and institutions.

Ideas and Interests

As mentioned above, while hardly anyone denies the role of ideas in shaping political life, many dispute whether ideas exert an independent influence on political outcomes or individual's choices and actions. The conventional perspectives give ideas an inferior status in comparison to material interests because the latter is considered to be the underlying motivation for political action. Here, as suggested by Hay (2011), the role of ideas, and indeed institutions, is secondary to that of interests and only comes to count when actors are faced with selecting among multiple strategies for maximizing their material self-interests. However, as Judith Goldstein puts it, "only in a world of perfect information could interests be perfectly congruent with strategies" (1993, p. 10). This conventional conception of the relationship between interests and ideas is rooted in the naturalist tradition of inquiry and its manifestation in Marxist materialism and rational choice institutionalism. These see ideas as simply echoing actors' deeper material interests and as such they are used instrumentally by actors to promote those interests. Here, ideas are considered to be "entirely epiphenomenal, reflections of material necessity without any causal power of their own" (Hay, 2011, p. 73).

By contrast, discursive institutionalism considers interests not as objective facts but as social and historical constructs. This constructivist understanding defines 'interests' as "social constructs that are open to redefinition through ideological contestation" (Blyth, 2002, p. 271), or through actors' *changing* perceptions of their *changing* environments. This echoes Lukes's radical power theory which points to the plurality of actors' interests and the lack of "a canonical set of … interests that will constitute the last word on the matter" (Lukes, 2005, p. 148). As Hay (2011, p. 80) asserts, the constructions of interests "are inherently normative and subjective/intersubjective conceptions of self-good … They are idealized extrapolations of subjective/intersubjective preferences and, as such, are different from immediate and/or particular desires". This means that our conceptions of our self-interests provide us with a cognitive filter through which we, in interaction with our environment, orient ourselves and choose a course of action (ibid.). The crucial point to note is that our conception of our self-interest is not determined by our institutional environment and is not dependent on our knowledge of that environment, but rather reflects our subjective/intersubjective preferences – that is, the things we value and the relative values we assign to the desires we can imagine (ibid.).

Discursive institutionalism considers the fragile balance of the relationship between ideas and interests, as well as emotions and desires, as multidirectional and fluid (Blyth, 2002). This dynamic interrelationship between ideas and interests demands a line of inquiry which is concerned with both change and continuity. So, on the one hand, analysts need to identify and examine how established ideas become codified and stabilized (albeit temporarily) through processes of institutionalization and normalization, and how does that affect actors interpretations of their environment and, hence, their conception of their self-interests. On the other hand, analysts need to examine the conditions under which established and institutionalized ideas (cognitive filters) become contested, and how ideational shifts can herald institutional change (Hay, 2011).

Ideas and Change

What is the role of ideas in constituting policy change? What is the power of persuasion in policy debate? These questions are at the heart of the relationship between ideas and change. According to Béland and Cox (2011, p. 11), "ideational explanations are richer than other explanations of change". This is particularly the case with regard to radical, path-departing change. For many new institutionalists, path-dependent change is the norm while radical change is an exception and it takes place when political systems are confronted with external forces that disrupt institutional stability and punctuate the equilibristic 'ecosystem' of interests. Political action is seen largely as a reaction or adaptation to changing environments and circumstances in much the same way as biological systems evolve (for a critique of the application of this evolutionary account to social domains, see Davoudi, 2012, 2016).

By contrast, the ideational approaches consider radical change as a response to new ideas and ways of thinking and doing that can be reactive or proactive. As such, ideational approaches put the emphasis on human agency and the choices they make (or are compelled to make), arguing that these "choices are shaped by the ideas people hold and debate with others" (Béland & Cox, 2011, p. 12), which in turn are based on their interpretation of the world as well as their experiences. The broad definition of ideas adopted here allows for an analytical distinction between the *sources* of ideas which can include, for example, perceived interests, ideologies, emotions, aspirations, experiences and practices.

Discursive institutionalists provide a distinctive explanation of how ideas may lead to institutional change. Schmidt (2008, 2011) uses two concepts to address these questions: *background ideational ability* and *foreground discursive ability*. The former describes individual cognitive processes and the latter describes the social processes. While separately they may be analytically useful, in practice they are interrelated. Background ideational ability is used as a generic concept to summarize a number of related concepts including John Searle's philosophical concept of 'background ability' (which makes us sensitive to constitutive rules), Bourdieu's sociological notion of 'habitus' (which refers to constituted and constitutive nature of our action), and some behavioural psychologists' theories of cognitive dissonance (which hold that human actions are often based on mental short cuts). These concepts highlight the fact that our actions do not always follow rules, be it rationalist, normative or path-dependent rules. Background ideational ability is internal to actors and allows them to make sense of their changing environment and its rationality in a given meaning context without necessarily following (consciously or unconsciously) the rules of their environment that are considered as 'external' to the actors by the three aforementioned types of new institutionalism (Schmidt, 2008, p. 314).

Foreground discursive ability is also used as a generic term that draws on Habermasian communicative action and its role in breaking up elite monopolies (Dryzek, 2010). Foreground discursive ability represents the logic of communication, as opposed to the logic of instrumentality or the logic of appropriateness. It enables actors to deliberate and communicate critically about institutions and their rules even, when they use them, to persuade one another to bring about institutional change by thinking, speaking and acting outside the institutions while they work in it. Discourse, seen as an interactive social process, allows actors to think and act outside the institutions even when they are operating within and constrained by their rules (Schmidt, 2011, p. 48).

The use of discourse highlights that the power of ideas in explaining change and continuity lies not only in what is said (substance) but also in the interactive processes through which what is said is conveyed – that is, who said what to whom, where, when, how, and why (Schmidt, 2008). Embedded in this understanding is the role of power relations which resonates with Foucault's power/knowledge dyad (1980) and his perspective on governmentality. Used in this way, ideas do not simply emerge from 'voices in the air'; nor do they belong exclusively to 'academic scribblers' as the quote from Keynes (1936) at the start of this chapter asserts. Instead, the discursive understanding of ideas and institutions resonate with a broader and more inclusive notion of knowing in which puzzling and powering are intricately entangled processes (Davoudi, 2015, 2016).

Successful Ideas

In his seminal work, Kingdon (1984) posed the question: "What makes an idea's time to come?" and more recently, Mehta (2011, p. 31) posed a related question: "when an idea's time is up?" Given the existence of competing ideas at any moment in time, what makes one idea more applicable than others, what factors and processes make one idea favourable over others; or in short, why do some ideas succeed and become adopted in policy (or bring about institutional change) while others fade away? According to Hall (1989), for an idea to be successful it should combine policy, political and administrative appeal and viability. He rejects the suggestion that the intrinsic worth of an idea is enough for its adoption. A point stressed by the critiques of evidence-based policy (Davoudi, 2006, 2015). Political viability can be interpreted in two opposing ways: first, a policy idea is successful only when it has the support of powerful interests, implying that it has no independent influence of its own. Second, a policy idea is successful because it provides a strong rationale which overrides powerful interests. Discursive institutionalists suggest that a policy idea is successful if it combines the two. As Mehta (2011) argues, a new policy idea can win political support by forging its own coalition or by convincing the opposing political groups to see their interests in new and different lights.

For Kingdon (1984), policy ideas succeed when three streams come together: problems, policy solutions and politics. The latter, which includes factors such as national mood, opens a 'window of opportunity' (or critical junctures as historical institutionalists call it) which is seized by 'policy entrepreneurs' and allows them to connect preferred solutions to existing problems – that is, solutions that sometimes precede the problem. This implies that like institutions, ideas can also be path dependent. An example from planning is the legacy of Green Belt policy in the UK which continues to feed the evaluation of current planning policies and proposals and affected their legitimacy.

Both Hall and Kingdon have provided valuable insights into the factors that determine why some ideas are adopted and others are not but none specify the mechanisms through which these factors interact and lead to a certain policy and particular political outcome. Discursive institutionalists attempt to fill that gap by arguing that for an idea to succeed it ought to be *seen as* convincing in cognitive terms (i.e. credible in framing the problem and presenting a solution), and persuasive in normative terms (i.e. fits into the dominant rationalities) (Mehta, 2011; Schmidt, 2008); it ought to be seen as working for both puzzling and powering. The term 'to be seen' is important because it stresses that the success of an idea may not be due to the intrinsic value or internal logic and coherence of that idea but because of the ways in which it is conveyed; the nature of the discursive interactions through which it is represented, deliberated and legitimated. Indeed, we cannot understand political or policy ideas by abstracting them from "the uses they are put to in argument" (Skinner, 2002).

A significant contribution to the understanding of the interactive processes has been made by Ernesto Laclau's discourse analysis and his emphasis on 'the signifiers'. Here, signification is an act of naming around which a presumably universalizing discourse is structured. Laclau famously refers to 'empty signifiers' that organize the myths at the foundation of all political actions (Laclau, 1996, p. 109). For discursive analysts, "politics is always about nomination. It is about naming a political subjectivity and organizing politically around that name" (Critchley, 2007, p. 103; see also Davoudi, 2016, for a discussion on the resilient self). Although signifiers, with which subjects identify, are not fixed, they can be hegemonic in the sense that they can temporarily stabilize meaning through nomination, and anchor and structure discourses.

Adding to Laclau's signification, Finlayson (2012) points to the critical role played by 'the argument', by which he means not only 'semiotic conditions' but also "the strategies of political actors as they express and embody their political thinking [idea] and communicate it to others" (Finlayson, 2012, p. 758). He calls this activity 'rhetoric' and argues that rhetoric includes not only Laclau's 'tropes of naming', but also rhetorical style and practices such as, "the skills of delivery, narrative arrangement and, most importantly, the 'invention' of reasons suitable for presentation to others" (Finlayson, 2012, p. 758). So, rhetorical thinking is about closing the gap between what we think we know to be the case and what we imagine others think to be the case. Rhetorical thinking is about persuading others to think as we think and to imagine as we imagine. It is through such persuasion that the cognitive and normative credibility of certain ideas is enacted so that they are seen as being superior, more coherent and more viable than other competing ideas. Finlayson (2012) considers three different modes of rhetorical appeals that are used to make ideas more convincing and persuasive: *ethos* or invocation of character, *pathos* or invocation emotions and *logos* or invocation of logic. Given the limited space available here, I focus on only one of these appeals, the ethos.

The rhetorical appeal to ethos endows an idea with credibility not because of what is said but because who said it, and whether the target audience trust and respect the messenger in terms of their perceived character, expertise and authority. What constitutes authority is not fixed. Indeed, a critical question in understanding why certain ideas succeed is how authorities are identified or sustained. It is worth elaborating on one source of authority that is perceived expertise. The perceived authority of experts, such as professional planners, in validating ideas has the potential to turn them into key agents of change. Drawing on such authority, they simultaneously 'describe' and prescribe perceived realities and dilemmas and make them thinkable and amenable to political deliberations (Bourdieu, 2003, p. 85).

In the UK, traditionally policy and planning experts operated largely from within the state institutions and included a great number of professionals and civil servants. In the abovementioned account of the shift from Keynesian to monetarist forms of macroeconomic regulations in the 1980s, Hall (1993) emphasizes that officials and in-house experts played a greater role in policy transformation than politicians. The same can be said about the role of public sector professional planners in generating ideas and shaping planning policies of the early twentieth century. In the last few decades, however, expertise has been outsourced, leading to an expanding marketplace of 'expert' ideas within which a myriad of institutions and think tanks have become actively engaged in puzzling and powering in the policymaking processes. However, in the current climate of the so-called post-truth politics, the place of expertise as an important source of ethos has been challenged; an indication of the dynamic nature of what constitutes 'authority' at a particular time and place. Instead, what is on the rise is the authority of populism and the appeal to *pathos* (emotions, desires and fears) through skilful use of media for making certain arguments convincing and persuasive.

Concluding Remarks

Discursive institutionalism has emerged from and is firmly based in the context of other types of new institutionalisms. The extent to which it differs from them is a matter of dispute. Some scholars argue that the relationship is complementary (Schmidt, 2008), while others suggest that the ontological and analytical assumptions of discursive (or constructivist) institutionalism are distinctive (Blyth, 2011; Hay, 2011). Despite this, both camps agree that discursive/constructivist approaches provide "an endogenous account of complex institutional evolution, adaptation, and innovation", and as such "represent a considerable advance on their rationalist and sociological predecessors" (Hay, 2011, p. 67).

While acknowledging that there is much to do to fully understand the different conceptions of political institutions, action and change, I concur with Hay's statement that a discursive institutional analyses of change and stability in planning policies, practices and institutions can be particularly insightful given the rich history of planning ideas. A line of inquiry that focuses on influential ideas in planning, explores their substantive contents, excavates the interactive processes through which they have been conveyed, and identifies the rhetorical appeals employed to produce, communicate and legitimate them will undoubtedly advance our understanding of how planning reforms happen and what purpose they serve.

References

Bates, R. H., de Figueiredo Jr, R. J. P., & Weingast, B. R. (1998). The politics of integration: Rationality, culture, and transition. *Politics and Society*, 26(2), 221–256.

Béland D., & Cox, R. H. (2011). Introduction, Ideas and Politics. In D. Béland & R. H. Cox (Eds.), *Ideas and Politics in Social Science Research* (pp. 3–20). Oxford: Oxford University Press.

Béland, D., & Hacker, J. S. (2004). Ideas, private institutions, and American welfare state 'exceptionalism': The case of health and old-age insurance in the United States, 1915–1965. *International Journal of Social Welfare*, 13(1), 42–54.

Bourdieu, P. (2003). *Firing Back: Against the Tyranny of the Market 2*. New York: The New Press.

Blyth, M. (2002). *Great Transformations: Economic Ideas and Institutional Change in the Twentieth Century*. New York: Cambridge University Press.

Blyth, M. (2011). Ideas, Uncertainty, and Evolution. In D. Béland & R. H. Cox (Eds.), *Ideas and Politics in Social Science Research* (pp. 83–101). Oxford: Oxford University Press.

Campbell, J. L. (2004). *Institutional Change and Globalization*. Princeton, NJ: Princeton University Press.

Critchley, S. (2007). *Infinitely Demanding: Ethics of Commitment, Politics of Resistance*. London: Verso.

Davoudi, S. (2006). Evidence-based planning: Rhetoric and reality. *disP: The Planning Review*, 165(2), 14–25.

Davoudi, S. (2012). Resilience: A bridging concept or a dead end? *Planning Theory and Practice*, 13(2), 299–307.

Davoudi, S. (2015). Planning as practice of knowing. *Planning Theory*, 14(3), 316–331.

Davoudi, S. (2016). Resilience and Governmentality of Unknowns. In M. Bevir (Ed.), *Governmentality after Neoliberalism* (pp. 152–171). New York: Routledge.

Davoudi, S., Crawford J., & Dilley, L. (2014). Energy consumption behaviour, rational or habitual? *disP The Planning Review*, 50(3), 11–19.

Davoudi, S., & Madanipour, A. (2015). Localism and post-social governmentality. In S. Davoudi & A. Madanipour (Eds.), *Reconsidering Localism* (pp. 77–103). London: Routledge.

Dolowitz, D., & Marsh, D. (2000). Learning from abroad: The role of policy transfer in contemporary policy-making. *Governance*, 13(1), 5–24.

Dryzek, J. S. (2010). Rhetoric in democracy: A systemic appreciation. *Political Theory*, 38(3), 319–339

Emmerij, L., Jolly, R., & Weiss, T. G. (2005). Economic and social thinking at the UN in historical perspective. *Development and Change*, 36(2), 211–235.

Finlayson, A. (2012). Rhetoric and the political theory of ideologies. *Political Studies*, 60(4), 751–767.

Fischer, F. (2003). *Reframing Public Policy: Discursive Politics and Deliberative Practices*. Oxford: Oxford University Press.

Foucault, M. (1980). *Power/Knowledge: Selected Interviews and Other Writings, 1972–1977*. C. Gordon (Ed.). New York: Pantheon.
Foucault, M. (1991). Questions of Method. In G. Burchell, C. Gordon & P. Miller (Eds.), *The Foucault Effect: Studies in Governmental Rationality* (pp. 73–86). Hemel Hempstead: Harvester-Wheatsheaf.
Foucault, M. (2000). *Power, Essential Works of Foucault, 1954–1984*. New York: New Press.
Goldstein, J. (1993). *Ideas, Institutions, and American Trade Policy*. Ithaca, NY: Cornell University Press.
Goldstein J., & Keohane, R. (1993). *Ideas and Foreign Policy: Beliefs, Institutions and Political Change*. Ithaca, NY: Cornell University Press.
Hall, P. A. (Ed.). (1989). *The Political Power of Economic Ideas: Keynesianism across Nations*. Princeton, NJ: Princeton University Press.
Hall, P. A. (1993). Policy paradigms, social learning and the state: The case of economic policymaking in Britain. *Comparative Politics*, 25(3), 275–296.
Hall, P. A., & Taylor, R. C. R. (1996). Political science and the three new institutionalisms. *Political Studies*, 44(5), 936–957.
Hay, C. (2001). The 'Crisis' of Keynesianism and the Rise of Neoliberalism in Britain: An Ideational Institutionalist Approach. In J. L. Campbell & O. K. Pedersen (Eds.), *The Rise of Neoliberalism and Institutional Analysis* (pp. 193–218). Princeton, NJ: Princeton University Press.
Hay, C. (2006). Constructivist Institutionalism. In R. A. W. Rhodes, S. Binder & B. Rockman (Eds.), *The Oxford Handbook of Political Institutions* (pp. 56–74). Oxford: Oxford University Press.
Hay, C. (2011). Ideas and the Construction of Interests. In D. Béland & R. H. Cox (Eds.), *Ideas and Politics in Social Science Research* (pp. 65–83). Oxford: Oxford University Press.
Heclo, H. (1974). *Modern Social Politics in Britain and Sweden*. New Haven, CT: Yale University Press
Jabko, N. (2006). *Playing the Market*. Ithaca, NY: Cornell University Press.
Keynes, J. M. (1936). *The General Theory of Unemployment, Interest and Money*. New York: Classic Books America.
Kingdon, J. W. (1984). *Agendas, Alternatives and Public Policies*. New York: Longman.
Lukes, S. (2005). *Power: A Radical View* (2nd ed.). Basingstoke: Palgrave.
Laclau, E. (1996). *Emancipation(s)*. London: Verso.
March, J. G., & Olsen, J. P. (1984). The new institutionalism: Organization factors in political life. *American Political Science Review*, 78(3), 734–749.
March, J. G., & Olsen, J. P. (1989). *Rediscovering Institutions: The Organizational Basis of Politics*. New York: Free Press.
March, J. G., & Olsen, J. P. (2008). Elaborating the 'New Institutionalism'. In S. A. Binder, A. W. Rhodes & B. A. Rockman (Eds.), *The Oxford Handbook of Political Institutions*. Oxford: Oxford University Press
Mehta, J. (2011). The Varied Roles of Ideas in Politics: From 'Whether' to 'How'. In D. Béland & R. H. Cox (Eds.), *Ideas and Politics in Social Science Research* (pp. 23–47). Oxford: Oxford University Press.
North, D. C. (2005). *Understanding the Process of Economic Change*. Princeton, NJ: Princeton University Press.
Parsons, C. (2003). *A Certain Idea of Europe*. Ithaca, NY: Cornell University Press.
Peters, B. G. (1998). *Institutional Theory in Political Science: The 'New Institutionalism'*. London: Pinter.
Roe, E. (1994). *Narrative Policy Analysis: Theory and Practice*. Durham, NC: Duke University Press.
Rothstein, B. (2005). *Social Traps and the Problem of Trust*. Cambridge: Cambridge University Press.
Schmidt, V. (2008). Discursive institutionalism: The explanatory power of ideas and discourse. *The Annual Review of Political Science*, 11, 303–326.
Schmidt, V. (2011). Reconciling Ideas and Institutions through Discursive Institutionalism. In D. Béland & R. H. Cox (Eds.), *Ideas and Politics in Social Science Research* (pp. 47–65). Oxford: Oxford University Press.
Schön, D. (1983). *The Reflective Practitioner: How Professionals Think in Action*. New York: Basic Books.
Skinner, Q. (2002). *Visions of Politics, Regarding Method*. Cambridge: Cambridge University Press.
Tannenwald, N. (2005). Ideas and explanation: Advancing the theoretical agenda. *Journal of Cold War Studies*, 7(2), 13–42.
Wendt, A. (1987). The agent-structure problem in international relations theory. *International Organization*, 41(3), 335–370.

5
INSTITUTIONS IN URBAN SPACE

Land, Infrastructure, and Governance in the Production of Urban Property

André Sorensen

Introduction

A basic function of local government is to regulate and manage the production and reproduction of urban space and property. These powers are embedded in complex sets of urban governance institutions, and demonstrate great diversity in jurisdictions around the world. The rules governing capital investment in urban property are particularly important during the current phase of global urbanization, as the world urban population is projected to increase by 2.5 billion to 6.3 billion by 2050 (UNDESA, 2014), and the total urban area is projected to more than double over the next two decades (Angel, 2012). Whatever the actual amount, the growth of urban area will be enormous, and urban property and infrastructure is currently one of the world's largest arenas of capital investment. A major claim of this chapter is that the rules in place during phases of urban growth have profound long-term implications for the urban property and space created.

This chapter follows on and extends the argument in my recent paper (Sorensen, 2015) that made the case for a serious engagement of planning historians with 'historical institutionalism'. Here I develop a 'historical institutionalist' approach to an examination of urban space and urban property, suggesting that municipal governance, infrastructure, and property institutions are particularly path dependent, and that a historical institutionalist approach provides valuable insights for both planning theory and planning practice. This project is intended to complement that of Patsy Healey, whose 'sociological institutionalist' approach provides a relational and social constructivist account of the actors involved in local governance processes, with particular focus on how institutions structure the ways actors produce meaning from complex social realities, and how groups of actors mobilize to achieve innovation and transformation of local governance in specific settings.

My contribution is to suggest that historical institutionalism is particularly suited to an analysis of what Healey refers to as "Formalised government (comprising the systems and organisations of formal law, politics and administration and the practices associated with this activity)" (see Healey, Chapter 2, in this volume). That is, while Healey's approach provides profound insights into the actors in the drama of urban governance and how they construct meaning and action, a historical institutionalist approach helps make sense of the institutional architectures specific to the formal structures of local government, planning, and infrastructure building that shape the production of urban property, and the path-dependent qualities of urban space and property itself. Neither of these approaches is particularly suited to the examination of property markets or developers, which constitute the third major element of the city-building trio of citizens, governance institutions, and markets, each of which has its own actors, institutionalized patterns of action, and change processes.

The focus here is therefore on the formal structures of local government including municipal laws and regulations, spatial planning systems, property ownership rules, taxation systems, development control rules, and infrastructure management and finance systems. Each city has a distinct set of constraints in the powers allowed by senior governments, and equally in its own history, geography, and its particular timing and sequencing of institutional and spatial development. I have argued elsewhere that planning institutions are path dependent, interdependent and socially constructed (Sorensen, 2015), and that they are commonly established during critical junctures of institution-making that are contingent and differentiated between jurisdictions (Sorensen, 2018a).

The production, regulation, protection, and servicing of urban property has been central to the emergence of municipal government institutions. Evolving from attempts by merchants in medieval Europe to usurp legal and political space for self-governance from feudal lords, the city corporation was created as a vehicle to share ownership and costs of municipal infrastructure, public spaces, defence, and self-management (Magnusson, 1996; Weber, 1958). The city corporation is also the origin of the modern business corporation, with the legal distinction between public and private corporate status only decided in the United States in the mid-nineteenth century (Frug, 1980).

Fundamental to the city's institutional DNA are the city corporation's powers to own property, provide services, build and maintain infrastructure, borrow capital, raise taxes, regulate private capital investment in property, regulate working and trading conditions, and record and register land transactions and divisions. The earliest municipal corporations established courts to adjudicate property disputes, and police powers to enforce property rules. Although increasingly subjected to control by nation states from the fifteenth century, this basic corporate institutional structure was spread around the world through conquest and colonization from the sixteenth to twentieth centuries (Home, 1997; King, 1990), and has become the globally dominant form, albeit with considerable variation in powers and autonomy. City governments have responsibility for management of the urban fabric, in which huge amounts of public and private capital is invested, and significantly, each city has monopoly control of municipal governance institutions within its territory. These powers and responsibilities are extraordinary, but have been so normalized that we scarcely notice their fundamental structuring role, particularly with regard to urban property.

This chapter develops a historical institutionalist analysis of urban governance, spatial planning practices, and urban property. Most historical institutionalist work ignores space and cities entirely, focusing instead on aspatial national and international policies and institutions, and there has been no systematic effort to incorporate historical institutionalism into planning theory, or to develop its insights for planning practice. A historical institutionalist approach provides a conceptual framework for understanding the political dynamics of urban institutional change, contributing to our understanding of the social production of space, and helping to explain the enduring diversity of planning systems and capacities in different jurisdictions. As Blomley (1998, p. 569) argued, "socially produced space is saturated with power relations". This paper develops a conceptual framework for analysis of the ways in which the sets of institutions that structure the production of property in cities are also socially produced, in processes that are similarly saturated with power relations.

The six core historical institutionalist concepts outlined below support a distinctive perspective on urban property and the institutions that structure and support it. The rules around property investment are contested and produce highly uneven distributional outcomes, and property institutions are characterized by densely co-evolutionary processes of institutional and spatial change over time. In these processes, the timing, sequencing, and conditions governing the creation of new units of property are key, as they create enduring spatial units of property and patterns of infrastructure. The claim is that this perspective helps us to understand urban property and the roles of planning and urban governance in structuring it, and generates new research questions and a robust method for comparative research.

The core argument of this chapter is that the spatially differentiated patterns of urban property, public space, infrastructure, and other forms of capital investment in cities are profoundly institutionalized. I propose that we group urban property institutions into three main categories:

1. *Urban land and property institutions*, including property laws and regulations, building codes, cadastral records systems, property taxes, financial systems, property markets, spatial planning systems that regulate changes to property and the creation of new property units, and others. Most of these are implemented by local governments, but some may be the responsibility of senior governments.
2. *Infrastructure institutions*, including the rules and systems structuring the creation, regulation, funding and maintenance of streets and other public spaces, transport systems, parks and green spaces, water supply and sewers, and schools, etc. Infrastructure is produced by a politically mediated and contested set of funding, management, and maintenance institutions that have specific geographies and relationships to property.
3. *Governance institutions* – including municipal governments and the senior governments that delegate powers to them and create the rules that they must follow – that establish and modify urban regulations, design, finance, and manage public infrastructure and services, regulate private activity, and enforce compliance. Local government powers are in most cases decided by senior governments, but their actual capacities, and the geographies of local government units is a product of their history. Local governments have many responsibilities, but the focus here is on the regulation of property.

Municipal governance territories and institutions tend to be quite varied in different cities even within countries, national systems are diverse, and once established these differences tend to exhibit the continuities over time associated with path-dependent systems. The evolving legacies of institutional choices made at the local level also produce a profound diversity of institutional arrangements between cities both because of contingent processes of institutional evolution and differences in underlying legal systems (Healey, 2006; Newman & Thornley, 1996; Salet, 2002).

The suggestion is that the interrelationships between these three sets of institutions tend to reinforce their path dependence, so that even if some aspects change, the overall configuration and function of the institutional matrix continues (see North, 1990). But even more important, every urban property parcel is shaped by and thus permanently imprinted with the set of rules that existed when it was created, because parcels are always embedded within sets of other parcels, public spaces, infrastructures, and governance systems. These spatially differentiated configurations are enduring and consequential. The impact of municipal governance on urban property is powerfully reinforced by the fact that each land parcel has a unique location and relationship to other urban spaces, has a distinct set of infrastructures and services available, and cannot be moved to another location.

In the next section I review the core concepts of historical institutionalism. I then apply this set of concepts to urban space, and outline the interrelationships between land, infrastructure, and governance institutions, and the spaces they regulate. The concluding discussion outlines some insights about urban property and planning that flow from this conceptual framework.

Core Concepts of Historical Institutionalism

This section defines 'institutions' and outlines six core historical institutionalist concepts that provide a conceptual framework for a historical institutionalist analysis of spatial planning: path dependence and positive feedback effects; critical junctures of institution formation; the unequal distributional impacts of institutions; structured processes of incremental institutional change; co-evolution processes among institutions; and the significant role of discourse and ideas in helping to frame alternative approaches (for a fuller exposition and literature reviews, see Sorensen, 2015, 2017).

The definition of institutions is important, and there are many approaches, depending on the focus of research. For the study of planning institutions and property, Streeck and Thelen's (2005, p. 9) definition of institutions as "collectively enforced expectations with respect to the behaviour of specific categories of actors or to the performance of certain activities" is useful. Remembering that many 'collectively enforced expectations' are informal, in spatial planning there are many relevant institutions in the form of laws and regulations that are routinely enforced by municipal governments and agencies.

It is useful to start with path dependence, the idea that some institutions become harder to change over time because they generate self-reinforcing 'positive feedback' effects. Path dependence is defined by Pierson as referring to "social processes that exhibit positive feedback and thus generate branching patterns of historical development" (Pierson, 2004, p. 21). Where positive feedback effects are present, particular critical junctures or institutional choices lead to the creation of new branches, and over time it becomes more difficult or more costly to jump from one branch to another, or to revert to a previously available option. A major form of positive feedback in governance processes is where individuals or groups who benefit from an institution have incentives to resist changes that will reduce their power or rewards (Hacker, 2002; Mahoney & Thelen, 2010; Pierson, 2004).

The suggestion is not that path dependence in cities means that institutions become frozen or that particular patterns are 'locked in'. Clearly the large sunk costs of investments in immoveable buildings and infrastructure is a significant source of continuity, but cities do continuously change and transform. Rather, the idea is that institutional choices early in a process can generate self-reinforcing feedback and may therefore be difficult to reverse, and that purely institutional facts may be equally or more path dependent than literally concrete ones. For example, a policy such as single-family-detached zoning of neighbourhoods is often vigorously defended when change is threatened, and similar political support for parks and green space and other urban amenities is common. Pierson's (2004, p. 30) particular insight is that political processes are often even more path dependent than market processes because of the necessity of collective action, the high density of institutions, positive returns to power, and their inherent complexity.

A second core historical institutionalist concept is the idea that institutions are often created during critical junctures or moments of crisis, times when established structures fail to provide either adequate solutions to pressing problems or convincing explanations of changing contexts. In such moments of crisis, actors seek new approaches. As Capoccia and Kelemen put it:

> During critical junctures change is substantially less constrained than it is during the phases of path dependence that precede and follow them. In critical junctures contingency is enhanced, as the structural constraints imposed on actors during the path-dependent phase are substantially relaxed.
>
> *(Capoccia & Kelemen, 2007, p. 368)*

The idea of contingency is that during critical junctures the particular choices made will depend on the circumstances, timing, power relations, and combinations of actors involved, so it is impossible to determine the outcome in advance. Such contingency does not mean that the choices made are random, but decisions have unavoidably to be made with less than full information, and dominant actors vary between places and times, so minor differences in conditions or timing may lead to very different outcomes. A prime example is the establishment of modern planning systems in all advanced countries at the beginning of the twentieth century in response to the nineteenth-century crisis of urban industrialization. There was significant variety in the new planning institutions that emerged in different jurisdictions, and these differences have produced enduringly distinct approaches (Booth, 1996; Sutcliffe, 1981).

A third claim is that institutions unavoidably distribute valued resources unequally, and that such unequal distributional effects can powerfully structure both political opportunity and political mobilization (Mahoney & Thelen, 2010). In this view, institutions are understood not as static sets of rules, but as dynamic products of political conflicts and as the legacy of past struggles. They are continually contested, as they shape political power, choices and behaviour, and can serve to mobilize action either for their reform, or in their defence. As Lowndes puts it: "institutional rules embody power relations by privileging certain positions and certain courses of action over others – they express 'patterns of distributional advantage'" (Lowndes, 2009, p. 95). It takes power to impose new sets of rules, but once established, those rules can sometimes be used to reinforce a position of advantage. This represents one form of positive feedback supporting institutional continuity.

A fourth major focus of historical institutionalism is on structured processes of incremental and endogenously driven institutional change. Much research over the last decade has been on incremental change (Hacker, 2004; Lowndes & Roberts, 2013; Mahoney & Thelen, 2010; Thelen, 2003). Institutions clearly do evolve outside of critical junctures, and such changes are shaped by characteristics of the institution in question, by institutional settings and revision procedures, and by the characteristics of the actors who seek change. Although obviously a simplification, this is easiest to express as a simple binary: change is most sought by those who were losers in previous rounds of institutional development, who have the most to gain from policy change, while those who benefit from existing arrangements are more likely to seek to further entrench or strengthen existing rules.

Many urban planning and governance institutions do see incremental change processes over time, and many urban institutions are open to significant levels of interpretation and discretion in enforcement. Even in a situation of stable rules, different interpretations of the rules, or strict or lax enforcement of them can lead in practice to institutional change (Mahoney & Thelen, 2010). The question is which sorts of institutions tend to see which types of incremental change processes, and how this can help us to better understand patterns and processes of incremental change in cities.

A fifth core concept is that institutions always operate in conjunction with multiple other institutions and are co-evolutionary. North (1990) described such complementary institutions as interdependent webs of an institutional matrix. Urban planning is a matrix of dozens or even hundreds of different institutions that have profound impacts on the others' operation and implementation processes. The concept of co-evolution is that incremental change and mutual adaptation over time affects all the institutions in a matrix. Such interdependence and co-evolution is well explained by Van Assche et al., "the relations between the different institutions and between actors and institutions can be conceptualized as interdependencies. Each step on a governance path is conditioned, not only by the previous steps, but also by the pattern of actors and institutions that evolved over time" (Van Assche et al., 2015, p. 30, see also Van Assche et al., 2017 forthcoming). Institutional co-evolution increases the likelihood of significant differences emerging between jurisdictions, because in each jurisdiction the particular sets of institutions that co-evolve most closely and the circumstances that trigger change are likely to be different, with environmental challenges prominent in one place, economic processes dominating change in another, or a particular disaster or risk driving change in a third.

A sixth core concept is that ideas and discourses can be powerful institutions (Blyth, 2002; Hay, 2004; Schmidt, 2008; Taylor, 2013). As Blyth (2002) argued, ideas matter because they shape people's conceptions of their own self-interest, structure their conceptions of possible and desirable change, and serve as powerful tools in contests over urban policies. Urban ideas include changing normative conceptions of 'good urban form' that have been influential in anti-sprawl and smart growth campaigns, but also in conceptions of desirable housing (or marketable from the point of view of the developer), safe investments, risky places, and possible and desirable interventions by the state. Existing spatial patterns are also facts-on-the-ground that shape conceivable interventions, potential for change, profitability of further investment, and local opposition to or support for changed policies.

Ideas have profound impacts on urban infrastructure, through concepts of best management practice ranging from municipal ownership to contemporary demands for privatization, from expectations for universal service delivery to various profit-making approaches. And similar to urban form, existing infrastructure approaches can powerfully constrain what most people conceive to be possible, in areas from energy supply to transport infrastructure.

But the structuring and enabling role of ideas is possibly most profound in the realm of urban governance. Planning interventions are profoundly and always constrained by conceptions of legitimate governance interventions. Ideas about the appropriate division of powers and responsibilities between state, market and civil society are quite different in different places and at different times (Healey & Upton, 2010; Sanyal, 2005), and while ideas change, they can have long-lasting impacts in the particular choices of governance institutions that are made during critical junctures, that themselves often turn out to be highly path dependent even if the dominant ideas that helped to shape those particular compromises themselves lose power and are discarded. Part of urban governance, especially for those with particular agendas to advance, is to attempt to shape and re-shape concepts of good policy, legitimate interventions, and possible futures.

Institutions and Urban Space

This section proposes a conceptual framework for applying historical institutionalism to urban space and property. Historical institutionalism urges a greater attention in social science to issues associated with temporality in social processes (Pierson, 2004; Thelen & Mahoney, 2015). For the institutional study of cities, we must also pay careful attention to issues of space, and the issues specific to the production, maintenance, and governance of urban space over both short and long time horizons.

There are significant conceptual challenges related to the complexity and multiplicity of urban institutions, and to the related fact that cities usually consist of spatial patterns and investments that were created over extended periods. The solidity of buildings and the expense of major urban infrastructure create an illusion of permanence that is belied by the constant change seen in most cities. I suggest that the 'sunk costs' of facts-on-the-ground of existing built forms and structures are important, but that path dependence in urban space is much more varied in its origins than sunk costs, and is in particular shaped by the urban institutional matrices that regulate capital investment in property. Evolving approaches to planning and the regulation of urban development over the course of the twentieth century meant that systems regulating the production of property have changed over time, and therefore the geographies and specifications of property created at different times have also evolved, creating differentiated landscapes of property (see Blomley (1998) for a valuable conception of landscapes of property) that vary across geographical space by time and place of development.

I have proposed three main categories of urban property institution: (1) Urban land and property institutions, (2) Urban infrastructure institutions, and (3) Urban governance institutions, as defined above. All three are necessary components of every urban system. The fact that changes to urban property institutions, to urban infrastructure institutions, or to urban governance institutions can powerfully influence property values generates dynamism – and intense conflicts over changes to the rules – and creates significant interrelationships between the three categories. All three are highly path dependent, but in different ways, with their own evolutionary processes, actors, reform mechanisms, veto points, and veto players. It is worth discussing each of these categories separately, while remembering that they are in practice interdependent, co-constitutive, and co-evolutionary parts of an institutional matrix, and are embedded in every urban parcel, as discussed below.

Urban Property Institutions

It makes sense to start with property institutions, as urban property gives rise to the need both for infrastructure – at minimum a street network but usually much more – and some form of legal authority to regulate and maintain that infrastructure and to regulate property itself.

Urban property institutions are powerfully shaped by the distinctive characteristics of landed property (including both land and structures). First, each land parcel has a unique location, and cannot be moved, so has enduring and consequential relationships with other properties, public spaces, infrastructures, and governance systems. For example, the value and meaning of a property within a single-family-home neighbourhood is fundamentally different from an otherwise identical property located in an industrial district, or near a city centre, and these are influenced both by the sets of neighbouring uses and nearby infrastructures, and the potential for significant change in use or intensity. The urban pattern of streets and parcels is, in practice, difficult and costly to change, so in most cases street networks and parcel boundaries change very slowly, even while buildings are demolished and rebuilt, and parcels are sometimes assembled into larger units or further subdivided. Every urban property is thus profoundly structured by the sets of rules and ideas that determined the pattern of streets and parcels around it.

Second, changes to the rules, and public and private investments in urban space, can have powerful impacts on urban property values throughout a city (the classic study is Hagman & Misczynski, 1978). The structural incentive to maintain or increase property values means that institutional and material changes that may lower property values will usually face opposition. Incentives favour changes from lower to higher land values, from less to more fragmented property, and from less to more dense and complex patterns of infrastructure and institutionalization. Such changes are inherently difficult to reverse, both because of the enhanced property values created, and because of the complex matrices of institutions that are established in the process.

The case of a new residential subdivision is useful as an illustration. When farmland is developed, it is much more than just surveying a site, dividing it into parcels, and building houses. In fact it is also a complex process of institutionalization, and what is being sold is not just houses, but legally defined parcels with street access, guarantees that those streets will be maintained, that fresh water will be delivered through pipes and waste water removed and treated, that schools and other municipal services will be available, that garbage will be collected, police will protect against trespassing, and that a scrapyard will not locate next door. Although it is conceivable from a construction point of view that the process could be reversed, houses demolished, pipes and streets removed, and properties reassembled, that almost never happens. This is not just because of the huge expense and loss of property value inherent in reversal, but also because it is difficult or impossible to get all the new property owners to agree, and to undo the new institutional fabric.

The redevelopment of an inner city parcel such as a former factory site to a high-rise condominium property is a comparable process of transformation from a less densely to more densely institutionalized space, with more complex property rights, and higher aggregate property value. Although it is technically possible to reverse this process, that is extremely rare. Condominium is also a particularly path-dependent form of property ownership because of the by-laws and covenants that regulate shared ownership and present significant obstacles to major change. For simplicity these are both examples of physical changes, but legal, political and policy changes can also shift the meaning of the built environment in material ways without implying any physical change at all, as for example in a rezoning, or even a change to a building code. For example, in Japan the central government dramatically increased permitted building heights and floor area ratio (FAR) throughout the country by changing the rules for FAR calculations in the building code (Sorensen et al., 2010). A regulatory change to allow increased development capacity is normally unidirectional in the sense that moves in the opposite direction to reduce permitted development could trigger demands for compensation.

Seen this way it becomes clear that urban property is embedded in a complex mesh of interlinked rights, obligations, guarantees, and risks. Some of these are formally recognized in title deeds, some are contracts between property owners and municipal governments, some are unwritten and customary, while others are generated merely by proximity (see Fennell, 2009). Property owners have powerful incentives to prevent changes that will lower the resale value of their property, so such changes are often vigorously opposed by NIMBY movements. Such 'defensive localism' is a fundamental driver of urban politics (Cox, 2002; Dear, 1992).

We should therefore see capital investment in urban property not merely as a construction process, but as a highly complex process of urban institutionalization, in which dense new networks of rights, obligations, relationships, and expectations are established. Urban property development can be understood as a *spatial critical juncture* in which new place-related facts are created, including land parcels and the property rights and values associated with them, the varied infrastructures that support them, and the city governance promises that enable and protect them. These processes should be examined with careful regard to their timing and sequencing, the actors involved, and the particular sets of power relations, values, and configurations that are embedded in the new urban forms.

The particular aggregations of property that are produced in different jurisdictions always create significant positive feedback effects and long-term links to other urban institutions that will vary depending on the nature of the property produced. The particular sets of property that are produced at a given place and time will vary based on the then-dominant rules and ideas, and these vary in time and place. The spatial and institutional patterns created vary over time, are enduring, and have different meanings and potential for future change.

Urban Infrastructure Institutions

A second set of highly path-dependent institutions is associated with urban infrastructure networks and their ongoing management and maintenance requirements. Investments in water supply, sewers, subways, and roads are usually expensive, so the most obviously enduring characteristic of urban infrastructure is a result of large capital costs, usually referred to as 'sunk costs' because most such investments cannot be moved, and multiple other locational choices are then based on the existence of the system. Early choices and locations get reinforced. While this factor is worth keeping in view in any analysis of path dependence in cities, as it may influence many other choices, three other characteristics of urban infrastructure may generate more important path dependencies.

First is that fact that many urban infrastructures are networks that have significant 'natural monopoly' characteristics because the high initial costs of building the network mean that it is wasteful to build duplicate competing systems. The obvious example is that of water supply and wastewater removal, but city gas systems, electricity grids, municipal waste collection, streets and streetlights, transit systems, and other network infrastructure have similar properties. As a result they have usually been provided either by municipal governments, or by selling long-term monopoly franchises to private investors. Such natural monopoly services (whether publicly or privately delivered) are likely for multiple reasons to be more path dependent (without making any claims about efficiency) than cases where multiple competing providers can engage in continuous competitive innovation in service delivery (see Sorensen, 2015 for the detailed argument and references).

Second is the fact that the early establishment of a particular infrastructural choice can block the subsequent emergence of other potentially equally viable or better alternatives. For example, Quitzau (2007) examines flush toilets and waterborne sewer systems, and points to the strongly path-dependent character of modern sewage technologies. Although in many water-scarce regions using six litres of drinking water to flush small amounts of human waste is deeply problematic, it has proven difficult to introduce alternative technologies such as composting toilets. This is in part because universal flush toilet use makes it inexpensive relative to other options because of economies of scale, in part because municipal by-laws and building codes frequently mandate flush toilet use for new building projects, and in part because many people have come to accept flush toilets as a marker of cleanliness, civility, and minimum sanitary practice. This is a clear case of the early dominance of a particular technology leading to a path-dependent trajectory, even though more locally appropriate technologies have since been developed.

An equally important case is automobile dominance of urban transportation systems. During the last 60 years, a radically new urban form was deliberately created in order to accommodate mass automobile use, initially in North America and subsequently in cities around the world. Auto-dominant urban areas tend to have much lower population densities than before, see rapid expansion into peripheral areas, have hierarchical road systems, and much larger single-use areas of housing, employment, and retail uses.

Automobile dominance is path dependent in part because the urban forms of automobile-oriented cities make it difficult to run cost-effective and viable public transit services (Filion, 2010; Miller & Soberman, 2003); at the same time the automobile-related industrial complex generated huge profits and powerful political forces in support of automobile-related infrastructure (Dunn, 1998; Urry, 2004), boosted the administrative capacity of the road building bureaucracy while management and fiscal capacity in the public transit sector declined (Low & Astle, 2009), and automobile use became increasingly normalized and seemingly inevitable.

Third, the management bodies established to deliver, finance, and maintain urban infrastructure are themselves often highly path dependent. Different cities have adopted different approaches to the ownership, management, finance and policy-making for municipal infrastructure and service delivery, and such approaches can have profound distributional consequences in terms of overall quality of life, costs, environmental impacts, and the distribution of costs and benefits. Such systems and choices embody the power relations existing at the time they were established, and those choices frequently have long legacies.

A clear example is the shift to special service districts for the delivery of services such as water and wastewater, schools, and parks in most US cities during the Progressive Era before and after the First World War. The goal was to professionalize and depoliticize such services and reduce corruption at city hall. Such service districts have taxation powers, often have directly elected managers, and borrow large amounts of capital from financial markets to finance the building and maintenance of infrastructure networks. This has proven to be a highly path-dependent institutional innovation which is difficult to reverse. It has also profoundly influenced municipal governance, as sewer and water districts are independent of municipal government and often include much larger territories. Whereas in Canadian cities municipal governments manage water and sewers directly, and have used them as an effective tool of growth management, that is impossible for most US cities as service districts are self-governing and self-financing (Tarr & Konvitz, 1987).

Urban Governance Institutions

The third category of urban institutions are those related to urban governance, including municipal governments and their decision systems, the senior governments that delegate powers to them, planning systems and property laws, and the territorial division of space into different municipal jurisdictions. Urban governance institutions overlap significantly with both property institutions and infrastructure institutions, and the three categories work together to form interdependent institutional matrices. But it is useful to consider separately some of the characteristics of path dependency in urban governance institutions.

Municipal governments occupy a defined territory. Such territories can be changed, for example by annexing adjacent suburbs, or by amalgamation with adjacent municipalities whether voluntarily or forcibly by a senior government, but normally municipal boundaries are relatively stable. Municipalities are not able to move somewhere that has a better climate, or a more congenial central government that allows them more powers or revenues. And in most countries rules around annexation tend in most cases to make it relatively difficult to accomplish, especially if the target area is already partly urban with its own urban property, infrastructure, and governance institutions.

Yet the location, size, and geography of any given municipality is profoundly important for urban fortunes. In the United States tightly bounded central cities lost tax revenues as the middle class moved out to the suburbs, and small suburban municipalities have protected their autonomy fiercely. The result has been highly fragmented and sprawling metropolitan regions that see major regional inequities in access to schools, jobs, and quality urban services (Orfield,

1997; Rusk, 2003). Conditions vary widely between jurisdictions, and have major impacts on the capacity of local governance institutions. Contingent choices fix the geographies of municipal boundaries, whether they include whole functional urban regions or are fragmented, and the particular mix of powers, resources, and responsibilities they exercise, which are almost always decided by senior levels of government.

Local government capacities are also always constrained by their own past choices of undertaking some initiatives and not others, and the pattern of spaces, institutions, and actors that emerged. Since there are always limited resources and capacity, then investing heavily in one approach such as expressways or parks means that other choices such as public transit or social housing get less. These choices have long-term impacts including maintenance costs and opportunities not created. As is clear from the United States, where municipal revenues depend primarily on taxes based on the value of property, jurisdictions with low and/or declining property values experience different fiscal conditions than those with high and/or rising property values. If all municipalities had a similar mix of rich and poor and similar legacies of prior infrastructure investment, historical patterns of development would differentiate cities less, but in fact these are highly variable. The set of properties in any given municipal territory thus has self-reinforcing qualities that reinforce path dependency in many cases. A poor city with a collection of small ageing houses on small lots and limited services cannot easily transform itself into a wealthy city with mansions on large lots and high quality services.

Similarly, contingent choices in the development of governance institutions and spatial planning policies and laws generate quite varied outcomes in different jurisdictions. Both the systems regulating the creation of new property, and the forms and specifications of the property they produce are extremely varied, even when the built form of buildings is superficially similar. For example, a condominium property built in Florida in the 1970s has different property rights from one built in 2010 because of intervening changes in condominium law, and that in turn has different property rights and obligations from one built in the same years in Ontario, or Japan, or Malaysia, because of differing legal regimes and traditions. Similarly, the extensive areas of informal development outside São Paulo or Mexico City that have been regularized and granted legal title have a fundamentally different set of property rights and protections, and relationships to the state than do planned suburbs outside Phoenix, Nanjing, or Bangalore. Urban property is a highly differentiated set of products that generate distinct political dynamics and path-dependent trajectories in different cities and under differing legal and governance regimes.

The point is that urban jurisdictions are governed through hundreds of interdependent institutions that co-evolve because they impact each other in multiple and continuous ways. Jurisdictions have profoundly different histories, institutions and capacities, and these have had powerful impacts on the institutions that have developed, the mix and varieties of property that have been created, the actors that are engaged in urban governance processes, and the meaning of urban space.

Interdependence of the Three Categories

These three categories of urban institution are interdependent in their structuration of urban property, as illustrated in Figure 5.1.

Urban property is always embedded in a triangular relationship with specific sets of infrastructure and governance institutions, in a particular municipal jurisdiction with a unique geography and history. In this perspective, urban property is a bundle not only of property rights associated with a specific property, but also of relationships with surrounding public and private property, and with specific infrastructures and governance institutions.

Institutions in Urban Space

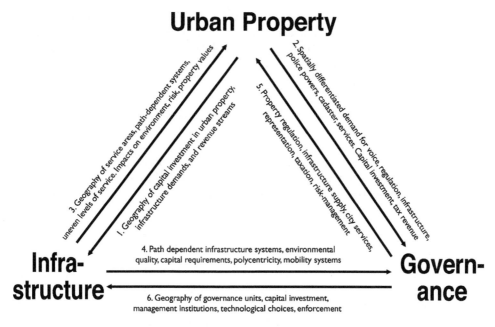

Figure 5.1 The urban property triangle: Relationships between categories of urban institutions
Source: Sorensen (2018b)

The analysis in Figure 5.1 starts from the premise that spatiality is fundamental to the distinctive patterns of positive feedback in cities. Urban property institutions, infrastructure institutions, and governance institutions in each jurisdiction are tightly linked and co-evolutionary, and likely to be path dependent. But in each jurisdiction they are also profoundly related to the existing sets of property, infrastructure, and government units that they support, as existing institutions shape patterns on the ground, and patterns on the ground generate spatially differentiated feedback effects that are likely to powerfully influence processes of institutional stability and change. The paragraph numbers correspond to those in the Figure 5.1 indicating the direction of influence of one category on another.

(1) Existing spatially differentiated patterns of urban property generate important positive feedback effects on infrastructure management and financing institutions by structuring demands for continued/improved service, and by supplying spatially differentiated revenue streams to infrastructure suppliers. This works partly through the aggregation of particular sets of property into territories where service provision is mandated, and areas outside the territory where no such obligation exists, but also by creating differential levels of services and revenues in different areas.

(2) Spatially differentiated patterns of property generate parallel impacts on governance institutions, by aggregating political demands for regulatory protection or services for particular areas, reinforcing long-lasting political boundaries and sometimes sharp divisions between rich and poor districts or jurisdictions, and as a result of the emergence of particular political and planning cultures and capacities in different places during specific past conjunctures. The social capital to enhance or protect local place qualities is highly variable, tends to be embedded in particular places, and can be self-reinforcing where local governance episodes lead to the emergence of governance cultures that support the continued development of local governance capacity (Healey, 2006).

(3) Infrastructure systems, by structuring the provision of essential services to urban property, impact property in spatially differentiated ways, most prominently through geographical boundaries of service districts, through path-dependent choices of particular technologies and capacities and not others within particular territories, and by imposing long-term cost/benefit structures that have profound impacts on property values and development potential.
(4) Infrastructure systems affect governance processes by making some choices obvious and rendering others unthinkable; and generating demands for continued services, or for continued growth to pay for earlier choices. Where infrastructure provision has been established independently of municipal governments as in much of the United States the available set of city planning tools is circumscribed, or shifted to the level of intergovernmental affairs, from one of inter-departmental coordination.
(5) Geographically differentiated municipal governments structure urban property by defining and enforcing the expectations associated with particular collections of urban property; by levying taxes and providing services; and by regulating and sometimes actively pursuing development projects that seek to change those patterns. Political boundaries aggregate certain collections of property, costs and revenues, and actors, and exclude others. Municipal government actors develop and enhance some governance capacities and neglect others.
(6) Similarly, geographically differentiated municipal governments impact infrastructure institutions by setting territorial boundaries and infrastructure standards, regulating property, providing services and enforcement, mandating and/or investing in new infrastructure, and setting liability and risk-management standards, among many others.

The sets of property, infrastructure and governance institutions in each municipality are profoundly interdependent and necessarily co-evolve over time because of their relationships to spatially differentiated sets of urban property. Each type of institution also has its own actors, processes and veto points for rule changes, implementation and enforcement approaches, and developmental pathways. At the same time, urban property is one of the largest and most lucrative repositories of capital, which can be transformative in its impacts on particular places. Mediating arising conflicts is a traditional task of planning, and of municipal corporations long before modern planning emerged.

This triangular relationship of urban property institutions, infrastructure institutions, and governance institutions appears highly likely to be path dependent. There are three main aspects of path dependence to consider: First is that sets of property are forever linked together in space and to a particular jurisdiction. Property and its supporting institutions work together as a matrix, so changes to any aspect of the system affect all the others to a greater or lesser degree. Institutional matrices are more likely to be path dependent because interdependence limits the range of possible change that can occur without undermining the function of the system as a whole.

Second, property owners, infrastructure suppliers, and local governments all have powerful incentives to prevent changes that might threaten property values. While the built form of property is immobile and usually changes incrementally, the value of property can shift rapidly and radically with fluctuations in demand. As cities are reliant on continued property investment, there are incentives to avoid changes that increase short or long-term uncertainty, so paradoxically, the very liquidity of property markets is likely to promote institutional stability.

A third form of positive feedback is seen in self-reinforcing spirals of decline and spirals of growth. As has been shown so often in the United States – where municipalities are dependent primarily on property taxes for revenue and are fragmented into relatively small units – self-reinforcing processes of growth or decline are common. Some contingent factor such as a large new investment or the closure of a major industry can tip a jurisdiction either into a positive cycle of increased property values, better municipal revenues and services, and greater attractiveness to new investments, or the reverse. Either way the benefits or costs to local residents and businesses can be substantial. Such tendencies exist everywhere, but tend to be less dramatic and visible where higher levels of government pay for a larger share of municipal expenditures, and where municipal territories are large or include whole functional urban regions. Self-reinforcing spirals of growth and decline are of particular concern because of their powerfully regressive redistributive impacts, with locations where poor people live much more likely to suffer spirals of decline, while those with more wealth can choose to live in places with a much greater likelihood of long-term increases in asset values.

Discussion

This chapter is a contribution to an institutionalist analysis of urban property that draws on historical institutionalist approaches to examine the logics of urban property as institutionalized space. I argue that urban property, infrastructure, and governance institutions play a central role in regulating capital investment in cities, shaping the kinds of property that can be created, and servicing, protecting, and structuring its long-term meanings and values.

This approach suggests that there are profound and enduring variations between jurisdictions, that urban institutions are produced during contingent moments of crisis when new approaches are demanded, that urban property systems are evolutionary and over time become increasingly densely institutionalized and complex, and that spatial patterns of property and infrastructure are both enduring and profoundly important for long-term function and value. Urban politics is fundamentally about contests over the power to change the institutions that structure property in the city, understanding that changing the rules and services for existing property and how it may be taxed and invested in will always impact the value of all property in a jurisdiction to a greater or lesser degree.

Cities can thus be understood as path-dependent landscapes of property that are differentiated primarily by the enduring imprint of the governance and infrastructure institutions that produce them. These institutions have tended to evolve over time in most jurisdictions, so the urban space that is produced during one period tends to be different from the space that is produced during a subsequent period, and necessarily reflects the dominant social, political, and economic powers and values of the time and jurisdiction where it is produced. As Pred (1984) put it, the making of place is a complex and contingent historical process of the sedimentation of existing power relations into new patterns in space. And particular choices mean that other possibilities are excluded.

Significantly, the spatial layout of property parcels and streets is a powerful aspect of the institutional design of property, as spatial patterns structure possibilities for both current use and future change. The spatial design and layout of new urban developments is, however, precisely the area where radical new institutional designs have repeatedly been attempted. An example is the new pattern of suburban development created in North America in the 1950s with carefully separated land uses and looping roads in residential areas instead of the grids and mixed land uses of the pre-war period. The meaning of residential property in these new suburbs is quite different from that under the former pattern. Suburban residential property in the post-war period was also deliberately designed to be highly resistant to incremental change through exclusive residential zoning, and with physical designs that inhibited non-residential uses. By facilitating universal automobile use for travel, these new designs made other modes of travel less viable, and fundamentally transformed urban life.

There are therefore two distinct but related aspects of cities that each appear profoundly path dependent: first is the set of formal local government, planning, and infrastructure building institutions that shape the production of urban property, which is highly variable between countries and even between cities within a country because of multiple contingent choices made over time (see Sorensen, 2015). Second are the spatially differentiated patterns of property that exist in a jurisdiction that are shaped by the institutions in place when they were first created or later changed, and which exhibit both physical continuities and significant positive feedback effects on the institutions that created them. This chapter has focused primarily on these enduring characteristics of urban space and property.

The claim of path dependence, however, begs the question: if formal urban institutions and spatial patterns are path dependent, how do we understand change processes? I suggest that these two aspects have quite different patterns and processes of change. The formal structures of local government, planning, and infrastructure building change primarily through contested political processes in which political and economic power, as well as the norms, policy, and meaning-producing engagements studied by Healey (2006 and Chapter 2 in this volume) play prominent roles. Conflict over changes to these rules is therefore explicitly power-political, and changes are potentially lucrative. Here the exclusive jurisdiction of municipal governments within their own territories is key, as winning coalitions can exercise political authority and losers often have limited exit options (Pierson, 2015). A large urban politics literature is devoted to analysis of such processes of change, and cannot be examined here.

It is significant, however, that existing spatially differentiated properties and their supporting infrastructures exhibit quite different rules, processes, and modes of change. Changes to urban space are made not only through changes to the rules, but also through urban investment that either changes existing property or creates new units of urban property ownership. Such changes are in most jurisdictions regulated by planning systems, building codes, legal systems, property taxes, and infrastructure capacities, among other things. But in most cities investment in urban space and property is continuous, even where no new units of property are created, as property changes hands or is maintained. The fact that urban property requires continued reinvestment both by new owners of existing properties and for maintenance means that change in market conditions can exert rapid and profound change to property values. Change is also generated by new ideas and approaches to property development, changing building technologies, and changing economic conditions. Through all these changes, however, earlier structures and patterns of property have enduring and self-reinforcing influences, as described above.

This perspective on urban property suggests that the production of new sets of urban property (whether green field or as redevelopment) is a decisive process, in which the spatial configurations of property parcels and of public spaces such as streets and parks, and particular property types and infrastructure systems are established. The regulation of development capacity, property type, land use, spatial patterns, and infrastructure standards should therefore be seen as a profoundly important act of institutional design that has enduring consequences for the meaning of the property produced, and for the places where it is located.

As the development of new property is such an important process, produces enduring consequences, and is relatively open to radical innovation in terms of spatial layouts, planners should be very careful to consider the long-term implications of new approaches. The spatial design of post-war, low-density suburbia has proven expensive, wasteful of land, automobile dependent, and extremely hard to incrementally reform. Similarly, condominium property is a new form of property ownership that has spread since the 1960s, which brings serious long-term management and maintenance challenges, and generates enormous numbers of civil suits in places like Florida (Poliakoff, 1992). These two are simply extreme examples of the broader point that the design, layout, and specification of new property development has profound consequences. Municipal governments are liable for the long-term management of property in their jurisdiction, long after developers have sold their product and moved on. Institutional designs which are highly inflexible should be understood as potentially bringing higher long-term risks than those which can be adapted to changing conditions.

Finally, planners are faced with recurring and insistent calls to dismantle, reform, and simplify the complex institutional compromises that have evolved to regulate the production of property, and often lack clear answers that are based on a deep understanding of the institutions that structure the creation of urban property, how they came to be, how they have changed over time, and how they work together to produce urban space and property. The claim here is that a historical institutional approach offers significant conceptual leverage for understanding both urban property and the structures that create it.

More generally, city building and the regulation of urban investment should be understood as a complex and unavoidable process of detailed institutional design, in which the role of city government is central. Urban property is necessarily embedded in and sustained by municipal governance, services, and infrastructures. As Polanyi (1944) argued, a 'self-regulating free market' apart from government action does not and cannot exist. The suggestion here is that this is doubly the case in urban space.

Acknowledgements

This chapter is adapted from the article 'Institutions in urban space: Land, infrastructure, and governance in the production of urban property' by André Sorensen, in *Planning Theory and Practice* (2018b), available online at: http://dx.doi.org/10.1080/14649357.2017.1408136. Thank you to participants at Willem Salet's *Institutions in Action* workshop for feedback and critical comments. I am also grateful for the comments of Wendy Burton, Robert Freestone, John Friedmann, Patsy Healey, Bharat Punjabi, Lake Sagaris, Willem Salet, and Zack Taylor on earlier drafts. I alone am responsible for any errors and omissions.

References

Angel, S. (2012). *Planet of Cities*. Cambridge, MA: Lincoln Institute of Land Policy.
Blomley, N. K. (1998). Landscapes of property. *Law & Society Review*, 32(3), 567–612.
Blyth, M. (2002). *Great Transformations: Economic Ideas and Institutional Change in the Twentieth Century*. Cambridge/New York: Cambridge University Press.
Booth, P. (1996). *Controlling Development: Certainty, Discretion in Europe, the USA and Hong Kong*. London: UCL Press.
Capoccia, G., & Kelemen, R. D. (2007). The study of critical junctures: Theory, narrative, and counterfactuals in historical institutionalism. *World Politics*, 59(3), 341–369.
Cox, K. R. (2002). *Political Geography: Territory, State, and Society*. Oxford/Malden, MA: Blackwell.
Dear, M. (1992). Understanding and overcoming the NIMBY syndrome. *Journal of the American Planning Association*, 58(3), 288–300.
Dunn, J. A. (1998). *Driving Forces: The Automobile, Its Enemies, and the Politics of Mobility*. Washington, DC: Brookings Institution Press.
Fennell, L. A. (2009). *The Unbounded Home: Property Values Beyond Property Lines*. New Haven, CT: Yale University Press.
Filion, P. (2010). Reorienting urban development? Structural obstruction to new urban forms. *International Journal of Urban and Regional Research*, 34(1), 1–19.
Fischel, W. A. (2001). *The Homevoter Hypothesis: How Home Values Influence Local Government Taxation, School Finance, and Land-Use Policies*. Cambridge, MA: Harvard University Press.
Frug, G. E. (1980). The city as a legal construct. *The Harvard Law Review*, 93(6), 1057–1154.

Hacker, J. S. (2002). *The Divided Welfare State: The Battle Over Public and Private Social Benefits in the United States.* New York: Cambridge University Press.

Hacker, J. S. (2004). Privatizing risk without privatizing the welfare state: The hidden politics of social policy retrenchment in the United States. *American Political Science Review*, 98(2), 243–260.

Hagman, D., & Misczynski, D. (1978). *Windfalls for Wipeouts: Land Value Capture and Compensation.* Chicago, IL: American Society of Planning Officials.

Hay, C. (2004). Ideas, interests and institutions in the comparative political economy of great transformations. *Review of International Political Economy*, 11(1), 204–226.

Healey, P. (2006). Transforming governance: Challenges of institutional adaptation and a new politics of space. *European Planning Studies*, 14(3), 299–320.

Healey, P., & Upton, R. (Eds.). (2010). *Crossing Borders: International Exchange and Planning Practices.* London/New York: Routledge.

Home, R. K. (1997). *Of Planting and Planning: The Making of British Colonial Cities.* London/New York: Spon.

King, A. D. (1990). *Urbanism, Colonialism, and the World Economy: Cultural and Spatial Foundations of the World Urban System.* London: Routledge & Kegan Paul.

Low, N., & Astle, R. (2009). Path dependence in urban transport: An institutional analysis of urban passenger transport in Melbourne, Australia, 1956–2006. *Transport Policy*, 16, 47–58.

Lowndes, V. (2009). New Institutionalism and Urban Politics. In J. S. Davies & D. L. Imbroscio (Eds.), *Theories of Urban Politics* (pp. 91–105). Los Angeles, CA: Sage.

Lowndes, V., & Roberts, M. (2013). *Why Institutions Matter: The New Institutionalism in Political Science.* Houndmills: Palgrave Macmillan.

Magnusson, W. (1996). *The Search for Political Space: Globalization, Social Movements, and the Urban Political Experience.* Toronto: University of Toronto Press.

Mahoney, J., & Thelen, K. A. (2010). *Explaining Institutional Change: Ambiguity, Agency, and Power.* Cambridge/New York: Cambridge University Press.

Miller, E. J., & Soberman, R. M. (2003). *Travel Demand and Urban Form.* Toronto: Neptis Foundation.

Newman, P., & Thornley, A. (1996). *Urban Planning in Europe: International Competition, National Systems, and Planning Projects.* London/New York: Routledge.

North, D. C. (1990). *Institutions, Institutional Change, and Economic Performance.* Cambridge/New York: Cambridge University Press.

Orfield, M. (1997). *Metropolitics: A Regional Agenda for Community and Stability.* Washington, DC/Cambridge, MA: Brookings Institution Press, Lincoln Institute of Land Policy.

Pierson, P. (2004). *Politics in Time: History, Institutions, and Social Analysis.* Princeton, NJ Princeton University Press.

Pierson, P. (2015). Power and Path Dependence. In J. Mahoney & K. Thelen (Eds.), *Advances in Comparative-Historical Analysis* (pp. 123–146). Cambridge: Cambridge University Press.

Polanyi, K. (1944). *The Great Transformation: The Political and Economic Origins of Our Time.* New York: Farrar & Rinehart.

Poliakoff, G. A. (1992). The Florida Condominium Act. *Nova Law Review*, 16(1), 471–513.

Pred, A. (1984). Place as historically contingent process: Structuration and the time-geography of becoming places. *Annals of the Association of American Geographers*, 74(2), 279–297.

Quitzau, M.-B. (2007). Water-flushing toilets: Systemic development and path-dependent characteristics and their bearing on technological alternatives. *Technology and Society*, 29, 351–360.

Rusk, D. (2003). *Cities Without Suburbs.* Washington, DC: Woodrow Wilson Center Press.

Salet, W. G. M. (2002). Evolving insitutions: An international exploration into planning and law. *Journal of Planning Education and Research*, 22(1), 26–35.

Sanyal, B. (2005). *Comparative Planning Cultures.* New York: Routledge.

Schmidt, V. (2008). Discursive institutionalism: The explanatory power of ideas and discourse. *Annual Review of Political Science*, 11, 303–326.

Sorensen, A. (2015). Taking path dependence seriously: An historical institutionalist research agenda in planning history. *Planning Perspectives*, 30(1), 17–38.

Sorensen, A. (2017). New Institutionalism and Planning Theory. In M. Gunder, A. Madanipour & V. Watson (Eds.), *Routledge Handbook of Planning Theory.* London/New York: Routledge.

Sorensen, A. (2018a). Global Suburbanization in Planning History. In C. Hein (Ed.), *Routledge Handbook of Planning History.* London/New York: Routledge.

Sorensen, A. (2018b). Institutions in urban space: Land, infrastructure and governance in the production of urban property. *Planning Theory and Practice*, 19(1), 21–38.

Sorensen, A., Okata, J., & Fuji, S. (2010). Urban renaissance as intensification: Building regulation and the rescaling of place governance in Tokyo's high-rise manshon boom. *Urban Studies*, 47(3), 556–584.

Streeck, W., & Thelen, K. (2005). Introduction: Institutional Change in Advanced Political Economies. In W. Streeck & K. Thelen (Eds.), *Beyond Continuity: Institutional Change in Advanced Political Economies* (pp. 1–39). Oxford: Oxford University Press.

Sutcliffe, A. (1981). *Towards the Planned City: Germany, Britain, the United States and France, 1780–1914*. Oxford: Basil Blackwell.

Tarr, J. A., & Konvitz, J. W. (1987). Patterns in the Development of Urban Infrastructure. In H. Gillete & Z. L. Miller (Eds.), *American Urbanism: A Historiographical Review* (pp. 195–226). New York: Greenwood Press.

Taylor, Z. (2013). Rethinking planning culture: A new institutionalist approach. *Town Planning Review*, 84(6), 683–702.

Thelen, K. (2003). How Institutions Evolve: Insights from Comparative-Historical Analysis. In J. Mahoney & D. Rueschemeyer (Eds.), *Comparative-Historical Analysis in the Social Sciences* (pp. 208–240). Cambridge: Cambridge University Press.

Thelen, K., & Mahoney, J. (2015). Comparative-Historical Analysis in Contemporary Political Science. In J. Mahoney & K. Thelen (Eds.), *Advances in Comparative-Historical Analysis* (pp. 3–36). Cambridge: Cambridge University Press.

UNDESA. (2014). *World Urbanization Prospects: The 2014 Revision*. New York: United Nations Department of Economic and Social Affairs.

Urry, J. (2004). The 'system' of automobility. *Theory, Culture & Society*, 21(4/5), 25–39.

Van Assche, K., Duineveld M., & Beunen, R. (2015). *Evolutionary Governance Theory: Theory and Applications*. New York: Springer Berlin Heidelberg.

Van Assche, K., Duineveld M., & Beunen, R. (2017). Co-Evolutionary Planning Theory: Evolutionary Governance Theory and Its Relatives. In M. Gunder, A. Madanipour & V. Watson (Eds.), *Routledge Handbook of Planning Theory*. London/New York: Routledge.

Weber, M. (1958). *The City*. Toronto: The Free Press, Collier-Macmillan.

6
MOVING TOWARDS A FLAT ONTOLOGY OF INSTITUTIONAL INNOVATION

Actor-Relational Lessons Learned from Early Water Management Perspectives

Luuk Boelens

Institutional Innovation

The dictionary defines innovation simply as a new idea, device, or method (Merriam-Webster, 2016). It is also viewed as the application of better products or solutions that meet new requirements, markets, or unarticulated needs (Maryville, 1992). The latter points to a future situation we are not aware of yet, but which we will, supposedly, eagerly want when innovation has occurred. Recent economic theories analyse innovation within the economic system itself, as an endogenous force for growth. In this respect, innovation is as important a cause as is the outcome of that economic process (ESF, 2012). Likewise, evolutionary biologists regard innovation as one of the most contentious issues for species to survive in a changing environment (Erwin, 2015; Nitecki, 1990). In turn, social innovation is expected not only to meet social needs, but also to strengthen and extend civil society towards greater resilience (Drucker, 1985; Tempels, 2016). As such, innovation has also been regarded as a prerequisite of modern times; it drives us towards an ongoing condition of *not yet, but already gone* (Bollerey, 1988). At first sight, institutions seem to hold the opposite viewpoint. Institutions are generally regarded as following the mutually agreed upon rules of the game, focusing on a relative stability and valued, recurring patterns of behaviour (Huntington, 1965). Institutions have traditionally been used to explain stability in an ongoing world of flux (Greenwood et al., 1996). Over time, through structuration (Giddens, 1984), even primary or meta-institutions evolve – such as family, culture, religion, the democratic society, etc. – which guarantee even more stability and structure. They are broad enough to encompass many other institutions and societal changes. Williamson (2000) even distinguishes four levels of institutions, each with their own levels of robustness in specific time-frames.[1] Each of these institutions reduces our transaction costs, in economic, social and political terms. They are expected to make our lives easier, but are not needed to negotiate every decision or step we take.

Nevertheless, in a time and place in need of fundamental and radical transformation, institutional frames are often experienced as a major restraint for innovation (Boelens & Goethals,

2015). This is especially the case when we are in need of new answers and solutions dealing with for instance climate change, energy transition, circular economy, sustainable food production, nearshoring, demographic ageing, shared mobility and so on. In other words, it is a transition from a classic (hardware) growth model, towards a better and more efficient utilization and reorganization (soft/orgware) model of space. However, present planning and other institutions are often structured according to the age-old nineteenth- and twentieth-century reality of growth: expansion and functional differentiation (Janssen-Jansen, 2004). For example, zoning plans serve specific property rights, rationalization and segmentation of space as a platform, rather than the actual and increasing mutable daily use, which shapes and gives meaning to space, as it is shaped by that space (Massey, 2005). For real innovation, there is a need to lift institutional restraints, at least temporarily, to experiment with new ideas and regimes (Bey, 1991; Bolo'bolo, 1995; Gewest Vlaanderen, 2012; Urhahn, 2010; Vromraad, 2009). These experiments (especially within planning and in the accompanying sectors of planning such as housing, mobility, farming, etc.) remain just that. They even scour institutional innovations, which are more focused on generic and all-encompassing rules than on situational differences (Boelens, 2015). That's why I agree with Willem Salet's refocus on pragmatism next to institutional innovations (see Salet, Chapter 1, in this volume). However, the actual dynamics, a-linearity, and volatilities of present-day society spread to such an extent, that the actual institutional innovations – even the most pragmatic ones – can't keep track anymore. In fact, both worlds (the complex dynamic world of our daily lives and the longer path-dependent institutional world) grow ever more apart, in such a way that various institutions don't provide useful or efficient path-dependent behaviour anymore. It seems they have turned into a lock-in instead (Arthur, 1989).

At the same time, pleas for institutional free zones are pleas to grant exceptions for a specific development or group of stake and shareholders, within a grand middle-of-the-road institutional narrative without real, engaged innovation. But while those differences and pleas for exceptional treatment have become more common, it is no longer institutional structure that rules with some exception, but exceptions have become the rule, serving to further fragment and differentiate. Institutional innovation can hardly build on former path-dependent and all-encompassing foundations anymore. It must remould itself differentially and situationally from within as a continuous adaptive actor-relational force. But how can we guarantee certain overall values and reduction of transaction costs within those volatile and dynamic situations? How can social reflexivity be guaranteed, which is essential for social interaction within a fragmented world? How can we guarantee agents' capacity to engage in learning and to reflect on context for their actions, beyond the mere pragmatic exception?

A Flat Ontology

I will use a flat ontology to analyse some institutional innovations of our time. This ontology rejects any pre-given, transcendent or hierarchical meaning, but stresses that these meanings must always be fought or strived for in specific assemblages (DeLanda, 2006). The usefulness and/or efficiency of norms, morals, rules, contracts, and so on, are always the outcome of interactions between involved and conscious actors in specific locatable dynamic settings, and never *a priori* given. When those outcomes have been achieved, they will affect the 'conscious actors' and 'locatable settings', which in turn drive change. Therefore institutions and agencies have history and co-evolve in a positive or a negative way. Institutions (whether subject or object) are never 'closed' but always in a state of '(undefined) becoming' and therefore always in a 'condition of (potential or actual) innovation'. Those innovations can never be generic, but are always situational in time and space. Even seemingly universal norms and meta-institutions like 'thou shalt not kill' or 'thou shalt love your neighbour', will get various explanations in different parts of the world, or are temporarily postponed in times of war, famine, or otherwise (Hampshire, 1983). Institutional innovations can have different paces or even directions, at various places, next to each other. Consequently, institutional innovation becomes, if not plural, at least layered or 'rhizomized' in thousands of plateaux of possibilities and progressions (Deleuze & Guattari, 1980).

To deal with this hard-to-define and ongoing (layered) fragmentation, it is helpful to refer to Luhmann's system theory of social innovation. Although Luhmann can't be accused of being 'rhizomatic flat' and his methods are structured and ordered, for Luhmann there is no point in society from which society can be observed in its totality. Society is simply too complex, a-linear, and volatile. To deal with this kind of complexity, Luhmann (1997) regards it as essential to approach the complex reality with a number of autonomous and distinct subsystems, like the economic system, the legal system, the system of science, education, art, mass media, etc. These subsystems are operationally closed by reducing the complexity of the environment, according to the structure and the internal and self-defined (institutional) codes of that subsystem. Even more, Luhmann shows that through those codes of identification, modern society develops ever more differentiation in various layers and subsystems: *die Gesellschaft der Gesellschaften*; or in other words 'a profound differential institutional system'. Modern society is more and more without an *apex* or *centre* (Luhmann, 1990, p. 31), thus making it flat or horizontal. But for Luhmann, that doesn't mean that modern society would only be highly fragmented in various distinct subsystems. On the contrary, like Derrida and Deleuze, Luhmann regards reality as highly relational. Whereas context shapes identity, elements structure reciprocally the other way around; both realms of reality (system and context) are to be considered as the outcome of transformations, and the starting point for new ones (Pottage, 1998). This would mean that each subsystem also evolves in its changing surroundings or other subsystems, just like the economic system would respond to changes in the political system, the law on morality and mass media on innovations in art. A specific institution is just one subsystem next to the other, and responds or adapts to changing circumstances, needs or interests in those other subsystems. Although those turns, changes or innovations would always accord to the internal codes of institutional self-reference, institutions could adapt and innovate themselves to exceptional situations, or hold to their own path-dependent behaviour and perspectives as well. Changes in their surroundings could therefore expand and strengthen institutions towards a better fit with the surroundings.

That would come very near to complexity theories and ideas on complex adaptive systems (De Roo et al., 2012; Miller & Scott, 2007). Halsall (2012) shows convincingly that although Luhmann's sociology is often accused of being anti- or post-human (focusing on the structure of subsystems and their internal codes of reduced complexity), the human bodies and their aspirations play a prominent role in his thinking. The same goes for things. Subjects and objects can interpenetrate other subsystems with the codes and self-reference of their subsystems or they can irritate them by making pronouncements or innovations, which need to be incorporated into those other subsystems to survive. Moreover, Luhmann focuses on the translating networks, or 'communication' between objects and subjects, and on the autopoiesis of various subsystems in society, analysing those systems as 'operational' wholes in themselves, but also organically in reference to each other (Arnoldi, 2001). In fact, Luhmann comes very near to actor-network theorists like Law, Callon and Latour. Actors and agencies matter (even the non-human ones), but the specific networking (or according to Actor-Network Theory better 'worknetting') between them would be most important for gaining meaning, importance or impact. Even more recently Borch (2005) and Van Assche, Duineveld and Beunen (2014) have argued that there are many similarities in the approaches on power by Luhmann, Foucault, Deleuze and (I might add) Actor-Network Theory. Power is not so much conceived in causal classical terms (A has power over B, thus A's behaviour causes B's behaviour), but as an interaction between subject and environment, or subsystem and other subsystems, which can also become internalized (either in a positive uplifting, or in a negative, sanctioning way). The premium position of one actor above the other, or one system above the other, only becomes apparent as power *in actu*; in that specific place, in that specific time and for this specific subject as a result of those assemblages (for better or worse).

Considering the subject of institutions in action, these ideas also resonate with Bob Jessop's (2001) relational approach of institutional (re)turns. Although Jessop is often characterized as a political, and specifically state, theorist coming from a Marxist background, his 'strategic-relational approach' to concepts such as capital or state regards these concepts not as mere things but as social relations more than the narrow monolithic view of economic or political power. For Jessop (2008), as well as Michel Foucault (1975) or Nico Poulantzas (1978) for that matter, the state is a complex ensemble of various parts, interests and ambitions, institutionalized in various state apparatus, rules and laws, which in some way relate to and mirror the struggles and quarrels of real life. Thus, the state (being a capitalist state, military power, theocratic regime, representative democracy or otherwise) is never finished, but always a distinct, ongoing ensemble of institutions and organizations whose socially accepted function is to define and enforce collectively binding decisions on a given population in the name of their 'common interest' or 'general will' (Jessop, 1990, p. 341). It always has to reproduce its legitimacy. As Luhmann theorized, a state is not only operationally closed and situational, with different liabilities or vulnerabilities in specific societies, but especially in our times of cross-bordering network societies, dependent on the acceptability of other states or regimes. In other words, the state is marked by its double relative autonomy depending on its differential ability to pursue interests and strategies in specific contexts and on its strategic ties and networks within an increasingly complex interstate system of an emerging world society (Jessop, 2008, p. 6). In these cases, political decisions are always strategically selective in origin and impact.

The same goes for institutional innovation. Jessop's ideas of institutions never exist outside of specific action contexts, nor do they form bigger environments. They matter only in terms of their structurally inscribed strategic selectivity: *institutions build on and select behaviour* (Jessop, 2001, p. 1226). Institutions not only frame action, but are also framed by it, while actors still have room to manoeuvre in choosing specific paths of action for that specific case or situation and to reflect on it. For Jessop, that reflexivity would reconstitute institutions and their resultant framing. Institutions would then be connected to specific forms of power and domination, but they could also redefine the power geometries with diverse ways of organizing and institutionalizing social interaction. Moreover, as such institutions would be inevitably spatio-temporal; they emerge in specific places and at specific times, to operate on one or more particular actor-relational spaces and with specific temporal horizons. However, institutions could also be remoulded and stretched over time. For Jessop, a short-term constraint for a given agent or set of agents could become a 'conjunctural opportunity' over a longer time horizon for different strategies, with shifting focus points and objectives. According to Jessop (2001, 1227) structural constraints and conjunctural opportunities could also be determined in a relational manner. Constraints and opportunities, conservatism and innovation would then become both sides of one coin. For Jessop's strategic-relational approach to society, or state for that matter, two specific but interrelated methods would matter: (a) an institutional turn and (b) an evolutionary turn. The institutional turn could help to analyse the importance of the reduction of transaction costs, common values and some form of stability in times of change whereas the evolutionary turn would highlight the contingencies of progress generated by the semiosis of the new, and the path dependency of selection, variation and retention (Jessop, 2008, p. 242). So not only the specific situation place and experiment matter, but also the long run of history, not in the sense of simple fatalism, but as a social force that could intervene to co-evolve towards various, but related trajectories over time.

What would this flat, relational, ontological view mean for our subject of institutional innovation? First, when institutions can be regarded as following the black-boxed common agreed upon *rules of the game* at a given time, they could also be modified over time as the result of, and dependent on, actant-relational needs, incentives and aspiration in specific spatio-temporal settings. It would mean that there is no such thing as *the* institutional innovation, but that there are lots of institutional innovations in various directions at the same time. Analysing institutions in action would focus on specific institutional turns, for specific purposes and subsystems. Second, this would mean that those innovations hardly emerge from within, but are interpenetrated or irritated from the outside-in by changing circumstances (factors of importance) or conscious (human) actors in the environment, often operating from a different subsystem or lines of progress. Third, it means that through those processes institutions could expand, enlarge, renew or in other words innovate themselves, which would have an impact on (the number or focus of) the actors involved, or the progress of things, such as factors of importance in an affirming or restrictive manner. Actors, factors and institutions in specific spatio-temporal situations (re)constitute each other in their surroundings. And fourth, it would show that institutions should be analysed as complex emergent phenomena built on actor-factor (or actant) networks, whose reproduction is always incomplete, provisional and unstable, and who co-evolve with a range of other complex emergent phenomena (see Figure 6.1). Institutions in each subsystem could also

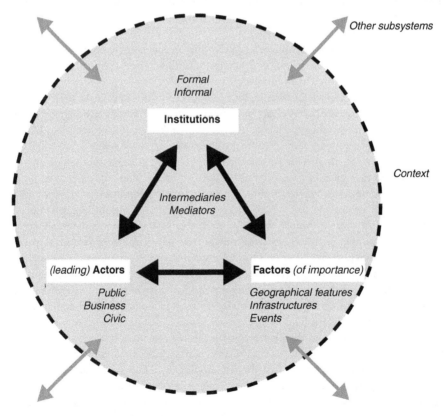

Figure 6.1 Ontological scheme
Source: Luuk Boelens composition

interpenetrate or irritate other subsystems, which in turn would have to assimilate or innovate to survive. Thus, institutions could reconstruct themselves within their own sector or subsystem, but could also move and influence other sectors and subsystems towards a greater and better fit within specific places at a given time. This wouldn't refer to the hierarchical vertical structuring of institutional assemblages of Williamson (2000) mentioned before, but rather to a subtler horizontal constellation, which is upheld by historical relational networks, rather than by the elements itself. Following the relational networks rather than the elements or actors themselves is therefore of main importance.

Waterings and Polders

From this relational flat background, I will analyse the birth of institutionalized water management in the Eurodelta (the delta of the Rhine, Meuse and Scheldt, comprising parts of present-day Flanders, the Netherlands and Lower Westphalia). With the perspective of a dynamic progress between factors, actors, institutional innovation, factors and so on, of always becoming, it is not easy to decide where to start. But in the tenth and eleventh century AD, the centuries-old and ongoing struggle of men against the regular flooding in the Eurodelta became somewhat collectively organized. This struggle even gained new meaning since the British historian Simon Schama (1987) interpreted it as 'a moral geography', a breeding ground to foster regional or national consensus about general codes of social behaviour, innovative entrepreneurship, and patterns of formal and informal political-cultural (thus institutional) framing. According to Schama, in delta areas (like the Eurodelta) this organized struggle against the water to make new spaces resulted in an elaborate self-institutionalization not only about water management, but about various realms of the agrarian and urban society. In accordance, the ideological, economic and political constitutions of these 'low countries' are often described as 'federal or decentralized unitary states', grounded on self- or co-government (see Zonneveld, 2010). This kind of governance would become most distinct in the Dutch and Flemish policy of *polderen*, which would refer to the noun 'polder', being the quintessential water management unit of most of the Netherlands and parts of Flanders. Reclaiming land from the sea would only be possible through cooperation and balancing different interests on the level of the polder, bottom-up, and not by grand top-down schemes. It would represent the institutional uniqueness of deltas, or at least that of the Eurodelta. Although insightful, that kind of analysis remains too superficial. Moreover, it stays nicely within an age-old and unproductive vertical ontology: consequently moving in two-dimensional directions from top-down incentives towards bottom-up innovations or vice versa. It includes everything in between, even up to present managerial days. Subsequently, ideas on institutional innovation remain framed within that kind of vertical ideology, with all its impact on the analysis of recent and upcoming ideas on self-organization, adaptive management, and participation as exceptions and not as a general rule (Boonstra & Rauws, 2016). However, analysing the birth of offensive land reclamation in the Eurodelta more profoundly (which originally took shape in West-Flanders and not in the Netherlands by the way) offers more nuanced and elaborated ideas on flat institutions in action.

At the time of this birth, there was a remarkable conjuncture of several events in the coastal area of what is modern-day Belgium. First, during the nineth and especially the tenth and eleventh centuries, the former Flemish peers of the Kingdom of France privatized themselves more and more, and tried to establish an independent county of their own. At first the King of France allowed this appropriation of an almost abandoned area to establish a buffer against the raids of the Vikings. But soon the assertive Flemish counts started expanding their

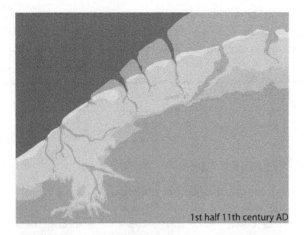

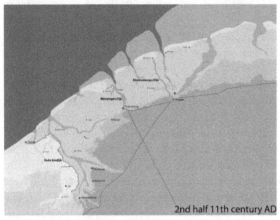

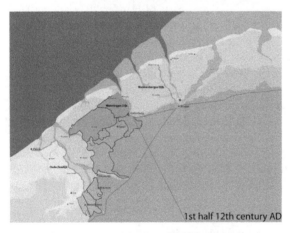

Figure 6.2 Overview of water management in West-Flanders from the tenth until the thirteenth century AD
Source: Luuk Boelens

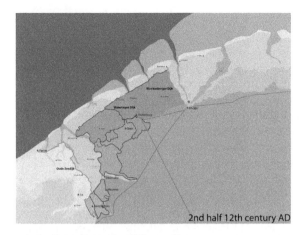

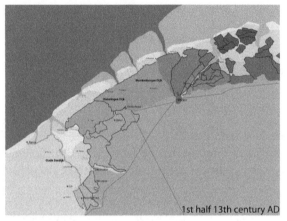

Figure 6.2 (Continued)

influence over the neighbouring areas, until the King of France established their claims as an independent county officially in 1237. Secondly, at the time, the sea regularly flooded the area, resulting in various tidal gutters perpendicular to the coastline (Verhulst, 2000). But especially during the first half of the eleventh century, the climate warmed up remarkably, resulting in the drying up of parts of the marshland (Prak & Luiten van Zanden, 2013). At first, Christian monasteries started to use this land for sheep breeding, which in turn endangered the scarce vegetation, promoting the squirting of the small dunes and affecting their protection against floods. Furthermore, still occurring north-western storm floods, such as those recorded in 1014, 1042 and 1134, attacked the new land, leaving behind an infertile soil for agriculture. However, the most important problem to deal with was the regular rainfall and the rise of the (sometimes salty) groundwater. For both purposes, monks erected earthworks, small in height but sometimes of important length, minding the north-western storms mostly in south-east lines deepening the main natural gutters mentioned above. For instance, the *Oude Zeedijk* next to the *Avekapellegeul*, the *Wateringen Dijk* next to the *Bredena* and the *Blankenbergse Dijk* next to the *Sincfal* (see Figure 6.2). However, next to their defensive meaning, these ditches, gutters and earthworks mainly served the drainage of the hinterland, hence the word 'watering'.

This resulted in periodic quarrels between neighbouring farmers and landowners about how much water needed to be drained, and how much gutters needed to be deepened. At first custom law decided this. The claim to drain water and to carry out earth and water management infrastructures depended on who was first in the area, and on what (after a while) had always been done. These customs officially became institutionalized in so-called 'artisanal courts', responsible for fertile land issues and thus decisions about conflicts concerning the course of the water drainage (Soens, 2009, p. 25).

However, the Flemish counts also experimented with other organizations, probably due to the malfunctioning of those artisanal courts or convinced by other windows of opportunity. For instance, in 1161 the Flemish Count Filips van den Elzas agreed with the Saint Pieters abbey of Oudenburg that they could develop and maintain drainage ditches towards the sea and as a result gained the responsibility to deal with the quarrels of the adjoining land users by giving them the right to cultivate the area and fish in the drainage ditches. In return the abbey got the right to erect and claim new agricultural land from the mudflats by offensive damming (Verhulst, 1998, p. 13). The first 'polres' or polders were born. It meant a new beginning in the history of the Eurodelta, where man proactively tried to tame the dynamic and free forces of the sea. This process started in the southern parts of West-Flanders, around the estuary of the Yser river, but over the years it gradually evolved towards the northern parts of West-Flanders as well. At first this was sanctioned by preliminary contracts between two parties, on the one side the count of Flanders and on the other side the abbot of the involved monasteries. It was done according to private law, sustained in documents and if necessary enforced by neighbouring kings and counts or the Pope himself.

However due to the prosperous impact on a more regular and efficient agricultural production, the (grand)sons of Filips van den Elzas continued in the footsteps of their (grand) father and organized similar arrangements with other (slave-)farmers, still serving the noble men, but trying to improve their living conditions with additional income. If they organized themselves within a group they could receive similar arrangements from the count. This induced an enormous incentive to reclaim land from the sea by building new polders, obtaining the right from the count to use the land according to their own wishes and ideas. In return they had to maintain the dykes, polders and locks, and serve the count with new products or other (military) services. This was formalized in specific, situational, public-private group-contracts with the involved 'nascent farmers'. The main element was the so-called *verhoefslaging*, whereby each farmer according to the size of his farm had to maintain a certain length of the dyke and the ditches of the polder. Among the polder-community, periodically a *primus inter pares* was elected – the so-called *dyke-earls* or *dyke-sheriffs* ('dijkgraven' in Dutch) – which checked that each of the farmers executed his duties sufficiently and on time. This was institutionalized in so-called Waterboards, where each of the polders where organized according to their own *heme law*: often unwritten and orally agreed upon or by handshake, but always highly situational.

This model proved to be so successful and widely distributed that soon there was a need to coordinate the (private and heme law) polders themselves. Therefore, this birth of collective water management coincided with major innovations on a governmental level too. During the eleventh century, the Flemish counts had already replaced the Carolingian district system with that of a military chancellery around medieval castles and strongholds, probably as a defensive system against the offensive Franks. The biggest and most important one was the chancellery organized around the burg of Bruges. But due to the prosperous land reclamation, the environments of the burg received more and more special rights from the Flemish counts to organize themselves as well. Eventually in 1127, this countryside even received its first domestic government in land issues, the so-called *Brugse Vrije*. Here the magistrates of the involved villages and estates received more or less direct control of the area of the *Vrije* under the aegis of the count, much sooner than any other medieval town. The *Vrije* was organized around three parts: a) the real countryside divided into 35 jurisdiction areas (the so-called 'ambachten') each consisting of one or more parishes, b) the so-called 'belongers' ('de appendanten') consisting of around 30 manors spread over the countryside with each of their own lower courts, and c) the so-called 'contributors' ('de contribuanten') of seven adjoining manors who upheld their own high and low courts, but cooperated with the *Vrije* on taxing. All of these partners could somewhat democratically decide about the future affairs of their common land in a general meeting once a year. Next to that, the main task of the *Brugse Vrije* was not only to collect taxes for the count, but also to mediate between the individual quarrels about 'watering' (or the right to discharge surplus water over neighbouring fields) and the coordination of the land reclamation of the communal 'Waterboards'. That they weren't always successful is proven by the increase of land reclamations resulting in the silting of the open access of Bruges towards the sea. Several canals and even new outposts of Bruges had to be erected to safeguard Flemish trade. Moreover even bigger locks between the sea and the inland rivers and polders were necessary. This even became a self-enforcing process, while these grand waterworks became the responsibility of the *Brugse Vrije* again, thus inducing a fairly coherent whole of enforceable agreements, ordinances, regulations, democratic voting systems and so on (Huys, 1998).

As a result, in and around Bruges/West-Flanders, several competitive institutional regimes co-evolved, each as a 'flat' distinct subsystem, but also in reference to each other: sometimes according to common law, at other times or places according to private, heme or public law. Periodically the magistrates of the *Vrije* tried to incorporate the artisanal courts, private contracts and polder boards into their own organization. But they hardly succeeded; perhaps partly because for the Flemish counts, these multi-institutional systems were highly profitable: the project and cooperative organized polder system could (re)claim new land (and subsequently tax and services) at practically no cost by contracting polder pioneers, and the custom organized 'waterings' and the *heme law* could decide about disputable debates decisively and eliminate free riders.

Thus by the end of the twelfth century a coherent coastal dyke system evolved in the corner of a small stronghold, later known as Bruges, who prospered highly from this stable and efficient agricultural production in its country side, evolving to the biggest trade post and metropolis of Western Europe at the time. As such they were backed up even more intensively by the new counts of Flanders. These counts even started to attract a new kind of project managers ('locatores') among the lower noble men to mediate between the various pioneering farmers, to mutually develop dykes and drainage canals. These managers (or better still 'intermediaries') became eventually the domestic notables of each polder and village, next to the dyke-earls who regarded their position over time as a kind of heritable right. But more importantly, due to their ongoing welfare and the prosperity of Bruges, some of the farmers moved towards the city and left the daily work on the farm to their servants or renters, and the maintenance of their part of the dyke to professional experts. At the same time, wealthy citizens in Bruges recognized the opportunities of the countryside and bought up land for (trade) production and properties for leisure. As a result, the traditional duties regarding dyke-maintenance and payment in kind changed to professional polder and water management organizations, financed by a new system of polder taxing. Small and poor farmers, who couldn't pay the rising polder taxes, had to abandon their plots, which were subsequently divided among the polder-members who could continue to (additionally) pay their share. As a result, during the fourteenth and fifteenth centuries, a dramatic decline of small ownership and in turn a professionalization in agriculture and water management occurred: while 75% of farms were less than five hectares

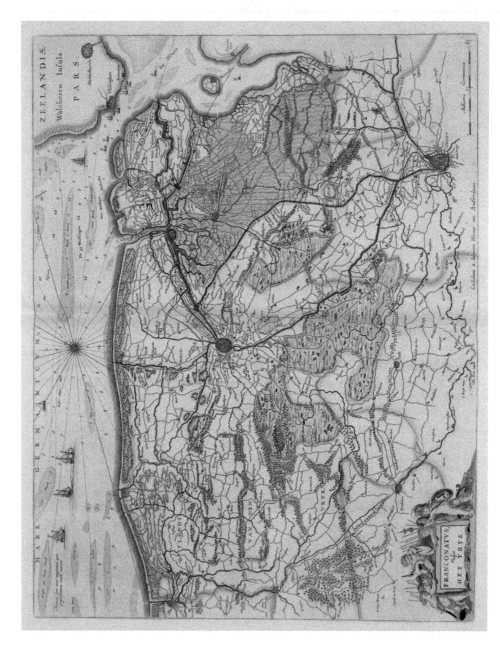

Figure 6.3 Map of the Brugse Vrije
Source: Luuk Boelens, based on based on the Map of the Brugse Vrije in 1664, from Willem Janszoon Blaeu

in the mid-fourteenth century, less than 25% of those small, individual farms existed by mid-fifteenth century. Hence and in reference to the new professionalization and tax system, the custom and private law had to be translated into a new kind of *public law* according to a specific mix with the domestic *common and heme law* to serve the domestic might of the notables in the villages (Soens, 2009). In this (co)evolving mix of institutional becoming, the professional 'locatores' played a dominant role by tuning the developments with other water management initiatives, fishermen and interests of the adjoining landowners. Furthermore, after cultivation they often served their ongoing mediating role in the management of the 'waterings' and polder administrations, thus pragmatically interconnecting various institutional subsystems from their differing roles in water management.

A Moral Geography?

Due to its success, this multi-institutional model of flat organized subsystems and conditional self-organization was soon broadly copied, not only by the count of Flanders himself (in the region of Veurne or Ghent), but also elsewhere, in the northern corners of the Eurodelta (like Zeeland and Holland) and even in other parts of North-West Europe, such as Bremen, Hamburg and Danzig (Prak & Luiten van Zanden, 2013). Moreover it also served organizational innovations within other parts of the delta society. The first medieval cities were regularly organized by the model of elected prominent civilians and a mayor appointed by the count. Later, when cities got more prominent economic and political status, these *primi inter pares* were periodically appointed by the local community itself.

Furthermore, to defend themselves against raids and robberies during travels, and to overcome the unpredictable whims and tolls of numerous regional lords, merchants started to organize themselves according to different production sectors or trade-routes in *amicitia* ('friendships or guilds'). That was also the ground for the further elaboration of the merchant city-network of the Hanze, operational for more than four centuries from the fourteenth century onwards, and which stretched at one time from Bruges in the south-west towards Novogorod in the north-east, including more than 200 European cities (d'Haenens, 1984).

Next, in the era of global trade and colonization from the sixteenth until the nineteenth century, the Oostendse, and West- and East-India Companies were loosely organized as somewhat of an open merchant-city-network, under the aegis of national governments. Moreover, unlike previously established counterparts elsewhere (such as the Company of Merchant Adventurers, or the Eastland and Levant Companies in London) these Eurodelta trading companies obtained the political and military power to act on foreign shores on behalf of the governments in their motherland. But they only received this right to reign and exploit the areas overseas when they upheld the custom laws of the motherland (Prince, 2006).

Other realms of urban life, like agriculture, social housing, labour unions, industrial and financial corporations and even political coalition strategies, were organized in the nineteenth and twentieth centuries according to this model of self-organization, within the realm of a co-operating and co-evolving identity, thus influencing Eurodelta urbanization from various realms. Some have referred to this schizophrenic situation as a kind of 'com-coll mentality': *com*peting against each other where possible, and *coll*aborating when necessary (Boelens & Taverne, 2012). It even serves the maritime and industrial strategies of some entrepreneurial organizations until the present day (see the year report 2015 of the Port Authority of Rotterdam, Havenbedrijf Rotterdam, 2016).

Simon Schama (1987) explained the enormous differentiation of Protestant churches in the Low Lands from the Flemish and Dutch polder landscape. Each polder remained relatively isolated and therefore served its own God. Nevertheless, instead of a 'geographical determinism', (see also Schama, 1995) due to the flat ontology, I take a more nuanced point of view. I interpret the Dutch polders not so much as a moral geographical landscape, but as a networked actor-factor-institutional assemblage, meaning that actors and institutions have an impact on the geographical space itself, vice versa, and operate in a bigger environment. For instance, Schama neglects the idea that the Protestant churches in the Low Lands were not only organized from the bottom-up, but also gained meaning and importance through the centuries-long struggle against the domination of Catholic Spain (De Winne, 1903) and the periodic synods from 1559 onwards, which have upheld central Protestant customs and morals through the ages. Institution in action therefore means a plural or at least a multi-level approach: co-evolving path dependencies and new innovations at the same time, serving stability and renewal in a flat relational way.

Discussion

The dichotomous Wateringen/Polder/Vrije, or custom/private/public institutional model of water management served as a kind of *dispositif* in the terminology of Foucault (1977) – 'an institutional mechanism or apparatus' to enhance and maintain power in several realms of society. Nevertheless, this 'dispositif' hasn't remained the same, fixed over time or the same in various realms of society; it has proven to be not only highly spatio-temporal but also subject-object focused. Therefore, I prefer Jessop's idea of conjunctural innovation, co-evolving with historic institutional constraints towards a better fit, or consistency, with other realms of institutional innovation. Although it stems in general from the same core idea, the custom/private/public model gets different institutional translations within the Low Lands management of social housing, Protestantism, polder politics, entrepreneurialism, and so on. So institution in action becomes flat: dependent on specific actor-factor constellations for specific purposes, at specific places, in specific times. Moreover, in Low Lands' history, this dependent institutionalization has proven to be highly efficient, functional and resilient. In reference to other metropolitan areas, the Eurodelta has received a relatively high level of welfare and (socio-geographic) security at relatively low costs and (public) expenditures.

More astonishingly, during the last 50 years, and perhaps under the pressure of further neo-liberal globalization, this more pronounced, situational and sophisticated model of custom-private institutionalization seems to be under ongoing pressure. While in the mid-twentieth century there were still some 3,000 Waterboards functional in the Low Lands, there are hardly a handful left, incorporated into just a few public services at the regional or provincial level. The recent Dutch and Belgian Water Management Laws not only established a more uniform system of water governance with specific responsibilities through various scales, but also altered the electoral procedure to be adjusted to the more general (and hardly spatio-temporal) features of representative democracy, with all its accompanying misfits (Boelens, 2009). Furthermore, social housing co-operations were still acting for and on behalf of their members in the first half of the twentieth century, but they have now become an exclusive dissemination unit of public policies framed in representative policy objectives (Strijland, 2006). Even the political polder model has become representative for disputing the middle of the road, and avoiding decisions in real, pressing social issues of everyday lives (Fortuyn, 2002). Despite the ongoing window-dressing of co-production, crowd-funding, self-organization and the rest, the public-private law, the unitarian, so-called representative rule seems to have won, leaving behind the more interesting multifocal and adaptive tensions between the individual and the collective, customs and group formation, the big and the small. In my view this is very unfortunate as the challenges of tomorrow need that multi-institutional vocality again, now more than ever. For instance, a real energy transition is only possible through major behavioural changes from flat organized actors or common agencies themselves, but only when these are backed up by real changes in more generic energy path dependencies at the same time (such as the final abandonment of nuclear energy, coal and (shale) gas). Slow-food production would only be possible if in our direct environment new possibilities go beyond generic existent zoning plans and realize new ecosystem services based on situational autarkic inventions. A real and decisive smart mobility would only be possible if the major stakeholders in the travel, transport and traffic markets would endorse the translations towards new concepts such as Mobility as a Service (MaaS), backed up by new technologies, major restrictions on the free use of public space, and the abandonment of path dependencies focused on the liberalization of the poor and minorities through mobilization, and so on. Real institutionalization in action would therefore be plural and relational to other intents and aspirations in a dynamic actor-relational environment.

When planning enhances this flat institutionalization in action, it doesn't mean it would ignore the existing institutional frames and power relations, but it would regard them as outcomes and would reveal their existing or lost relational understanding for the real differential world. It would mean that planning would need to go beyond the vertical public-private dichotomy and become flat relational starting from different angles and multi-vocal roles in real societal interactions (see Boelens, 2015; Boonstra, 2015). Planners could enhance interest or help to refocus the actors involved towards a better fit with their aspirations. Planners could serve as an intermediary for or mediate between factors and things, by putting them on the agenda or by giving them new meaning by analysing them or by new interpretations. Planners could facilitate institutional adaptations or innovations, or propose new cross-overs and networks between institutions-actors-factors in their surroundings towards a better fit, resilience or consistency. For Luhmann, no one could really oversee this manifold process, let alone know beforehand how it would end. For Jessop, it would mean that the institution-actor-factor assemblage should be deconstructed, rather than reified. In my view, it would mean that there would be a need for a multi-planner planning of undefined spatio-institutional becoming. It doesn't mean that planners wouldn't have intent, visions or even utopias, but these intents, visions and ideas would serve to (inter)mediate, not to be realized. Moreover, instead of focusing on the actors, factors, institutions and their surroundings themselves, in a flat ontology the relations and networks between these elements would become the principal focus of planners, not the elements themselves. In a flat ontology, the tactical utilization of the opportunities in a specific place or time would be of more importance than the strategic establishment of a place over time. Utopias would become a dynamic network towards an ongoing adapting fit of actors, factors and institutions of becoming, rather than the static ideal or vision at the horizon itself. Institutionalization in action would therefore become undefined and engaged again; probably only a visionary attitude of ongoing adaptive becoming.

Note

1 (a) Religions, belief systems, ideologies and the like with a highly socio-cultural *embeddedness* and with a rate of change of between 100–1,000 years; (b) political, legal, cultural frameworks functioning as *rules of the game* with a rate of change of between 10–100 years; (c) governance structures, organizational rules and the like serving as *the play of the game* with a rate of change of between 1–10 years; and d) resource allocations like *customs* which change continuously.

References

Arnoldi, J. (2001). Niklas Luhmann: An introduction. *Theory, Culture & Society*, 18(1), 1–13.
Arthur, B. (1989). Competing technologies, increasing returns, and lock-in by historical events. *The Economic Journal*, 99(394), 116–131.
Bey, H. (1991). *The Temporary Autonomous Zone*. New York: Autonomedia.
Blockmans, W. (2010). *Metropolen aan de Noordzee. Geschiedenis van Nederland, 1100–1555*. Amsterdam: Prometheus.
Boelens, L. (2009). *The Urban Connection: An Actor-Relational Approach to Urban Planning*. Rotterdam: O10-Publishers.
Boelens, L., & Taverne, E. (2012). Why Cities Prosper as Deltas: The Urbanisation of the Eurodelta, In. L. Lucassen & W. Willems (Eds.), *Living in the City: Urban Institutions in the Low Countries, 1200–2010* (pp. 192–215). New York/London: Routledge.
Boelens, L. (2015). Governance of Mobile Complexity: Co-evolutionary Management Towards a Resilient Mobility in Flanders. In L. Boelens, D. Lauwers & F. Witlox (Eds.), *Adaptive Mobility: A New Policy and Research Agenda on Mobility in Horizontal Metropolises* (pp. 191–209). Groningen: InPlanning.
Boelens, L., & Goethals, M. (2015). Planning Tactics of Undefined Becoming: Applications within Urban Living Labs of Flanders' N16 Corridor. In Y. Rydin & L. Tate (Eds.), *Materiality and Planning: Exploring the Influence of Actor-Network Theory* (pp. 186–203). London: Routledge.
Bolo'bolo (1995). *P.M.* Zürich: Paranoia City Verlag.
Bollerey, F. (1988). Noch nicht und schon gewesen – Zeichen der Wende. *Beeld, Amsterdam juni 1988*.
Boonstra, B. (2015). *Planning Strategies in an Age of Active Citizenship*. Groningen: InPlanning.
Boonstra, B., & Rauws, W. S. (2016). Conceptualizing Self-organization in Urban Planning: Turning Diverging Paths into Consistency. Paper Presented on the Conference on Complex Systems, 19–22 September 2016. Amsterdam: Beurs Van Berlage.
Borch, C. (2005). Systemic power: Luhmann, Foucault and analytical power. *Acta Sociologica*, 48(2), 155–167.
DeLanda, M. (2006). *A New Philosophy of Society: Assemblage Theory and Social Complexity*. London: Continuum International Publishing Group.
Deleuze, G., & Guattari, F. (1980). *Mille Plateaux: Capitalisme et Schizophrénie*. Paris: Editions de Minuit.
de Roo, G., Hillier, J., & Van Wezemael, J. (2012). *Planning & Complexity: Systems, Assemblages and Simulations*. Farnham: Ashgate Publishing.
de Roo, G., & Silva, E. A. (2010). *A Planners' Encounter with Complexity*. Farnham: Ashgate Publishing.
De Winne, A. (1903). *Door Arm Vlaanderen*. Ghent: Samenwerkende Volksdrukkerij.
D'Haenens, A. (1984). *De Wereld van de Hanze*. Brussels: Mercatorfonds.
Drucker, P. (1985). *Innovation and Entrepreneurship*. New York: HarperCollins Publishers.
Erwin, D. (2015). A public goods approach to major eveolutionary innovations. *Geobiology*, 13(4), 308–315.
ESF. (2012). *The Science of Innovation: ESF-STOA policy brief*. Strassbourg: European Science Foundation.
Fortuyn, P. (2002). *De puinhopen van acht jaar paars*. Rotterdam: Karakter.
Foucault, M. (1975). *Surveiller et punir: Naissance de la prison*. Paris: Gallimard.
Foucault, M. (1997). The Confession of the Flesh. In C. Gordon (Ed.), *Power/Knowledge Selected Interviews and Other Writings* (pp. 194–228).
FTM. (2015). *Het definitieve einde van de coöperatie Rabobank*. Retrieved from: www.ftm.nl/dossier/cooperatie-rabobank.
Gewest Vlaanderen. (2012). *Beleidsplan Ruimte Vlaanderen*. Groenboek, Brussel: Vlaams Gewest.
Giddens, A. (1984). *The Constitution of Society: Outline of the Theory of Structuration*. Cambridge: Polity Press.
Greenwood, R., & Hinings, C. R. (1996). Understanding radical organizational change: Bringing together the old and the new institutionalism. *The Academy of Management Review*, 21(4), 1022–1054.
Halsall, F. (2012). Niklas Luhmann and the body: Irritating social systems. *The New Bioethics*, 18(1), 4–20.
Hampshire, S. (1983). *Morality and Conflict Stuart Hampshire*. Cambridge, MA: Harvard University Press.
Havenbedrijf Rotterdam. (2016). *Jaarverslag 2015*. Rotterdam: Havenbedrijf Rotterdam NV.
Huntington, S. (1965). Political development and political decay. *World Politics*, 17(3), 386–430.
Huys, E. (1998). *Polders en wateringen: rechtsbronnen*. Oostende: Vlaams Instituut voor de Zee.
Janssen-Jansen, L. B. (2004). *Regio's uitgedaagd: Growth management ter inspiratie voor nieuwe paden van pro-actieve ruimtelijke planning*. Utrecht: Universiteit van Utrecht.
Jessop, B. (1990). *State Theory: Putting the Capitalist State in Its Place*. Cambridge: Polity Press.
Jessop, B. (2001). Institutional (re)turns and the strategic-relational approach. *Environment and Planning A*, 33(7), 1213–1235.

Jessop, B. (2008). *State Power: A Strategic-Relational Approach*. Cambridge: Polity Press.
Luhmann, N. (1990). *Essays on Self-Reference*. New York: Columbia University Press.
Luhmann, N. (1997). *Die Gesellschaft der Gesellschaft*. Frankfurt: Suhrkamp.
Maryville, S. (1992). Entrepreneurship in the business curriculum. *Journal of Education for Business*, 68(1), 27–31.
Massey, D. (2005). *For Space*. London: Sage Publications.
Miller, J., & Scott, E. (2007). *Complex Adaptive Systems: An Introduction to Computational Models of Social Life*. Princeton, NJ: Princeton University Press.
Merriam-Webster. (2016). *Open Dictionary*. Martinsburg: Quad Graphics.
Nitecki, M. (Ed.). (1990). *Evolutionary Innovations*. Chicago, IL: University of Chicago Press Books.
Pottage, A. (1998). Power as an art of contingency: Luhmann, Deleuze, Foucault. *Economy and Society*, 27, 1–27.
Poulantzas, N. (1978). *State, Power, Socialism*. London: NLB.
Prak, M., & Luiten van Zanden, J. (2013). *Nederland en het poldermodel. Sociaal-economische geschiedenis van Nederland, 1000–2000*. Amsterdam: Uitgeverij Bert Bakker.
Prince, G. (2006). De Commerciële Revolutie en het Wereldsysteem. In W. Frijhoff & L. Wessels (Eds.), *Veelvormige Dynamiek: Europa in het Ancien Régime, 1450–1800*. Amsterdam: Sun.
Schama, S. (1987). *The Embarrassment of Riches: An Interpretation of Dutch Culture in the Golden Age*. New York: Knopf.
Schama, S. (1995). *Landscape & Memory*. London: HarperCollins Publishers.
Soens, T. (2009). *De spade in de dijk? Waterbeheer en rurale samenleving in de Vlaamse kustvlakte (1280–1580)*. Ghent: Academia Press.
Strijland, R. (2006). Tweede privatiseringsronde corporaties noodzakelijk. *Cobouw*, September 2006.
Tempels, B. (2016). *Flood Resilience: A Co-Evolutionary Approach*. Groningen: InPlanning.
Urhahn, G. (2010). *The Spontaneous City*. Amsterdam: BIS Publishers.
Van Assche, K., Duineveld, M., & Beunen, R. (2014). Power and contingency in planning. *Environment and Planning A*, 46(10), 2385–2400.
Verhulst, A. (1998). *Polders en Wateringen in Vlaanderen: Status Questiones van het Historisch Onderzoek*. Oostende: Vlaams Instituut voor de Zee.
Verhulst, A. (2000). Historische ontwikkeling van het kustlandschap. *Met zicht op zee. Vlaanderen: Tweemaandelijks Tijdschrift voor Kunst en Cultuur*, 49(3), 7–10.
Vromraad. (2009). *Stad en wijk verweven. Schakelen, verbinden, verankeren in de stad*. Advies Juli 2009. Den Haag: SDU.
Williamson, O. (2000). The new institutional economics: Taking stock, looking ahead. *Journal of Economic Literature*, 38(3), 595–613.
Zonneveld, W. (2010). Governing a Complex Delta. In H. Meyer, I. Bobbink & S. Nijhuis (Eds.), *Delta Urbanism: The Netherlands* (pp. 100–113). Chicago, IL: American Planning Association.

7
PLANNING AND THE POLITICS OF HOPE

A Critical Inquiry

Jonathan Metzger

Introduction

The purpose of this essay is to investigate the relationship between hope and experience within the type of policy work that much of planning practice pertains to. Due to the radically situated circumstances of planning work, Rittel & Webber (1973, p. 163) have argued that every planning intervention must be considered an experimental "one-shot operation". However, what one sometimes may ask oneself is how mindful the practitioners that plan and direct these interventions really are of the conditions under which the experiments themselves unfold – and what the risks are of failing to reflect upon this. To understand these dynamics and their consequences better, I will in this essay focus on the foundation that underpins all social experiments: a sense of *hope*, not only as a recognition of the possibility of change, but also of improvement or 'progress'. Anderson (2006, p. 733) has suggested that hope and hoping are "taken-for-granted parts of the affective fabric of contemporary Western everyday life" and that "[t]he circulation, and distribution, of hope animates and dampens social and cultural life across numerous scales: from the minutiae of hopes that pleat together everyday life to the larger scale flows of hope that enact various collectivities".

Nonetheless, it has repeatedly been suggested that the topic of hope *per se* has received surprisingly little attention from contemporary philosophers and social scientists (McGeer, 2004, p. 101; see also Bovens, 1999). However, the deep relationship between hope and planning in the generic sense of these terms has long been recognized (see Moltmann, 1971). More strictly, in relation to the professional sphere of planning, John Forester has even suggested that the practice of planning can fundamentally be understood to be "the organization of hope" (Forester, 1989, p. 20, citing S. Blum; see also Baum, 1997). In a similar way, hope, as well as an experimentalist attitude towards social intervention (see Salet, Chapter 1, in this volume), has also been highlighted as a cornerstone of pragmatist philosophy. This affinity between pragmatism and planning theory should perhaps come as no surprise. Both are underpinned by a strong Promethean ideal – the idea that humans can change the world and take their fate into their own hands. The Promethean ideal and its related hopeful attitude can even be considered fundamental to much of 'Western', and particularly 'modern' culture (Brunsson, 2006, p. 22); the cultural context from which traditional planning theory as well as pragmatist philosophy have emerged from and in various ways are enmeshed in.

If we consider a hopeful attitude towards 'progress' and purposeful improvement of human existence as deeply embedded in widely diffused Western cultural notions, this also helps explain why contemporary invocations of hope today seem to convey a general, albeit somewhat fuzzy 'feel-good' sentiment. All sorts of ambitions and projects are connected to associations of hope, including – among many other things – a controversial housing program (HOPE VI) and a whole US presidential bid. Based on a quick analysis of such broad cultural tendencies, it would seem as if hope currently is understood as a taken for granted good-in-itself. You simply do not question appeals to hope unless you are prepared to come across as nothing but a complete misanthrope and cynic. This positive understanding of hope chimes well with the ancient Greek myth of Pandora. According to Greek mythology, Pandora was the first woman on Earth, and was tricked into opening a jar containing all the evils of the world. When the evils had all been let loose and she finally managed to close the container, there was only one meagre spirit left – the spirit of hope – *Elpis*. Traditionally, the interpretation of this myth has been that hope is the only good thing humanity has left to hold onto in a world full of rampaging evil.[1] However, in contrast to this positive appreciation of hope, the old Norse tradition had a very different understanding of the cosmic function of hope. In the Icelandic sagas 'hope' (*Ván*) was the name of the river formed by the flowing froth from the mouth of the world-destroying *Fenris* wolf. Thus, if you allowed the path of 'hope' to guide your steps it would carry you straight to the jaws of doom.

Juxtaposing the two classical myths about hope shows that there is not one, but many different ways to understand the function and ethical valence of hope. Based on such an intuition I will in this chapter conduct a critical inquiry into the relationship between hope and contemporary planning practices.[2] I will do so primarily by relating to scholarly literature on hope deriving from the two different traditions that form the thematic of this book, namely philosophical pragmatism on the one hand and institutionalist social science on the other. In very general terms, one could claim that much of the pragmatist tradition maps onto the Greek, Pandoran appreciation of hope-in-itself, while the institutionalist perspectives perhaps tend to lean more towards the bleaker, Norse-style understanding of the social and political functions of hope.

In the discussion of pragmatist conceptions of hope I will primarily be highlighting the work of the two philosophers in this tradition for whom the idea of hope has been most central to their philosophical projects: the classical pragmatist John Dewey and his more contemporary neo-pragmatist interpreter, Richard Rorty. With regards to the institutional theories, inspiration is primarily drawn from political economy and from the work of Nils Brunsson. Brunsson is generally considered to be a leading representative for the strand of research that with time has become known as 'Scandinavian institutionalism' (see also Boxenbaum & Pedersen, 2009; Czarniawska & Sévon, 1996; Lægreid, 2007). This body of work has grown out of the sociological 'new institutionalism' in organizational theory, which urges investigators of social phenomena to pay attention to how action is always situated, and thus unfolds within complex simultaneously overlapping and fragmented cultural and organizational contexts that create both possibilities and restraints. Based on such an intuition, research in the Scandinavian institutionalist tradition takes a particular interest in the concrete mechanisms and practices that produce variegated effects of change and stability at different times and places. Its style of research tends towards rich theorizations based upon situated, qualitative studies of organizational practice – that is, an "explicit combination of a theoretical ambition and detailed empirical studies of 'living' organizations" (Christensen & Lægreid, 2013, p. 94). In these case studies, particular interest is often directed towards the practices and arrangements that serve to uphold, subvert or transform local organizational cultures and behaviours. Thus, somewhat crudely put, one could argue that whereas most institutional analysis tends to pay attention to the stability of institutional patterns, and pragmatism-inclined work tends to take an explicit interest in the production of agency and novelty, Scandinavian institutionalism fills a function 'in between'; not by attempting to mediate between the former phenomena like, for example, Giddensian structuration theory, but by asking questions about how both stability and novelty are produced as practical achievements through an explicit focus on the 'how'.[3]

Due to lack of space, I will admittedly be painting the provided picture with broad brushstrokes – but the ideas presented here are nonetheless based on numerous years of close engagement with various types of contemporary urban, regional and environmental planning work, both as a researcher and as a planning practitioner. In the next part of the chapter, I will proceed to review some of the existing philosophical and social scientific literature that in one way or another focuses on substantially analysing the societal function of hope, with a particular (but not exclusive) focus on the work of Dewey, Rorty and Brunsson. After this, I move on to discuss the role that hope has come to play in contemporary planning contexts, with a particular focus on developments during the last four decades in Western capitalist societies. Based on this account I will argue in the final part of the chapter that the link between hope and positive change may not be as general and solid as often seems to be assumed, and that hope under certain conditions actually may come to function more as a stabilizing factor that inhibits learning from experience, and thus effectively blocks the development of more fertile strategies for desired change.

In conclusion, I suggest that the concrete social role that hope comes to play in any given planning process depends on the wider social and political context that this hope is articulated within. Therefore, when hope is in play, there is always a 'politics of hope' that needs to be taken into consideration which influences how hope is articulated and mobilized with variegated social and political effects – sometimes so as to effectuate radical change, but at other times so as to effectively suppress or block it. Therefore the social function of hope must always be analysed relationally, with due attention to how it is interwoven in intricate – always politically charged – webs of assumptions, aspirations, actions and expectations. Finally, I round off with some suggestions concerning how one can go about beginning to 'unpack' the political functions of hope, and in the process, perhaps even learn to begin to "hope well" (McGeer, 2004), in the sense of developing a sober and intellectually mature attitude that imagines hope not as a transcendent good-in-itself that cannot be questioned, but rather understood as a social fact of variable political function and ethical valence.

The Concept of Hope

Within philosophy, a hopeful position is known as 'meliorism' and is to be understood in contrast to fundamental optimism on the one hand, and pessimism on the other. A meliorist position recognizes that in the ongoing saga of humanity, things can go well – but also badly. The future is yet to be written, so it is still possible that our choices and actions may affect how it unfolds. Given this, meliorism can be understood as a philosophical position diametrically opposed to determinism. Meliorism is not unique to the philosophical tradition of pragmatism, but it has nonetheless been repeatedly argued that it is particularly central to this school of thought (see Dendeen, 1999; Fishman & McCarthy, 2005).[4] The link between hope and pragmatism is perhaps particularly central to the work of John Dewey, one of the leading proponents of classical pragmatist thought. Somewhat peculiarly, even though the idea of hope was so important to Dewey's philosophical project, he himself nonetheless never explicitly addressed the phenomenon of hope *per se* in his writings (Fishman & McCarthy, 2005, p. 675); instead he repeatedly came to discuss the subject of hope tangentially and in relation to various other issues and questions (which may not be so strange after all, given the emphasis in his philosophical project on the need to always relate vague, general concepts to specificities). However, this lacuna hasn't precluded others from 'excavating' or 'constructing' a Deweyan theory of hope based on the numerous scattered passages in which he addresses this phenomenon throughout his works. Perhaps most famous among these commentators is Richard Rorty, he himself also a leading neo-pragmatist in his own right.

According to Rorty's interpretation, Deweyan hope is a vague ethical calling to have faith in the possibility of social change towards a better future. However, in Rorty's view, the articulation of such hope must never become too precise. Otherwise one risks circumscribing and limiting the vistas for possible social change so as to encompass only those developments that are easily imaginable from the viewpoint of the present, and hence risk locking down trajectories of development into pre-existing, and perhaps uninventive, modes of thought. Therefore, in the words of Rorty, Deweyan hope must by necessity be "criterionless", wherefore "Deweyans" by necessity must limit themselves to offering "inspiring narratives and fuzzy utopias" infusing their audience with the "ability to believe that the future will be unspecifiably different from, and unspecifiably freer than the past" (Rorty, 1999, p. 120). For Dewey, at least in Rorty's reading, such unspecified hope was the necessary ground for that which Dewey considered to be the only goal of intrinsic value, "growth", defined as "developing, not only physically but intellectually and morally" (Dewey, 1938, p. 19). Dewey's belief in the possibility of achieving such 'growth' rests on two fundamental tenets of (secular) faith: firstly, that ventures of collective human intelligence will lead to ever new discoveries of the nature of the world, and secondly that these "secrets of nature, once disclosed, will prove nothing but beneficial to human moral ends" (Dendeen, 1999, p. 592).[5]

In relation to Dewey's thoughts on hope and growth, Dendeen (1999) has pointed out the curious paradox that although Dewey's political philosophy is explicitly anti-foundationalist, it nonetheless rests upon a foundation of faith in the human capacity to master its environment, and to purposely alter it in ways that will be beneficial for its future development or growth. Hence, at a deeper level, Dewey's philosophical ideas about human growth are founded upon a faith in the existence of "a process of continual improvement and mastery – a process with no necessary culmination, but one in which even acts of horrible barbarism are viewed solely as 'setbacks', not as intractable manifestations of human depravity" (Dendeen, 1999, p. 601). Thus, even if Deweyan pragmatism has become broadly known in philosophical circles as the meliorist philosophy *par excellence*, a more careful reading discloses that Dewey's understanding of hope more comes across as a fundamental *optimism*, the belief that even though specific things can sometimes go bad, in the long run, they will turn out for the better and inevitably progress towards a somehow qualitatively better future to come. The only thing that is required for this to happen is that humans do not give up their faith and commitment to such progress.

The deep, albeit fuzzy faith in the universal goodness of hope that underpins Dewey's and Rorty's pragmatist philosophies may come across as somewhat idiosyncratic when carefully scrutinized. However, the pragmatists are in no way alone in leaning upon such an uncritical, optimistic embrace of hope as a good-in-itself. When carefully examined from this perspective, leading contemporary social theorists appear to share the same habit of mind and pen. To give but a few brief examples, Arjun Appadurai's (2007) understanding of hope seems to circle around a somewhat vague and patient aspiration for a materially more prosperous future, in Latour's *Pandora's Hope* (1999), the term is barely mentioned, let alone substantially discussed, and in David Harvey's *Spaces of Hope* (2000), the discussion on the concept of hope is so scant that the word itself doesn't even appear in the index. Only marginally better is Castells's (2012) *Networks of Outrage and Hope*, and what overall seems to unite all these otherwise extremely diverse leading social theorists is their apparent acceptance of the phenomenon of hope as something of a self-evident and undifferentiated good – of such obvious social and political benefit that this barely needs to be explained, let alone argued.[6]

In contrast to these more current social theorists' somewhat cavalier treatment of the concept of hope, the neo-marxist philosopher Ernst Bloch dedicated his academic life to a substantial inquiry into the phenomenon in his encyclopedic three-tome magnum opus *The Principle of Hope* (Bloch, 1995). Although to a newcomer Bloch's way of reasoning may come across as a somewhat curious blend of arcane mysticism and Marxist dogmatism, *The Principle of Hope* must nonetheless be considered an obligatory passage point for any social scientific work dealing with the topic of hope. It is also interesting to note that although Bloch's philosophical position can also be described as broadly meliorist, there are both interesting similarities and differences between his thinking and that of pragmatists such as Dewey and Rorty. However, what is of particular interest in the context of this chapter is the differentiation Bloch makes, in contrast to Dewey and Rorty, between different kinds of hope. Already in the introduction to the first volume, Bloch makes a distinction between "stale" daydreams that easily become "booty for swindlers" and radical forms of hope, where the latter needs to be very carefully and thoughtfully cultivated and developed to live up to their potential for societal transformation (Bloch, 1995, Vol. 1, p. 4). The purpose of Bloch's argument is to distinguish between 'true' and 'false' forms of hope. Even if one does not follow him in this endeavour, it is interesting to note how he in this process calls to attention that hope can have many different social functions, and that it further is important to be vigilant of both the contents and functions of hope (Bloch, 1995, Vol. 1, p. 7).

The work of Nils Brunsson on the 'mechanisms of hope' leads in a similar direction, albeit from a very different starting point. In his research, Brunsson has for many decades focused on studying the practical implementation of ostensibly rational reforms in both private and public organizations. In *Mechanisms of Hope* (Brunsson, 2006), Brunsson tries to grapple with the conundrum concerning why the urge to repeatedly try on new rationalizing reforms never seems to falter – even though such reforms constantly seem to fail to produce the desired effects. Further, Brunsson also relates this issue to the more general question concerning "how we can preserve our hope for a better world, even in the presence of discouraging evidence" (Brunsson, 2006, p. 1). In his study Brunsson noticed that within the organizations he studied the failure of reforms to achieve the stipulated goals never seemed to be attributed to deficiencies in the principles guiding the reforms, but to the contrary, only seemed to have functioned to reinforce the reformers conviction to re-embark on further reform ventures that once again "try to redo the same thing" (Brunsson, 2006, p. 143). Thus, Brunsson notes, the reformers and their organizations did not seem to learn anything from experience, except from reinforcing their faith that they were right from the start, and that there was nothing wrong with the ambitions they kept pursuing – at least not in principle. Thus, the reformers did not waiver in their faith in the principle that rational reform was good and necessary, even if they repeatedly failed to implement it.

In his study, Brunsson outlines a number of 'mechanisms' that allowed the reformers to sustain their hope for future success – even in the face of discouraging evidence in the form of prior experiences. The three main types of mechanisms that Brunsson describes were: (a) avoiding considering practical experiences and consequences, (b) addressing only practices that did not threaten hope, and (c) interpreting practice in such a way that hope was not threatened (Brunsson, 2006, p. 186). Relating to the first point, Brunsson notes that in the organizations he had studied, reformers took very little interest in hearing about others' experiences from similar reforms, and – perhaps somewhat surprisingly – were also quite uninterested in the outcomes of their own reforms too. All they payed attention to was to ensure that they had been 'implemented': "which turned out to mean that the reform had led to people writing things that were roughly in accordance with the intentions. There was little interest now in the effects on operations and their management, which had been emphasized in an abstract fashion at the launch of the reforms" (Brunsson, 2006, p. 191). Regarding the second point, Brunsson notes that the reformers generally only focused on easy targets, or 'low-hanging fruit', that did not challenge any of the more fundamental structures of the organizations. And finally, relating to the third, he notes that the reformers constantly seemed to interpret obvious failures as successes – or else always had an excuse in stock so as to explain why this one particular reform measure seemed to have failed (but would be successful if tried once again, in a correct manner). Finally, Brunsson also concludes that the explanation behind how these mechanisms can be upheld rests upon three foundations: a strong faith in the goodness of the principle (rationality), the abstractness and malleability of the principle itself, and finally the attitude that the principle primarily applies to the work of others, not oneself.

In his conclusions, Brunsson assumes a somewhat agnostic stance regarding the value of hope, noting that "[i]t is difficult to provide a general answer to the question of whether it is good or bad to preserve one's hope" (Brunsson, 2006, p. 211). What he does suggest, however, is that the function of hope in relation to the mechanisms of hope may not at all be the one that we normally assume: "[h]ope may seem to be connected to change. But continued hope is an instance of stability, and the mechanisms of hope that I have presented are all mechanisms of stability rather than change" (Brunsson, 2006, p. 225). However, the *belief* that change was occurring, or at least about to occur, also filled a function in itself – it in effect blocked the possibility of learning from experience (see also Tängh Wrangel, 2017, p. 9, on "amnesiac hope"). Since the present and the future were imagined to be so different (changed/changing) from the past, prior experiences were deemed to be of no real relevance to present endeavours. As a consequence, Brunsson notes, "[p]aradoxically, then, we can see that this belief in change has increased stability – the same ideas have lived on. The impression of change and novelty leads to stability" (Brunsson, 2006, p. 226). Finally Brunsson reasons that the mechanisms of hope appear to fill a very important psychological function for the reformers he has studied, by functioning as "means of ... avoiding a confrontation between the notion of one's own importance and a conspicuously less grand reality". Simply, in order to find the energy to conduct one's daily work, "it helps to assume that we can change things in the desired way" (Brunsson, 2006, p. 223).

The Function of Hope in Planning Work

What Brunsson's work on the mechanisms of hope to a large extent speaks to is the troubled relationship between hope and experience. Somewhat more specifically, it puts its finger on how hope that does not learn from experience may come to serve functions completely adverse to those professed or intended, for instance as a stabilizing factor rather than an agent of change. This also resonates with John Law and Karel Williams's (2014) discussion of the "state of unlearning" that according to them characterizes the thirty-odd-year neo-liberal policy experiment in the UK in general, and England in particular. Regarding the notion of 'experimenting' in English public policy, Law & Williams pull no punches:

> The assumption was that the economy would prosper if markets were allowed to work properly. The idea was that competition would deliver efficiency and better services. The problem is that thirty-five years on government is still blindly running the same

> experiment even when its results are catastrophic. As a part of this, manifest failures in industrial policy are explained away by saying that the experiment is not working because it is incomplete ... Against this, our argument is that government has stopped learning because it is incapable of thinking constructively about the limits to its own assumptions and its experimental frame. After thirty years of centralised economic and industrial experiments and an increasing litany of failure, by now we are living in a state of non-learning.
>
> *(Law & Williams, 2014, p. 2)*

Law and Williams further suggest that even though consecutive UK governments have recognized that the outcomes of their experiments have been unsuccessful, none of them have really questioned the assumptions that have underpinned these reforms or the market-oriented framework in which they have been performed. Instead, the accumulating evidence of failure is framed as a consequence of insufficient application of the framework, leading to calls for new reforms in the same grain and direction as the previous failures. This, the authors describe as a "state of profound non-learning" in which it is assumed that the given response to obvious failures is "that the experiment be properly conducted and that the framing be more thoroughly applied" (Law & Williams, 2014, p. 7).

Law and Williams's argument focuses on the UK. However, even though the timeframe may vary, give or take a decade or so, it can nonetheless be forcefully argued that at the present time most of the so-called 'Global North' (and South, for that matter) is today substantially also part of the neo-liberal policy experiment and correlate 'state of non-learning'. *Pace* Brunsson, it may well be that many of the policy professionals working within the frame of these experiments are driven by an individual and/or collective urge to facilitate 'progressive' change. Nonetheless, quite tragically, their work constantly in effect turns out to produce the opposite: a reasonably stable neo-liberal policy framework in which questioning of the primacy of deregulated market forms of economic exchange is completely out of bounds. In a way, it thus appears as if many of these, in their own eyes perhaps 'progressive', policy professionals are stuck in something akin to a neo-liberal time-warp, unable to confront the underlying conditions and seemingly taken-for-granted assumptions that set the context and action space for their work – and which they hence also contribute to reproducing.

Institutionalized planning work is inevitably a type of governmental policy practice, and one which I would argue very much falls into the frame of Law and Williams's argument about the 'state of non-learning'. Relating to this observation, one can here also draw a parallel to David Harvey's classical critique of the role of planning within capitalist societies, 'Planning – The Ideology of Planning' (Harvey, 1985; reproduced in Hillier & Healey, 2008). In the essay, originally put forth in 1978 (and republished as Harvey, 1985), Harvey performs an analysis of the social and economic function of that which somewhat crudely could be called 'really existing planning'. He begins by posing the question about the role of planners within societies founded upon capitalist principles of economic exchange. Do planners generally challenge the reproduction of such fundamental societal relations and frameworks of order? No, says Harvey. In practice, planning serves just as much to reproduce them, particularly through alleviating inherent tensions within capitalism and the particular conflicts these produce in urban environments. In the words of Harvey himself:

> The planner's task is to contribute to the processes of social reproduction and that in so doing the planner is equipped with powers vis-à-vis the production, maintenance and management of the built environment which permits him or her to intervene in order to stabilize, to create the conditions for 'balanced growth', to contain civil strife

and factional struggles by repression, cooptation, or integration. And to fulfil these goals successfully, the planning process as a whole (in which the planner fulfils only one set of tasks) must be relatively open.

(Harvey, 1985, p. 176)

Further, Harvey admits that his analysis may appear "unduly simplistic", however he still maintains that any "down-to-earth analysis of what planners actually do, as opposed to what the mandarins of the planning fraternity think they do" will actually prove him right, further adding that "the history of those who seek to depart radically from this fairly circumscribed path suggests that they either encounter frustration or else give up the role of planner entirely" (Harvey, 1985, p. 176).

Harvey's quite extreme generalizations warrant some comments, to say the least. To begin with, it has long been recognized that even markedly capitalist economies are founded upon a bulk of socio-economic relations that in themselves cannot in any way be argued to be capitalist (see Gibson-Graham, 1996; Law & Williams, 2014). Further, Harvey provocatively provides absolutely no empirical backing to his claims. Nonetheless, somewhat dishearteningly, it can now, almost 40 years on, be concluded that over four decades of planning research offer very little evidence to challenge his central thesis: that planning practice generally shies away from challenging the fundamental dynamics of capital accumulation. However, it can quite convincingly be argued that even though the power of the planner may generally be less impressive today than at the time when Harvey originally penned his argument, the market-supporting function of planning is on the other hand even more nakedly apparent in the vast majority of cases (see Allmendinger, 2016).

A particularly pertinent aspect of Harvey's argumentation in relation to the topic of this chapter, is how he is very clear in pointing out that the planner's role does not imply that she is always a "mere defender of the status quo" (Harvey, 1985, p. 177). On the contrary, the function of the planner is to pre-empt and ward off the inevitable social frictions that result from the dynamics of capital accumulation in the built environment. "In fact", Harvey notes, "the whole tradition of planning is progressive in the sense that the planner's commitment to the ideology of social harmony – unless it is perverted or corrupted in some way – always puts the planner in the role of 'righter of wrongs', 'corrector of imbalances', and 'defender of the public interest'" (Harvey, 1985, p. 177). However, "[t]he limits of this progressive stance are clearly set ... by the fact that the definitions of the public interest, of imbalance, and of inequity are set according to the requirements for the reproduction of the social order, which is, whether we like the term, or not, a distinctively capitalistic social order" (Harvey, 1985, p. 177).

To be able to fulfil their function as a resolver of tensions and manager of conflicts within the urban manifestations of capital dynamics, planners and planning scholars constantly come up with new theoretical concepts and ideas that both assist planners in focusing their work and in legitimizing what they do. Therefore, for Harvey, 'planning theory' emerges as the ever-evolving and variegated pool of concepts and ideas that help planners tell themselves that they are actually doing some other work, and contributing to some other societal function, than that which they in effect serve (e.g. understood as promoting sustainable development, social equity, resilience, etc.). However, Harvey suggests, the one question that the majority of planners and planning theorists repeatedly seem to fail to ask themselves is "why the planner seems doomed to a life of perpetual frustration, why the high-sounding ideals of planning theory are so frequently translated into grubby practices on the ground", and facing up to "how the shifts in world view and in ideological stance are social products rather than freely chosen" (Harvey, 1985, p. 184). None of this will change, according to Harvey, until the day that planners can address what we today could call 'the elephant in the planning office': that planners operate in a capitalist system which produces gross social tensions, economic inequalities and ecological harm. And to Harvey the issue is clear-cut: planners will not be able to really do anything to stop these destructive tendencies until they recognize and confront the roots of the problem, that is, the dynamics of capital accumulation and circulation. Until that day, they will merely be providing what Slavoj Žižek dismissively has referred to as "palliative damage-control measures within the global capitalist framework" (Žižek, 2000, p. 321).

To bring this recapitulation of Harvey's critical analysis back into the fold of the overarching objective of this chapter, one could thus argue that even though many contemporary planners perhaps imagine themselves to be agents of change towards more equal, sustainable, or in some way more 'progressive' societies; the function their profession has filled over the past decades has generally been completely the opposite. Through their labours they have contributed to the reproduction and extension of a capital-driven development of urban environments that very much has exacerbated all the ills that planners generally see themselves to be combatting. This by no means implies a claim that planning has somehow been 'inefficient'. On the contrary, it has contributed to facilitating urban transformations on the grandest of scales. However, in doing so, it has generally not achieved the societal goals it has set before itself to contribute towards. Nonetheless, we repeatedly hear from planners and planning theorists that we needn't be disheartened by the 'grubby reality' of what planning is today, because there is so much else, so many good things planning *could be* – if we just keep trying, again and again. The articulations of such claims are however deeply reminiscent of the 'mechanisms of hope', seeing that it builds upon the assumption of that if we just keep doing roughly the same thing again – only better, with better conceptual direction and in more informed ways – everything will work out well!

Brunsson argued that the mechanisms of hope perhaps primarily serve the function of allowing their enactors to avoid confrontation with a 'less grand reality' than what they wish to see. In relation to contemporary planning practice, perhaps this less grand reality is the fact that while things ostensibly (and sometimes, extensively) change in contemporary urban environments, much also stays the same. New rail lines, roads and houses are planned and built – but that which was supposed to change for the better as a result of these projects – social and economic inequality, environmental harm, etc. – appears to remain elusively obdurate, or is even aggravated by the manifest changes that are achieved. So what planners in effect appear to be contributing to in most cases is a form of change that in practice contributes to stabilizing social and economic meta-patterns of inequality. This change is part of and contributes to the smooth operation of an enormous social machine that produces these inequalities by constantly contributing with an illusion of change, that 'progress is being made', but which in effect amounts to a "change of no change" (Marres, 2011) or to paraphrase Schön (1971), a *conservative dynamism*, which at best (or rather, worst) contributes to a local geographical and temporal warding-off or outsourcing of negative effects to distant places or future generations, 'out of sight, out of mind' (see Hillier, 2009).

Given all the above, it seems as if it may be important not just to stare ourselves blind on what changes through planning endeavours, but to also pay critical attention to that which persists – or is even exacerbated – throughout changes, seeing that it is hope that is the fuel of the experimental state of non-learning and 'roll-out' neo-liberalism (see also Allmendinger & Haughton, 2013), which today perhaps even more insidiously than ever harnesses the mechanisms of hope in the enrolling of professionals and citizens through participatory or 'self-organizing' governance ideas such as 'social entrepreneurship', 'DIY urbanism' and 'sustainable lifestyles' (Savini, 2018, forthcoming). All these planning ideas articulate hope for 'enabling' change 'from below' in a manner that however does not at all question the overarching framework of capital accumulation and circulation within which these initiatives unfold; a framework that they for the most part will contribute to stabilizing and reproducing through alleviating concrete social and economic tensions and conflicts in urban environments, which themselves to quite some extent are effects of those aforementioned dynamics.

When planning work and thought all too naively focus on the possibilities of facilitating 'the organization of hope', based on a self-image as agents of change, it thus appears as if there is a substantial risk that one forgets to pay attention to that which remains relatively (albeit, dynamically) stable throughout all the commotion. That is, to be specific, the 'elephant in the planning office' that is so seldom pointed out: capitalism. Arguably, capitalism isn't the only ill of the world, but when it comes to urban development it is today evident that unfettered, 'feral' capital dynamics is one of the greatest culprits in producing social and economic inequalities and ecological harm (Steele, 2015). One may therefore ask oneself when 'progressively' styled planners will be able to shift out of their 'state of unlearning' and face up to the collected mass of evidence which suggests that their professional practice, whether they like it or not, generally fills completely other functions than those they wish to imagine themselves involved in. When will they look beyond the apparently ungrounded hope that they will be able to effectuate any form of fundamental contestation of the production of social, economic and ecological harms without confronting or at least questioning the overarching conditions and mechanisms that serve to recurrently produce these devastating effects?

Learning to Hope Well

It has been argued that it is important for social scientists to stay attentive to the functioning of "institutions of hope", understood as the "enabling institutions that offset, loosen, or challenge the constraints imposed by regulatory institutions" (Braithwaite, 2004, p. 7). Complementing this rather rosy understanding of the social functions of hope, one may perhaps in light of the previous discussions also suggest that we may do wisely to also add to that list all those social mechanisms that co-opt, enrol or even prey on hope in ways that produce effects that we might not find ethically or politically appealing. For, as has been noted by McManus (2011, n. 5), the role of hope as a counterforce to oppression is well known, "but what of, conversely, the role of hope in the reproduction of hegemonic relations? When should a skeptical eye be cast upon the colluding capacities of affirmative affect?" Relating to such a suspicious intuition regarding the social and political function of specific, situated articulations of hope, the work of institutionally inclined social scientists such as David Harvey and Nils Brunsson invites us to not only consider the contextually situated outcomes of specific modes of hoping, but also to direct our attention to the more general problem of the relationship between hope and experience.

The utopianist Bloch considered experience (or, as he termed it, 'memory') to be the sworn enemy of true hope, whereas Brunsson and Harvey appear to suggest that hope that fails to learn from experience is naïve, contributes to social obduracy rather than change (Brunsson), and is also easily manipulated (Harvey). Contrary to Brunsson and Harvey, commentators have noticed that Rorty appears to have assumed a similar position to that of Bloch, in seeing experience ('knowledge') as opposed to hope. Or as formulated by Sami Pihlström (2010, p. 6), "Rorty's dichotomy between hope and knowledge is one of the dualisms he – as many critics have pointed out – is unpragmatically committed to, despite his pragmatic urge to destroy dichotomies". However, perhaps the classical pragmatists were less dismissive about the necessity of a tempered balance between hope and experience than what comes across in Rorty's interpretations. For instance, regarding the work of the founding member of the pragmatist school, C. S. Peirce, Cooke (2005, p. 653) suggests that for Peirce "[t]he value of hope depends on its ability to be checked by experience; otherwise it is mere wishful thinking". Similarly, Fishman and McCarthy (2005) suggest that for Dewey, hope in effect amounted to a form of vigilant curiosity, rather than the vague optimism that Rorty – among others – has later made it out to be. In their reading of Dewey, he very much urges his readers not only to turn their attention to vague hope itself, but rather towards the substantial content of our hope – with a specific focus on "what price others … must pay for the goals we choose" (Fishman & McCarthy, 2005, p. 697).

So perhaps the classical pragmatists would nonetheless have agreed with those who today call for the need of paying close and critical attention to the dynamics that we, in lack of a better term, perhaps could call 'the politics of hope'. An attention to the politics of hope would not proceed from a taken-for-granted assumption that all articulations of hope have some form of 'progressive' political function effectuating progress or change towards some obvious 'better'. As noted by McManus (2011), "hope does not entail a political orientation, and competing visions of the future invoke 'hope' to compel allegiance and direct political agency" (see also Duggan & Muñoz, 2009; Mouffe & Laclau, 2002, p. 125). As further highlighted by Drahos (2004, p. 36), hope is also susceptible to purposeful manipulation, through which public injunctions towards hope can allow actors to "harness emotionally collectivities to economic and social agendas that are poorly understood by those collectivities and that are ultimately destructive of the social institutions upon which actual private and collective hopes depend". Thus, as Valerie Braithwaite (2004, p. 8) puts it somewhat dramatically, hope can be "spooned out to mass publics by those who command our institutions – as a sedative to injustice and abuse and as a means of delaying, even circumventing, calls for social change".

Proceeding from the above insights, it is certainly possible to agree with Bloch (1995) that hope is a mobilizing emotion, but at the same time it becomes clear that it is perhaps a bit spurious to assume that hope exists in a binary opposition to anxiety and fear, like he does. Rather, what we are now confronting in many places around the world are quite elaborate attempts at enacting political choreographies of both fear and hope, in which the evocation of fear for certain things (immigrants, Muslims, desolate poverty) interplays with the channelling of hope towards quite specific political ambitions and projects. Accordingly, hope must always be understood to be produced in a field of social and political relations in which "power cannot be divorced from the question of whose hopes will dominate and be realized" (Courville & Piper, 2004), and further leading towards Ananya Roy's conclusion that, following John Forester's assertion that one should never conduct an analysis of power without an analysis of hope, one should conversely also never provide an analysis of hope without an analysis of power.

Following on from the above, it appears that we would be wise to heed Susan McManus's (2011) suggestion to always ask ourselves how a specific articulation of hope is "produced, sustained, and circulated", and what are the content and effects of different "modalities of hope". With regards to the recent history of the professional practice of planning, it is perhaps of particular importance to remain vigilant of how hope can function both as a driver of change and as a basis for stability, depending on how it is articulated within a particular social and political context at a given time and place. In relation to the last few decades of really existing planning practice there actually appears to be good reasons to suspect that many articulations of hope in contemporary planning endeavours in practice more or less function as mechanisms of co-optation of more radical transformative impulses, harnessing the mobilizing potential of hope and enrolling 'progressive' planning idealism in a way that it comes to serve as a system-stabilizer rather than the system-transforming force many proponents perhaps would like to see it be.

To begin to round off, we may remind ourselves that according to Dante, those who were condemned to eternal torture and suffering were greeted with the words 'Abandon all hope, you who enter here' written above the Gates of Hell. And perhaps Dante was right in that when giving up hope wholesale, we also give up something of our humanity (or even, more generally, of what it means to be alive). Relatedly, on a more collective level, the harnessing and channelling of hope may well be the fuel that keeps any given social machine in motion. However, it is therefore also of crucial importance to recognize that these machines can be of very different kinds, and in turn therefore also produce dramatically variegated outputs. But, as Valerie Braithwaite (2004, p. 7) has noted, if we accept that hope may be "at the core of our being", that inevitably leads to the question of how we may hope in better and worse ways, both as individuals and as collectives (see also McGeer, 2004).[7] The point here is thus not that we in some way should 'abandon all hope' and give in to despair, but rather it is an appeal for the need to be conscious and savvy about how hope can be manipulated, and can come to perform functions quite contrary to the aspirations and expectations of those who articulate or are mobilized through it. In turn, this calls for a certain suspicious caution towards the goals and processes in which we invest our hopes and desires, and what we, by way of a careful weighing of experiences and aspirations, imagine that they can realistically lead to within the contexts that we act. This would amount to an engagement in 'the politics of hope' that is not merely naively assertive ('we need to hope!'), but instead performed in a more inquisitive manner, akin to Healey's call for the development of an ability to both 'zoom in' and 'zoom out' in the analysis of the practical function of hope in episodes of situated planning practice (see Healey, Chapter 2, in this volume). Overall, such a stance would eventually hopefully lead towards the emergence of a somewhat more sober relationship to hope in our endeavours as planning academics and practitioners, which does not take for granted that any articulation of hope is a granted good-in-itself.

Based on such an intuition, one may perhaps agree with John Forester in his assertion that planning work organizes hope; but if so, it is then also of crucial importance that we pay very careful attention towards what objectives our hope is organized, and to what concrete effects. Thus, even if we agree with Rorty's assertion that "[t]he utopian social hope which sprang up in nineteenth-century Europe is still the noblest imaginative creation of which we have on record" (Rorty, 1999, p. 277), we may nonetheless do well to be suspicious of his demand for an unwavering faith in the goodness of hope, and particularly his demand that we adhere to the conviction that "the future will be unspecifiably different from, and unspecifiably freer than the past". Or more generally put: even if we agree with the productivity of certain hopes, this by no means implies that we have to uncritically assume that any and every expression of hope will serve our ideals. One must recognize that it is possible to hope for innumerable different things, some of which may be compatible with Rorty's 'noblest imaginative creation', and some that most certainly run completely contrary to it. From such a vantage point, an intelligent way of hoping, what Bloch called *docta spes* ('educated hope'), must constantly remind itself to ask not only whether there is hope or not, but also to be constantly (critically) vigilant of what this hope is directed towards, what contextual effects it has, how it is imagined to be realized – and at what price.

Notes

1 However, there are of course also alternative interpretations of this myth, arguing for instance that *Elpis* ('hope') in fact was an evil (why else was she in the jar?) and/or that by closing the jar, Pandora, in effect, sealed off and withheld hope from humanity (see Verdenius, 1985).
2 'Critical' should in this context be read as 'scrutinizing', but not necessarily 'dismissive'. Also note that Roy (2008) articulates a similar ambition but then takes a somewhat different tack compared to the line of inquiry pursued in this chapter. However I do consider Roy's argument and the present argument to be mutually reinforcing.

3 Scandinavian institutionalism appears to share a strong family resemblance with Patsy Healey's approach to sociological institutionalism, as presented in this book (see Healey, Chapter 2, in this volume); particularly where Healey points out that "Institutional change is not the puzzle ... Instead, it becomes important to understand whether and how stabilities are created through time".
4 For a well-grounded, distinctively meliorist position in contemporary social theory grounded in a different tradition, see Hall (1986).
5 It can be argued that Rorty, and perhaps also Dendeen to some degree, vulgarizes and misconstrues Dewey's notions of 'hope' and 'growth', and that these ideas are actually much more nuanced and multi-layered in the context of Dewey's thinking than what Rorty makes justice of in his interpretations. (For alternative readings of these aspects of Dewey's work, see Johnston, 2006, pp. 106–107; Saito, 2005, p. 5; see also the concluding part of this chapter.)
6 Eagleton (2015) however comes across as a recent exception to this light-handed treatment of the concept of hope among leading contemporary philosophers and social scientists.
7 However it can be argued that it is far too simplistic and crude to try to differentiate between supposedly good 'collective' hope and evil 'public' hope in the way Braithwaite (2004) attempts to do.

References

Allmendinger, P. (2016). *Neoliberal Spatial Governance*. London: Routledge.
Allmendinger, P., & Haughton, G. (2013). The evolution and trajectories of English spatial governance: 'Neoliberal' episodes in planning. *Planning Practice & Research*, 28(1), 6–26.
Anderson, B. (2006). Becoming and being hopeful: Towards a theory of affect. *Environment and Planning D: Society and Space*, 24(5), 733–752.
Appadurai, A. (2007). Hope and democracy. *Public Culture*, 19(1), 29–34.
Baum, H. (1997). *The Organization of Hope*. Albany, NY: State University Press.
Bloch, E. (1995). *The Principle of Hope* (Vols. 1–3). Cambridge, MA: MIT Press.
Bovens, L. (1999). The value of hope. *Philosophy and Phenomenological Research*, 59(3), 667–681.
Boxenbaum, E., & Strandgaard Pedersen, J. (2009). Scandinavian Institutionalism – A Case of Institutional Work. In T. B. Lawrence, R. Suddaby & B. Leca (Eds.), *Institutional Work*. Cambridge: Cambridge University Press.
Braithwaite, V. (2004). Collective hope. *The ANNALS of the American Academy of Political and Social Science*, 592, 6–15.
Brunsson, N. (2006). *Mechanisms of Hope: Maintaining the Dream of the Rational Organization*. Malmö: Liber.
Castells, M. (2012). *Networks of Outrage and Hope: Social Movements in the Internet Age*. Cambridge: Polity Press.
Christensen, T., & Lægreid, P. (2013). SCANCOR and Norwegian public administration research development. *Nordiske Organisasjonsstudier*, 15(4), 91–110.
Cooke, E. (2005). Transcendental hope: Peirce, Hookway, and Pihlström on the conditions for inquiry. *Transactions of the Charles S. Peirce Society: A Quarterly Journal in American Philosophy*, 41(3), 651–674.
Courville, S., & Piper, N. (2004). Harnessing hope through NGO activism. *The ANNALS of the American Academy of Political and Social Science*, 592(1), 39–61.
Czarniawska, B., & Sévon, G. (1996). Introduction. In B. Czarniawska & G. Sévon (Eds.), *Translating Organizational Change*. Berlin: de Gruyter.
Dendeen, P. (1999). The politics of hope and optimism: Rorty, Havel, and the democratic faith of John Dewey. *Social Research*, 66(2), 577–609.
Dewey, J. (1938). *Experience and Education*. New York: Macmillan.
Drahos, P. (2004). Trading in public hope. *The ANNALS of the American Academy of Political and Social Science*, 592, 18–38.
Duggan, L., & Muñoz, J. E. (2009). Hope and hopelessness: A dialogue. *Women and Performance: A Journal of Feminist Theory*, 19(2), 275–283.
Eagleton, T. (2015). *Hope without Optimism*. Charlottesville, VA: University of Virginia Press.
Fishman, S. M., & McCarthy, L. (2005). The morality and politics of hope: John Dewey and positive psychology in dialogue. *Transactions of the Charles S. Peirce Society: A Quarterly Journal in American Philosophy*, 41(3), 675–701.
Forester, J. (1989). *Planning in the Face of Power*. Berkeley, CA: University of California Press.
Gibson-Graham, J. K. (1996). *The End of Capitalism (As We Knew It): A Feminist Critique of Political Economy*. Cambridge, MA: Blackwell Publishers.

Hall, S. (1986). The problem of ideology-Marxism without guarantees. *Journal of Communication Inquiry*, 10(2), 28–44.

Harvey, D. (2000). *Spaces of Hope*. Edinburgh: Edinburgh University Press.

Harvey, D. (1985). On Planning: The Ideology of Planning. In J. Hillier & P. Healey (Eds.), *Critical Essays in Planning Theory, Vol. 2: Political Economy, Diversity and Pragmatism*. Aldershot: Ashgate.

Hillier, J., & Healey, P. (Eds.). (2008). *Critical Essays in Planning Theory, Vol. 2: Political Economy, Diversity and Pragmatism*. Aldershot: Ashgate.

Hillier, J. (2009). Assemblages of justice: The 'ghost ships' of Graythorp. *International Journal of Urban and Regional Research*, 33(3), 640–661.

Johnston, J. S. (2006). *Inquiry and Education: John Dewey and the Quest for Democracy*. Albany, NY: State University Press.

Latour, B. (1999). *Pandora's Hope: Essays on the Reality of Science Studies*. Cambridge, MA: Harvard University Press.

Lægreid, P. (2007). Organization theory – the Scandinavian way. *Nordiske Organisasjonsstudier*, 9(1), 77–82.

Law, J., & Williams, K. (2014). *State of Unlearning? Government as Experiment*. Manchester: CRESC Working Paper 134.

Marres, N. (2011). The costs of public involvement: Everyday devices of carbon accounting and the materialization of participation. *Economy and Society*, 40(4), 510–533.

McGeer, V. (2004). The art of good hope. *The ANNALS of the American Academy of Political and Social Science*, 592(1), 100–127.

McManus, S. (2011). Hope, fear and the politics of affective agency. *Theory & Event* 14(4).

Moltmann, J. (1971). *Hope and Planning*. New York: Harper & Row.

Mouffe, C., & Laclau, E. (2002). Hope, Passion, Politics. In M. Zournazi (Ed.), *Hope: New Philosophies for Change*. London: Lawrence and Wishart.

Pihlström, S. (2010). Rorty on faith and hope: Comparative perspectives on neopragmatist philosophy of religion. *Pragmatism Today*, 1(1).

Rittel, H. W., & Webber, M. M. (1973). Dilemmas in a general theory of planning. *Policy Sciences*, 4(2), 155–169.

Rorty, R. (1999). *Philosophy and Social Hope*. London: Penguin.

Roy, A. (2008). Post-liberalism: On the ethico-politics of planning. *Planning Theory*, 7(1), 92–102.

Saito, N. (2005). *The Gleam of Light: Moral Perfectionism and Education in Dewey and Emerson*. New York: Fordham University Press.

Savini, F. (2018, forthc.). Self-organization and urban development: Disaggregating the city-region, deconstructing urbanity in Amsterdam. *International Journal of Urban and Regional Research*.

Schön, D. A. (1971). *Beyond the Stable State: Public and Private Learning in a Changing Society*. London: Maurice Temple Smith.

Steele, W. (2015). Planning Wild Cities. In J. Hillier & J. Metzger (Eds.), *Connections: Exploring Contemporary Planning Theory and Practice with Patsy Healey* (pp. 179–188). Aldershot: Ashgate.

Tängh Wrangel, C. (2017). Recognising hope: US global development discourse and the promise of despair. *Environment and Planning D: Society and Space*, 35(5), 875–892.

Verdenius, W. J. (1985). *A Commentary on Hesiod Works and Days, vv. 1–382*. Leiden: E. J. Brill.

Žižek, S. (2000). Holding the Place. In J. Butler, E. Laclau & S. Žižek (Eds.), *Contingency, Hegemony, Universality: Contemporary Dialogues on the Left* (pp. 308–329). London: Verso.

PART 3

Pragmatism

The Dimension of Action

8
ADAPTING DIFFERENT PLANNING THEORIES FOR PRACTICAL JUDGEMENT

Charles Hoch

Pragmatist Planning Theory

Spatial planning scholars and analysts treat planning theory as a collection of ideas about spatial planning drawn from different disciplines and doctrines. Friedmann sought to classify and order many of these in his magnum opus, *Planning in the Public Domain* (Friedmann, 1987), while Klosterman catalogued the disparate collection of ideas that planning faculty have used for teaching planning theory courses over three decades (Klosterman, 2011). I think students of planning theory too quickly sort the work of planning theory scholars into disciplinary or ideological camps without exploring how their ideas might prove useful for understanding spatial plans and planning.

Hillier and Healey valiantly and competently compiled three volumes of planning theory essays and an additional compendium of solicited work (Hillier & Healey, 2010). They found no epistemic convergence towards some underlying truth about spatial planning theory. However, both concluded the differences do not so much diverge as parallel one another. The many theories about spatial planning make sense for scholars and practitioners if read as complementary conceptions informing practical inquiry about plans and planning for complex places (Hillier & Healey, 2010, pp. 24–25). I agree with that conclusion (Hoch, 2011).

I have long argued that planning scholars and practitioners should adopt a pragmatist approach to understanding planning practice (Hoch, 1984, 1994, 2002, 2012). The pragmatist approach treats planning as a crucial practical resource for any thoughtful and purposeful judgement about the future. Persons learn to make plans as part of their cognitive development. A pragmatist approach to spatial planning theory does not offer a philosophical foundation for an activity people already do. Pragmatist planning theory focuses instead on how to improve the efficacy of plan making and planning for complex spatial problems. The many theoretical ideas about spatial planning offer an opportunity for improved learning. Putting aside the misleading quest for a theory that correctly comprehends the reality for planning as it is, pragmatic theory focuses on the consequences of different theories for spatial planning and what these differences mean for understanding and improving practical consequences for people and the world.

I use a pragmatist approach to characterize and compare the work of two prominent planning theorists whose work taps very different disciplinary streams: Lew Hopkins and Bob

Beauregard. I want to show how following pragmatist arguments in each can help us recognize complementary conceptions of spatial planning threading through their work. Establishing some conceptual kinship enables me to show how we can use differences in their work as we read and compare spatial plans; in this instance watershed plans in Metropolitan Chicago.

The current plan for flood control in Chicago remains tied to a centralized district that uses rational plans to reduce flood risk for portions of the region. The plans ignore the growing uncertainty generated by the interaction effects of continued urban sprawl and increasing climate-change-induced storm intensity. A pragmatist critique reconceives the problem proposing institutional changes that introduce decentralized practical flood-prevention practices that spread responsibility. I show how Hopkins and Beauregard offer very different ways to conceive adaptive water planning.

A Pragmatist Interpretation of Spatial Planning Theory by Beauregard and Hopkins

Hopkins

Lew Hopkins would relieve regional planners of the burden of including all plans within a single comprehensive scope (Hopkins, 2012). He reminds us that most of the people involved in urban development plans do not work as professional planners for government agencies. Hopkins focuses on the logic of plans – how they represent an order for arranging and coordinating future decisions and actions. He identifies different tools for planning judgement that offer different kinds of order. We can make plans using lists to set an agenda, sequencing and prioritizing future tasks. We may conceive a vision that describes specific features for a place set in the future. We may compose a design that proposes how we might develop a prototype for the future. Plans may include an array of policies combined to yield alternative combinations worth comparing and choosing. Finally, a plan may anticipate the interests and intentions of others offering strategic options.

Professional planners should not try to include or otherwise subordinate all the private and public plans guiding land development for a metropolitan region into a plan. They should instead identify the plans in play and develop planning tools and tasks that will improve coordination among these. This holistic coordination of many plans breaks with the notion of creating a single comprehensive plan for a region or city. Professionals should make plans for places offering provisional and iterative conceptions of future development rather than periodic and cumulative assessments of goal achievement. Hopkins adopts a pragmatic conception of plans that recognizes the inherent complexity of urban development and how coordination among these plans may help agents adjust to the ensuing uncertainty. Theories provide tools professionals might use to improve their efforts making and using plans for specific spatial situations.

Hopkins (with Kierhan Donaghy) argues for coherence across different theoretical conceptions for spatial planning (Donaghy & Hopkins, 2006), including those focusing on comprehensive plans (Kelly et al., 1999), collective choice (Saeger, 2002), markets (Webster & Lai, 2003) and communication (Forester, 1999; Innes, 1996). Professional planners working for a regional agency may use what they learn from freight-transportation plans as well as plans for public education reform and affordable housing even when doing so yields no consistent interplay among them. Plans that offer distinct, inconsistent and even conflicting representations may hang together less as a nested hierarchy and more as part of an emerging web for practical planning inquiry and decision making. Focusing on what these plans propose and what the imagined consequences mean for different organizational, institutional and locational interests may improve coordination as the agents with these interests use plans to adjust their strategies. Relevance displaces consistency and nested hierarchy as the conceptual resource for using and joining the emerging web (Verma, 1998).

Hopkins has designed and built a database system that encodes information from plans detailing place relevant arguments about problems and causes as well as specific proposals for future changes. He has studied how digital information using database software, geographic information systems (GIS) and other visualization display software enables users to access and view related plan information for specific topical issues tied to specific places. This information can fill gaps as planning agents access and use the data to identify how current plan proposals for the same sites interact with overlapping or adjoining plans by other agents. Hopkins hopes that professional planners might deploy this type of system in ways that discourage wasteful duplication and encourage complementary substitutability. If plans inform intentions, then learning about the confluence of specific plan proposals as they emerge may enable those making different plans relevant for the future of the same place to better coordinate their plans. This may contribute to improved outcomes from deliberations within democratic collaborations among those making plans, and it may also improve spatial planning outcomes in adversarial situations of political contest, economic competition or legal dispute; or perhaps less contentious public settings where expert access to respective plans improves plan adjustments that reduce cost and improve benefits. Hopkins recognizes that using the database tool does not assure success.

Hopkins and Knaap argue that professionals who scan the web of plans should consider the plans not only as sources of information about different conceptions detailing local problems and proposals for change, but understand how these signal the intentions of different agents (specific developers, governments, agencies and organizations) (Hopkins & Knaap, 2016). The meaning of the signals varies with the audience: a single organization, all stakeholders touched by the plan proposals, all organizations interdependently tied to the plan or among coalitions of organizations. Plans may signal intentions to other relevant actors or agents. This plan focusing approach encourages those planning for different agents facing interdependent uncertainty to make specific plans that signal intent; and for professionals working with coalitions of such agencies to seek to communicate these signals and coordinate the response in their own more inclusive scenario planning. Instead of communicating plan goals and seeking consensus, this approach articulates diverse planning possibilities and compares the contingent plausibility of pursuing different strategies.

The encoding of intentions and interdependence among actions in plans offers heuristic support for reasoning among plans. Hopkins mentions substitutability and complementarity as principles in play as different agents consider and compare plans for the same situation or place. Judging whether an action proposed for one plan may substitute or complement the action proposed in another requires an understanding of imagined interaction effects for a specific situation and place. Asking what these differences mean will prove more useful if the plans compare future effects for robust, flexible and contingent strategies as scenarios rather than prescribe recommended actions (Chakraborty et al., 2011).

Beauregard

Beauregard challenges the idea that plans fill a gap between knowledge and action. Taking a pragmatist turn, he treats planning as an active future-focused form of inquiry. Planning conceives problems by assessing relevant causal influences while anticipating plausible solutions. Good spatial plans do not fit a doctrine or rule, but help inform practical judgements about the value and meaning of expected consequences for a place and the lives of those tied to it.

Beauregard, using insights from Bruno Latour (1999, 2005) and John Dewey (1954/1927), shows how the conception of consequences for plan making does more than offer instrumental benefits (Beauregard, 2016). Spatial planning done democratically enables participants to reconsider prior beliefs and commitments and so pave the way for new ones. How does this work? Beauregard uses Anthony Giddens's four criteria for practical judgement (Giddens, 1984): intentional, reasonable, accountable and responsible as a guide. These criteria closely match the pragmatic speech norms proposed by Habermas (1979, 1984) and made popular for planning analysts by Forester (1989): sincere, truthful, comprehensible and legitimate. Spatial planning informed by this purposeful pragmatic approach treats plans for the world not as windows to the future, but as tools for improving practical judgements about problems for specific places. This includes not only discourse but visual, gestural and physical manipulation as well.[1]

Beauregard makes an important distinction among spatial site, context and setting. Site refers to the provisional conception of a geographic location that provides the spatial focus for the plan. Context refers to the confluence of social, cultural, economic and physical conventions and institutions that shape the place. Setting describes the domain for planning practice. Professionals conceive sites using principles that combine moral and technical judgements offering abstract conceptions of good practice. In contrast, context refers to the meanings geographic locations possess for the people who inhabit and use a place. Many physical, environmental, social and symbolic features compose the reality of a place, even as different actors and agents (including professional planners) conceive competing interpretations about the future of that place (multiple truths). Setting is the concept that describes the domain where the contributions of spatial planners and plans encounter the obdurate context of place. Spatial planners make plans not as rules reflecting a structural or normative doctrine, but as practical guides composing and comparing site configurations and their imagined effects in and for different specific settings. The efficacy of good spatial planning relies crucially on tapping the diversity of causal interactions among non-humans and humans that together compose a place. For instance, the planning principle of sustainability attends to how specific non-human features of the world like water or more complex organic ecosystems like marshes interact with specific human practices and policies. The entanglements of human and non-human features populate the settings that professionals use to compose spatial plans for a place. Good professional planning deploys democracy to assure legitimacy that accompanies the inclusion of diverse voices from and for a place that may offer an improved understanding of the spatial features of site and place.

Beauregard focuses on the rhetorical dimensions of planning arguing that professional planners rely upon practical principles that propose a kind of moral order that evokes meaningful future possibilities for their audience. Like those who write fiction, planners craft plans that link the truth of possible changes with the complex reality of everyday experience. Beauregard admits that attention to planning principles leads spatial planners to focus on the truth of possibilities while abstracting the messy realities. Planners often compose plans that embrace possibility, but are bereft of the kind of meaningful experiential details that inspire belief and hope and evoke doubt and despair. Beauregard wants professionals to make plans that translate the truths about possibility as narratives that offer specific accounts of the impacts on the lives of people likely to be touched by the plan.

The places that professionals plan include embedded human social conventions, routines and non-human infrastructure, topographic variation and a myriad of species life-cycle events. The most obdurate resist purposeful change even in the face of troubling disruption. Beauregard warns spatial planners that any planning effort will likely fall short of expectations as the various parties resist – human actors disagree with proposed goals or policies and non-human actors resist too rigid and one-dimensional physical constraints. Political conflict persists no matter how analytically objective the approach or neutral the setting. Seemingly intractable entanglements binding a place to past decisions can start to unwind. Professional planners may contribute to such change by identifying problems for a local context and identifying possibilities for improvements where none seemed relevant before plan making got underway. Such critical insight flows from a pragmatist sensibility that combines sensitivity to experiential frustrations tied to environmental causes with practical inquiry assessing the consequences of current entanglements for human and non-human agents. Beauregard wants professional planners to make plans that inform the existing, emerging and potential publics that form around efforts to shape future consequences that appear as real possibilities. This means treating time less as a sequence from plan to action and more as a series of events with uncertain effects. The contingency and complexity of spatial change cannot be captured well in a rational plan with fixed goals, but requires spatial planning that responds imaginatively and is provisionally guided by a sense of purposeful practical hope.

Beauregard explores how plans inspire commitments. Planning professionals in their occupational and organizational settings mediate contract disputes, apply for grants, adjust regulations, prepare capital budgets, evaluate and assess project impacts. These activities are done in relation to many overlapping plans and planning efforts by other agents with a stake in the future of a place. Practical democratic reconciliation can bind together plans and intentions in ways that make commitment less distant. As the professional involves other actors as sponsors, clients, partners and colleagues in the conduct of these activities, this involvement may reduce scepticism or indifference. It may also lead to conflict. Professionals do not implement a plan like following a blueprint, but articulate through politically sensitive and practically embedded spatial judgements what provisional imagined outcomes can and might mean from diverse points of view. Beauregard calls this baroque enunciation. Progress and ambitious social goals emerge as joint compromises taking shape in the complex reconstruction and use of sites that ultimately compose the places where we live and work. These efforts may fail to inspire coordination and collaboration as they often do. The plan may be responsible for reasons of faulty analysis or social exclusion. It offered bad advice. But other causes might account for the failure. Beauregard offers insight about the links between non-human and human relationships for spatial plans that improve our ability to tell the difference.

Important Differences for Assessing Spatial Plans

Both Hopkins and Beauregard share a pragmatist conception of social learning. They conceive of professional spatial planning as offering advice using democratic institutional norms and practices; even when many other agents making plans for places may ignore or violate these norms. Both treat plans as purposeful provisional products composed to guide practical judgement in the face of problems. The value of a spatial plan flows from its usefulness in comparing and assessing the future effects of imagined changes for a place. Real plans inform intention and so enjoin commitment. Professional spatial planners should aspire to make plans for places democratically and provisionally.

Table 8.1 maps my interpretation of important differences in how each think about plans. For Hopkins, plans serve intentions. Plans speak about different human agencies and what each expects to do in the future. Beauregard also envisions a plurality of human actors, but adds non-human agency – modern technical system behaviour. Problems for Hopkins take shape as situations formed by frustrated purposes among actors focusing on a place. Beauregard attends to the stories people compose about local issues, but also how professionals can craft narratives that include non-human complications as well. When it comes to composing plan alternatives Hopkins focuses on the logic of plan making, ordering temporally and spatially

Table 8.1 Differences between Hopkins and Beauregard

Pragmatist Plan Elements	Hopkins	Beauregard
Plan author, agent & audience	Include all human actors shaping future for a place in situation	Include human and non-human agents shaping a place
Setting problems democratically	Many agents justify their interests for the future of a place	Contested narratives link causes and purposes for sites in a place
Composing alternatives comparing future effects	Identify type of plan and use the relevant logic to order options	Translate principles for future place possibilities into plausible realities
Informing responsible & feasible intentions to act	Signal intentions among strategic actors enhancing coordination	Inspire commitment among informed publics to follow a plan

Source: Hoch

limited information about intentions that include decisions, related actions, possible futures and plausible outcomes. The logic varies for him depending on the kind of use: agenda, vision, design, policy or strategy. Beauregard offers a more poetic conception that has professionals translate principles about future possibilities for a place into plausible realities. Good plans show imagined effects that integrate fact and value as practical judgements about relevant options. Hopkins envisions professionals as information cowboys wrangling information for ongoing planning efforts for a place. Professionals act responsibly and democratically as they improve access to valid information for the plans, improving their coherence and the prospects for communicating intentions more clearly and collaboratively. Beauregard focuses on plans as tools that serve democratic publics as these emerge to cope with problems for a place. He expects professional planners to foster forms of democratic learning that inspire commitment to practical options serving a progressive liberalism.

Reading Plans

I believe plans communicate advice, but not like the messages that animate the attention of consumers viewing advertisements, commercials and social media. Nor do they compare strategic choices like those used by armies and private corporations. Hopkins convinced me that places take shape based on many different plans – some coordinated, many not (Hopkins, 2001). The professional planner should in his view seek to identify and coordinate these plans using all the clever technical tools for visualizing and communicating information. Seymour Mandelbaum and Brent Ryan helped me learn how plans provide vehicles for cultural ideas as well as testimonials to predominant values at the time they are made (Mandelbaum, 2000; Ryan, 2011). Ryan, along with my mentor Peter Marris, taught me that if we misinterpret the meaning of a plan we cannot adequately (validly) or accurately (reliably) evaluate its moral significance and practical impact (Marris, 1996). Seymour Mandelbaum imagined three kinds of interpretative approaches to reading a plan: policy argument, design opportunity or story. Ryan urges us to expand our scope to include the visual, gestural and tactile sensibilities we use to comprehend, imagine and project ideas conceiving future changes for a place. Comparative attention to the change in the craft of professional plan making and sensitivity to socioeconomic context and current beliefs should always offer specific innovative place related problem-solving proposals using attractive graphic display. Beauregard's theoretical work inspires reading in a similar critical vein.

Hopkins reads plans as messages that signal intent. He breaks the conventional spatial plans into logical components subject to classification as information available for cognitive review. Plans do not persuade so much as direct and focus attention on priorities and comparisons that are subject to empirical examination and conceptual review. Beauregard embeds plan making as part of an expansive place making enterprise to which we all contribute. Professional spatial planners tap political traditions and domains of practical craft to identify principles that guide the composition of future possibilities into specific proposals that the audience for the plan finds credible and feasible. Plans involve emotional commitments as well as cognitive understanding. So how would each read and evaluate plans for the same place? First I will describe the case and then conduct the analysis comparing how each author would read the plan.

The Case of Water Planning: Compromising with Complexity

Rational Water Planning

Water binds each of us to planet earth. But the forms water takes and its complex contributions to geophysical forces, geographic landscapes, living organisms and climate overwhelm any effort to keep these relationships firmly in mind. Conceptions of water use do not just refer to knowledge about the flow of water, but the diversity of symbolic tools used to represent the flow and the many kinds of physical facilities and structures used to alter and amend that flow. The water plans for the Chicago region offer an excellent account of how making a modern metropolis like Chicago relies upon a multitude of pumps, conduits, channels, lakes, dams and containers. The current infrastructure systems engineered to capture, store and distribute water for irrigation, industrial production, household consumption and flood control were planned as projects for specific places at different scales. The success of these projects encourages increased local water use, pollution and control that yields negative cumulative effects for a wider region. Ironically, the tens of thousands of plans and decisions that make each pump, pipe and container improve the predictability of local water flow has increased uncertainty for neighbouring communities and ecosystems. Solving water problems for each local place generates complex interaction effects for other places requiring spatial planning.

Those responsible for planning water provision, quality and impact at federal, state and regional scales point to the uncoordinated multiplicity of local plans by developers, authorities and municipalities as the cause of emerging water problems: aquifer depletion, flooding and pollution. Comprehensive planning at the regional scale appears to be the most attractive approach promising to combine rational analysis with broad public authority to enforce a unified approach. Such promises have proven ephemeral in practice in the United States and across the globe (Milly et al., 2008; Ostrom, 2005).

I selected a regional plan by the most powerful regional water planning agency in Illinois, the Metropolitan Water Reclamation District (MWRD). The district has taxing and land use authority delegated by the state (Environmental Protection Agency, 2014). It has a large geographic scope that includes Chicago and most of the suburban areas in the surrounding Cook County. MWRD completed a comprehensive storm water plan in 2014 (Metropolitan Water Reclamation District of Greater Chicago, 2014). I briefly summarize their approach and focus on the plan for one watershed. I then compare how I think we might use the insights about plans from Hopkins and Beauregard using each of the four pragmatist plan elements in Table 8.1.

Metropolitan Water Reclamation District's Approach to Plan Making

The Illinois legislature passed a law in 2004 authorizing the Metropolitan Water Reclamation District to prepare watershed plans, finance storm water infrastructure and manage storm water related regulations within Cook County. MWRD was authorized to work with other organizations, including local governments to manage storm water and was charged to create a storm water management ordinance regulating flood plain and storm water streams, channels and basins. The ordinance was passed in 2014. The MWRD water management plan (Metropolitan Water Reclamation District of Greater Chicago, 2014) describes goals and tasks largely in terms of legal authority and engineering responsibility.

The MWRD adopts a countywide (and beyond) scope for water planning. The state has authorized storm water planning, regulation and financing in one agency. The legislation included local councils composed of elected officials from municipalities. The 2014 plan distinguishes local from regional responsibility for storm water management. MWRD takes responsibility for preparing watershed plans including the north branch of the Chicago River.

The outline for the plan focuses on estimating future storm water levels based on historic data using updated geographic information. This is combined with flood reports from prior storm events detailing flood levels and damages to property. The plan focuses on engineering responses to regional infrastructure difficulties and failures during major storms.

The alternatives focus exclusively on MWRD-sponsored projects targeted at locations where recent flood events proved most damaging. The problems follow the contours of authority and engineering capacity of one agency. The involvement of the watershed councils focuses on advice about specific flood-related problems and setting priorities for limited funds for improvements to different types of storm water management. The plan was prepared by an engineering firm (HDR Engineering, 2011) that subcontracted with seven more specialized engineering consultants (2IM Group, LLC Cushing and Company Fluid Clarity, Ltd., Huff & Huff, Inc., Lin Engineering, Ltd., MPR Engineering, Corp., Inc., V3 Companies of Illinois Ltd). No planning, environmental or landscape consultants were hired.

The project evaluation scheme identifies technical physical improvements to problems for locations using model simulation data and local flood reports. These describe problems and plan option solutions as physical improvements to the current flood control system paying attention to the concerns of local municipalities in each watershed within Cook County. The plan includes a long list of alternative project improvements for each watershed including cost–benefit estimates for each. The comparative ranking of projects by cost–benefit score provides the analytical rationale for selection.

The MWRD Plan for the North Branch of the Chicago River

Decades ago the MWRD prepared region wide plans that imposed flood control through the deployment of massive infrastructure development. The plans focused on engineering expertise and the public activity was about how to raise funds to pay for these adequately and fairly. Since 2004, the MWRD has divided its jurisdictional domain into watershed areas that include local government officials and other public actors responsible for storm water management. The MWRD engineers and state hydrologists use models of future storm events to look for leaks in the large (regional) waterways within a vast storm water infrastructure system always under construction.

The MWRD prepared a storm water plan for the north branch of the Chicago River in 2011. The engineers consulted with appointed members of the watershed council selected to represent the local governments whose jurisdictions overlap some portion of the watershed. The plan includes a massive amount of flood information for hundreds of waterway locations where storm water damage was reported. The engineers prepared locational assessments detailing the flood problems and alternatives for each regional level waterway site including a cost–benefit analysis for different physical improvements to alleviate the inundation for that location. The most cost-effective project among the many studied in the report focused on reservoir storage improvements. The storm water control projects recommended for adoption in the north branch of the Chicago River in Cook County had the highest net-benefit scores. The information includes the cost–benefit ratio, estimated project cost and local governments affected by the project improvement.

Comparative Analysis of the MWRD Plan

Plan Author, Agent and Audience

Hopkins would direct our attention to the links among the many existing water plans already in play and underway across the Chicago metropolitan area. The MWRD looked at the other local government water plans for input, but did not consider how these agencies might act using information from the MWRD plan. The MWRD plan offloads responsibility for 'local' water problems to local government while taking responsibility for regional waterway flood problems. Centralizing the watershed plans within a single agency creating a single plan makes it difficult for other agents pursuing plans with impacts on storm water to recognize what their efforts might mean for others pursuing their plans. The plan offers justification for the selection and recommendation of engineering improvements to the MWRD board using watershed councils composed of local government representatives to offer some democratic legitimacy for the recommended projects.

Beauregard would frame the MWRD as only one of many agencies responsible for water planning in the Chicago region. He would alert us to the misplaced confidence in flood control that engineers possess because they believe that their tools can tame the social and environmental complexity of water flows. Beauregard would identify the political opponents of MWRD practices: local homeowners and businesses in neighbourhoods experiencing unexpected inundation, local governments seeking regional solutions to local flooding events and advocacy groups challenging MWRD practices documenting systemic failures during major storm events that lead to the discharge of polluted storm water into Lake Michigan (the source of drinking water for Chicago and many suburbs). Others take advantage of shifting policy initiatives of federal and state agencies embracing a sustainability agenda. Practical attention comes from actors in these organizations whose experience and expertise with various water problem events motivates their participation. Advocates from environmental movement organizations offer research findings, sustainability policies and practices from other places calling for solutions that challenge conventional land development. The physical infrastructure system becomes an active partner for understanding the actors and an audience for change.

Setting Problems Democratically

Hopkins would note that the plan systematically identifies flood locations based on prior and existing data. The engineers use hydrology models to simulate major storm events in order to forecast potential locations and estimate future flood damage. They combine model data with flood report data to analyse alternative physical improvements for each local problem site using project cost–benefit estimates. Hopkins would point out that creating a set of decomposed project priorities in a single plan does not address the encompassing complexity of interactions among changing land development activity, environmental conditions and climate change storm events. The MWRD engineers cast the plan as a design – a blueprint for discrete physical solutions to breakdowns in the current infrastructure system. This approach works fine if future conditions fit forecast assumptions. But this will likely not hold given the evidence of increased storm intensity and the interaction with local government storm water efforts. The MWRD cast the problem too narrowly and vertically.

Beauregard would point out how the planning narrative excludes the crucial role of the existing infrastructure that MWRD manages and the characteristics of the places vulnerable to flooding from major storms. The narrative tells an abstract tale of MWRD provision of predictable flood control infrastructure facing occasional local breakdowns during major storm events. The engineers possess the competence to analyse local flood problem reports together with storm event water flow simulations identifying gaps and creating fixes. Functional arguments turn each place into projects valued as equivalent cost–benefit scores. The lurking uncertainty of ecological damage or complex interaction effects disappear in the reassuring analysis of cumulative efficiencies. Beauregard would introduce the plans of other agencies, organizations and groups whose plans include MWRD practices as an important part of the watershed problems. Some organizations focus on water conservation and shift the narrative from just channelling water to changing the use of land to absorb and retain much greater amounts of storm water. Others focusing on water quality and long-term sustainability propose even more dramatic shifts away from reliance on infrastructure, substituting more ecologically resilient forms of land development and use. The rhetoric of watershed plans prepared by planners for the regional planning agency and non-profit advocacy organizations do just this (Chicago Metropolitan Agency for Planning, 2010; Openlands Project, 2005).

Beauregard would argue that the 2004 legislation that authorized watershed planning by MWRD was a political response to the agency indifference to the growing concerns of local governments whose residents experienced increased frequency and damage from flooding. The matter-of-fact rhetoric of the watershed plans provides more excuses than guidance. MWRD remains deeply wedded to building massive storm water collection and storage capacity as the solution to major storm events. This effort is not mentioned in the watershed narrative. The protections of legal representation are not enough to ensure water plans for the watershed that offer more complete stories about uncertainty and accountability.

Composing Alternatives: Comparing Future Effects

Hopkins might urge the MWRD planners to consider using models that invite those local agencies and groups with plans to view alternative displays of flooding effects with and without their plans. The MWRD engineers cannot know as well as the locals what land use changes will likely happen. Instead of experts composing alternatives on their own using historical forecast data, they would involve locals in simulation assessments of flood locations, testing interaction effects from future development changes. Hopkins would encourage professionals to offer an institutional framework for the display and frequent updating of watershed plan components that enable users to review and adjust their expectations relative to what others propose. This would shift the focus from design to strategy. The plan would identify flood risk areas jointly conceived and encourage collaborative flood control strategies for the watershed as well as vulnerable locations within it.

Beauregard would focus more on how well the plan translated the practical possibilities for improved water conservation and recycling into proposals that reconcile the problems for the human and non-human stakeholders most vulnerable to drought and flooding. These could take shape as Hopkins describes – a policy or a strategy for instance. But for Beauregard they would need to include enough narrative details to link causal attribution and moral responsibility for the imagined and proposed consequences. The professionals making the spatial plans translate the possibilities for local storm water safety, offering images of imagined future effects with specific proposals detailing plausible improvements.

Informing Responsible & Feasible Intentions to Act

Hopkins recognizes that plans need be revealed strategically to influence audiences at specific times (Kaza & Hopkins, 2009). MWRD and other agencies responsible for flood control face a dilemma in making plans that identify property likely to flood in the event of a major storm. But environmental advocacy groups can use MWRD data to make plans that identify the geographic areas at risk. MWRD and other agencies trying to cope with flooding can then use these plans to justify conservation measures that they could not propose without raising public protest or political resistance from elected board members.

Hopkins would recognize the value of the watershed councils, but instead of convening these groups to build consensus for MWRD watershed plans, MWRD planners should study the storm water plans for these governments as well as the plans by land developers, builders, municipal governments, park districts, water authorities, conservation organizations, environmental activist groups, neighbourhood associations and homeowner groups with spatial ties to the watershed area. He would have planners collect, compile and map the specific proposals for change proposed in these plans. They would then share the information with these actors offering an analysis that could help to identify potential redundancies, conflicts and opportunities for substitution and complementarity within and beyond the watershed.

Hopkins directs our attention to the many plans and how we can organize and display this information about current plans more clearly and usefully (Finn et al., 2007). Local government plans do not include water authority plans or the plans of developers proposing new subdivisions. The focus on rules and regulations distracts MWRD from considering the plans underway across the region and how these may impact the infrastructure system they control. The scope and complexity of the decisions across so many jurisdictional arenas, sectors, scales and levels makes any unified and comprehensive plan more of an excuse than a guide. Hopkins argues that professional planners should improve access and uptake of plan intentions enabling the actors to modify and improve their plans. This will not remove uncertainty, but it may improve the prospects for coordination and collaboration among actors as they anticipate and prepare for future flooding.

Beauregard would not find much inspiration from the list of project recommendations. He would not dismiss the practical value of plugging gaps, but he would urge the substitution of this approach for a consideration of proposals that address the contribution of the infrastructure design to the uncertainty of storm events. The plan does not inspire publics to form who can recognize in some set of proposals how their interests for the future of the place may be realized. The plan as is offers a bad compromise with the future – one that remains too wedded to current water retention practices that favour human protection at the expense of non-human ecological integrity. He would likely point out how the attachment to the demands of physical obsolescence and the precedent of engineering prowess blinds the analysts and the officials they advise to the real uncertainty of future water flows.

Beauregard would envision a more politically engaged planning. Water shortage problems recast as sustainability problems should reflect the public engagement of environmental advocacy groups whose plans offer more ambitious goals about the relationship with non-human ecological agents. These plans include more demanding solutions because they require changes to social habits, indifferent to the reality of organic interdependence. These efforts are underway in the Chicago region coordinated by CMAP (Chicago Metropolitan Agency for Planning, 2010) and other civic non-profits (Openlands Project, 2005).

Conclusion

Instead of multiplying planning theories that offer substitutes for one another, I urge the adoption of a pragmatist approach that seeks to assimilate and reconcile planning theories. This does not mean imposing a pragmatist theoretical doctrine, but searching for the practical significance that different planning theories offer for making and using spatial plans. Trade in the philosophical quest for ontological or epistemic certainty and work hard to study and use competing and complementary ideas about the meaning and use of spatial plans and planning. This already happens frequently as scholars and practitioners adopt theoretical ideas as they make and study plans for places.

I showed how the planning theory ideas from two very different authors might be put to practical use comprehending a watershed plan for a place in the Chicago region. I do not believe either Hopkins or Beauregard would identify as pragmatists, but I argue that using pragmatist ideas can uncover complementary insights that may improve practical judgements about making, reading and using plans. The pragmatist sensibility can enhance the assimilation and use of diverse theoretical ideas rather than displace or subordinate them.

Pragmatists envision institutional design as purposeful, developmental and situational. They invent new institutions in the face of disruptive situations where routines continue to fail after repair. Pragmatists alter both means and ends, but rarely start from scratch. Testing options in the context of specific historical and spatial contexts enables pragmatists to assess effects, revise expectations and improve learning. New habits improve responses to earlier trouble and offer an understanding of ourselves and the world. In this way institutions adapt and so may progress.

The institutional design for the organization of collective decisions has a developmental focus for pragmatists. Charles Lindblom's incremental muddling through (Lindblom, 1959) captured the situational relativity of pragmatist inquiry, but without the critical experimentalism that stimulates and fosters expansive compromise; compromise that includes more people as relevant agents in shaping their own destiny. People invent, debate and adopt policies, conventions and rules to guide conduct for place building and living. But people also make plans that detail projects for dwellings and businesses, infrastructure and plazas, estuaries and solar panels and all the vast complex combinations of physical and institutional constructions that bind people and other animate and inanimate things together in places. Students of spatial planning offer contested interpretations of what planning includes and how it is and should be done. Instead of having to choose one of these, the pragmatist tries to include their ideas in the planning conversation inspiring practical plan innovations susceptible to theoretical critique and empirical examination (Hoch, 2016).

Note

1 Latour would likely note how both Giddens and Habermas do social theory still burdened with that structure–agent dualism, even as both offer pragmatist inspired conceptions to show how inquiry can escape the inevitability of lurking structural forces (Latour, 2005). Latour insists we cannot get outside the

bounds of practical inquiry to obtain theoretical assurance. These 'norms' are not a touchstone or transcendent foundation for rational judgement, but reminders as we conduct inquiry that to make sense of the results – the test of consequences – we need to pay attention to what others have done before us and to the results they experienced. Most of this we thankfully take for granted as we are embedded in the social habits and conventions we each learn to follow growing up. These habits have become part of the landscape we take for granted even as each of us keep them going. Latour wants sociologists to focus on problems or concerns that emerge where we face disruptions or difficulty in these routines. Beauregard taps into that critical approach, even if at times he wants theoretical reassurance that Latour rejects.

References

Beauregard, R. (2016). *Planning Matter Acting with Things*. Chicago, IL: University of Chicago Press.
Chakraborty, A., Kaza, N., Knaap, G.-J., & Deal, B. (2011). Robust plans and contingent plans. *Journal of the American Planning Association*, 77(3), 251–266. Retrieved from: http://dx.doi.org/10.1080/01944363.2011.582394.
Chicago Metropolitan Agency for Planning. (2010). *Water 2050: Northeastern Illinois Regional Water Supply/Demand Plan*. Chicago, IL: Chicago Metropolitan Agency for Planning.
Dewey, J. (1954/1927). *The Public and Its Problems*. Athens, OH: Swallow Press.
Donaghy, K. P., & Hopkins, L. D. (2006). Coherentist theories of planning are possible and useful. *Planning Theory*, 5(2), 173–202.
Finn, D., Hopkins, L. D., & Wempe, M. (2007). The information system of plans approach: Using and making plans for landscape protection. *Landscape and Urban Planning*, 81, 132–145.
Environmental Protection Agency. (2014). *Clean Water Act Enforcement Cases*. Retrieved from: www.epa.gov/enforcement/2014-major-criminal-cases#Clean Water Act.
Forester, J. (1989). *Planning in the Face of Power*. Berkeley, CA: University of California Press.
Forester, J. (1999). *The Deliberative Practitioner*. Cambridge, MA: MIT Press.
Friedmann, J. (1987). *Planning in the Public Domain*. Princeton, NJ: Princeton University Press.
Giddens, A. (1984). *The Constitution of Society*. Berkeley, CA: University of California Press.
Habermas, J. (1979). *Communication and the Evolution of Society*. T. McCarthy (Trans.) [German, 1976]. Boston, MA: Beacon.
Habermas, J. (1984). *The Theory of Communicative Action. Vol. I: Reason and the Rationalization of Society*. T. McCarthy (Trans.) [German, 1981]. Boston, MA: Beacon.
HDR Engineering. (2011). *Detailed Watershed Plan for the North Branch of the Chicago River and Lake Michigan Watershed*. Chicago, IL: Metropolitan Water Reclamation District of Greater Chicago. Retrieved from: www.mwrd.org/irj/portal/anonymous/stormwateroverview.
Healey, P., & Hillier, J. (2008). *Critical Essays in Planning Theory, Vol. 1 – Foundations of the Planning Enterprise; Vol. 2 – Political Economy, Diversity and Pragmatism; Vol. 3 – Contemporary Movements in Planning Theory*. Aldershot: Ashgate.
Hillier, J., & Healey, P. (2010). *The Ashgate Research Companion to Planning Theory*. Farnham: Ashgate.
Hoch, C. (1984). Doing good and being right: The pragmatic connection in planning theory. *Journal of the American Planning Association*, 50(3), 335–345.
Hoch, C. (1994). *What Planners Do*. Chicago, IL: Planners Press.
Hoch, C. (2002). Evaluating plans pragmatically. *Planning Theory*, 1(1), 53–76.
Hoch, C. (2011). The planning research agenda: Planning theory for practice. *Town Planning Review*, 82(2), vii–xv.
Hoch, C. (2012). Making Plans. In R. Weber & R. Crane (Eds.), *Urban Planning Handbook* (pp. 241–258). New York: Oxford University Press.
Hoch, C. (2016). Utopia, scenario, plan: A pragmatic integration. *Planning Theory*, 15(1), 6–22.
Hopkins, L. D. (2001). *Urban Development: The Logic of Making Plans*. Washington, DC: Island Press.
Hopkins, L. D. (2012). Plan Assessment: Making and Using Plans Well. In R. Weber & R. Crane (Eds.), *The Oxford Handbook of Urban Planning* (pp. 803–822). New York: Oxford University Press.
Hopkins, L. D., & Knaap, G. J. (2016). Autonomous planning: Using plans as signals. *Planning Theory*. Retrieved from: http://dx.doi.org/10.1177/1473095216669868, 30 September.
Innes, J. (1996). Planning through consensus building: A new view of the comprehensive ideal. *Journal of the American Planning Association*, 62(4), 460–472.
Kaza, N., & Hopkins, L. D. (2009). In what circumstances should plans be public? *Journal of Planning Education and Research*, 28(4), 491–502.

Kelly, E. D., Becker, B., & So, F. (1999). *Community Planning: An Introduction to The Comprehensive Plan*. Washington, DC: Island Press.

Klosterman, R. E. (2011). Planning theory education: A thirty-year review. *Journal of Planning Education and Research*, 31(3), 319–331.

Latour, B. (1999). *Pandora's Hope: Essays on the Reality of Science Studies*. Cambridge, MA: Harvard University Press.

Latour, B. (2005). *Reassembling the Social: An Introduction to Actor-Network Theory*. Cambridge, MA: Oxford University Press.

Lindblom, C. (1959). The science of 'muddling through'. *Public Administration Review*, 19(2), 79–88.

Mandelbaum, S. (2000). *Open Moral Communities*. Cambridge, MA: MIT Press.

Marris, P. (1996). *The Politics of Uncertainty, Attachment in Private and Public Life*. New York: Routledge.

Metropolitan Water Reclamation District of Greater Chicago. (2014). *Cook County Storm Water Management Plan*. Chicago, IL: MWRD. Retrieved from: www.mwrd.org/irj/portal/anonymous?NavigationTarget=navurl://f8a113b72db46b1b8972a3ceae1e170f.

Milly, P. C. D., Betancourt, J., Falkenmark, M., Hirsch, R. M., Kundzewicz, Z. W., Lettenmaier, D. P., & Stouffer, R. J. (2008). Stationarity is dead: Whither water management? *Science*, 319, 573–574.

Openlands Project. (2005). *Changing Course: Recommendations for Balancing Regional Growth and Water Resources in Northeastern Illinois*. Chicago, IL: Openlands.

Ostrom, E. (2005). *Understanding Institutional Diversity*. Princeton, NJ: Princeton University Press.

Ryan, B. (2011). Reading through a plan. *Journal of the American Planning Association*, 1(77), 309–327.

Saeger, T. (2002). *Democratic Planning and Social Choice Dilemmas: Prelude to Institutional Planning Theory*. Hampshire: Ashgate.

Verma, N. (1998). *Similarities, Connections and Systems*. New York: Lexington.

Webster, C., & Lai, C. (2003). *Property Rights, Planning and Markets*. Cheltenham: Edward Elgar.

9
FROM GARBAGE IN THE STREETS TO ORGANIZERS' OPPORTUNITIES

Navigating the Institutional Pragmatics of Democratic Inter-Subjectivity

John Forester[1]

Community organizers, we know, work pragmatically in the face of institutional power. They typically have little money to work with, still less capital to invest, and even less formal authority to exercise. Somehow, when they get things done, they do things with words, but of course not just with words. We will see that pragmatism—as an approach seeking to make a difference in the world and to learn by doing too—requires an institutionalist analysis if it is to become more than a set of good intentions. At the same time, an institutionalist framework—anticipating both formal and informal norms and routines—requires a pragmatic component if it is to include an account of growth and change (Hysing & Olsson, 2017).

In the story of an organizer's power play that follows, we will integrate pragmatic and institutional analyses with a particular purpose: to refine and develop agonistic theories of conflict and democratic politics. We will argue that agonistic accounts are right (political conflict is unavoidable and ineradicable) and yet not right enough (they remain too silent about qualities and pragmatics of democratic interactions). Responding to accounts such as those of Aletta Norval (2007) and Mark Purcell (2008), we will conduct a close political reading of a community organizer's confrontation with a representative of the local state. In particular, we will try to distinguish, recognize the politics of, and assess practically not just (a) the constitution of political agents' democratic subjectivities but also (b) the elements of the more fluid, performative and, of course, always contingent enactments of those agents' actual interactions, their democratic inter-subjectivity (Forester, 2014, 2017a).

To be sure, these distinctions reflect matters of emphasis. Subjectivity will always grow out of a matrix of subject-subject, inter-subjective relationships, from birth onwards, including processes of individuation (Wagenaar, 2011). Conversely, inter-subjective relationships could not illuminate shared conventions, regulations, or norms if these did not always pertain to actual institutionally situated subjects.

Nevertheless, if either term collapses into the other, pathology results: subjectivity without inter-subjectivity would reflect an atomistic world of solipsists unable to understand, much less recognize one another at all. Inter-subjectivity without distinct subjectivities would reflect a world of a homogenized, singular communitarian identity subsuming or erasing any difference (Tully, 2008).

This seems simple enough, and who could object to a respectful treatment of democratic subjectivity? The problem, we suggest, is that in the context of democratic politics, and in the contest of democratic politics, we need to be careful not to miss the action: how subjects treat each other, what they do to and with each other, how acting politically can transform the world of relationships for better or worse, in freeing or oppressive ways (Forester, 2017b; Warren, 2013; Wheeler, 2013).

To that end, not to miss the action in democratic politics, we take a close look at a small example of urban politics, a small example that provides a large political-theoretical lesson. Democratic politics must be about more than what we want and what we think about ourselves and Others. Agonistic political theory threatens to be like a courtship in which nothing happens, nothing but the day-dreaming of potential lovers. Let us turn, then, from the mere facts of plural wants and perspectives to actual actions, the pragmatics of institutionally situated democratic politics.

Setting the Scene of Urban Democratic Conflict

We begin with a passage from a discussion of "vital citizenship" in which Ted van de Wijdeven and Frank Hendriks (2007) reconstruct a fascinating exchange between a municipal official and a local neighborhood's citizen activist (even though an earlier essay of Hendriks and Tops (2005) provides a slightly different translation). We follow the more recent version simply as a plausible and striking example of the way that a practical discourse analysis can reveal the interplay of an institutionalist analysis with a pragmatism performed both for political ends and learning by doing too. Van de Wijdeven and Hendriks form their example of vital citizenship this way:

> Sometimes a confrontation can solve a dead lock. A "classic" example ... describes a confrontation between the head of the municipal department in charge of street-sweeping and Arie Schagen – director of ... a neighborhood development organization – who had the idea of the sweeping crew project on the Weimarstraat.
>
> *(Hendriks & Tops, 2007)*

According to the oral reports, the following conversation took place between the official and Arie Schagen:

> CITY OFFICIAL: *So, you are going to sweep the street.*
> SCHAGEN: *Yes. It's a good idea, don't you think?*
> CITY OFFICIAL: *Yes, but you just can't do that.*
> SCHAGEN: *Why not?*
> CITY OFFICIAL: *You have to have a permit for that.*
> SCHAGEN: *And you're going to arrange that for me, right?*
> CITY OFFICIAL: *I don't think so.*
> SCHAGEN: *I do think so.*
> CITY OFFICIAL: *If you start sweeping without a permit, then you'll be in violation, and I'll have to call the police.*
> SCHAGEN: *You just do that. I'll invite the press. That would make great headlines: "Police arrest citizens for sweeping the street on their own initiative!"*

CITY OFFICIAL: *And if you want to sweep in the Weimarstraat, what do you plan to do with the garbage?*

SCHAGEN: *We'll put it in the dumpsters there.*

CITY OFFICIAL: *Then it becomes industrial waste, and you have to pay a lot of money to dump industrial waste.*

SCHAGEN: *Oh, yes. Then we'll just have to dump this "industrial waste" in the front yard of the alderman in charge. You know that we've done things like that before, so if you don't cooperate a little here, things can get pretty tough for you.*

Wijdeven and Hendriks continue:

> It all worked out eventually. The sweeping crew was able to get to work. The circle of those involved became broader. A solution to the "industrial waste problem" was found within the city budget. The city official on duty left. Noticeably better cooperative relations developed with officials that had agreed with the value of the street-sweeping initiative. Confrontation eventually turned into cooperation and co-production.

The Analysis of the Institutional Pragmatics of Democratic Struggles

We see here a pragmatic struggle over both institutional possibilities and institutional change. How does the organizer prevail over the representative of the local state? If we look closely at this quoted material, we can distinguish, first, the formation and construction of democratic subjectivities, from, second, the pragmatic enactment of a complex democratic inter-subjectivity found here too (Barrett, 2012).

We find that the authors have framed the conversation provocatively as a "confrontation," one that somehow "solved" what they called a "dead lock." What makes this a "classic" example for them remains unclear, but we can infer a rough imbalance of resources: typically, the head of an operational municipal department will have staff, budget, and political and administrative connections that will dwarf those of the head of a community organization.

That resource imbalance, of course, sets the stage, in part, for the drama that follows. We might well wonder how "the confrontation" might play out in ways that are not boringly predictable with the stronger party simply dominating the weaker one. How might any so-called "solution" to "the dead lock" emerge in a way that does not simply solve the problem for the city and impose the costs on the weaker neighborhood party? Even the authors' lead-in provides a sense of contingency as we read not the logical claim that "confrontation can solve a dead lock" but that "sometimes" that can be true—so we find ourselves wondering, of course, just when that might be true and just what contingencies might be involved politically.

So, we want to know, in light of the resource imbalance, given the promise of a contingent political solution to the past dead lock, what happened? We anticipate a dramatic confrontation, a struggle pitting interest against interest, and we expect the story now to unfold for us, as the actors perform and interact, not just against the backdrop of the historical "dead lock."

We know that the characters are not just isolated, wholly autonomous individuals, for they are political actors, one a municipal agency director with obvious status and responsibilities, the other a community organization's director and one of some imagination, one we're told "who had the idea of the sweeping crew project on the Weimarstraat." So, we might expect in this example not just a "conversation" about a dead lock, but a dramatic "confrontation" and somehow even more, a surprising resolution to emerge from this struggle that we're about to witness. So, what actually happened? Hendriks and Tops quote the oral reports as beginning:

> CITY OFFICIAL: *So, you are going to sweep the street.*
> SCHAGEN: *Yes. It's a good idea, don't you think?*

The city official began with a bit of self-importance, "So," announcing that he has an observation or a point to make, and he then declares that he understands rather than needs to ask what the other's about to do, "you are going to sweep the street." We see perhaps just a hint of doubt about the activist's subjective intentions, in an inquiry that tests, in effect, if this is really what he's planning to do, to "sweep the street"?

The activist doesn't respond to the test in a worried way—Why do you ask? Is that OK? Do you, Mr. Official, approve? Instead, he replies with crisp confidence in one precise word: "Yes," I am going to. But the activist refuses to make this interchange, or his plans, simply a personal or psychological matter: "It's a good idea," he asserts, speaking to the publically assessable merits of the idea, not merely someone's subjective preferences. Only then, with his own subjective commitment and strategic plan asserted with his "Yes," and his suggestion of the objective merits, "it's a good idea," does he then not just plant his feet in alluding to the merits, but he deliberately re-engages the official, "don't you think?"

Notice that the activist's question does more than ask for an opinion on the part of the official: it asks for his cooperation and agreement or, lacking that, for his cooperation in taking the idea seriously and then explaining, in his official capacity, why he might not think "it's a good idea." So, the activist tries here, it seems, neither to argue the point nor to dismiss the official's views as irrelevant, but rather to find a way to gain the official's institutional support for the citizens' initiative to sweep the street.

Drawn in, the official seems not only ambivalent but pulled in politically contradictory directions, for he says:

> CITY OFFICIAL: *Yes, but you just can't do that.*
> SCHAGEN: *Why not?*

It's a good idea, right? "Yes," the official begins, as if he's no more capable of arguing against street sweeping than against motherhood. Of course, sweeping one's street is a good idea. Except that there's a "but" coming, and so in the "Yes, but ..." the official already shows his own and a broader public ambivalence, his own and a broader institutional duality of commitment. It might be indeed a publically recognizable, good idea, "but you just can't do that." It's a good idea, but the official invokes some higher reason to try to show that "you just can't," that what the activist thought he could do he cannot after all do, that what the activist thought was institutionally possible is really going to be impossible after all. Yes, yes, great idea, but ... not so much, "you just can't"—and why, he hasn't yet explained.

The activist follows the logic and the mystery of the official's self-contradictory claim—it's a good idea to do it, but it's impossible (so how can it be a good idea?)—and so he asks, "Why not?" apparently asking the official for an authoritative judgment and explanation that might make sense of things.

The city official is unperturbed by the contradiction, by his own ambivalence, by his own weak diplomatic effort to compliment the activist's nice idea while explaining why that idea's not really very good at all. So, he says,

CITY OFFICIAL: *You have to have a permit for that.*
SCHAGEN: *And you're going to arrange that for me, right?*

The official tries to resolve the problem by invoking the rule of law, or at least the rule of administrative regulation and corresponding public obligation. So, he tries simultaneously to depersonalize the situation, to make it a matter of standing institutional norms, and to take it out of Schagen's control. He points out that the activist may think this is a great idea, but this isn't about me or you, really, it's about the regulations, the institutional setting, so, "You have to have a permit for that." But, of course, he re-personalizes his point too. He's not speaking in general about street sweeping or urban services; he's very direct, "You have to," you, Mr. Activist, in this situation that you're really not understanding, with this great idea of yours, you "have to"—must, are obligated to— "have a permit for that."

He appeals to an impersonal, non-particularistic system of rules, and he does not merely observe, if Schagen's interested, that there are rules about this kind of thing—but he does much more. He invokes those rules and his own authority as someone knowledgeable about the rules "for that," for street sweeping. His power play, "You have to have a permit for that," tries to reassert his authority and simultaneously the activist's inability to act as he wishes; the activist's being subject to the impersonal rule of law in their city.

But the activist now turns the official's appeal to power and authority around, not by challenging the claim about needing a permit, not by challenging the established system of law and regulation, but by pressing for the official's own (official) cooperation: Yes, I will need a permit, "And you're going to arrange that"—and not just arrange that in general, but arrange that *for me*, a power play in turn, softened only a bit by the question to check, "right?"

We seem that we have come back to a dead lock, each telling the other what they will and won't do:

CITY OFFICIAL: *I don't think so.*
SCHAGEN: *I do think so.*

Am I, the official finds himself asked, going to help this activist get the permit that I know he needs? Hardly, and so he says, "I don't think so"! Here we have come back to the official's subjective willingness to help arrange a permit. Is he ready to do this? Apparently not.

Does the activist take the official at his personal word? Hardly, for he seems to have something else in mind, a way to gain the official's institutional help, even if the official is now claiming quite explicitly quite the contrary, and so, listening to the official's refusal, Schagen presses on nevertheless, "I do think so."

We seem stuck at an impasse: No I won't; Yes, you will. No I won't; Yes, you will.

What's more, the city official doesn't seem to like, or appreciate, either being told what to do, or being directly contradicted, or both. So, he makes a further power play, this time by making a direct and precise threat, and a personal one at that:

CITY OFFICIAL: *If you start sweeping without a permit, then you'll be in violation, and I'll have to call the police.*

The threat is contingent, of course: "If you start sweeping without a permit" identifies the conditionality of the threat, and it combines universalistic and particularistic elements: you (or anyone sweeping without a permit) will be "in violation," and then as a municipal agency director knowledgeable about street sweeping, the official continues, "I'll (officially, not personally) have to call the police" (to come and take care of you!).

Notice that there is no logical or political (or even moral) necessity for the official to move from "you'll be in violation" to "I'll have to call the police." The "I'll have to" seems quite disingenuous here, for the official does not work for the police, and his calling the police would call for an exercise of his discretion somewhat like the one we might make if we called the police when we saw another motorist on the highway traveling in violation of the posted speed limit. The official threatens to "call the police" if, and only if, the activist starts "sweeping without a permit," and why, because, he says, "you'll be in violation" of city regulations.

The activist sees that the official's threat is purely discretionary, a matter of personal choice and even gamesmanship, and the activist seems unfazed, unimpressed, and he suggests that he too has discretion to employ, even if it's quite unconventional. Two can play this game, he suggests:

> SCHAGEN: *You just do that. I'll invite the press. That would make great headlines: "Police arrest citizens for sweeping the street on their own initiative!"*

The activist does not bother with argument at all about needing a permit. Instead, he focuses attention on the broader institutional interests—and the vulnerabilities!—of the city and its officials. Yes, the official may wish to follow bureaucratic protocols and standard operating procedures, that's expectable enough—but surely, it has been the inadequacies of just those status quo procedures that have led to the need for sweeping the street in the first place! So, what else matters, Schagen seems to have asked, to city officials? Perhaps they care too about public reputation, public opinion, respect, and support?

So, the activist does not take the bait of arguing about institutional permits and obligations and violations and police—he debates none of that!—and he responds to the threat of the official's calling the police by assessing the possible consequences for the city official himself, as he would subject the city's administrative performance to public ridicule, "That would make great headlines ... ."

The activist invokes the power of publicity: let's not make this an argument between us, let's not make this an argument (as individuals, as psychological subjects) about regulations, let's see what the public thinks about institutional officials who call the police to arrest citizens for sweeping their own streets!

Recognizing and Appreciating the Relational Interactions of Democratic Inter-subjectivity

Notice that the activist responds here less to the official's subjective or personal feelings of authority or his deliberate, intentional power play, his threat to call the police, than to that official's institutional relationship to a potentially interested and watchful public, a public to whom, the activist bets, the official may be in part accountable. Responding to the official's subjective intentions would have been the wrong move, the activist suggests; responding instead to the official's inter-subjective interdependence and vulnerability, the official's interrelationship to the public in whose name the official is "official" in the first place, provides the activist with the leverage of a countermove: if you call the police, they'll arrest us, and the newspapers, whom we will have called, will make fine headlines for you!

So, the city official seems less eager to make the news after all, and he changes course. He does not say, Go ahead and try it! He wishes to avoid such headlines and institutional damage, and so he explores another avenue to dissuade Schagen from his plans:

CITY OFFICIAL: *And if you want to sweep in the Weimarstraat, what do you plan to do with the garbage?*
SCHAGEN: *We'll put it in the dumpsters there.*

The official puts the permit question aside and returns to the activist's proposed actions and intentions: What do you have in mind? What will you do with the garbage then? The official explores intentions and searches for vulnerabilities and weaknesses in the activist's plans. The official's questions probe power relationships, and as we soon see, the activist has power plays of his own in mind. So, the official learns from the activist's matter of fact response, you want to put the garbage in the dumpsters! That leads to further problems, he suggests:

CITY OFFICIAL: *Then it becomes industrial waste, and you have to pay a lot of money to dump industrial waste.*

Notice that the official no longer speaks of "garbage" any more, for now, taking space in these dumpsters, what he had called "garbage" swept up from the street has become "industrial waste"—for that's what the dumpsters collect and contain, as a matter of administrative designation and corresponding regulation—and as a result, then, were he to transform "garbage" into "industrial waste" by placing it in the dumpsters, the activist would now face further institutional, not personal—inter-subjective, not subjective—obligations, "to pay a lot of money" to dump that "industrial waste."

But notice now that the official appeals not just to one change of identity but two, all as part of his power play. Not only will mere "garbage" change its identity to become "industrial waste," the official argues, but the performance of the activist's street-sweeping that "garbage" into those receptacles, the dumpsters, will—prospectively—also transform the activist himself from an ordinary citizen sweeping up his or her streets into one now having "to pay a lot of money" for what he's done with that "industrial waste"!

But two can play this game of power and threatening consequences, the activist shows us:

SCHAGEN: *Oh, yes. Then we'll just have to dump this "industrial waste" in the front yard of the alderman in charge. You know that we've done things like that before, so if you don't cooperate a little here, things can get pretty tough for you.*

Again, the activist does not argue about rights or rules or regulations, he agrees— "Oh, yes," he says—and he practically reframes and changes the game. He does not debate the transformation of garbage into industrial waste, and he does not argue about fee schedules regulating the disposal of such waste. Indeed, he agrees to call that garbage "industrial waste" and he suggests now that he might dump it not into the dumpsters after all, but—again for publicity purposes—now in "the front yard of the alderman in charge."

The activist doesn't work out the consequences of that action, but quite clearly the official in charge of waste collection would now have some complex "explaining to do" to the alderman. Why, after all, would citizens willing to sweep their own streets be driven to dump their collected garbage or waste onto the alderman's front yard? Whether the activist would pay with some sort of legal prosecution or not, the resulting publicity would once again make the city and its agencies and politicians all look bad, perhaps incompetent, in the public eye. The activist recognizes the possible legal penalties and so makes very clear the credibility of his hypothetical scenario, "You know that we've done things like that before."

But all of this hypothetically anticipated future story depends on the official's cooperation, the official's help that might enable the activist's organization to sweep their own street. The activist persists in at least two ways: first, not arguing with the official's points, and second, making clear how the community organization's efforts could easily call embarrassing publicity and negative public attention to municipal non-cooperation. Pragmatism, here—pointing to the consequences and differences made by publicity—and not conceptual debate, arguing the merits of the official's words point by point, leverages institutional norms and the prospects of embarrassment to, and public disfavor and withdrawal of support for, city officials.

The official's power plays appeal to law and regulation, the need for permits and the obligation to "pay a lot of money." The activist engages in a series of power plays as well, appealing not to legal representation, not to any alternative reading of, or debate about, the regulations, but instead to the official's and the city's *need* to maintain positive public opinion or, alternatively, to avoid public embarrassment. The activist focuses not on the official's subjectivity or personal qualities, but on his institutional, inter-subjective identity, position, and vulnerability.

Move by move, claim by claim, the official and the activist set forth what they care about, what they might and might not do with respect to each other. The official comes to see that the standard procedures will not suffice in this case. The activist comes to see that several approaches could have serious costs: legal or economic, for example.

Finally, though, the authors tell us that after this parrying:

> It all worked out eventually. The sweeping crew was able to get to work. The circle of those involved became broader. A solution to the "industrial waste problem" was found within the city budget. The city official on duty left. Noticeably better cooperative relations developed with officials that had agreed with the value of the street-sweeping initiative.
>
> *(Hendriks & Tops, 2007)*

This exchange involves power, inequality, negotiation, threats, and more. The two speakers stand in for others: the official represents a public agency and the political administration in power, and the activist represents a community organization concerned about their neighborhood.

For our purposes, however, we should notice that the speakers not only read one another's subjectivities, one another's identities, wishes, intentions, and interests, but the official and activist also invoke complex inter-subjective relationships as well—one invokes regulations and obligations, for example, and the other invokes the significance of public opinion and the accountability of public officials and aldermen to a broader electorate. The pair speak both, then, to democratic subject formation—the construction of intentions and hopes, of identity and interests and wishes and plans—and as crucially and pragmatically, to democratic inter-subjectivity, not just to the relationships potentially enacted between community members and existing regulatory regimes or between officials and publics, but also to the complex interactions that we typically call "threats" or "questions" or even "statements of obligation."

Exploring the Pragmatics of Relational Interactions in a Democratic Inter-subjectivity

Since recent studies have paid relatively more attention to "subject formation" than the character of democratic inter-subjectivity, we turn now briefly to examine more specifically the inter-subjective character of his exchange. In particular, we seek to show how a focus primarily upon subject formation would blind us and prevent our understanding of significant moments of social and political action.

Rules and Permits as Leverage

We can begin, for example, with the official's bald statement in response to the activist's claim, "It's a good idea": the official claims in turn, "Yes, but you just can't do that." The official here does not threaten, does not command, does not instruct, but he tries to construct the impossibility of what the activist has proposed, an impossibility he will go on to explain in the administrative terms of permit requirements that he claims will pertain to anyone seeking to sweep a public street.

If we ignored the inter-subjective action here, we would be left with a simple prediction that the activist will not be able *within the rules* to do what he's said. But the official's actual claim does far more than predict: it invokes as authoritative and binding a particular institutional framework of rules and obligations that he suggests to be objectively and inter-subjectively shared. The official's not just subjectively recommending or endorsing those rules.

Similarly, the official's "You have to have a permit for that," works not simply as a true or false description of the facts, as innocent as that might be. Instead, in saying that, he invokes the activist's membership in a political system in which members have not only rights but responsibilities, not only autonomy but obligations. The official recognizes and invokes not simply the other's subjective identity—you wish to do A, you care about B, you have interests in C—but he recognizes and invokes the activist's inter-subjective, normatively salient relationships as they will be enacted, for better or worse: if you begin to sweep, you will need a permit for that; if you don't get a permit, you'll be in violation, and I'll have to call the police … if you put garbage into the dumpster, it becomes "industrial waste" and you need to pay a lot of money for that.

As a matter of subject formation, a networked actor expresses a disposition: as a *city official*, not as my mother's son, I'll have to call the police, for that's who *I* am—relationally, not simply subjectively! —the official says. Similarly, the activist counters, effectively: in my relational capacity as the *community organization's agent*, I'll have to call the press, for that's who *I* am. The official and activist express and recognize these relational, as well as felt, subjective identities clearly enough; neither asks Why in the world would you do that? They do recognize one another's subjective identities, their subject formation, but we should not fail to see that they do very much more than that too!

So, this exchange shows us a great deal more than democratic or agonistic subject formation, however intentionally opposed these subjects' requests, claims, and demands may be. The power play—the oppositional political negotiation—that the official and the activist engage in shows us that without a fine sensitivity to the politically nuanced inter-subjective and institutional matrix that makes relational, interactive, and pragmatic sense of each actor's place, role, and subject position, only simplistic statements of will and self-description remain.

Refusals

Consider another example. The official tells the activist that a permit will be necessary. The activist says, "And you're going to arrange that for me, right?" The official then replies, "I don't think so."

Taken as a matter of subject formation, "I don't think so" is a vivid description of the official's own analysis, interpretation, evolving (negative) commitment, his self-understanding, his characterization of his own feelings, and his (un)willingness to act. Each word matters, for with the "I" he speaks for himself; with the "don't" he disavows a line of consideration and approach;

with "think" he refers to his own ability to evaluate and judge the case at hand; and with "so" he takes a stance with respect to the course of action at hand. We learn clearly as a listener that this official has no intention of helping the activist obtain the permit: that's his "position," his feeling, and even decision about the matter, that's who he is in this practical instance.

But notice that "I don't think so" is not simply a self-referential description, although it seems literally to be that. For as a pragmatic matter of inter-subjective action, saying that sends a practical signal and makes an instrumental claim in response: that utterance is far more than subjective self-description, it is a political refusal, an outright rejection of the activist's suggestion. "I don't think so" is literally and superficially an act of democratic subject formation, but it is far more than that too. It enacts a political, relational, pragmatic refusal taking form both as an interpersonal one between practical actors and as an official, institutional one: a refusal enacted by a member of a political administration toward a member of the public body to whom that administration may be contingently accountable.

Only if we take "I don't think so" as more than expressing evidence of subject formation, as more too than as enacting that subject formation directly and performatively, only then can we understand that "I don't think so" reconstitutes inter-subjective relationships as well as subjective ones, enacts inter-subjective non-cooperation pragmatically where the activist had just raised the political possibility of emergent cooperation. "I don't think so" changes (reaffirms the position of) not only the speaker (that's the work of subject formation), but the speaker's world as well, the way that speaker relates to others, what others can expect of the speaker not just as an Other (subject) but as an interlocutor, as an inter-actor, as someone who's just taken a distinctive relational position and enacted not just a "presentation of self," but a particular interactive relationship, here one of refusal and non-cooperation.

Threats and Warnings

We could make a similar case, to take yet another example, for the activist's plain-spoken, self-referential, "we've done things like that before." Taken as a matter of subject formation, this claims a performative history of what we've done before, an identity based not just upon intentions or aspirations but upon concrete past practices, a record for all to see of past actions. This, the activist says, shows who we are; this recollection from practical memory shows, he claims now, who we are. So much for subject formation, once again: now we have the activist claiming an identity not just for himself but for his organization, for a "we" that has "done things" like dump garbage on an alderman's lawn before—and so, he suggests, "we" might do that again: "we," surely, having done it before, are therefore subjectively, even objectively, capable of doing it again. But that alone misses the action in the here and now, in the dawning future.

For only if we take these very same words in this same utterance in this same claim as a matter of inter-subjective performance can we appreciate the activist's political power play here. Taken inter-subjectively, the claim not only refers to an organization's activist identity but it establishes the credibility of the pragmatic threat to do it again, to dump the waste in the alderman's front yard. "We've done things like that before" does not only self-describe as a matter of subject formation, but it pragmatically warns the official: we are not just talking about ourselves here, but, in effect, this is what we're prepared to do again, if you want us to, or if you put us in the position of doing so. Taken inter-subjectively and institutionally, the same claim both (a) does the work of subject formation and (b) enacts a relationship, changes an interactive world, for it says to the official, we are talking here not only about the community organization's past but about our—the official's and activist's—joint future, our joint and contingent future, the future that, the activist threatens, the official might usher in if he does not act carefully.

Here we move far beyond democratic subject formation and the creation or enactment of identity to the creation, enactment, and production of new inter-subjective, politically contingent, institutional relationships, both informal and formal: not only have we dumped garbage on a politician's lawn before, not only are we fully prepared to do it again, but we're giving you warning about, allowing you to anticipate, what can well happen "if you don't cooperate a little here."

Appreciating Democratic Subjects, Recognizing Democratic Interactions

Of course, the work of subject formation, properly understood, must always take place in historical, inter-subjective settings. But a view of actors that privileges subject formation, an overly self-referential if not epistemological view of actors as knowers constructing worlds, can limit our view to the contingencies of self-understanding and identity-formation at the expense of our understanding the contingencies and performativity of inter-subjective relationships, practical political interdependence, practical political negotiations, and power plays that can account for political and institutional change, both formal and informal (Laws, 2013; Laws & Forester, 2015; see also Forester, 2017b).

Finally, notice that if we only pay attention to subjects, we are at an impasse, for we will then miss the interactions and contingencies and responsiveness as political actions seek to change their worlds. Both our subjectivities and our relationships are contingent. Put more politically, we can change our subjectivities *and* we can act to change our relationships with one another. When we act pragmatically, we not only try to make a difference, but we learn, grow, and change, by doing as well. We not only express oppositional sentiments, we act to change our circumstances, changing ourselves and others practically in the process. Notice the diverse practical moves, acts, and tactics found in our exchange above: probing the other, testing for the others' assent, assenting, sanctioning, challenging, invoking the other's obligations, soliciting cooperation, refusing cooperation, insisting upon cooperation, warning and threatening, calling a bluff and warning and threatening in turn, countering the other's strategy, making the strategy plausible and credible, invoking new obligation, threatening a new strategy and its costs to the Other—among others. All these relational acts could well be *missed* if we attend primarily to democratic subject formation, to oppositional aspirations however earnestly or righteously expressed, to the subjects without their practical interactions. With all due regard and respect for democratic subjects and contingent subjectivity, then, we need to attend just as much to democratic inter-subjectivity—the relational, world-changing actions we perform pragmatically and institutionally as we deal with our ineradicable differences, as we confront those differences in deed as well as in oppositional, however sincere, intentions.

Note

1 This essay is a revision of an earlier draft written at the University of Amsterdam where the author served as a Nicis fellow doing the research that culminated in (Laws & Forester, 2015). It builds upon the author's *Dealing with Differences: Dramas of Mediating Public Disputes* (Oxford University Press, 2009), his *Planning in the Face of Conflict* (American Planning Association Press, 2013) and Forester (2014).

References

Barrett, F. (2012). *Yes to the Mess: Surprising Leadership Lessons from Jazz*. Cambridge, MA: Harvard Business School.
Forester, J. (2009). *Dealing with Differences: Dramas of Mediating Public Disputes*. New York: Oxford University Press.

Forester, J. (2013). *Planning in the Face of Conflict: Surprising Possibilities of Facilitative Leadership*. Chicago, IL: American Planning Association Press.

Forester, J. (2014). Learning Through Conflict. In S. Griggs, A. Norval & H. Wagenaar (Eds.), *Practices of Freedom*. Cambridge: Cambridge University Press.

Forester, J. (2017a). On the Evolution of a Critical Pragmatism. In B. Haselsberger (Ed.), *The Evolution of Planning Thought*. London: Routledge.

Forester, J. (2017b). Deliberative Democracy, Not Smothering Invention. In A. Bächtiger, J. Dryzek, J. Mansbridge & M. Warren (Eds.), *Oxford Handbook of Deliberative Democracy*. New York: Oxford University Press.

Hendriks, F., & Tops, P. (2005). Everyday fixers as local heroes: A case study of vital interaction. *Local Government Studies*, 31(4), 475–490.

Hysing, E., & Olsson, J. (2017). *Green Inside Activism for Sustainable Development: Political Agency and Institutional Change*. New York: Palgrave Macmillan.

Laws, D. (2013). *Negotiating Community: The Role of Conflict and Difference in Improvising Urban Democracy. Forum Essay*. Utrecht, Holland: Forum: Institute for Multicultural Affairs.

Laws, D., & Forester, J. (2015). *Conflict, Improvisation, Governance*. New York: Routledge.

Norval, A. (2007). *Aversive Democracy*. Cambridge: Cambridge University Press.

Purcell, M. (2008). *Recapturing Democracy: Neoliberalization and the Struggle for Alternative Urban Futures*. New York: Routledge.

Tully, J. (2008). *Public Philosophy in a New Key: Volume I, Democracy and Civic Freedom*. Cambridge: Cambridge University Press.

Van de Wijdeven, T., & Hendriks, F. (2007). *Real-Life Expressions of Vital Citizenship: Present-Day Community Participation in Dutch City Neighbourhoods*. Paper presented at the Vital City conference 2007, available from Tilburg School of Politics and Public Administration.

Wagenaar, H. (2011). *Meaning in Action: Interpretation and Dialogue in Policy Analysis*. London: M. E. Sharpe.

Warren, M. (2013). Governance-Driven Democratization. In S. Griggs, A. Norval & H. Wagenaar (Eds.), *Practices of Freedom*. Cambridge: Cambridge University Press.

Wheeler, M. (2013). *The Art of Negotiation: How to Improvise Agreement in a Chaotic World*. New York: Simon and Schuster.

10
WHAT CAN WE LEARN FROM EVOLUTIONARY THEORY WHEN CONFRONTING THE DEEP CHALLENGES OF OUR TIMES?

Luca Bertolini

Deep Challenges

Contemporary societies are confronted by an array of 'deep' challenges: there is broad agreement about the need to act – and act urgently – but consensus about what and how to do in practice is lacking. Even when tentative unity regarding possible solutions exists, the interventions face ostensibly unsurmountable resistance to change under the status quo. The list of challenges that share these characteristics is long and diverse. It includes daunting ones such as the need to cope with climate change; the need to shift to an environmentally sustainable economy; the need to drastically reduce if not eliminate economic, social, cultural, ethnic, gender and other forms of inequality and discrimination; and the need to lessen the tensions and realize the coexistence potentials between different cultures and identities. Many of these challenges are not new, but today they display heightened intensity, urgency and complexity – in short, the problems have become much 'deeper'. The overarching question is how can societies change in the face of a widely felt perception of the need to change, but also under the irreducible uncertainty about what and how to change.

Many attempts to cope with these and similar challenges, and also hopeful success stories (Solnit, 2016), can be noted, but a conclusive 'solution' is nowhere in sight. Accordingly, there is intense debate about which approach to follow, within society in general and especially within the policymaking field. Looking at the latter, two ends of the spectrum can be broadly identified. On the one end are policy approaches based on long-term strategies and far-reaching coordination of stakeholders, with a focus on established institutions as the main agents of change (as in 'strategic planning': Albrechts, 2010; Albrechts & Balducci, 2013). Critics point, however, at the severe difficulty of implementing such consensus-based approaches in the face of fundamental disagreement about what does and does not work, or even about the desirable outcome (see Boelens & De Roo, 2016; Salet et al., 2013).

Others wonder whether established institutions could ever act as agents of change, due to their vested interests in the status quo (Purcell, 2009). At the other end of the spectrum are policy approaches based on incremental interventions and innovative, disruptive practices as the main agents of change (as in 'government by experiments': Bulkeley & Castán Broto, 2013). Some key limitations highlighted by critics are the inadequacy of the scope of change relative to the scope of the challenge, the insufficient leverage vis-à-vis broader societal structures, and the risk of lock-in (i.e. of reaching a situation that is not desirable, but where no further change is possible) (Savini et al., 2015). There are also emerging, intriguing visions of hybrids between the two: top-down approaches open to bottom-up experimentation, and bottom-up approaches that are able to impact top-down structures (as in 'transition governance': Grin et al., 2010). At a more general, epistemological level, the very goal of this book – enabling a dialogue or even integration between institutionalist and pragmatist views of planning (see Salet, Chapter 1, in this volume) – can be also seen as such a hybrid, and the chapters by Healey (Chapter 2) and Boelens (Chapter 6) highlight potential pathways to realize it.

In order to help structure and advance this debate, and further articulate hybrid approaches, this chapter looks for inspiration in the theory and empirical evidence of biological evolution. Underlying the intellectual project is the observation that biological evolution is a quintessential process of adaptation to emerging threats and opportunities, in the absence of knowledge about what does and does not work, and without a projected end state. In other words, evolution can be seen as an unparalleled depositary of responses to 'deep' challenges like those identified above: urgent, but with no predetermined path to a solution and facing systemic resistance to any fundamental change of course. As such, it can be expected to have a high heuristic value when looking for ways of coping with such challenges. The prime aim of this chapter is to explore this heuristic potential. The application of evolutionary insights in the policymaking domain is not new (see Bertolini, 2010; Mehmood, 2010; Moroni, 2010); however, many or even most of these applications do not acknowledge the great enrichment of evolutionary theories in the last decades. Evolutionary theories have moved far beyond their original, narrow Neo-Darwinian features (Laland et al., 2014). Thus, the second and more general aim of this chapter is to bring this enrichment to bear on applications of evolutionary theories in the policymaking domain.

In what follows, I will first summarize this extended view of evolution. An underlying, central concern will be the identification of potential dynamics to accelerate evolution in the face of emerging environmental threats and opportunities. Next, I will adapt this extended view to the policymaking domain and illustrate its heuristic potential by applying it to a deep challenge in the field of urban planning. Urban planning is a particularly relevant field of application because by definition it is oriented towards the future – a crucial difference from other social sciences and practices. As Myers (2001, p. 366) notes: "[t]he future is the only topic that other professions have ceded to planners as relatively uncontested turf". For urban planning, therefore, confronting emerging threats and opportunities is a central and defining task. Furthermore, the chief object of urban planning is the social and spatial arrangement of cities, and today's rapidly urbanizing cities are the locations where the deep challenges mentioned above are most intensely felt, and finding approaches to cope is a most pressing issue (Barber, 2013). Finally, the contribution aims to stimulate a debate within the urban planning field itself. In particular, it explores what a planning oriented towards enabling transformative societal change could entail. The specific urban planning challenge considered in this chapter is the transition to sustainable urban mobility. This challenge is directly related to a number of the broader societal challenges named in the opening paragraph (Bertolini, 2012).

Evolutionary Theory beyond Narrow Neo-Darwinism

In its essence, the Neo-Darwinian view of biological evolution centres on processes of variation of the hereditary characteristics of individual organisms determined by random and blind genetic mutations, and the selection of these characteristics by an exogenous natural environment. During the past several decades, new insights have enriched this view in three important respects (Jablonka & Lamb, 2014). First, current research does not only focus on processes of variation and inheritance at the genetic level, but also at three additional levels: the developmental or 'epigenetic' level of organism development, the level of animal behaviour, and the level of human culture. Second, they do not only focus on processes of blind and random mutation, but also on processes of more focused, 'directed' variation. Third, they do not see the environment as exogenous to processes of variation and inheritance but as co-determined by them – that is, they characterize the relationship between organisms and environment as one of co-evolution. This extended view of biological evolution is summarized below. The account is mainly based on the comprehensive overview by Jablonka and Lamb (2014). It is important to stress that, for the sake of clarity, the presentation is simplified by schematically contrasting a 'narrow' and an 'extended' view of biological evolution. This simplification does not do justice to the many nuances and lively debates among evolutionary biologists (see Laland et al., 2014). The aim is not to highlight all of these nuances or to take a stance in the debate but rather to identify the widest possible range of evolutionary dynamics, as a basis for exploring their potential significance in the social and policy domains.

Determination and Transmission of Characteristics

A basic prerequisite for evolution is the existence of variable characteristics that can be transmitted between different entities. In the narrow Neo-Darwinian view of evolution these are the variable characteristics of individual organisms, as determined by the genetic code contained in their DNA and as transmitted by their reproduction process. More recent views of evolution add three other potential levels of determination and transmission of characteristics.

First is the developmental or 'epigenetic' level. This is the level where during the development of an organism from its embryonal to its mature state, cells diversify and reproduce, activating or deactivating genes in the process (hence the term 'epigenetic'). According to the narrow Neo-Darwinian view of biological evolution, these acquired characteristics cannot be transmitted to descendants. However, there is increasing evidence that at least in some cases they could be. While there is heated debate among biologists around the evolutionary significance of these processes (see the sceptic's view of Dickins & Rahman, 2012; and the response by Mesoudi et al., 2013), conceptually they add an important evolutionary path. This is because developmental/epigenetic processes are sensitive to environmental conditions and provide a much more directed response to a change in the environment than random and blind processes of genetic mutation, and thus a pathway for accelerating evolution when the need or the opportunity arises. This acknowledgment of the potential role of development in evolution has branded its advocates as 'Neo-Lamarckians' and the view 'Neo-Lamarckian', adding another twist to a long-standing debate (Bowler, 1983, 1988).

A second additional level of the determination and transmission of the characteristics of living organisms is provided by behavioural processes in the animal world, resulting in so-called 'animal traditions' (Avital & Jablonka, 2000). A typical evolutionary pathway involves the discovery of a better fitting behaviour for the environment, either by accident or by trial and error, and its transmission by means of imitation. Examples include the discovery and diffusion of strategies for procuring food or for escaping predators.

At a third level characteristics are determined and transmitted through human cultural processes – that is, symbols. A prominent and well-researched example is the evolution of language; however, in any area of human life there is evidence of individual and group characteristics determined and transmitted by means of cultural processes: from raising children, to work practices, to care and leisure in adulthood, to the relationships people have with others, and to the very values and norms driving individual and group choices (Mesoudi, 2011). What human cultural processes add to animal behavioural processes is the possibility to imagine the future, and thus bring expectations of potential outcomes to bear on present choices. It should be immediately emphasized that imagining the future is by no means equal to predicting it and that potential outcomes do not necessarily evolve into actual outcomes.

The evolutionary significance of behavioural and cultural processes is less heatedly debated among evolutionary biologists than that of developmental, epigenetic processes. However, their implications for evolutionary pathways are also far-reaching. Again, they open up additional and fundamentally different pathways of evolutionary change. Animal behavioural processes add the possibility of determining and transmitting characteristics that do not require any changes in the nature of the organisms, either of their genetic or of their developmental characteristics. Furthermore, and related to this point, they add the possibility of the horizontal transmission of characteristics (as in learning among individuals of the same generation) next to vertical transmission (as in genetic and epigenetic processes, and in learning from one generation to the other). Animal behavioural processes thus provide the possibility of a much more directed and rapid response to emerging environmental threats and opportunities than random and blind genetic mutation. Human cultural processes dramatically increase the range and reach of potential responses, as they allow the exploration of yet non-existing realities. However, they also introduce the possibility of a deliberate negation of real environmental cues, with potentially disastrous consequences (for a thought-provoking account, see Diamond, 2005).

Next to the consideration of processes at different levels, in the extended view of evolution there is also a lot of attention paid to the interaction between levels, for instance between genetic and cultural processes (Laland et al., 2010). What these interrelations add to the general picture is the relevance of positive and negative feedback among a great array of processes, and their potential to greatly accelerate (in the case of positive feedback) or constrain (in the case of negative feedback) evolutionary change.

Variation

Evolution requires varied traits to be produced and transmitted. In the narrow Neo-Darwinist view, the key sources of variation are random and blind genetic mutations; however, emerging views of evolution are broadening this notion. Already at the genetic level, there is evidence of varying and non-random rates of mutation, with environmental stress both inducing an intensification of mutation rates and localizing this intensification in specific genes. Variation at the developmental, epigenetic level is by definition directed (it is directed towards reaching the mature state of an organism). However, next to this built-in directionality of the organism's developmental process, there is also the possibility of variation that responds to the environment and changes therein, be it inside or outside the egg or womb (e.g. the embryo's responses to the eating and drinking patterns of the mother during pregnancy). The latter is particularly relevant, as it entails the possibility of an adaptive variation – a variation better fit to the environment. Variation at the behavioural and cultural level is also a process that involves directionality. It is perhaps best summarized by the notion that it is by and large a goal-directed process, geared towards the achievement of a particular goal (e.g. procuring food, avoiding predators, preserving a social order or creating a new one).

Altogether these sources of variation show that next to random and blind genetic mutation more directed processes of variation may also take place: either by focusing variation at specific times and locations or by directing variation towards addressing specific challenges, real or imagined (in the case of cultural variation). This does by no means imply that such variations will be successful (i.e. adaptive), but it can be argued that they might increase the chance that when faced with emerging environmental threats and opportunities, species or communities might adapt more rapidly.

Selection Environment

The third and final basic component of evolution is the selection environment. In the narrow Neo-Darwinian view, the environment and its changes are by and large exogenous to the processes of variation of individual organisms and communities. The extended view of evolution adopts a much more bi-directional stance, where individual organisms and communities construct 'environmental niches' which in turn will shape their further development, in a co-evolutionary process fuelled by self-reinforcing feedback cycles (Laland et al., 2010; Odling-Smee et al., 2003). In some conceptualizations the distinction between the environment and living organisms almost entirely blurs. In these more extreme conceptualizations the environment is seen as the sum of the organisms it contains, and all organisms evolve following interaction with the environment – that is, interaction with all other organisms. Perhaps the most suggestive example of such a view is the so-called Gaia hypothesis, which applies this logic to the whole planet (Lovelock, 1988).

The philosophical and practical implications are profound. Philosophically, it suggests a continuous and interconnected development of organisms and the environment rather than an environment that separately 'is', and organisms that separately 'become'. Practically, this perspective opens the possibility of evolution by means of actively shaping the selection environment by the very entities being selected by it.

A Plurality of Evolutionary Dynamics

The evolutionary dynamics highlighted in the discussion above can be summarized in the following way.

First, evolution unfolds at several, interrelated levels. Characteristics are determined and transmitted through genetic, developmental/epigenetic, behavioural and cultural processes, and these processes are interrelated. This greatly enlarges the array of elements and processes involved in evolution, multiplying the range of evolutionary paths available.

Second, next to blind and random genetic mutation, there is also more directed variation (i.e. variation more directly responsive to a specific environmental stimulus), both in terms of rate, timing and location (also in the case of genetic mutation), and in terms of scope (in the case of developmental/epigenetic, behavioural and cultural variation). This directionality amounts to an additional possibility to accelerate evolution in the face of environmental change. This possibility does not, however, imply a certainty, as there is still no prior guarantee that the variation will be successful (i.e. adaptive). Furthermore, in the case of cultural variation, the possibility opens up of deliberately negating an environmental signal – that is, deliberately blocking the evolutionary process (e.g. if it is not seen as consistent with the prevailing social values and norms).

Third, the selection environment is not exogenous to processes of genetic, developmental/epigenetic, behavioural and cultural variation, but is also shaped by them through co-evolution. This process identifies a distinct evolutionary pathway, in which individual organisms or communities may contribute to creating an environmental niche, which in turn will facilitate and condition their further development. For humans, this pathway opens up the option to try and deliberately shape a selection environment consistent with their present culture. It also, however, entails the risk of overestimating the degree to which it is desirable and feasible.

Altogether, these evolutionary dynamics and pathways document many ways of accelerating evolution in response to emerging environmental threats and opportunities. In the biological domain, this provides potential additional explanations for the richness and speed of evolution (Jablonka & Lamb, 2014). In the social and policy domain, this arsenal of dynamics might provide many sources of inspiration for pathways to realizing change in the face of uncertainty and resistance (which are explored below).

Insights from Evolutionary Processes for Coping with Deep Societal Challenges

Figure 10.1 synthesizes the evolutionary dynamics described above, and adapts them to the social domain. It is important to underline that this adaptation from the natural to the social is not intended to be literal, nor does it imply direct equivalences between elements and processes. Rather, it aims to provide a conceptual framework for exploring potential analogies between the dynamics of stability and change at a meta-systemic level. The translation is inspired by sociological theories positing a two-way relationship between social structure and social agency, most characteristically captured by Giddens's (1984) structuration theory (see also Healey, Chapter 2, and Boelens, Chapter 6, in this volume). In the natural world (Figure 10.1, left half) living organisms with varying and interrelated genetic, epigenetic/developmental, behavioural, and cultural characteristics are selected by the natural environment and at the same time produce it (through processes of niche creation). In the social world (Figure 10.1, right half) instead of living organisms there are social practices (i.e. 'what people do' on an everyday basis: Reckwitz, 2002). Instead of the natural environment there are social institutions (i.e. 'patterns of social norms' as defined by Salet, Chapter 1, in this volume) and human artefacts, such as the physical fabric of settlements. Analogously to the natural world, in the social world social practices with varying and interrelated characteristics

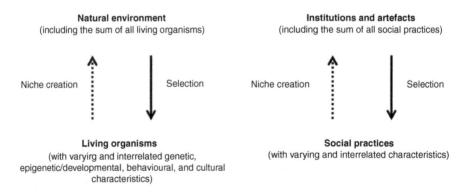

Figure 10.1 Dynamics of biological evolution (left) and translation to the social domain (right)
Source: Bertolini

are both selected by institutions and artefacts (in the sense that institutions and artefacts shape the conditions that facilitate or hamper the performance of social practices) and produce them through processes analogous to niche creation.

Figure 10.2 further articulates this framework with a focus on the dynamics of system stability and change. Key sources of inspiration are studies of socio-technical transitions, in particular the idea that niche–regime interactions are at the core of processes of social and technical change (Geels, 2005; Rip & Kemp, 1998; Schot, 1998). This inspiration also extends to more recent proposals of how to integrate social practices within this socio-technical dynamic (Shove & Walker, 2010; Watson, 2012; see also on both points Healey, Chapter 2, in this volume). The framework in Figure 10.2 distinguishes on the one hand between 'prevailing' and 'niche' institutions and artefacts, and on the other hand between 'conformist' and 'non-conformist' social practices. These distinctions give rise to a variety of potential evolutionary processes. 'Conformist' social practices are both enabled (i.e. positively selected) by prevailing institutions and artefacts, and reproduce them. 'Non-conformist' social practices are both hampered (i.e. negatively selected) by the prevailing institutions and artefacts, and contest them. 'Non-conformist' social practices have instead a positive, two-way relationship with consonant institution and artefact niches: they are both enabled by and reproduce them. These conflicting and contradictory dynamics can produce systemic stability (the more common outcome, as the niche disappears or remains marginal) or systemic change (a niche becoming prevailing, which happens much less frequently).

Moving from this framework, how can the evolutionary processes, discussed above, be translated to the social and policy domains? And more specifically, how can the evolution

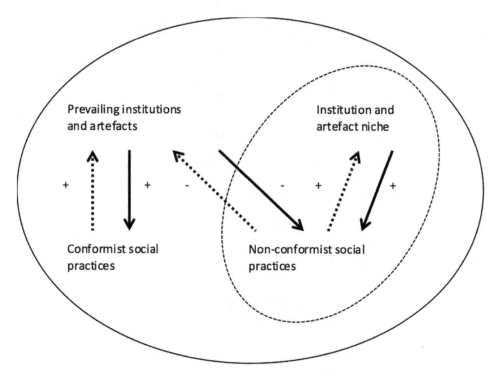

Figure 10.2 Dynamics of stability and change in the social domain
Source: Bertolini

of social practices, institutions and artefacts be accelerated in the face of the deep challenges outlined in the introduction? Let us look at each of the three ways in which biological evolution is being reconceptualized, and what each implies for the answer to the latter question. The argument in this section is mainly conceptual, supplemented by more concrete illustrations in the next section.

Determination and Transmission of Characteristics in the Social Domain

In the biological domain, according to the extended view, evolution is determined and can be accelerated by processes at different and interrelated levels (genetic, developmental/epigenetic, behavioural and cultural/symbolic). By analogy, in the social domain, evolution is determined and can be accelerated by varying/experimenting at the same time with different and interrelated social practices, in order to find new and self-reinforcing combinations of them. For example, by varying/experimenting with both different work and different care practices (such as working less and spending more time to care for relatives or neighbours), new and self-reinforcing work and care combinations can be found (new solidarity arrangements within a family or the community).

Variation in the Social Domain

While the role of accidental change/variation in fuelling evolution should be always acknowledged (as with contingent events in path dependency theory: Mahoney, 2000), also more directed change/variation is a source of evolution, and might be an essential condition for accelerating it. This would require increasing variation/experiments in times of crisis and at most affected locations (geographical and functional). It would also mean that variation/experiments should match the scope of the challenge – that is, should provide a plausible potential solution. While this last point might seem obvious, one can recall how many policy interventions have the declared aim of addressing the challenges mentioned in the introduction but do not have the potential, even if successful, to provide adequate answers.

Selection Environment in the Social Domain

Two notions are central here. First, the complex, undetermined and undeterminable interplay of variation and selection remains the key process in producing evolutionary outcomes. This means that in the face of deep challenges such as climate change, sustainable development, social inequality or cultural diversity, naïve (i.e. deterministic) planning or design approaches are not likely to succeed, or worse, risk being the superimposition of the will of the few on the lives of the many (see e.g. Scott, 1998). Second, the selection environment is not external but rather is co-shaped by social practices; implying that institutional and artefact niches can be deliberately created to allow experimentation with non-conformist social practices (cf. Figure 10.2).

Without changes in institutions and artefacts it is unlikely that very different practices will develop. On the other hand, changes in institutions and artefacts are likely to elicit different practices (even though unpredictably so). Furthermore, following the relations outlined in Figure 10.2, social practices are not only shaped by but can in part also shape institutions and artefacts (as institutions and artefacts are, in fact, the accumulation and consolidation of those practices). New social practices can thus also try and create institutional and artefact niches where they can develop further.

An Evolutionary Approach to the Deep Challenge of Achieving Sustainable Urban Mobility

The processes described in the preceding section together provide cues for possible ways to achieve the acceleration of the evolution of social institutions, artefacts and practices to address the deep challenges of today. But how would this process play out in a specific case? What kinds of concrete policy interventions might it demand? The following paragraphs outline a few possible directions in the case of sustainable urban mobility.

Varying/Experimenting with Different and Related Social Practices

In urban mobility, varying/experimenting with different and related social practices demands that not only different ways of transporting people and goods should be experimented with, but also different ways of related practices such as working, shopping, spending leisure time or socializing. Practically this would imply not only, for instance, promoting more walking and cycling, but also reducing the need to travel long distances by encouraging more proximate types of working, shopping, leisure time and socializing activities.

This timely and consistent change in multiple related social practices is important because of the strong interrelation between mobility and other human activity domains such as work, education, leisure and socialization. This deep interrelatedness has led some to speak of the present car-based urban mobility model as a 'system of automobility' (Urry, 2004). The difficulty of changing such a highly interrelated system has prompted others to highlight the current 'automobile/car dependency' (Jeekel, 2013; Newman & Kenworthy, 2015). On the bright side, it means that when change in multiple related practices is timely and consistent, the chance of creating positive, self-reinforcing feedback loops with potentially disruptive impacts on the dominant system will be greatly enhanced. One example of such a process currently underway is the interrelation between the rediscovery of urban living and the increased use of alternative modes of transport to the personal motor vehicle (Newman & Kenworthy, 2015).

Increasing the Rate of Variation/Experiments in Times and Places of Crisis

Urban mobility is everywhere in a state of crisis: no city can claim to have 'squared the circle' between on one side the dependency on high mobility of contemporary lifestyles and business models and on the other side the lack of sustainability of contemporary urban mobility patterns (Bertolini, 2012). In response to this crisis, every city faces the need to increase the rate of urban mobility variations/experiments, with some locations facing a more deeply felt urgency (most notably the rapidly growing, congestion- and pollution-ridden cites in China, India and other urbanizing countries). In these places both the need and the opportunity to experiment with different mobility arrangements are arguably the highest. It is, however, also a matter of perception. Cities are essentially created by the people who live there, and unless the inhabitants can start worrying more about their health, quality of life and the climate than about getting a job, a house or even just food for the day, the urban mobility crisis will not, in fact, exist. Conversely, in cities with an apparently much less dramatic situation, the urgency of change away from prevailing urban mobility might be more deeply felt; perhaps because more basic problems have been solved for many, and a shift in priorities has taken place (think about several European cities).

The point that the urban mobility experiments/variations should match the scope of the challenge is a very relevant one. While some cities might claim to have policies in place that are leading them towards solutions to some transport-related problems (e.g. safety, pollution, congestion), many cannot. Furthermore, no city can claim success in the face of more complex urban mobility challenges like mitigating climate change, or reversing the depletion of non-renewable natural resources. The sustainable urban mobility discourse is often not matched by outcomes (Boussauw & Vanoutrive, 2017). Let us look at some concrete examples of what matching the scope of the challenge might mean.

If air pollution or noise is the problem, a shift to transport that reduces air pollution or noise, as with electric or human-powered vehicles, is essential. Marginal improvements of present, fossil fuel-based car technology will arguably not do, and yet they are often advanced as solutions. If greenhouse gas emissions are the problem, the primary energy source is crucial (it should not be fossil-based, even in the case of electricity), but arguably, using less energy (e.g. shifting to collective and non-motorized modes, or travelling shorter distances) is essential, because non-fossil energy sources are not yet widely or readily available. Again, marginal efficiency improvements in fossil fuel-powered engines will not do, in spite of their many advocates. If congestion and the encroachment of public space are the problem, a shift in the type of transport used (e.g. from using cars to taking public transport or cycling or walking) means that significantly less space is needed. Marginal adaptations of the car-based transportation system (e.g. more temporal spreading of trips, higher car occupancy, or even self-driving cars and car sharing) will not do, whatever the contentions to the contrary. There is a common thread throughout the argument and examples above: in many, if not most cases, improvements in car technology will not be sufficient, and the reliance on cars needs to be reduced. This scope is not matched, however, by most present policy approaches.

Creating Institution and Artefact Niches for New Social Practices

Institutional niches could be places (for instance a street or an entire neighbourhood) and time periods (for instance for a few months or during the weekend) where radically different rules for the use of street space can be tested. For instance, motorized traffic can be greatly curtailed or entirely prohibited; local residents and businesses, instead of the city council, can decide how to use street space. But institutional niches could also be less geographically and more functionally defined, such as a set of incentives to actively lower car use by workers in an organization (as in intra-firm competitions for who drives less, coupled with information on and improvement of alternatives, and salary benefits favouring more sustainable modes of transport). There could also be a road pricing scheme in a city, a different urban parking regime, and other financial or fiscal incentives. Empirical evidence shows that under such conditions behavioural change can exceed expectations and be of a different order of magnitude than the predictions of transport models that assume an unchanged institutional context (e.g. EPOMM, 2013).

Artefact niches could be areas in a city with a different transport provision (e.g. more cycle lanes and fewer parking spaces) and urban fabric (focused on non-motorized and/or public transport, rather than being car-oriented). An example of what this might achieve if other favourable environmental conditions are in place, such as an urban fabric that allows reaching many destinations within short distances, is the impact of the provision of bicycle lanes, which is proven to induce a dramatic surge in cycling virtually in every mixed-use city district where it is implemented (Buehler & Dill, 2016).

It is important to emphasize that institutional and artefact niches need not to be benign, and not all demonstrate or even seek possible ways of coping with the deep challenge of urban mobility. However, even 'perverse' niches could still be instructive, as they might show what not coping with the dilemma of mobility might imply. Let us take the example of North

American or Australian cities. Sprawling North American or Australian cities are much more car dependent than the majority of cities in the world, and in that sense form a planetary, 'perverse' niche. They are a model that cannot be seemingly extended to the entire planet if challenges such as climate change or the depletion of non-renewable energy and other finite natural resources (such as land) are to be dealt with. From this vantage point, there are reasons to try and contain, if not counter this extremely car-dependent niche. However, this already sizeable niche could instead grow, and even become prevalent, as cities in rapidly urbanizing countries follow this model instead of the European or Asian models (or their own, new, non-car-dependent model).

A final observation should be made here. While the argument has focused on the creation of new, alternative institutional and artefact niches, it is also conceivable that existing, prevailing institutions and artefacts are marginally changed from the inside through 'reformist' policies. While these actions might be easier to implement, and might have a wider impact, they also might – and often do – result in a degree of change that does not match the scope of the challenge, pointing to an interesting and recurring theme for the debate.

An Illustration: The Living Street Initiative in Ghent, Belgium

An example from Ghent, Belgium provides an illustration of a concrete urban mobility policy initiative that innovatively and uniquely expresses many of the directions identified so far. The 'living street' is an initiative that envisages the temporary but extended closure (for one or two months) of residential streets to motorized traffic so that they can be used for other purposes. During the closure, alternative mobility options to the private car are promoted or offered, such as car sharing and cargo bikes. The initiative was taken by the inhabitants of the streets and was facilitated by a civic organization, the Lab van Troje, and the city council.[1]

It started in 2013 with just two streets, and has expanded each year to involve 19 streets in 2016. It is being followed-up elsewhere – for instance, in Rotterdam, Utrecht and Amsterdam in the Netherlands. The initiative is part of a broader ambition of the City of Ghent to explore the real-life conditions in a carbon-free city, and the barriers and opportunities for scaling-up from individual streets to the entire city.

The living street initiative is distinctive in several ways that sets it apart from mainstream urban mobility policy practices. First, and with reference to the first of the three clusters of insights mentioned above, it experiments at the same time with different ways of moving around and transporting goods (by non-motorized modes of transport and shared vehicles) and with different interrelated social practices (playing, socializing, working, shopping, running a business). As a result, there is a higher chance to create an interconnected whole, or a system where the components reinforce each other through positive feedback loops. This sets it apart from a recurring feature of mainstream urban mobility policy, where typically only some of these elements are altered or elements are not changed consistently, with negative, status quo maintaining feedback loops ultimately prevailing (see, for some telling cases, Boussauw & Vanoutrive, 2017).

Second, Ghent is an example of how the perception of a crisis might count more than the crude facts. At the local level, mobility in Ghent is not especially problematic, particularly when compared to megacities in emerging economies, for example. However, there is a shared awareness of the highly problematic planetary implications of the present local mobility patterns, as highlighted by the aim of becoming a carbon-neutral city. Furthermore, with respect to the scope matching the challenge, mobility practices during the living street experiment aimed – and to a large extent succeeded – to drastically reduce their environmental footprint.

Importantly, while still temporary and local in nature, they are explicitly seen as practices that could become permanent and extended to the entire city, and beyond.

Third, perhaps some of the most interesting and distinctive features of the living street initiative are related to how it succeeds in creating an effective institutional and artefact niche. Institutionally, a niche is created because other, exceptional decision-making procedures and regulatory regimes apply: inhabitants take the initiative; a civic organization facilitates the process; the city supports but does not lead and allows non-conforming regulations for the use of street space to be temporarily implemented. There are also signs of different norms, with the value of localism and sociability rising at the expense of the value of footlessness and detachment. An artefact niche is created by means of a different allocation of street space and the availability of different mobility options.

Overall, and as a result of all the above, the living street initiative is distinctive because it seamlessly couples transformative ambitions with an experimental attitude, thus possibly showing a way to bridge the gap between top-down and bottom-up approaches to change.

Summary and Research Agenda

Summary

In this chapter, an emerging, extended theory of biological evolution was used as a reference to identify ways of addressing the deep societal challenges of our time, characterized by a broad consensus on the need to act, but profound disagreement about what to do and endemic resistance to change. Building on this understanding of evolutionary processes, a number of potential coping strategies have been discussed:

- Vary/experiment at the same time with different and interrelated social practices;
- Increase the rate of variations/experiments in situation of crisis (and conversely enhance the very perception of crisis), and make variations/experiments match the scope of the challenge;
- Create institutional and artefact niches where new, non-conformist social practices can develop (or possibly modify prevailing institutions and artefacts to allow for the incremental adaptation of conformist practices).

The case of urban mobility and the example of the living street initiative in Ghent were used to illustrate the possible implications of these strategies in real-life practice.

Altogether, I suggest that these strategies might show a way of reconciling the tension between 'top-down' and 'bottom-up' approaches to policymaking, and help further articulate a 'hybrid' approach. On a more abstract level, I suggest that the overall conceptualization introduced in this chapter, and visualized in Figures 10.1 and 10.2, can offer a way to connect pragmatist and institutionalist views of planning. Institutionalist and pragmatist views of planning can be seen as pointing at distinct but interrelated components of an evolutionary process where social practices are conditioned by social institutions and artefacts (the institutionalist view) and also produce social institutions and artefacts (the pragmatist view).

Research Agenda

The conceptualization, strategies and illustrations in this chapter also reveal several possible themes for a research agenda, most importantly including:

- Refining and testing hypotheses about the effectiveness and workings of the suggested strategies by comparing the transformational impacts of policy experiments with different characteristics, and of policy approaches not based on experimentation;
- Looking into institutional and artefact conditions that enable or hamper transformation of social practices by experimentation, and into opportunities for modifying such conditions.

Last but not least, in the chapter there was no discussion of the interrelations between the processes of natural and social evolution. Simply, one process was seen as providing an analogy for the other. However, the two processes are not separate: humans are not only an integral part of biological evolution, but also play an increasing crucial role in shaping it (as recently captured by the notion of the Anthropocene: Bonneuil & Fressoz, 2016). In fact, many of the noted societal challenges concern this interrelation and the growing tensions between natural environments and prevailing social institutions, artefacts and practices. These natural–social interrelations should be given a more central place in future conceptualizations.

Note

1 For further information see the following three webpages: www.labvantroje.be/, last accessed 1 April 2018; www.leefstraat.be/, last accessed 1 April 2018; www.klimaat.stad.gent/, last accessed 1 April 2018.

References

Albrechts, L. (2010). More of the same is not enough! How could strategic spatial planning be instrumental in dealing with the challenges ahead? *Environment and Planning B: Planning and Design*, 37(6), 1115–1127.

Albrechts, L., & Balducci, A. (2013). Practicing strategic planning: In search of critical features to explain the strategic character of plans. *disP—The Planning Review*, 49(3), 16–27.

Avital, E., & Jablonka, E. (2000). *Animal Traditions: Behavioural Inheritance in Evolution*. Cambridge: Cambridge University Press.

Barber, B. R. (2013). *If Mayors Ruled the World: Dysfunctional Nations, Rising Cities*. New Haven, CT: Yale University Press.

Bertolini, L. (2010). Coping with the Irreducible Uncertainties of Planning: An Evolutionary Approach. In P. Healey & J. Hillier (Eds.), *Ashgate Research Companion To Planning Theory: Conceptual Challenges For Spatial Planning* (pp. 413–424). Aldershot: Ashgate.

Bertolini, L (2012). Integrating mobility and urban development agendas: A manifesto. *disP—The Planning Review*, 188(1), 16–26.

Boelens, L., & De Roo, G. (2016). Planning of undefined becoming: First encounters of planners beyond the plan. *Planning Theory*, 15(1), 42–67.

Bonneuil, C., & Fressoz, J.-B. (2016). *The Shock of the Anthropocene: The Earth, History, and Us*. London/Brooklyn: Verso.

Boussauw, K., & Vanoutrive, T. (2017). Transport policy in Belgium: Translating sustainability discourses into unsustainable outcomes. *Transport Policy*, 53, 11–19.

Bowler, P. J. (1983). *The Eclipse of Darwinism: Anti-Darwinian Evolution Theories in the Decades Around 1900*. Baltimore, MD: Johns Hopkins University Press.

Bowler, P. J. (1988). *The Non-Darwinian Revolution: Reinterpreting a Historical Myth*. Baltimore, MD: Johns Hopkins University Press.

Buehler, R., & Dill, J. (2016). Bikeway networks: A review of effects on cycling. *Transport Reviews*, 36(1), 9–27.

Bulkeley, H., & Castán Broto, V. (2013). Government by experiment? Global cities and the governing of climate change. *Transactions of the Institute of British Geographers*, 38(3), 361–375.

Diamond, J. (2005). *Collapse: How Societies Choose to Fail or Succeed*. New York: Penguin.

Dickins, T. E., & Rahman, Q. (2012). The extended evolutionary synthesis and the role of soft inheritance in evolution. *Proceedings of the Royal Society, B*, 279(1740), 2913–2921.

EPOMM – European Platform on Mobility Management. (2013). *Mobility Management: The Smart Way to Sustainable Mobility in European Countries, Regions and Cities.* Brussels: EPOMM.

Geels, F. W. (2005). Processes and patterns in transitions and system innovations: Refining the co-evolutionary multi-level perspective. *Technological Forecasting & Social Change,* 72(6), 681–696.

Giddens, A. (1984). *The Constitution of Society: Outline of the Theory of Structuration.* Cambridge: Polity Press.

Grin, J., Rotmans, J., & Schot, J. (Eds.). (2010). *Transitions to Sustainable Development: New Directions in the Study of Long-Term Transformative Change.* New York/London: Routledge.

Jablonka, E., & Lamb, M. J. (2014). *Evolution in Four Dimensions: Genetic, Epigenetic, Behavioral, and Symbolic Variation in the History of Life* (Revised ed.). Cambridge/London: The MIT Press.

Jeekel, H. (2013). *The Car-Dependent Society: A European Perspective.* Aldershot: Ashgate.

Laland, K. N., Odling-Smee, J., & Myles, S. (2010). How culture shaped the human genome: Bringing genetics and the human sciences together. *Nature Reviews Genetics,* 11(2), 137–148.

Laland, K., Uller, T., Feldman, M., Sterelny, K., Müller, G. B., Moczek, A., … Strassmann, J. E. (2014). Does evolutionary theory need a rethink? *Nature,* 514(7521), 161–164.

Lovelock, J. (1988). *The Ages of Gaia: A Biography of Our Living Earth.* New York: W.W. Norton & Company.

Mahoney, J. (2000). Path dependence in historical sociology. *Theory and Society,* 29(4), 507–548.

Mehmood, A. (2010). On the history and potentials of evolutionary metaphors in urban planning. *Planning Theory,* 9(1), 63–87.

Mesoudi, A. (2011). *Cultural Evolution: How Darwinian Theory Can Explain Human Culture and Synthesize the Social Sciences.* Chicago, IL: University of Chicago.

Mesoudi, A., Blanchet, S., Charmantier, A., Danchin, E., Fogarty, L., Jablonka, E., … Benoît, B. (2013). Is non-genetic inheritance just a proximate mechanism? A corroboration of the extended evolutionary synthesis. *Biological Theory,* 7(3), 189–195.

Moroni, S. (2010). An evolutionary theory of institutions and a dynamic approach to reform. *Planning Theory,* 9(4), 275–297.

Myers, D. (2001). Introduction. *APA Journal,* 67(4), 365–367.

Newman, P., & Kenworthy, J. (2015). *The End of Automobile Dependence: How Cities Are Moving Beyond Car-Based Planning.* Washington, DC: Island Press.

Odling-Smee, F. J., Laland, K. N., & Feldman, M. W. (2003). *Niche Construction: The Neglected Process in Evolution.* Princeton, NJ: Princeton University Press.

Purcell, M. (2009). Resisting neoliberalization: Communicative planning or counter-hegemonic movements? *Planning Theory,* 8(2), 140–165.

Reckwitz, A. (2002). Toward a theory of social practices: A development in culturalist theorizing. *European Journal of Social Theory,* 5(2), 243–263.

Rip, A., & Kemp, R. (1998). Technological Change. In S. Rayner & E. L. Malone (Eds.), *Human Choice and Climate Change* (pp. 327–399). Columbus, OH: Batelle Press.

Salet, W., Bertolini, L., & Giezen, M. (2013). Complexity and uncertainty: Problem or asset in decision making of mega infrastructure projects? *International Journal of Urban and Regional Research,* 37(6), 1984–2000.

Savini, F., Majoor, S., & Salet, W. (2015). Dilemmas of planning: Intervention, regulation, and investment. *Planning Theory,* 14(3), 296–315.

Schot, J. (1998). The usefulness of evolutionary models for explaining innovation: The case of the Netherlands in the nineteenth century. *History and Technology,* 14(3), 173–200.

Scott, J. C. (1998). *Seeing Like a State: How Certain Schemes to Improve the Human Condition Have Failed.* New Haven, CT: Yale University Press.

Shove, E., & Walker, G. (2010). Governing transitions in the sustainability of everyday life. *Research Policy,* 39(4), 471–476.

Solnit, R. (2016). *Hope in the Dark Untold Histories, Wild Possibilities* (updated ed.). Chicago, IL: Haymarket Books.

Urry, J. (2004). The 'system' of automobility. *Theory Culture & Society,* 21(4–5), 25–39.

Watson, M. (2012). How theories of practice can inform transition to a decarbonised transport system. *Journal of Transport Geography,* 24, 488–496.

11
LEARNING AND GOVERNANCE CULTURE IN PLANNING PRACTICE
The Case of Otaniemi

Raine Mäntysalo, Kaisa Schmidt-Thomé & Simo Syrman[1]

Introduction

This chapter sets off by discussing the relationship between pragmatism and planning research from the perspective of the broad scientific tradition of *Organization Development*. This tradition has applied systems-theoretical views on the development of organizations (Friedmann, 1987, pp. 56–57). Organization Development is a spin-off of *Scientific Management*, which developed after 1945 mainly to serve large private corporations. Chris Argyris, Donald Schön, Peter Senge, Ikujirō Nonaka and Hirotaka Takeuchi, and others, moved the field gradually away from profit as the sole criterion of management, and brought forth humanistic values and the motive of psychological self-development (Friedmann, 1987, pp. 56–57). American pragmatism (James, Peirce, Dewey, Mead) has had a strong influence on Organization Development, and it has provided a specific flavour to the latter's systems-theoretical approach.

In line with pragmatism, the Organization Development tradition works with a process concept of knowledge: knowledge is not seen as pre-existing in libraries, agency documents, computer files, or in the expert's 'head'; it is rather *designed* by small task-oriented groups of both experts and clients. Knowledge is the product of a *social learning process*, bringing mutual understanding of a problematic situation and providing, at the same time, means to alter that situation. Knowledge is bound to specific real-life contexts and problems and goals that are relevant in those contexts. What is generalizable is not knowledge itself, but the collective learning processes that generate knowledge. The research interest is thus on advancing organizations as *learning systems*.

When applied to the field of planning and its organizations, we argue that this theoretical tradition needs further development, in order to grasp the learning challenges of planning practices that are posed by long-standing dilemmas in governance culture. Such dilemmas are often connected to institutional conditions that frame individual planning tasks. While, following pragmatism, the focus in the Organization Development tradition has been on learning to cope with individual problem situations; it has failed to identify dilemmas that may have developed in the governance culture over a long period of time, framing the reflectivity on individual problem situations in counterproductive ways. Such dilemmas concern, for example, institutional ambiguity and the related lack of institutional trust. By drawing on Gregory Bateson's learning theory and organizational learning theories that have applied it, we aim to offer theoretical insights on learning in planning, in the face of such dilemmas.

This theoretical approach relates interestingly to the dialectic between pragmatism and institutionalism outlined by Willem Salet in Chapter 1 in this volume. Salet suggests a 'normative double strategy' for planning research that would integrate reflectively both perspectives: the pragmatist purposiveness of situated planning action, and the institutionalist consideration of the norms and rules that guarantee the legitimacy and validity of this action, in view of roles taken, authority claimed and commitments made. In turn, the Batesonian systemic view challenges this set-up of alternating between two mutually incompatible theoretical perspectives. The Batesonian approach to learning incorporates both lower levels of learning corresponding to pragmatist 'reflection-in-action' (see Schön, 1983) and a higher level of learning addressing institutionalist reflection, integrating all these levels in a single systemic view of learning.

As an example to illustrate our theoretical discussion, we will examine a recent participatory urban planning process in the district of Otaniemi, in the city of Espoo, Finland. We will begin our account by introducing the Batesonian learning theory in relation to the learning system approach to planning. Next we will present the Otaniemi case, and then proceed to analyse the development of the Otaniemi planning process with different incidents of learning and related challenges and opportunities. In our analysis, we will connect our observations of learning at different levels to a theoretical discussion on the concept of the *trading zone* and the dialectics between ambiguity and uncertainty, input and output legitimacy, government and governance and institutional and interpersonal trust. In the final part of the chapter, we will draw conclusions on the implications and relevance of our theoretical argument to the Organization Development and social learning discourses in planning research and to the pragmatism/institutionalism dialectic of this book. Situated reflectivity needs to be combined with institutional reflectivity when dealing with long-standing dilemmas in planning practice, but our claim is that this combination can be achieved within a single theoretical framework.

The Three Levels of Learning

A widely applied model of learning system is provided by Chris Argyris and Donald Schön (1978). It is based on the idea of the learning system as a self-corrective cybernetic system that is able to redirect its actions on the reception of feedback of its former actions, thus reacting to unexpected consequences. In the simplest case, such self-corrective learning proceeds through *single-loop learning* that corresponds with a 'trial-and-error' type of learning: if *this* action is found not to produce the intended consequences, then *that* action is tried, and repeated until the intended consequences are hopefully achieved. Single-loop learning is problem-solving within the context of a given habit or technical practice. In Argyris and Schön's terms, there is a given set of *governing variables* that determines the identification of the problem and the available choices for its resolution.

However, not all problems can be resolved by relying on existing habitual approaches, but require 'thinking out of the box'. Argyris and Schön's *double-loop learning* represents this type of 'higher' learning. Double-loop learning occurs when mismatches are corrected by first examining and altering the 'governing variables', or prevailing contextual assumptions that determine the approach to the problem, and then the actions (see Figure 11.1). Double-loop learning is *learning to learn* in the sense of learning a new approach to solving problems, when the former approach is found to be unsatisfactory.

Learning and Governance Culture

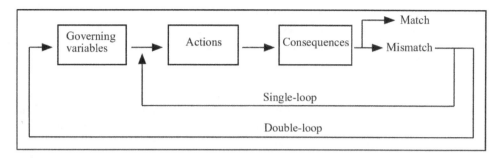

Figure 11.1 Argyris and Schön's cybernetic model of single-loop and double-loop learning
Source: Argyris and Schön (1978)

Argyris and Schön's theory of single- and double-loop learning was largely based on Gregory Bateson's learning theory, in which Bateson identified two levels of learning: *proto-learning* and *deutero-learning* (Bateson, 1972/1987, pp. 166–167, pp. 292–293). It was also related to John Dewey's (1910/1960) distinction between *empirical learning* and *experimental learning* (see also Engeström, 1995, pp. 82–84). However, Bateson later systematized his learning theory (Bateson, 1972/1987) and added a *third* level of learning – *Learning III* – which Argyris and Schön's theory does not address, not at least in its full extent (Engeström, 1995, p. 86).

A key concept in understanding Bateson's Learning III is his concept of *double bind*. The concept stems from Bateson's theory of schizophrenia (Bateson, 1972/1987). According to Bateson, a double-bind situation occurs:

- when *two orders of messages* – messages conveyed through actions and messages explaining these actions – are being communicated in the same self-explaining activity;
- the messages are *mutually contradictory*;
- the actor is unable to comment on the orders of messages being communicated, to correct his/her discrimination of what order of message to respond to (Bateson, 1972/1987, pp. 206–209).

In planning, a double-bind situation may occur, for example, when planning activity that is not really strategic is self-explained in planning communication as such, and the actors involved are not provided with proper means to grasp this self-contradiction. While bringing action into self-contradiction, the double-bind situation inhibits reflective learning on this self-contradiction. Ad hoc and incremental planning is repeatedly, even ritually, confirmed to be strategic. A discordance between single-loop and double-loop learning is generated. In a double-bind situation, no changes in actions and their governing variables seem to help in the face of recurring mismatches (Bateson, 1972/1987, p. 302). Yet again an unexpected and disturbing planning decision has been made while (allegedly) following the strategy. One is faced with problems, each of which appears to be so specific that no general lessons on how to deal with them can be drawn. Each new problem is as difficult to solve as were the former ones. In a double-bind situation, learning acts follow one another, but no improvement in terms of capability building takes place. In such conditions, the learning system has developed pathological routines for addressing problems that no longer enhance its learning but seem to lead to unexpected situations and deviating phenomena over and over again. In his later work, Argyris described such pathological behaviour in organizations by using the terms "skilled incompetence" and "defensive routines" (Argyris, 1993; see also Hytönen et al., 2016; Mäntysalo et al., 2011b).

The planning organization becomes skilled in routinely practising self-contradictory strategic planning and develops defensive routines to prohibit reflectivity on these self-contradictions. Bent Flyvbjerg's (1998) famous Aalborg case is a good example.

The most difficult problems for the learning system – the double-bind situations – are not posed by the unexpectedly behaving 'outer' environment in problem situations, but by the *pathological way* the learning system has *learned* to approach its environment, through double-loop learning (Mäntysalo, 2000; see also Schmidt-Thomé & Mäntysalo, 2014). Being focused on individual problem situations, Argyris and Schön's theory of single- and double-loop learning does not adequately describe how organizations should deal with their cultural pathologies (Engeström, 1995, p. 86). While growing initially from immediate problem situations, the cultural pathologies are a consequence of a long historical process of contradictory handlings and aspirations. In order to deal with its pathologies, the political-administrative system of an organization needs the capability to reflect on its *own governance culture*, including its institutional path dependencies. Such a capability is provided by the kind of learning that reaches Learning III.[2] It involves grasping reflectively the forces and causalities that more or less together constitute the pathologies of practice behind the regular management of affairs within the organization.

These insights are refined in Yrjö Engeström's theory of organizational learning that is based, in part, on Bateson's theory of three learning levels (Engeström, 1987). In broader terms, Engeström's theory builds on the *Cultural-Historical Activity Theory* (CHAT) – a theoretical framework that Engeström himself helped to develop. It is closely related to American pragmatism, despite drawing on the work of Soviet(!) psychologists, Lev Vygotsky and A N Leontyev (Engeström, 1995). A central difference, however, is CHAT's approach to social practice as a collective activity system, the nature of which cannot be understood without a historical perspective to the trajectories behind current practice, with its social, psychological, cultural and institutional dimensions (see Leontyev, 1981). This extension of perspective provided by CHAT in relation to pragmatism challenges the pragmatism/institutionalism dialectic discussed in this book. How should we proceed from acknowledging the insufficiency of the pragmatist approach? Should we complement it with the uneasily matching institutionalist approach, or could CHAT provide a broader framework incorporating the necessary considerations of both approaches?

Otaniemi Case

Otaniemi is a peninsular district in the city of Espoo, Finland, roughly 7 km west of the city centre of Helsinki, the capital of Finland. The history and built environment of Otaniemi is closely related to Aalto University (until 2010 Helsinki University of Technology), whose campus and student community has been developed gradually since the 1940s in the previously rural peninsula. Today, the Otaniemi district has around 4,000 residents, most of them students. However, the daily population of Otaniemi is far greater with 14,000 students and 11,000 employees. The low-density campus structure, with lots of open space and buildings with cultural-historical value, is based on the plan by Alvar Aalto. Most of the land is owned by the real estate companies of the university and the Government of Finland. The planning of Otaniemi by the City of Espoo has been done as a part of wider Southern Espoo partial master plan with small-scale detailed plans inside the campus area. However, with the university relocating activities from its two Helsinki campuses to Otaniemi, the western metro line being under construction and general pressure for urban intensification, the need for a more strategic land use vision for the whole Otaniemi area has been increasingly acknowledged by the City of Espoo.

The current planning debate in Otaniemi has its origins in the plan of the new building for two of the Schools of Aalto University, which is also connected to the new metro station and forms the nucleus of the intensified campus. The architectural competition for the building and its immediate surroundings was followed by a process of detailed planning, which gave the two main landowners, the university's real estate company Aalto University Properties Ltd and the state-owned Senate Properties, an opportunity to envisage an even wider area of development in Otaniemi. The landowners prepared a strategic land use vision for the Otaniemi district, thus taking the role of the initiator in the planning process, ahead of the City of Espoo. The vision was labelled *Kokokuva* ('The whole picture') as it provided an overview and touched upon a number of themes from land use restrictions to innovation promotion and opportunities to introduce mixed-use development. However, it also promoted vast new development, clearly in the economic interest of the landowners. The landowners' scheme was prepared by an architectural bureau, A-Konsultit, which has been involved in the planning of Otaniemi on behalf of the landowners for more than 20 years.

The publication of the Kokokuva vision in spring 2014 caused protest among the local students and other residents. The opposing groups did not settle for a conventional reactive role in the process but started to prepare alternative plans for the area. The City of Espoo, now confronted with competing visions outside the legitimate planning system, asked the researchers of Aalto University to help in facilitating the planning discussions between the stakeholders. The chosen facilitators of the *Otaniemi OK* process, as it was named, represent the Aalto University Built Environment Lab,[3] which is a project and a room equipped with immersive virtual reality technology and visualization equipment, located in the premises of Urban Mill[4] in the Aalto University campus. The Aalto Built Environment Lab was established in order to bring the different stakeholders involved in urban development together in a space, which could also be characterized as a 'decision theatre'. Facilitating Otaniemi OK is one of the Aalto Built Environment Lab's pilot studies.[5]

Between December 2014 and November 2015 there were three meetings that count as Otaniemi OK gatherings. They all took place in the premises of Aalto Built Environment Lab, which represents a rather neutral ground from the perspective of most stakeholders. It is also located within the area currently under scrutiny, making it easily accessible for all stakeholder groups. The Aalto Built Environment Lab personnel documented the discussions in the meetings and made the memos and other background material available to the participants of the meetings. We took part in the sessions in terms of participatory observation and had access to the detailed transcripts of the sessions.

The first meeting, in December 2014, was planned as a joint fact-finding session. The facilitators had collected a large amount of information on the different aspects that would have to be taken into account in planning the area. These pieces of information on actual conditions and future trends followed the list of planning principles agreed upon by the City Planning Board of Espoo.[6] The information was meant to support the situation awareness of the participants – and to find out whether the stakeholders could identify a common 'operating environment', to have a shared understanding of the present conditions and issues in Otaniemi, while orienting the design towards the future. The different stakeholders were also asked to present their visions and ideas about Otaniemi's desired future. There was also some time for general discussion and agreeing on the next steps.

The second meeting, in April 2015, started with a summary of the first meeting discussions, followed by general reflections and a discussion on the role of Kokokuva. Next, there was a substance-related discussion on whether there should be a new housing development targeted at 'outsiders' – people who neither study nor work in Otaniemi. Then the facilitators gave

Figure 11.2 The student union representative presenting the locations of student housing and private housing in the Otakaari area in their alternative scheme, in the second Otaniemi OK meeting
Source: Photo taken by Maria Viitanen

their presentations. They had worked out a joint visualization of the stakeholders' visions, in order to identify focus areas for new development that seemed the least controversial. Then one of the 'unproblematic' focus areas was examined under closer scrutiny, as the students' representative gave a presentation on the Otakaari area. One of the most surprising moments of the meeting was the statement by a representative of one of the two major landowners, Aalto University Properties Ltd. He mentioned that there was a lot of empty office/laboratory space within the campus area and suggested that demolishing some of these (impractical/outdated) buildings, and thus allowing more flexibility for new development, would be an option worthy of examination.

The third meeting was held in late November, 2015. As stated by the main facilitator at the end of the previous meeting, the intention was to report back on how the discussions on each focus area had proceeded and to continue the discussion on the planning approach. The degree of formality of planning – whether or not a statutory land use plan was needed for the whole district – had opened for discussion towards the end of the second meeting. In the third meeting, the City of Espoo seemed to be willing to provide its own answer to this question and suggested the preparation of an unofficial *zoning framework* ('kaavarunko') for the Otaniemi district. A part of the session was then allocated to related group discussions about gathering material for this flexible and informal strategic document. Instead of returning to the focus areas identified by the facilitators in the second session, this session included short updates from the perspective of each stakeholder. The facilitators also presented their considerations about the different zones and routes, as well as green corridors, within the area.

Three stakeholder groups had elaborated their visions of future Otaniemi by the time of the first meeting. In addition to the Kokokuva of the landowners, both residents and students had prepared their statements. In order to narrow down the technical head start of the planning professionals, the students and residents had been assisted by the Aalto Built Environment Lab personnel in visualizing their planning schemes in the first meeting.

The *residents' vision* for the area was very plain, underlining the key priorities which are few. In their view, the open shoreline should be developed as a recreation zone and as an important section of Rantaraitti (Shore route[7]), which the City of Espoo has been upgrading during the past two decades. The residents did not make many statements about the development of other areas outside of their spatially concentrated area of dwelling and its immediate surroundings. They held that the future of Otaniemi should be steered by the needs of the university. Other major developments were not welcomed as they would allegedly endanger the natural and cultural heritage of the area. However, the residents' hope of Otaniemi not becoming too attractive for development stood in slight contrast with their wish to retain some services at the old shopping mall instead of losing them to the more distant metro station area.

The *student activists' scheme*, representing the official student union point of view, was geographically more substantive than the residents' version. The main agenda of the students was to increase the amount of student housing in the Otaniemi area. In addition, the students also welcomed other residents. Whereas new student housing would be built in a manner that fosters the student community, other housing projects could be targeted at residents seeking peaceful but well-connected areas. The students proposed four areas for new development, none of which stood in strong contrast to the residents' scheme.

The vision prepared by *Aalto University* was still under preparation at the time of the second meeting. This fourth vision started to emerge as Aalto University assigned one vice president post to campus development issues. In the second meeting, the vice president shared some information on the planned projects within the campus area, but referred to the third meeting as a possible occasion to tell more about Aalto's intentions. By the time of the third meeting, things had changed considerably as Aalto University's real estate services had been reorganized. The university's real estate company heightened its profile in the Otaniemi planning debate, leaving the state-owned Senate Properties, the other major landowner in the area, somewhat alone with the Kokokuva process. By the time of the third meeting, the university's real estate company was already in the position to talk about concrete projects instead of presenting a vision only. As a proactive stakeholder operating in the core areas of Otaniemi, it seemed to have an edge over the less central and less agile stakeholders. However, this also made the position of the university's real estate company somewhat more unpredictable when compared to the previous agendas of the Kokokuva alliance.

Prior to the meetings, the City of Espoo had complied with its tradition to give landowners ample room for manoeuvre in initiating and proposing new developments (see Maisala, 2008; Mäntysalo et al., 2016). In the case of Kokokuva, there was even some confusion about the 'ownership' of the vision. The landowners proposed the Kokokuva scheme; the City of Espoo welcomed it and started to call the planning process by the same name. The Kokokuva materials were kept in the same material bank with the material produced by the City, and the intention was to add further material there along the way. One could say that the City backed the landowners' strong first move. As the chief city planning official said in the second meeting, "Espoo is only a passenger in the [Otaniemi OK] process", they could have equally said the same about the Kokokuva process, at least at the point of mounting that train in 2014. This kind of passive reactivity to landowner and developer initiatives is not a standard approach in land use planning in Finland, especially in cities, where the local authorities often utilize their considerably strong power granted by the statutes. Later on in the process, the City of Espoo changed its track: it took a step back, leaving the landowners alone in their windy pole position and searched for a new round of discussions, albeit indirectly, with the help of facilitators.

There are a number of commonalities in the visions presented by the different stakeholders. Every party endorsed built heritage and natural environment values. Every scheme acknowledged the need for intensification, new housing and services. Even the residents, being the most critical of intensification and new housing, did not rule that option out but rather expressed doubts about the attractiveness of the area for people other than students and university employees.

In terms of discrepancies, one can say that the closer to the shoreline the focus moves, the more the land use schemes start to diverge from each other. The residents defended strongly the existing coastal area arrangements and opposed housing in the vicinity of their apartments, which currently have an open access to the shoreline and views to the sea. The sites where the students' scheme hoped to see more student life, at the boat harbour area and beyond, were not seen as a threat to the residents' aims. The landowners' proposal, in turn, with a considerable amount of new development, including landfills in the bay area, was clearly the strongest source of discontent for the residents, making that shore the most crucial zone in terms of conflict potential.

Overall, however, there were surprisingly few major disputes between the stakeholder groups. In addition to the shoreline discrepancy between the residents and landowners, another issue of some controversy was the residents' reluctance towards new non-student housing. But, as the facilitators brought up in the third meeting, no one seemed to oppose general development in the western fringe towards the Tapiola district. However, this was minor comfort as the more pivotal central and coastal areas were more problematic. For instance, in the zone around the core university campus area, the built heritage and landscape protection legislation sets strict limits, and in the forest-dominated student village, the habitat questions (e.g. the protected flying squirrel and old forest sections) bring in a number of restrictions.

We have identified a number of turning points – or critical thresholds – in this process as a learning system. We may not be in the position to say on which side of the threshold the process currently stands, but we can ponder the implications each position would have. Next, we will elaborate the occasions and challenges of learning in the Otaniemi OK process, in connection with our theoretical discussion of local governance and planning as a learning system – a system that, on the one hand, has to deal with contemporary challenges of institutional ambiguity and questioning of legitimacy and trust, and, on the other hand, has the capability to utilize new facilities and tools of boundary-crossing planning communication.

The Generation of Trading Zones as Double-Loop Learning in the Otaniemi Case

In the Otaniemi case, the incidents of double-loop learning emerged with the facilitation of planning negotiations and with the City of Espoo starting to reclaim its own planning stance against the traditional reliance on developers. Interestingly, this happened indirectly, by allowing a third party to facilitate the negotiations. The governing variables were reworked or at least adjusted through 'inter-cultural' communication that emerged through planning facilitation. This was enabled by the use of the Aalto Built Environment Lab facilities and personnel for the facilitation of planning negotiations between the different stakeholders – that turned out to be exceptionally astute and resourceful in devising their own alternative planning proposals to back up their arguments. An associated incident of double-loop learning was the realization by the City of Espoo that in the Otaniemi case it had gone too far in its reliance on landowner-oriented planning, to the extent that it had become difficult to discern the City's own planning documentation and related aims from those of the two major landowner-developers. In part, the Otaniemi OK process was launched in December 2014 to clarify this issue.

The Aalto Built Environment Lab is a specifically equipped meeting room utilizing immersive virtual reality and visualization technology, to enable richer and more easily perceptible visualization of plans and analyses regarding urban development in Espoo, especially Otaniemi, where the Aalto Built Environment Lab is located. In the Otaniemi OK process, it enabled more even and contributory planning discussions across different stakeholder groups, as the stakeholders were relatively equally equipped, with the help of the Aalto Built Environment Lab personnel, to present and visualize their own alternative plans.

The Aalto Built Environment Lab provided a kind of *trading zone* platform for the different stakeholders in their scheming and debating the future planning of Otaniemi. The concept of a trading zone was coined by Peter Galison. In his ground-breaking study (1997), Galison examined the interaction between theorists, experimentalists and instrumentalists in particle physics, conceiving each as a subculture of its own. Galison identified local "infrastructures" of shared concepts, laboratory equipment and spatial settings that had facilitated exchange of information and services between the different 'social worlds' of particle physics. These infrastructures had functioned as platforms for the generation of localized "exchange languages". Such exchange languages had enabled the mutual "out-talk" between members of different sub-cultures, transforming highly elaborate and complicated issues into "thin descriptions". As boundary-crossing communication platforms, trading zones *evolve* and may go through different developmental stages, such as evolving from scientific jargon to 'pidgin' and further to 'creole', a living hybrid interlanguage of science, such as nanotechnology and biochemistry (see Galison, 2010).

Mäntysalo et al., (2011a; see also Balducci & Mäntysalo, 2013) have outlined the so-called *trading zone approach* as a potential method for dealing with complex urban planning problems with multiple stakeholders. Leino (2008, 2012) has further studied the organizational aspects of participatory planning as *boundary work*. In the field of Sociological Studies of Science different kinds of cooperative constellations have been identified to emerge as facilitators of knowledge transfer between research, politics and business. Some may be quite fixed 'boundary organizations' (Guston, 1999), while others may be 'hybrids' that may change their form rapidly (Miller, 2001). In urban planning we have witnessed the recent emergence of different *'urban living labs'* (see Wallin & Staffans, 2015; Wallin et al., 2016) that may be perceived as some kind of hybrid platforms in managing boundary work in urban planning and development. The Aalto Built Environment Lab in Otaniemi provides an example (Mäntysalo, 2016).

The generation of a boundary-crossing platform with trading zone characteristics indicates double-loop learning, when it provides a resolution to communication problems between culturally and linguistically differentiated groups. When the stakeholders are not able to convey their ideas and views on the planning issue to each other, they are faced with the need to rework the 'governing variables' of their communication. The generation of the trading zone is such reworking as it changes the situation from the "muted coexistence" of differentiated and exclusive languages to having a joint platform for mutual out-talk.

In this sense, the use of the Aalto Built Environment Lab in the Otaniemi OK process represents a case of double-loop learning, as it changed the governing variables of planning and policy communication and introduced new means for 'inter-cultural' communication. In the Aalto Built Environment Lab environment it was possible for the stakeholders to prepare themselves for the meetings together with the staff and to engage in the discussions as equally recognized partners. The juxtaposition between 'the Plan' and its opponents – which is very common in events of alleged participatory planning – could be alleviated with 'inter-cultural' communication emerging through the process. The governing variables were at least adjusted if not fully reworked. In our view, this was illustrated, for instance, by the residents' courage to make a major move in the second meeting. They stated that they would refrain from opposing the plans on the condition that the piece of Rantaraitti (Shore route) adjacent to their housing area was left untouched. Also the students chose a proactive stance through their engagement with the Otakaari area.

Actually it seemed that the residents and students used the available 'political space' in a more efficient manner than the landowners did, indicating their double-loop learning. The landowners lost their head start as they visualized 'too many' details but in an ambivalent way. They did not spell out their own interests as clearly as the others but went 'hiding' behind the overview that was supposedly providing all necessary tools for the development of the area. In a certain sense, the mere presence of the landowners in the Otaniemi OK meetings seemed to imply that no single stakeholder could impose its plan for the area.

The immediacy of the planning discussions played an interesting role in the process. Bringing people into a joint space meant that the stakeholders were confronted with each other as individuals. It was clear that some felt comfortable during confrontational situations, but others preferred to ease the pressure somewhat by retreating from their original position or by opening up completely new discussions. We do not know whether the residents' decision to present their 'ultimatum' had been previously decided or had emerged spontaneously in the meeting, but the latter seemed to hold true for the Aalto University real estate company representative coming up with the demolition card. Considering that this statement was made by a partner of the Kokokuva process, such a sudden statement might have been unwelcome news for the state-owned Senate Properties, as questioning the need for new office space somewhat equalled pulling the rug from under their feet.

Uncertainty and Ambiguity

Communication problems can become crucial obstacles when there would otherwise be potential for political agreement on planning and governance goals between the stakeholders. However, when there is deep political disagreement, it can hardly be resolved by enabling better mutual communication on the disagreement (see Kanninen et al., 2013). Using John Forester's (1993) categorization, communication problems can be seen to belong to the *technical dimension* of planning problems. In broader terms, the technical dimension refers to the lack of information of the planned object in its present and some future state, and the lack of time, resources and cognitive and organizational capabilities for the rational programming of planning work. These are problems of *uncertainty*. Communication problems, too, are problems of uncertainty, and they call for a sort of technical reworking of 'syntax and semantics', so that the stakeholders can be more certain on what each means by different proposals and documents.

But, according to Forester (1993), there is also the *political dimension* that concerns the *legitimacy* of the ends and means of planning. Legitimacy is the moral justification of an entity in wielding political power (Buchanan, 2002, pp. 689–690). In a democracy, the authority of public planning rests on legitimacy (Sager, 2013, p. 3). Rather than focusing on individual planning processes and decisions, legitimacy, as a concept, addresses the institutional level of the political-administrative system itself. As noted by Sager (2013, p. 8), legitimacy is mainly addressed to sources of political authority: the governments, institutions and regimes making political decisions. Problems of legitimacy in planning have to do with *political ambiguity*, according to Forester (1993). Whereas uncertainty rather concerns questions about the current *object* of planning, ambiguity has to do with more general questions on *who* gets to define the planning object and decide upon it in the first place, with what jurisdiction and on what terms, and who else should be involved in the process.

A distinction has also been made between *input legitimacy* and *output legitimacy* (Scharpf, 1999; see also Mäntysalo & Saglie, 2010). While input legitimacy focuses on the general acceptability of political processes, output legitimacy focuses on the acceptability of the outcomes of specific political decisions and policies. Whereas the former is concerned with the democratic quality of decision-making processes, the latter is concerned with the effective achievement of common good in implementing the decisions made. Input legitimacy is thus more focused on the general institutional justification of governance provided by adherence to norms and rules, while output legitimacy is more focused on pragmatic justification brought by reference to specific planning outcomes. Output legitimacy has become more emphasized in the ongoing transformation of governance culture in the public sector, often referred to as change from government to (network) governance (e.g. Pollitt & Bouckaert, 2011; Rosenau, 1992). Bang and Esmark (2009) even argue that the new conditions of globalized and networked society require a reorientation from politics-centred (input) to policy-centred (output) public governance. Following Castells, they emphasize the forward mapping of policy risks and challenges, rather than backward mapping of how conflicting interests and identities acquire free and equal access to, and recognition in, democratic politics (Bang & Esmark, 2009, pp. 16–17).

However, regarding change from government to governance, it is important not to overlook the institutional path dependency of 'government' in the legislative system and governance culture (see Mahoney, 2000; North, 1990; Pierson, 2000). With such persistence of 'government', the governance reform may only lead to shallow changes and may thus become a source of various sorts of ambiguities in politico-administrative processes. A complex reality of governing may result in which different understandings of the determinants of legitimate conduct, due policy process, and the professional identities and roles of different actors coexist and compete with one another. Embedded in the institutionalized structures and normative prescriptions of 'good governance', the deep-seated regulative model of planning and the associated model of representative democracy are still holding fast, framing what is possible or even conceivable. Government actors are still central agents in public governance networks and they have their own 'institutional baggage' with them when operating in governance networks. The given roles, legal duties and formal authority relations, between the political decision-makers, public administrators and non-government actors, are carved deep into these institutional structures, and these inscriptions can be very difficult to overwrite with the new governance ideas.

Moreover, the institutional level is not to be considered as a mere hindrance to governance reforms, but as a necessary provider of continuity in such reforms. In the form of legally based normative rules or norms it enables action in conditions of uncertainty. The normative rules establish the codes of behaviour that enable people to orientate to each other with expectations of mutual reliability (see Salet, Chapter 1, in this volume; Van Rijswick & Salet, 2012). On such orientations the governance networks ultimately rest, too.

With the coexistence of different governance perspectives (government *and* governance), the issue of political ambiguity enters the level of governance cultures and institutions, beyond individual planning problems. This level of political ambiguity is grasped by Maarten Hajer's concept of *institutional ambiguity* (Hajer, 2003, 2006, 2009). Hajer has coined the concept to describe the emergence of 'new political spaces' that challenge the existing classical-modernist and nation-state-based political institutions. The globalization of markets and the associated dependence of localities on (global) investments, as well as digitalization, providing new opportunities for active citizenship and entrepreneurship, put pressure on local governments to develop more proactive and networked forms of governance. Instead of approaching the private sector and civil actors merely as actors to be regulated, they are also increasingly perceived as partners in (co-productive) governance – as economic growth, the basis of welfarist redistribution, is no longer self-evident, but needs to be actively fostered by the public sector, to enable its own redistributive performance. In Europe, the EU encourages this development.

Hajer's concept of institutional ambiguity suggests that we are not actually dealing with a historical shift from one mode of governance to another, but rather with *hybridization of governance*. The classical-modernist political institutions, embodying the idea of nation-state, continue to provide the necessary legal-administrative mechanisms for the legitimacy of political decisions and the related use of public power, although the realm of politics (and public administration as well) has had to stretch beyond these institutional boundaries to reach the 'new political spaces' and utilize them. Hajer's own examples of such new political spaces mostly deal with civil society development that has given rise to political movements and pressure groups that transcend institutional and national boundaries, such as Greenpeace and the Occupy movement. Such political activism challenges the existing political institutions both at the local and the national level, often simultaneously.

So, the political institutions are challenged both by their economic dependence on private (global) investments and the emergence of (glocal) civil society movements. While the two forces pull the political institutions in different directions (success in global economic competition, open and inclusive political processes), they cannot rid themselves from their own legitimacy-guaranteeing institutionalized operations. Especially, when the interests of economic competitiveness and opening up of political processes are in conflict, the procedures of the existing political institutions are needed to settle the conflict in a legitimate manner.

In our view, the hybridization of governance poses a challenge that cannot be settled once and for all with a certain model; instead it requires governance that would reach the capability of continuous reflectivity. This calls for learning that would reach even beyond the level of double-loop learning.

Learning III in the Otaniemi Case

In the Otaniemi OK process, we identified (the potential for) Learning III at least on three occasions. The first occasion was associated with the decision to launch the Otaniemi OK process in the first place. The landowner-oriented planning that Espoo has traditionally relied on seemed to have gone too far as it had become difficult to discern the City's own planning documentation and related aims from the scheme of the two major landowner-developers. Had the City of Espoo not realized this in time and had the landowner-developers taken major steps towards binding plans, we might have seen both major confusion and conflicts. But the stakeholders trusted that a joint forum would make a difference. The residents and students expected true opportunities for involvement, instead of being put to a position of hearing about plans that had already been fixed.

The second occasion showing potential for Learning III is associated with the City of Espoo admitting that it cannot handle the ambiguous situation on its own. As it decided to test a new approach in Otaniemi and resorted to facilitators, its capability to act increased, albeit indirectly. The researchers acted as facilitators in the process, which helped to broaden the basic setting of the planning process. The question was no longer about whether to utilize Kokokuva as the starting point of both the City and the landowners but rather about having multiple perspectives that do not need to be mutually exclusive. Now that the discussion around Otaniemi planning was more participatory, it could also better cope with the fact that the City of Espoo was no single actor but an organization with many interfaces with Otaniemi.

The third occasion where Learning III was emerging related to the question of how to proceed forward from the second meeting. The proposal put forward by the Aalto Built Environment Lab staff was to gather small groups to discuss the chosen focus areas and to come together again in the third meeting with related findings. The residents did not accept this but called for a clear definition of the sub-areas and land uses that are to be preserved from development. They requested an overall plan to set the limits of development for the whole district. Thereby they wanted to avoid an indefinite setting of having in the future successive piecemeal detailed land use plans that would gradually extend to the areas they wanted to protect. This statement reflected their lack of trust towards the City and the landowners. The comfort zone provided by the Otaniemi OK process was too informal from the perspective of the residents. We will now turn to the concept of trust and its implications for Learning III.

Interpersonal and Institutional Trust

In our view, coping with institutional ambiguity and hybridization of governance requires from the local political-administrative system the capability of reaching Learning III. Failing in this could lead to a loss of *trust* in local governance. For a political-administrative system, a loss of trust implies a double-bind situation when it reaches the institutional level of the system itself. Then the legitimacy of the system is in question. This is an existential question for the political-administrative system, since, as noted by Bang and Esmark, "[t]he fact of political community is that political authorities could not make and implement authoritative decisions unless laypeople would accept and recognize themselves as bound by them" (Bang & Esmark, 2009, p. 20). Such system-level trust can be called *institutional trust*.

Institutional trust is a category of trust that is far less known than trust between persons, and even its very existence has been debated among scholars.[8] The most familiar type of trust is *interpersonal trust*. It denotes a relationship between the truster and the trustee, in which the truster relies on the trustee to fulfil his/her expectations in the future, and the trustee is aware of the truster's reliance on him/her, which makes their relationship reciprocal. (e.g. Offe, 1999; Patterson, 1999; Sztompka, 1999). According to Laurian, interpersonal trust addresses "the extent to which we rely on the signs of trustworthiness in others" (Laurian, 2009, p. 371). Thus the focus is "on factors involved in creating trust: how past interactions and reputation shape perceptions of the trustee's benevolent motivations, credibility, competence, objectivity, consistency and procedural fairness" (Laurian, 2009, p. 371).

Yet, according to Offe (1999), many of the problems of social coordination in our complex societies call for the kind of trust that is not interpersonal and reciprocal but between "me" and "everyone else", without a personal dimension. With institutional trust, large-scale social institutions can also be built. Trusting an institution, instead of one's neighbour, means in Offe's (1999) view that one has sufficient understanding of the 'basic idea' or 'good' of the institution, acknowledges it and is thereby motivated to obey the institution's rules. "Knowing the repertoire of meaning and justification that is being generated by institutions allows 'me', the participant observer, to determine the measure of trust I can extend to those who, although strangers, are still co-residents within an institutional regime and whose patterns of behavior 'I' have reasons to expect to be shaped and informed by the evident meaning that is inherent in an institution" (Offe, 1999, p. 71).

According to Laurian, institutional trust "protects social order and institutions and is essential to the stability of social systems. It is a condition for stable rules of exchange and claims to rights and justice. It is also necessary for the legitimacy of systems that allocate power, prestige and wealth, define the public good and regulate the distribution of public goods. When institutional trust fails, social crises erupt" (Laurian, 2009, p. 372). According to Laurian (2009), institutional trust is also essential for political freedom, as without it we would be doomed to prisoner's dilemma-type calculations in our interactions. In international comparison, the institutional trust dimension is relatively strong in Finnish public governance (see Hytönen, 2016; Puustinen et al., 2017).

However, interpersonal trust is essential, too, as institutional and interpersonal trust are dynamically intertwined. As representatives or gatekeepers of their institutions, the public administrators (e.g. planners) affect institutional trust through gaining or losing trust at the personal level in their everyday work (Sztompka, 1999, p. 48). According to Warren, "Institutions work well when they take into account the 'thick' context of interpersonal relations, habits, and customs that determine the meanings and associated expectations of formal rules" (Warren, 1999, p. 15). The pragmatist approach tends to overlook institutional trust, while the institutionalist approach accordingly tends to dismiss interpersonal trust. But the dichotomy of these approaches needs to be transgressed, since both dimensions of trust are systemically interdependent. Hence, the issue is not about which category of trust to choose, but how to nurture both of them in order to improve the performance capability of local urban governance. The gradual building of interpersonal trust reproduces institutional trust, which, in turn, equips the local planners and politicians as 'trustees'. Laurian stresses the importance of 'facework': "Since public trust in a system is strongly affected by citizens' experiences at access points, planners are in a position to build public trust in local land management and development processes through their facework" (Laurian, 2009, p. 373). Managing both dimensions of trust, the institutional and the interpersonal, is required if the planner is to gain sustained jurisdiction in managing planning processes coherently. The hybridization of governance should utilize both dimensions of trust.

In the Otaniemi OK process, the residents' association's lack of institutional trust became evident in the second discussion event in the Aalto Built Environment Lab, in April 2015. Despite apparent consensus on many sub-areas to be developed, landowner-oriented planning piece by piece, starting from these sub-areas, was not supported by the representative of the residents' association, as discussed above. As stated by the chief city planning official in the second event, the regional state organ supervising the local governments in their planning[9] had suggested the making of a legally binding partial master plan for the Otaniemi area, before engaging in piecemeal planning of the area in terms of detailed land use plans.

Naturally, the discussions in the Otaniemi OK process also reflect the experiences and attitudes gained in earlier sessions of planning and development of Otaniemi, and Espoo more broadly. While as a 'new political space', the Otaniemi OK process opened new possibilities for making initiatives and reaching agreement by using richer means of visualization than traditional planning, the lack of institutional trust, evident in the residents' association representative's comment, hindered the utilization of these possibilities. When institutional trust is lacking, the use of legally binding land use planning instruments is called for.

Hybrid Governance as Strategic Activity

Regarding the development of urban planning, the hybridization of governance implies strategic use of both institutional planning arenas and informal planning platforms, such as the Otaniemi OK platform (see Mäntysalo et al., 2015). The second discussion event approached such a strategic setting, when, in the closing part of the event, the coordinator (university researcher) opened the discussion on whether the use of more flexible planning instruments should be tested in the Otaniemi case. Thereby the question was discussed, whether a statutory overall (partial master) plan was needed for the area, to guide detailed land use planning, and, if so, whether it could be made in a less comprehensive and burdensome format and with a more selective focus. Within the frame of such an official plan, the detailed planning of the area could then be carried out in a more project-oriented manner. Planning at each level would proceed through the institutional procedures of the local government, but the strategic management of their relationship would be broadened to accommodate such 'new political spaces' as the Otaniemi OK platform.

The political weight of such an unofficial platform would depend on how it is utilized in building trust and shared means of communication (trading zone). The political and administrative leadership of the local government needs to address these platforms as extensions of local political forums that are essential for the institutional reproduction of local government, while acknowledging that they cannot replace 'government'. The unofficial platforms may provide crucial occasions for interpersonal facework in reproducing institutional trust, and, further, richer communicative means for generating trading zones for the mutual 'out-talk' between the different 'sub-cultures' of stakeholder groups (see Balducci & Mäntysalo, 2013; Galison, 1997). Such hybridization of governance ultimately relies on trust.

Here, the idea of hybrid governance reveals its strategic nature. It means utilizing *governance* type of policy measures and informal planning instruments to build networks and partnerships in conditions of agreement and trust, and relying on *government* decisions and official planning instruments to guarantee the formal legitimacy of such governance, and as a necessary channel to cope with political conflict and distrust. Such hybrid governance as strategic activity entails the capability of reaching Learning III.

In the case of Otaniemi, this kind of learning is only emerging – it is not easy to change or adjust the prevailing governance culture. All kinds of learning – single-loop, double-loop and Learning III – constitute steps of capability building. Some are just small steps, which may still be important for the stakeholder group in question. Others represent (actual/potential) major leaps, systemic advancements in terms of capability building.

Conclusion

We have examined the planning process of Otaniemi OK gained from the decision to open up the planning process with the help of university researchers, who facilitated the discussion in a neutral and specifically equipped space. Each stakeholder gained new capabilities to act during the process, which was not to the detriment of the City of Espoo. Rather, opening up the discussion contributed to trust formation. As multiple stakeholders were given a mandate, they were in the position to hope for a smooth continuation of the open process, a kind of a planning game, instead of being forced to object to some fixed deal from the outside. However, as long as the binding decisions about building rights are pending, the situation remains unpredictable and the small players vulnerable. Although thus far the City of Espoo has acknowledged the importance of not lining up with the major landowners and recognized the voices of the students' association and the residents, the wind might turn as soon as the building right questions are formally resolved as the process proceeds.

Lack of trust can clearly be an impediment in attempting to utilize the full potential of the 'new political spaces', such as Otaniemi OK. How could the situation be improved? As we hope to have shown, cities need to exercise continuous reflectivity on their governance cultures in order to deal with institutional ambiguity and hybridization of governance – and related problems of legitimacy and trust. In order to cope with these challenges, such organizational learning is needed that exceeds the level of individual planning tasks. Hence, the pragmatist perspectives of Organization Development need to be broadened by insights, developed by

Cultural-Historical Activity Theory, on the crucial role of historical and institutional trajectories in organizational learning.

The dialectic between institutionalism and pragmatism discussed in this book correlates interestingly with the dialectics that we have observed between ambiguity and uncertainty, government and governance, input and output legitimacy and institutional and interpersonal trust. Building on Bateson's systemic learning theory and its application in the Cultural-Historical Activity Theory, we have stressed the systemic interconnectedness of the strands brought together by these dialectics. We suggest that this theoretical framework has the potential for bridging the strengths of both institutionalist and pragmatist approaches. Here the concept of double bind is key. On the one hand we have the results-oriented pragmatism of tackling uncertainties and building situated governance networks, interpersonal trust and output legitimacy. But, on the other hand, this pragmatism becomes systemically incapacitated, when a double-bind situation occurs with the institutional ambiguity of neglecting government and its related capacity-building resources of institutional trust and input legitimacy. Indeed, with the concept of double bind, the need of planning activity to maintain its institutional reflectivity beyond mere situated reflection-in-action can be explained.

Notes

1. The paper is based on the authors' research in the project SASUI, reported in Mäntysalo et al. (2016). The research was funded by TEKES and Academy of Finland (project no. 288848).
2. Kolb's theory of experimental learning includes "integrative learning" that is based on "third-order feedback" (Kolb, 1984, pp. 156–160, and pp. 224–228), but the theory does not involve a description of whether and how such learning would contribute to the resolution of the type of dilemmas that have a double-bind character.
3. http://abe.aalto.fi/en/.
4. http://urbanmill.org/.
5. The related projects include EUE (Energizing Urban Ecosystems, RYM-SHOK funding) and PEKA (Rule-based urban planning and agent-based modelling, TEKES funding).
6. "Kaupunkisuunnittelulautakunnan teesit" http://espoo04.hosting.documenta.fi/kokous/2014297235.PDF and http://espoo04.hosting.documenta.fi/kokous/2013283381-10.PDF
7. A public route for pedestrians and cyclists along the shores of Espoo. The city has a goal to connect the whole shoreline for public use. The existing route includes both urban and natural environments, the section around Otaniemi being almost completely in a natural state.
8. See the debate between Hardin (1999) and Offe (1999).
9. The Uusimaa Centre for Economic Development, Transport and Environment.

References

Argyris, C. (1993). *On Organizational Learning*. Cambridge, MA: Blackwell.
Argyris C., & Schön D. (1978). *Organizational Learning: A Theory of Action Perspective*. Reading, MA: Addison-Wesley.
Balducci, A., & Mäntysalo, R. (Eds.). (2013). *Urban Planning as a Trading Zone*. Dordrecht: Springer.
Bang, H., & Esmark, A. (2009). Good governance in network society: Reconfiguring the political from politics to policy. *Administrative Theory & Praxis*, 31(1), 7–37.
Bateson, G. (1972/1987). *Steps to an Ecology of Mind*. Northvale, NJ: Jason Aronson.
Buchanan, A. (2002). Political legitimacy and democracy. *Ethics*, 112(4), 689–719.
Engeström, Y. (1987). *Learning by Expanding*. Helsinki: Orienta-konsultit.
Engeström, Y. (1995). *Kehittävä työntutkimus. Perusteita, tuloksia ja haasteita*. Helsinki: Hallinnon kehittämiskeskus.
Flyvbjerg, B. (1998). *Rationality and Power: Democracy in Practice*. Chicago, IL: The University of Chicago Press.
Forester, J. (1993). *Critical Theory, Public Policy, and Planning Practice*. Albany, NY: State University of New York Press.
Friedmann, J. (1987). *Planning in the Public Domain*. Princeton, NJ: Princeton University Press.

Galison, P. (1997). *Image and Logic: A Material Culture of Microphysics*. Chicago, IL: University of Chicago Press.

Galison, P. (2010). Trading with the Enemy. In M. E. Gorman (Ed.), *Trading Zones and Interactional Expertise: Creating New Kinds of Collaboration* (pp. 25–52). Cambridge, MA: The MIT Press.

Guston, D. H. (1999). Stabilizing the boundary between US politics and science: The role of the Office of Technology Transfer as a boundary organization. *Social Studies of Science*, 29(1), 87–112.

Hajer, M. (2003). Policy without polity? Policy analysis and the institutional void. *Policy Sciences*, 36, 175–195.

Hajer, M. (2006). The living institutions of the EU: Analysing governance as performance. *Perspectives on European Politics and Society*, 7(1), 41–55.

Hajer, M. (2009). *Authoritative Governance: Policy Making in the Age of Mediatization*. Oxford: Oxford University Press.

Hardin, R. (1999). Do We Want to Trust in Government? In M. E. Warren (Ed.), *Democracy and Trust* (pp. 22–41). Cambridge: Cambridge University Press.

Hytönen, J. (2016). The problematic relationship of communicative planning theory and Nordic legal culture. *Planning Theory*, 15(3), 223–238.

Hytönen, J., Mäntysalo, R., Peltonen, L., Kanninen, V., Niemi, P., & Simanainen, M. (2016). Defensive routines in land use policy steering in Finnish urban regions. *European Urban and Regional Studies*, 23(1), 40–55.

Kanninen, V., Bäcklund, P., & Mäntysalo, R. (2013). Trading Zone and the Complexity of Planning. In A. Balducci & R. Mäntysalo (Eds.), *Urban Planning as a Trading Zone* (pp. 159–178). Dordrecht: Springer.

Kolb, D. A. (1984). *Experiential Learning: Experience as the Source of Learning and Development*. Englewood Cliffs, NJ: Prentice-Hall.

Laurian, L. (2009). Trust in planning: Theoretical and practical considerations for participatory and deliberative planning. *Planning Theory & Practice*, 10(3), 369–391.

Leino, H. (2008). Kansalaisosallistuminen kaupunkisuunnittelussa: rajaorganisaatioita vai hybridien hallintaa? *Alue ja ympäristö*, 37(2), 41–48.

Leino, H. (2012). Boundary interaction in emerging scenes: Two participatory planning cases from Finland. *Planning Theory and Practice*, 13(3), 383–396.

Leontyev, A. N. (1981). *Problems of the Development of the Mind*. Moscow: Progress Publishers.

Mahoney, J. (2000). Path dependency in historical sociology. *Theory and Society*, 29(4), 507–548.

Maisala, P. (2008). *Espoo – oma lukunsa. Kaupunkisuunnittelun, kaupunkirakentamisen ja kaavoitushallinnon kehitys vuoteen 2000*. Helsinki: Espoo City Planning Department.

Mäntysalo, R. (2000). *Land-Use Planning as Inter-Organizational Learning*. Oulu: Acta Universitatis Ouluensis Technica C 155.

Mäntysalo, R. (2016). From Public-Private-People Partnerships to Trading Zones in Gaining Co-coordinative Capability in Urban Planning. In G. Concilio & F. Rizzo (Eds.), *Human Smart Cities*. Dordrecht: Springer.

Mäntysalo, R., Tuppurainen, S., & Wallin, S. (2016). Keilaniemi, Espoo. A Large Scale Solution Seeking a Problem, and Facing Dilemmas. In F. Savini & W. Salet (Eds.), *Planning Projects in Transition – Interventions, Regulations and Investements* (pp. 156–173). Berlin: Jovis.

Mäntysalo, R., Balducci, A., & Kangasoja, J. (2011a). Planning as agonistic communication in a trading zone. *Planning Theory*, 10(3), 257–272.

Mäntysalo, R., Kangasoja, J. K., & Kanninen, V. (2015). The paradox of strategic spatial planning: A theoretical outline with a view on Finland. *Planning Theory and Practice*, 16(2), 257–272.

Mäntysalo, R., Saglie, I.-L., & Cars, G. (2011b). Between input legitimacy and output efficiency: Defensive routines and agonistic reflectivity in Nordic land-use planning. *European Planning Studies*, 19(12), 2109–2126.

Mäntysalo, R., & Saglie, I.-L. (2010). Private influence preceding public involvement. *Planning Theory and Practice*, 11(3), 317–338.

Miller, C. (2001). Hybrid management: Boundary organizations, science policy, and environmental governance in the climate regime. *Science, Technology & Human Values*, 26(4), 478–500.

North, D. C. (1990). Institutions. *Journal of Economic Perspectives*, 5(1), 97–112.

Offe, K. (1999). How Can We Trust Our Fellow Citizens? In M. E. Warren (Ed.), *Democracy and Trust* (pp. 42–87). Cambridge: Cambridge University Press.

Patterson, O. (1999). Liberty Against the Democratic State: On the Historical and Contemporary Sources of American Distrust. In M. E. Warren (Ed.), *Democracy and Trust* (pp. 151–207). Cambridge: Cambridge University Press.

Pierson, P. (2000). Increasing returns, path dependence, and the study of politics. *The American Political Science Review*, 94(2), 251–267.
Pollitt, C., & Bouckaert, G. (2011). *Public Management Reform: A Comparative Analysis. New Public Management, Governance and the Neo-Weberian State.* Oxford: Oxford University Press.
Puustinen, S., Mäntysalo, R., Hytönen, J., & Jarenko, K. (2017). The 'deliberative bureaucrat'. Deliberative democracy and institutional trust in the jurisdiction of the Finnish planner. *Planning Theory and Practice*, 18(1), 71–88. Retrieved from: http://dx.doi.org/10.1080/14649357.2016.1245437.
Rosenau, J. N. (1992). Governance, Order, and Change in World Politics. In J. N. Rosenau & E.-O. Czempel (Eds.), *Governance Without Government: Order and Change in World Politics* (pp. 3–6). Cambridge: Cambridge University Press.
Sager, T. (2013). *Reviving Critical Planning Theory: Dealing With Pressure, Neo-Liberalism, and Responsibility in Communicative Planning.* London: Routledge.
Scharpf, F. (1999). *Governing in Europe: Effective and Democratic?* Oxford: Oxford University Press.
Schmidt-Thomé, K., & Mäntysalo, R. (2014). Interplay of power and learning in planning processes: A dynamic view. *Planning Theory*, 13(2), 115–135.
Schön, D. A. (1983). *The Reflective Practitioner.* New York: Basic Books.
Sztompka, P. (1999). *Trust: A Sociological Theory.* Cambridge: Cambridge University Press.
Van Rijswick, M., & Salet, W. (2012). Enabling the contextualization of legal rules in responsive strategies to climate change. *Ecology and Society*, 17(2), 1–8.
Wallin, S., Horelli, L., & Engberg, L. (2016). Urban Living Labs: Experimentations with Visualizing, Anticipating and Steering Urban Development. In F. Savini & W. Salet (Eds.), *Planning Projects in Transition – Interventions, Regulations and Investements* (pp. 26–43). Berlin: Jovis.
Wallin, S., & Staffans, A. (2015). From Statutory Urban Planning to Living Labs. In P. Lappalainen, M. Markkula & H. Kune (Eds.), *Orchestrating Regional Innovation Ecosystems: Espoo Innovation Garden* (pp. 69–280). Espoo: Aalto University in Cooperation with Laurea University of Applied Sciences and Built Environment Innovations, RYM Ltd.
Warren, M. E. (1999). Introduction. In M. E. Warren (Ed.), *Democracy and Trust* (pp. 1–21). Cambridge: Cambridge University Press.

PART 4

On Justification

12
CONSTITUTIONS, LAWS AND PRACTICES
Ethics of Planning and Ethics of Planners

Stefano Moroni

Introduction

In planning theory – but also in political science – it seems that for some time certain misunderstandings have arisen (leading to unsatisfactory indications for practice, and slowing progress of the debate) because different *levels* or *stages* of the discourse have not been clearly distinguished. The recent – and opportune – interest in the question of the institutions in planning theory (Cars et al., 2002; Gualini, 2001; Healey, 1997; Salet & Faludi, 2000; Verma, 2007) seems to provide a good opportunity to try and establish some order. In this regard, the first part of the chapter distinguishes five different decisional levels. The second part re-examines three classic problems of policy analysis and planning theory in light of the proposed distinction among levels. The final part draws some conclusions.

Five Decisional Levels

Assuming that we are considering a constitutional democracy,[1] I suggest distinguishing among five different decisional levels (the word 'decision' is used here in a very broad sense to denote deliberative standpoints). The five levels or stages are the following:

1. The pre-constitutional level;
2. The constitutional level;
3. The legislative level;
4. The administrative level;
5. The civil society level.[2]

The schema can be interpreted as a framework within which we can deal with issues regarding decision-making and decision-taking at various levels. It moves from the most abstract to the most concrete. At the first level, the requirement is to operate behind a thick *veil of ignorance* (Rawls, 1971) or *veil of uncertainty* (Brennan & Buchanan, 2000; Buchanan & Congleton, 2003). The 'veil' conceals the concrete and contingent characteristics of the various real individuals (their social position and status, their particular and contingent preferences, etc.), and the very specific features of the social and economic reality in which they live. The thickness of the veil of ignorance/uncertainty relative to the concrete characteristics of the social and economic reality progressively decreases (i.e. the veil is partially removed) on passing from the pre-constitutional level to the constitutional and post-constitutional ones: in other words, limitations on knowledge regarding the characteristics of society and the economy can be progressively relaxed. The first level is clearly 'fictional' (a thought-experiment whose purpose is to help self-clarification and public-clarification: Rawls, 1993), while the other four are real-world situations. Each individual layer may be further subdivided and specified, but for the purposes of the discussion on planning (and planners) that I intend to conduct here, the division into five stages is sufficient.

The first level is what we may call *pre-constitutional* – that is, a level exemplified by the Rawlsian idea of the 'original position'. We may note that every theory of justice has in fact, explicitly or implicitly, its own version of the original position (Barry, 1989, pp. 320–353; Scanlon, 2003, pp. 124–150). The original position is an analytical device: it is the situation in which we hypothesize that imaginary individuals decide on the principles to be adopted in writing a good constitution. The original position is therefore (a) *hypothetical* (we ask what the parties, appropriately characterized, could, or would, agree to, and not what the parties have agreed to) and (b) *non-historical* (we do not suppose that the agreement among the parties has actually taken place) (Rawls, 1993, pp. 273–274 and 2001, pp. 16–17). In the original position, the parties are supposed to have strongly limited knowledge: they have only very general knowledge of social and economic facts, and no knowledge of their specific situation and of individual particularities.

The second level is the *constitutional* one – that is, the level at which real individuals write a constitution (in light of the principles which they have supposedly chosen in the original position). The constitution is a permanent, or quasi-permanent, framework within which political life and social interaction has to take place. At this stage, the central problem is that of *constitutional design* (Epstein, 2014; Lijphart & Waisman, 1996; Maravall & Przeworski, 2003; Schneier, 2006). The veil of ignorance is partially lifted. The delegates to the constitutional convention know the relevant facts about the natural circumstances and the social situation; but they still lack information about the positions and statuses of individuals and groups. A constitution, as a framework of meta-rules, has two important functions: first, it constitutes in the strict sense the public institutions and their role (it founds and establishes power); second, it constrains the power conferred on those institutions. The constitutional constraints on state power should be of two kinds: substantive and procedural (Kurrild-Klitgaard, 2005). The *substantive* constraints set insurmountable barriers on the action of the state and define its duties; these constraints directly affect the content (possible and impossible) of public decisions. The *procedural* constraints instead concern 'who' can make certain decisions (e.g. here the separation-of-powers mechanism comes into play) and 'how' such decisions are made (e.g. what are the process rules to be respected in actual public decision-making – voting procedures, decision times, etc.). Procedural constraints act directly on the modes and forms of public decisions and only indirectly on their content. A constitutional framework is the indispensable prerequisite of an acceptable and viable form of democracy. In other words, democratic decision procedures can start only after a constitutional framework has been established, and only within the limits it sets (Buchanan, 1975; Riker, 1988). Constitutional government *is* "limited government" (Schneier, 2006, p. 3). Accepting constitutional constraints means accepting that "some issues are beyond politics" (Gaus, 1996, p. 213). Limitations on public action do not necessarily constitute a weakening of that action. In some cases, indeed, they may represent a strength able to mobilize attention and public resources in the most appropriate direction (Holmes, 1995). Observe that beneficially working markets also need appropriate constitutional constraints (Vanberg, 2001).

Thirdly we have the *legislative level* (central and local) – that is, the level at which real individuals (members of parliament or local councils) introduce laws and regulations in compliance with the substantive and procedural constraints defined in the constitution. It is assumed that the veil of ignorance will be further reduced for those who decide on laws and regulations. They know the specific economic, social and technological circumstances, but they are still required to act in ignorance of individual positions. The latter requirement reflects the traditional requisite of "equal treatment by the law" (Moroni, 2007).

In the fourth place, we have the *administrative level* – that is, the stage at which public officials apply and implement law and regulations. Here all the facts are known, but public officials must still avoid taking individual statuses and positions directly into consideration. In this case, the issue is not yet equal treatment by the law – already granted at the previous level – but 'equality before the law' (equality under the law).

In fifth place we have the *civil society level*. At this stage no limits on knowledge and accessible information remain. I shall use the term 'civil society' in the broad sense to denote the set of activities that individuals perform in society – whether market activities or otherwise. At this level we find, for instance, entrepreneurs who take economic and financial decisions, and ordinary citizens who take all kinds of everyday-life decisions – both groups doing so in compliance with the previous normative framework.

To conclude, observe that the five levels are in hierarchical order: at each new stage the options are subject to the standards and constraints introduced at the earlier stages. Some standards and constraints will be substantive and immediately cogent for the subsequent levels; others will introduce procedures to follow. In particular, "legislative majorities may be acting *within the rules* (the political constitution) that constrain their own behavior *in changing the rules* that constrain the behavior of persons in their private capacities" (Brennan & Buchanan, 2000, p. 9). The doctrine of unqualified, absolute, parliamentary sovereignty is therefore rejected. And observe also how the presence of the first stage (i.e. the original position) implicitly refutes the modern positivistic tendency to define law as anything stated by the public authority.

Here a specification is important before the discussion continues. In this chapter, for the sake of simplicity, I consider the entire question from a predominantly synchronic standpoint (which might give the impression that the schema is excessively rigid; as well as the impression that it is solely top-down). In a broader perspective, which considers the diachronic dimension too (i.e. *also* the evolution in time of the various stages), certain dynamic matters should also be taken into account (e.g. the fact that pressures to reform certain aspects of 'higher' levels, even the constitutional one, may arise from the 'lower' levels, such as civil society). As said, I shall not address this issue here (but in this regard, see Moroni, 2010).

Three Main Questions

The foregoing discussion allows clearer reconsideration of some recurrent problems in planning theory and political science. Here I focus on three questions: (i) To which decisional level do principles of justice apply? (ii) What or who do certain principles concern? (iii) What are the relevant virtues at each level? I have decided to focus on these problems because they seem particularly relevant to the issues discussed in this book.

Principles of Justice at What Level?

First, we may wonder as to the level at which certain principles of justice apply. For example, is Rawls's *difference principle* used only to design the constitution or also to define specific policies and planning practices? As well known, the difference principle states that "social and economic inequalities ... are to be to the greatest benefit of the least advantaged members of society" (Rawls, 1993, p. 6). (The difference principle, combined with an overriding principle of liberty, is the fulcrum of the famous Rawlsian theory of *justice as fairness*).

Almost all the planning theory and practice that has adopted a Rawlsian approach (e.g. Beatley, 1988; Berry & Steiker, 1974; Kiernan, 1983; Krumholz, 1982, 1994; Krumholz, Cogger & Linner, 1975, 1978; Marlin, 1995; McConnell, 1981, 1995) maintains that the difference principle should be applied directly to individual policies and plans.[3]

By contrast, Rawls (1971, p. 7) states that the two principles – adopted by the parties in the original position – should be applied primarily to the *basic structure of society* (i.e. the way in which the major social institutions distribute fundamental rights and duties) and that they should not necessarily concern every individual public choice. The basic structure consists of the *ground rules* – that is, the main institutional scheme – that shape the social system (Pogge, 1989, p. 22). The focus here is on what might be called *structural coercion* (Williams, 2005, p. 57). That the primary object of justice is the basic structure of society suggests moreover "the idea of treating the question of distributive shares as a matter of pure procedural justice. The intuitive idea is to design the social system so that the outcome is just whatever it happens to be" (Rawls, 1971, pp. 84–85). Rawls specifies: "Pure procedural justice obtains when there is no independent criterion for the right result: instead there is a correct or fair procedure such that the outcome is likewise correct or fair, whatever it is, provided that the procedure has been properly followed" (Rawls, 1971, p. 86). This point is also stressed many times in his subsequent works, for instance: "The two principles of justice ... incorporate an important element of pure procedural justice in the actual determination of distributive shares. They apply to the basic structure ...; within appropriate limits, whatever distributive shares result are just" (Rawls, 1993, p. 282). He also writes:

> Taking the basic structure as the primary subject enables us to regard distributive justice as a case of pure background procedural justice: when everyone follows the publicly recognized rules of cooperation, the particular distribution that results is acceptable as just whatever that distribution turns out to be ... This allows us to abstract from the enormous complexities of the innumerable transactions of daily life and frees us from having to keep track of the changing relative positions of particular individuals.
>
> *(Rawls, 2001, p. 54)*

Regardless of the interpretation of Rawls that one deems more credible, the fundamental problem is that planning theory and practice should not forget that the theories of justice which usually inspire them are always and, above all, theories regarding the basic structure of society (Barry, 1989; Höffe, 1987). Their application to policies and plans is therefore neither straightforward nor immediate.

A problem similar to the one discussed in relation to Rawls arises for the *ideal speech situation* and the *discourse principle* of Jürgen Habermas (1983, 1991). Many planning theorists who have adopted the Habermasian perspective have taken them to be immediately and directly relevant to planning practices. As Pauline McGuirk observes:

> Communicative planning theory draws on the Habermasian concepts of 'communicative distortion' and 'ideal speech situations' ... Distortion is said to occur when groups

seek to extend their power by attempting to restrict argumentation by excluding participants, making unfounded appeals to rationality, strategically obscuring issues, or manipulating opinion ... In contrast, communicative planning theory would minimise communicative distortions which have enabled powerful groups to maintain positions of power ... and thus achieve power neutrality by approximating Habermas's 'ideal speech situation'.

(McGuirk, 2001, p. 197)

In fact, the idea of the *ideal speech situation* is relevant at a meta-theoretical level. It suggests that if we, as participants in a discourse, do not accept the validity of certain preconditions we get entangled in performative self-contradictions. "This notion of an 'ideal speech situation' presupposed in discourse is central to Habermas's efforts to provide moral-practical foundations for critical theory" (McCarthy, 1984, p. 307). It is "an unavoidable supposition ... of discourse ... This supposition is usually (and perhaps even always) counterfactual. Nevertheless it is made, and must be made, whenever we enter into discourse ... It is intrinsic to the very sense of doing so" (McCarthy, 1984, p. 309). But, in the attempt to utilize the idea of the ideal speech situation and the discourse principle in the context of political theory and policies there is still a long way to go (Pedersen, 2012, p. 415). Actually, Habermas's central idea is to apply the discourse principle "to the legal form, and subsequently to point out how this will yield a system of rights that will give equal weight to private and public autonomy, and which will have the principle of democracy at its core" (Pedersen, 2012, p. 416). The same point is stressed by Hanna Mattila (2016, p. 360): "Habermas ... has not purported his theories to be applied in everyday administrative contexts but in democratic processes of law-making and in processes where formal institutional designs are laid out".[4]

To conclude: the problem is not simply that theories of justice like those of Rawls (1971, 1993) and Habermas (1991, 1992)[5] are mainly centred on the pre-constitutional and constitutional levels (as aptly pointed out by Campbell, 2006, p. 93: "Neither Rawls nor Habermas intended his constitutional-level conceptualizations of justice to be applied to the everyday situated judgments with which planning and many other areas of policy making are concerned"). The problem is also that if we imagine a constitutional democracy, any theory of justice can only indicate the framework within which there will be a (partially) autonomous role for democratic choices made in a particular sequence and according to specific procedures. In other words, it is not only a problem of non-immediate translatability (see again Campbell, 2006, p. 93: The concerns of many philosophical theories of justice "are with the constitutional essentials of whole societies ... Their horizons are therefore broader than a subsection of public policymaking concerned with the creation of place and the mediation of space. This is not to dismiss this hugely significant body of work but to caution the appropriateness of direct translation"). The main problem is that theories of justice for a constitutional democracy are partly open. A theory of justice intended for a constitutional democratic state is therefore not *indeterminate* but partially *underdeterminate*.

Principles for Institutions and Principles for Individuals

Secondly, we should distinguish between *principles for individuals* (i.e. principles which apply to agents in particular roles or situations), and *principles for institutions* (i.e. principles which apply to the basic structure of society, such as the two famous Rawlsian principles of justice as fairness, which comprise the difference principle). The distinction is made clear by the fact that sometimes, to solve certain social problems, we need to *change conduct*; at other times, to solve different problems, we have to *reform institutions*. For example, if a single police officer commits an offence, we can accuse him/her of misconduct and have him/her dismissed; if, however, such behaviour is common among police officers, being not only allowed but indeed covered by institutional forms, it is the institutions that are indicted and must be reformed.

According to Rawls (1971, p. 110), both kinds of principles (i.e. principles for institutions and principles for individuals) are chosen in the original position: but principles for individuals are adopted after those for institutions; in fact, individuals' political obligations and duties presuppose a moral conception of institutions. This aspect of Rawls's approach – principles for individual – has often been overlooked, but it is a crucial part of his theory of justice (Farrelly, 2000).

A rather similar position is taken by Russell Hardin with specific reference to office holders:

> Once the institution's morality is defined, we may infer or deduce the morality of individual office holders in the institution as derivative from the purpose of the institution. Or, we may say, the rules and procedures that guide the actions of individual officeholders are determined by the functional relation of their actions to the general purposes of the institution.
>
> *(Hardin, 1996, p. 127)*

Principles for institutions are therefore principles that political structures and law must fulfil. Principles for individuals are instead principles with which individuals are required to comply. These latter comprise, firstly, *principles of political obligation*, which entail compliance with the laws and decisions of just institutions.[6] (As Rawls, 1971, p. 112, observes, people are not bound to unjust institutions; in particular, they do not have an obligation to arbitrary and autocratic forms of government. In short: loyalty is not unconditioned.) Secondly, there are principles which introduce more *specific duties* (i.e. 'to do our part') according to the role covered (e.g. public officials, professionals, etc.). These are responsibilities and tasks assigned to certain positions: their content is therefore defined by institutions or practices the rules of which define what it is that a person is required to do.

Failure to take account of the previous distinction often creates confusion in the discussion on the work and role of planners; for planners – as public officials, for instance – do not have to comply directly with principles for institutions, but rather with principles for individuals.

Not considering the above distinction creates confusion in particular between the ethics of planning and the ethics of planners. The *ethics of planning* – for example, in relation to land ownership – is discussed by considering principles for institutions; it is no coincidence that many questions of this kind involve constitutional issues and rulings by constitutional courts: the problem of expropriation for public utility, taking issues, discriminatory zoning, etc. (Siegan, 1997). The *ethics of planners* (as public officers in particular: for example, their relationship with elected members, colleagues or subordinates, relations with the public, use of their margins of discretion) is discussed by considering principles for individuals. For instance, on considering the role of planners as (non-elected) civil servants, Elizabeth Howe (1994) observes that the most basic ethical principles for them are the following: first, respect (legitimate) law; second, adhere to duties of justice (i.e. honesty: no theft, no bribery, avoid doing political favours, do not use the power of office to obtain special personal benefits, be fair with colleagues and subordinates; try to do quality work: use appropriate methods, provide accurate information; and truthfulness: be free from pressures of any kind on planning judgements, keep promises); third, be accountable (be responsive to the public, grant procedural openness and transparency).[7] The fact that behaving in this way is not always self-evidently clear, and that a public official must often discover along the way how best to do his/her duty (Moore, 1985), does not change the basic point.[8]

All these duties are also crucial for the existence of *trust*. In this regard, Stanley Stein and Thomas Harper (2003, p. 135) aptly underscore that the widespread idea that understanding the planning world only requires understanding power relations is reductive: as they observe, there is another crucial vocabulary that has not been given much attention but is of equal importance particularly to planners: that is, the vocabulary of *trust*.[9]

Here I take it for granted that planners are not mere technicians applying only quantitative formulaic methods (as endlessly stressed by recent planning theory: Howe, 1992). This is not, however, to forget that (a) they must nevertheless make some kind of technical contribution (in terms of suggestions like "if you do X, you get Y": Chiodelli, 2012; Mazza, 1995) and (b) if they work as public officials, they are still non-elected subjects. We can therefore also stress the political nature of their work and their actions as moral agents (Bolan, 1985), provided that we do so in light of precise theoretical conditions and restrictions.

Repositioning Virtues: The Example of Altruism

The multi-level schema is also useful for re-examining the role and meaning of certain 'virtues'. The term 'altruism', for instance, is often used in a confused manner, also in planning theory, to denote a certain institutional task and a particular individual behaviour simultaneously. However, it seems necessary to clarify a crucial point in this regard.

At the level of the original position, it is better not to conceptualize individuals as altruistic. John Rawls (1971, p. 144) proposes to characterize them as endowed with mutually disinterested rationality. That is, the parties seek to reach the agreement that will ensure the best conditions in which to pursue their ideas of life without seeking to confer benefits – or to impose any injury – on one another. This not only seems more appropriate to the particular nature of the original position; it also makes the argument more cogent because it is not based on motivations which are already *in themselves* charitable. Also James Buchanan (2005) noted that reciprocity is the crucial aspect at the original position level. The principles of justice adopted at this level involve mutual respect: they reflect *reciprocity* rather than *compassion* (Buchanan, 2005, p. 43). In other words: "A person does not agree to be bound by constitutional rules because of some expressed interest in the well-being of others ... The 'constitutional moment' is one of mutual gain ... rather than some upswelling of recognized utility interdependence" (Buchanan, 2005, pp. 43–44). The same point is stressed also by James Buchanan and Roger Congleton:

> The person who advances an argument in support of one particular rule (or set of rules) must invoke criteria that take on elements of general or public interest. An argument may claim that this or that rule is indeed in the 'general' interest (as defined by the anonymity of the veil), and that such a rule is supported, not from altruism, but from the necessary coincidence between the individual and general interest.
> *(Buchanan & Congleton, 2003, p. 9)*

Principles selected at the level of the original position involving an institutional system designed to combat poverty are therefore not expressions of altruism, solidarity or charity (of the parties in the original position) but insurance against the possibility that *anyone* may find themselves in difficulties in the future. In short, the institutions that take care of the weak are not 'altruistic' but 'just'; altruists may be individuals who act in society. To conclude: just institutions ought to take care of *potential* poverty; altruistic individuals may take care of *real* poverty.

Final Remarks: Towards a More Layered Approach

The issues discussed above are only some examples of those that can be more clearly and consciously addressed once the idea of the 'multiple levels' is accepted. My concern in this chapter has been not so much to take specific positions with respect to the substantive questions raised as to formulate them in clearer terms. The proposed schema offers both a reconstruction of the way in which a constitutional democracy functions, and a framework in which to evaluate actual decisions: each level represents an appropriate point of view from which certain kinds of issues have to be assessed. In general, the proposed schema suggests that we need, in planning theory, too, a *more layered* approach to decision issues that recognizes the *different kinds of public problems* that emerge at different levels. And it also suggests that a strictly 'instrumental' view of institutions and the law – as a means to achieve specific outcomes directly – is inadequate (Salet, 2002; Van Rijswick & Salet, 2012): appropriate institutions and laws instead create a multi-scalar structure fundamental in creating the conditions for plural co-possible individual actions (Moroni, 2011). They are not *shaping-devices*; rather, they are mainly *filter-devices* (Moroni, 2015).

Notes

1 The idea of constitutional democracy obviously entails certain normative values, such as the importance of the separation of powers, the need to constrain the power of majorities, etc., which are not examined – and defended – here (on this see Allan, 2001).
2 I follow, in part, the idea of the four-stage sequence put forward by Rawls (1971, pp. 195–201). However, I divide the levels in a somewhat different manner by also taking account of the idea of the three-stage-problems sequence in Barnett (1998); the idea of different justificatory levels in Gaus (1996, pp. 195–245); and the distinction between first-level and second-level political justice and first-level and second-level personal justice in Höffe (1987). On Rawls's four-stage sequence – possible uses, limits, etc. – see, for instance, Nowell-Smith (1973), Scanlon (2004), Shelby (2004), Ron (2006), Baker (2008), Hedrick (2010), Bedi (2014).
3 For instance, Kiernan (1983, p. 83) after quoting Rawls's difference principle and asking how, concretely, might this normative principle be translated into action through the day-to-day activities of planning practitioners, suggests the following: "The planner's first task ... is to raise to the level of explicitness the question of who benefits and who loses from whatever planning proposal is under consideration. Having done this ... it is my view that planners ought to practise the politics of positive discrimination ... In other words, the first test of any planning proposal would be the extent to which it contributed to the alleviation of social and economic disparity. Planners would consciously structure their own proposals and their adjudication of those emanating from the private sector according to this principle ... What is being advocated is the systematic and disproportionate allocation of the benefits of future planning proposals to ensure that both the absolute and the relative position of the disadvantaged is improved".
4 Some doubts about the immediate relevance of Habermas's notion of ideal speech situation to planning theory and practice were first raised by Forester (1990, pp. 52–53, and 1993, p. 3, p. 138).
5 But also, for example, of Nozick 1974 (see Pogge, 1989, pp. 24–25).
6 For an overview of the theoretical questions underlying the reasons for political obligation see Raphael (1990, pp. 175–209).
7 Compare with Elcock's (2012) discussion. Here I shall not pay particular attention to the issue of professional codes of conduct (with specific reference to planning, see Bickenbach & Hendler, 1994; Howe, 1992; Taylor, 1992). I regard them as roughly coincident with ordinary ethics (or, at least, functionally related with it), and partially overlapping with the principles of justice for individuals. Good professional codes may contribute to reinforcing trust: see the discussion that follows.
8 Some misunderstandings are perhaps created here by *another* problem (that the proposed schema can help to clarify): if institutions are 'just' according to some principles for institutions, then the planner as a public official must simply follow certain (ethical) principles for individuals (in this case the appropriate deliberative standpoint is the administrative level); but, if the institutions are 'unjust', the planner

can more actively think and act to promote change and institutional reform (in this case the appropriate view to adopt is a 'superior' one).
9 For critical discussions on trust in planning, see Höppner (2009), Tait (2011) and Talvitie (2011). For a more general description on the role of trust in the city, see Ikeda (2004).

References

Allan, T. R. S. (2001). *Constitutional Justice*. Oxford: Oxford University Press.
Baker, C. E. (2008). Rawls, equality, and democracy. *Philosophy & Social Criticism*, 34(3), 203–246.
Barnett, R. (1998). *The Structure of Liberty: Justice and the Rule of Law*. Oxford: Oxford University Press.
Barry, B. (1989). *Theories of Justice*. London: Harvester-Wheatsheaf.
Beatley, T. (1988). Equity and Distributional Issues in Infrastructure Planning: A Theoretical Perspective. In J. M. Stein (Ed.), *Public Infrastructure Planning and Management* (pp. 208–226). Newbury Park: Sage.
Bedi, S. (2014). The scope of formal equality of opportunity: The horizontal effect of rights in a liberal constitution. *Political Theory*, 42(6), 716–738.
Berry, D., & Steiker, G. (1974). The concept of justice in regional planning: Justice as fairness. *Journal of the American Institute of Planners*, 40(6), 414–421.
Bickenbach, J. E., & Hendler, S. (1994). The Moral Mandate of the 'Profession' of Planning. In H. Thomas (Ed.), *Values and Planning* (pp. 162–177). Aldershot: Avebury.
Bolan, R. (1985). The Structure of Ethical Choice in Planning Practice. In M. Wachs (Ed.), *Ethics and Planning* (pp. 70–89). New Brunswick: The Center for Urban Policy Research.
Brennan, G., & Buchanan, J. (2000). *The Reason of Rules: Constitutional Political Economy*. Indianapolis, IN: Liberty Fund.
Buchanan, J. (1975). *The Limits of Liberty*. Chicago, IL: The University of Chicago Press.
Buchanan, J. (2005). *Why I, Too, Am Not a Conservative*. Cheltenham: Edward Elgar.
Buchanan, J., & Congleton, R. D. (2003). *Politics by Principle, Not Interest. Towards Nondiscriminatory Democracy*. Indianapolis, IN: Liberty Fund.
Campbell, H. (2006). Just planning: The art of situated ethical judgment. *Journal of Planning Education and Research*, 26, 92–106.
Cars, G., Healey, P., Madanipour, A., & De Magalhaes, C. (Eds.). (2002). *Urban Governance, Institutional Capacity and Social Milieux*. Aldershot: Ashgate.
Chiodelli, F. (2012). Re-politicizing space through technical rules. *Planning Theory*, 11(2), 115–127.
Elcock, H. (2012). Ethics and the public interest: A question of morality. *Teaching Public Administration*, 30(2), 115–123.
Epstein, R. A. (2014). *The Classical Liberal Constitution: The Uncertain Quest for Limited Government*. Cambridge, MA: Harvard University Press.
Farrelly, C. (2000). Incentives and the natural duties of justice. *Politics*, 20(1), 19–24.
Forester, J. (1990). Reply to my critics… *Planning Theory Newsletter*, 4, 43–60.
Forester, J. (1993). *Critical Theory, Public Policy, and Planning Practice*. New York: State University of New York Press.
Gaus, G. F. (1996). *Justificatory Liberalism: An Essay in Epistemology and Political Theory*. Oxford: Oxford University Press.
Gualini, E. (2001). *Planning and the Intelligence of Institutions*. Aldershot: Ashgate.
Habermas, J. (1983). *Moralbewußtsein und kommunikatives Handeln*. Frankfurt am Main: Suhrkamp.
Habermas, J. (1991). *Erläuterungen zur Diskursethik*. Frankfurt am Main: Suhrkamp.
Habermas, J. (1992). *Faktizität und Geltung. Beiträge zur Diskurstheorie des Rechts und des demokratischen Rechtsstaats*. Frankfurt am Main: Suhrkamp.
Hardin, R. (1996). Institutional Morality. In R. E. Goodin (Ed.), *The Theory of Institutional Design* (pp. 126–153). Cambridge: Cambridge University Press.
Healey, P. (1997). *Collaborative Planning*. London: Macmillan.
Hedrick, T. (2010). Coping with constitutional indeterminacy. *Philosophy & Social Criticism*, 36(2), 183–208.
Höffe, O. (1987). *Politische Gerechtigkeit*. Frankfurt am Main: Suhrkamp.
Holmes, S. (1995). *Passions and Constraint*. Chicago, IL: University of Chicago Press.
Höppner, C. (2009). Trust – A monolithic panacea in land use planning? *Land Use Policy*, 26, 1046–1054.
Howe, E. (1992). Professional roles and the public interest in planning. *Journal of Planning Literature*, 6(3), 230–248.

Howe, E. (1994). *Acting on Ethics in City Planning*. New Brunswick, NJ: The Center for Urban Policy Research.
Ikeda, S. (2004). Urban interventionism and local knowledge. *The Review of Austrian Economics*, 17(2–3), 247–264.
Kiernan, M. J. (1983). Ideology, politics, and planning: Reflections on the theory and practice of urban planning. *Environment and Planning B*, 10, 71–87.
Krumholz, N. (1982). A retrospective view of equity planning: Cleveland, 1969–1979. *Journal of the American Planning Association*, 48(2), 163–174.
Krumholz, N. (1994). Dilemmas of equity planning: A personal memoir. *Planning Theory*, 10(11), 45–56.
Krumholz, N., Cogger, J. M., & Linner, J. H. (1975). The Cleveland policy planning report. *Journal of the American Institute of Planners*, 41(5), 298–304.
Krumholz, N., Cogger, J. M., & Linner, J. H. (1978). Make No Big Plans… Planning in Cleveland in the 1970s. In R. W. Burchell & G. Sternlieb (Eds.), *Planning Theory in the 1980s* (pp. 29–40). New Brunswick, NJ: The Center for Urban Policy Research.
Kurrild-Klitgaard, P. (2005). Ulysses and the Rent-Seekers: The Benefits and Challenges of Constitutional Constraints on Leviathan. In P. Kurrild-Klitgaard (Ed.), *The Dynamics of Intervention* (pp. 245–278). Amsterdam: Elsevier.
Lijphart, A., & Waisman, C. H. (Eds.). (1996). *Institutional Design in New Democracies*. Boulder, CO: Westview Press.
Maravall, J. M., & Przeworski, A. (Eds.). (2003). *Democracy and the Rule of Law*. Cambridge: Cambridge University Press.
Marlin, R. (1995). Rawlsian Justice and Community Planning. In S. Hendler (Ed.), *Planning Ethics* (pp. 141–153). New Brunswick, NJ: The Center for Urban Policy Research.
Mattila, H. (2016). Can collaborative planning go beyond locally focused notions of the 'public interest'? The potential of Habermas's concept of 'generalizable interest' in pluralist and trans-scalar planning discourses. *Planning Theory*, 15(4), 344–365.
Mazza, L. (1995). Technical knowledge, practical reason and the planner's responsibility. *Town Planning Review*, 66(4), 389–409.
McCarthy, T. (1984). *The Critical Theory of Jürgen Habermas*. Cambridge: Polity Press.
McConnell, S. (1981). *Theories for Planning*. London: Heinemann.
McConnell, S. (1995). Rawlsian Planning Theory. In S. Hendler (Ed.), *Planning Ethics* (pp. 30–48). New Brunswick, NJ: The Center for Urban Policy Research.
McGuirk, P. M. (2001). Situating communicative planning theory: Context, power, and knowledge. *Environment and Planning A*, 33, 195–217.
Moore, M. H. (1985). Realms of Obligation and Virtue. In M. Wachs (Ed.), *Ethics and Planning* (pp. 90–117). New Brunswick, NJ: The Center for Urban Policy Research.
Moroni, S. (2007). Planning, liberty and the rule of law. *Planning Theory*, 6(2), 146–163.
Moroni, S. (2010). An evolutionary theory of institutions and a dynamic approach to reform. *Planning Theory*, 9(4), 275–297.
Moroni, S. (2011). The role of deliberate intervention on organizations and institutions. *Planning Theory*, 10(2), 190–197.
Moroni, S. (2015). Complexity and the inherent limits of explanation and prediction: Urban codes for self-organizing cities. *Planning Theory*, 14(3), 248–267.
Nowell-Smith, P. H. (1973). A theory of justice? *Philosophy of the Social Sciences*, 3(1), 315–329.
Nozick, R. (1974). *Anarchy, State and Utopia*. New York: Basic Books.
Pedersen, J. (2012). Justification and the application: The revival of the Rawls-Habermas debate. *Philosophy of the Social Sciences*, 42(3), 399–432.
Pogge, T. W. (1989). *Realizing Rawls*. Ithaca, NY: Cornell University Press.
Raphael, D. D. (1990). *Problems of Political Philosophy*. London: Macmillan.
Rawls, J. (1971). *A Theory of Justice*. Cambridge, MA: Harvard University Press.
Rawls, J. (1993). *Political Liberalism*. New York: Columbia University Press.
Rawls, J. (2001). *Justice as Fairness: A Restatement*. Cambridge, MA: Harvard University Press.
Riker, W. H. (1988). *Liberalism against Populism*. Long Grove, IL: Waveland.
Ron, A. (2006). Rawls as a critical theorist: Reflective equilibrium after the 'deliberative turn'. *Philosophy & Social Criticism*, 32(2), 173–191.
Salet, W. (2002). Evolving institutions: An international exploration into planning and law. *Journal of Planning Education and Research*, 22, 26–33.

Salet, W., & Faludi, A. (Eds.). (2000). *The Revival of Strategic Spatial Planning*. Amsterdam: Royal Netherlands Academy of Arts and Sciences.

Scanlon, T. (2003). *The Difficulty of Tolerance*. Cambridge: Cambridge University Press.

Scanlon, T. (2004). Adjusting rights and balancing values. *Fordham Law Review*, 72(5), 1476–1486.

Schneier, E. (2006). *Crafting Constitutional Democracies: The Politics of Institutional Design*. Lanham, MD: Rowman & Littlefield.

Shelby, T. (2004). Race and ethnicity, race and social justice: Rawlsian considerations. *Fordham Law Review*, 72(5), 1696–1714.

Siegan, B. (1997). *Property and Freedom: The Constitution, the Courts, and Land-Use Regulation*. New Brunswick, NJ: Transaction.

Stein, S. M., & Harper, T. L. (2003). Power, trust, and planning. *Journal of Planning Education and Research*, 23, 125–139.

Tait, M. (2011). Trust and the public interest in the micropolitics of planning practice. *Journal of Planning Education and Research*, 31(2), 151–171.

Talvitie, T. (2011). The problem of trust in planning. *Planning Theory*, 11(3), 257–278.

Taylor, N. (1992). Professional ethics in town planning. What is a code of professional conduct for? *Town Planning Review*, 63(3), 227–241.

Vanberg, V. (2001). *The Constitution of Markets*. London: Routledge.

Van Rijswick, M., & Salet, W. (2012). Enabling the contextualization of legal rules in responsible strategies to climate change. *Ecology and Society*, 17(2), 1–8.

Verma, N. (Ed.). (2007). *Institutions and Planning*. Amsterdam: Elsevier.

Williams, J. A. (2005). *Liberalism and the Limit of Power*. Basingstoke: Macmillan.

13
HOW TO CONTEXTUALIZE LEGAL NORMS IN PRACTICES OF SUSTAINABLE DEVELOPMENT? DISTINGUISHING PRINCIPLES, RULES AND PROCEDURAL NORMS

Anoeska Buijze, Willem Salet & Marleen van Rijswick

Introduction

This chapter addresses the question of how different kinds of central regulation affect the ability of local actors to achieve legitimate and effective sustainable solutions through governance processes. We assume central rule must allow for legal contextualization. With legal contextualization we mean the activation of generic norms in practices where involved subjects actively interpret their normative meaning in very specific contexts and hold each other to this meaning, while unfolding their own activities. We recognize that central regulation is needed to normatively guide and enable urban processes of sustainable area development while at the same time the success of this development depends on the commitment and governance of bottom-up configurations. We consider the legitimate and effective interplay between central norms and bottom-up practices of policy invention as crucial in the search for legitimate and effective contextualization. This perspective is especially relevant to sustainable urban development. The transition to a sustainable society is pre-eminently a project where the classic top-down hierarchical approach is thought to be destined to fail, with the input of other subjects and agencies being a requirement for success, in addition to a condition-setting role of public authorities (Cramer, 2012, pp. 19–20, p. 23).

This chapter explores the quality requirements of central regulation that make this interplay more legitimate and effective. The structure of the chapter is as follows. First, the perspective of central regulation is considered from the underlying dimension of social self-regulation. Next, we will discuss the merits of various forms of central regulation. We will focus in particular on the potential for successful contextualization in material norms (both at the level of principles and at the level of rules). Finally, we will discuss the potential of procedural norms of justice. The statements will be briefly illustrated with relevant examples of policymaking and law from five empirical case studies that were conducted in the Netherlands.

The Underlying Dimension of Social Self-Regulation in Central Rule

Our starting point is the self-regulating potential of society. Central norms are not omnipotent in a plural and partly non-regulated society but once established they are critical in the processes of policy discovery and negotiation, both enabling and constraining specific practices of normative assessment and action (North, 1990). Yet, the validation of central ruling is not in central hands and it would become extremely vulnerable if its enforcement would depend on the span of central control. The challenge of legal contextualization is to condition and to enable the power of local self-regulation for sustainable development. Social subjects perceive "incentives as the positive and negative changes in outcomes that are likely to result from particular actions taken within a set of rules in a particular physical and social context" (Ostrom et al., 1993, p. 8). Those incentives do not only include financial rewards or legal penalties but also opportunities for prestige, power, pride, personal comfort and feeling of participation (ibid, p. 8). Ostrom identified – by way of analytical distinction – the reasoning of individual subjects as the motor of all regulation (Ostrom, 1990). She focuses on the rationalizing of action: Why would social subjects invest their energy and resources in norms regarding sustainable development? She claims that subjects will do so if they expect the benefits to exceed the costs and the efforts.

Ostrom adapted this pure economic reasoning to social and ecological incentives to allow for the fact that the benefits and costs of investing social energy are perceived completely differently by individuals. Individuals have internalized very different norms and the discount rates of their norms are highly different. Nevertheless, the rationalizing principle of action as such provides a clue for understanding the underlying dimension of *self-regulation* in regulation. The position of methodological individualism is not uncontested in the social sciences in particular because of the imputed naivety of assuming that we are 'free choosing and optimizing individuals'. Scientific researchers take many different positions with regard to this. One of the more sophisticated positions comes from Pierre Bourdieu who proposes a deliberate recombination of social subjectivism and objectivism as drivers of social action (Bourdieu, 1989). In this chapter we will not delve into the different configurations of social rationality, we will use the rationalizing principle of action purely in a methodological sense (Coleman, 1990) in order to understand that in regulation – also in central rule – there is an autonomous space for participating social subjects to rationalize whether it does or does not make sense for them to commit and validate the norms, and whether they tend to do this in a structural way.

Taking this analytical perspective on regulation, it becomes possible to critically analyse the potential and the limits of central ruling when it has to be materialized in different local settings of sustainable area development. Ostrom used this model to analyse social arrangements of self-regulating common-pool resources as substitutes for central control but the model can be applied to local arenas of decision-making more generally. Ostrom berates the simplification of hierarchy and central ruling as *deus ex machina* (Ostrom, 1990, p. 10). Getting the central authority right is not self-evident but, rather, difficult to achieve, time-consuming and conflict ridden. The threat of non-commitment is always there (the continuing story of 'tragic escape'). Central rule's largest challenge is to become known and recognized in order to become a more active part of social interaction where subjects might make it reality. The social subjects are the experts on the local situation; they are the knowers, the main enforcers and the sanctioners.

The rulings have to shape and reshape the very situations within which individuals must make decisions and bear the consequences of actions taken on a day-to-day basis (Ostrom, 1990, p. 185; see also Ostrom, 2008). Thus, the variables of a particular context are crucial in analysing the effectiveness and legitimacy of central rule.

Thus, central regulation should take into account the underlying dimension of knowable and reasoning social subjects that make their own selections under the particular spatial and temporal conditions of different contexts. Paradoxically, attempts at central rule with the aim to promote sustainable development may hinder and even destroy the potential of sustainable development if these requirements are neglected when the rule/norm is first drafted. Specifying conditions of action at the central level that do not match with particular contexts can in practice be a disincentive for sustainable action, as is prescribing the specific pathways of action instead of regulating the required outcome levels of environmental quality. Central rule usually requires specification on the spot – when applied to a concrete case, rules must leave room to take into account the particularities of the current local context – rather than fix all detail at central level. Ostrom and colleagues investigated a large number of cases and summarized the empirical findings as follows:

> National governments can help or hinder local self-organization. 'Higher' levels of government can facilitate the assembly of users of a common-pool resource in organizational meetings, provide information that helps identify the problem and possible solutions, and legitimize and help enforce agreements reached by local users. National government can also hinder local self-organization by defending rights that lead to overuse or maintaining that the state has ultimate control over resources without actually monitoring and enforcing existing regulations ... Participants are more likely to adopt effective rules in macro-regimes that facilitate their efforts than in regimes that ignore resource problems entirely or that presume that central authorities should make all decisions.
>
> *(Ostrom et al., 1999, p. 291)*

Addressing central regulation from the perspective of contextualization requires the establishment of legal norms and policies that build upon existing norms in society and active processes of internalization. It also requires a parsimonious selection of the norms that should be established at central level. Over-inclusivity of norms (by including local specifics and its differentiation in central norms) may easily become a problem in local practices. Central rule demarcates the scope of norms precisely in order to clarify the conditions for local action while allowing for alternative ways of performance. Clarifying the boundaries of local action in this way creates space for policy innovation that can be used in active ways (constraining margins does not only prohibit behaviour but it also creates space for action). Next we consider it prudent to focus on conditioning material norms rather than on the production of services.

Below, we will address some strategies adopted by the legislator to optimize the interplay between law and governance and their potential impact upon governance processes. Ideally, legislation should build upon existing social structures and not undermine their success. Because the success of specific legislative methods is highly dependent on the characteristics of a country's (legal) culture, we will illustrate our argument mostly with examples from a single jurisdiction – the Dutch one. Although the categorization of norms can function irrespective of jurisdiction, the manner in which such norms function within a jurisdiction – and the manner in which they will impact governance processes – will differ.

Tradition versus Innovation: Governance and the Law

One of the instruments that public authorities have to steer developments in society is to include behavioural norms in legislation. Legal norms are defined here as valid, binding propositions which impose an obligation to either perform or refrain from performing a certain action upon an addressee, with an optional conditionality requirement (Hage, 2007, p. 99; Klanderman, 2007, pp. 113–115). Legalistic approaches to steering society are often argued to lack the characteristics required for a successful transition to a sustainable society. They focus too much on instrumentality and lack flexibility, rely heavily on public authorities initiating and steering developments, and are ill-suited to deal with innovation (Bardach & Kagan, 1982; Coglianese & Kagan, 2007; Majone, 1994). An alternative is to rely solely on the self-regulating potential of society. Governance is argued to be a better method for steering society, due to its flexibility and potential for bottom-up initiatives (Olsson et al., 2004; see also Folke et al., 2005; Gunderson & Light, 2006).

Adaptive governance and central regulation are often presented as mutually exclusive, but there is nothing in their nature that necessarily makes them so (van Rijswick & Salet, 2012). By enacting contextualizable legal norms, the self-regulating potential of society can be used optimally, combining the safeguard-function of the law with the innovative potential of governance methods. Actors cooperate to determine the meaning of legislation in a given context to steer their own and each other's behaviour. Below, we will discuss several forms of central regulation, and the manner in which they may impact upon governance processes. First, we will address legal principles. Next, we will proceed with a discussion of the various kinds of substantive and procedural rules.

Contextualization as Principle-Based Adjudication

Theoretically, all norms can be contextualized in a way that builds upon existing practices and informal norms and values that exist in society, when principle-based methods of interpretation are used. This method works regardless of how complex, detailed and instrumental the rules that actually comprise the law are, because it relies on the fundamental principles and societal values these rules were originally based on. Principles are a subset of legal norms, which do not prescribe or prohibit specific behaviour, but rather oblige actors to act in a way which is congruent to the realization of a goal which the legal order as a whole recognizes as worthy of pursuit (Alexy, 2002; Ávila, 2007). Human rights are a classic example (Dworkin, 1977). Principles can be codified by a legislator, but they are an inherent part of the legal system, and can be derived from the rules within that system even when they cannot be found in its written law. Principles are juxtaposed with rules, which are more concrete and oblige their addressee to either take or refrain from taking specific actions, without immediate reference to the results of such behaviour (Ávila, 2007; Groussot, 2006).

With regard to the interpretation and application of the law to specific cases, taking into account all relevant legal and factual circumstances, Dworkin offers one description of how this process could take place (Dworkin, 1986). He argues that the ideal court decides cases based on a comprehensive analysis of the legal system. They then take the decision that 'fits' best with all previous decisions. Thus, if many of the rules in a given jurisdiction indicate that people should not profit from their crimes, the courts can decide that a murderer cannot inherit from his victim, even if there exists no previous rule to that effect (Dworkin, 1986). The application of rules will be sufficient to solve most cases, but if this would result in undesirable outcomes, the courts can refer to the principles underlying the rules to argue that the only right decision is in fact to reinterpret the rule in a way to make it confirm with those principles (ibid., 1986). Note that the court does not overrule the legislator, but instead discovers the law that is applicable to this specific case:

> What could be more unreasonable than to suppose that it was the legislative intention in the general laws passed for the orderly, peaceable and just devolution of property, that they should have operation in favor of one who murdered his ancestor that he might speedily come into the possession of his estate? Such an intention is inconceivable. We need not, therefore, be much troubled by the general language contained in the laws.
> (Riggs v. Palmer, 1889)

Legal principles are, at least according to *common law doctrine*, an important part of the legal system. They are a safeguard against the mindless application of rules that leads to injustice. They allow for all relevant aspects of a case to be taken into account, and balanced against one another. In addition, their interpretation and application will reflect the views of society as they have been ingrained in the legal system. This allows for adaptation to changing circumstances and values in society without intervention of the legislator. Legislation can build on existing norms and structures, and if due to unforeseen circumstances the strict application of a rule would go against these norms, it could be overturned.

Principles have limitations as well. They provide less legal certainty than rules, and their application is more difficult. Dworkin argues that principles are usually implicit; they only surface in hard cases (1986). Most cases are decided using rules. Identifying and applying principles is a Herculean task in terms of the effort required. Because principles reflect the values that underlie the legal system as a whole, enacting them is an inefficient way to accommodate changing values and stimulate transition. They are conservative in nature. Their weight will be determined by the importance attached by the legal system as a whole to the values they refer to (Ávila, 2007). If sustainability is not already ingrained as a value in the legal system, the application of legal principles will not lead to sustainable outcomes.

In addition, although principles can provide a correction to rules when the application of rules leads to perverse outcomes, they are dependent on the willingness of the *legal actors* in a system to apply them. We assume that sustainable development requires the involvement of private parties and can profit from the self-regulating potential of society. Thus, different actors should be able to contribute to the process where principles are used to contextualize the law. These parties include the legislator, the administration, the courts, the business sector, third parties with an interest, and civil society. Borgers shows that theoretically all these parties can be involved, which makes principle-based contextualization of legislation an attractive option (Borgers, 2012). However, because the official decision-making power on how norms are to be interpreted in concrete cases usually resides with the administration, or ultimately with the courts, their willingness to contextualize norms is a necessary condition for this process to function. In practice neither the Dutch Council of State nor the Dutch administration appears willing to utilize legal principles in this way.

The theory of principles as facilitators of contextualization has been developed mostly by scholars from common law jurisdictions, where the law is traditionally developed through case law, and new situations are easily resolved by applying the principles underlying the judgements in older cases. The doctrine of *stare decisis* is best understood as requiring the courts to decide new cases based on the same rationale as old ones, rather than by applying the same rule (Brouwer, 2013). Even in common law jurisdictions, though, where principle-based adjudication is a well-established part of the legal system, the approach is not without its downsides. The amount of case law that needs to be processed by legal professionals is enormous, and for laymen it is an insurmountable obstacle to navigating the legal landscape (van Rijswick & Salet, 2012). Other jurisdictions may prove less enthusiastic about principle-based adjudication: it gives a very central role to the courts, and diminishes the importance of the legislator. Forcing principle-based adjudication upon these jurisdictions is unlikely to work, because it does not fit with their constitutional systems. Thus, it is unlikely that a one-size-fits-all approach to inject the law with flexibility will work.

In the Netherlands, the courts traditionally have a different role than in common law jurisdictions. There is a strict divide between policy and law: policy decisions are made by the administration, the judge merely reviews whether those decisions comply with the law, and will not interfere with the policy choices the administration makes (van der Hoeven, 1989). The courts are expected not to interfere with policy matters and must practise restraint when reviewing administrative decisions (Schlössels & Zijlstra, 2010). Although they do contribute to the development of the law, the basic premise is that they merely apply rules, both to ensure a proper working of the law and to solve individual conflicts, preferably in a consistent and efficient way. The other powers (the legislature and the executive) are quite concerned with the courts staying in their proper place (van Kemenade, 1997). The Dutch legislator refrained from including principles in its new water law to prevent them from 'affecting the law' (van Rijswick & Havekes, 2012, p. 81). The lack of a constitutional court in the Netherlands contributes to this view of what courts are and are not supposed to do. The final arbiter of whether legislation is in compliance with the public interests and the goals of the legal system as a whole is parliament (Belinfante & de Reede, 2009, p. 15). This means that in practice, principles play a very modest role in Dutch adjudication. They do however play a role in policy documents and plans, and can be used by the administration to motivate decisions that are more innovative or sustainable than usual (van Rijswick, 2012).

On the other hand, in EU law principles serve an important function. Environmental principles of a substantive nature are included in, for example, article 191 TFEU (Havekes & Van Rijswick, 2012, p. 80). These principles are elaborated upon in directives and affect the law of the member states. One would expect the inclusion of principles to be helpful in correctly implementing the directives into national law, since they clarify the intention of the legislator, while still allowing significant room for national and local authorities to interpret them in concrete situations. The EU environmental principles are also used to interpret secondary EU legislation. Indeed, it has been observed that the European Court of Justice has much in common with the Dworkinian court (Groussot, 2006, p. 137). The 'polluter-pays' principle has for instance had a large impact on the interpretation of liability rules in the Water Framework Directive (Bleeker, 2009).

We conclude that all norms can be contextualized referencing the underlying principles, regardless of legislative quality. Principle-based legislation should be particularly easy to contextualize. This process could potentially involve all actors, but its success is dependent on the willingness of the administration and the courts to apply the law in this manner. This willingness is absent in some jurisdictions, indicating that a principle-based interpretation and application of legislation to allow for contextualization does not offer a one-size-fits-all solution. Alternative methods to promote contextualization are needed. We must turn to rules then to stimulate sustainable development. Their potential is clear: rules provide legal certainty and can help prevent and resolve conflict. They can ensure that actors can be held accountable for their actions (Ostrom, 1986). They are also, as will be shown below, difficult to do right.

Exemplary Legislation: General Rules

As we have seen, the quality of legislation matters. In theory, criteria for good legislation are easily given. Fuller, after decades of experience as a judge, argued that good legislation should meet the requirements of generality, promulgation, non-retroactivity, clarity, non-contradiction, not asking the impossible, durability, and congruence between rules and official action (Fuller, 1964). These kinds of rules offer normative guidance in the abstract, and can help realize the self-regulating potential of society to its fullest extent (van Rijswick & Salet, 2012, p. 18). They are in some ways similar to principles, because although they do prescribe or prohibit behaviour, they do so in a fairly abstract way, and the underlying values are easy to distinguish.

In practice, these ideal rules are seldom enacted, and if they are, they don't often last. Authorities draft new legislation in response to urgent societal needs, and tailor it to the specific problems society faces at the time. The abstraction to general rules is often avoided. In addition, generality and clarity may conflict, as general terms leave room for doubt over their interpretation in specific cases (Diver, 1983, pp. 70–71). General rules, like principles, have the potential to be contextualized because of their abstract nature, but it is not necessarily easy to do so. By enacting more detailed rules, central authorities give local legal actors a surer footing when applying those rules in a local context, at the price of creating a legal system consisting of more precise and more instrumental rules. Such rules, although helpful in tackling current issues, may obscure the general values underlying the legal system as a whole. Thus, they make it harder for local actors to come up with innovative solutions that are in compliance with those general values.

It is often assumed the resulting legislation makes laws more difficult to apply, but little is known about how different sorts of legislation affect processes of contextualization. Below, we will discuss some problems and advantages of different legislative choices.

Discretionary Powers and Open Norms

The classic approach to facilitating a more bottom-up approach is to award discretionary powers to the administration. Discretionary powers have become increasingly prevalent as the government has become responsible for the provision of a growing number of services, and it became abundantly clear that the legislator lacked the foresight to create rules that would lead to appropriate outcomes in all circumstances (De Haan et al., 1976). The exact meaning of the concept of 'discretionary room' varies between jurisdictions (Forowicz, 2011, pp. 4–7). Some common distinctions made between different types of discretionary power may prove useful to our research. The first is *classic discretion*, the equivalent to Dutch 'beleidsvrijheid' and German 'Ermessen'. The second is *jurisdictional discretion*, similar to Dutch 'beoordelingsruimte' and German 'Beurteilingsspielraum' (Craig, 2012, pp. 403–405).

The first category is the most straightforward. Norms of this kind allow their addressee to do something, or to refrain from doing something, but leave the final decision on whether to act upon this permission up to him. An example can be found in article 16(1) of the Habitats Directive, which includes some conditions under which member states *may* derogate from the norms in the directive. However, they are under no obligation to do so. Thus, member states can set their own priorities and are able to balance different interests with the importance of nature conservation (van Holten & van Rijswick, 2014). By their nature, these kinds of norms give competences, but little substantive guidance on how to use them. They do little to correct the weaknesses inherent in governance processes. What they do is allocate decision-making power to public authorities. At best, this would give those authorities the possibility to use their powers in harmony with social norms and self-regulatory practices. At worst, it takes away power from social actors, diminishing their sense of responsibility and their ability to ensure compliance within their own community.

The second category does not give the norm's addressee the freedom to balance interests when deciding whether to use a power. Instead, it imposes an obligation. Public authorities *have to* do something. They cannot choose whether or not to use the power they have been given. However, the conditions that should be met for the obligation to apply or the exact nature of the obligation that is imposed are open to further interpretation. Article 37 of the Dutch Soil Protection Act (1986) imposes an obligation upon the provincial executive to determine whether a current or intended use of the soil will lead to "such a risk for humans, plants, or animals, that speedy decontamination is necessary". This requires the provincial executive to determine when the risk is no longer acceptable. The provision itself gives some guidance as to what factors should be taken into account when making this decision, but does not provide a solution for individual cases. The norm must be contextualized: it is up to the provincial executive to determine if there is a risk that requires swift decontamination or, in other words, if the conditions for the applicability of the norm are met.

Such norms can be further subdivided into two categories, dependent on who has the final responsibility for their interpretation. Sometimes, this will fall to the administration. In such cases, the courts, when confronted with a case, will accept the administration's interpretation. At other times, the responsibility will be the courts. In those cases, the courts will fully review the administration's interpretation of a norm, and may replace it with their own interpretation if they disagree. The legislator can indicate its intent to leave the interpretation of a particular rule to the administration by using certain terminology. Courts also tend to practise restraint when the administration has to make complicated economic and social decisions, and when it lacks the specific knowledge necessary to evaluate the situation – knowledge that the administration possesses (Caranta, 2008, p. 194). However, the power to decide whether a vague norm is intended to convey true discretionary jurisdiction to the administration, or is merely a 'vague' norm in need of interpretation but subject to full judicial review resides with the courts (Schlössels & Zijlstra, 2010, p. 170). This creates a lack of certainty about the acceptability of innovative interpretations, which works as a disincentive for novel solutions. The risks of a court ruling quashing the decision are born primarily by the administration, which provides an incentive to stick to conservative interpretations of the law (Buijze, 2013, p. 42). Open norms, whether they are principles or vague norms that imply jurisdictional discretion, are often operationalized in policy rules, lower level regulation, or guiding documents for decision-making authorities (e.g. the circular soil decontamination which operationalizes norms from the Soil Protection Act (Buijze, 2013, p. 44) and the Association of Netherlands Municipalities' (VNG's) guidelines for environmental zoning around businesses (Dembski, 2013, p. 28)). Reliance on policy rules, circulars and guidance documents lowers administrative authorities' workload and the risk of decisions being quashed. There is little incentive to deviate from these norms, even when they are not binding, because deviating requires an extensive motivation and compliance with the principle of carefulness, which requires public authorities to chart and take into account all relevant interests, and because the courts may rely on them when reviewing decisions (Bröring & Geertjes, 2013). Thus, open norms can close up regardless of the intentions of the originator of the norms.

Even when there is discretionary room in the true sense of the word, that is, classic discretion, administrative authorities have to comply with a host of general procedural and substantive obligations. These must observe human rights law and often also the general principles of EU law. At the national level, Dutch authorities must observe the general principles of proper administration. France has the similar *principes generaux du droit administrative* (Langbroek, 2003). These rules limit the range of substantive decisions they can take, and regulate the decision-making procedure. Although these rules will tend to be general in their scope, they might be problematic due to uncertainty about their interpretation by the courts or because of the stringent demands they place on decision-making procedures. Poignant examples are the principle of due care, which requires the administration to take into account all relevant interests and information when making a decision, and the duty to give reasons, which requires the administration to motivate any decision it takes.[1] More substantive examples are the principle of proportionality, the principle of equality and the principle of legal certainty.

To conclude: rules that award discretionary room move decision-making power away from the national legislator and put it in the hands of either the administration or the courts. Some brands of discretionary power do a better job at providing normative guidance than others. The extent to which these rules will allow for contextualization and whether they are an asset rather than a hindrance for local governance will depend on the constellation of the legal system and several cultural factors, in particular the willingness of administrative authorities to condition rather than control decision-making, and the judicial review of administrative decisions.

Procedural Justice as an Alternative to Normative Guidance

In the absence of norms that provide normative guidance, the legislator or the courts can attempt to ensure procedural justice. According to the compensation theory the principles of proper administration were introduced by the courts to allow judicial review of administrative decisions even though the discretionary room awarded to the administration was steadily increasing. A lack of substantive rules was compensated by the introduction of procedural rules (Nicolaï, 1990, p. 212). They aim to ensure just and legitimate outcomes where discretionary powers have been awarded because the legislator could not prescribe a substantive outcome (Schlössels & Zijlstra, 2010, p. 388). The EU is increasingly using this method in lieu of substantive norms, to allow member states to take local circumstances into account when setting standards (Howarth, 2009). This increased freedom is paid for with procedural demands, monitoring and reporting obligations (Scott, 2010, p. 273). A prime example is the environmental impact assessment, which aims to ensure that environmental interests are taken into account at an early stage and which requires public authorities to gather a large amount of information. The effect on decision-making is not guaranteed though. Authorities must take the results of the assessment into account when taking decisions, but the directive contains no substantive norms that must be met. A similar approach is seen in the Water Framework Directive, which instead of setting down a universal standard for the entire EU allows member states to set some standards for their territory by themselves, provided they comply with procedural obligations included in the annexes to the directive. In particular, standards must be subject to peer review and public consultation (Annex V, table 1.2.6 to Directive 2000/60/EC, 2000; see also van Holten & van Rijswick, 2014). In both cases, the legislator does not provide principles, or even the substantive rules that are derived from these principles, but rather enacts procedural rules that the governance process has to comply with. Such rules aim to counter the weaknesses of governance processes, and seek to guarantee that all interests are represented and have a say. They have the benefit that they do not prescribe goods to be realized, and instead leave it to societal actors to determine what is good for society, allowing local authorities to build upon existing norms and social practices. The pitfalls of unregulated governance are thought to be avoided through mandatory consultations or participation of interest groups. The success of such mechanisms in guaranteeing a positive outcome is disputed (Curtin & Meijer, 2006; Scott,

2010, p. 273; van Holten & van Rijswick, 2014). In addition, procedural rules detract from the flexibility and spontaneity of the governance process. Complying with procedural norms like the principle of carefulness requires a lot of resources and can lead to a tendency to tick the boxes rather than to take carefully considered decisions (Dembski, 2013, p. 55).

Contextualization in Dutch Practices: Focus on Exemptions to Create Flexibility

In practice, the process of contextualization does not function well in the Dutch jurisdiction. The courts are reluctant to adopt it and are actively discouraged to do so. The administration tends to bind itself with substantive rules and policy guidance documents, and is bound by procedural rules originating from the courts and the legislator. Thus, the legislator often tries to meet the need for flexibility by including exceptions and procedures for deviating from the rules. Such legislation is related to the process of contextualization in one of two ways.

First, the legislator can attempt to contextualize the principles underlying the legislation by itself, coming up with situations where applying existing rules leads to undesirable outcomes, and creating new rules for that specific situation. This approach falls short because the legislator is not omniscient. It will create new rules to meet specific situations that arise, which will lead to an increasingly intricate set of rules and a decrease in transparency (Diver, 1983). An alternative is the inclusion of a general equivalence clause, as included in article 1.3 of the *Bouwbesluit 2012* ('Building Decree 2012'). This article stipulates that one does not have to meet any of the requirements in the Bouwbesluit if one uses another method that guarantees at least the same level of safety, protection of health, usability, energy efficiency and environmental protection as the one that a particular requirement aims to achieve. Although this allows for made-to-measure decisions, it can lead to confusion about how to establish whether a proposed method is equivalent to the one the legislator came up with (Nijmeijer, 2013).

Second, the legislator can try to regulate the process of contextualization, by enacting procedures or conditions for deviating from the rules like in the Dutch Crisis and Recovery Act. This is different from proceduralization because substantive rules still apply to standard cases. If the proper procedures are followed, the outcome of the decision-making process is deemed to be legitimate. Compared to a situation without substantive rules for standard cases, legal certainty is increased and high decision-making costs are, most of the time, avoided. The underlying rationale for such procedures can vary. Often, the following of the proper procedures is thought to lead to a decision of high quality that does in fact help to bring the utopian situation embodied in the principles that underlie legislation closer. The doctrine that public participation and access to decision-making procedures will actually lead to better substantive decisions that respect environmental interests is seen most clearly in the Aarhus Convention and its implementing legislation (Mason, 2010, p. 16). At other times, the values underlying the legislation are lost sight of, and the legitimacy of the decision is guaranteed only by adherence to the doctrine of procedural justice, with little or no regard for the substance of the decision that is the outcome of the procedure.

Way Forward: Stimulating Contextualization in Achieving Sustainability Values

Neither legislation nor governance will necessarily lead to sustainable bottom-up governance which makes optimal use of the self-regulating potential of societal actors. The legal system as a whole rather than the manner in which specific legal norms are drafted provides incentives against contextualization in favour of risk-averse behaviour. The legislator has several means at its disposal to stimulate legal actors to engage in contextualization regardless. Contextualization of legal rules is always a possibility. Principles are always present, and help contextualize rules when their straightforward application would lead to perverse results. Note that the presence of detailed rules does not, in theory, hamper the process of contextualization, although they do make the legal system less transparent. In a case study concerning the restructuring of Utrecht's railway station area, the detailed rules in the Soil Protection Act did not prevent the municipality from implementing its novel method of soil decontamination, but they did pose a challenge in terms of how that solution could be fit into the legal framework. The case study suggests that this kind of contextualization will only take place under exceptional circumstances, where the gain of a non-traditional interpretation offsets the time, effort, and risks of departing from the conventional way of doing things (Buijze, 2013, p. 46). The common law approach to principle-based adjudication has not taken hold in the Netherlands. Although the *contra-legem* application of principles is not unheard of, it is exceedingly rare (Schlössels & Zijlstra, 2010, p. 434). Therefore, there is a need for different strategies to ensure that the law achieves the results it was meant to achieve. Many of the classic methods of creating flexibility fail to bridge the gap between central norms and bottom-up practices, though, and do not allow for successful contextualization. They sometimes restrict more than intended, while at other times they fail to provide normative guidance. A more promising strategy is to enact substantive rules that can be applied in standard situations, and to stimulate legal actors to contextualize the underlying principles when these rules fall short. This can be done in several ways.

First, legislation can include a so-called principle of equivalence in addition to instrumental rules which aim to realize a clearly identified goal. Such a provision allows the use of alternative methods to realize this goal if the initiator of a project can show that they are as effective as the means the law prescribes. This approach provides clear guidance in standard situations, while awarding flexibility when needed. In the latter case, the decision-making process will be more elaborate and time-consuming, but this will be the exception rather than the rule. Because the goal that must be realized is clearly delineated, substantive review of the decision is made possible, and the necessity to rely on procedural review is diminished.

Second, legislation can contain procedures for allowing exceptions to rules. In this case, the rules included in the law can be set aside if the proper procedure is followed. The legitimacy of the decision is achieved by following certain procedural guarantees. Although this method provides flexibility, it foregoes normative guidance, and the public interest may be insufficiently protected as a result. It seems preferable to relying exclusively on procedural norms though. The costs of forced contextualization are limited, because the rules can be relied on in standard situations. Using the exception will carry costs for both the administration and the initiator of a project, which ensures that it is only used if deviating from the norm carries a significant benefit. There is no guarantee it is a benefit to the public interest though. The danger of allowing for exceptions to rules as long as the proper procedure is followed is that the applicable standards are not contextualized, but in fact are simply lowered (Dieperink et al., 2012; Keessen et al., 2010).

Third, legislation can contain substantive exceptions. In such cases, the law allows deviation from the rules if their straightforward application would not result in the realization of the goals that inspired that law, or lead to otherwise perverse outcomes. This is similar to the principle of equivalence, except that it allows for the possibility that the law's goal cannot be realized at all in a given situation, and has similar benefits.

A concrete option that could allow for contextualization is the 'area-based approach', also called the 'programmatic approach'. With this approach, the appropriate standard is deemed to be met if an area as a whole meets that standard, even if specific parts of it do not (Backes & van

Rijswick, 2013; Boeve & van den Broek, 2012; Groothuijse & Uylenburg, 2014). The upside of this approach is that it can allow large-scale solutions to problems that cannot be resolved on a smaller scale, like in the Utrecht and Markermeer cases (see Chapter 24 in this volume; see also Buijze, 2013; Waterhout et al., 2013). The downside is that it may lead to the lowering of standards. Simple minimum standards do not exclude a varying quality within an area, and the purpose of the area-based approach may simply be to justify not meeting minimum standards at one place with an excellent performance in another (Bontje, 2013). When properly applied though, the area-based approach is an example of a substantive exception, where the goals underlying the legislation are thought to be better served by a different approach. The approach has been used with some success in the United States, where it has arguably improved environmental quality and saved both time and money (Greer & Som, 2010, p. 234).

Likewise, legal regimes that require mitigation or compensation are substantive exceptions to general rules.[2] Following the standard rules will lead to an undesirable outcome, and taking mitigating or compensating measures is thought to lead to a better outcome in terms of the goals society wants to realize (McGillivray, 2012, p. 418).

These options seem attractive, but they are not without problems of their own. When applying substantive exceptions or a principle of equivalence, there is bound to be a certain degree of uncertainty about whether the substantive goal will be better achieved by deviating from the standard rule. This kind of uncertainty opens the door for endless discussions on the validity of information-gathering methods, and the subsequent development – most likely through case law – of a host of procedural rules that regulate this process. This is reflected in the abundance of research obligations and impact assessments. It would therefore be advisable to think about whether we could devise a relatively simple way to deal with such situations.

Likewise, trying to achieve justice, either substantive or merely procedural, by following proper procedure opens the door to endless discussions about proper modes of participation and information gathering (Scott, 2010, pp. 267–271). Because certainty is impossible, decisions will never be motivated convincingly enough in the eyes of their opponents. The procedural review of the Council of State has resulted in a host of rules on how to conduct decision-making procedures. Although merely regulating decision-making processes rather than the substance of decisions does allow for more flexibility with regard to outcome, it also leads to lengthy procedures and to uncertainty about the acceptability of that outcome, to an even greater extent than when substantive norms provide guidance about what the outcome of the process should be.

Thus, substantive rules for standard cases are both inevitable and desirable. They circumvent the process of contextualization of the underlying principles, which is costly and time-consuming. In addition, principles will inevitably breed rules. If rules are insufficient, or lead to undesirable outcomes, principles can come to the rescue. Because the Dutch legal culture is not naturally welcoming to this phenomenon, the legislator should take action to stimulate this process where necessary. It can do this by providing substantive conditions for deviating from rules safeguarding that the public goals and values will be realized and respected. Alternatively, the legislator can create a procedure which, when followed, allows the administration to make an exception to the standard rules. Instead of regulating the outcome of the decision-making process, the legislator regulates the process itself. This appears to lead to costly investigative duties and detailed procedures to guarantee procedural justice, which may or may not be achieved. A possible downside of this approach is that rules can be circumvented even when their application would not lead to a perverse outcome, and also when powerful actors disagree with the legislation and the importance of the respective values that inspired it.

Conclusion

Generally speaking, all legislation can be contextualized. The law is built on a set of substantive principles that can be uncovered and used to guide the interpretation and application of the law in concrete situations, especially when unforeseen or changing circumstances are involved. This process of interpretation can potentially involve all actors, but its success is dependent on the willingness of the administration and the courts to apply the law in this manner. The institutions that have the final say over the interpretation of the law can reject a particular agreed-upon interpretation in favour of their own. The willingness to involve other actors in this process, or at least to transfer any real decision-making power to them, is absent in some jurisdictions. Hence, the principle-based interpretation and application of existing rules will not always lead to effective contextualization. The quality of legislation does matter: principle-based adjudication makes all manner of rules contextualizable, but that does not detract from the fact that some methods of legislating stimulate the process more than others. We must formulate rules in a manner that stimulates sustainable development through contextualization. To achieve this, the abstract normative values that underlie legislation must be clearly visible. This can be done by making the underlying principles explicit, or by enacting sufficiently abstract rules. These rules can be elaborated upon and be made more concrete. If more concrete legislation is called for, clear substantive rules work best for standard cases. If unforeseen circumstances come up, more flexible forms of regulation may allow for better contextualization. In almost all cases though, legislation can either interfere with or provide a focal point for processes of self-regulation: whether legislation interferes with or stimulates self-rule is not just dependent on how the legislation is drafted, but also on other aspects of legal culture. In the Netherlands, to stimulate contextualization the legislator has to overcome a legal culture that is adverse to it. There is a strong tendency to create legal certainty that leads to rigidity and blanket solutions for cases that deserve tailor-made solutions, even in the absence of restrictive national and EU norms. Moreover, discretionary room is compensated by stringent procedural rules which are experienced as even more limiting than substantive rules. The legislator has various possibilities to counteract these tendencies, but must make a choice between flexibility in outcome and ease of decision-making. Principle-based regulation is a must, but rules for standard cases cannot be missed.

Acknowledgements

The authors would like to thank the researchers of the NWO CONTEXT project for their comments on earlier versions of this paper. We are particularly grateful to Wil Zonneveld and Sebastian Dembski for their helpful contributions.

Funding

This work was supported by the Netherlands Council for Scientific Research [438-11-006].

Notes

1 Note that these are not principles in the Dworkinian sense, but rather rules that apply generally.
2 See Trevisanut & van Rijswick (2014), special issue on compensation in nature conservation and water law.

References

Alexy, R. (2002). *A Theory of Constitutional Rights*. Oxford: Oxford University Press.
Ávila, H. (2007). *Theory of Legal Principles*. Dordrecht: Springer.

Backes, C., & van Rijswick, M. (2013). Effective Environmental Protection: Towards a Better Understanding of Environmental Quality Standards in Environmental Legislation. In L. Gipperth & C. Zetterberg (Eds.), *Miljörättsliga perspektiv och tankevändor, Vänbok till Jan Darpö & Gabriel Michanek* (pp. 19–50). Uppsala: Iustus Förlag AB.

Bardach, E., & Kagan, R. A. (1982). *Going by the Book: The Problem of Regulatory Unreasonableness.* Philadelphia, PA: Temple University Press.

Belinfante, A. D., & de Reede, J. L. (2009). *Beginselen van het Nederlandse Staatsrecht* (16th revised ed.). Deventer: Kluwer.

Bleeker, A. (2009). Does the polluter pay? The polluter-pays principle in the case law of the European Court of Justice. *European Energy and Environmental Law Review*, 6, 289–306.

Boeve, M., & van den Broek, G. M. (2012). The programmatic approach: A flexible and complex tool to achieve environmental quality standards. *Utrecht Law Review*, 8(3), 74–85.

Bontje, N. (2013). *Case Study Utrecht Station Area, the Netherlands: Legal Contextualization as a Suitable Solution for Air Quality* (CONTEXT Report 9). Amsterdam: AISSR Programme Group Urban Planning.

Borgers, H. C. (2012). *Duurzaam handelen: Een onderzoek naar een normatieve grondslag van het milieurecht.* The Hague: Sdu.

Bourdieu, P. (1989). Social space and symbolic power. *Sociological Theory*, 7, 14–25.

Bröring, H. E., & Geertjes, G. J. A. (2013). Bestuursrechtelijke soft law in Nederland, Duitsland en Engeland. *Nederlands Tijdschrift voor Bestuursrecht*, 12, 74–87.

Brouwer, R. (2013). *On the Interdisciplinary Nature of the Study of Law.* Paper presented at the Methodology Seminar, Faculty of Law, Utrecht.

Brunnée, J., & Toope, S. T. (2010). *Legitimacy and Legality in International Law: An Interactional Account.* Cambridge: Cambridge University Press.

Buijze, A. (2013). *Case Study Utrecht Station Area, the Netherlands: How PPPs Restructured a Station, a Shopping Mall and the Law* (CONTEXT Report 4). Amsterdam: AISSR Programme Group Urban Planning.

Caranta, R. (2008). On Discretion. In S. Prechal (Ed.), *The Coherence of EU Law: The Search for Coherence in Divergent Concepts.* Oxford: Oxford University Press.

Case Law. (1889). *Riggs vs Palmer, 115 NY 506.*

Craig, P. P. (2012). *EU Administrative Law.* Oxford: Oxford University Press.

Coglianese, C., & Kagan, R. A. (2007). *Regulation and Regulatory Processes.* Aldershot: Ashgate.

Coleman, J. S. (1990). *The Foundations of Social Theory.* Cambridge, MA: The Belknap Press of Harvard University Press.

Cramer, J. (2012). De bijdrage van milieurecht aan duurzame ontwikkeling. In N. Teesing (Ed.), *De toekomst van het milieurecht: eenvoudig beter?* The Hague: Boom Juridische Uitgevers.

Curtin, D. M., & A. Meijer. (2006). Does transparency strenghten legitimacy? *Information Policy*, 11, 109–122.

Dembski, S. (2013). *Case Study Amsterdam Buiksloterham, the Netherlands: The Challenge of Planning Organic Transformation* (CONTEXT Report 2). Amsterdam: AISSR Programme Group Urban Planning.

Dieperink, C., Raadgever, G. T., Driessen, P. P. J, Smit, A. A. H., & van Rijswick, H. F. M. W. (2012). Ecological ambitions and complications in the regional implementation of the Water Framework Directive in the Netherlands. *Water Policy*, 14, 160–173.

Diver, C. S. (1983). The optimal precision of administrative rules. *Yale Law Journal*, 93, 65–109.

Dworkin, R. M. (1977). *Taking Rights Seriously.* Cambridge, MA: Harvard University Press.

Dworkin, R. (1986). *Law's Empire.* Cambridge, MA: Harvard University Press.

European Parliament. (2000). Directive 2000/60/EC of the European Parliament and of the Council establishing a framework for the Community action in the field of water policy, OJ L 327, 22 December 2000, pp. 1–73.

Folke, C., Hahn, T., Olsson, P., & Norberg, J. (2005). Adaptive governance of social-ecological systems. *Annual Review of Environment and Resources*, 30, 441–473. Retrieved from: http://dx.doi.org/10.1146/annurev.energy.30.050504.144511.

Forowicz, M. (2011). *State Discretion as a Paradox of EU Evolution.* EUI Working Paper 2011/27.

Fuller, L. L. (1964). *The Morality of Law.* New Haven/London: Yale University Press.

Greer, K., & Som, M. (2010). Breaking the environmental gridlock: Advance mitigation programs for ecological impacts. *Environmental Practice*, 12, 227–236.

Groothuijse, F., & Uylenburg, R. (2014). Everything According to Plan? Achieving Environmental Quality Standards by a Programmatic Approach. In M. Peeters & R. Uylenburg (Eds.), *EU Environmental Legislation: Legal Perspectives on Regulatory Strategies* (pp. 116–145). Cheltenham: Edward Elgar.

Groussot, X. (2006). *General Principles of Community Law.* Groningen: Europa Law Publishing.

Gunderson, L. H., & Light, S. S. (2006). Adaptive management and adaptive governance in the Everglades ecosystem. *Policy Sciences*, 39, 323–334. Retrieved from: http://dx.doi.org/10.1007/s11077-006-9027-2.

Haan, P. de, Drupsteen, T., & Fernhout, R. (1976). *Bestuursrecht in de sociale rechtsstaat*. Deventer: Kluwer.

Hage, J. (2007). Wat is een rechtsnorm? In J. Donkers et al. (Eds.), *Liber Amicorum ter gelegenheid van de 60ste verjaardag van Prof. Dr. J. Jaap van den Herik* (pp. 98–106). Maastricht: Maastricht ICT Competence Centre.

Hoeven, J. van der. (1989). *De drie dimensies van het bestuursrecht*. VAR-reeks no. 100. Alphen a/d Rijn: VAR Vereniging van Bestuurskunde.

Holten, S. van, & van Rijswick, M. (2014). The Consequences of a Governance Approach in European Environmental Directives for Flexibility, Effectiveness and Legitimacy. In M. Peeters & R. Uylenburg (Eds.), *EU Environmental Legislation: Legal Perspectives on Regulatory Strategies* (pp. 13–47). Cheltenham: Edward Elgar.

Howarth, W. (2009). Aspirations and realities under the Water Framework Directive: Proceduralisation, participation and practicalities. *Journal of Environmental Law*, 21(3), 391–417.

Keessen, A. M., van Kempen, J. J. H., van Rijswick, M., Robbe, J., & Backes, C. W. (2010). European river basin districts: Are they swimming in the same implementation pool? *Journal of Environmental Law*, 22(2), 197–222.

Kemenade, J. A. van. (1997). *Bestuur in het geding; rapport van de Werkgroep inzake terugdringing van de juridisering van het openbaar bestuur*. Haarlem: Provincie Noord-Holland, Servicepunt Facilitair Bedrijf.

Klanderman, J. (2007). Normativiteit, gelding en handhaving van rechtsnormen. In H. T. M. Kloosterhuis, P. W. Brouwer, M. M. Henkel & A. M. Hol (Eds.), *Drie dimensies van recht*. (107–127). Den Haag: Boom Juridische Uitgaven.

Langbroek, P. M. (2003). *General Principles of Proper Administration and the General Administrative Law Act in the Netherlands*. New York City: World Bank Workshop.

Majone, D. (1994). The rise of the regulatory state in Europe. *West European Politics*, 17(3), 77–101. Retrieved from: http://dx.doi.org/10.1080/01402389408425031.

Mason, M. (2010). Information disclosure and environmental rights: The Aarhus Convention. *Global Environmental Politics*, 69, 263–279.

McGillivray, D. (2012). Compensating biodiversity loss: The EU Commission's approach to compensation under Article 6 of the Habitats Directive. *Journal of Environmental Law*, 24(3), 417–450.

Nicolaï, P. (1990). *Beginselen van behoorlijk bestuur*. Deventer: Kluwer.

Nijmeijer, A. G. A. (2013). Het gelijkwaardigheidsbeginsel in de omgevingswet. *Milieu en Recht*, 10(135), 646–651.

North, D. C. (1990). *Institutions, Institutional Change and Economic Performance*. Cambridge: Cambridge University Press.

Olsson, P., Folke, C., & Berkes, F. 2004. Adaptive comanagement for building resilience in social-ecological systems. *Environmental Management*, 34(1), 75–90. Retrieved from: http://dx.doi.org/10.1007/s00267-003-0101-7.

Ostrom, E., Schroeder, L., & Wynne, S. (1993). *Institutional Incentives and Sustainable Development: Infrastructure Policies in Perspective*. Boulder, CO: Westview Press.

Ostrom, E. (2008). Twenty years into our common future: The challenge of common-pool resources. *Environment*, 50(4), 8–21. Retrieved from: http://dx.doi.org/10.3200/ENVT.50.4.8-21.

Ostrom, E., Burger, J., Field, C. B., Norgaard, R. B., & Policansky, D. (1999). Revisiting the commons: local lessons, global challenges. *Science*, 284(5412), 278–282. Retrieved from: www.jstor.org/stable/2898207.

Ostrom, E. (1990). *Governing the Commons: The Evolution of Institutions for Collective Action*. Cambridge, MA: Cambridge University Press.

Ostrom, E. (1986). An agenda for the study of institutions. *Public Choice*, 48(1), 3–25.

Rijswick, H. F. M. W. van. (2012). Een normatief kader voor het omgevingsrecht. In C. W. Backes, N. S. J. Koeman, F. C. M. A. Michiels, A. G. A. Nijmeijer, H. F. M. W. van Rijswick, B. J. Schueler ... R. Uylenburg (Eds.), (2012). *Naar een nieuw Omgevingsrecht, Preadvies voor de Vereniging voor Bouwrecht* (pp. 5–29). Den Haag: Instituut voor Bouwrecht.

Rijswick, H. F. M. W. van, & Havekes, H. J. M. (2012). *European and Dutch Water Law*. Groningen: Europa Law Publishing.

Rijswick, H. F. M. W. van, & Salet, W. G. M. (2012). Enabling the contextualization of legal rules in responsive strategies to climate change. *Ecology and Society*, 17(2), 18.

Schlössels, R., & Zijlstra, S. (2010). *Bestuursrecht in de sociale rechtsstaat*. Deventer: Kluwer.

Scott, J. (2010). Flexibility, 'Proceduralization', and Environmental Governance in the EU. In G. D. De Búrca & J. Scott (Eds.), *Constitutional Change in the EU*. Oxford: Hart Publishing.
Soil Protection Act. (1986). Wet van 3 juli 1986, houdende regelen inzake bescherming van de bodem, Stb. 1986, 374.
Trevisanut, S., & Rijswick, H. F. M. W. van (2014). Critical issues in water, oceans and sustainability law. *Utrecht Law Review*, special issue, 10(2).
Waterhout, B., Zonneveld, W., & Louw, E. (2013). *Case Study Markermeer-IJmeer, the Netherlands: Emerging Contextualization and Governance Complexity* (CONTEXT Report 5). Amsterdam: AISSR Programme Group Urban Planning.

14
INTERPRETING PLANNING AS ACTIONS 'IN PLURAL'
From Democratic Claim to Diverse Institutional Change

Monika De Frantz

Planning between Agency and Institutions: Interpreting Collaboration

The theme of this book, 'institutions in action', invites a closer look at how planning is situated between urban studies and political science. Urban studies have moved from empirical sociology to diverse normative critiques of globalization, embracing political-economic, culturalist and new institutional perspectives. Political sciences have turned from normative state theory and policy analysis towards new institutionalism, opening government to governance of space, diversity, private actors and everyday politics. Influenced in various ways by the critique of modernity and positivism, their shared focus on justice and legitimacy opens a field of interdisciplinary inquiry about political power in social and economic transformations. Planning, on the other hand, long considered a technocratic craft, has turned to research, theoretical controversy and normative engagement. To deal with the crisis of social sciences and democracy through concrete problems, planners now draw on pragmatic philosophy and new institutionalism. But in this complex and contested interdisciplinary field, planning faces questions about the relations of power, knowledge and social practices in urban space. How do new institutional theories contribute to understanding power structures and agency in planning? How does planning contribute to institutional continuity and change through practical responses to urban problems?

Planning is a policy that intervenes directly in physical spaces with the aim to control, mediate and regulate the territorial effects of governmental policies, markets and everyday social practices. As social inequality, cultural differences and complex transnational networks prove territorial governance limited, planning has turned from top-down implementation to collaborative practice. The different power functions of collaborative planning have resulted in a theoretical and methodological controversy between deliberative and participative or contentious approaches (Innes & Booher, 2014; Marcuse et al., 2014). To bridge this divide, Healey (2012, p. 19) has claimed that planning not only enacts larger policies of democratic government in concrete local contexts, but also engages in 'democratic micro practices'. By initiating community initiative and civic enterprise, planning as 'democracy in action' can contribute to transform these larger structures of urban governance (Healey, 2012; see also Wagenaar et al., 2015). Drawing on Giddens' sociological institutional approach, Healey (2006) conceived of structures and agency as mutually constituted in planning practice. Planning as 'communicative rationality' (Healey, 1993) introduced Hajer's discursive policy analysis as a collaborative method to reflect and overcome structural difference. Interpretative methods would further serve to translate the changing meanings of "transnational flows of planning ideas and practices" between different local contexts (Healey, 2013, p. 1510). Then, Healey (2015a) embedded the historical emergence of different normative ideas guiding planning policies in the different institutional and intellectual contexts of their time and place. Planning for a more "people-centred democracy", "micro practices of 'democracy in action'" draw on "knowledge and values in a plurality of claims" to "generate transformative change in place qualities and political culture" (Healey, 2012, p. 20).

Thus, the interpretative approach embedded planning as collaborative action in an open-ended institutional context to overcome the structural opposition between civic society and government, public interest and markets. But such a plural and differentiated conception of structure–agency dynamics turns Healey's civic claim into a research question with open-ended and contextually differentiated outcomes. The diversity of the institutional context also implies a plurality of claims, which reduces the specific civic ideal of the planner to one of many normative values applied and reinterpreted in the collaborative process. As community interest is contested by diverse civic claims, the model of a "more people-centred democracy" also becomes one of many potential institutional outcomes of the interpretative interactions. Political plurality is what constitutes a democratic process, and collaborative planners have the task to elaborate strategies considered legitimate "by the many, and not just the few" (Healey, 2015b, p. 169). But such interpretative interactions can also involve claims and outcomes which planners would consider less appropriate to their normative democratic ideal. These may range from reiteration of a dominant neo-liberal consensus to 'non-civic' populist ideas which are exclusive of minorities or divisive for the 'people', up to solutions that are considered implausible by experts or even unfeasible. Alternatively, the interpretative interactions may give rise to mobilization processes that involve such a broad spectrum of meanings, claimants and publics that collaborative closure cannot be found and institutional instability prevails. In sum, the mere institutional diversity which opens structural positions to interpretative interactions also leads us to question the connection between collaborative planning and a more 'people-centred' democracy.

My research on the *Museumsquartier* in Vienna and the *Schlossplatz* in Berlin (e.g. De Frantz, 2005, 2011, 2013) showed that structural political or economic explanations did not grasp the complex planning processes and urban transformations. Culture-led urban regeneration aims to 'make places' (Philo & Kearns, 1993) by way of material reconstruction, as well as by using cultural activities, symbolic meanings and political discourse to change the associations with collective belonging. But rather than a public choice response or a local community alternative to market competition, the two contested symbolic projects showed that planning is a plural political process. Top-down planning initiated political cycles of public contention of urban symbols which gave rise to discursive interactions. Their contextual, plural and opened-ended character stressed the diversity of the urban context, which challenged, opened and changed the legitimacy of institutional power, though in open and unpredictable ways. But the interactions were also framed by institutional paths which were reflectively changed, as governmental actors joined their institutional resources to integrate elements of the various emerging cultural spectrum into a concrete implementation plan. Partially shared and incoherent, these visions manifested institutional transformations connecting the socio-cultural diversification of community identities with the European transformations and globalization of democratic government.

Further elaborating on this interpretative conception of urban politics, in De Frantz (2007, 2008, 2014), I gave an overview of the political debate about European cities, which originally introduced the new institutional approach to urban studies, and – important for this book – elaborated the action perspective. At the time, the dominant political-economic perspectives in urban studies conceived power – affirmatively or critically – as market driven. The debate on European cities introduced new institutionalism as a political model of urban collective action based on the assumption of the structural coherency of civic society, local state and urban space (e.g. Le Galès, 2002). Questioning this coherent institutional model of an urban polity, I distinguished the multiple institutional formations framing urban practices in the European context of state-building and transformation (De Frantz, 2007, 2008). Drawing also on regionalism and social constructivist EU integration theory, I introduced the different approaches within new institutionalism to analyse these multi-facetted institutional dimensions of structures and agency. Distinguishing the European city as a normative model from either an analytical ideal type or a historical reality required discussion of the potential practical implications of such urban ideals. In conclusion, the different political aspects of 'doing knowledge' led me to conceive the reflective agency of the researcher as an interpreter between different institutional dimensions. As the postcolonial critique claimed cosmopolitan difference in urban globalization, in De Frantz (2014), I proposed the new institutional conception as a diverse theoretical approach to intersubjective legitimacies in comparative urban politics. By opening civic institutions to diversity and open-endedness, my conception of political agency in the urban context also helps in understanding planning research between practice and institutions.

To elaborate on the question of collaborative planning as civic empowerment for democratic change, my previous research on urban politics offers some relevant lessons on new institutionalism and interpretative politics. To take stock now of the practical relevance for planning, my various research contributions referred to the debates on 'institutions and action' in the urban and political disciplines. In order to link this book's contributions from planning to the relevant ongoing debates on agency in new institutionalism, cross-fertilization with these neighbouring disciplines embeds practical experience in a larger perspective of power and space. After a short introduction to the comparative case study of 'Capital City Cultures', this chapter critically reflects on the new institutional debate about European cities and then introduces interpretative politics to elaborate agency. The experience from Vienna and Berlin will serve to discuss the various institutional structure–agency dimensions in these interpretative processes to draw some lessons for planning. In conclusion, I argue that planning as democratic action needs to open civic community claims as well as markets and government to institutional diversity as interpretative political interaction with plural, open-ended and differentiated – potentially 'uncivic' – outcomes.

Capital City Cultures: A Case Study of 'Planning Turned Politics' in Vienna and Berlin

The *Museumsquartier* in Vienna and the *Humboldt Forum* on the *Schlossplatz* in Berlin can be seen as symbolic political projects of culture-led urban regeneration where planning emerged as contested local processes of institutional transformation. Situated in European capital cities with similar heritage and government, both constituted a political response to urban contexts shaken by a diverse spectrum of transformation pressures. The necessary reconstruction of run-down buildings in the city centres, up until then mere administrative matters of urban planning and heritage protection, offered opportunities for large-scale political projects. Rather than being left to market mechanisms or civic engagement, these symbolic cultural initiatives combined various political objectives of redefining the urban locations from the top down. But the planned interventions provoked protest and contentious interactions that postponed the implementation, influenced the planning processes and ultimately changed the outcomes of the projects. Thus, in response to external transformation challenges, planning turned into a political process where urban leaders struggled for a shared vision and collective strategy for the city.

Located in the historic centre right next to the imperial palace and other historic monuments of the capital city, the *Museumsquartier* represents Vienna's most ambitious cultural project in recent decades. Inaugurated in 2001, the complex combines a broad variety of cultural offers including museums, an exhibition hall, a contemporary dance venue, two event halls, offices and workspaces for international artists and local initiatives, as well as cafes, restaurants and shops. However, the planning of the project confronted extended protests led by several prominent experts, journalists and the right-populist Freedom party, who formed a citizens' initiative in defence of the historic cityscape. The evolving controversy about architectural design and cultural use concept addressed Vienna's diverse identity as a national and European capital – from the imperial heritage and National Socialism to a small republican state, globalization pressures and opportunities of European transformations. The political controversy inhibited the realization of the project and allowed for a flourishing local arts scene to develop autonomously in the abandoned complex. Ultimately, a series of political and administrative personnel changes prepared the way for a compromise. In 1996, the municipal parliament transferred its political responsibility back to the federal bureaucracy, which mandated an expert commission for the preservation of the cultural heritage. The redesigned plans made the new buildings smaller and removed the symbolic towers so as not to interfere with the historic sight axes of the cityscape. The heritage protection was extended to include not only the baroque architecture but also the nineteenth-century buildings in the complex. As a result, the whole inner city of Vienna was approved as a UNESCO World Heritage landmark. Doing away also with many of the small local initiatives but including more contemporary programming by larger public institutions, the new cultural district was inaugurated in June 2001. Despite the long preparation phase, it has been marketed highly professionally since and is mostly well accepted by tourists and local residents.

While many of the sites included in Berlin's urban reconstruction process of the 1990s constituted part of the city's economic restructuring, some of the new buildings also served the symbolic representation of reunified Germany's new capital city. Whereas, by the turn of the twenty-first century, most of these new developments were realized successfully, the *Schlossplatz* represented the focal point of a highly emotional public controversy about Berlin's identity. Constructed by the German Democratic Republic (GDR) regime in 1973 at the site of the city castle of the Prussian Hohenzollern kings (*Stadtschloss*), which was demolished by the GDR in 1951, the *Palast der Republik* emerged as a contested site of German reunification. The symbolic building had contained the – largely powerless – GDR parliament and, in 1990/1991, the post-Communist transitional parliament of Eastern Germany. But more importantly than any political symbolisms, the Palace of the Republic held for many East Berliners memories of their everyday lives during the GDR period. As the official cultural centre, the palace had offered concerts, theatres, restaurants, a discotheque and other facilities used for entertainment, recreation and celebratory events. After its closure in 1990 due to asbestos contamination, the GDR building stood as an empty ruin. In 2002, the federal parliament voted for building a cultural centre on the site, the so-called *Humboldt Forum*, with the reconstructed form and facade of the former baroque castle. This plan aimed to symbolize German reunification: materially through the elimination of most of the built GDR heritage; symbolically, through the acknowledgement of the need for a shared representation of the heterogeneity of Germany's national heritage in a historically continuous form; and procedurally, through an agreement between the city and the federal government on governing mechanisms for planning the new capital city. However, only in 2006 did the now conservative-led federal government enact the demolition of the palace and, in 2007–2008, the architectural competition resulted in a strictly historicist design resembling the former baroque castle. Neighbouring and complementing the old national museums on the *Museumsinsel*, the cultural complex will contain the extra European collection of the Prussian Heritage Foundation, parts of the Humboldt University's libraries and the Berlin municipal library. The major financial share being carried by the federal government, the new *Humboldt Forum* has been under construction since 2013 and, following a series of delays, is due to open in 2019.

My research complemented the urban debate by focusing on a previously neglected aspect of institutional transformation: the role of culture as a contested issue of public mobilization and discursive agency in the local policy process. Urban culture was not a *tabula rasa* to be newly defined at will, so that the political mobilization strategies necessarily intervened in long-established identity structures. Over more than ten years during the 1990s and early 2000s, the ensuing public controversies offered rich empirical material disclosing the discursive dynamics influencing the political decision-processes. Interpreting, tracing and comparing these discursive processes, I approached the blurred concept of urban culture by linking the imagination of meaning with institutional innovation, material construction of cultural symbols – architecture, museums, cultural programming – with urban identity structures, and political legitimacy with social contention. The discursive meanings associated urbanity in general, such as discussed in the academic debate, with the specific contexts of Vienna and Berlin, the planning of the projects and the histories of the sites.

In both cities, the political decisions constructing urban culture showed highly complex and contentious discursive interactions. Incapable of controlling the evolving public mobilizations, the political leaders followed rather unintentional and informal institutional paths. The emerging sets of meanings remained quite incoherent, yet they transformed the normative legitimacy of what should be built and what was considered a shared cultural understanding in policy as well as society. At the same time, these transformations were still influenced by established meanings and practices in the local contexts, manifested by the physical form, symbolisms, cultural programs and management structures. The more consolidated institutions of Vienna and the fragmented post-reunification context of Berlin further influenced the planning processes, their timely duration as well as the political and cultural outcomes. Vienna's leaders ultimately returned to their consociational traditions and settled for a pragmatic compromise that was mostly orientated at external representation. But during the extended transition period when Berlin's intergovernmental institutions were not yet fully functional, the discursive style was more deliberative and accepting of public conflict in view of reaching internal understanding and consensus. Due to the weakness of local political leadership, ultimately, both state governments regained control of the urban arenas – with major changes to the projects, some normative adjustments in the cultural fields, but minimal effects – mainly in Berlin – upon the formal institutions. These multi-dimensional dynamics of normative structures and interpretative agency constituted institutional transformation in addition to material culture as collective good, economic capital and product of urban regeneration.

New Institutionalism: Debating Structures and Agency in European Cities

Against the economic bias of North American and British urban political economy as general theories of globalization, the new institutional approach stresses the different institutional capacities of public planning for urban cohesion (e.g. Le Galès, 2002; see also De Frantz, 2008; Zimmermann, 2012). Also in Europe, recent transformations of urban government, economic deregulation, state decentralization, and EU integration have increased competition pressures and a turn to 'neo-liberal' urban policies. Thus, the cultural heritage of European cities has gained importance as a locational advantage in the competition for investment and economic development, resulting in commercial pressures, social exclusion and spatial transformations. But most European cities still appear rather lively and robust, with relatively intact urban centres, and less affected by urban decline than many American cases. As a good institutional fit with global state transformation, Weberian urbanists hypothesized the heritage of bourgeois city-states as a shared resource to mobilize civic society, government and markets for urban collective action (Le Galès, 2002). Thus reversing the Marxist-influenced conception of culture and policy as a representation of material power, the historical path dependency of civic and political institutions merged the state versus market dichotomy within the local state. As I distinguished critically, Weber's analytical ideal type was thus turned into a normative theoretical model, a historical myth, and a political ideology guiding actions in congruent ways (De Frantz, 2008). As Le Galès (2011) conferred later, some claims for European cities as a coherent institutional model, a separate urban category or a bounded territorial unit have been overstated. But now the recent reception in planning shows new institutionalism again at risk of a similar misinterpretation as a collaborative model that embeds democracy in civil society.

Empirical comparison of the diverse local responses to political and economic transformations gave rise to various institutional explanations of European difference. The European context with its complex historical state-building and present transformations illustrates a broad and diverse institutional spectrum of the social and political processes embedding urban political economies. A diversity of relatively small towns with old – medieval, early modern, up to industrial – roots share the history and characteristics of a pre-national urban system (Le Galès, 2002). Based on the diverse role of cities in state-building, the importance of town planning is embedded in varying local and national frameworks. European states show various structures of national, metropolitan and local government, centralized and decentralized local competences, executive and legislative power, party and corporatist systems (Wollmann, 2004). European urban policies tend to be driven more by political parties and less by business lobbies, more by social or environmentalist objectives and less by economic pressure groups. The governments tend to provide for social welfare and infrastructural services, and local constituencies are less dependent on autonomous financial resources than in the US (Harding, 2009). In addition, various transnational, intergovernmental regimes and particularly the supranational EU constitute a multifaceted and multi-level framework that regulates market integration, promotes state reforms and offers post-national frames of identification. Europeanization, along with various national policies of state decentralization and privatization, has resulted in local convergence towards informal and horizontal forms of governance and public–private partnership and a strengthening of local executives (Wollman, 2004). Cultural policy in particular is rooted in old national legacies that now meet, merge or conflict with local economic strategies for the promotion of cultural industries and city marketing (Bianchini, 1993).

Thus, diverse concepts explained or defined local institutions, such as thick networks, place or community, social capital or trust, the local state or the bourgeois civic heritage of the medieval city, public–private partnership or governance and recently the intrinsic logic of cities.

Apart from a mere normative claim for difference and reaffirmation of public space that had long been implicit to the urban debate, new institutionalism offers indeed an appropriate epistemological approach to conceptualize urbanity. It understands societal power as a historical process embedding politics, society and economy in different forms of legitimacy beyond the nation-state. These new institutional extensions to the 'old' studies of legal rules and formal government take account of the informally established practices, norms, values and frames of local governance and civil society. The new institutional paradigm comprises a broad range of different hypotheses, roughly associated with rational choice, historical, social constructivist and discursive approaches. These different conceptions of structures and agency serve to ask different questions, namely, how rational actors establish institutions based on mutual interest; how such initially functional structures, once established, can guide individual practices along more permanent paths despite a changing context; and how actors contribute to institutional stability or change by interpreting, reflectively responding to and thus interacting with an incoherent context of multiple institutional sets (Hall & Taylor, 1996). Instead of a coherent theoretical model, the different institutional elements and concepts may rather be understood as variable components of a mutually constitutive, open-ended, differentiated process with more or less stable institutional outcomes. Different conceptions of power serve to analyse different aspects of institutional processes in different empirical fields and result in often contradictory explanations of their form, origin, effect, persistence and change.

Summarizing the various empirical observations and institutional concepts within a common model implies the risk of 'black box' explanations that tend to essentialize certain ideal notions of European urbanity, local state, community or civic society. Most recently, the German concept of *Eigenlogik* (Zimmermann, 2012) explained different patterns of collective action based on locally bundled sets of values, meanings and practices of socialization. But again, this historic institutional conception of the city merges the unit of analysis, explanatory variable and outcome by presupposing local institutions as a relatively separate polity. Empirically, some institutional structures of Europe's urban system may indeed facilitate more cohesive local strategies in smaller and medium-sized towns with strong historical roots or municipal autonomy (Le Galès, 2002). However, plural interactions such as in the contested symbolic politics of the case studies do not speak of an absence or fragmentation of institutions in these capital cities either (De Frantz, 2005, 2011, 2013). Introducing the new institutional question about structure and agency merely shifted the structural focus on global markets in urban political economy to the continuities of local institutions. But without a more refined analytical conception of local agency as diverse, open-ended and transformative power, the European claim for historical institutions thus repeats the structural–functionalist bias it started out to criticize. Therefore, a political counterhypothesis to economic globalization requires an agency-based conception of institutional legitimacy that conceives diversity and open-ended, differentiated outcomes within and between different urban contexts (De Frantz, 2008, 2014).

Interpretative Politics: Discursive Agency and Legitimacy in Knowledge and Practice

Discursive institutionalism added a dynamic approach to institutional change through ideas and discourse of policies, programs and philosophies constituting interests and power structures as cognitive and normative constructs internal to agents' logics of communication (Schmidt, 2008). The new institutional debate thus turned discourse from a methodological tool into an epistemological understanding of power as an open-ended process being mutually constituted by knowledge and societal legitimacy. Focusing on agency in the institutional dynamics of structural continuities and change, interpretative policy analysis (e.g. Fischer, 2009; Hajer, 2002, 2009) conceives policy as a discursive process of claims-making and interactive reframing. The fundamental rethinking of the normative power in the policy process and research itself helps think of the planning endeavour as 'institutions in action'.

The interpretative approach derives authority from the characteristics of social interaction itself, through the discursive construction of political issues, actors' interpretative strategies and societal institutions. Beyond a mere representation or reproduction of power structures, discourse is also a reflective process that interactively reconstructs problems as well as context. Discourse analysis can clarify the actors' various perspectives, their engagement with the policy process, and link their argumentative strategies with larger structures of societal discourse, norms and routines. It relates the narrative production of reality with social practices that create, represent, elaborate and correct meanings across a sequence of settings. By interpreting political performance in addition to discursive deliberation, story lines can be traced from language to social norms and routines as well as non-verbal aesthetic and symbolic aspects of communication. When policy is experienced as a sense of collective participation, this joint experience – beyond the reasoned elaboration itself – can build legitimacy. Hajer's (2002) concept of discourse coalition describes a group of actors who share a social construct to give meaning to ambiguous social circumstances. If it is found that various policy issues and fields are integrated, discourse structuration describes a policy outcome where a specific set of discourse dominates society's overall conceptualization of the world. Discourse institutionalization happens when such a dominant discourse becomes attached to an organizational practice or a traditional way of reasoning about legitimacy (Hajer, 2009). But in an increasingly mediatized public sphere, meanings meander and evolve through a string of enactments by multiple actors at various stages and with specific settings, establishing varying relationships between problems, publics and political decisions. Politics is staged as a drama and performed in particular settings, which challenges the legitimacy of conventional deliberation procedures of representative government and policy planning (Hajer, 2009).

Interpretative policy analysis includes the researcher as a normative actor in the political field and the research activities as a participative practice situated in specific institutional contexts. The researcher turns from an outside observer and provider of substantive expertise to an active participant as claims-maker and mediator in the policy process. Understanding theoretical models as normative ideas instead of presentations of truth opens institutional power to practical enquiry of the cultural effects of interpretative claims. Beyond value neutrality and context-independence of policy-expertise, post-empiricist approaches consider the sociocultural context of how knowledge is obtained and discursively constructed. In reflecting academic knowledge through practical experience, the researcher turns from an objective analyst into a political actor between different institutional spheres and knowledge cultures. Thus, collaborative approaches appreciate the contributions of lay, local and experiential knowledge as well as the exchange between experts and practitioners for collective learning. However, not only the power differentials between the participants but also the different epistemological assumptions and rules of deliberation inhibit such collaborative practice. Faced with increasingly complex urban problems, citizens are in need of specialized expertise but have lost trust in planning experts as disinterested facilitators and competent knowledge authorities. To empower citizens, deliberative planners need to analyse the 'policy epistemics' of expert–citizen/client relationships and act as interpreters between different knowledge cultures, policy fields and perspectives of social actors. Dialogue about differences enables stakeholders' self-transformative learning of the tacit knowledge concepts that constitute their value positions. Political research can contribute to designing deliberative procedures in experimental ways to provide space for intersubjective reflection of the rules and for emotional performativity. By interpreting the social and normative foundations of power, experts can thus contribute to institutional change of democratic legitimacy (Fischer, 2009).

Drawing also on Dewey's (1933) and Schön's (1983) concept of reflective practice, the interpretative turn in policy studies originated from theoretical reflection of practical planning experience. But the focus has been on environmental policy, science and technology as well as human-nature relations more than on urban planning as such. Building on Hajer's (1989) earlier work, the 'ground zero' in NYC exemplified a pilot study of performative planning (Hajer, 2009). Rydin (2005) stressed the argumentative turn in geography, and recently again, Healey (2013) proposed interpretative policy analysis for knowledge transfer in planning. Having moved from a science-based technocratic endeavour to theoretical controversy, participative mobilization and reflective learning, the planning discipline is at the core of a broad spectrum of interventionist research practices. By overcoming mindsets that induce suffering and marginality or otherwise ineffective behaviour, reflective intervention has been applied to social change in community mobilization, movements, social work, health, individual empowerment, organizations and international development. Recently, collaborative planning has joined forces with science and technology studies to feed emerging pragmatic references in critical urban studies to the city as a 'democratic laboratory' (Karvonen & Heur, 2014). Despite the frequent side-references, critical urban studies have not fully received the implications of philosophical pragmatism and interpretative policy analysis for political economy.

Extending interpretative policy analysis to the field of urban culture, in De Frantz (2005, 2011, 2013) I compared two contested planning cases showing how public discourse mediates and reconstructs institutions and agency. By combining discursive interpretation with process tracing, I related the project plans to the broader institutional context of their political emergence and the diverse symbolic meanings and contested issues of urban culture for public legitimacies. The political and economic opportunity structures were identified by various electoral changes of the local and national governments, the cities' economic performance and broader changes in the European and global environment. These structural changes to the institutional contexts were related to the changing issues and discursive strategies claimed by the different actors and coalitions in the course of the processes. Tracing the political debates leading to each of the decisions produced an extract of the main arguments legitimating the political outcomes. Various topics of scholarly debate could be identified through the cultural issues and discursive arguments of different opinion leaders. Those topics most often repeated in either affirmative or destructive argumentations served as evidence for the issues at stake and showed the contested meanings of the urban themes in different contexts. The evolution of these meanings illustrated the interactive repositioning of conflicting interests and/or their possible integration into shared urban visions. The debates focused on the period between 1990 until 2002, partly extended in the case of Berlin until 2010. The sources stemmed mainly from newspapers (e.g. *Der Standard*, *Die Presse*, *Kurier*, *Kronenzeitung* in Vienna; *Berliner Zeitung*, *Der Tagesspiegel*, *Berliner Morgenpost*, *Berliner Kurier* in Berlin), complemented by weekly magazines (*Profil*, *Falter* in Vienna; *Spiegel*, *Zeit* in Berlin), official documents (e.g. parliamentary protocols of *Deutscher Bundestag*), interviews with decision makers and bureaucrats and public podium discussions. In addition, specialized monographs, grey literature, guide books and city marketing brochures framed the urban contexts.

Interpreting Vienna and Berlin: Some Lessons on Institutional Agency for Planning

My comparative case study of the *Museumsquartier* in Vienna and the *Schlossplatz* in Berlin compared the institutional contexts and discursive politics which ultimately constructed these symbolic sites of 'Capital City Cultures' (De Frantz, 2005, 2011, 2013). In the complex European transformation of the 1990s, the cultural projects were planned as representations of democratic states that combined a competitive economy with contemporary urban lifestyles. The governmental plans thus aimed to symbolize a democratic response to 'network governance' and to draw – more or less successfully – on private resources in addition to intergovernmental cooperation. But in many ways, the study also posed an opposite case to Healey's civic claim of democratization through collaborative planning because the mere size and symbolism of the projects required top-down planning by the governments. Only at a late stage and upon pressures of public contention, the planning processes were made more collaborative but still limited to expert deliberation. Therefore, the projects actually speak a lot about the failure of planning and the consequences of the absence of a guided collaborative approach. Also the outcomes showed little formal empowerment of civil society or the municipality as such. Ultimately the federal governments took control of the symbolically important decisions about cultural planning in the capital cities and civic participation was mostly excluded from the final cultural projects. Yet, the findings showed a civic impact on institutional change, though more indirect and multifaceted than implied by Healey's (2012) collaborative planning for a 'people-centred democracy'.

Even though the interactions were more contentious than collaborative, the planning decisions were constituted by collective action processes which involved civic claims. Collective action emerged through contentious cycles of public discursive interaction as well as the real manifestation of civic and artistic initiatives in public space. These contentious actions had an impact on civic empowerment and on the political outcomes. First, the public debates inhibited the implementation of the initial government plans for holistic representations of urban cultural innovation. Second, the engagement of diverse new actors in the political debate changed their political influence on the planning process. Some ended up being offered official positions in cultural policymaking; others lost their jobs in the process. The contentious interactions also changed the public identifications with the sites and the political decisions on cultural programming and physical architecture. Beyond the immediate projects, the debates impacted cultural policy by reconstructing the collective legitimacy of urban culture, and – in Berlin – the formal institutional procedures. Overall, the long controversies anchored urban culture as an issue and arena of political claims-making and representation in shared public legitimacies. The public contentions turned into discursive interactions where parts of the claims were integrated into collaborative processes that changed and legitimized the political decisions. While the projects were planned as governmental responses to political and economic transformation pressures, the political institutions incorporated the public claims – though partially and in incoherent ways – to reflect the changing social contexts within these cities.

The mediating effect of planning between democratic micro practices and larger institutional transformations (Healey, 2012) was not a simple structure–agency relation between local context and government. Indeed, urban policy responded to the external challenges by mobilizing different political, economic and cultural resources for urban transformation. But external restructuring challenges were not directly transformed into an optimum public choice. The institutional base was not a homogeneous, static essence of place unifying the political elites either in support or in resistance to capitalist globalization. Nor were the actors clearly polarized between growth and anti-growth interests, winners and losers of globalization, party-political coalitions or any enduring cultural cleavages. Contrary also to a hyper-pluralist fragmentation ensuing from urban diversity, the interpretation and renegotiation of shared sites and symbols turned the local contexts into contested arenas. Beyond either merely a collective good, a unitary power representation, a common value or social practice, urban culture became a construct of various identifications and power claims. These plural political responses interacted with the institutional practices through dynamic and open-ended processes constituting the public debate as a civic realm of collaborative learning. Thus, the planning processes involved political choices, reflective agency and public politics as bottom-up state transformation.

Even planners working for the government need not only find technical or legal solutions for urban problems but they must also deal with potentially contentious political issues arising from the diversification of political institutions and social relations. As Healey (2015b, p. 442) elaborated, "planners … combine a strategic grasp of the contextual dynamics" and "the particularity of moments and opportunities in which cracks can open in institutional discourses and practices". In an open urban context of multi-level governance and cultural diversity, the sources of power and identity are plural and stakeholders not necessarily limited to those defined by political or territorial rules. Institutional and cultural diversity can give rise to complex relational dynamics and even fragmentation effects that make particularly large urban centres seem ungovernable. On the other side, this diversity is what distinguishes 'urbanity' as a specifically innovative milieu that might also serve as an endogenous local resource. As functional and symbolic centres that transcend territorial government, cities are places of creative struggles over space that is not only materially sparse but also highly symbolical. As centres of European statehood, capital cities certainly constitute particularly symbolic and contested contexts to illustrate urban politics as a plural field. While Vienna was more path dependent and Berlin more affected by changes, other cities may even be more unitary and consolidated or more plural and fragmented. But the open and diverse character of contemporary cities implies that most combine these different tendencies in various ways, highlighting plural politics as a shared condition of urban planning.

Approaching collaborative planning as 'communicative rationality', Healey (1993) proposed discourse analysis to overcome institutional barriers in network governance. But questioning the ideal of community participation in planning, civic claims-making implied interactive reframing through a plural process that involved conflict and contention as well as integration. As the issues themselves were contested and redefined, planning emerged as a non-linear process of mobilization of bias by framing political problems. Therefore, the conventional differentiation in planning between the various stages of problem identification, policy formulation and implementation were blurred (Hajer, 2009). The affected publics of planning interventions only emerged in the process and the stakeholders were thus hard to define for a deliberative collaboration. The institutional roles of planning experts not only differed (Marcuse et al., 2014) but in some cases even changed from political advisors to private contractors, public claimants, citizen representatives and political actors. These discursive interactions led planning beyond political-economic functions or community claims towards plural and open-ended political processes.

Hajer's discursive structuration would serve Healey (2006) to diffuse planning interventions from civic episode to different levels of democratic power. Therefore, I traced the planning processes "from conscious actor invention and mobilization to routinization as accepted practices, and to broadly accepted cultural norms and values" (ibid., p. 303). But the case studies showed the discursive mobilizations difficult to control which rendered the planning processes quite unpredictable. The various situational outcomes of the interactions were diverse – from social fragmentation and exclusion to conflictive escalation, civic empowerment and institutional adaptation. Some powerful forces – in these cases the federal states more than markets – came to reassert dominant influence that locked these urban processes into more permanent plans for implementation. Yet, this involved institutional transformations as a result of the reorientation of diverse objectives within the cultural field in accordance with some partially shared urban visions. It also resulted in coordinated institutional action across various policy fields, as well as an opening of governmental dominance to local claims. But institutional power relations remained open-ended with only intermediately stable situations and conflicts re-emerging on different occasions.

The "micro practices of 'democracy in action'" draw on "knowledge and values in a plurality of claims" to "generate transformative change in place qualities and political culture" (Healey, 2012, p. 20). This plurality of claims stemmed from the diverse ways that knowledge was interpreted as different values and policy alternatives in the urban contexts. But planning knowledge itself includes different normative models proposing different epistemologies of knowledge and ontologies of power reflecting their institutional and intellectual contexts of time and place (Healey, 2015a). Given the institutional failure in the case studies, a search for new models and policy claims led to a close interaction of politicians and experts. Translating transnational knowledge (Healey, 2013), various cultural models – the 'Guggenheim effect' of Bilbao, the Paris Louvre or the mutual examples of Berlin's modernity and Vienna's cohesion – offered norms for policymaking. These models were not implemented on a one-to-one basis, but elements of them were reinterpreted in specific contexts to mobilize collective action or provoke contention. Planning practitioners, researchers, and decision makers legitimated their political values by applying various knowledge tropes to concrete local contexts as well as reinterpreting societal interest in light of these models. By reflecting on the validity of powerful legitimacies between knowledge and practice, the actors interactively reconstructed the future visions of their cities and thus the normative bases of planning.

Beyond limiting discourse analysis to a methodological tool, the interpretative policy approach shifts the focus to the plural discursive constitution of the research activity in the politics of planning. 'Doing research' in planning implies diverse relations to practice – as a source of 'ideas', the 'field', the institutional and organizational contexts of place, the object of research and impact, and the multiple roles and positionings of the researcher (Silva et al., 2015, p. xxxv). This action orientated approach also attributes an ethical responsibility to the planning experts for addressing the societal role of academic discourse as meta-theory and real social intervention in a so-called 'knowledge society'. I thus offer my research intervention by contributing my interpretation to the political and academic discourse. The intersubjective intent of my systematic methodology distinguishes my work from postmodern subjectivism and from normative power critique. By conceiving discursive agency as a potential source of change beyond the mere reproduction or contention of structural power, I have shed a local, contextual perspective on the institutional changes constituting urban transformations. I thus aim to indicate a democratic potential for engaging in diverse political alternatives to a planning practice exclusively determined by government or left to global market forces. Instead of merely criticizing the top-down policies of government or the structural constraints of markets, planning as practical research implies the societal responsibility to mobilize civic society and empower the less advantaged to participate. Therefore, the case studies served to identify structural opportunities for collective action, intervene in the institutional processes and elaborate alternative legitimacies as diverse sources of plural civic action.

Interpreting Planning Practice as Institutions in Action: A Democratic Potential?

Following Healey's (2012; also in Wagenaar et al., 2015) claim for a 'more people-centred democracy', I asked how planning can actually empower citizens to act for urban change beyond dominant strategies of government and markets. To embed Healey's (1993, 2006, 2013, 2015b) interpretative and sociological conception of the institutional dynamics of planning between power structures and civic agency, I have introduced the debates on the institutional capacities of European cities and interpretative policy analysis. Applying these theoretical insights, the case study exemplified the multifaceted dynamics of institutional structures and interpretative agency in highly contested urban contexts. These lessons from urban and political studies served to help us understand the planning discipline as knowledge practice that responds to concrete problems by facilitating citizens' collective action for democratic institutional change in response to network governance.

Conceiving urban regeneration as institutional change, the contested cultural projects from Vienna and Berlin served to elucidate the normative power of discourse as ideas, values and practices in the planning process. This triadic relation between academic knowledge, social and political institutions, and physical and medial space replaces cultural essentialism and structural determinism by reflective agency as endogenous to the urban context (De Frantz, 2013). All three, the academic-ideational, the socio-political and the material-symbolic realm can show structural openings from transformation pressures upon path-dependent institutions. While actors may respond rationally to each of these structural opportunities, practical problems concern complex situations with diverse and contingent structure–agency relations. Moreover, individual socialization and cultural context contribute to different perspectives of the problems at stake and their contention gives rise to the interactive reinterpretation of political issues. Thus, complementing political-economic and historical perspectives by a normative-discursive approach to urban collective action turns urbanity from a universal claim or local characteristic into diverse and contextual interpretations. I thus conceived urban research as political agency through comparative interpretative reflection of urbanity as analytical ideal type, historic civic-political paths and normative-political values (De Frantz, 2008).

Applied to collaborative planning, democratic action is to be distinguished between an 'empirical' description of a specific practical experience, a normative claim for specific 'civic' values, and an intersubjective practice of reflective learning. In a concrete planning situation, these different dimensions will take diverse forms and interact in various and contingent ways which may be hard to distinguish in the evolving processes. But this distinction is important for understanding collaborative planning as a diverse interpretative process where democratic change evolves from plural politics. Otherwise, the planner risks to impose their subjective interpretation of an assumed homogenous community interest on the diverse and complex social relations constituting the civic realm. While intending to challenge the power of government and markets, this idealistic conception of local community (Young, 1986) merely introduces another structural dimension. By excluding diversity, agency would merely result from institutional functions or structural contradictions, but not from a collective action such as intended by collaborative planning. Moving from discursive methods to an ontological understanding of planning as interpretative politics can help to avoid the structural–functionalist trap and constitute agency as a plural political process. Understanding interpretation as constitutive of planning, collective action may emerge from a diverse, intersubjective and open-ended collaboration process.

Though acknowledging diversity, such opening of institutions by itself does not yet lead to democratic change. It is important to understand that actors need to seize the structural opportunities to develop strategies and build coalitions to mobilize support for their implementation. But as planners embrace democratic ideals, collaborative endeavours often fail due to the sheer plurality of stakes, technical complexity, power differences and interest conflicts involved (Fischer, 2009). The controversy between deliberative and contentious planning (Innes & Booher, 2014; Marcuse et al., 2014) highlights the multiple expectations of the practical task. Particularly in central sites, collaboration may be further complicated, as symbolic identifications and functional relations extend public mobilization beyond a limited range of stakeholders (Amin, 2011). But turning the conflicting professional roles into a structural opportunity, planners also act as institutional gatekeepers of the material resources and social legitimacies required for collective action. When Healey (2015b, p. 442) asks to 'use perceptions of instabilities and crisis in a strategic way', this should concern not only the 'field' but also the institutional context of planning. Thus, reflecting their different power positions and functional purposes opens a structural 'crack' for the planner to interpret their role. Beyond a detached mediation between political, economic and civic interests or a normative critique of top-down and bottom-up interaction, this intervention is more complex than the choice between rebel or bureaucrat (Marcuse et al., 2014). Interpreting their varying tasks in practice, the planner acts from a personal perspective of the normative criteria to be applied to the problem definition, collaborative process and appropriate response. Also the evaluation of interest conflicts, of who wins or loses from specific outcomes, differs between different issues, situations and the changing positionings of the participants – including the planner – in the process. Instead of merely supporting or contesting established power structures, such interpretative interactions can give rise to reflective learning about the self and the collective. Ideally, reflective learning from collaboration then leads to a shared understanding of the issues, turning the field from object into subject of collective action in a larger institutional context.

In view of an interdisciplinary dialogue with urban studies and political science, the 'coevolution' of new institutionalism and pragmatism (see Salet, Chapter 1, in this volume) carries particular relevance for planning. Contrary to a complex reality that may evolve independently of social experience, the postfoundational core of the new institutional debate is the intersubjective constitution of power and knowledge through social practice. Thus, institutional research is not merely about analysing institutions as organizational instruments, actors or objects of planning, but a way of thinking about power relations as intersubjective legitimacies. New institutionalism is a broad and diverse debate, involving different knowledge approaches, definitions, methods and subject disciplines. These different perspectives pose different questions and result in incoherent findings about the institutional conditions of the planning process. Institutions as rules, norms and routines, which are collectively accepted and re-enacted in practice, are not only 'out there in the field', but constitute what is valid knowledge as the power context of planning practice. To avoid that planners justify their various interpretations of specific situational problems as functionally optimal solutions, it is important to understand knowledge paradigms as value based research assumptions. Questioning the epistemological foundations of structural assumptions in urban political economy, local government and cultural studies, the social constructivist approach opens institutional power to diverse interpretation.

Not only normatively but also ontologically and epistemologically, it is important to conceptualize planning as a diverse structure–agency dynamic in an open-ended institutional process. As neo-liberal hegemony interpretations tend to overemphasize structuring mechanisms, Healey's (2012) civic action claim gains relevance as a democratic counter model. From a new institutional perspective, even markets are constituted by normative legitimacies which vary and change in different contexts. The quasi-natural requirement of economic development is thus reduced to merely one of many normative models which may guide planning. As diverse legitimacies claim the civic realm of the city, these plural interactions challenge governmental institutions as the political side of globalization. In this process, institutional change – whether large or small – is not a result of structural contradictions or functional dissemination, but of confronting assumptions about normalcy with different experiential perspectives. Extending Healey's (ibid.) critique of structural instrumental logics to local community, this diverse civic empowerment can initiate plural political claims – from social justice to nationalist populism or culturalist escalation. While interpretative interventions can thus give rise to institutional changes, the political outcomes are diverse, uncertain and do not necessarily comply with the planner's democratic ideal. To give space to a plurality of claims beyond a predefined civic interest, the planner can act as interpretator between different knowledge cultures. Including those considered 'uncivic' by the norms of society increases the risk of obtaining diverse, potentially unexpected or undesired outcomes. Yet, facilitating an awareness of power relations and a mutual understanding of difference is a precondition for institutional openness in a plural society. Only an open-ended, diverse, contextually situated and relational understanding of the planner's role, the socio-phyiscal field and the governance institutions can provide for a pluralist collaboration process. For a truly democratic action, the civic claim involves not only a political but also an ethical role for the planner in guiding the plural processes towards the elaboration of mutually accepted and thus democratic legitimacies.

References

Amin, A. (2011). Urban Planning in an Uncertain World. In G. Bridge & S. Watson (Eds.), *The New Blackwell Companion to the City* (pp. 631–642). New York: Wiley-Blackwell.

Bianchini, F. (1993). Remaking European Cities: The Role of Cultural Policies. In F. Bianchini & M. Parkinson (Eds.), *Cultural Policy and Urban Regeneration: The West European Experience*. Manchester: Manchester University Press.

De Frantz, M. (2005). From cultural regeneration to discursive governance: Constructing the flagship of the 'Museumsquartier Vienna' as a plural symbol of change. *International Journal of Urban and Regional Research*, 29(1), 50–66.

De Frantz, M. (2007). 'The City Without Qualities': Political Theories of European Urbanity and Globalization. EUI Working Paper. Florence: European University Institute.

De Frantz, M. (2008). Contemporary political theories of the European city: Questioning institutions. *European Journal of Social Theory*, 11(4), 443–463.

De Frantz, M. (2011). *Capital City Cultures: Reconstructing Contemporary Europe in Vienna and Berlin (Book Series 'Multiple Europes')*. Brussels: Peter Lang.

De Frantz, M. (2013). Culture-Led Urban Regeneration: The Discursive Politics of Institutional Change. In M. Leary & J. McCarthy (Eds.), *Routledge Companion to Urban Regeneration: Global Constraints, Local Opportunities*. London/New York City: Routledge.

De Frantz, M. (2014). The Cosmopolitan Politics of Comparative Urbanism: A European Contribution. In J. Boyer & B. Molden (Eds.), *EUtROPEs: The Paradox of European Empire*. Paris/Chicago: University of Chicago.

Dewey, J. (1993). *How We Think: A Restatement of the Relation of Reflective Thinking to the Educational Process*. Lexington, MA: Heath.

Fischer, F. (2009). *Democracy and Expertise: Reorienting Policy Inquiry*. Oxford: Oxford University Press.

Hajer, M. (1989). *City Politics: Hegemonic Projects and Discourse*. Avebury: Aldershot.

Hajer, M. (2002). Discourse analysis and the study of policy making. *European Political Science*, 2(1), 61–65.

Hajer, M. (2009). *Authoritative Governance: Policy Making in the Age of Mediatization*. Oxford: Oxford University Press.

Hall, P., & Taylor, R. (1996). Political science and the three new institutionalisms. *Political Studies*, 44(5), 936–957.

Harding, A. (2009). The History of Community Power. In J. Davies & D. Imbroscio (Eds.), *Theories of Urban Politics*. Los Angeles, CA: Sage.

Healey, P. (1993). Performing Place Governance Collaboratively: Planning as a Communicative Process. In F. Fischer & J. Forester (Eds.), *The Argumentative Turn in Policy Analysis and Planning*. Durham/London: Duke University Press.

Healey, P. (2006). Transforming governance: Challenges of institutional adaptation and a new politics of space. *European Planning Studies*, 14(3), 299–320.

Healey, P. (2012). Re-enchanting democracy as a mode of governance. *Critical Policy Studies*, 6(1), 19–39.

Healey, P. (2013). Circuits of knowledge and techniques: The transnational flow of planning ideas and practices. *International Journal of Urban and Regional Research*, 37(5), 1510–1526.

Healey, P. (2015a). Planning theory: The good city and its governance. *International Encyclopedia of the Social & Behavioral Sciences* (2nd ed.), 18, 202–207.

Healey, P. (2015b). Rethinking the Relations Between Planning, State and Market in Unstable Times. In J. Hillier & J. Metzger (Eds.), *Connections: Exploring Contemporary Planning Theory and Practice with Patsy Healey*. Aldershot: Ashgate.

Innes, J., & Booher D. (2014). A turning point for planning theory? Overcoming dividing discourses. *Planning Theory*, 14(2), 195–213.

Karvonen, A., & Heur, B. (2014). Urban laboratories: Experiments in reworking cities. *International Journal of Urban and Regional Research*, 38(2), 379–392.

Le Galès, P. (2002). *European Cities: Social Conflicts and Governance*. Oxford: Oxford University Press.

Le Galès, P. (2011). Urban Governance in Europe: What is Governed? *The New Blackwell Companion to the City* (pp. 747–758). New York: Wiley-Blackwell.

Marcuse, P., Imbroscio, D., Parker, S., Davies, J. S., & Magnusson, W. (2014). Critical urban theory versus critical urban studies: A review debate. *International Journal of Urban and Regional Research*, 38(5), 1904–1917.

Philo, C., & Kearns, G. (1993). *Selling Places: The City as Cultural Capital, Past and Present*. Oxford: Pergamon Press.

Rydin, Y. (2005). Geographical knowledge and policy: The positive contribution of discourse studies. *Area*, 37(1), 73–78.

Schmidt, V. (2008). Discursive institutionalism: The explanatory power of ideas and discourse. *Annual Review of Political Science*, 11, 303–326.

Schön, D. (1983). *The Reflective Practitioner: How Professionals Think in Action*. London: Temple Smith.

Silva, E., Healey, P., Harris, N., & Broeck P. van den. (2015). Introduction: The Craft of 'Doing Research' in Spatial and Regional Planning, In *The Routledge Handbook of Planning Research Methods*. New York: Routledge.

Wagenaar, H., Healey, P., Laino, G., Vigar, G., Isern, S. R., Honeck, T., ... Beunderman, J. (2015). The transformative potential of civic enterprise. *Planning Theory & Practice*, 16(4), 557–585.

Wollmann, H. (2004). Local government reforms in Great Britain, Sweden, Germany and France: Between multi-function and single-purpose organisations. *Local Government Studies*, 30(4), 639–665.

Young, I. M. (1986). The ideal of community and the politics of difference. *Social theory and practice*, 12(1), 1–26.

Zimmermann, K. (2012). Eigenlogik of cities – Introduction to the themed section. *Urban Research & Practice*, 5(3), 299–302.

15
PROVENANCE, IDEOLOGY AND THE PUBLIC INTEREST IN PLANNING

Leonie Janssen-Jansen[1] & Greg Lloyd[2]

The collective body of the people, if at any time their power shall predominate, ought above all things to insist on a just regulation of property in land. It belongs to the community to establish rules by which this general right might become definite; but not to recognise such a right at all, not to have established any rules by which its claims maybe ascertained and complied with, ought to be accounted essentially unjust. Means may certainly be discovered by which this general right of the community in the property of the soil may be clearly and practically ascertained.
(William Ogilvie, 1781, paragraph 4, quoted in Hardy, 1999)

He mentions Profit, Progress, Enterprise, as if they are his personal Muses. Ours has been a village of Enough, but he proposes it will be a settlement of More, when finally he's fenced and quick-thorned all the land and turned everything – our fields, our commons and the 'wasted woods' – into 'gallant sheep country'.
(Crace, 2013, p. 186)

Introduction – The Spirit and Purpose of Planning

Planning is a complex and deliberate action (or set of actions) of governance with the goal of reconciling private and public interests in the use and development of land. Planning is a mandatory government function with a statutory land use planning system. Planning and planning decisions inevitably rest on power relations around policy and property rules – and they operate in a highly convoluted context. There is a marked distinction between anticipating the needs of society and individual communities in periods of economic growth and then in times of industrial restructuring and contraction. Planning is even more challenged when growth and decline take place across different spaces at the same time. There is a need then to understand both the nature of planning as a deliberate form of intervention to secure a wider public interest and to appreciate the emergent rules of engagement in terms of societal and political metrics. A messy context indeed!

Land use planning has always raised important questions for different societies and communities, landed interests, property rights, interest groups and individuals. The latter, of course, can act collectively – as neighbourhoods or communities. This convoluted state of affairs holds in the face of the clear benefits to society of deliberate planning which enables the orderly, connected and efficient regulation of land. Planning has been a technocratic and democratic conduit ensuing that land resources have been used appropriately in the wider common weal.

In practice, planning involves a composite of different forms of regulation concerning land use and development, providing forward-looking schemes for different forms of development (at various scales of governance – national, regional and local) and the financial arrangements to enable land assembly, provision of infrastructure and community facilities, and visioning for the future use of land in light of projected demographic trends and environmental and economic conditions. Land use planning is further complicated by the scales at which it operates, its ambitions (the spatial planning agenda being an example of this broader connectivity remit) and societal expectations. Here the emphasis on a better quality of life, standards of services and accessibility for all groups is important. This specific focus has become more pronounced in recent decades as planning has (by default?) been charged with meeting wider and more complex economic and social challenges, including the provision of affordable housing, securing health and welfare advances and addressing the effects of economic and industrial restructuring and contraction.

Today, land use planning is as much concerned with attracting inward investment, promoting social inclusion and securing adaptation to climate change and flooding as regulating the design of individual property development schemes. How planning is understood in such circumstances is important. Over time there have been different models of understanding planning. Planning started from a positivist perspective, building on the narrow grounds of neoclassical economics. The neoclassical economic construct offered a technocratic interpretation of planning intervention to correct perceived market failures. These were related to the external effects of land development, the provision of infrastructure and ensuring that monopoly effects from land ownership were avoided. This relatively simplistic model of understanding did not incorporate the importance of power relations, and ownership and control in land and property.

Over the years planning evolved into a science of normative actions that provided a more nuanced way of understanding the dynamics and complexities of land matters (Salet, 2002, p. 28). As this edited volume evidences, this shift boosted different approaches in the planning literature, such as the communicative approach, the turn to collaborative and consensus thinking specifically and also the institutional approach. An institutional approach seeks to explore the complex and contested interpretations of the relations between economic interests, the associated spatialities of change and the importance of understanding the appropriateness of different institutional forms within which change may be understood and planned. This provided a relatively more holistic understanding of the layering discipline in the institutions in planning and development.

An institutional model of understanding is alert to change – questioning what learning or morphological change has taken place in context and planning. Attention should be drawn to the formal arrangements in place which set a parameter to planning together with the informal or customary practices in planning and development. These considerations are dynamic – stressing the reciprocal relations involved and allowing for specific circumstances to be acknowledged. Thus, there is not one planning model but variations reflecting history, tradition, cultures, legal arrangements and ways of doing (Dembski & Salet, 2010). Strategic planning and intervention is a complex process that stresses the importance of strategic capacity which involves strategic ambiguity (the tension between different purposes and goals), redundancy (having more options than necessary from an efficiency perspective) and resilience (is the process reactively or proactively resilient to outside demands?). An institutional perspective rejects any tendency to a reductive approach which seeks to simplify rather than grapple with the underlying material complexities. Today, for example, the political advocacy of austerity (driven by neoliberal metrics) encourages a simplistic explanation of change and prescription to action (Blyth, 2013).

Following the broad narrative of institutional thinking, the importance of history, experience and culture cannot be overestimated. Such matters establish the context for the formal rules of the game, the informal relations and the outcomes that result. Understanding the strands of such a context also creates opportunities to appreciate the importance of addressing the deficit around power evident in public and private actions in planning matters. Institutional understanding can then promote relatively more focussed interventions and influence the design of appropriate arrangements such as explicit policy coupling – bringing together compatible planning objectives, such as economic development and flood prevention (Peel & Lloyd, 2010). As a consequence of neglecting the provenance of planning, the normalisation of neoliberal values and the powerful critiques of planning and its performance, we argue that planning is out of step with the real world (Janssen-Jansen & van der Veen, 2017; Lloyd, 2015). Yet it remains a bedrock for managing change in complex societal circumstances. Reconciling these tensions is its essential challenge, creating planning's 'normal' operating theatre, making it even more vulnerable to critique and misunderstanding.

Provenance

Provenance refers to the origins of the land and land use planning question, and its changing meanings or social constructions through time. It refers to the pedigree of the various facets of the land question, including its ownership, tenure, use and development. The introductory quotations to this chapter capture the essence of the complex provenance of the land question. Provenance involves the importance of the passage of time, the history of ideas, the iteration and maturation of ideas, and the ways in which specific measures carry with them deeply embedded values, assumptions and metrics which are then exposed to changing contexts. Time and intellectual timelines are often neglected facets of understanding the land use planning system.

This concept of provenance of the land use planning system has an important role in reconciling private and public interests in the use and development of land in order to inform the circumstances leading to the contradictory positions about planning. Provenance refers to the complex warp and weft of ideas, experience, innovation and changing contexts over time. What may be appropriate at one time may be out of sync at another time. Yet this broader dynamic appears to be a lost factor in considering the specific conditions around space and place over and through time. The history of ideas and practice, for example, is often ignored even though the exogenous and endogenous conditions are changing, new conflicts are being engendered and the social construction of the public interest is rendered more abstract and obtuse. Indeed, it is possible that planning suffers from a path dependency in failing to innovate in its approach to regulating property development, mediating between vested interests and securing the public interest. In effect, planning was devised and executed at a particular time and within a particular context. It achieved its early objectives and evolved in terms of its procedures and instruments. Yet, planning then continued to operate in very different conditions and its provenance has been overlooked or has been deliberately misconstrued.

The only way to explain, understand and devise appropriate planning responses is to consider the provenance of planning. Provenance is not simply the past. It involves a deeper understanding of the origins of planning, its guiding theoretical principles which provided its rationale for intervention in a world of private property and private interests. It involves an appreciation of the changing social constructions of planning in different epochs (theoretical and applied) – there is the critical thinking associated with the planning experience and then engagement with the ways in which any progressive change had an effect. Strategic planning – its rise and fall, rise and fall again – is a case in point. Provenance is about the institutional analysis of planning ideology – the assertion and dominance of the private property rights hegemony. Provenance is about the characteristics of planning (in theoretical terms its reliance on positivist values and assumptions articulated mainly through neoclassical economic values). That is the basis of planning – a limited expression of a liberal and limited mode of intervention to address monopoly interests in land, externalities, public goods and to provide some equity considerations. A narrow positivist basis of planning remains notwithstanding the layered intellectual and normative cul de sacs associated with collaborative planning theories and the turn to stress processes in planning rather than outcomes.

The concept of provenance is influenced by drawing on a wide range of influences – specifically the dynamics between ideas, political institutions and agents, and how they interact and inform an understanding of change. In particular, attention is paid to the imperative of the social constructions of cultures, values, and property rights as well as the inter-relations of institutions and organisations in seeking to understand change and behaviours (Williamson, 1994, 2000). Alongside the formal institutions, governance and practices of planning, for example, attention must also be paid to the informal influences – the cultures, norms, customs and traditions associated with land. To this end, provenance considers the import of time, the history of ideas and the timeline within which land use planning operates. This chapter suggests that a deeper appreciation of institutions, interests and property rights can contribute to a deeper understanding of this planning predicament.

Provenance captures the essence of time, experiential learning, maturation and rejection of ideas and changing contexts in which land use planning operates. The complexity of these factors is vividly evident – but often overlooked – with respect to the land question. Provenance seeks to incorporate alternative thinking around, for example, the radical transformation of economic ideas over time (Fine & Milonakis, 2008) which serve to further distort our social constructions of change. Provenance also stresses the importance of locating change in its appropriate time – its historical niche which incorporates a package of ideas, values, metrics and behaviours at that point – as illustrated by a contemporary literary account of the rise of private property rights (Crace, 2013). The contextual changes for planning have been dynamic and complex, including the rise of globalisation and multinational capital mobility, the spread of new ideological ideas, the mobility of policy measures, shifting state-market-civil relations, political uncertainties and new economic, social and environmental parameters. Central to this is time and the pockets of ideas, values and experiences which may or may not transfer across spaces and places.

The Critiques of Planning

Land use planning is a contested and (frequently) misunderstood concept and function of government and governance. This is primarily a consequence of its multiple dimensions. Planning is contested as it effectively intervenes in, and redistributes, prevailing property rights and can affect the balance of interests around private land holdings and associated land and property values. Here, the spirit and purpose rests on a very particularly constructed understanding of land.

Land is a fundamental factor of production. Yet it is more than an economic commodity, it embodies foundational historical, cultural and community values – it is the *sine qua non* of a stable, ordered society. Without land there would be nothing. The complexities of seeking to understand the host of legal, practical and emotional issues around the land question – the natural resource itself, its bundles of diverse and complex property rights, the associated power relations and political machinations, and the arrangements for planning, governance and regulation of the resource are profound. Yet, perspectives on those property rights relations tend to be partial and static (Massey & Catalano, 1978). This particular social construction of land has inhibited a wider understanding of the dynamic characteristics of the land question and the role of the land use planning system. Conflicts over the use and development, ownership and control of land arise constantly – national versus local, development versus conservation, economic versus community, economic versus environment, development versus preservation of rural areas – and these tend to be presented as aberrations rather than an endemic feature of the sector. In particular, the land use planning system attracts particular opprobrium from all sectors: property development, communities, environmental groups and government itself. Why should this be?

The antagonism towards the statutory land use planning system emanates from a wide array of protagonists, including builders and property developers, think tanks, politicians, communities, environmental groups and other vested interests. Planning is at once misunderstood and vilified yet it has played, does play and has a progressive role to play in light of the future conditions facing many nation states. Over and above the criticism there is the practical contestation regarding the spirit and purpose of the statutory land use planning system in which land use planning is framed as a simplistic activity by the state to secure an appropriate balance of development. This context means that the work of the statutory land use planning system is nearly always polarised with respect to the preparation of development plans, its regulation through development management, enforcement, the devising of strategic planning policy priorities and its relationship to other areas of the public sector domain. In intellectual terms there is a constant battle for ideas and in terms of practice the statutory land use planning system operates in an adversarial context with different communities of interest or place or identity seeking to capture the deliberations of the planning process – including some notable interfaces such as conservation versus development, builders versus local communities, energy companies versus local authorities, environmental bodies versus planning authorities, and even the proposed designation of high-quality areas are resisted by farming and fishing interests.

Two conflicting perspectives on planning exist. On the one hand, it is self-evident that an unfettered land and property development market would be at once inefficient, ineffective and inequitable. There would be a proliferation of social, economic and environmental costs leading inevitably to high conflict – likely to be discharged in the courts and legal systems – and thereby creating another layer of cost, uncertainty and inconsistency. As a consequence, there would be marked divisions in communities and localities, particularly as development takes place driven by specific and uneven power groups. That dystopic scenario is the very one that planning was intended to avoid. It follows that there is a strong intellectual rationale for land use planning in mitigating and adapting to societal needs and private sector interests in land and property development. This begs the question as to the intellectual foundation of planning in addressing these agendas.

On the other hand, the intellectual case for land use planning has been subject to sustained criticism for some time in political, business, community and environmental-sector circles. This liberal and neoliberal well of critique on planning is long standing and suggests a deep mistrust of the implications of land use planning from the very start. This strikes at the very core of assumed behaviours and relations between state, market and civil society. The relatively early contribution of Sorensen & Day (1981), for example, represented an example of countervailing critique in the early neoliberal phase – drawing on the philosophical thinking associated with libertarianism and offering a resolute dismissal of the spirit and purpose of the then relatively well-established land use planning system. This line of reasoning suggests there is an embedded fault line deep in the substance and philosophy of land use planning.

Yet, we perceive that the politics of land and property development and land use planning in terms of power, control and influence are overlooked. North (2011), for example, observed that "the tools we use to translate understanding into a framework are institutions composed of formal rules, informal norms, and enforcement characteristics. Institutions are very blunt instruments to deal with very complex issues. Perhaps because the norms of behaviour and the formal rules do not work or because enforcement is imperfect, the problems are still unresolved. Underlying the economic and social institutions must be a political framework. In order to understand that framework and how societies work, we need a theory of politics, which does not exist".

This insight is helpful as it uncovers the complex political relations associated with land and property development and the role of land use planning regulation – it drives to the central issue – that of challenges to, and the redistribution of power and control around the land resource itself. Here, Prior (2005), for example, in considering a regulationist interpretation of changes in the (more contemporary) planning system points to the dominance of private property and the land and property development sectors in determining the outcomes for new regulation arrangements. This suggests a sharp interface of values, motives and behaviours in institutional and organisational terms. Furthermore, Broadbent (1977) described this tension in terms of a lopsided political balance in which the public sector or the land use planning system was essentially caught in a cleft stick in determining outcomes for land and property development proposals.

Today, there is an awakening interest in re-examining the land question. As Bleischwitz (2001) points out, there was a shift away from land as a reference point for measuring productivity in the economy, and this would appear to have obscured the property rights dimension to debates around land and property development. This is an important point. It may be interpreted as the market commodification of land resources, a change that carried with it considerable conflict over what was held to be the wider public interest. Indeed, Gibb argues in a more contemporary setting:

> This new clear sighting of the great but suppressed truth of our human situation can be found beginning to grow in almost every sphere of human life. But, unfortunately, only in almost every sphere, and the deficiency is critical; for it is in that most fundamental social matter – that of our society's instituted relationship with the land.
>
> *(Gibb, 1997, p. 14)*

The underlying property rights strata underpinning the use and development of land is key to understanding this position. The intellectual context here is the early writings of William Ogilvie, a Scottish intellectual who published an anonymous political treatise advocating the rethinking of land ownership and control in the 1780s (Lloyd & Peel, 2008a). Drawing on this provenance, Gibb asserts further:

> Axially defining our societies is the point of relationship between the community and the individual. In one direction, the relationship is manifested as the restrictions

society places on the individual (that is, what is permitted to take from him, such as consents to act, or social dues): simultaneously, in the other direction, the relationship is defined by the extent to which, and means by which, the individual empowers the social community and enables it to act. We see that the way society makes provision for its common expenses is a matter of central importance to it. In the arrangement adopted, potentially lies the key to embodying, at a deep level within our human social systems, that sought-for natural order.

(Gibb, 1997, p. 15)

This then rests on the complex nature of the land resource itself which creates a very uneven intellectual, practical and political context within which land use planning has to operate. Moreover, this extends to the appreciation of what constitutes the public interest. Rolling forward this notion creates a contested relationship between property rules and policy rules – a long established experiential context for the planning system. Today, this messiness is compounded by changing economic conditions, responses to those conditions (such as austerity), ideology (witness the nefarious effects of neoliberalism, libertarianism and authoritarianism), and the various scales of planning engagement. This holds in various ways across the different planning institutional arrangements in Europe; we take the UK as example.

Neoliberalism and the Public Interest

Neoliberal thinking has transformed the planning landscape in many ways. As argued in the previous section, the land use planning system has operated in the context of a complex material resource – the land question. This is not simply another good or service which may be codified in abstract market terms. Yet in practical terms land carries with it highly distinctive characteristics relating to ownership, tenure, use and development potential (Davy, 2012). Conventional neoclassical land economics – on which planning is founded – however, asserts that land is fixed in absolute supply, is fixed in location, is subject to happenstance in terms of floating potential development values, is of variable quality, is dominated by private interests but carries with it a complex of communal, social and public property interest. These accounts suggest an emphasis on the formal aspects of institutions which tend to articulate private property interests. This intellectual basis of planning intervention predicated on neoclassical micro-economics – monopoly, externalities, public goods and justice – is the bedrock on which planning stands and falls. This exposes it to criticism on a number of fronts. There is an array of informal characteristics (or institutions) to the land question – a rich and complex history of ownership and tenure, conflict and private and social expectations. The embedded property rights, power relations and vested interests – together with the potential betterment in land values to be secured through land and property development – all contribute to a challenging operational context for securing regulation and forward planning in the public interest.

Against this detached relationship of people and land, the ascendancy of private property and public participation has had powerful consequences for our understandings of the public interest. Following Hall (1999) it is imperative that in seeking to understand this (unintended?) consequence there is a need to be vigilant about maintaining a cognisance of context – particularly with respect to ideology, technology, economic restructuring, social expectations and political metrics. These create a set of related questions as to why the UK land use planning system has struggled since its formal introduction in 1947. Why and how did private property rights prevail in terms of political influence and control? Why has public participation served to compound discourses around wider understandings of a common well-being of the land resource? Why has the public interest been eroded so deleteriously?

The erosion, dilution and labile nature of the public interest has not helped as it has served to isolate land use planning from its principal objectives in seeking to create positive and progressive economic, social and environmental purposes. Provenance is everything here. The concept of the public interest was created in a very specific set of conditions associated with the maturation of democracy, the maturing of political thinking and argument, the evolving forms of representative and participative political organisation and the articulation of private property rights (Dunn, 2005). The social construction of the public interest is bound up with the prevailing and inherited culture in society, with the mediation and expression of power, of the construction of knowledge, of ideology and political thinking, of property rights, and rules of law (Campbell & Marshall, 2002).

In tandem with this economic contraction and uncertainty there have been radical shifts in the prevailing ideological contexts. In part coinciding with the beginnings of economic and industrial crises, the shift from social democratic values and priorities to neoliberalism has proven to be profound for conventional land use planning. It has been argued, for example, that the practical concept of the public interest was an early casualty of this ideological shift – in both economic and political terms (Marquand, 2004). In effect a new private property economy has been explicitly and deliberately asserted and sustained. Marquand (2014) has described this as the laying down of a new moral economy. The extent to which this has transformed the context in which state, market and civil relations are conducted is a radical one. Here, Fine & Milonakis (2008) have documented the changing basis of economic philosophy over time from moral philosophy and political economy to economics – a changing lexicon that hides dramatic shifts in perception, understanding, observation and prescription.

Judt (2010) and Sandel (2012) argue that the UK is now dominated by agendas of libertarianism, short termism, policy fragmentation and thinking and where decision making is overwhelmed by monetised values and templates. Moreover, Klein (2007) demonstrated how neoliberal thinking has been exported aggressively across global governance. This underlines the point that land use planning in seeking to discharge its initial remit has been undermined by radically different values. This goes further than the eroded understandings and social constructions of the public interest. Fundamental shifts have taken place in the approach to understanding state, market and civil relations. In terms of future scenarios there is little respite. Shutt (2014), for example, argues that neoliberalism has operated and been adopted and perpetuated in such a way so as to normalise its metrics and values. Indeed, Mirowski (2013) has shown how neoliberalism works to secure its future – this is a force to be reckoned with. In essence, the private sector interests are now dominant and this bounded context creates powerful challenges to notions of planning and the public interest which were born in a different space, place and time.

Reflecting this transient intellectual and material environment, the world of land use planning itself – its endogenous environment – has undergone considerable shifts in theorising and conceptualising planning ideas, practices and the nature of the public interest (Tewdwr-Jones, 2011). There have been shifts from viewing planning as a necessary corrective to embedded market failures in private land and property development, to stressing the need for greater understanding of process and collaborative action, to the assertion of power and influence and at the present time an interest in resilience to address future challenges for society, the economy and the natural environment.

Think Tanks and the Social Re-Construction of Planning

In the UK in particular the normalisation of neoliberal values and thinking may be illustrated by the critical advocacy of the think tank community. Think tanks play an important role in contemporary governance. In terms of provenance, however, think tanks are relatively recent agents in political debates but their velocity with respect to influence is remarkable. Think tanks can contribute new or fresh thinking to political and policy debates, challenge conventional ideas or even support public policy implementation (Cockett, 1995). While the various organisations may reflect different political values, the dominant arguments over the last 30 years have tended to reflect neoliberal values and business interests. Arguably, the business-oriented think tank community has become more vociferous and visible under the neoliberal regime – demonstrating Mirowski's (2013) argument that neoliberalism seeks to create its own survival. While cutting across vast swathes of public policy, including health and education, this market-led criticism is increasingly the case with respect to different aspects of land use planning. Taken together these provide a challenging market-based perspective of established land use planning practices and thinking. It is not possible to present a comprehensive review of the documentation here. Some examples demonstrate the ferocity of the sustained attacks on the conventional land use planning system which remains in pursuit of the public interest in very different circumstances and values.

Drawing on the market-oriented think tanks in the UK, a recent advocacy document calls for the scaling back of established land use planning arrangements (Boyfield & Greenberg, 2014), asserting that the UK planning system is not fit for purpose. Evidence for this claim rests on the perceived chronic housing shortage in the UK and the perceived costs associated with an unwieldy planning system which serves to stifle economic growth. Moreover, it has been suggested that planning legislation is poorly understood and that local authorities are best described as a 'planning leviathan'. This description is couched in negative terms. Boyfield & Greenberg (2014) call for further consolidation and simplification of land use planning through the designation of Pink Zones to provide relatively more diluted regulatory regimes. The proposal contains a number of ideas relating to local government finance, compensation and legislative reform and reflects a continuing antagonism towards the established land use planning system.

The intellectual scope and focus of the general critique of planning by such think tanks are important. The generic anti-interventionist stance embraces sectors related to land use planning – including housing provision and design standards (Evans & Hartwich, 2005a) – and appeals for lessons to be learned from international comparative practice (Evans & Hartwich, 2005b). Reference is made to the ideas related to new institutional economics where alternative private property models are advocated (Webster, 2005). This market-infused advocacy is highly nuanced. On the one hand, Pennington & Miers (2006), for example, acknowledge the need for land use planning as a contextual prism in which orderly investment in land and property development can be secured. This acknowledges the security offered to property investors and developers by a comprehensive set of recognisable land regulations. On the other hand, Pennington & Miers (2006) advocate a radical reform of planning arrangements and posit alternatives based on a different, market-based and private property system. Here reference is made to the designation of Business Improvement Districts which involve the transfer of public space to a new form of sub-municipal governance of business interests (Lloyd & Peel, 2008b). To date, Business Improvement Districts have been established in town centres or industrial parks – places of concentrated economic activity. Recently, however, the argument to replace public sector governance with one based on private arrangements has been extended to community parks in urban areas (Policy Exchange, 2014). This demonstrates the point that neoliberal-infused think tanks exercise considerable influence in convincing the state, businesses and sections of civil society that land use planning is the problem not the solution. In effect, the neoliberal critique is challenging even the narrow intellectual basis of planning itself.

Path Dependence

Neglecting provenance has had a dramatic effect. While the aims and objectives of the UK statutory land use planning system have remained relatively constant since its establishment, it has increasingly been wrong-footed. External economic conditions, political priorities, ideologies, development ambitions, regional geographies, social and community conditions, environmental vulnerabilities, governmental and governance forms, state-market-civil relations and expectations have served to create the conditions in which planning has come under profound criticism. As a consequence of its systemic structural flaws around private property and public interest considerations, its tendency to path dependency and the over-arching cultures and attitudes towards the land question, planning has become the target for opprobrium, disappointment and criticism from all quarters.

Path dependency implies that the form and content of action is constrained by decisions made in the past (Sorensen, 2015). This can be the result of positive feedback (Pierson, 2000) – for example, in the case that zoning for green results in the creation of a popular park that consequently restricts rezoning for other purposes (Sorensen, 2015). Yet, path dependency also exists when past circumstances are no longer relevant, or are even counter-productive: a situation of a 'lock in' emerges. If this is the case, often some of the actors involved have a strong interest in the protraction of the situation.

Essentially a failure to appreciate the deeper provenance of planning's provenance has resulted in an extraordinary tendency to 'lock in' and 'path dependency'. It has led to the gladiatorial nature of debates about planning, the political positions taken regarding its perceived role, the ideologically infused criticism of its work and the business-infused advocacy for alternative, market-based positions.

Three determining factors may be identified. First, understandings of the very land question itself have been obscured by a failure to appreciate its importance in society. The land resource is now viewed as a market commodity and its inherent cultures and histories have been forgotten. Land is viewed as a vehicle for speculative development and financial gain rather than as a common asset with wider societal values. Thus, even when the intellectual rationale for statutory land use planning is asserted as serving, or seeking to secure the public interest, the private metrics predominate. Statutory land use planning has then had to operate in a defensive manner.

Second, the external conditions in which the land question has been addressed and the context in which the statutory land use planning system operates have changed. In general terms, the genesis of the UK planning system took place in the post-war recovery phase when active reflation of the economy was in train. The early work of the planning system and its achievements was conducted in the context of public sector expenditure, a post-war boom and investment in the necessary infrastructure. Moreover, that early phase of the statutory land use planning system involved expectations that growth would continue. In other words, planning as a regulatory means of securing the public interest was broadly accepted. Driving these circumstances was a social democratic milieu which was sympathetic to active intervention and planning regulation. From the late 1970s, however, there has been a general tendency to economic downturns, contraction in public expenditures and an ideological turn to neoliberal values. This latter point is critical as it is distrustful of government intervention and planning and more minded to promote the interests of business and private property. Certainly, this transformation in context is exemplified by the market-infused think tanks which advocate a small state and more simplified planning. This is predicated on a support for private interests rather than a notion of a broader public interest – of government failure as opposed to market failure.

Finally, and reflecting these powerful exogenous contextual changes, the internal practices of the statutory land use planning system have changed. The focus and lexicon of planning has shifted from growth, regulation and investment in infrastructure, for example, to agendas around regeneration – at regional, subregional and local scales. This has created a variation in planning practice – in some instances there is a tendency to focus on process. As statutory land use planning comes under increased criticism it becomes more defensive. Over and above these features, devolution has encouraged experimentation in different ways – in each case seeking to respond to the prevailing conditions in each devolved state.

Conclusions – Progress through Institutional Reform

A clichéd expression of modern times is 'going forward'. This rhetorical expression carries with it quite material implications and is deployed in many contexts – political, policy and administrative. It suggests a sense of progressive action from a standing start or the present position, through a deliberate set of steps to overcome adversity, avoid a problem, secure greater stability and security, and achieve a position of more positive well-being. In general terms, the tenor of the cliché is a positive one. The term is deployed in various contexts – and can involve different forms, including physical relocation or institutional or organisational change. It implies a deliberate step to start a new momentum to a more certain (and yet often ill-defined) perceived nirvana. The practical myopia of going forward is encouraged by the increasingly normalised neoliberal political economy which has transformed the context for planning within which problems are defined, priorities set and the role of planning perceived.

It is in the nature of things that going forward into the future involves a starting place. That starting place is the here and now. It is static and often associated with a catalogue of problematic conditions or issues which must then be resolved in the future – in effect, a solution will be found going forward. Thus, for example, there are strident demands on planning to devise solutions to urgent issues – such as securing appropriate housing supply, affordable housing, new settlements and economic regeneration. Climate-change agendas are the most recent. It is frequently the case that the statutory land use planning system is under considerable stress to devise appropriate solutions and is exposed to myriad forms of criticism and vehemence as to its performance and outcomes. The emphasis is on the here and now – the issue at hand – and the focus translates to devising alternative ways forward for the political system to consider. The danger is that the past, its associated experiential learning and experience, is forgotten because of the clamour to push forward to a solution.

The radically changed world now presents very specific economic, ideological and political conditions which have encouraged the formidable questioning of the role of planning in this market-dominated context. Neoliberalism is suspicious of government intervention in general and land use planning in particular and fosters a campaign of criticism and the advocacy of business-infused alternatives. It is clear that this serves to undermine the provenance of the planning system in terms of the negative impacts on its traditions, experiences and public interest values, its formal institutions and organisations, its governance and the actual operation of planning on the ground, as well as in the context of informal institutions. It is also argued that the new moral economy is creating differentiated effects – as is suggested is the case in the context of strategic planning – and new forms of contractual relations in planning (Janssen-Jansen

& van der Veen, 2017). The concept of provenance helps demonstrate that the mobility of planning ideas over time, its informal elements, the planning architecture and the behaviours of involved interests are proving inadequate to the new context.

This position is highly complicated. Experience and practice suggests that the statutory land use planning system has benefitted society. Land uses, property development, the provision of housing, retailing and commercial space, industrial infrastructure and the use of land for recreational and conservation purposes have been secured in a way that enhances society's well-being and quality of life. In simple terms, the statutory land use planning system does its job. It secures the outputs and outcomes expected of it. Basic infrastructure has been laid out, community facilities provided for, improved accessibility and connectivity ensured between communities of interest, place and identities, and higher standards of construction executed. Given the febrile nature of change, however, the processes and decisions by the planning system are contested. This is a profound area. The political nature of the land question – in terms of power, influence, the spectrum of gainers and losers – together with the financial potential of land and property development – renders the role of the statutory land use planning system a complex and sensitive one. There is much to gain and lose from the outcomes of statutory land use planning by society at large and communities and localities in particular. It is at once a technocratic activity and responsibility of government based on narrowly defined neoclassical economic criteria and is expected to deliver a democratic function of that government. Institutional change needs to address the rationale for planning and not focus on processes and aspirations which cannot be delivered in a world of private property rights, neoliberal values and the normalisation of the government failure motif.

As a consequence of ignoring provenance, always starting from here (besieged by a strident clamour for solutions), and faced with an uncertain and threatening neoliberal/austerity landscape, it is not surprising that planning remains misunderstood and contested. Why is that? There is a theoretical vacuum. Post-positivism offers much, yet contributes little tangible substance to provide planning with the capital it needs to fully discharge its role. As a result, planning (operating in a post-modernist world) rests on its positivist values to justify its existence and to predetermine its limits for action. The neoliberal policy agenda wants action (solutions) *now*, yet planning theory (in terms of post-positivist thinking) remains abstract and wanting. A fetish with solutionism is not ideal (Milne, 2012) yet it is what the world wants/demands. Therefore, planning fails – its theory diminishes its practical contributions.

Land use planning was introduced at a particular point in time, characterised by specific ideological influences, political and economic ambitions, social circumstances and defined expectations for its contribution to the considered public interest. These combined to create the provenance of planning and the intrinsic narratives and actions of planning which have remained intact ever since. Essentially, neglecting planning's provenance has resulted in an extraordinary tendency to 'lock in' and 'path dependency'. This chapter contends that, as a consequence, planning has not managed to mature, evolve or learn sufficiently to operate within very radically changed ideological, economic, social, political and environmental conditions. Essentially, planning is at odds with reality and this creates the tensions which lead to the ongoing criticism of the planning system. There is a case to re-engage with the promise of planning in the public interest with a deliberate recognition that planning's role is very different within the prevailing neoliberal norms. There is a need for society to have a conversation about a potential fundamental reform of institutional arrangements for securing a public interest in land policy. Public and private matters can exist in a neoliberal world and it is time to acknowledge the case for change by recalling the provenance of planning. This is needed in planning education, policy debates, political manifestos and in social conversations at large.

Notes

1 To our deep regret Professor Leonie Janssen-Jansen passed away on 11 April 2018 after completing this chapter and during production of this book.
2 This chapter builds on the authors' articles in the Dutch Rooilijn journal (Janssen-Jansen, 2016; Lloyd, 2016).

References

Bleischwitz, R. (2001). Rethinking productivity: Why has productivity focussed on labour instead of natural resources? *Environment and Resource Economics*, 19(1), 23–36
Blyth, M. (2013). *Austerity: The History of a Dangerous Idea*. Oxford: Oxford University Press.
Boyfield, K., & Greenberg, D. (2014). *Pink Planning*. London: Centre for Policy Studies, November.
Broadbent, T. A. (1977). *Planning and Profit in the Urban Economy*. London: Routledge.
Campbell, H., & Marshall, R. (2002). Utilitarianism's bad breath? A re-evaluation of the public interest justification for planning. *Planning Theory*, 1(2), 163–187.
Cockett, R. (1995). *Thinking the Unthinkable: Think-Tanks and the Economic Counter-Revolution, 1931–1983*. London: Harper Collins Publishers.
Crace, J. (2013). *Harvest*. London: Picador.
Davy, B. (2012). *Land Policy: Planning and the Spatial Consequences of Property*. London: Ashgate Publishing, Ltd.
Dembski, S., & Salet, W. (2010). The transformative potential of institutions: How symbolic markers can institute new social meaning in changing cities. *Environmental Planning A*, 42, 611–625.
Dunn, J. (2005). *Setting the People Free – The Story of Democracy*. London: Atlantic Books.
Evans, A. W., & Hartwich, O. M. (2005a). *Unaffordable Housing: Fables and Myths*. London: Policy Exchange, June.
Evans, A. W., & Hartwich, O. M. (2005b). *Bigger Better Faster More: Why Some Countries Plan Better than Others*. London: Policy Exchange, June.
Fine, B., & Milonakis, D. (2008). *From Political Economy to Economics: Method, the Social and the Historical in the Evolution of Economic Theory*. London: Routledge.
Gibb, P. (1997). *William Ogilvie's Birthright in Land*. London: Othila Press.
Hall, P. (1999). *Cities in Civilisation: Cultures, Innovation and World Order*. London: Phoenix.
Hardy, S. A. (1999). *Birthright in Land and the State of Scotland*. Pitlochry: Peregrine Press.
Janssen-Jansen, L. B. (2016). Stromen van institutionele verandering. *Rooilijn*, 49(5), 378–381.
Janssen-Jansen, L. B., & Veen, M. van der. (2017). Contracting communities: Conceptualizing community benefits agreements to improve citizen involvement in urban development projects. *Environment and Planning A*, 49(1), 205–225.
Judt, T. (2010). *Ill Fares The Land: A Treatise On Our Present Discontents*. London: Penguin.
Klein, N. (2007). *The Shock Doctrine: The Rise of Disaster Capitalism*. London: Penguin.
Lawson, J. (2016). Reacting or re-shaping institutions. *Rooilijn*, 49(5), 374–377.
Lloyd, M. G. (2015). *Provenance, Planning and New Parameters*. Amsterdam: University of Amsterdam Press.
Lloyd, M. G. (2016). Understanding institutions in metropolitan governance? *Rooilijn*, 49(5), 332–335.
Lloyd, M. G., & Peel, D. (2008a). *The Public Interest: Expropriation of Property Rights – A Historical Perspective*. Paper presented to the Association of European Schools of Planning (AESOP) International Academic Forum Thematic Group Meeting 'Planning, Law and Property Rights' Second Symposium, Warsaw, 14–15 February.
Lloyd, M. G., & Peel, D. (2008b). From Town Centre Management to the Business Improvement District Model in Britain: Towards a New Contractualism? In G. Morçöl, L. Hoyt, J. Meek & U. Zimmermann (Eds.), *Business Improvement Districts: Research, Theories, and Controversies* (pp. 71–94). New York: Taylor & Francis.
Marquand, D. (2004). *Decline of the Public: The Hollowing Out of Citizenship*. Cambridge: Polity Press
Marquand, D. (2014). *Mammon's Kingdom: An Essay on Britain, Now*. London: Allen Lane.
Massey, D. B., & Catalano, A. (1978). *Capital and Land: Landownership by Capital in Great Britain*. London: Edward Arnold.
Milne, S. (2012). *The Revenge of History: The Battle for the Twenty-First Century*. London: Verso.
Mirowski, P. (2013). *Never Let a Serious Crisis Go to Waste: How Neoliberalism Survived the Financial Meltdown*. London: Verso.
North, D. C. (2011). Foreword. In D. Cole & E. Ostrom (Eds.), *Property in Land and Other Resources*. Boston, MA: Lincoln Institute.

Ogilvie, W. (1781). An Essay on the Right of Property in Land, paragraph 4. Quoted in S.-A. Hardy. (1999). *Birthright in Land*. Pitlochry: Peregrine Press.

Peel, D., & Lloyd, M. G. (2006). The twisting paths to planning reform in Scotland. *International Planning Studies*, 11(2), 89–107.

Peel, D., & Lloyd, M. G. (2007). Neo-traditional planning: Towards a new ethos for land use planning? *Land Use Policy*, 24(2), 396–403.

Peel, D., & Lloyd, M. G. (2010). Strategic regeneration: An integrated planning approach to managing a coastal resort in South Wales. *Environmental Hazards: Human and Policy Dimensions*, 9(3), 301–318.

Pennington, M., & Miers, T. (2006). *The New Land Economy: A New Approach to Planning, Development, Conservation and Infrastructure*. Edinburgh: The Policy Institute, December.

Pierson, P. (2000). Increasing returns, path dependence, and the study of politics. *American Political Science Review*, 94(2), 251–267.

Prior, A. (2005). UK planning reform: A regulationist interpretation. *Planning Theory & Practice*, 6(4), 465–484.

Policy Exchange. (2014). *Green Society: Policies to Improve the UK's Urban Green Spaces*. London: Policy Exchange.

Salet, W. G. M. (2002). Evolving institutions: An international exploration into planning and law. *Journal of Planning Education and Research*, 22(1), 26–35.

Sandel, M. (2012). *What Money Can't Buy: The Moral Limits of Markets*. London: Allen Lane.

Shutt, H. (2014). Responding to the great disintegration: Denial or renewal? Retrieved from: http://harryshutt.com/2014/11/27/responding-to-the-great-disintegration-denial-or-renewal.

Sorensen, A. (2015). Taking path dependence seriously: An historical institutionalist research agenda in planning history. *Planning Perspectives*, 30(1), 17–38.

Sorensen, A. D., & Day, R. A. (1981). Libertarian planning. *Town Planning Review*, 52(4), 390–402.

Tewdwr-Jones, M. (2011). *Urban Reflections: Narratives of Place, Planning and Change*. Bristol: Policy Press.

Webster, C. (2005). The new institutional economics and the evolution of modern urban planning: Insights, issues and lessons. *Town Planning Review*, 76(4), 455–484.

Williamson, O. (1994). Transaction Cost Economics and Organization Theory. In N. Smelser & R. Swedberg (Eds.), *The Handbook of Economic Sociology* (pp. 77–107). New York: Russell Sage Foundation.

Williamson, O. (2000). The new institutional economics: Taking stock, looking ahead. *Journal of Economic Literature*, 38(3), 595–613.

PART 5

Cultural and Political Institutions in Action

16
CONTEXTUALIZING INSTITUTIONAL MEANING THROUGH AESTHETIC RELATIONS
A Pragmatist Understanding of Local Action

Julie-Anne Boudreau[1]

Institutions take various forms: patent letters, organizational charts, job descriptions, budgets, inputs and outputs. These are generally the artefact considered to study them. What is of interest to us in this chapter is a too-often neglected institutional form: their embodiment. Institutions are made of actors and artefacts who interact, do and feel things in specific moments and places.[2]

When institutions come to life through these specific situations, we are faced with more than a simple analytical divide between policymaking and policy implementation. Much of the literature on policy implementation, or on 'street-level bureaucracy', emphasizes the gap between policy on paper and policy in action. Through a pragmatist, situated and ethnographic approach, one can see more than a gap. Institutions participate in the unfolding of specific "universes of operation" shaped through the interaction of macro, meso and micro temporalities. In order to understand local institutional action, this chapter argues that we need to be sensitive to various registers of action, from the visceral feeling that something is happening without being able to cognitively process the situation, to strategically planned moves more typical of institutional analysis. These visceral registers are what we will call here aesthetic relations: action through non-verbalized means, through our bodies and feelings. Let me illustrate this with ethnographic vignettes from the Saint-Michel neighbourhood in Montreal before developing more systematically in conclusion this theoretical argument.

Mike was about 24 years old when I met him near the Louis-Joseph-Papineau high school in the northern part of the neighbourhood.

> I have seen police officers speaking to youths, bla, bla, bla … they try to explain to them how to behave, how not to behave, [Mike doesn't like police officers] but me, personally, I never had contacts with police officers. In fact, for me it's only Rodney

to whom I spoke because we were together at the barbershop. But police officers and I are not really friends because I try to make ... I try to find a parallel way with others, like we will never cross them in fact.

(Interview, 6 April 2011)

Paul, a tall white police officer and Rodney, a shorter black police officer with a contagious smile, are central characters of the Saint-Michel neighbourhood in Montreal. Rodney meets many young men at the barbershop. One day, as he was enjoying his hamburger at McDonald's with two young men from the neighbourhood, they confided in him about violent acts they were planning to do. As Rodney was telling me this story he was making wide gestures with his arms, smiling out of amazement: "They didn't remember that I was wearing my shirt!" Sophie is one of Rodney's young colleagues, white skin, dark hair, she likes biking around the neighbourhood when patrolling. When a young woman ran away from home, Rodney recalls, she sent an SMS to Sophie: "Mme Sophie, I am running away, but don't worry".

While Sophie is newer to Saint-Michel, Paul and Rodney's names were mentioned to us by almost all youths we met there. Paul arrived in the poste de police 30 (PDQ 30 – local police station) 25 years ago. Before community policing became a formal policy, he changed his approach to policing. During the violent 1990s, he used repressive measures to try to control gang activities. One day, he told me, a drive-by-shooting killed two innocent victims (including a pregnant woman), and this is when he said: "That's enough". He was morally outraged, sat down and reflected on his work and changed his approach, while maintaining repression when necessary. He began to see youths in their milieu, working with various local partners. Moral outrage is still what drives his action. In this more recent example he speaks of a young woman who was mugged by gang members and his reaction:

> And then I went to see the guys and I said: "If I see another one trying that, trying to hit a young girl like that for nothing, I will be the first one to come and get you. He [pointing at the aggressor] is a big idiot and I don't want that anymore". And the guys, they didn't even say a word. They were about 30 guys there, and they didn't even say: "But why [did you arrest our friend]?" It's the prevention we make, the relations we create that enable us, even when we have to do repression, to get the message through. And the message was clear.

He gave us another example where one of his colleagues was saved from being circled by gang members when he was responding to a call because a young man recognized him and stopped his friends from pushing the police officer in a corner. The man remembered that he had "come once in his living room" to speak with his mother and estimated that this officer deserved respect because of that. Paul is still surprised by the strength of human relations:

> In the long term, you're a winner all the way. This time, he helped us avoid a confrontation because one day we went to sit in his mother's living room. Special, no? No, no, it makes me flip each time. And it's always anecdotes like that that come back.

Neither Paul nor Rodney grew up nor reside in the neighbourhood, but they are very involved personally beyond police work. They are doing work that is much appreciated by community organizations in Saint-Michel.

As Stéphane told us:

There are many nuances to make you see, because each police officer, each person, it's different. However, the system as such makes it that heavy trends – and it's also like a group dynamic that police officers live, you see. And there's a real fraternity within the police as such, so many times they will put themselves in a position of strength against us: It's them against us, if you know what I mean.

Stéphane was 22 years old when I met him at his house in April 2011. He likes sports; he likes to "express my ethnicity with, for example, my hair, my dreads". Like most youths in Saint-Michel (as elsewhere I might add), he does not like the police institution. Yet, he distinguishes between the institution and certain individuals such as Paul and Rodney.

We heard an anecdote concerning a new local police officer. The freshly graduated police officer who did not know Montreal very well, let alone Saint-Michel, was patrolling on Jean-Talon Street. He suddenly puts in a call for backup. Panicking, he says: "There's a huge crowd of Arabs taking over the street!" He was afraid the crowd would get out of control and that he would not be able to contain it alone. He had no clue why the street was suddenly flooded by joyful bodies. As we were told this story, Paul and Rodney were quietly smiling: "It's the end of the Ramadan! It's normal, don't worry".

Their objective in recounting this story is to emphasize the need to learn about Saint-Michel's diverse population in order to be able to do good police work. This involves human relations and constant embodied engagement. But beyond this message, the anecdote illustrates the power of an aesthetic appearance which speaks to the new police officer's affect more than his cognitive capacity to analyse the situation. An aesthetic appearance is when we are faced with something that speaks to our senses, when we cannot name it (recognize it as something we know). We can simply 'admit' that it is touching us. The intensity of this experience is generally neglected from political analysis because it cannot be described with words and thus articulated as ideology or interests. "Under the pressures of immediacy," Panagia writes, "we lose access to the kinds of conditions that make it possible to determine things like motivation, use, or belief—all forces that constitute the nature of interest" (Panagia, 2009, p. 27).

This officer felt afraid and overwhelmed by the appearance of the crowd on the street to celebrate the end of the Ramadan. The circulation of artefacts such as North African flags, or the chattering noise coming from the numerous cafés on Jean-Talon Street, the smell from the feast, provoked intense effects on the police officer unaware of the custom. He could not cognitively make sense of what was happening, but he could certainly feel the aesthetic of the situation, which was strange to him. Beyond the very many times he heard that Saint-Michel is a multicultural neighbourhood, feeling it aesthetically in a very embodied way had a very different effect than what he knew cognitively, namely that the neighbourhood is home to diverse cultures.

With these short ethnographic vignettes from the Saint-Michel neighbourhood in Montreal, I wish to contribute the following reflections to the idea of 'institutions in action'.

1. With its quotidian, situational outlook, ethnography uncovers how institutions, in this case the police, work in the field. They work through experimentation, adaptation and affective human relations. Local contexts such as Saint-Michel are "universes of operation" that we can properly see only if we adopt what AbdouMaliq Simone (2010) calls an "epistemology of blackness".
2. Action unfolds on various registers, from the visceral to the cognitive. Even if it was not intended or planned, an act always has consequences. Studying action, therefore, requires

attention to the labour through which an affectively sensed ordeal is translated into a publicly hearable problem. Action is not simply motivated by will or interest.
3. The normative quality of institutions is productively revealed in moments of transgression. In the contemporary context of urbanity, such moments are frequent and tend to precipitate institutional innovation.

In order to expand on these points, let me continue the story of police innovation in Saint-Michel.

Policing Protocols and Police Action: A 'Blackness' Analysis

Simone suggests that blackness is "a means of tying together the various situations and tactics that have been at work in the long history of African people moving out into and around a larger urban world" (2010, p. 268). Because black people have historically moved across various cities, through their "multiple and discrete sojourns and implantations" (ibid., p. 280), such as in Saint-Michel, they have invented a "universe of operation" (ibid., p. 297). Whether Saint-Michel youths actually move physically or not in the present is not as important as the legacy of movement by their ancestors who have learned to "bring an increasing heterogeneity of calculations, livelihoods, and organizational logics into a relationship with each other" (ibid., p. 279) as they implanted themselves in specific neighbourhoods.

Saint-Michel is a neighbourhood of approximately 54,000 residents, largely of immigrant origin (most notably from Haiti and more recently North Africa). It is, as Giulio, a tall white man of Italian origins, describes, "like a big chilling spot". Élisabeth's post on the mapcollab.org website[3] synthesizes wonderfully how many youths wish to speak of Saint-Michel. It captures with a simple image, that of the subway line, and a simple number, 67 (the bus line running on Saint-Michel boulevard), the importance of mobility for this neighbourhood. Élisabeth also mentions other important sites of the neighbourhood: Louvain street; the McDonald's near the subway station; the two French-language high schools, Jean-François Perrault (j.f.p) and Louis Joseph Papineau (l.j.p); the Maison d'Haïti; and the local police station (poste 30) (see Figure 16.1). Or as Ouali, 20 years old, who arrived in Canada from Algeria only 11 months before we began the workshops in Saint-Michel, describes: "Arabs, Haitians, Québéckers, and South Americans play together". He speaks of Saint-Michel as a "*quartier libre*" ('a free neighbourhood'). "It's like medication," he says, "my neighbourhood is my life". For him, Saint-Michel is a "welcoming land". He feels at home, particularly because of the Petit Maghreb, the portion of Jean-Talon Street we discussed above, formally called as such because of its concentration of North African businesses (for a detailed history of how this appellation came about, see Manai, 2015).

Blackness is "a device for affirming and engaging forms of articulation among different cities and urban experiences that otherwise would have no readily available means of conceptualization" (Simone, 2010, p. 279). The epistemology of blackness enables us to see the arbitrary instead of focusing on the institutional norm. Rather than assigning Saint-Michel youths identities and stereotypical representations based on their skin colour and where they live, the epistemology of blackness invites a focus on their gestures, on what they do, where, when and how. It is, in other words, a pragmatist epistemology.

Blackness does not belong exclusively to black people. It is a way of living in the city which builds on what black people have constructed in the neighbourhoods where they have sojourned. Young Saint-Michel residents identify strongly with the neighbourhood, so do local police officers. Paul explains that

A Pragmatist Understanding of Local Action

Figure 16.1 Élisabeth's online post, mapCollab project, October 2014
Source: www.mapcollab.org

here at the 30th [poste de quartier 30], I would say, we are a big family. And perhaps we don't work as elsewhere. You know, we have our way and as I was saying earlier, there are partners and the police is not better than the other partners. We are all equal.

Police officers' attachment to their neighbourhood quarter mirrors youths' attachment to their neighbourhood. Saint-Michel has its own universe of operation, shared by youths and police officers. There are specific ways of doing police work here, linked to the population, economic and institutional history of the neighbourhood.

Blackness is about saying "something about the city that nobody else can [say], and if we are really prepared to listen, we could not rest at ease with the theories of the city being put into play today" (Simone, 2015, p. 8). Indeed, most academic and mainstream knowledge about the city, the people inhabiting its spaces and its history, rest on controlling what is said by certain people (racialized youths) and showcasing what is said by others (academics, planners, police officers, journalists). The idea of institutions in action forces us to articulate academic, planner, journalist tales of the city with personal tales (Finnegan, 1998). Lipsky's (1980) seminal work on various police officers' different street-level attitudes demonstrates how successful institutional action requires a fine-grained and culturally sensitive understanding of the context in which institutions operate. And in order to understand this context, we need to be sensitive to various narratives by inhabitants and not only actors performing their institutional tasks. We also need to be sensitive not only to what people tell us, but also to what they do, how their bodies speak.

Police work in Saint-Michel does not simply follow protocol. We saw in the opening vignettes how Paul and Rodney work, interpret and adapt protocols. We saw how moral outrage and empathy are central to their work with youths. These are registers of action to which youths are highly sensitive. Local contexts such as Saint-Michel are "universes of operation" that we can properly understand only if we remain attuned to these affective registers. This is something the new recruit, scared because of the outpour of "Arabs" on Jean-Talon Street, did not yet understand.

Quotidian Ordeal: Racialized Bodies Scanned through Risk-Management Programs

The mapCollab guide to Saint-Michel created by youths during our workshops seek to move visitors not only with a physical tour of the neighbourhoods, but also and mostly by appealing to affective aesthetics.[4] Analysing these youth worlds as 'anti-social' or 'at-risk', as the media and public policies do, blinds us from seeing what is being constructed on a daily basis in these universes of operation. We saw with Simone how an epistemology of blackness based on the legacy of black mobilities and their ability to create a "universe of operation" in the neighbourhood where they sojourned enables us to see the arbitrary, the unexpected ways through which people articulate their daily lives in complex normative environments.

Institutional prevention measures, ranging from community policing to public subsidies for community projects aimed at keeping youths away from street gangs (in the 2000s) or [religious] radicalization (in the 2010s), are based on practices of racial profiling. Such practice does the opposite of blackness. Instead of revealing the unexpected, it imposes patterns and predictability on certain bodies. Prevention programs work with an actuarial logic. On paper, profiling means using probabilistic calculations to establish risk factors. In this approach, youths are conceived as statistical aggregates; their behaviour is 'predicted' by their concentration of risk factors, race being one of them. In my interviews, I constantly heard local actors appropriating the institutional risk-factor discourse to describe the neighbourhood or their own social work. For instance, the local police commander exposes youth vulnerability, while hesitating to use the actual words:

> They are youths who unfortunately have less means, more challenges. So, they are youths – I don't want to say they are at-risk, but they are youths who weren't unfortunately ... spoiled by destiny, I don't know.

If we ethnographically examine what local civil and police actors actually do with youths, or ask them how they perceive them, responses are not always coherent with the institutional risk-factor discourse. They speak less in terms of vulnerability and more in terms of empowerment, although this distinction is more or less intense according to who is speaking. For instance, there was a gendered and job distinction between the more maternal discourses of community relations police officers who (in Saint-Michel) are female, and the more respect-driven discourse of police patrollers, such as Paul and Rodney, who are mainly male. Compare these two excerpts, the first by Julie, who was the community relations police officer at the Saint-Michel police station, and the second by Paul:

> It's all true, it's disadvantaged, yes, in comparison to other neighbourhoods, but this does not mean there is less potential. We need to give these youngsters confidence [in a maternal tone, she sometimes speaks of "my" youths], the possibility to do other things. This is the opportunity: when they do sports, when they are engaged in projects.

They [youths] will respect the individual; they will respect you. You know them well and you are going to say [to gang youths]: "Me, guys, it's me who organizes this thing, please". The guys will say: "I respect you, no problem, you can do what you want, nothing will happen".

The contrast here cannot simply be explained by gender, but the mandate corresponding to each position must also be taken into account. Community relations police officers work exclusively on prevention, mainly in schools (elementary and secondary). They work with youths in general, and not so much with criminalized youths. Police patrollers have a repressive as well as a preventive mandate. They work with older criminalized youths who are not really seen as vulnerable. Rather, the relationship developed between Paul, Rodney and gang veterans is one of equal forces and mutual respect.

Despite these differences, the logic of prevention based on profiling techniques (identifying risk factors) remains racialized. Although the police keep insisting that criminal profiling and racial profiling are not the same thing, on the ground, these profiles are generally amalgamated and have important effects on youths. Racial profiling has been publicly contested since at least 2003, when a working group on the issue was created locally, followed by various consultative commissions at the provincial level. Following the 2008 revolts in Montréal-Nord, a neighbourhood adjacent to Saint-Michel, the Montreal police service began a public reflection on racial profiling. Following the death of a young man of Latino origins named Freddy Villanueva, murdered by a police officer, the Montreal police faced the need to explain the controversial anti-gang operations of the Eclipse squad. This is when, in conjunction with a shift of priorities at the federal and provincial levels, the term 'street gang' gradually disappeared from the public scene (public consultation by the Commission on Public Security, May 2011), to be soon replaced by 'radicalization'. Although certain initiatives were taken such as awareness workshops for police officers, racial-profiling techniques persist at the local level, while the provincial public debate is openly targeting racialized youths with their radicalization prevention programs.

Profiling relies on the statistical identification of patterns. Racism, on the other hand, involves embodied and affective relations of attraction and/or revulsion.

> So here we are passing through the parking lot, recalls Stéphane, [this day he was returning home from school with two friends] and then there is an old woman there in her car and all, and who says: "Hey there, hey! We're not in Africa here. We don't eat on the street". See what I mean – situations you see … very very eeeeeehhh … that … racism that that expresses itself like that, you see. [Stéphane hesitates to use the word racism in this conversation with my student, who is also of Haitian origins.] So we are three youths you see: Me who is smiling, the other who runs and tries to hit the car, and the other who doesn't do anything.
>
> *(Interview, 3 April 2011).*

Stéphane describes a situation of racism (revulsion based on certain bodily characteristics) and racialization (generalization about someone's expected behaviour based on stereotypical understanding of race – as in the affirmation that in Africa people eat in certain ways) that has an effect on the three friends. Racism is a modality of power relations playing on the affective register. Racialization is a form of power relation mobilizing the cognitive register in very similar ways to the institutional technique of profiling. In the situation described by Stéphane, the friends engage in different political gestures in response to the woman's racist comment: smiling, hitting, freezing. Her comment about Africa and eating habits had the effects of excluding them from Montreal's normative 'civility'.

From police profiling techniques to daily experiences of racism and racialization, action unfolds on various registers, from the visceral to the cognitive. Even if it was not intended or planned, an act always has consequences. This is why, following the French pragmatist school of sociology, I find it particularly useful to reflect on the labour required to translate an ordeal operating on a visceral register into a publicly legitimate form of action operating on a cognitive register. The strange feeling we experience when 'something is happening' in our daily whereabouts can progressively be transformed into a publicly defined citizenship conflict (Breviglieri & Trom, 2003). Inhabiting the city signifies feeling a place with our body, knowing its universe of operation. It means we know the place; we know it enough to sense when something is 'happening'. We can perceive changes in the environment because our body is accustomed to certain odors, sounds, shadows. When we sense that something is unusual, we become more attentive to our urban environment. When the woman in the car senses that Stéphane and his friends do something 'unusual' like eating on the street, she begins to observe more intently. This 'trouble', this 'something is happening', puts her urban knowledge to test (Breviglieri & Trom, 2003). The strange feeling that something is wrong pushes her to find adjustments to the situation. She qualifies the situation with her available repertoire of explanations, which in her case is based on racialization: "Black people do things differently, they are therefore threatening and out of place".

Breviglieri and Trom (2003) suggest that inhabiting a place and being able to perceive these 'troubles' moves people from the 'familiar register' of inhabitant to the 'public register' of citizen. The multiple situations of trouble perceived by our bodies in urban settings require complex micro-labour to match the sensation of trouble with a repertoire of urban problems. By explaining what she senses with problems such as how we live together in difference, the woman in the car is generalizing the circumstantial character of the 'trouble' and makes it a publicly shared problem of civility. Unfortunately, her voice is much louder than Stéphane's.

Urbanity requires these constant adjustments between the micro-experience of inhabiting and the public discourses available to understanding them as political problems. With its intensity and diversity, urban life imposes numerous perceptive reorientations that we then categorize as urban political problems with various levels of government. When 'trouble' is perceived in relation to something foreign, it gives consistency to ambient xenophobic discourse. Young black men are seen as 'different' because they bring new elements to the routine perception of the dominant city.

Conceiving of political action on these various registers opens the door to integrating various forms of distributed agency in the analysis and creates a better understanding of truly creative political moments. Connolly (2011) speaks of the interrelation of the "proto-agency" of non-human actors which disrupts our sense of perception through unexpected vibrations and "complex agency" (what is generally recognized as public action). According to him, complex agency (public action) cannot become creative and innovative unless something disturbs our sense of perception. This something comes from proto-agents. Unfortunately, institutional analysis tends to ignore this proto-agency. In Stéphane's story, proto-agents are the smell of the food he was eating, or perhaps more importantly, the impact of his appearance (his dreads), the clothes he was wearing and the image projected by three black bodies in the parking lot. In this story, complex agency is absent. The woman in the car blatantly proffered a racist gesture and apparently did not even realize it. The variety of reactions on the part of Stéphane and his friends (smiling, hitting, freezing) did not lead to innovation. It was rather a sterile interaction between the woman and the three youngsters. In many ways, however, it was a moment of transgression that revealed the power of social (racist) norms.

The Moment of Transgression

Most studies of urban governance and social regulations start with institutions, looking at how decisions are made, policies developed and laws enforced. While this institutionalist approach is important, combining it with pragmatist insights is my privileged starting point with a focus on the lived micro-experience of regulation as a lens to studying governance. What happens in specific urban spaces when a norm governing its usage or meaning is challenged? This is what the woman in the car expresses. Why is the norm transgressed by Stéphane and his friends? Or is it a transgression? For whom and by whom? How do youths commit to, or refute, social norms? And what does this tell us about institutional innovation? Police work consists of regulating transgression. This is why I find youth–police interaction revealing.

Transgressing involves distorting, disturbing and stretching the norm. Most of the literature exploring transgressive practices either adopt a 'deviance' approach (sociology of deviance) or a 'cure and care' approach (psychology, medicine, social work, criminology). The former approach seeks to understand why and how certain social groups or urban spaces become deviant (Cohen, 1959; Sutherland, 1924; Tanner, 1996). In doing so, it begins with a moral representation of 'deviant' practices understood as being outside the norm (Becker, 1963/1997). The sociology of deviance tends to explain transgression by emphasizing that marginalization produces specific sets of needs and behaviours. In turn, the latter approach, with its pathological rather than moralist stance, focuses on risk prevention and the eradication of transgressive practices from public spaces (Andrews et al., 1990; Bonell, 2004; Young et al., 2006). This is what risk-prevention programs such as those in Saint-Michel aim to accomplish.

Both these perspectives have been criticized for ignoring power relations. They question the reasons why the norm is transgressed (deviance approach) and how transgression can be managed (cure and care approach), but never whose interest the norm and transgression serve. For instance, what does curing and caring mean for the agency of young black men in Saint-Michel? I understand transgression as the expression of conflict with the norm, the law or the authorities. Expressing conflict does not necessarily entail a direct confrontation. Transgressing can also be seen as a game (to test the limits) or a quest for pleasure (Lyng, 1990), for autonomy (Parazelli, 2009) or for justice.

Transgression is increasingly visible and valorized as a force of social change, especially so in urban settings (e.g. the Black Lives Matter movement). As Taussig (1999, p. 142) puts it, following Bataille (1957), "[t]ransgression *suspends* the taboo without suppressing it". It does not negate the rule but makes it more visible and salient. The moment of transgression is thus particularly rich to reveal institutional norms and produce innovation. Urban spaces of transgression (including our own transgressive bodies) affect our very understanding of the private and the public, shifting from the confidential to the revealed, from the intimate to the visible. Youth practices are often seen as transgressive because they challenge this fundamental norm.

How can the epistemology of blackness work against racialization and contribute to institutional innovation? Or in other words, how can emphasizing what is constructed in these neighbourhoods through the transgression of civil and institutional norms attune our sensitivity to the unpredictable, rather than the actuarial logic of racial profiling and patterning? Tivon, a participant in Little Burgundy, another Montreal neighbourhood, explains this brilliantly:

> This is the south side of Elgin Terrace. The two blocks surrounding these backyards are ram-packed with low-income-housing project buildings and houses. I used one camera to take these two pictures. While taking these pictures I was being watched by six different cameras. Due to past crime in the area, the city and the police decided

to secure Little Burgundy with over 50 surveillance cameras. The areas you see in the pictures above have approximately eight cameras alone. Privacy is not your backyard.

(www.mapcollab.org)

His use of the camera is personalized and expresses his world in all its arbitrariness and messiness, while surveillance cameras work more like scanners: looking for patterns and regularity. The epistemology of blackness works with Tivon's transgressive camera; institutional prevention programs work with surveillance cameras.

The fruitful combination of institutional norms revealed through moments of transgression work through various cognitive and affective registers. In her raging critique (in bell hook's sense, 1995) of the lack of punishment for the white young man who stabbed someone else at school in 2005, Élisabeth expresses injustice: "We cannot be teenagers here because of the neighbourhood". "Why," she asks, "are the media immediately here when something happens, and transform the neighbourhood into an *affaire de clowns* ('a circus')?" Because of stigmatization, youths cannot be transgressive like youths normally are. Their race is always used to explain their youthful behaviour. Creative agency, combining visceral with cognitive registers, can emerge from transgressive moments. Interpreting these moments sheds light on institutional norms and their transformation.

Conclusion

As suggested by Salet (Chapter 1, in this volume), institutions in action are institutions whose legitimacy relies on the ongoing process of trial and ordeal in specific situations. The police institution in Saint-Michel is dependent upon Paul and Rodney's constant situational interactions with youths, with the neighbourhood, and with specific artefacts (internal memos, orders, protocols, their uniform, etc.). One of the strongest and most valid critiques of the pragmatist approach is its reductive, immediate, lens that neglects longer processes of normative stabilization, which could be represented here in specific police protocols such as the practice of profiling. This is why I find it revealing to focus, not on any types of situations, but on moments of transgression. Transgression, by definition, implies a tensed relation to a set of norms. Taussig's (1999) anthropological work on difficult moments of "defacement" shows how transgression makes the norm visible. These micro-situations of transgressive action are then articulated with the longer meso-history of institutional norms. Macro-structural forces of globalization, urbanization and international migration are equally affecting institutional transformation.

This chapter sought to rehabilitate ethnographic methods in institutional analysis because such methods shed light on how institutions actually work in the field, as we saw with Rodney and Paul, and the many youngsters who spoke of them. Ethnography, however, should not mean being unable to theorize and generalize. This is why I find it useful to combine various timeframes, from micro-situations to History with a capital H, including the relatively long period of institutional stabilization that we may call the meso timeframe. Concepts such as a universe of operation work on the macro level of History. A universe of operation such as Saint-Michel developed through the combination of deindustrialization, racialization, the constant mobility of the Haitian population, and the development of a local response through a vibrant tissue of community organizations, whereas programs such as gang prevention and police protocols function at the meso level of institutional stabilization. I like the term stabilization, which I borrow from urban regime theory, because it emphasizes the temporariness of institutional arrangements that have real effects on specific daily situations, as we have seen with racial profiling. Yet, only a pragmatist approach can help us understand how the pain felt by

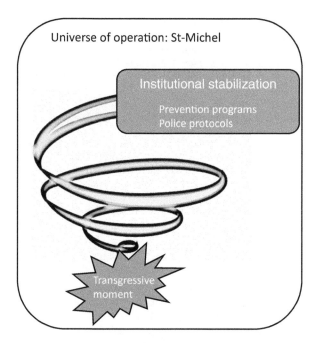

Figure 16.2 Contextualizing institutional meaning through aesthetic
Source: Boudreau

Stéphane and his friends upon hearing the old woman's racist comment during this transgressive moment, contributes to shaping their opinion about racial profiling and the police work of Paul and Rodney (Figure 16.2). This in turns productively reveals the weaknesses of a specific institutional stabilization and helps anchor them in specific universes of operations that form over a longer time period.

Notes

1. This text is based on ethnographic elements taken from Boudreau & Rondeau, *The Aesthetic of Political Action: Youth Urban Worlds in Montreal* (forthcoming). It also uses a reworked version of chapter 3 in Boudreau, *Global Urban Politics: Informalization of the State* (2017).
2. This work is inspired by the very stimulating approach developed by Schwenkel (2015) where she explores the affective role of bureaucratic artefacts in the life of a high-rise building in Vietnam.
3. Most of this empirical material was collected through a collaborative research project with youths in Montreal and on the periphery of Paris (funded by the Social Sciences and Humanities Research Council of Canada; the project is called mapCollab).
4. Through 30 hours of discussion and co-creation over seven weeks, youths produced a multimedia guide of their neighbourhoods (their work is available at www.mapcollab.org if you wish to immerse yourselves in their aesthetic world while walking in these places).

References

Andrews, D. A., Zinger, I., Hoge, R. D., Bonta, J., Gendreau, P., & Cullen, F. T. (1990). Does correctional treatment work? A clinically relevant and psychologically informed meta-analysis. *Criminology*, 28(3), 369–404.
Bataille, G. (1957). *L'Érotisme*. Paris: Éditions de Minuit.
Becker, H. S. (1963/1997). *Outsiders: Studies in the Sociology of Deviance*. New York: The Free Press.

bell hooks. (1995). *Killing Rage: Ending Racism*. New York: An Owl Book.
Bonell, C. (2004). Why is teenage pregnancy conceptualized as a social problem? A review of quantitative research from the USA and UK. *Culture, Health and Sexuality*, 6(3), 255–272.
Boudreau, J. A. (2017). *Global Urban Politics: Informalization of the State*. Cambridge: Polity Press.
Boudreau, J. A., & Rondeau, D. (2018, forthc.). *The Aesthetic of Political Action: Youth Urban Worlds in Montreal*. London: Wiley.
Breviglieri, M., & Trom, D. (2003). Troubles et tensions en milieu urbain. Les épreuves citadines et habitantes de la ville. In D. Cefai & D. Pasquier (Eds.), *Les sens du public: publics politiques et médiatiques* (pp. 399–416). Paris: Presses Universitaires de France.
Cohen, A. K. (1959). The Study of Social Disorganization and *Deviant* Behavior. In R. K. Merton, L. Broom & L. S. Cottrell (Eds.), *Sociology Today: Problems and Prospects* (pp. 461–484). New York: Basic Books.
Connolly, W. E. (2011). *A World of Becoming*. Durham, NC/London: Duke University Press.
Finnegan, R. (1998). *Tales of the City: A Study of Narrative and Urban Life*. Cambridge: Cambridge University Press.
Lipsky, M. (1980). *Street-Level Bureaucracy: Dilemmas of the Individual in Public Services*. New York: Russell Sage Foundation.
Lyng, S. (1990). Edgework: A social psychological analysis of voluntary risk taking. *American Journal of Sociology*, 95(4), 851–886.
Manai, B. (2015). *La 'mise en scène' de l'ethnicité maghrébine à Montréal* (Unpublished dissertation, Institut National de la Recherche Scientifique, Montréal).
Panagia, D. (2009). *The Political Life of Sensation*. Durham, NC/London: Duke University Press.
Parazelli, M. (2009). Existe-t-il une 'morale globale' de la régulation de la rue? Réflexions autour de l'hypothèse d'un imaginaire écosanitaire. *Géographie et Cultures*, 71, 91–111.
Schwenkel, C. (2015). Reclaiming rights to the post/socialist city: Bureaucratic artefacts and the affective appeal of petitions. *South East Asia Research*, 23(2), 205–225.
Simone, A. (2010). *City Life from Jakarta to Dakar: Movements at the Crossroads*. London: Routledge.
Simone, A. (2015). It's just the city after all. *International Journal of Urban and Regional Research*, 40, 210–218.
Sutherland, E. (1924). *Principles of Criminology*. Chicago, IL: University of Chicago Press.
Tanner, J. (1996). *Teenage Troubles: Youth and Deviance in Canada*. Oxford: Oxford University Press.
Taussig, M. (1999). *Defacement: Public Secrecy and the Labor of the Negative*. Stanford, CA: Stanford University Press.
Trasher, F. (1927). *The Gang: A Study of 1,313 Gangs in Chicago*. Chicago, IL: University of Chicago Press.
Young, R., Sweeting, H., & West, P. (2006). Prevalence of deliberate self harm and attempted suicide within contemporary goth youth subculture: Longitudinal cohort study. *Bmj*, 332(7549), 1058–1061.

17
'LONDON'S VATICAN'
The Role of the City's New Architectural Icons as Institutional Imaginaries

Maria Kaika[1,2]

Introduction

In recent years academic inquiry in planning, geography and sociology has built up an impressive body of research on tall buildings, examining the social and political conflict involved in their commissioning and construction (Imrie et al., 2008; Jacobs, 2006; Merrifield, 1993) or analysing them as signifiers of social, economic and political power (McNeill, 2002; Sklair, 2005). Focusing empirically on the proliferation of iconic buildings in London's financial centre (the City), I offer a new approach to understanding these commissions: not as signifiers of economic boosterism and power, but as a symptoms of a deep crisis in the institutions that promote them, notably the Corporation of London, the institution that runs the City.

Despite its importance in London's economic and spatial development, the Corporation of London (henceforth referred to as 'the Corporation') has received relatively little attention as an object of academic enquiry, with the exception of Kynaston's historical magnum opus (2005), the monographs by Roberts and Kynaston (2001), and Ian Gordon et al.'s analysis of the City in economic geography (2005). Equally little attention has been paid to the role of the Corporation in shaping physical space in and around London, despite the fact that the Corporation is not only a powerful business networking institution, but also an important planning authority that until recently had sole planning jurisdiction in and over the City. In much other work on London, the Corporation features only as a peripheral actor in shaping London's urban space, rather than as a theme of enquiry in its own right. Powell's (2005) monograph on London's new architecture maps the City's transformed skyline, but does not engage with the politics and economics that produce it. Burdett and Hadidian (1987) analyse the choreography of power between developers, English Heritage and the Corporation in the redevelopment of Paternoster Square, but do so from an architectural critic's perspective. Some geographers, however, have considered the role of the Corporation in shaping the City's spatialities. Budd (1992), Zukin (1992), Merrifield (1993), Fainstein, Gordon and Harloe (1992) and Fainstein (1994), for example, addressed the role of the Corporation as a key player in developing London's housing and planning policies; Jacobs (2006) and Power (1998) offered an in-depth understanding of the Corporation's conservative strategies; while Jacobs (1994), McNeill (2002, 2005, 2006), McNeill and Tewdwr-Jones, (2003) and Imrie et al. (2008) brought new insights concerning the power relations between the Corporation, the Mayor's office, English Heritage and developers.

Over the last decade or so, however, the Corporation's planning strategy underwent radical change. Its time honoured conservation oriented policy was replaced by a new planning framework that allowed for a massive expansion of commissions for tall office buildings in the City. McNeill's (2002) work details insightfully the Corporation's new and intricate relationship to the Mayor's Office, and scrutinizes the Corporation's role as part of a broader framework of spatial change in London. However, as this chapter will argue, the radical changes in the Corporation's planning strategies are also linked to important internal institutional changes that are less well documented in the literature. Indeed, there is no analytical framework linking these institutional changes to recent changes in the Corporation's spatial policies.

Standing on the shoulders of the aforementioned authors, this chapter fills this gap and chronicles how the Corporation's untouchable character was dented not only by the Docklands development in the 1980s, but also by less documented but arguably more significant European competition, and by open threats for abolition from the government in the 1990s. These threats led to internal restructuring, and to a voting reform in 2002 (City of London Corporation, 2002). Detailing how the Corporation of London had to reinvent itself and its identity after three long decades of disputes with the government and developers, the chapter puts this period of institutional crisis at centre stage. By doing so, the argument presented here departs from the interpretation of London's recent 'iconic' developments as signifiers of London's international economic success, and exposes them instead as signifiers of mutations in the structure of London's elites, and in the role of the Corporation as the reigning authority for the Square Mile. Unlike the City's traditional place-loyal elites, the City's new transnational elites (Sklair, 2005) enjoy the amenities and kudos that a City location may offer, and take advantage of recent favourable planning regulations, but by no means commit themselves to staying in London (Sennett, 2001). London's new footloose architectural patronage has given rise to a new relationship between the architectural landmark and the city. If the modernist object of architecture was the city as a whole, the object of today's architectural patronage is the individual building in and for itself. Although the City's earlier landmarks could easily be identified with the City's traditional institutions, the City's contemporary 'icons' operate more as branding objects for transnational corporations (TNCs), or as speculative objects for real estate developers.

The research for this chapter was conducted and the chapter was written before the global financial crisis; the recent developments in global finance, however, make it more topical and more relevant than ever before. The research reported here draws on material collected from the following key sources:

- The Hansard Debates archive (period 1980–2007);
- The Royal Institute of British Architects archives (period 1970–2007);
- Fifteen interviews with key informants (Corporation of London employees, Architects, Planners, NGOs, quangos, and academics) conducted between September – December 2007 and June – September 2008;
- Fifty interviews with City workers conducted between June – September 2008.

London's Vatican

The City "is a constitutional anomaly that, for the main part, has outlived its usefulness".
(Hansard Debates, 1999, Col. 178)

The City of London (henceforth referred to as 'the City') is not only London's financial heart, but also its historical centre, the original walled city around which contemporary London has evolved. It covers an area of more or less one square mile (hence, often referred to as 'the Square Mile'). The heart of trade and banking during the 'glorious years' of the British Empire, this part of London evolved during the twentieth century into the centre of business and financial activities, a "concentration of international expertise and capital, with a supportive legal and regulatory system" (Corporation of London, 2008). However, the institutions and rituals that govern and administer the City of London have hardly evolved, and their roots are lost deep back in time and still veiled in an air of myth and mystery.

The Corporation of London is the administrative body that runs 'the City' and holds a unique institutional and political status. A hub for global business and power networking activities, the Corporation is an institution older than the British Parliament. It was established in 1132, when Henry I recognized full County status for the City (Roberts & Kynaston, 2001). Although today the Corporation is treated by local government legislation as one of London's boroughs, in strictly legislative terms it is not, as its establishment predates by many centuries the 1963 London Government Act. Since the Corporation predates Parliament, the latter does not have the power to dictate terms to the Corporation or to make institutional, administrative, or other changes in the City (Mr. Sawford, MP, in Hansard Debates, 1999, 2 November 1999; Col. 183). In short, the Corporation is a local authority unlike any other, a state within a state, with a unique privileged status that can only be compared to that of Rome's Vatican. The role of London's very own Vatican, however, is not to serve god, but "the needs of international business" (Corporation of London, 2008). The Corporation is a non-party political authority whose electorate comprises not citizens, but businesses that physically occupy premises in the Square Mile (Roberts & Kynaston, 2001), and is "committed to maintaining and enhancing the status of [London's City] as the world's leading international financial and business centre through the policies it pursues" (Corporation of London, 2008); it is an agglomeration of business leaders, bankers and brokers that provides global business networking services. However, apart from being a powerful business networking institution, the Corporation also functions as a planning authority, and is a significant real estate proprietor, as it owns about a third of all the freeholds in the Square Mile (Martin, 1993), and manages open and public spaces in London, including Epping Forest, Hampstead Heath, and the Barbican Arts Centre (Corporation of London, 2008).

A Fetishized Urban Space to Match a Fetishized Institution

"The City is more than a financial network – it expresses national character: the City is 'characteristically English'".
(Cohen-Portheim, 1935, p. 1, cited in Kynaston, 2005)

Over the many centuries of its existence, the Corporation's institutional structure, organization and role as the reigning authority of the City of London underwent very little renewal.

And so did the signifiers of this authority. When, in the early twentieth century, American capital found in the skyscraper the symbol of its expanding world power (Twombly, 1996), the Corporation of London clung to its past and remained primarily inward looking and English-focused (Cohen-Portheim, 1935; Kynaston, 2005). The Royal Exchange and St Paul's Cathedral have been symbols of the City and of the rise to power of the British Empire and are protected heritage sites. Even the views towards St Paul's Cathedral are protected since 1938 (Wynne Rees, 2002, pp. 171–173; see also Mayor of London, 2001). Over the years, the protected "strategic views" to St Paul's have become a strategy in themselves that the Corporation has used very effectively to tell developers where, what and how to build (Markham, 2008). As London's global economic dominance declined in the twentieth century, the Corporation mobilized its glorious imperial past as a means of securing its future, and guarded itself closely against the 'intrusion' of both foreign companies and architectural styles in the Square Mile. Proposals for modernizing the City institutionally and architecturally met with resistance from the part of the Corporation that saw change as hostile and damaging to the veneered traditions of the City. The Corporation's 'Englishness' and archaeolatry extended not only to the City's institutional arrangements, but also to the City's spatial arrangements. Resisting modernism became a matter of imperial pride. Fending off foreign 'intruders' from entering its exclusive club also extended to 'protecting' the Square Mile from the intrusion of modernist architectural design. As Jacobs (1994) documents beautifully, in the 1980s and after a long dispute with developers, the City succeeded in fending off the 'intrusion' of the international style in Bank Junction and thus missed the opportunity to have a Mies van der Rohe design, in favour of a more 'traditional English' design by Sterling. In its adamant pursuit of conservation the Corporation became one of English Heritage's best friends in promoting conservation policies in the Square Mile.

Although the City's isolationism arguably served well the interests of the British Empire for many centuries, after the 1970s the City's exclusive club character and an increasingly globalized economy proved to be bad bedfellows. When the City proved damagingly slow in opening up to global finance and in adapting to the requirements of a global economy, the Corporation's isolationism came under close scrutiny for the first time in a serious manner. In what follows, I shall document how the Corporation's resistance to adapt to changes in the global economy after the 1970s brought about a deep crisis not only in London's economy, but also in the Corporation's identity and institutional role.

Change? Why Change? Dismal Performance and the 'Invasion of the Real'

During the 1970s, the Heath (1970–1974) and subsequently the Thatcher (1979–1990) governments' aggressive policies led to the UK economy's expansion at "twice the rate of the average of the previous six years … [at the same time as] the unemployment total reached seven figures for the first time since 1947" (Kynaston, 2005, p. 452). This was an explosive combination that, as the *Financial Times* noted, "gave enough reason for a revolution to overthrow capitalism" (cited in Kynaston, 2005, p. 452). During this period, pressures for the internationalization of the UK economy were coming from all directions, and foreign capital was 'besieging' the City of London. By the early 1970s "US commercial banks, led by Citibank, achieved 25 per cent penetration of the UK large corporate loan business … and by the middle of the 1970s, London hosted three dozen consortium Banks" (Kynaston, 2005, p. 447). However, these institutions operated only under the City's "reluctant tolerance" (ibid.) as the Corporation was determined not to allow officially foreign companies to enter its exclusive territory. In a racist rant against admitting foreigners into this club, Peter Swan (from Phillips and Drew) proudly asserted the City's xenophobia and hostility towards foreign intrusion:

Over the years, we have built up and are improving our high standard of business conduct. For these reasons the City and the Stock Exchange receive a large amount of overseas business because people abroad like to deal with us and trust the way in which we operate ... I am worried for the future of the Stock Exchange if the restriction is moved because whilst a foreigner may no doubt pass his examinations, he may come from a country which does not have the same standards that we have built up in the City. Also, please do bear in mind that he will have two loyalties.

(Peter Swan quoted in Kynaston, 2005, p. 449)

During this period, the City's business isolationism was matched by mounting spatial isolationism. The Square Mile became literally the castle within which the old City boys guarded themselves against a world that was rapidly changing around them. In the 1980s, the Corporation was resisting office renewal to such an extent that, as *The Times* noted, it was "stifling the City's lifeblood in its conservation oriented draft development plan" (*The Times*, 31 October 1985, cited in Jacobs, 1994). During the 1990s, fending off alien intruders (real or imaginary) from the City's spatial territory tightened further when the City constructed its infamous 'ring of steel' as a response to the 1993 Bishopsgate bombing. The ring of steel gave material form in the most dramatic manner to the City's isolationism. Security was tightened even further after the South Quay blast in 1996, with City police and armed police officers on 24 hours patrol (Bennetto & Rentoul, 1996).

Inevitably, the two crucial decades of isolationism in the midst of global internationalization had dismal effects for London's economy. During the 1990s, the London Clearing House failed to strengthen the City's status as an international financial centre: "The Bank of England was less than impressed by this policy of benign neglect, particularly at a time of dramatic growth in the trading of derivatives of all kinds" (Bourse Consult, 2007, p. 28). During the same period, the London Stock Exchange (LSE) also registered a tumultuous performance, not only because it was missing opportunities by remaining closed to a large number of international businesses, but also because it moved only at a very slow pace to a full-scale electronic trading system, and failed to complete a series of 'modernizing' ventures. The promising Transfer and Automated Registration of Uncertified Stock (TAURUS) programme that was meant to bring the LSE into the twentieth century met with endless delays, and was ditched after 12 years and 400 million GBP of spending[3] (Kynaston, 2005, p. 742). The LSE's dismal performance during the 15 years that followed the 1986 'Big Bang' brought it from being the pre-eminent exchange in Europe to one largely surpassed by its European competitors (Bourse Consult, 2007, p. 28).

There was, however, a big success story in the 1980s and early 1990s for the City with the opening of the London International Financial Futures and Options Exchange (LIFFE), which took off in 1982, after long debates and speculation, and rapidly ascended to the third largest in the world (Kynaston, 2005, 740). Kynaston characterizes LIFFE in the 1990s as the 'fourth pillar' of the City, "the first three being the Bank of England, the Stock Exchange and Lloyd's" (Kynaston, 2005, p. 741). However, even this success story soon turned sour after a series of mismanagements on the part of the City, notably the decision not to go ahead with electronic trading but to stick instead to the open outcry system. *The Independent* characterized this decision as "a victory of vested interests over technological and commercial reality" (*The Independent*, 10 July 1997, cited in Kynaston, 2005, p. 780). The decision to preserve the – literally – colourful open outcry system was a key error of judgement on the part of the City that contributed to LIFFE losing its supremacy over other Futures exchange markets. When LIFFE was later taken over, this was done by Euronext rather than by the London Stock Exchange

(Bourse Consult, 2007, p. 28). By that time both of London's main competitors, Paris and Frankfurt had "outstripped the LSE in terms of breadth of products traded, size and market value" (Bourse Consult, 2007, p. 28; see also Head, 2001).

But the big blow for the City came in 1993, when, despite the City's optimistic expectations, it was decided that the European Central Bank (ECB) would locate its headquarters in Frankfurt instead of London. The 'loss' of the ECB to Frankfurt came as a serious blow to the City's self-importance. It signalled the end of the 'blind optimism' of the 1980s (Kynaston, 2005) and the beginning of the realization that the Corporation had to adjust to reality (Interview with Anonymous City Administrator, January 2007). Up until that moment, and despite strong signals that the Corporation's strategies were negatively affecting London's international expansion, the Corporation was too powerful an institution to be touched by anyone. The loss of the ECB to Frankfurt was the moment of the 'invasion of the real' for the Corporation (Žižek, 1989), a reality check that abruptly shattered the Corporation's fantasy of continuous world supremacy, and the moment when the Corporation woke up to the twentieth century. As a response to the Corporation's performance, by the end of the 1990s the government was putting increasing pressure on the Corporation for reform, modernization and infrastructure renewal, and launched open threats to abolish the Corporation in its existing form. The threats, combined with the loss of economic optimism and the constitution of the Greater London Authority, meant that the time had come for the Corporation to be literally whipped into redemption.

A Reformed City: The Beginning of the End of Business Isolationism

"[The City is] a rotten borough".
(John McDonnell, Labour MP, Hansard Debates, 1999, Col. 171)

The events of the 1990s threatened to dent the Corporation's reign as the all-powerful authority of the Square Mile. The open hostility towards the Corporation from the part of the government was no secret, and was expressed resolutely in John McDonnell's (Labour MP) speech during the parliamentary debate over the Corporation's electoral reform in November 1999:

> [The] City Corporation should not be confused with the City itself ... The Corporation is a group of hangers-on, who create what is known as the best dining club in the City. They bear no relationship to the creation of wealth by the City ... Labour was from its earliest days committed to the abolition of the City Corporation as constituted ... it should be replaced with a democratic institution ... It is argued that we have ... called for democratic reform of the City Corporation and its finances because we are seeking to blackmail the corporation into spending more money in London. I suppose we are doing that: we are trying to open the books of the City Corporation and to ensure that they are accountable to the City of London overall. Without democratic reform of the City Corporation, the City will never pull its weight in supporting our capital. It will remain the self-interested, isolated dining club that it has been for the past century.
> *(John McDonnell, Labour MP, Hansard Debates, 1999, Col. 169–174)*

Faced with unprecedented hostility and threats not only from the government, but also from developers, the media and foreign investors, the Corporation was quick to adopt a fight back survival strategy.

From 1992 onwards, the City Corporation realised that the prospect of a Labour Government put privilege at risk, so every resource and sinew of connection and influence were mobilized by the Corporation's elite to bring Labour to heel. The Corporation established a public relations team, set aside resources and started a long-term lobbying strategy ... The tragedy is that New Labour was all too ready to become an adornment of the Corporation. All it took was a few phone calls and a couple of dinner parties and, in the 1997 manifesto, the Labour party sought, not abolition or democratic reform, but only reform.
(John McDonnell, Labour MP, Hansard Debates, 1999, Col. 171)

The Corporation's defensive strategy, however, extended well beyond a few dinner parties. Either because of government threats, or because of the shock of the European Union's decision to locate the ECB in Frankfurt, the Corporation devised a survival strategy in the 1990s, and championed a new identity for themselves. They knew they had to be seen to be:

- 'opening up' to the surrounding boroughs;
- 'reaching out' to the world;
- acting positively towards keeping international businesses in London.

As part of their 'opening up' strategy, the Corporation launched an unprecedented number of charitable organizations whose benefits aimed, uncharacteristically, to 'reach beyond the Square Mile'. *The City Bridge Trust* was founded in 1995 and became the grant-making arm of Bridge House Estates, whose sole trustee is the Corporation. It is "committed to making grants of £15 million a year to charitable projects benefiting the inhabitants of Greater London" (The City Bridge Trust, 2008). In 2008 the Trust funded projects supporting better access for disabled people, projects for maintaining local shopping areas in London, programmes against alcohol and domestic abuse, and projects for improving services for older people. The *City Action for Community Development* was established in 1998 and is an employee volunteering service whose aim is to establish partnerships between City business and local community organizations and schools in the City and seven surrounding boroughs: Camden, Hackney, Islington, Lambeth, Southwark, Tower Hamlets and Westminster (City Action for Community Development, 2008). The *Heart of the City*, a charity registered in 2000, is also housed and funded by the Corporation. Its role is to "enlarge the number of firms in the City and City fringes which participate in Corporate Social Responsibility" (Heart of the City, 2008). In 2007, the London Development Agency pumped funds into the *Heart of the City* in order to expand their programme for Corporate Social Responsibility to the City fringes, i.e. Southwark, Lambeth, Tower Hamlets, Hackney, Islington and Camden. The *Local Procurement Project*, established in 2003, encourages competitive procurement from small- and medium-sized enterprises in the boroughs immediately adjacent to the Square Mile (Local Procurement Project, 2008). The two most recent additions to these programmes are: *The City of London Volunteering Employee Programme*, which offers City staff the entitlement to take "two working days per year to volunteer with community groups in the City and its neighbouring boroughs ... in approved volunteering activities" (City of London Employee Volunteering Programme, 2008); and the Corporation's *Partnerships Programme* (2008) which "assists City businesses looking to engage young people through introducing them to City-type careers; and works with City businesses to maximize access to employment opportunities for City fringe residents" (City of London Corporation, 2008a).

The extent to which the Corporation's charitable activities are benefiting the surrounding boroughs, or act more as a means of expanding the City's influence outside the Square Mile, by gearing local education programmes, business and physical planning towards the needs of the City, is an open and important question, which, however, lies outside the scope of this chapter. What is central to the debate in this contribution is that the majority of the City's charitable activities were established in response to strong pressures for City reform. Through these activities, the Corporation wished to promote itself as a socially responsible organization and to distance itself from its traditional image as an exclusive boys' club.

The proliferation of charitable activities in the 1990s was accompanied by the launch of an unprecedented media campaign that aimed to change the image that the Corporation projected to the outside world. The campaign was championed by Michael Cassidy, chairman of the Policy and Resources committee at the Corporation of London between 1991 and 1997 (later President of the London Chamber of Commerce). The *Independent on Sunday* alone, counts 329 articles mentioning Michael Cassidy during his time as chairman of the Policy and Resources committee (Bowen, 1997).

As part of the same strategy of 'reaching out', during the 1990s, the Corporation also launched a controversial electoral reform. Like all its statutes, the Corporation's electoral system is unique. Currently, the City serves around 8,000 residents and 300,000 workers, with only four of the City's 25 wards being residential: Aldersgate, Cripplegate, Portsoken and Queenhithe (City of London Corporation, 2008b). Given its peculiarity of hosting more business than residential population, the City was not reformed by the Municipal Corporations Act 1835, or by any other subsequent legislation. Hence, when the non-residential vote (or business vote), was abolished in the rest of the country in 1969, it was retained for the City of London, thus making businesses rather than residents the key electoral body for the City.

The 2002 Act introduced two key innovations. Firstly, it extended City voting rights to "[a]ny incorporated[4] or unincorporated[5] body [who] physically occupy premises in the City on the qualifying date of 1 September in the year prior to the ward elections. This includes banks, insurance companies, stockbrokers and other financial institutions, limited liability partnerships, charities, trade associations, livery companies, churches and other religious bodies, and hospital trusts" (City of London Corporation, 2002, c. vi: 1). Secondly, it linked voting rights for City-located businesses according to the size of the corporations, by decreeing that "qualifying bodies that occupy premises in the City receive a number of voting entitlements based on the number of employees based at those premises. The basis of entitlement is one voter for every five members of the workforce up to 50 with an additional voter for every 50 thereafter, as follows".

In the Corporation's own words, the 2002 electoral reform was a means of democratizing its voting system, as it enabled a greater number of businesses to register for voting (City of London Corporation, 2002, c. vi: 1). However, as Mr John McDonnell, Labour MP noted:

[The Ward Act] does not bring about universal suffrage based on one person, one vote, but maintains business votes based on ownership. It goes further – it is regressive, introducing a system whereby the buying of votes by more business is facilitated. Under the proposed system, the extension of votes is up for sale, depending on how much land in the City can be bought.

(McDonnell, Hansard Debates, 1999, Col. 171)

For this reason, another Labour MP, Mr. David Heath (Labour MP for Somerton and Frome), compared publicly the arrangements in the Bill with those "in the so-called functional constituencies in Hong Kong, which were roundly condemned by the British Government and many others as being totally undemocratic [and] were devised by the Chinese Government as a way of avoiding universal franchise in Hong Kong" (Hansard Debates, 1999, Col. 171).

Indeed, the agenda and scope of the 2002 electoral reform extended beyond the noble task of allowing "the City of London to extend the City's franchise to a wider range of businesses and organizations in the Square Mile" (City of London Corporation, 2002, c. vi: 1). It was also a response to pressures for increasing the number of residents in the Square Mile. When, in the late 1990s, the Corporation reluctantly succumbed to pressures to expand residential numbers and to maintain the dominance of residents over businesses in the City's four residential wards, the electoral reform became a cunning way to secure the dominance of business over residents in the City's electorate as a whole, by changing significantly the proportion of residential to business votes, in favour of the latter.

Spatial Habits Die Harder than Institutional Habits

The previous sections detailed how, during the 1990s the Corporation fathomed – the hard way – that the isolationism that served it well for many decades, had become damaging for the City and launched institutional and strategic changes. However, if the Corporation were to keep business in place, institutional changes had to be matched by a new spatial strategy and the Corporation's reinvented identity had to be matched by an image makeover. But the Corporation's spatial isolationism proved much more difficult to tackle than its business and institutional isolationism. Despite the City's urgent need for hi-spec office space, its planning system remained stuck in the past, preoccupied with preserving heritage and protecting strategic views to St. Paul's. Even the development of Canary Wharf as a rival business location in the 1980s, and the loss of many of the City's traditional banking and media institutions[6] to this new rival did not stir a change in the Corporation's planning policies (Daniels & Bobe, 1993; Merrifield, 1993). The 1984 City Plan that could have initiated the much-desired change proved a missed opportunity, as it ignored the need for office expansion in the Square Mile and focused instead on further expansion of conservation areas and building restrictions.

At the time, only a handful of people in the Corporation emphasized the need to move away from a policy framework oriented towards heritage and conservation (Martin, 1993). Michael Cassidy was among this enlightened minority and, acting as chairman of the City's planning committee in 1986, asserted the need to treat the planning system not "as a prophylactic, but as a catalyst" (cited in Martin, 1993, p. 24). Cassidy was instrumental in implementing the Corporation's first –reluctant – agreement to increase plot ratios to a single figure of 5:5:1 as an 'emergency measure' in 1985 (Martin, 1993). Although the 1985 emergency measures did allow for a 20 per cent increase in the size of new buildings in the Square Mile, this was not enough to enable the realization of the City's much needed image makeover. It was only in the late 1990s, in the midst of the national threats and international pressures documented above, that the Corporation finally revised its planning restrictions. The 2002 Unitary Development Plan finally replaced the City's antiquated planning framework, and decreed that the Corporation would "permit high buildings where they would enhance the City's skyline and not adversely affect the character or amenities of their surroundings or the City's environment to an unacceptable degree" (Wynne Rees, 2002, p. 145). The Unitary Development Plan "allows for Tall buildings in the Square Mile, while at the same time asserting (in a non-committal way) the protection of the skyline of features of historic landmarks, including: Cannon Street Station (Towers), Central Criminal Court (Cupola), Christchurch, Spitalfields, City Temple (Tower) Guildhall (Roof and fleche), HMS Belfast, Old Port of London Authority Building (Tower), Royal Exchange (Campanile), Southwark Cathedral (Northern transept and tower), Tower Bridge" (Wynne Rees, 2002, p. 223).

Although the new plan allows for a potential expansion of office space in the Square Mile, all new tall buildings still remain subject to restrictions posed by St Paul's strategic views, viewing corridors, and conservation areas (Markham, 2008; see also Hebbert & McKellar, 2008). In fact, after all restrictions are taken into consideration, there are only a few small clusters left where high-rise buildings are possible (Wynne Rees, 2002), p. 167). For this reason most of the "expanded plot ratios will be realized on the fringe of the Square Mile" (Eley, 1986), while conservation areas around the Bank will remain intact (Wynne Rees, 2002, p. 169). The expanded plot ratios centre around the East and Tower 42 (25 Old Broad Street, formerly the "NatWest" Tower); and the North-Central area, around 125 London Wall (Wynne Rees, 2002).

As anticipated, after the new planning regulations became operational, the Corporation's planning office received a great number of applications for tall buildings and many were granted planning permission to appear in London's skyline; among them: 30 St Mary Axe (formely the Swiss Re building), The Shard at 32 London Bridge St, Broadgate Tower at 201 Bishopsgate, One Blackfriars Road Tower (scheduled for completion in 2018), and The Leadenhall Building at 122 Leadenhall Street.

A New Image for a New Identity, or a Visual *Coup d'État*?

The new generation of office towers in the Square Mile were commissioned under the promise to bring London's skyline into the twenty-first century. Over the past decade, mass media and architectural critics have bestowed great praise on these buildings and presented them as signifiers of the City's global financial dominance and power. "In our hot-wired economy, developers want this kind of dynamism" wrote Jay Merrick in *The Independent* in 2006, in an article titled 'the sky's the limit' that hailed London's iconic buildings as the best partner to the City's boosterism (Merrick, 2004). However, as I argued in this chapter, the Corporation's shift of focus from conservation to high-rise was not the consolidation of a glorious period of success, but instead a strategic response to a period of crisis in the Corporation's relations to the outside world, a response to a long string of events that shook the foundations of the Corporation and threatened its traditional institutional structure.

Encouraging the production of spectacular architecture at moments of crisis or institutional decline is of course not a strategy invented by the Corporation of London. Schnapp (1992) argues that an overproduction of aesthetic images and signs in the form of architecture, movies, paintings, posters, etc., is necessary to settle questions of identity of a society or an institution in crisis. Throughout history, periods of crisis or decline have given birth to remarkable architecture. Castoriadis (1987) too, identified the overproduction of the aesthetic, combined with the overdetermination of symbols (a situation whereby one single signifier can be attached to a signified multiplicity) as symptoms of a crisis and corrosion in the institutions and elites that hold society together, indicative of an urgent need to institute a new social imagery. The overproduction of cultural signs and symbols covers up the hollow core of a society or institution in need of a new identity. The overproduction of iconic architecture in the Square Mile is no exception. I shall argue that the City's contemporary iconic architecture complements the lack of a clear vision for the future of urban space and urban society (see also Bell, 1976) and provides the symbol for an urban society in search of a new identity, of corporations in need of re-branding, of institutions in need of renewal.

Indeed, although at a material level London's new landmarks fulfil London's urgent need for infrastructure renewal, for keeping businesses in place and for attracting international investment, at a symbolic level it could be argued that these buildings mark a dent in the Corporation's authority over London's Square Mile, as they signify the Corporation's defeat after three decades

Iconic Design as Institutional Imaginary

Figure 17.1 St Paul's Heights views protection
Source: Copyright: Maria Kaika

of battling in favour of conservation policies and against high-rise office renewal (Jacobs, 1994). Towering over the Corporation's traditional signifiers (Figure 17.1), these buildings constitute a visual *coup d'état*, a thorn in the Corporation's age-old heritage-oriented planning policies. To the Corporation, the new buildings are a necessary evil, rather than a desirable virtue, an acknowledgement of the City's need to re-brand itself.

Depoliticized Footloose Elites and Curious Architectural Objects

After three decades of fending off international businesses, the Corporation had to undergo an image makeover, in order to convince international investors that they are welcome to conduct their businesses in the City. Despite the Corporation's *grand* rhetoric about London's supremacy, London has quite a way to go to convince the international business community not so much of its primacy as a business location, but more of its primacy as a desirable living and working place. Although the City's primacy in global business networking activities remains undisputed, London's desirability as a place to live and work fails to top the charts. Indeed, while London stands at the apex of the global financial centres in business indicators, and remains the city with the highest Direct Real Estate Transaction Volumes and the highest office occupancy rates (at 20,475 US$ per workstation per annum in 2007 (Z/Yen Group Limited et al., 2007, p. 53), it lags behind in quality of life indicators, despite the Corporation's claims that London is "the best party on the planet" (Interview with Peter Wynne Rees, 4 September 2007). Mercer's 2007 survey rated London 23rd among 27 global cities in quality of life indicators (with Zurich at the top) (Z/Yen Group Limited et al., 2007, p. 35). Within this framework, the new iconic buildings in the Square Mile signify the need to construct a new imaginary identity for the City and for London, pretty much the same way that the Guggenheim became a way of raising Bilbao's global profile (Moulaert et al., 2003), or megastructures became a means of upgrading Dubai's international kudos (Davis, 2006).

Although most of the debate around the City's new buildings has been consumed over issues of heights and architectural style, I shall argue that the most significant innovation in the way these buildings are commissioned lies beyond style and height; it lies with the role these buildings perform as signifiers of a particular historical moment. The City's earlier landmarks could easily be identified with the City's traditional institutions. The Bank of England, the Royal Exchange, etc., borrowed a neo-classical architectural vocabulary to instil imperial pride and primacy. Even when the Corporation gave its first reluctant consent to modern buildings in the 1970s, the first constructions to go up, the NatWest Tower (1971–1979) and the Lloyd's building (1978–1986), were still clear signifiers of place-loyal British institutions, committed to the Corporation's traditions. The piece-by-piece transfer of the eighteenth-century Lloyd's dining-room from the old to the new Lloyd's building was an eloquent symbolic gesture affirming Lloyd's loyalty to the veneered traditions of the Corporation, despite their modernizing efforts (Kynaston, 2005). In contrast, the City's contemporary signifiers operate more as branding objects for multinational corporations or as speculative objects for real estate developers. The Swiss Re building (opened May 2004) the first of many towers to be erected against London's skyline was commissioned by a Swiss-based TNC, an 'alien' with no prior links or history of loyalty to the City of London, and with no particular interest to forge such links in the future. Indeed, Swiss Re sold the tower in 2007, only three years after its inauguration, at a profit of approximately 200 million GBP, a venture that boosted the company's net profit for that year by 54 per cent (Simonian, 2007). The sale was hailed as yet another success story for London's economic boosterism, with the *Financial Times* stating, in what retrospectively appears to be the utmost irony, that London's commercial property market is "supported in the same manner as the residential housing market by a wall of foreign and City money" (Warner, 2004).

However, unlike the City's traditional institutions and traditional elites, who remained loyal to the Corporation and maintained their City-based signifiers often at great financial cost, the new generation of urban elites falls into a category that Sklair dubbed the "Transnational Capitalist Class" (Sklair, 2005). They enjoy the amenities and kudos that a City location may offer, but by no means commit themselves to staying there (Sennett, 2001). They take advantage of the Corporation's new planning framework to boost their real estate speculation practices and profits, but care little about the politics and development of the City itself and of London in general. However, although Sennett (2001) laments this loss of place loyalty as a loss of the driving force behind urban renewal and urban splendour, Peter Wynne Rees, former head of planning at the Corporation asserts that the footloose character of London's new elites is not something to be lamented, but, instead, something to be celebrated (Interview with Peter Wynne Rees, 4 September 2007). According to Wynne Rees, the footloose character of London's new elites is precisely what the Corporation needs at this moment. The fact that they come to London because "it offers the best free sex in the world", and leave after a couple of years, after having consumed urban life, and without 'interfering' in the city's political life, is an asset, rather than a defect in the Corporation's eyes (Interview with Peter Wynne Rees, 4 September 2007). This lack of interest in urban political life makes the Corporation's planning policies much easier to implement. The Corporation's fierce opposition to admitting residents in the Square Mile is part of the same logic. The City has always been a black hole in Londoner's cognitive maps, and the Corporation wishes to keep it this way. To the Corporation, residents are an alien species whose numbers should be kept to a minimum, in order to maintain the Square Mile's function as an exclusive business hub. If the Corporation were to admit more residents in the Square Mile, they would have to divert their role and energy from providing business networking services, to providing essential services, schools, medical care, etc. Insofar, however, as the Corporation recently had to consent to admitting more residents in the Square Mile under heavy pressures from the central government, transnational elites are the least evil option for the Corporation. Their single-family structure and footloose existence do not pose a serious threat to the Corporation's plans, as they are the perfect depoliticized subject.

This new type of footloose architectural patronage has given rise to a new way of producing architecture, and a new relationship between the architectural landmark and the city. If the modernist object of architecture was the city as a whole, the object of today's architectural practice and architectural patronage is the individual building in itself and for itself. Contemporary urban signifiers standalone like self-contained Machines (Tafuri, 1973/1999), resembling what Baudrillard calls Monster Architecture (Baudrillard & Nouvel, 2002).

London's new landmarks are, above everything else, functional objects of capital accumulation and real estate speculation. Although star architects are also employed today to design the new global landmarks, what they actually produce is a kind of chain-store architecture; a repetition of successful commercial forms whose role is to please their clients, the public, the media and the authorities. For all its innovative elements, Guggenheim's Bilbao loses some of its iconic status and magic when its successful form is repeated in Los Angeles, New York, Chicago, etc. Within this context, the nineteenth-century idea of the unimpeded artist creator, free to pursue his/her own dream and creative impulse and impose it on 'the masses' (Bell, 1976) is replaced by the conformist architect whose creativity is checked by his/her clients (Imrie, 2006; Imrie & Street, 2006). The global star status of Norman Foster did not protect Foster + Partners from having their creativity checked by their clients, Swiss Re, who, after having commissioned Foster + Partners to design the building's shell, they awarded the building's interior design to a different company, Bennett Interior Design, following a competition with 32 participants, including Foster + Partners (von Arx & Schorr, 2005).

While more and more examples of this type of architecture rise against urban skylines, not only are these incapable in themselves to restore any meaning or synthesis to our cities, they have even abandoned any effort to do so (Tafuri, 1973/1999, p. 6). Without a clear signified authority to refer to, these buildings stand as empty signifiers in search of their signified, as forms without utopia, as the curious objects of global design competitions. And cities become something of a curiosity shop, a backdrop for architectural experimentation and for the display of these curious objects. Indeed, as new signifiers seem to be rising in London's skyline in search of their signified, it appears that London's public has a hard time not only to access them physically, but also to read them as signs and symbols of something that is meaningful for them. Perhaps indicative of the public's puzzlement towards these new urban objects is the nicknaming of these buildings. In an effort, on the part of the public or the media to make them part of the urban imagery, the Swiss Re Tower became famous as London's Gherkin, the Leadenhall Street Tower became the Cheese Grater, 20 Fenchurch Street Tower became the Walkie Talkie, and London Bridge Tower became The Shard, etc. Charles Jencks has performed his own search for meaning behind these signifiers and has found it outside of anything that has to do with the city in which they belong but rather in the 'cosmic, supernatural order' that we humble humans could not possibly relate to (Jencks, 2004). Madelon Vriesendorp in her excellent illustrations of Jenck's *Iconic Buildings* performed her own ironic and playful search for meaning and found that the Swiss Re building in London can signify a number of objects: the screw, the gherkin, the phallus (in Jencks, 2004, p. 186). In short, contemporary urban signifiers could signify a number of different things, all irrelevant to the city within which they are located. They have 'Cultural Objects' for mass entertainment to feed on (Arendt, 1961), the perfect neo-liberal objects for real estate speculation assisted by global media, arts and architectural networks.

Conclusion

In this chapter, I linked the recent architectural commissions in London's Square Mile to a period of institutional crisis for the Corporation and to the social, political and economic pressures under which the City's planning policies underwent a radical change. By documenting the dramatic institutional and structural changes that the Corporation of London went through since the 1970s, I departed from the dominant perception of London's new architecture as a signifier of success and world supremacy, and revealed the efforts to improve the City's skyline as a spasmodic response on the part of an uneasy institution (the Corporation) who tries to re-brand itself and to forge a new identity in order to survive in an ever-changing world. Corresponding to changes in the City's constitution (from British-based to international) and to the Corporation's institutional identity, the City's new buildings differ from previous landmarks in the City not only in height and style, but primarily in the role they place as urban signifiers. While the City's traditional buildings were expressions of the dominance of British institutions, the City's contemporary landmarks constitute a visual *coup d'état* against the Corporation's traditional anglo-centrism and conservation strategies.

The City's new skyline has become a symbol of the Corporation's institutional changes: a Corporation that has moved a long way away from their 1970s and 1980s policies that refused foreigners' entry to their exclusive club. As expected, the internationalization of businesses in the City benefited the UK economy (Oxford Economics Ltd., 2007, pp. 48–49). "[Today,] there [is] little concern if the institutions themselves [are] non-UK owned, as long as any overseas ownership [does] not produce a related intrusion of foreign regulation" (Michael Snyder, Chairman of Policy and Resources Committee, City of London, quoted in Oxford Economics Ltd., 2007, p. 2). However, despite its strategic plans to 'open up' and despite the radical change in its planning policy, the dent in the Corporation's status during the 1990s was significant, and the City's *raison d'être* as an exclusive business location remains disputed in the twenty-first century.

> Clearly the original reasons for the concentration of infrastructure providers in one location have long gone … The major City investment banks indicated to us that they needed to be physically close to other intermediaries and support services such as lawyers, but that they could cope with being a little more distant from the managers of infrastructure providers (especially the regulators).
>
> *(Oxford Economics Ltd., 2007, p. 46)*

The most recent blow for the City was JP Morgan's decision, in August 2008, to pull out of negotiations to occupy 90,000 square metres in the Square Mile[7] and to locate its European Headquarters at Canary Wharf instead (Pickard, 2007). The decision fuelled, once again, debates on the "beginning of the end of the City as a financial district", and "the City [not being] big enough to accommodate the mega-banks any more" (Cruise, 2008).

Therefore, it remains an imperative for the Corporation to sustain and promote its image as a prime global institution that still reigns supreme over the Square Mile. The City's new landmark commissions have been an expression of this aspiration. As the Corporation's own consultants put it: "If one piece of iconic infrastructure were missing, the perception of the power of the centre would be significantly diminished" (Bourse Consult, 2007). However, as noted in the previous section, although these buildings are successful as branding objects for TNCs and/ or as objects of real estate speculation and mass entertainment, they fail to perform a role as underwriters of the power of the centre, i.e. the Corporation, insofar as the Corporation aimed to use them as part of a strategy to reinvent a new identity for itself and to promote a new global status for the City. These buildings stand as empty signifiers, forms without utopia, turning the City into a curiosity shop, arguably even more alienating than it ever was. The failure of these buildings to produce in themselves the desired new urban imaginary for the City of London, stands witness to the fact that spatial arrangements are never sufficient to produce meaningful social or institutional change, and meaningful urban space.

Notes

1 Many thanks to the editors of *Transactions of the Institute of British Geographers* Journal and to John Wiley & Sons publishers for granting permission to reproduce material for this chapter from the article: Kaika, Maria (2010). 'Architecture and Crisis: Re-Inventing the Icon, Re-Imag(in)Ing London and Re-Branding the City'. *Transactions of the Institute of British Geographers*, 35(4), 453–474.
2 The research for this chapter was supported by the British Academy, award number SG: 45263.
3 TAURUS was eventually replaced by the successful CREST, in 1996 (Kynaston, 2005).
4 "An *incorporated company* is a legal person in its own right, able to own property and to sue and be sued in its own name. A company may have limited liability (a limited company), so that the liability of the members for the company's debts is limited. An unlimited company is one in which the liability of the members is not limited in any way" ("company", *A Dictionary of Finance and Banking*. Ed. Jonathan Law and John Smullen. Oxford University Press, 2008. *Oxford Reference Online*. Oxford University Press, 14 January 2009, www.oxfordreference.com/views/ENTRY.html?subview=Main&entry=t20.e726). "In the USA firms which offer limited liability to stock holders are designated by *inc.* or *corporation*. In the UK, either *limited, LTD., Ltd., public limited company* or *PLC (plc)*" ("incorporated", *The Handbook of International Financial Terms*. Peter Moles and Nicholas Terry. Oxford University Press, 1997. *Oxford Reference Online*. Oxford University Press, 14 January 2009, www.oxfordreference.com/views/ENTRY.html?subview=Main&entry=t181.e3911).
5 "*Unincorporated business* is a privately owned business, usually owned by one person, that is not legally registered or recognized as a company. The sole owner has unlimited liability for any debts he or she may incur" ("unincorporated business", *A Dictionary of Finance and Banking*. Ed. Jonathan Law and John Smullen. Oxford University Press, 2008. Oxford Reference Online. Oxford University Press, 14 January 2009, www.oxfordreference.com/views/ENTRY.html?subview=Main&entry=t20.e3954).
6 Fleet Street gradually lost all of its traditional media occupants to accountants and lawyers, with *The Times* and *The Daily Telegraph* being the first, and *Reuters* the last to resettle in Canary Wharf in 2003.
7 The deal was negotiated with Hammerson, Britain's fourth-largest property company, and concerned JP Morgan potentially occupying a building on the site of St Alphage House.

References

Arendt. H. (1961). Society and Culture. In N. Jacobs (Ed.), *Culture for the Millions? Mass Media in Modern Society* (pp. 43–53). Princeton, NJ: D. Van Nostrand Co.
Arx, M., von & Schorr, S. (2005). *Building the Gherkin*. Switzerland: Ican films.
Baudrillard, J., & Nouvel, J. (2002). *The Singular Objects of Architecture*. Minneapolis, MN: University of Minnesota Press.

BBC News. (2003). Reuters Says Goodbye to Fleet Street. London.
Bell, D. (1976). *The Cultural Contradictions of Capitalism.* New York: Basic Books.
Bennetto, J., & Rentoul, J. (1996). 'Ring of Steel' around City set to Tighten. London: The Independent.
Bourse Consult, Cox, P., & Jones, L. (2007). *The Competitive Impact of London's Financial Market Infrastructure.* London: City of London Corporation.
Bowen, D. (1997). Ready to Carry the Can of Worms. London: *The Independent on Sunday*, 12 January 1997, 4.
Budd, L. (1992). An Urban Narrative and the Imperatives of the City. In L. Budd & S. Whimster (Eds.), *Global Finance and Urban Living: A Study of Metropolitan Change* (pp. 260–281). New York: Routledge.
Burdett, R., & Hadidian, M. (1987). *Paternoster Square: Urban Design Competition.* London: RIBA Report.
Castoriadis, C. (1987). *The Imaginary Institution of Society.* Cambridge: Polity Press.
City Action for Community Development. (2008). *City Action for Community Development.* Retrieved from: www.city-action.org (15 August 2008).
City of London Corporation. (2002). *City of London Ward Elections Act 2002.* Printed in the UK by the Stationery Office Limited under the authority and superintendence of Carol Tullo, Controller of Her Majesty's Stationery Office and Queen's Printer of Acts of Parliament, Crown Copyright, 2002.
City of London Corporation. (2008a). *Corporate Responsibility.* Retrieved from: www.cityoflondon.gov.uk/Corporation/LGNL_Services/Environment_and_planning/Regeneration/Corporate_responsibility (20 July 2008).
City of London Corporation. (2008b). *The Voting System.* Retrieved from: www.cityoflondon.gov.uk/Corporation/LGNL_Services/Council_and_democracy/Councillors_democracy_and_elections/appointment_proccess.htm.
City of London Employee Volunteering Programme. (2008). *City of London Employee Volunteering Programme.* Retrieved from: www.cityoflondon.gov.uk/Corporation/LGNL_Services/Environment_and_planning/Regeneration/Corporate_responsibility/emp_vol.htm (20 August 2008).
Cohen-Portheim, P. (1935). *The Spirit of London.* London: B.T. Batsford.
Corporation of London. (2008). *City of London: Business.* Retrieved from: www.cityoflondon.gov.uk/Corporation/LGNL_Services/Business (20 July 2008).
Cruise, S. (2008). J. P. Morgan Spurns London's Square Mile. New York/London: Reuters.
Daniels, P.W., & Bobe, J. M. (1993). Extending the boundary of the City of London – The development of Canary Wharf. *Environment and Planning A*, 25, 539–552.
Davis, M. (2006). Fear and money in Dubai. *New Left Review*, 41, 47–70.
Eley, P. (1986). Manifesto for the city: Building for the Square Mile. *Architects' Journal*, 183, 28–32.
Fainstein, S. S., Gordon, I., & Harloe, M. (1992). *Divided Cities: New York & London in the Contemporary World.* Oxford: Blackwell.
Fainstein, S.S. (1994). *The City Builders: Property, Politics & Planning in London and New York.* Oxford: Blackwell.
Financial Times. (2007). Swiss Re confirms £600m Gherkin sale. London: Financial Times.
Gordon, I., Haslam, C., McCann, P., & Scott-Quinn, B. (2005). *Off-Shoring and the City of London.* Reading: Corporation of London.
Hansard Debates, House of Commons. (1999). *Hansard Debates for 2 November 1999.* London: House of Commons Archives.
Head, C. (2001). *TAURUS and CREST: Failure and Success in Technology Project Management.* Cranfield: ECCH, the case for learning.
Heart of the City. (2008). *Heart of the City.* Retrieved from: www.theheartofthecity.com/who_we_are/index.htm (20 July 2008).
Hebbert, M., & McKellar, E. (2008). Tall buildings in the London landscape. *The London Journal*, 33, 199–200.
Imrie, R. (2006). *The Interrelationships between Building Regulations and Architects' Practices.* London: King's College London, Dept. for Geography.
Imrie, R., Lees, L., & Raco, M. (2008). *Regenerating London: Governance, Sustainability and Community.* London: Routledge.
Imrie, R., & Street, E. (2006). *The Attitudes of Architects towards Planning Regulation and Control.* London: King's College London, Dept. for Geography.
Jacobs, J. M. (1994). Negotiating the heart: Heritage, development and identity in postimperial London. *Environment and Planning D: Society and Space*, 12, 751–772.
Jacobs, J. M. (2006). A geography of big things. *Cultural Geographies*, 13, 1–27.
Jencks, C. (2004). *The Iconic Building: The Power of Enigma.* London: Frances Lincoln.

Kaika, M. (2010). Architecture and crisis: Re-inventing the icon, re-imag(in)ing London and re-branding the City. *Transactions of the Institute of British Geographers*, 35(4), 453–474.

Kynaston, D. (2005). *The City of London, Vol. 4: A Club No More, 1945–2000*. London: Pimlico.

Local Procurement Project. (2008). *Local Procurement Project*. Retrieved from: www.cityoflondon.gov.uk/Corporation/LGNL_Services/Business/Tenders_and_contracts/local_procurement.htm (20 August 2008).

Markham, L. (2008). The protection of views of St Paul's Cathedral and its influence on the London landscape. *The London Journal*, 33, 271–287.

Martin. I. (1993). The policy maker in the City. Michael Cassidy, chairman of the City's policy committee is bringing an interventionist approach to the development of the Square Mile. *Architects' Journal*, 197, 24–25.

Mayor of London. (2001). Interim strategic planning guidance on tall buildings, strategic views and the skyline in London. London: Greater London Authority.

McNeill, D. (2002). The mayor and the world city skyline: London's tall buildings debate. *International Planning Studies*, 7, 325–334.

McNeill, D. (2005). Dysfunctional urbanism. *International Journal of Urban and Regional Research*, 29: 201–204.

McNeill, D. (2006). Globalization and the ethics of architectural design. *City*, 10, 49–58.

McNeill, D., & Tewdwr-Jones, M. (2003). Architecture, banal nationalism and re-territorialization. *International Journal of Urban and Regional Research*, 27, 738–743.

Merrick, J. (2004). The Sky's the Limit. London: *The Independent* (11 February, 12).

Merrifield, A. (1993). The Canary Wharf debacle: From 'TINA' – there is no alternative – to 'THEMBA' – there must be an alternative. *Environment and Planning A*, 25, 1247–1265.

Moulaert, F., Swyngedouw, E., & Rodriguez, A. (Eds.). (2003). *The Globalized City*. Oxford: Oxford University Press.

Oxford Economics Ltd. (2007). *London's Place in the UK Economy, 2007–2008*. London: City of London.

Pickard, J. (2007). Eye-Catching Schemes in Pipeline for City. London: *Financial Times*, (16 July, 4).

Powell, K. (2005). *New London Architecture*. London: Merrell.

Power, D. (1998). *The Alienation of the Public in the City of London* (Thesis D. Phil). Oxford: University of Oxford, Faculty of Anthropology and Geography.

Roberts, R., & Kynaston, D. (2001). *City State: A Contemporary History of the City of London and How Money Triumphed*. London: Profile Books.

Schnapp, J. T. (1992). Architecture and culture in fascist Italy: Fascism's museum in motion. *Journal of Architectural Education*, 45, 87–97.

Sennett, R. (2001). A Flexible City of Strangers. Paris: *Le Monde Diplomatique*, February 2001 issue. Retrieved from: https://mondediplo.com/2001/02/16cities (14 March 2017).

Simonian, H. (2007). Gherkin Sale Helps Swiss Re Beat Estimates. London: *Financial Times*.

Sklair, L. (2005). The transnational capitalist class and contemporary architecture in globalizing cities. *International Journal of Urban and Regional Research*, 29, 485–500.

Tafuri, M. (1973/1999). *Architecture and Utopia: Design and Capitalist Development*. Cambridge, MA: MIT Press.

The City Bridge Trust. (2008). *The City Bridge Trust*. Retrieved from: www.citybridgetrust.org.uk/citybridgetrust.

Twombly, R. C. (1996). *Power and Style: A Critique of Twentieth-Century Architecture in the United States*. New York: Hill and Wang.

Warner, J. (2004). Gherkin Sold: London's Commercial Property Market is Booming, and with Good Reason. London: *The Financial Times* (20 October, Business, 36).

Whimster, S. (2008). *Global Finance and Urban Living: A Study of Metropolitan Change* (pp. 260–281). New York: Routledge.

Wynne Rees, P. (2002). City of London Unitary Development Plan 2002. London: City of London, Transportation Department.

Žižek, S. (1989). *The Sublime Object of Ideology*. London: Verso.

Zukin, S. (1992). The City as a Landscape of Power: London and New York as Global Financial Capitals. In L. Budd & S. Whimster (Eds.), *Global Finance and Urban Living: A Study of Metropolitan Change*. New York: Routledge.

Z/Yen Group Limited, Yeandle, M., Mainelli, M., & Harris, I. (2007). *The Global Financial Centres Index 2*. London: City of London Corporation.

18
THE POLITICAL NATURE OF SYMBOLS
Explaining Institutional Inertia and Change

Federico Savini & Sebastian Dembski

Introduction

The relationship between spatially embedded social norms and politically biased, purpose-led, urban intervention is very complex and hard to disentangle. Institutional change occurs from a complexity of social, cultural and political dynamics. In this chapter, we focus exclusively and deliberately on one (partial but important) explanatory variable of institutional change: the role of political coalitions in re-constructing meaning. Institutions have an intrinsic nature of durability and resistance to change. Internalised norms are, by definition, durable. Yet, institutional change occurs at certain places and times. This change is always structured around a process of interpretation, confirmation and modification of meaning by social formations and individuals. Among these formations, we see political coalitions of powerful actors. Our view is that planning is embedded within these structures of powers which reflect particular social norms, and that change also occurs as a process of symbolic mobilisation that enacts a re-construction of social meanings.

The industrial crisis in the 1970s caused a fundamental spatial restructuring of Western cities that continues until today. Cities followed quite diverging development strategies to tackle the resulting urban crisis, be it market- or state-led (Evans, 2009; Savitch & Kantor, 2002; Zukin, 1996). While the early days of urban restructuring were characterised by large-scale projects catering for the new urban economy (Fainstein, 2008; Salet & Gualini, 2007), the new generation of urban transformation projects is increasingly concerned with the adaptation of the existing urban fabric, often from a small-scale and sustainability oriented perspective. Current urban interventions often embody discourses and narratives that emphasise co-production, self-regulated urbanism and self-organised governance (Iveson, 2013; McFarlane, 2012; Rauws et al., 2016). These narratives underline a widespread optimism on tactical, experimental and innovative interventions, especially at the urban level. Yet, the extent to which these practices offer a new institutional base of urban planning remains unclear. Critics point out that these practices might offer a new scalar and spatial fix of the capitalist economy (Brenner, 2015; Peck, 2012), while others are much more optimistic about the transformative potential of these experiences (Bulkeley & Castán Broto, 2013; Evans et al., 2016).

A closer look at these contemporary practices in urban experimentalism shows that considerable energy is invested in building new discourses and imaginaries of urban change.

Planners make extensive use of metaphors, iconic architecture and celebratory events to convey the innovative character of episodic initiatives. These practices also play an important role in reshaping mainstream discourses and political narratives about how cities will (and should) change. Symbolic markers, as we define them, encompass a broad set of symbolic practices mobilised in space. These are rhetorical, physical and narrative elements, instrumentally used by planners and political elites in concrete spatial interventions.

The symbolic mobilisation of new imaginaries, habits, decision-making procedures and broad ideals of spatial use is never free of conflict. Institutional change is a political phenomenon and this is often not fully appreciated in both pragmatist and sociological institutional thought. A common misunderstanding among planning practitioners is that symbolic strategies of urban restructuring are 'power-free', simply reflecting a state of local society and responding to an existing demand for change, transition or transformation towards a more sustainable and inclusive city. Critical urban theory has instead showed that this view is symptomatic of a 'post-political' condition of urban change, because it tends to define institutional (and environmental or social) change as a 'matter of fact', a 'natural evolution of cities' or an 'inevitable consequence' of environmental and technological improvements (Allmendinger & Haughton, 2012; Metzger et al., 2015; Swyngedouw, 2009). This critique urges us to problematise the relation between institutions and the political, purpose-led nature of planning interventions, and to understand how the latter links to the former (Campbell, 2001; Salet & Savini, 2015).

In this chapter, we conceptualise and provide a view on the political logics of institutional change, scrutinising how symbols are mobilised by political coalitions to trigger socio-economic change in cities. We first argue that the historical viscosity of institutions is (partly) the result of the power-holding nature of coalitions that have a vested interest in maintaining these norms. Secondly, we define the meaning and role of symbolic narratives, acts and artefacts in the dynamic of institutional change, building on literature on semiotics and framing. Thirdly, we provide an illustrative case to show how institutional change has occurred in the transformation of the Northern IJ Bank in Amsterdam over the past two decades. Formerly a location for shipbuilding and other heavy industries, this area has evolved as a hotspot for the creative sector since the 1980s and has been subject to redevelopment since the 2000s. In the concluding section, we reflect on the political responsibility of planning and the pitfalls of institutional determinism, and problematise the democratic value of symbols.

Institutional Inertia: The Role of Political Agency and Coalitions

Planning is a transformative practice that (generally) aims at creating a better society by setting the social, spatial and political conditions for the common good. This highly ambitious goal is also the cause for one of the biggest frustrations within the discipline. Turning 'knowledge to action' (Friedmann, 1987) requires more than proposing the best technical-rational solution to a problem. The implementation deficit of rational planning has been widely acknowledged (Hajer & Zonneveld, 2000; Salet, 2018), and part of the answer can be found in the way rational approaches insufficiently understand and appreciate how institutions, intended as socially produced norms, evolve. Institutions not only establish social expectations about what to expect of individuals and their collectives, but also organise relationships of power which inevitably favour certain groups of society. These are vested interests in maintaining particular orders, discourses and ways of doing things (for an overview see Salet, Chapter 1, in this volume). That is also why many of planning's successful transformative policies, which at some point managed to break the inertia, have themselves become part of institutional norms and have developed into barriers to change. Examples range from green belts to regulations for housing quality standards. Policies create and reproduce a particular community of interest, which inherently is interested in maintaining the status quo (Sorensen, 2015). This is a totally natural process in how institutions work: new institutions are produced and consolidated by practices contextualised in time and space, but in turn become frameworks of reference for new practices.

This tension between stability and change, between the individual and the collective, is essential to human action. In planning, this is perhaps best illustrated in Faludi's idea of a planning doctrine, describing the powerful set of core ideas relating to spatial organisation and the way planning is organised that have guided spatial planning in the Netherlands over several decades (Faludi & Van der Valk, 1994). It served particular interests and enabled the survival of certain ideas, in spite of criticism that some planning concepts may no longer be fit for purpose (Hajer & Zonneveld, 2000). The main difficulty in planning studies concerned with institutions is the need to conceptualise how change occurs despite this natural viscosity of norms. In contrast, there is much more evidence of how planning agency reproduces and reinforces pre-existing institutional order over time (Mahoney & Thelen, 2010; Sorensen, 2015. These views on institutional change strongly emphasise the risks perceived by incumbent actors (Pierson, 2000), the long-term advantages of complying with habits, routines and existing norms, and the pre-emptive capacity of regimes to co-opt change (Avelino et al., 2016), but are much less clear on why change occurs (or simply argue that it comes from 'external' conditions).

Planning practice and theory is very much concerned with transformative agency, widely discussing the role of discursive, legal and financial norms in enabling or constraining spatial practices and imagination (Healey, 1992; Savini et al., 2015). Along this line of reasoning, we propose three main meanings of planning with regard to institutional change. First, planning is always a practice of interpretation, modification, mobilisation and 'stretching' of meaning. This means that this change of meaning is (mostly) gradual and connected to some past understanding of future society. Secondly, as a practice of interpretation, planning is always embedded in a particular context, which it aims to change from within. Context is both spatial and temporal. Thirdly, and most importantly, this interpretation in context is always politically biased exactly because context itself is a field that establishes power relations and preferences. This latter point urges us to understand planning as a politicised practice of interpretation of the past and imagination of the future.

Political agents, such as local governments, planners and political parties, not only respond to contextual trends but also operate as purpose-led agents of institutional change, which stimulate certain patterns rather than others. Nevertheless, these active tactics of changing courses of action and norms tend to remain somehow 'elusive' in most institutional research, and agency has remained unproblematised as a theoretical object of institutional analysis (Dembski & Salet, 2010; Emirbayer & Mische, 1998). In planning research in particular, the role of designers, architects, planners and developers, in combination with that of political elites, is central in explaining institutional change as a result of a reorganisation of collective action around spatial visions (Fainstein, 1994; Salet, 2008; Savini, 2014). Planning is often regarded as a practice of active institutional design (Innes, 1995) and planners are 'instigators of change' (Alexander, 1992 in Taylor, 2013, p. 691), but the political bias of this active imagination, and their contextualisation, has to be better conceptualised.

In a study of the political nature of institutions, March and Olsen (1989) argue that politics is an *institutionalising* process, a practice of organising and distributing different systems of meanings in society. Politics provides 'interpretations of life' (March & Olsen, 1989, p. 47) and occurs through the establishment of frames of appropriateness in a democratic process.

This view understands institutions not only as a *frame of* political agency but as a *political act* itself, carried out as the organisation of socio-economic interests and around particular *normative* agendas. These normative agendas are expressions of particular regimes of power, namely constellations of public, private and civic actors that convey particular meanings to the present, past and future of urban economies (DiGaetano & Strom, 2003; Savitch & Kantor, 2002). Not surprisingly, the notion of 'regime' is still today a black box of institutional research, referring to the power-laden, durable systems of norms that represent a particular politico economic organisation of society. Political regimes are resistant because their *raison d'être* is the (re)production of an institutional framework as a source of legitimacy (Pierre, 2014; Stone, 1989). As institutional agents, coalitions have the tendency to resist change. They have the capacity of 'pre-empting' new norms to be established by excluding particular views and demands (Stone, 1988). Institutional capacity is accordingly understood as the ability to mobilise different systems of meanings by organising different sets of actors.

Regime theory offers a fruitful, analytical approach to unpack the inner political mechanics of institutional resistance and change. Regimes have a natural tendency to persist once they have become established, because coalition building involves high start-up costs in gaining political power, mobilising polities, building narratives and organising leadership (Sorensen, 2015). Governing coalitions are strange agents: on the one hand, they are inherently conservative because they are born in a particular institutional context which reflects their power interest. On the other, because this context is in perpetual change, they also need to adapt to it. First, coalitions need stability to act and they are motivated by the necessity to minimise political and economic risks, avoiding losing electoral consensus and hence legitimacy. The risk to destabilise existent polities and consensus is often perceived to be higher than the advantages, especially when they require the reorganisation of a large set of regulations and bureaucracies (Hirschman, 1970; Taylor, 2013). Secondly, political coalitions are not detached from changing socio-economic contexts. They also recursively react to social dynamics to reinforce consensus and structure new political demands. The use of symbols explains how the conservative nature of coalitions often matches with practices that convey new meanings and institutions (Mossberger & Stoker, 2001). Symbolic acts are recursively used to displace attention, filter policies, camouflage the social implications of agendas or justify the financial and social costs of experimental policies. To hold power against institutional change, politicians operate through the manipulation of attention, the identification of anomalies, shifting perceptions on risks, and by giving signs of success and failure (March & Olsen, 1989). In cases of political conflict, political elites convey institutional change as a 'drift' (Mahoney & Thelen, 2010). A drift is the result of a complex set of tactics deliberately oriented to manipulate the meaning of institutions through symbolic narratives, while maintaining the appearance of institutional, and thus power, continuity. These drifts can occur through low-profile stimuli that target particular norms. We define these as symbolic markers.

Institutional Change: The Political Use of Symbolic Markers

The fascination of symbolic markers lies in the capacity of symbols to project into a future state an existing nexus of institutionalised norms. Giddens has straightforwardly argued that symbols are the resources of signification in the structuration process of society, as they are intertwined within particular symbolic orders and allow the organisation, grouping and articulation of different institutional norms into systems of meaning and biases (Giddens, 1984). Institutional thought is full of references to the power of symbols in conveying meaning and substantiating the internalisation of institutions by individuals. Symbols are considered powerful because they are softer than contracts and formal legal or financial incentives, and they underlie the deeper meanings of durable norms, while simultaneously changing those meanings.

Symbols are fundamental for ensuring the existence of institutions as they can reinforce or legitimise certain social beliefs (Berger & Luckmann, 1966; Geertz, 1973; Lefebvre, 1991). They not only carry meaning, but also recreate new meaning (Yanow, 1996, p. 10). Symbols are extensively used by political actors because they have this inherent capacity of institutional re-construction. Based on the work of Castoriadis (1987), Kaika argues, for example, that iconic architecture is "not only a means of *expressing/signifying* existing elite power, but also one of the most effective means for *instituting* new elite power, and constituting new social relations as real or naturalised during moments of social, economic, or political change" (Kaika, 2011, p. 970, emphasis in original). On the other hand, to do so symbols need to refer to recognisable social values; when symbols are de-contextualised from the existing social and political views in certain places, they might generate conflict.

The working of symbols therefore depends on the way they both relate to context, and project this context into a different level of abstraction in space and time. Semiotics and semiology have profiled the relationship between the sign and the meaning to which it refers. Simply stated, "a sign is an image or an object produced so as to *intentionally* stand for something else, i.e., it is the unification of object and meaning" (Gottdiener, 1982, p. 140, emphasis in original). The process of signification, that is the intentional link between the sign and the signified, is a social process of building norms. Strictly speaking a linguistic theory, it has extended into architecture and urban form. Symbols may be 'born' as symbolic instruments, intentionally produced to signify condensed meaning, or may become symbols in their lifetime by practices of political adoption and narrative co-optation (see Gottdiener, 1982).

'Sign' and 'symbol' are at times used interchangeably in the semiotic literature, while others define symbols as higher-order signs. For instance, for Berger and Luckmann (1966, p. 95), "symbolic processes are processes of signification that refer to realities other than those of everyday experience". In a similar vein, Geertz laments that, "in some hands [symbol] is used for anything which signifies something else to someone", instead preferring to define symbols as "any object, act, event, quality, or relation which serves as a vehicle for a conception – the conception is the symbol's 'meaning'" (Geertz, 1973, p. 91).

All these symbolic communicative forms have in common that they represent norms in a condensed form. Symbols play an important role in the transmission of institutional knowledge, functioning as "mnemotechnic aids" (Berger & Luckmann, 1966, p. 71). Particularly in the process of institutional change, the symbolic display is vital to instituting new meaning. However, symbols do not institute meaning themselves; it is the underlying constellation of (more or less organised) actors that brings them to life through a process of affirmation (Berger & Luckmann, 1966; Bourdieu, 1991). This implies a view of institutions as dynamic and continuously evolving (Salet, 2002). In the transformation of existing urban fabric, the conflict between established and emerging practices occurs as a clash of systems of meanings and norms: this clash is what symbolic markers attempt to bridge (see Swidler, 1986).

Symbols are abstract "expressions of socially existing codes" (Geertz, 1973, p. 6). Therefore, the analysis of symbolic markers needs to be combined with an understanding of underlying social and political patterns. The social agents who launch symbols or interpret them are equipped with specific political resources (Giddens, 1984) and a specific socio-cultural bias which guides the way they see the world. In our view, this practice of association between spatial signs and new signifiers is a core factor in explaining how institutional change occurs endogenously, against the inherent resistance of political regimes. Political groups are active agents in establishing new symbols and discourses over the future of cities, and symbols allow the abstraction of their durable power into other systems of meaning without exacerbating conflict.

Planning practice has a rich tradition in mobilising communicative devices as a means of uniting stakeholders, silencing conflicts, building consensus and involving the public in visioning spatial futures. With the communicative turn in planning theory, scholars have placed lots of emphasis on storytelling (Fischer, 2003). Several authors have highlighted the power of visualisation, particularly through maps (Dühr, 2007; Zonneveld, 2005). "Cartographic representations can be powerful instruments in strategic planning processes and in communicating key objectives of the spatial strategy" (Dühr, 2007, p. 153). Spatial concepts, often in the form of metaphors and other linguistic tropes, have proven one of the most powerful tools in planning and defining space (Faludi, 1996). The role of iconic architecture is also crucial for place making and place marketing. For instance, Kaika (2010) demonstrated how London's dramatically altered skyline over the past decades can be related to the institutional crisis of the City of London Corporation. She argues that "iconic architecture produced under moments of restructuring can be understood as part of a system of significations (alongside language, images, public discourse, etc.) necessary to produce a new identity for élites or institutions in need of reinvention" (Kaika, 2010, p. 454). Gottdiener (1995) investigated the role of themes in practices of naming and architecture that appeal to consumers and investors as a means of increasing the value of a place. Cultural flagship investments have equally functioned as key symbolic markers in urban regeneration projects.

There is a broad variety of symbolic markers at the disposal of power coalitions. They can be categorised into symbolic *objects*, *languages* and *acts* (Yanow, 1996, 2000). Symbolic objects refer to the physical artefacts of urban development that have been charged with meaning beyond its pure functional uses. The Guggenheim Museum by Frank Gehry, in the Basque city of Bilbao, Spain, became symbolic for the regeneration of this industrial city and the transition of the city into a new political-economic regime (Vicario & Martínez Monje, 2003). Symbolic language underlies the metaphorical language of urban agendas. The Green Heart in the Netherlands is a famous example of a planning metaphor mobilised to protect the arable land in between the four major cities of the Netherlands, and was sustained by a national growth coalition (Terhorst & Van de Ven, 1995; Van Eten & Roe, 2000). Symbolic acts instead refer to staged events in the planning process. This may involve the launch of a project or regular committee meetings evidencing the progress of change, perhaps portrayed as public events. Finally, "All language, objects, and acts are *potential* carriers of meaning, open to interpretation" (Yanow, 1996, p. 9, emphasis added) by a range of actors, but not every building, word or activity has symbolic meaning.

Political regimes organise consensus and simultaneously aim at changing institutions by establishing symbolic meaning to acts, languages and artefacts in urban interventions. Figure 18.1 provides a synthesis of our framework for the political analysis of institutional change. A concentric representation allows the observer to view political coalition building as part of a broad process of institutionalisation. Coalitions build on consensus and legitimacy from polities, which are socio-spatial and political communities, made up of voters and social groups. Social norms establish systems of meaning by these communities. This whole process (arrows down) can be broadly understood as the Giddensean process of reproduction of social norms. On the other hand (arrows up), the process of re-construction of meanings and norms takes place as a politically bounded process. Political coalitions employ languages, acts and objects to substantiate interventions in space as meaningful. These symbols are embedded in institutional orders but also contribute to change them. These interventions impact on the social and spatial composition of communities, which in turn produces new meanings and norms. Obviously, the change

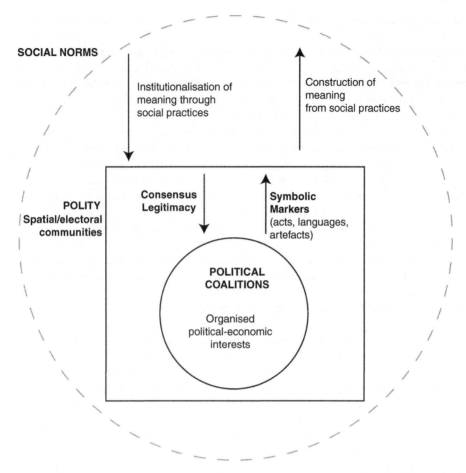

Figure 18.1 Visual representation of the relation between political coalitions (circle), social and electoral communities (square) and the complex system of norms (dashed circle)
Source: authors' own

of polities occurs continuously and is also impacted by other factors (e.g. technological innovation or global financial crises), but here we particularly problematise the political reactions to these other factors. In this framework, the use of symbolic markers is thus an expression of a political bias, a system of discursively constructed meaning that reflects the (re)organisation of political interests. This also explains the 'viscosity' of institutions: the establishment of a coalition is an *active part* of the inner mechanism of institutionalisation. In the following section, we will show how emergent political groups have operated through a careful mobilisation of symbols in order to trigger social, political and spatial change in Amsterdam-North.

Amsterdam-North: From Political Inertia to Institutional Change

Over the past decades, Amsterdam has transformed from a fundamentally social-democratic city into a city embracing the discourse of creativity (Engelen & Musterd, 2010; Peck, 2012; Uitermark, 2009). The Northern IJ Bank in the North district of Amsterdam is just the latest in a long series of working-class areas that have undergone profound transformation (Savini et al., 2016). Amsterdam-North is the only district on the 'other' side of the IJ waters, which was incorporated in the 1920s to accommodate Amsterdam's heavy industries. While being physically close to the city centre, the IJ forms a strong physical and mental boundary. For a long time, politics in Amsterdam-North were characterised by a social-democratic political class and a left-wing electorate that was interested in industrial jobs and a strong welfare state. This resulted in industrial policies that were strongly supported by the private sector and the trade unions. However, the industrial crisis of the 1970s and 1980s resulted in the closure of all mayor shipyards and turned the Northern IJ Bank into industrial wasteland. While initial attempts were made to continue with traditional politics, Amsterdam embarked on a more market-led approach in the 1980s (Engelen & Musterd, 2010; Peck, 2012; Uitermark, 2009; Van Gent, 2013), which also reached the self-governed district of Amsterdam-North. In the following section, we will analyse the role of symbolism in this remarkable transformation of a working-class district into the new creative hotspot of Amsterdam, focussing specifically on the Northern IJ Bank.

The role that symbols, rhetoric and new discourses have played in enabling this change in the long social-democratic tradition of Amsterdam's political landscape is highly important and became more evident when looking at specific projects such as the Northern IJ Bank. This area has gained large political centrality within the city council; it became a laboratory for experimental spatial policies and a breeding ground for new electoral groups. Politically, Amsterdam-North had traditionally seen strong left parties and industrial companies linked to the liberals, strategically positioned within a corporatist approach to economic policy based on solid coalitions between government, industrial groups and trade unions. Since 2002, however, the District Council of Amsterdam-North has shown a radical change in its developmental strategy, focussing on younger families and professionals and looking towards small and medium knowledge-intensive enterprises. The northern political landscape diversified, with a sharp increase of votes and seats for the progressive liberal party D66 (Democrats 66), a new centre-right group filling the space of the right-wing liberals of the VVD (People's Party for Freedom and Democracy), and an increase for the Greens in 2010, while the social-democratic PvdA (Labour Party) has lost support. This change also led to fundamental debates within the city council on the city's economic and social character (Savini, 2013). Political confrontations rotate around the conflicting relation between the surviving industrial productions (i.e. the harbour), the rising interest for knowledge economies in the area and the need of new homes for middle incomes instead of social housing.

The rise of 'the North' as a new hotspot for urban development, housing and urban creativity was surprising in light of its historical, physical and political detachment from the rest of the city. For many Amsterdammers, the North was not Amsterdam. It has been described as the 'Siberia of Amsterdam' (*De Groene Amsterdammer*, 2000) and the boringness of urban life is described in a song by Drukwerk with the refrain "I get so bored in North" (*Ik verveel me zo in Noord*). Politically, the North has been the area where the vanguard of the Labour Party (PvdA) and labour unions have been consolidated. The crisis of the 1970s and 1980s saw the last major shipyard closed in 1985. Amsterdam-North turned into an industrial wasteland. Today, "the water, the tough-looking industrial buildings, the quays, and the sheer scale in general, now form an inspiring décor, from which more and more urban dwellers and modern economic sectors derive their identity" (Gemeente Amsterdam, 2011, p. 60, authors' translation).

This new vision and meaning of the North, today almost unanimously agreed by companies, municipal planners and district politicians, is the result of a long path of political transition. Already in the mid-1990s, the IJ became a focal point for central city planning agencies, but most plans have looked at only the south side of the river, leaving the North untouched. In the early 1990s, the only activity of city-wide importance on the Northern IJ Bank was a yearly theatre festival, the 'Over het IJ Festival' on the site of the former NDSM shipyard. Amsterdam-North's urban agenda remained highly local in these early post-industrial years. In 1988, a first plan for the area (*Nota Tien Kilometre Noordelijke IJ-oever*) identified two scenarios: one where the North maintains its village-like structure and remains separated from Amsterdam; and an urban future, immediately juxtaposing visions of transformation into a mixed-use urban area against visions of conservation. Both these views entailed too high a risk for the consolidated electoral majority, as local communities feared the loss of work and the risk of marginalisation. The municipal structure plans of 1991 and 1996 continued to neglect the North as a transformation area. The strong political relevance of Amsterdam-North to the Labour Party (PvdA) and its weight in city politics did not offer the right conditions for a transformative agenda (see Dijkink & Mamadouh, 2003).

The main issues with the transformation of the North were political and institutional (Savini, 2013). Politically, the elected coalition of the Northern district was highly reluctant to approve a general masterplan of change. This was considered first too risky financially, but more importantly, local officials were fully aware that their electorate would have never approved this idea. The political risk of a radical change was too high, and local elected coalitions, as stated above, are inherently conservative. Yet, the option to abandon the idea of redevelopment was also not viable, in light of the social and economic change in the city. Such a change in the social and economic landscape of the city had to be dealt with in a way that was more contextual, more sensitive to the established meaning of the area. The constitution of a new process of gradual change was based on the so-called *Noordwaarts!* (Northwards!) a series of public meetings to discuss the future of the district and push for stronger city plans. This was a compelling symbolic act that allowed engagement within a broad series of planning processes, practices and initiatives that aimed at redefining the meaning of the area in the eyes of the whole city and of the local communities. It was primarily motivated by the need to react to the decision of the Royal Dutch Shell to leave vacant a 26.5 ha large site in Overhoeks, a prime location in the North. The elected coalition therefore had to deal with, on the one hand, the risk of losing 1,200 jobs in Amsterdam-North, and on the other, the ambition to maintain the internalised idea that the North was an industrial area. From 2000 to 2003, different plans were put forward: *Panorama Noord* (2000), which proposed a radical transformation into a mixed-use urban area, and an urban design masterplan, *Noord aan het IJ* (2003). These plans were the first attempts to trigger a strategy of transition, maintaining the image of a 'work city' to the eyes of its working-class polity but advancing the option of a more mixed-use development.

These ambitious plans met the resistance of the electorate in Amsterdam-North, which felt spatial change as de-contextual, unnatural and disrespectful of the social and cultural background of the area. This turned into a NIMBY movement that led to a change in the electoral composition of the local government. In 2002, the *Leefbaar Noord*, a populist local party linked to the national *Leefbaar* movement, won leadership of the district council, signalling a radical position of 'reject' by the local community to the proposed visions. It was this political volatility, triggered by the fear of institutional change that pushed the social-democratic coalitions to pursue a new strategy which could moderately advance a new meaning of the area without disrupting the local political consensus. The constitution of the Projectbureau Noordwaarts (Project Bureau Northwards) was the first symbolic act that represented a further 'drift' in the policy of the North: it was a political compromise between the local interests of the district and the city-wide politicians that worked as a symbolic act signalling an apparent change in the way the city was governing urban development. Beside its management rationale (which is debatable), this office represented a political agreement between the Labour Party constituency of the

North and the emerging progressive majority of the municipal council consisting of Greens and Labour (in favour of redevelopment). The mayor of Amsterdam and the district mayor chaired it jointly. More importantly, the office became an institutional space where a new developmental approach could be formulated. Labelled as 'organic', the new planning approach undertaken by the planners working for this new body, underlined the need to involve local groups, engage in experimental, contextual innovation and reduce the disruptive, top-down role of planning in changing the area.

Symbolic Markers and Tactics of Meaning Re-Construction

While many planners present this approach as experimental and rather open, such an organic approach is composed of a broad series of punctual interventions of institutional mobilisation to favour a gradual change in the area. This approach of selective mobilisation of meaning through symbols became the key to unlocking the existing political viscosity and inertia of the elected coalitions, both at the district and urban level. This approach therefore combined a set of symbolic acts, languages and artefacts, combined with a dense practice of daily negotiations with local groups and communities on the future of the area. Through this process, planners were able to reconstruct the 'meaning' of the North and to reposition it as creative cultural hotspot within the mental map of a dynamic city. Not surprisingly, because of the incredible success of this approach, the organic process of institutional change in the North was in fact benchmarked and transferred to many other areas in the city, and today it is almost an undisputed method of urban development. Below we closely look at the specific symbolic instruments used by political coalitions to convey a new meaning to the area and trigger spatial change.

From the very beginning the transformation rested on the symbolic language of two slogans that dominated the transformation of the Northern IJ Banks. First there was *Noordwaarts!*, the slogan of the public debate that led to the vision *Panorama Noord*, and that later became the name of the joint project office of the central city and the district. It emphasises the attractiveness of the North through an invitation to make the 'jump over the IJ', which in turn became the most recent label for the municipal investigation into a new transport connection over the IJ. *Noord aan het IJ* (North back to the IJ) and, related to that, *Y-sight* (the name of the internal project office until 2005), in contrast, are directed at the population of Amsterdam-North, highlighting the positive features of the urban development of the Northern IJ Bank. Both slogans represent two sides of the same coin. It is somehow reflective of the balancing act between the sentiments of local residents and of the other Amsterdam. One of the most obvious symbolic acts then was the establishment of Projectbureau Noordwaarts and its location in a newly developed office park on the Northern IJ Banks. This clearly signalled that decisions were not simply taken by the central city, but developed on site as a true co-production.

Co-optation of symbolic markers by the planning authorities was a common strategy and, in so doing, extended the coalition. The former NDSM shipyard has become one of the main icons of the transformation of Amsterdam-North. Artists discovered this abandoned space and started to occupy it from the early 1990s, successfully establishing an annual theatre festival (*Over het IJ Festival*). It was only much later that an artists' collective (*Kinetisch Noord*) managed to access municipal subsidies to establish NDSM as creative hotspot. By "embracing the artistic squatter" (Uitermark, 2004, p. 692), the district government ensured that this icon of the industrial North would function as a symbol that connects the past with the future. The built environment provided a rich pool of potential symbolic objects that would further combine the industrial heritage with the creative future, such as the spectacular transparent office building on a 270m-long concrete crane track over the water (*Kraanspoor*), designed by the architect Trude Hooykaas.

In the aftermath of the global financial crisis in 2008, which heavily affected the Dutch real estate market, the symbolic language of planners placed ever greater emphasis on the 'organic' character of the transformation driven by 'urban pioneers'. The North 'offered space' for development, literally by providing land, but also metaphorically, by enabling more freedom to develop without the strict urban design provisions of the rest of the city. This became epitomised in the organic development metaphor and extensive opportunities for self-building. A giant red shovel became the symbol for the pioneers, the celebrated *avant-garde* that makes the neighbourhood. This went along with symbolic acts such as 'self-build' markets staged by the local authority, in which interested individuals or collectives could select a parcel of land specifically made available for self-built dwellings. A self-installed 'quartermaster' (*kwartiermaker*) and the extensive self-documentation of the place making of Amsterdam-North on various websites, including the *Selfmade City*, pay testimony to what could be called the myth of organic development. Early residents considered themselves as pioneers and helped to frame the narrative of a bottom-up development process of the North. The Projectbureau enhanced this narrative of an open-ended and organic planning process, while in fact all forms of self-organisation were meticulously staged by the municipal planners via land use regulations and land policy (Dembski, 2013).

The Overhoeks project on the former Shell site almost seems exceptionally conventional in its development style. Developed by a large consortium, it constructed luxury apartments in sizeable blocks facing the waterfront. This new neighbourhood marks a stark architectural and social contrast with the traditional working-class neighbourhood next to it. Yet they picked up the idea from a local civic initiative (ANGSAW) to develop a cultural anchor at the waterfront. The futuristic building of the EYE film museum managed to attract masses of tourists to enjoy the views over the IJ, but more importantly it symbolised that the North was no longer a cultural desert. When the financial crisis hit, the site was opened for alternative ideas, and the Overhoeks Tower and the IJ Pavilion (the former Shell canteen) formed the décor for new cultural initiatives.

Amsterdam North is a successful case of a complete makeover of a neighbourhood within a timeframe of roughly a decade for the core interventions. The framing of Amsterdam-North cleverly aligned the interest of the ambitious district government with the emerging group of urban pioneers. The symbols were timed with a gradual shift in population composition. Companies, municipal planners and politicians today almost unanimously agree on this new future for the North. Yet, while this developmental vision might advance the claim to re-emphasise the specific characteristics of the North, it can also be understood as a process of 'colonisation' of the working-class areas by the wealthier residents living in other parts of the city (Oudenampsen, 2010, p. 36). In an essay, Oudenampsen (2010, p. 27) described the transformation of the Amsterdam-North as a change of strategy from the improvement of the local working classes towards place making, where the improvement occurs as the result of the influx of new residents. In this synthetic story of the North we demonstrated that institutional change was the effect of an active strategy pursued by local political elites. Yet, we might still wonder why the Labour Party deliberately pursued a policy that eventually led to the erosion of their very electoral base. Today a peculiar mix of Socialist Party and Liberal Democrats, as well as pockets of populist right wing support, represents the North.

Conclusions

There are two hypothetical and stereotypical views when trying to explain institutional change in cities. The first is to claim that institutional change is exclusively triggered by a changing landscape of conditions, technologies, global economic flows and environmental risks, or is instead hard to achieve because of institutionalised paths. The second is to emphasise the power of agency by individuals and their organised groups as the builders of their own future. The first case is an example of institutional determinism, where society is understood as something abstracted from individual agents, as a system of practices that are continuously affected by external conditions such as the global economy, international political institutions or environmental decay. The second is an example of uncritical instrumental pragmatism, where institutions are always produced, recursively changed and freely manipulated depending on the particular needs of time and place.

In urban practice and research, these views are (almost) always intertwined into a hybrid explanation of institutional change, which emphasises the transformative potential of practices without underestimating the broad socio-economic and political dynamics. Yet, in some cases, planners might tend either to underestimate or overestimate their role in this process. On the one hand, planning professionals, architects or engaged politicians might portray urban redevelopment and particular forms of ecological modernisation as something 'necessary' to react to socio-environmental changes that are beyond their control. Narratives of urgency and inevitability have often sustained discourses on smart and creative urban development. On the other hand, the same planners, professionals, designers and social activists might overestimate the innovative potential of individual choices and their social formations. They might look at self-organisation, do-it-yourself urbanism and local creations as the key to a changing society. This approach might not problematise the complex system of hierarchies and powers that establish a set of selective incentives and possibilities for those same practices to occur. Both these derivatives of planning have been correctly understood as expressions of a post-political condition of planning.

Institutional change is the result of a complex nexus of variables. In this chapter, we pointed at one particular element within those variables, which is often glossed over in planning research: the role of political coalitions. We do so in order to provide an understanding of institutional change which can be sensitive *both* to the viscosity, inertia and historical resistance of institutions, *and* to the capacity of endogenous agency to affect those frameworks *from within*. In our view, institutions are continuously reproduced and inherently resistant to change because they provide ways of understanding complex social interaction. They also do so in politics, providing structures that it make possible to organise collective decision making for complex societal changes. This capacity of endurance also explains why political coalitions in cities have an inherent tendency to conserve those regulatory frames that instrumentally reproduce established powers and interests. On the other hand, when coalitions do not react to social changes, they dissolve (or recur to authority to impose rules). This is why we see a permanent adaptation of power to new social conditions, a process that is hardly ever consensual and usually involves high potential for social and political conflict. This adaptation occurs through practices of active re-construction of institutions and the use of symbols to enable this process. The relation between sign and signifier entailed in a symbol perpetuates a particular established meaning of space while simultaneously stretching this meaning, drifting it towards other spatial or temporal formation. Giddens (1984) has called this process the 'regionalisation of localities' in his analysis of the structuration process. Yet, as constructed artefacts, symbols are politically biased and selective. They substantiate partisan dimensions of place to mobilise consensus around policies. Examples are numerous: the reuse of an industrial tower into a cultural tourist centre; the retrofitting of a factory building into a platform of cultural debate; the naming of certain development corporations after past industrial entrepreneurs. These are all practices of institutional reproduction of meaning through logics of symbolisation.

Planning is highly responsible for this process of signifying because it often attempts to link future and past understandings of place. This is also where the frustration of some planning-narcissists may come from, because space is always bounded to meanings, norms, habits and routines, and it cannot accommodate any utopian future that may be envisioned for it arbitrarily. Planning practice (and theory) thus have to problematise the political bias of these links between the past and future. Because of the intimate relation between institutions and political coalitions, symbols are never neutral. Politics unwinds through symbols, which selectively attain and nurture particular sets of institutional norms. Here, we have made a plea for the study of the political basis of symbolic practices in spatial planning, and for a careful analysis (and use by practitioners) of symbolic markers in their politically exclusive or inclusive effects. The following are therefore all crucial questions for a politically sensitive and socially engaged research on planning institutions: Can symbols be disruptive of established orders and produce radically new institutions? How do symbols differ in their social impact? How do symbols convey an inclusive and radically imaginative vision of cities?

References

Allmendinger, P., & Haughton, G. (2012). Post-political spatial planning in England: A crisis of consensus? *Transactions of the Institute of British Geographers*, 37(1), 89–103.

Avelino, F., Grin, J., Pel, B., & Jhagroe, S. (2016). The politics of sustainability transitions. *Journal of Environmental Policy and Planning*, 18(5), 557–567.

Berger, P. L., & Luckmann, T. (1966). *The Social Construction of Reality: A Treatise in the Sociology of Knowledge*. Garden City, NY: Doubleday.

Bourdieu, P. (1991). *Language and Symbolic Power*. Cambridge: Polity Press.

Brenner, N. (2015). Is 'Tactical Urbanism' an Alternative to Neoliberal Urbanism? *Post: Notes on Modern & Contemporary Art Around the Globe*. Retrieved from: http://post.at.moma.org/content_items/587-is-tactical-urbanism-an-alternative-to-neoliberal-urbanism.

Bulkeley, H., & Castán Broto, V. (2013). Government by experiment? Global cities and the governing of climate change. *Transactions of the Institute of British Geographers*, 38(3), 361–375.

Campbell, H. (2001). Planners and politicians: The pivotal planning relationship? *Planning Theory and Practice*, 2(1), 83–85.

Castoriadis, C. (1987). *The Imaginary Institution of Society*. Cambridge: Polity Press.

Dembski, S. (2013). *Case Study Amsterdam Buiksloterham, the Netherlands: The Challenge of Planning Organic Transformation*. Amsterdam: AISSR Programme Group Urban Planning.

Dembski, S., & Salet, W. (2010). The transformative potential of institutions: How symbolic markers can institute new social meaning in changing cities. *Environment and Planning A*, 42(3), 611–625.

De Groene Amsterdammer. (2000). Trek de grachtengordel door! Vergeten Amsterdam-Noord (17 February).

DiGaetano, A., & Strom, E. (2003). Comparative urban governance. *Urban Affairs Review*, 38(3), 356–395.

Dijkink, G., & Mamadouh, V. (2003). Identity and Legitimacy in the Amsterdam Region. In S. Musterd & W. Salet (Eds.), *Amsterdam Human Capital* (pp. 331–335). Amsterdam: Amsterdam University Press.

Dühr, S. (2007). *The Visual Language of Spatial Planning: Exploring Cartographic Representations for Spatial Planning in Europe*. Abingdon: Routledge.

Emirbayer, M., & Mische, A. (1998). What is agency? *American Journal of Sociology*, 103(4), 962–1023.

Engelen, E., & Musterd, S. (2010). Amsterdam in crisis: How the (local) state buffers and suffers. *International Journal of Urban and Regional Research*, 34(3), 701–708.

Evans, G. (2009). Creative cities, creative spaces and urban policy. *Urban Studies*, 46(5–6), 1003–1040.

Evans, J., Karvonen A., & Raven, R. (Eds.). (2016). *The Experimental City*. Abingdon: Routledge.

Fainstein, S. S. (1994). *The City Builders: Property, Politics and Planning in London and New York*. Oxford: Blackwell.

Fainstein, S. S. (2008). Mega-projects in New York, London and Amsterdam. *International Journal of Urban and Regional Research*, 32(4), 768–785.

Fischer, F. (2003). *Reframing Public Policy: Discursive Politics and Deliberative Practices*. Oxford: Oxford University Press.

Faludi, A. (1996). Framing with images. *Environment and Planning B: Planning and Design*, 23(1), 93–108.

Faludi, A., & Van der Valk, A. (1994). *Rule and Order Dutch Planning Doctrine in the Twentieth Century*. Dordrecht: Kluwer Academic.

Healey, P. (1992). Planning through debate: The communicative turn in planning theory. *The Town Planning Review*, 63(2), 143–162.

Friedmann, J. (1987). *Planning in the Public Domain: From Knowledge to Action*. Princeton, NJ: Princeton University Press.

Hirschman, A. O. (1970). *Exit, Voice and Loyalty: Responses to Decline in Firms, Organizations and States*. Cambridge, MA: Harvard University Press.

Geertz, C. (1973). *The Interpretation of Cultures: Essays in the Organization of Experience*. New York: Basic Books.

Gemeente Amsterdam. (2011). *Structuurvisie Amsterdam 2040: Economisch sterk en duurzaam*. Amsterdam: Gemeente Amsterdam.

Giddens, A. (1984). *The Constitution of Society: Outline of the Theory of Structuration*. Cambridge: Polity Press.

Gottdiener, M. (1982). Disneyland: A utopian urban space. *Journal of Contemporary Ethnography*, 11(2), 139–162.

Gottdiener, M. (1995). *Postmodern Semiotics: Material Culture and the Forms of Postmodern Life*. Oxford: Blackwell.

Hajer, M., & Zonneveld, W. (2000). Spatial planning in the network society – Rethinking the principles of planning in the Netherlands. *European Planning Studies*, 8(3), 337–355.

Innes, J. E. (1995). Planning theory's emerging paradigm: Communicative action and interactive practice. *Journal of Planning Education and Research*, 14(3), 183–189.

Iveson, K. (2013). Cities within the city: Do-It-Yourself urbanism and the right to the city. *International Journal of Urban and Regional Research*, 37(3), 941–956.

Kaika, M. (2010). Architecture and crisis: Re-inventing the icon, re-imag(in)ing London and re-branding the City. *Transactions of the Institute of British Geographers*, 35(4), 453–474.

Kaika, M. (2011). Autistic architecture: The fall of the icon and the rise of the serial object of architecture. *Environment and Planning D: Society and Space*, 29(6), 968–992.

Lefebvre, H. (1991). *The Production of Space*. Oxford: Blackwell.

Mahoney, J., & Thelen, K. A. (2010). *Explaining Institutional Change: Ambiguity Agency and Power*. Cambridge: Cambridge University Press.

March, J. G., & Olsen, J. P. (1989). *Rediscovering Institutions: The Organizational Basis of Politics*. New York: Free Press.

McFarlane, C. (2012). Rethinking informality: Politics, crisis, and the city. *Planning Theory and Practice*, 13(1), 89–108.

Metzger, J., Allmendinger, P., & Oosterlynck, S. (Eds.). (2015). *Planning Against the Political: Democratic Deficits in European Territorial Governance*. New York: Routledge.

Mossberger, K., & Stoker, G. (2001). The evolution of urban regime theory: The challenge of conceptualization. *Urban Affairs Review*, 36(6), 810–835.

Oudenampsen, M. (2010). Amsterdam Noord: van sociale naar ruimtelijke maakbaarheid. *Justitiële verkenningen*, 36(5), 27–40.

Peck, J. (2012). Recreative city: Amsterdam, vehicular ideas and the adaptive spaces of creativity policy. *International Journal of Urban and Regional Research*, 36(3), 462–485.

Pierre, J. (2014). Can urban regimes travel in time and space? Urban regime theory, urban governance theory, and comparative urban politics. *Urban Affairs Review*, 50(6), 864–889.

Pierson, P. (2000). Increasing returns, path dependence, and the study of politics. *The American Political Science Review*, 94(2), 251–267.

Rauws, W., De Roo, G., & Zhang, S. (2016). Self-organisation and spatial planning: An editorial introduction. *Town Planning Review*, 87(3), 241–251.

Salet, W. (2002). Evolving institutions: An international exploration into planning and law. *Journal of Planning Education and Research*, 22(1), 26–35.

Salet, W. (2008). Rethinking urban projects: Experiences in Europe. *Urban Studies*, 45(11), 2343–2363.

Salet, W. (2018). *Public Norms and Aspirations: The Turn to Institutions in Action*. New York: Routledge.

Salet, W., & Savini, F. (2015). The political governance of urban peripheries. *Environment and Planning C: Government and Policy*, 33(3), 448–456.

Salet, W., & Gualini, E. (Eds.). (2007). *Framing Strategic Urban Projects: Learning from Current Experiences in European Urban Regions*. Abingdon: Routledge.

Savini, F. (2013). Political dilemmas in peripheral development: Investment, regulation, and interventions in metropolitan Amsterdam. *Planning Theory and Practice*, 14(3), 333–348.

Savini, F. (2014). What happens to the urban periphery? The political tensions of postindustrial redevelopment in Milan. *Urban Affairs Review*, 50(2), 180–205.

Savini, F., Boterman, W. R., Van Gent, W. P. C., & Majoor, S. (2016). Amsterdam in the 21st century: Geography, housing, spatial development and politics. *Cities*, 52, 103–113.

Savini, F., Majoor, S., & Salet, W. (2015). Dilemmas of planning: Intervention, regulation and investments. *Planning Theory*, 14(3), 296–315.

Savitch, H. V., & Kantor, P. (2002). *Cities in the International Marketplace: The Political Economy of Urban Development in North America and Western Europe*. Princeton, NJ: Princeton University Press.

Sorensen, A. (2015). Taking path dependence seriously: An historical institutionalist research agenda in planning history. *Planning Perspectives*, 30(1), 17–38.

Stone, C. N. (1988). Preemptive power: Floyd Hunter's 'community power structure' reconsidered. *American Journal of Political Science*, 32(1), 82–104.

Stone, C. N. (1989). *Regime Politics: Governing Atlanta, 1946–1988*. Lawrence: University Press of Kansas.

Swidler, A. (1986). Culture in action: Symbols and strategies. *American Sociological Review*, 51(2), 273–286.

Swyngedouw, E. (2009). The antinomies of the postpolitical city: In search of a democratic politics of environmental production. *International Journal of Urban and Regional Research*, 33(3), 601–620.

Taylor, Z. (2013). Rethinking planning culture: A new institutionalist approach. *Town Planning Review*, 84(6), 683–702.

Terhorst, P., & Van de Ven, J. (1995). The national urban growth coalition in the Netherlands. *Political Geography*, 14(4), 343–361.

Uitermark, J. (2004). The co-optation of squatters in Amsterdam and the emergence of a movement meritocracy: A critical reply to Pruijt. *International Journal of Urban and Regional Research*, 28(3), 687–698.

Uitermark, J. (2009). An *in memoriam* for the just city of Amsterdam. *City*, 13(2–3), 347–361.

Van Eten, M., & Roe, E. (2000). When fiction conveys truth and authority: The Netherlands Green Heart planning controversy. *Journal of the American Planning Association*, 66(1), 58–67.

Van Gent, W. P. C. (2013). Neoliberalization, housing institutions and variegated gentrification: How the 'third wave' broke in Amsterdam. *International Journal of Urban and Regional Research*, 37(2), 503–522.

Vicario, L., & Martínez Monje, P. M. (2003). Another 'Guggenheim Effect'? The generation of a potentially gentrifiable neighbourhood in Bilbao. *Urban Studies*, 40(12), 2383–2400.

Yanow, D. (1996). *How Does a Policy Mean? Interpreting Policy and Organizational Actions*. Washington, DC: Georgetown University Press.

Yanow, D. (2000). *Conducting Interpretive Policy Analysis*. Thousand Oaks, CA: Sage.

Zonneveld, W. (2005). Multiple visioning: New ways of constructing transnational spatial visions. *Environment and Planning C: Government and Policy*, 23(11), 41–62.

Zukin, S. (1996). *The Culture of Cities*. Malden, MA: Blackwell.

19
THE URBAN COMMONS AND CULTURAL INDUSTRIES

An Exploration of the Institutional Embeddedness of Architectural Design in the Netherlands

Robert C. Kloosterman

The urban can never be simply conflated with a system of private property and competitive markets – indicative and normative ways – for diverse institutional arrangements both to deal with the technical market failures and to manage the common pool resources of the city as a whole.

(Scott, 2012, p. 25)

The market alone cannot meet our needs; nor can the state. Both, by rooting out attachment, help fuel the alienation, rage and anomie that breed extremism. One element has been conspicuously absent from the dominant ideologies, something that is neither market nor state: the commons.

(Monbiot, 2016)

The Quest for New Forms of Urban Governance

The urban environment has now become *the* typical milieu for Homo sapiens on a global scale. Accordingly, understanding how cities cope with social, economic and environmental issues is becoming ever more important. What, then, are the key conditions for liveable, sustainable and prosperous cities? And, more practically, which forms of governance can contribute to reaching these goals? The limits of allocation through markets, which was promoted as part of the neoliberal drive after 1980, have become much more manifest in the wake of the credit crisis of 2008 notably in the realm of social equity and climate change (Klein, 2014; Mason, 2015, Milanovic, 2016). A return to more statist approaches as in post-war Western Europe (Judt, 2005), it seems, is also not very feasible due the fundamental Hayekian problem of lack of knowledge which, arguably, has become even more serious with the increasing complexity and fragmentation of post-Fordist urban societies, and also because of the more mundane problem of lack of financial resources which many public actors face. There is, consequently, a quest for governance options which may counteract the obvious shortcomings of market allocation while avoiding some of the problems inherent in more statist approaches. There are many ways to look at urban governance – from the highly abstract to the detailed concrete and from the explicit normative to the descriptive and analytical empirical.

Below, I will use a rather modest window to analyse a specific case of the functioning of the so-called urban commons, the pool of resources in cities for which property rights are hard or even impossible to establish and therefore require forms of collective action. I will look briefly at how forms of collective action underpin a successful Dutch cultural industry, namely architectural design. The focus is on architectural design as an economic activity which can be seen as emblematic of advanced urban economies. Looking at architectural design may thus give us an understanding of how the urban commons function in relation to a wider set of economic activities. An outline of cities and the urban commons is given in the first part of this chapter. This is followed by an empirical illustration of a concrete example of a common pool of resources, based on earlier empirical research (Kloosterman, 2008, 2010a; see also Brandellero & Kloosterman, 2010; Heebels & Kloosterman, 2016; Stegmeijer et al., 2012). In the conclusion, some of the wider implications will be sketched.

Cities and the Urban Commons

Cities come in many shapes and sizes and quite a few attempts have been made to grasp what they have in common. Wilfully ignoring all kinds of finer distinctions and observations, cities can be seen, following Louis Wirth (1938), to boil down to a localised, sizeable human settlement with a relatively large population, which is densely populated. These complex interlocking man-made ecosystems comprise both durable physical parts, such as roads, buildings, sewage systems, internet infrastructure, and less tangible, but no less important and often also very durable, parts, such as governance systems, norms, values, financial transactions and cultural life. Myriad linkages between different parts exist in these relatively compact environments with a high population density, a refined division of labour and, related to this, an intricate social stratification. These parts interact thereby initiating a series of emergent effects, among them agglomeration economies, along path-dependent trajectories (Scott, 2012). From a spatial perspective, we can observe an elaborate mosaic of specialised land-uses containing social spaces where people live, production spaces, and circulation spaces (Scott, 1988, 2012; Scott & Storper, 2015). All cities, in principle, can be described in these rather abstract and general terms, but variations on this fundamental theme are both manifold and highly significant for the living standards, the quality of (everyday) life, the resilience and the spatial lay-out of cities (Fainstein, 2010; Kloosterman, 2010b; Kloosterman & Lambregts, 2007; Konvitz, 2016).

The long-term liveability and resilience of cities depends on meeting five basic requirements (see Hall, 1998):

(a) cities need a strong public authority which can guarantee the rule of law and public safety as well as being able to provide, directly or indirectly, basic services such as education, health care, garbage collection and physical network infrastructures;
(b) cities should have some kind of a democratic political system which allows for responsive, transparent and controllable governance in which the voice of citizens is heard and taken seriously;

(c) cities should be home to a set of competitive economic activities that provide jobs and generate incomes;
(d) cities have to be organised in an environmentally sustainable way with, among other things, clean water and air;
(e) cities must display at least some minimum degree of socio-economic equality both in terms of incomes and opportunity to achieve a certain level of social stability.

These very general requirements are sometimes conflicting in the short-term, and thus often demand a fine balancing act on behalf of the various relevant actors. Moreover, at least some of these essential requirements cannot be met through market allocation as property rights are hard if not impossible to establish, as in the case of much of the physical infrastructure, public safety, the environment, the underpinnings of competitiveness and social equality. They are, then, non-excludable and therefore prone to chronic undersupply. Some of these non-excludable resources are also non-rivalrous, which means that consumption does not affect the availability to others: using these resources is *non-substractive* as in the case of street lanterns (Ostrom, 1990/2011, p. 32). There are, however, also man-made resources and assets for which property rights are hard or even impossible to establish and, hence, difficult to exclude other users, but which are *rivalrous* in the sense that there is a limited stock which can be threatened by overuse as in the case of cities like Barcelona and Amsterdam where the large number of tourists tend to undermine the very quality of place which made them attractive in the first place.[1]

Although the distinction between 'pure public goods' which are non-rivalrous and common pool resources which are rivalrous makes analytically good sense, in practice they are not always easy to disentangle. What, for instance, may at first be seen as a pure public good, might turn into a rivalrous common pool resource if a certain threshold is reached as in the case of mass tourism where overuse is manifestly affecting other uses. It makes sense, therefore, to start an empirical analysis of the *urban commons* with the fundamental common characteristic of non-excludability and then proceed to define if and under which conditions these resources are rivalrous.

Given high costs or the impossibility to exclude users, these urban commons are liable to chronic undersupply if left alone to market forces thereby threatening the functioning of the city as a place to live, work and reside thus creating an inherent need for forms of collective action within the urban realm. In Allen Scott's view (2012, pp. 162–163), the very reproduction of capitalist society depends on these urban commons because:

1. markets cannot exist in the absence of legal and political structures;
2. unfettered markets are apt to give rise to many different kinds of corrosive outcomes (e.g. harsh labour conditions, pollution, recurrent crises);
3. markets are unable to deal in the long run with endemic political collusion between capital and labour over the distribution of the surplus into profits and wages.

(Scott, 2012, p. 163)

Seen this way, the presence and the reproduction of the effective urban commons are imperative for the survival of capitalist urban economies and not just based on a particular normative point of departure.

With respect to cities, Scott argues that the whole notion of markets and equilibria is not relevant for cities, because key elements – land-use and labour – tend to be inelastic and clustering "makes industries geographically lumpy and relatively hard to move" (Storper et al., 2015,

p. 22). Responses to external changes are often slow and cities develop along path-dependent (positive feedback) trajectories, contingent on particular points of departure and driven by increasing returns and positive feedbacks. Instead of viewing cities as a huge interlocking system of fluid and frictionless market transactions, they should be conceived as sets of gigantic urban commons of which agglomeration economies, the glue that holds cities together, constitute an essential part. What Scott proposes, then, is an ambitious urban research agenda in which forms of collective action may sustain and reproduce common pool resources straddling the field of urban studies with that of political economy and notably the path-breaking work by Elinor Ostrom, who has analysed the variegated landscape of institutional set-ups for providing these resources (1990/ 2011).[2]

The issue of common pool resources in urban contexts covers a wide range of aspects, which go far beyond the scope of this chapter.[3] I will seek to step down from the lofty heights of more abstract views and descend into the much less neat world of social reality and provide an empirically informed scan of the relationship between common pool resources and a specific economic activity. To be able to put this case in perspective, the next section goes into the role of knowledge in contemporary urban economies.

Cultural Industries, Architectural Design and Agglomeration Economies

Advanced urban economies thrive on the input of highly specialised knowledge. In an interesting approach Cesar Hidalgo (2015, p. 68), a statistical physicist, has conceptualised the economy as "a knowledge and know-how amplifier" where 'knowledge' involves the capacity to imagine and map more abstract relationships (as, for instance, in physics); and 'know-how' refers to the mostly tacit capacity to perform actions (ibid, pp. 6–7). In addition, he has coined the notions of 'person byte' and 'firm byte' which denote respectively the "maximum knowledge and know-how carrying capacity of a human" (Hidalgo, 2015, p. 82) and, *mutatis mutandis*, the maximum knowledge and know-how within one firm. Both are hard to quantify, but conceptualising these constraints sheds light on why networks of persons and firms are necessary to make complex products. Knowledge and know-how are sticky: they stick to persons, firms and networks. To be able to make complex products, many person bytes are needed and often they also transcend one firm byte and, hence, involve networks of firms. To reduce the transaction costs of the exchange of knowledge and know-how, persons and firms collaborating on a frequent basis tend to form spatial clusters of related economic activities.

This format also holds for cultural industries – economic activities concerned with producing and selling goods and services for which the main selling point is their aesthetic quality. Instead of competing just on price, many cultural industries markets display horizontal differentiation where products may differ along more dimensions within one price segment (Caves, 2000, p. 6). They are very much part and parcel of the economic profile of advanced cities, as nowadays a whole array of performing arts, consumer-oriented craft and artisanal industries, media and related industries as well specialised design industries, among which architectural design, generate a significant share of urban employment and income (Lipovetsky & Serroy, 2016; Scott, 2004). Their main production input is specialised knowledge to generate the aesthetic qualities and come up with stylistic and other innovations.

Cultural industries typically display a specific spatio-organisational format. Due to the volatility and unpredictability of demand, economies of scale are typically hard to reap and they tend to be vertically disintegrated forming spatially clustered networks of mainly small- to medium-sized firms often with one dominant large firm, a systems house (Scott, 2000), such as the Disney Corporation or LMVH which comprises among others, Dior, Marc Jacobs, Kenzo and Givenchy fashion brands (Lipovetsky & Serroy, 2016). Spatial concentration in specific urban areas, initiates recurrent processes of increasing agglomeration economies and increases both in size and in the social division of labour within these clusters along path-dependent trajectories. These agglomeration economies, "the principal force that makes activities geographically sticky" (Storper et al., 2015, p. 22), consist of the classic Marshallian triad of agglomeration economies: a localised pool of specialised labour, frequent exchange of knowledge and know-how and dedicated institutions dealing with, for instance, certification, product development and marketing.

Agglomeration economies are, by definition, spatially bounded *external* economies of scale. Many definitions of external economies abound, but they share the basic ideas that they cover gains or benefits of transactions accruing to third parties, that is, firms or persons which did not participate directly in those market exchanges, and these benefits are, hence, not reflected in the price (see Clark, 2003; www.businessdictionary.com/definition/externalities.html). They are, to use Alfred Marshall's (1919) dictum, "in the air". This famous observation does not just refer to their ubiquity in a certain place, but also to their elusiveness in terms of property rights: it is hard if not impossible to exclude users. Leaving the provision and reproduction of agglomeration economies just to market allocation would inevitably lead to undersupply. In some cases, the benefits of agglomeration economies can be qualified as non-rivalrous. This holds, for instance, in the case of the symbolic capital that a location may endow to specific products, such as fashion from Paris or Milan, music from Manchester or Nashville or architectural design from Rotterdam. They can, however, also refer to a subtractable pool of resources where use is rivalrous and overuse and even depletion of that particular stock is possible, such as in the case of a system of apprenticeships where there is a limited number of openings. This theoretical distinction between non-rivalrous 'pure' public goods and rivalrous common pool resources is anything but set in stone. In practice, there are all kinds of more blurred and rather dynamic situations requiring different institutional set-ups for provision and maintenance of these non-excludable resources. I will illustrate this by looking at the case of architectural design in the Netherlands.

Dutch design and notably Dutch architectural design – 'Superdutch' – are internationally renowned cultural industries (Kloosterman, 2008, 2010a, 2014; Lootsma, 2000; Rasterhoff & Kloosterman, 2014). From Marcel Wanders to Rem Koolhaas and from Piet Hein Eek's furniture to Ben van Berkel's UN Studio, Dutch design has made its name with daring stylistic innovations. High-end, innovative (*strong-idea*) and internationally oriented architectural design is concentrated in the two largest Dutch cities, Amsterdam and particularly in Rotterdam (Kloosterman, 2008; Kloosterman & Stegmeijer, 2004). Dutch architectural design was hard hit by the economic downturn after 2008 which led to a dramatic drop in domestic construction and, hence, demand for architectural design, but here we will briefly investigate the systems, the nature and the systems of provision of agglomeration economies. I specifically look at the localisation economies – those agglomeration economies which are more specifically related to one particular set of economic activities and leave out the more general urbanisation economies which, in principle, hold for all economic activities (see Jacobs, 2016). I follow the threefold division of a shared labour pool, exchange of knowledge, and dedicated institutions (see Storper et al., 2015).

A Shared Labour Pool

The presence of a sufficiently large labour pool of specialised workers constitutes a crucial agglomeration economy for many cultural industries. To be able to compete, innovative cultural industries are dependent on the input of highly qualified, specialised workers. In addition, they typically have to cope with rapid changes in demand and accordingly have to be able adjust their labour force. Being located in a place where it is relatively easy to attract extra, competent, workers at short notice is, therefore, of vital importance. In the case of strong-idea architectural design, (most) workers need to have formal qualifications from official schools of architecture to get a job. It turns out, however, that having an official diploma in architectural design is not sufficient. Part of the necessary skills in architectural design – as in many other cultural industries – are acquired through on-the-job training in intensive face-to-face settings: "Workers need to have not just the 'hard skills' (e.g. the ability to use complex 3D systems), but also the 'feeling' for particular styles and fashions … These soft skills are not very well codified and involve a lot of tacit knowledge" (Kloosterman, 2010a, p. 7). Transfer of this tacit know-how and knowledge and acquiring the *habitus* of an architect requires settings in which some kind of trust relationships exist (Fukuyama, 1995; Hidalgo, 2015; Kloosterman, 2008).

The creation and reproduction of the necessary skills is contingent on a local system of apprenticeships in which costs and benefits are not necessarily directly linked: one firm may invest in the soft skills of an apprentice, while another firm may reap the benefits while, later on, the first firm may benefit without having invested in that particular worker. Apprentices may, of course, also contribute right from the start to the firm – especially as they are usually paid only very meagre wages – but this is not a given. The overall benefits of the apprenticeship system are generated at the level of the cluster, and the irregular distribution of costs and benefits among individual firms make market allocation rather difficult. However, to be able to become officially certified as an architect in the Netherlands, an apprenticeship is mandatory (Heebels & Kloosterman, 2016). What has emerged is a bottom-up, organically grown system of apprenticeships resembling the pre-industrial guild system with its master–apprentice relationship (Banks, 2010; Epstein & Prak, 2008) and contributing to the reproduction of the localised pool of specialised labour – a crucial localisation economy (Kloosterman, 2008, 2010a). The stock of potential openings for apprenticeships is limited as became very clear during the downturn after 2008. The apprenticeship system in architectural design, therefore, displays the characteristics of a common pool resource: users (those who employ an architect after he or she has completed an apprenticeship) cannot be excluded while the use is rivalrous as the stock is subtractable.

The institutional set-up of this particular urban commons involves a hybrid of state-led regulation, informal arrangements among firms and a widely spread understanding of the long-term benefits of the apprenticeship system, probably partly based on the established architects own early career experiences.

Exchange of Knowledge

Innovative activities do not just thrive on the presence of talented workers, but they are also dependent on a more or less continuous exchange of all kinds of knowledge pertaining to stylistic and technological developments, to market and job opportunities, and, very prominently in cultural industries, to who is hot and who not. Clusters of related economic activities thus need conduits along which this embodied knowledge can be transferred. Much of this exchange in the architectural design cluster happens through workers moving from one architectural practice to another or setting up their own firm (Kloosterman, 2008). However, there are also other ways to exchange complex, context-dependent and topical knowledge. To put it somewhat more concretely: a cluster needs places or micro-spaces where workers can get together on a frequent basis and engage in conversations and identify the voice in the noise of the gossip (Kloosterman & Brandellero, 2016).

Our research has shown that architects of strong-idea firms in Amsterdam and Rotterdam do indeed frequently meet each other: "They often live within the same (cheap) apartment block in either Rotterdam or Amsterdam; go to the same lectures and also to parties of other architectural workers, and in many cases even have partners with the same background (mostly working for other practices)" (Kloosterman, 2008, p. 10). There is even a football competition for teams of Amsterdam- and Rotterdam-based architectural firms (www.archicup.nl/). These cluster-specific amenities fostering exchange of knowledge among workers in architectural design are then first and foremost bottom-up initiatives which then develop along path-dependent trajectories which are deeply intertwined with what Allen Scott (2000) calls "place-based communities". These communities comprise both the institutionalised places to meet and talk and the social networks based on trust to exchange this knowledge. Again, the knowledge is "in the air" but touches down selectively in concrete places where concrete people meet in trustful settings. The resource of knowledge itself is part of the urban commons and, in principle both non-excludable and non-rivalrous, but access to it is dependent on some kind of membership to relevant social networks, making it in practice more excludable and rivalrous, but, without the establishment of property rights. As with the maintenance of some fishing stocks, the presence of a small community with a strong social network and shared social norms is conducive to the reproduction of the combination of amenities and trust that enables the sharing of knowledge (Ostrom, 1990/2011).

Dedicated Institutions

These informal institutions enabling the exchange of knowledge form an important part of the "dedicated local institutional infrastructure" which also comprises public-sector instigated and publicly funded, local educational institutions (e.g. the Berlage Institute, the Department of Architecture and the Built Environment, Delft University, etc.) which reproduce, transfer and create knowledge. There are also other, not necessarily local, institutions which underpin the functioning of architectural design in the Netherlands, and in Amsterdam and Rotterdam in particular, by fostering competitiveness (along path-dependent lines) through the stimulation of R&D, quality control and the promotion of trust and exports. The national, publicly funded grant system selects innovative projects from architects and gives travel and project grants. This way, an institutional infrastructure is established which creates the conditions for innovation in a sector dominated by small firms where slack time is usually hard to come by (Brandellero & Kloosterman, 2010; Kloosterman, 2008). The highly diversified system of architectural prizes and competitions is not just a sector-specific system of quality control, but also establishes linkages promoting social networks and trust involving architects, critics, juries, customers and media.

More generally, what we observe in the case of Dutch architectural design is that the agglomeration economies are deeply intertwined and embedded in a rich, diversified sectoral institutional framework which weaves together excludable and non-excludable, as well as rivalrous and non-rivalrous resources. It is also an intricate combination of bottom-up, grass-roots initiatives; top-down state intervention; and formal and informal institutions. This lattice of relationships (Ostrom, 1990/2011) or, to use Bourdieu's terminology (Bourdieu, 2000), this *field* links producers and customers through intermediaries and enables the dissemination and reproduction of a specific habitus regarding quality and aesthetics comprising many institutional arrangements and actors. Much of these relationships are higher order emergent effects and help the cluster to generate increasing returns and move the cluster along a path-dependent trajectory.

The high level of organisation and institutionalisation of the field of Dutch architectural design, it can be argued, is also related to the *certification* of architects (Heebels & Kloosterman,

2016). The primary aim of professional certification is to set a minimum level of skill and knowledge for a certain profession: "with certification, any person can perform the relevant tasks, but the government or generally another non-profit agency administers an examination and certifies those who have passed, as well as identifies the level of skill and knowledge for certification" (Kleiner, 2006). Clients and the wider society are then up to some extent protected against incompetent practitioners and this should encourage demand for the services of certified professionals. From a more neoliberal perspective, certification is a form of protection which reduces competition and hence drives up prices. One could also take a broader view and look at how certification through the requirement of a minimum level of skills and knowledge contributes to the formation of a dense, multifaceted field which can also act as a forum for strategic choice and action (Scott, 2000) with permanent deliberation on different levels. Such an institutional setting allows for nuanced, interactive processes of "voice reaction", to quote Albert Hirschman (1992, p. 77), between practitioners, customers, educational institutions and others. In his view, success "of channelling individual voices requires members to join together, so that voice formation depends on the potential for collectice action" (Hirschman, 1992, p. 79). These processes of collective deliberation may strengthen the lattice or field even further. Without these conduits for "the articulation and channelling of opinion", actors face only two choices which are characteristic of the economic realm and arm's length market relations: go ahead with the deal or exit.

The relevance of architectural design for cities transcends that of merely providing employment and generating income. Using the communication channels that the field provides and by shifting the set of skills and knowledge that the certification of the profession stipulates, wider societal issues such as sustainability and liveability of cities which are related to the quality of the built environment and, therefore, to the quality of architectural design, may also be furthered (Heathcote, 2017; Heebels & Kloosterman, 2016).

Conclusions

We are, it could be argued, entering a new, though not necessarily brave, uncharted world regarding governance and public policies. The shortcomings of the relentless drive towards commodification and enlargement of the realm of market allocation excluding poorer segments of society from key services and even leading to debasing the very meaning and function of certain institutions essential for capitalism (e.g. rating agencies, reproduction of labour) have become very manifest. Social polarisation (Milanovic, 2016), growing uncertainty, environmental degradation and climate change, and, more generally, an erosion of trust in institutions and society at large are undermining the political stability of many societies. Populist revolts may threaten the rule of law and the very foundations of society. Notwithstanding the nostalgic views that some may have regarding the role of the state in Western countries during the "trente glorieuse" (the glorious 30 years from 1945 to 1975), there is no way back to post-war *dirigiste* statist policies. On the one hand, societies have become too fragmented, individualised and inserted in a myriad of global linkages to be governed in the way of the post-war reconstruction years. States, on the other hand, have seen their powers decline due to years of austerity and to their shrinking tax base as firms and rich people are transferring their money to offshore tax havens. Still, it is imperative that we find ways to protect and maintain common pool resources which underpin the social, economic and ecological sustainability of cities. To safeguard and enhance the quality of cities – "… simultaneously the most fragile of political achievements and the most necessary" (Mazower, 2017) – new forms of collective action and governance are needed. "How the commons can bring about a more ecologically sustainable, humane society" in order "to build human spaces in which the local, the distinctive, and the historical matter" is a concern David Bollier (2015, p. 2, p. 15) tries to address in his critique.

Above, an attempt was made to probe into how a competitive, knowledge-intensive activity is embedded in a wider framework which allows the generation of a whole array of resources which are out there, beyond the establishment of property rights. The window of entry, accordingly, has not been place- but sector-oriented. On the one hand, this has allowed a more focused identification of how the institutional framework may contribute to the emergence of agglomeration economies. On the other, this is inevitably a rather narrow approach and cities are, of course, much more than sets of economic activities and are confronted with issues which are much broader and more daunting than the competiveness of one particular cultural industry. However, there are more general lessons to be drawn from this particular case study.

A first lesson is that the generation of localisation economies – a pool of resources specifically for one set of economic activities – depends on a complex interplay of public and private actors with the former creating a broader framework in which the latter with bottom-up initiatives are able to thrive in an organic, interactive way. Secondly, the long-term development of such a shared political space is crucial in creating an effective field or lattice of relationships that is finely tuned and capable of enabling the creation of resources which are not provided through market allocation. Thirdly, it seems that it is not just that the provision falls outside the scope of market allocation, it also appears that crucial actors are motivated not just or primarily by profit maximisation but are intrinsically motivated to contribute to the field. Fourthly, the complexity and the significance of unintended emergent effects (second/third and higher order) and inevitable lack of knowledge of each individual actor makes targeted (instrumentalist) interventions difficult. This ties in with Willem Salet's view on institutional thinking: provide condition, focus on general norms rather than goals and solutions (see Salet, 2018 and Chapter 1 in this volume).

According to Allen Scott (2012, pp. 162–163) "… the continuation of capitalist society depends not only on individual action coordinated by markets, but also on wider institutions with the capacity and legitimacy to deal with the multiple breakdowns, failures, and lost opportunities that would inevitably undermine the viability of capitalism if individual decision-making and action alone were to prevail". What we now urgently need is a research agenda focusing on forms of collective action which are suitable for advanced urban economies thriving on knowledge and global linkages.

Notes

1 I owe this example to Jochem de Vries.
2 I am referring here not just to Allen Scott's book, *A World in Emergence*, but also to the lecture he gave on urban commons in Vienna, 26 August 2016, and I am much indebted to his insights.
3 This contribution is part of *The Urban Commons and Culture*, a larger research programme.

References

Banks, M. (2010). Craft labour and creative industries. *International Journal of Cultural Policy*, 16(3), 305–321.
Bollier, D. (2015). *Commoning as a Transformative Social Paradigm*. Retrieved from: http://thenextsystem.org/wp-content/uploads/2016/04/DavidBollier.pdf.
Bourdieu, P. (2000). *Les structures sociales de l'economie*. Paris: Seuil.
Brandellero, A. M. C., & Kloosterman, R. C. (2010). Keeping the market at bay: Exploring the loci of innovation in the cultural industries. *Creative Industries Journal*, 3(1), 61–77.
Caves, R. E. (2000). *Creative Industries; Contracts between Art and Commerce*. Cambridge, MA: Harvard University Press.
Clark, A. N. (2003). *The Penguin Dictionary of Geography* (3rd ed.). London: Penguin Books.

Epstein, S., & Prak, M. (2008). Introduction. In M. Prak & S. Epstein (Eds.), *Guilds, Innovation, and the European Economy, 1400–1800* (pp. 1–24). Cambridge: Cambridge University Press.

Fainstein, S. S. (2010). *The Just City*. Ithaca, NY: Cornell University Press.

Fukuyama, F. (1995). *Trust: The Social Virtues and the Creation of Prosperity*. London: Penguin Books.

Hall, P. (1998). *Cities in Civilization*. London: Pantheon.

Heathcote, E. (2017). Creature comforts: Buildings designed for humans and animals. London: Financial Times FT Weekend (4–5 March, 16–17).

Heebels, B., & Kloosterman, R. C. (2016). *Van binnen naar buiten: Een onderzoek naar de rol van de wettelijke titelbescherming voor interieurarchitecten*. Den Haag: Ministerie van Onderwijs, Cultuur en Wetenschap en Atelier Rijksbouwmeester.

Hidalgo, C. (2015). *Why Information Grows: The Evolution of Order, from Atoms to Economics*. London: Allen Lane.

Hirschman, A. O. (1992). *Rival Views of Market Society and Other Recent Essays*. Cambridge, MA: Harvard University Press.

Jacobs, J. (2016). *The Economy of Cities*. New York: Vintage.

Judt, T. (2005). *Postwar: A History of Europe Since 1945*. Harmondsworth: Penguin.

Klein, N. (2014). *This Changes Everything: Capitalism vs the Climate*. London: Penguin Books.

Kleiner, M. M. (2006). *Licensing Occupations: Ensuring Quality or Restricting Competition*. Kalamazoo: W. E. Upjohn Institute for Employment Research.

Kloosterman, R. C. (2008). Walls and bridges: Knowledge spillover between 'superdutch' architectural firms. *Journal of Economic Geography*, 8(4), 545–563.

Kloosterman, R. C. (2010a). Building a career: Labour practices and cluster reproduction in Dutch architectural design. *Regional Studies*, 44(7), 859–871.

Kloosterman, R. C. (2010b). This is not America: Embedding the cognitive-cultural urban economy. *Geografiska Annaler: Series B, Human Geography*, 92(2), 131–143.

Kloosterman, R. C., & Brandellero, A. M. C. (2016). 'All these places have their moments': Exploring the micro-geography of music scenes: The Indica Gallery and the Chelsea Hotel. *M/C Journal*, 19(3). Retrieved from: http://journal.media-culture.org.au/index.php/mcjournal/article/view/1105.

Kloosterman, R. C., & Lambregts, B. (2007). Between accumulation and concentration of capital: Toward a framework for comparing long-term trajectories of urban systems. *Urban Geography*, 28(1), 54–73.

Kloosterman, R. C., & Stegmeijer, E. S. (2004). Cultural industries in the Netherlands – path-dependent patterns and institutional contexts: The case of architecture in Rotterdam. *Petermanns Geographische Mitteilungen*, 148(4), 66–73.

Konvitz, J. W. (2016). *Cities and Crisis*. Manchester: Manchester University Press.

Lipovetsky, G., & Serroy, J. (2016). *L'esthétisation du monde. Vivre à l'âge du capitalisme artiste*. Paris: Editions Gallimard.

Lootsma, B. (2000). *Superdutch, de Tweede Moderniteit van de Nederlandse Architectuur*. Nijmegen: Sun.

Marshall, A. (1919). *Industry and Trade: A Study of Industrial Technique and Business Organization*. London: Macmillan.

Mason, P. (2015). *Postcapitalism: A Guide To Our Future*. London: Penguin Books.

Mazower, M. (2017). The endless exodus. London: Financial Times FT Weekend: The Best of 2016–2017 (1–2 April, 31).

Milanovic, B. (2016). *Global Inequality: A New Approach for the Age of Globalization*. Cambridge, MA: The Belknap Press of Harvard University Press.

Monbiot, G. (2016). The case for despair is made. Now let's start to get out of the mess we're in. London: The Guardian. Retrieved from: www.theguardian.com/commentisfree/2016/dec/13/despair-mess-commons-transform-society?CMP=share_btn_link.

Ostrom, E. (1990/2011). *Governing the Commons: The Evolution of Institutions for Collective Action*. Cambridge: Cambridge University Press.

Rasterhoff, C., & Kloosterman, R. C. (2014). *Designing Value: Modes of Production and Modes of Valuation in Dutch Design*. Paper presented at International Conference of Culture and Creativity, National Cheng Kung University, Tainan, Taiwan (4 December 2014).

Salet, W. G. M. (2018, forthc.). *Public Norms and Aspirations*. London: Routledge.

Scott, A. J. (1988). *Metropolis: From the Division of Labor to Urban Form*. Berkeley, CA : University of California Press.

Scott, A. J. (2000). *The Cultural Economy of Cities: Essays on the Geography of Image-Producing Industries*. London/Thousand Oaks/New Delhi: Sage Publications.

Scott, A. J. (2004). Cultural-products industries and urban economic development prospects for growth and market contestation in global context. *Urban Affairs Review*, 39(4), 461–490.

Scott, A. J. (2012). *A World in Emergence: Cities and Regions in the 21st century*. Cheltenham/Northampton, MA: Edward Elgar Publishing.

Scott, A. J., & Storper, M. (2015). The nature of cities: The scope and limits of urban theory. *International Journal of Urban and Regional Research*, 39(1), 1–15.

Stegmeijer, E., Kloosterman, R. C., & Lupi, T. (2012). *Bouwen op een sterk fundament: Een tussenevaluatie van het architectuurbeleid in opdracht van de ministeries van IenM en OCW*. Den Haag: NICIS Institute/Platform 31.

Storper, M., Kemeny, T., Makarem, N., & Osman T. (2015). *The Rise and Fall of Urban Economies: Lessons from San Francisco and Los Angeles*. Stanford, CA: Stanford University Press.

Wirth, L. (1938). Urbanism as a way of life. *American Journal of Sociology*, 44(1), 1–24.

PART 6

Institutions and Urban Transition

20
PRAGMATISM AND INSTITUTIONAL ACTIONS IN PLANNING THE METROPOLITAN AREA OF MILAN

Alessandro Balducci

Introduction

In this chapter, I will reflect on the story of planning in the city-region of Milan from the perspective of pragmatism and institutional thinking. Metropolitan planning is a theme on which I have done much research (and have extensive practical experience) and it can perhaps benefit from my peculiar perspective. Looking at planning at the metropolitan level means to deal with the problem of sustainability through one of the most important dimensions which is the capacity to address the issue of continuous urbanisation that has completely transformed the city-region creating congestion, pollution and resources dissipation.

The traditional method of managing urban growth and dealing with the problems that beset the ancient administrative subdivisions in Italy had been, for a long time, the annexation of municipalities surrounding the central cities. This happened recurrently in Italian history until the 17 March 1927, when the fascist regime of that time promulgated a law (Law 383) authorising the government to redesign the administrative subdivisions. This led initially to the reduction of the number of municipalities (decreasing from 9,200 to 7,000 in that year).[1] It was during the 1950s that the theme of metropolitan government assumed a new character. Post-war economic growth concentrated population and activities in urban poles in such a way that it became impossible to think of any kind of administrative fusion. The areas of influence of cities such as Milan and Naples, but also Genoa, Palermo and Rome,[2] became so wide that they even included municipalities belonging to different provincial areas.

The history of governing institutions for city regions is a continuous saga of attempts and failures. Municipal local government has always been the fundamental structure of territorial governance. But Italy has now about 8,000 municipalities, among them three with a population of more than one million – Rome, Milan and Naples. Even though the Italian Constitution of 1947 foresaw the creation of regional governments (indicating also the fields of autonomous legislative powers), until the 1970s the Italian institutional architecture, beyond municipal level, was based upon two hierarchical levels of government: the national and the provincial. During the long period of fast economic growth after the Second World War, both the traditional levels were criticised and challenged for their inadequacy to support the needs of modernisation and development in the country.

During the 1960s, widespread debate on the restructuring of the central state led finally to the institution of a regional tier of government in 1970. This grew in power following the decentralisation of public health, territorial planning, economic development, environmental policies and many others from the central state. Italian regions now number 20, including those with a special statute of autonomy (Trentino – Alto Adige, Friuli –Venezia Giulia, Valle d'Aosta, Sicilia and Sardegna). Around the same period the power of the provinces was also under discussion (Allione, 1976).

This debate gave way in some regions to the definition of a new tier of local government in the mid-seventies: the *Comprensori* ('territorial districts') – an institutional level less extended than the provinces, to be placed between regions and municipalities. The hope was that the Comprensori would have superseded the old provinces. However, after a short phase of experimentation at the beginning of the eighties, the idea of the new level of government was abandoned in favour of a redefinition of the role of the provinces both in territorial terms, with the institution of eight new provinces, and in functional terms, trying to revive the old provincial institutions. These provincial institutions were traditionally active in very specific areas such as road construction and management, education infrastructures and public assistance. With the reform law of 1990 (Law 142), the provinces were also granted planning powers. The same law also introduced *Città Metropolitane* ('metropolitan cities' – a new administrative division of Italy) in the most important city regions. These were intended to replace the provinces in metropolitan areas with a new institution that would also have taken powers away from the municipalities. But the institution of the Città Metropolitane wasn't implemented for a very long time. After a number of attempts to turn around the obstacles which prevented the implementation of a legislative decision, the process entered a phase of acceleration between 2013 and 2014 when the Renzi government decided to institute directly the new metropolitan authorities in the cities of Rome, Turin, Milan, Venice, Genoa, Bologna, Florence, Bari, Naples and Reggio Calabria, simultaneously abolishing the old provincial institutions.

In order to properly understand the complex process of bottom-up and top-down initiatives in creating planning institutions for the metropolitan authorities, I will use the case of Milan as an example of the conflict between a pragmatist approach and an institutional approach to the critical theme.

An Initiative from Below: The General Urban Plan

In the 1950s, after the frenetic period of post-war reconstruction began to slow down and the mass internal migration brought hundreds of thousands of people to Milan, the Municipality of Milan proposed to the Ministry of Public Works (the competent authority for the matter at that time) the institution of a *Piano Intercomunale* ('general urban plan') to include 79 municipalities around the central city. They realised that it was impossible to take planning decisions without trying to influence the surrounding territories, where problems often originated or had far-reaching impacts.[3] After a long phase of negotiation, the Ministry of Public Works decided, in 1959, to assign to the Municipality of Milan the task of preparing a general urban plan, including only 35 outer municipalities. However some of these municipalities opposed the ministerial decision, seeing it as interference by the central city into the powers of the small municipalities of the surrounding area. The conflict[4] led, in 1961, to the constitution of a voluntary consortium among all the municipalities of the Milanese area – called the *Piano Intercomunale Milanese*

(PIM) – organised upon a general assembly of mayors and an executive committee to enforce its decisions. This innovative solution, which guaranteed the same rights concerning planning decisions (and veto power) to even the smallest municipalities, was a way out of the initial conflict. A technical staff was established, funded by all the municipalities, assuming the task to design an intercommunal plan to be approved by the municipalities. The objectives of the new territorial plan were established in a chart licensed by the assembly of mayors at the outset "to define in comprehensive and far-reaching terms the territorial development in relation to the objective of man's welfare" and "to give to all the citizens of the metropolitan area equal opportunities to enjoy the advantages of living in a great city without suffering the disadvantages".

In 1963, the assembly of mayors approved the extension of the PIM area to 94 municipalities, and between 1963 and 1965 a very intense debate about the future form and character of the metropolitan area took place. This was the result of the popularity that the idea of metropolitan planning was conquering on the ground, even if there wasn't any formal authority of the PIM. Different planning schemes were developed and proposed by personalities who also represented different political orientations. The left-wing technicians, guided by Giancarlo De Carlo, proposed a scheme called 'the Turbine', which stressed the need to interrupt the oil-stain pattern of growth, consolidating external poles along the 'blades' of the Turbine represented by the radial infrastructure system. In contrast, the group of technicians linked to the Christian Democratic Party proposed a scheme of linear east-west development, with the intention of containing urban development in the rural, southern part of the area and in the already congested north, concentrating growth along the axis linking Milan with Turin to the west and Venice to the east.[5] Cultural positions were also influenced by the interests of political parties keen to attract development in the municipalities that they controlled, and this reinforced the divergence.[6] This new type of conflict gave rise to other issues: firstly, it became evident that a consensus on a unique general plan for the area would have not been reached through discussion among technicians or within the assembly of mayors because too many conflicting interests and objectives existed; secondly, the conflict was ascribed, by many technical and political actors, to the voluntary character of the institution that was obliged to follow the unanimity principle of decision making. Therefore, it became a widely shared conviction that the only way of having a general urban plan for the metropolitan area was to solve the deep weakness of the PIM – that is, by creating a new intermediate institution, directly elected, with power over territorial planning, following the model of British structural planning. While this, all too quickly, became an incontrovertible truth for which to engage the political arena, the attempt to solve practical problems in the short term, took two directions:

- The first focussed on reducing the expectations – arising from a general urban plan – by all the municipalities to a series of guidelines capable of gathering a general consensus in the assembly of mayors;
- The second aimed at giving more weight to the formal vertices of the organisation – the board of direction of the internal technical staff and the executive committee – that were quite strictly controlled by political parties (the only actors capable at this time of informally integrating decisions at the metropolitan level). Political parties in fact controlled mayors and planning officers in the municipalities, and so the nominations for the board of directors and for the executive committee of the PIM.

In 1967 a planning document was approved by the assembly of mayors entitled 'General Planning Scheme and Priority Implementation Guidelines'. This was not so much a compromise between the two main opposing schemes, but rather a less ambitious attempt to arrive at a general consensus among the conflicting parties and to set general objectives inspired by a rationalisation of the development pattern of the metropolitan area. The consensus was also reached because some of the real choices were postponed to a successive phase of detailed planning. The plan of 1967 remained as a kind of general statement that was not followed by formal decisions and this was seen by all the actors as a failure in accomplishing the mission of the PIM. This situation led to a new phase that began at the end of the sixties, characterised by different levels of effectiveness of the PIM, if only at an informal level.

While the internal technical structure was engaged in a never-ending process of producing the new binding metropolitan plan, the same structure played an important role in reviewing the local plans of the municipalities and trying to implement the general indications of the General Planning Scheme. This, however, was in the more uncertain framework of a voluntary and informal relationship. At the same time, the technical structure of the PIM was capable of promoting a series of sectorial projects. Among others it is possible to cite:

- The *Passante ferroviario* – a railway junction between all lines arriving at the city as the basis for a regional railway transport system, to be developed successively;
- The various proposals for the creation of metropolitan parks, particularly the *Parco Nord* ('North Park') and *Parco Sud* ('South Park'), two new parks with diverse characters – the first totally public and with an essentially recreational nature, and the second non-public and essentially devoted to the preservation of the agricultural environment – that would have been implemented in successive years;
- The constitution of a new consortium for planning and managing areas for low-income housing (CIMEP). This has continued to be a powerful institution for managing important portions of metropolitan growth.

This delegation of roles of assistance to municipalities, the promotion of new ideas and projects and the establishment of a new culture of planning among administrators have always been considered by the relevant PIM technical and political officers merely as by-products of the main activity of designing the plan to be formally approved. But the PIM was also the place where, through top political and technical management, political parties negotiated informally, behind the scenes, the opportunities for development that were put forward at the metropolitan level (Bellaviti & Fareri, 1984). And in this period, it is worth noting, a system of political corruption linked to development opportunities was growing silently. One of the most active property developers in the area at this time was Silvio Berlusconi – former prime minister and previous leader of the opposition. Among some relevant 'content'[7] innovations, he introduced the practice of informally obtaining the agreement of all political parties for his initiatives, at the highest possible level, in order to ensure approval for his plans despite frequent changes in the political colour of the various administrations. Of course, these negotiations were frequently contradictory to the PIM's role as planning authority. For example, Silvio Berlusconi's Milano 3 – a new town for 10,000 people – was built in the heart of the proposed Parco Sud under a proposed 'agricultural green' land-use designation. This highlights a problem of informal negotiation, as the initiative was only discussed within the vertices of the PIM controlled by political parties.

An Initiative from Above: The Institution of Territorial Districts and Metropolitan Authorities

Thus far, we have shown the main lines of development for the PIM. The anticipatory experience of a voluntary institution for planning and governing the city-region has all too quickly been liquidated. While at the same time and within the same institution, we have seen the development of many informal coordination activities that produced interesting effects of governance. The two tendencies are contradictory and even conflicting. The PIM fought for the creation of a new intermediate institution that could assume, among others, the powers of planning. During 1975 this process and perspective saw important changes in the context of action:

- A regional law was prepared and approved by *Regione Lombardia* ('Lombardy region') that started the *Comprensori* ('territorial districts'); the area of the PIM was identified as *Comprensorio 21* ('district 21'), and its technical structure became the Planning Bureau of the newly set institution;
- Given the perspective of the new institution, the process of elaboration of the new plan accelerated; the new proposal was voted by the assembly of mayors in April 1975.

However, the informal activity of integrating the decision-making processes, operated particularly by political parties, continued and strengthened as a consequence of a situation in which development opportunities were revealed as being less than they first appeared. Also, a new equilibrium between political parties of the left and centre imposed the need for negotiation. Until the beginning of the 1980s, *Comprensorio 21* ('district 21') and the PIM were at the centre of these rather schizophrenic processes of attempting to give form and content to the new intermediate institution and the process of informally offering an arena for negotiation among the political parties and between the public and private sectors.

The new decade marked a deep change in both these roles. In keeping with the deregulation ideology of the time, in 1981 the *Comprensori* ('territorial districts') were abolished after just a few years of operation. The PIM lost its institutional position, being obliged to resuscitate the voluntary organisation to survive. The territorial district plan quickly disappeared after two or three successive versions. In the political and technical debate the stakes were no longer planning the city-region, but rather the ability of Milan and its metropolitan area to keep pace with European competition. This required policies for the development of infrastructure, urban projects capable of sustaining investment in the inner city, and moving away from the logic of equilibrium, decentralisation and central planning of which the PIM had been one of the main supporters. At the same time, and partly for the same reasons, the central supra-local arena for informal negotiation of development projects became less and less necessary. This was partly because the more interesting projects were reconcentrated in Milan, but also because the political parties had learned to negotiate outside of metropolitan institutions. Another important change at this time can be represented by the multiplication of institutions that were active in the process of governing the city-region: legislation of the 1970s and 1980s created new institutions in many different fields, including public health, parks and green space, public instruction, environmental policies and many others. Governing the city-region became a process of working with many different actors and institutions, something which at this time was impossible to centralise in a pluralistic society such as that of Milan. After a decade of institutional uncertainty, while the urban region was growing even outside provincial and regional borders, a process of institutional reform at the national level arrived to a point with the implementation of Law 142 (1990) which for the first time recognised metropolitan cities.

In synthesis, Law 142 (1990) foresaw the establishment of metropolitan authorities with a special regime for the areas of Turin, Milan, Venice, Genoa, Bologna, Florence, Rome, Bari and Naples. The delimitation of each metropolitan area was assigned to the regions which would have to decide within one year, after consultation with the municipalities and provinces concerned.

The role of the regions was therefore decisive, while municipalities would have been only consulted. The options for the delimitation were quite varied, ranging from large boundaries substantially corresponding to the existing provincial jurisdictions, or restricted to the first urban belt. Moreover, the core city itself could remain as it was, or split into more municipalities to reduce the traditional disparity between the central municipality and those of the hinterland.

Apparently this looked a rational design, but it has since been blocked by resistance from the municipalities to losing their substantive powers, by the difficulties of regions in deciding the delimitation of new metropolitan authorities, by resistance from the provinces to disappear. Therefore metropolitan authorities in application of the Law 142 (1990) were never instituted.

The same Law 142 (1990), in the process of re-ordering of local powers, attributed territorial planning functions to the provincial authorities with the task of developing Territorial Coordination Plans, binding documents that should have been imposed on municipal authorities in the fields of growth control, environmental protection and infrastructure design. The first attempts to define the plan failed repeatedly due to the over-regulatory approach of the provincial government and the resistance of municipalities. The first Territorial Coordination Plan was approved in 2003 by a right-wing government; the following year, in 2004, the elected left-wing government started a process of radical revision of the plan which did not conclude its approval process. The following coalition government, again right-wing, in 2009, started the formation of a new plan which was approved in 2014, just before the abolishment of the provinces and the institution in its place of the new metropolitan authorities.

New Initiatives from Below: Municipal Activism and the Strategic Plan for the 'City of Cities'

In the second half of the nineties the municipalities of the urban region have been quite active in experimenting with new forms of cooperation. The themes were economic development, environmental policies and the institution of new parks, sharing of common services in various sectors like social assistance, waste treatment, transport and mobility (Pasqui & Bolocan, 1998). In some instances this form of cooperation was also inspired by the attempt not to be perceived only as the undifferentiated hinterland of Milan, but to be recognised, through cooperation, as multi-municipal 'cities' with a relevant population and a strong economic base. Some of them, starting from the positive experience of functional cooperation, developed their own strategic plan at the level of intermediate aggregations: Nord Milano, Adda Martesana, Alto Milanese, Magentino Abbiatense.

Drawing from this rich background, during the period 2004–2009 there has been also an interesting experience of preparing a strategic plan by the Province of Milan. Trying to overcome tensions between provincial and municipal authorities concerning growth control, and in order to sustain a cooperative approach on strategic issues, the newly elected provincial government decided to establish a new department for strategic planning and to start a process for the construction of a non-binding, innovative instrument to be produced together with municipalities of the area. Taking inspiration from the original positive experience of the PIM as a voluntary association, the strategic plan was developed with the technical assistance of the *Politecnico di Milano* ('Polytechnic University of Milan') (Balducci, 2003). The planning process was organised in many different streams of action (Balducci et al., 2011) based upon the idea of boosting sustainability and of favouring cooperation among municipalities in the 'city of cities'.

- The opening move was a document entitled 'City of Cities, a Strategic Project for the Milan Urban Region' presented as part of a public initiative in February 2006. A kind of white

paper on the themes of change in the urban region, rich in data and information, which launched the theme of *habitability* and presented the vision and the strategy.
- The second move was a *call for projects and good practices* which could contribute to the improvement of habitability in Milan's urban region. The idea of the competition as a planning tool was inspired by the German experience of the IBA Emscher Park.[8] The province received a huge response from Milanese society: foundations, universities, associations, individual or joint communes, non-profit organisations and private citizens all participated. There were 259 entries for good practices and new projects that covered various facets of *habitability* and portrayed a rich and lively local community that was keen to enter into a relationship with institutions in order to contribute to the development of relevant public programs.
- The third move was the preparation of an *atlas of policies and projects for habitability in the Province of Milan*, the outcome of a dialogue with the other 14 *assessori* ('councillors') and their managers. This was on the one hand an exercise in self-reflection and reciprocal internal information sharing within the provincial structure and across the sectors, and on the other hand an exercise in external communication and collecting information about what the province was already doing in the field of habitability. In total, 52 projects and policies were composed which could interface with the network of projects and practices coming from the competition.
- The fourth action was the launch of a limited number of *pilot projects*, designed to intervene in particularly relevant areas, such as the realisation of a peri-urban woodland, the trying out of innovative policies for housing access and a project for upgrading industrial spaces.
- The fifth step was organising an exhibition at the *Triennale di Milano*, an internationally recognised institution for the promotion of planning, architecture and design. The exhibition was held in the period May–July 2007 and provided information about the changes in the Milan urban region to a wider audience (10,000 people visited the exhibition) and translated the objectives of the project into a communicative language. At the core of the exhibition was the 'City of Cities Theatre', a meeting place where for two months an uninterrupted series of initiatives were held to construct, both literally and metaphorically, an arena in which people and decision-makers could meet and discuss the future of the urban region.
- The final move was the presentation, in June 2007, of a document entitled 'For the Habitable City: Scenarios, Visions and Ideas' in which all the actions initiated in the planning process were presented at the conclusion of this first phase, to illustrate what had been achieved at the different levels and to consolidate what the project aims were for the future.

The process has been really intense and with a great participation of municipal politicians and officers, local associations, private and public subjects. The *Città di Città* ('City of Cities') has experimented a new approach to planning based upon co-design, the involvement of different stakeholders and on the overturning of the usual hierarchical relations between governmental tiers. The limit again, as in the spontaneous forms of strategic cooperation between municipalities, has been due to the fragility of the informal process. In 2009, the elections brought to power a different coalition and all the work and the capital which had been produced during the previous five years has been set aside.

Back to Institutional Reform: The Real Establishment of New Metropolitan Authorities

Between 2013 and 2014 there has been a sudden acceleration in the realisation of the institutional reform which led to the creation of metropolitan authorities. This happened in the framework of cutting public expenditure with the abolition of provinces as directly elected institutions. Starting from a proposal of the previous government, President Renzi supported the approval of Law 56 (2014), which directly instituted ten metropolitan cities by 1 January 2015, together with the transformation of all the provinces into a lighter intermediate coordination body, non-directly elected, in those contexts in which they were not replaced by metropolitan cities. The issue of the definition of the boundaries of the new metropolitan authorities was solved by the identification of the borders of the provincial authorities. The mayor of the metropolitan cities is identified with the mayor of the capital city and the council is composed by the mayor and 24 councillors in the case of metropolitan cities with more than three million inhabitants, elected by the municipal councillors of the area. The law considers the possibility of a direct election only in metropolitan cities with more than three million inhabitants and only if the capital city is subdivided into districts with direct powers. Beyond the council, there is a Metropolitan Conference composed of the president and all the mayors of the municipalities that belong to the metropolitan city.

All the institutional roles are not paid in accordance with the principle of cost-cutting.

The metropolitan cities inherit the competences and roles of the former provinces (coordination) but they are also charged with new functions:

- to promote economic development;
- to integrate management of facilities, infrastructures and communication at the level of the entire area;
- to establish relations with other cities and metropolitan areas in Europe.

The instruments for the implementation of these ambitious objectives are a three-year strategic plan, which is the main guiding act; a territorial plan with a formal binding power towards municipalities; the management of public facilities at the metropolitan level; a mobility and road networks plan; the promotion of economic and social development. Regions and municipalities may assign to metropolitan cities further functions. In this complex situation, metropolitan cities have inherited a number of problematic issues from the provinces they have been forced to replace:

- a very critical budgetary condition, linked to the fact that the addition of new important functions has gone together with cuts of the finance from the state;
- a territorial configuration which is unable to embrace the real urban regions;
- a grey and opaque image of the old provincial institution whose structure they have assumed;
- a situation of competition with the regional institutions.

Nevertheless, there are also significant innovations introduced by the reform: different metropolitan cities may define their own statute; there is a strong accent on strategic action rather than on a traditional planning approach; they could even redefine via negotiation the total area included in the new authority. So far this freedom and innovative aspects have not been practised by the new institutions. The weight of the budgetary problems and the effort of dismantling the old provincial institutions have overwhelmed the capacity for innovation. One of the main problems, as in all the previous attempts, has been the idea of dealing with all the different metropolitan cities with the same norm. We know that metropolitan areas in Italy are very different. Milan is in a post-metropolitan phase with a provincial territory which includes only a minimal part of the vast urban region around it. Turin has an opposite situation: a provincial area that is much larger than the real metropolitan area. Bologna, Venice and Florence show an urbanisation structure based upon a linear development which still has little to do with the old provincial boundaries.

In Milan, after a troubled year dedicated to putting in place the new institution and dealing with the risk of financial default, some first moves have been made: the identification of homogeneous zones reinterpreting the territorial subdivisions of previous experiences, the preparation of the strategic plan which has been produced through a process of consultation with the municipalities organised in homogeneous areas. A document which is still quite abstract and light entitled 'Milan Real Metropolis, Possible Metropolis' wants to emphasise the realistic and pragmatic approach of an institution weakened by the difficult institutional transition.

Some Reflections about the Limits of Bottom-Up and Top-Down Initiatives

The Milanese planning culture has always been considered 'pragmatic' in a generic and lay sense. Most of the innovations in the planning culture in Italy stem from Milan experiments. This happened recurrently in the last 60 years: Milan has not experienced illegal development, like many other southern Italian cities including Rome, because the public administration has been able to adapt planning tools in order to allow rapid changes to the land-use regulations established in the 1960s (Graziosi & Viganò, 1970). Milan was the city which first introduced informal planning documents that changed the dispositions of the general urban plan:

- Documento direttore delle aree Industriali dismesse ('Framework plan for the abandoned industrial areas');
- Documento direttore del Progetto Passante ('Framework plan for the railway junction project');
- Documento di Inquadramento delle Politiche urbanistiche ('Framework document of urban planning policies');
- Programmi integrati di Intervento ('Integrated urban programmes').

All these instruments have been ways of coping with the rigidity of the statutory planning documents in a city which has been facing a rapid urban development.

If we look at the history of metropolitan planning we can see that, since the end of the 1950s, there has been the awareness of the metropolitan dimension as a crucial character of the city, and a pragmatic approach which has tried to solve the problem of coordinating decisions among the many municipalities through various means:

- The proposal to the central government of instituting a new planning authority;
- The organisation of a voluntary association when the formal solution was demonstrated to be impracticable;
- The exercise of the very important role of producing strategic visions, of making proposals and projects at the metropolitan scale (like the railway junction and the great metropolitan parks);
- The role exercised by political parties (through the board of directors of PIM), which has been a pragmatic solution to the problem of establishing an arena of negotiation for the development opportunities in the metropolitan area. Though questionable in terms of the formal legitimacy, this role has been able to solve problems of coordination and negotiations, in the spirit of the pragmatic approach. As noted by Salet, "the pragmatist orientation is essentially intentional, problem-led and solution focused … It does not delve into historical causes, ideologies, underlying social structures of action …" (Chapter 1 in this volume).

More recently the experience of strategic coalitions among the municipalities for dealing with problems of intermediate coordination and to claim the recognition as 'cities', and not as just hinterland, marked this pragmatic approach. The same could be said for the innovative experience of the strategic plan Città di Città launched by the province in 2004–2009, which led to a form of planning strongly based upon co-design and interaction, without any binding power.

But as we have seen in the story that I have described, the limit of this pragmatic approach is its fragility. All the efforts to solve problems with a pragmatic approach clash with the difficulty of conceiving a planning action which is not based upon legal authority. Voluntary initiatives are difficult and demanding because they must always rely on commitment to act and to cooperate. Therefore the escape from the fragility of these 'soft spaces' (Allmendinger et al., 2015) has always been sought in the direction of formal powers, institutionalisation and traditional forms of planning.

On the other extreme, the institutional approach is always rigid, abstract and unable to take into consideration differences. Moreover, it is always inspired by rational thought either in terms of planning epistemology or in terms of the idea of power implied. We have seen that the the institution of the *Comprensori* ('territorial districts') (1975–1980) was a flash in the pan which wasn't able to address the problem of renewing the idea of the intermediate tier of government for the resistance of existing provinces. The same happened with the institutional reform of 1990 with the establishment of metropolitan authorities which has been a complete failure at the national level, caught between the difficulty of defining the borders of the new authorities and the resistance of existing governments which would have been affected by the reform.

Even the last reform initiative, Law 56 (2014), which had the advantage of directly deciding to institute the new metropolitan authorities and to abolish at the same time the provincial governments, has suffered from this rigid approach. The metropolitan authorities are defined with the same characteristics and rules in ten different metropolitan areas of Italy which are profoundly different and some of them, like the *Reggio Calabria* ('Calabria region'), are even difficult to define as metropolitan. All these reform processes follow the myth of a rational approach (Webber, 1983) which clashes with the speed of change, the decreasing possibility of applying the same model to very different urban regions, the inability to go beyond a traditional idea of planning and the absolute failure in identifying the real urban region with the borders of the old province.

It seems that the pragmatic approach fails because of its fragility, and the institutional approach fails because of its rigidity. The issue at hand is how to reconcile the two perspectives since this seems to be increasingly necessary (see Salet, Chapter 1, in this volume).

The key question is what kind of institutionalisation is compatible with a pragmatic approach.

The planning literature has for a long time explored this direction, from the first reflections of Melvin Webber (Rittel & Webber, 1973) and Lindblom (1975) to the work of Judith Innes et al. (1993), Patsy Healey (2007), Jean Hillier (2007) and many others. But this rich reflection has only marginally penetrated institutional thought. Looking at the case study of Milan, it seems that when an institutional reform is proposed there is always a premature assumption of knowing what to do and a premature assumption of agreement between the different actors involved (Christensen, 1985). When the pragmatic approach recognises its limits, it strives for a traditional institutionalisation and is not able to look at innovative forms of institutionalisation. Informal, voluntary, bottom-up experiences need to be sustained by institutional support but not to be distorted and adapted to an abstract order that does not work. Institutional approaches need to become more flexible and able to contemplate differences, capable of becoming permissive rather than authoritarian (Webber, 1969), open to experimentation (Christensen, 1985), exploration and non-predetermined evolution. This would be the kind of institutional support that bottom-up pragmatic innovation needs to find.

In the last 20 years we have seen many signs of crisis both in the model of voluntary, informal pragmatic initiatives and in the top-down institutional approach. The time has come to practise a new relation between these two perspectives, only apparently in contradiction.

Notes

1 After the end of Second World War in 1945, many municipalities previously (compulsorily) suppressed or incorporated were restored passing from 7,681 to 8,102 in 1948, but this did not affect the great urban municipalities.
2 Rome is a very particular case: the municipality has a very wide territory (1,507.6 sq. km) that is eight times wider than the territory of Milan (181.7 sq. km), or more than 11 times wider than the territory of the Municipality of Turin (130.2 sq. km).
3 Even the Liberal Party that in 1956 proposed a project for establishing a new Provincia-Metropoli-Ambrosiana in order to cope with the problem of planning and governing a city-region that stretches from Milan to the northern province of Varese (Sernini, 1979).
4 The conflict was also characterised by the opposite political colour of the moderate Milan government and the red administrations of the surrounding municipalities.
5 A third scheme, proposed by the economist Mario Talamona (close to the Socialist Party), was based essentially upon a methodological proposal, rather than upon an image of development.
6 The 'Turbine' model gave the opportunity to assign important quotes of development to the southern *red* part of the metropolitan area that was at that time still untouched by the sprawl effect that had affected the northen part of the region, while the linear development concentrated the opportunities of development only upon the east-west *white* part of the metropolitan area.
7 Silvio Berlusconi invented the formula of the middle-class gated communities in Milan. With this model he realised two developments called Milano 2 and Milano 3 (each with a population of 10,000 people). His media empire had its origins in a private cable TV network, offered as a service to residents in his 'new towns'.
8 The innovative initiative of the Lander Renania Westphalia for the regeneration of the Ruhr-area, a basin with about five million inhabitants, which suffered due to massive de-industrialisation and environmental deterioration, was realised between 1989 and 1999 through a series of competitions that successively selected 100 projects (Kunzmann, 1995). The author wants to thank *Taylor & Francis* and *disP* journal for the permission granted to reuse in this different context some of the material describing the vicissitudes of metropolitan planning published in the article 'Policies, Plans and Projects: Governing the City-Region of Milan' (2003).

References

Allione, M. (1976). *La Pianificazione in Italia*. Padova: Marsilio.
Allmendinger, P., Haughton, G., Knieling, J., & Othengrafen, F. (2015). *Soft Spaces of Governance in Europe: A Comparative Perspective*. London: Routledge.
Balducci, A. (2003). Policies, plans and projects: Governing the city-region of Milan. *disP*, 152(1), 59–70.
Balducci, A., Fedeli, V., & Pasqui, G. (2011). *Strategic Planning for Contemporary Urban Regions*. Aldershot: Ashgate.
Bellaviti, P., & Fareri, P. (1984). La formazione del governo metropolitano: il caso del Pim tra decisione e legittimazione (1951–1971). In B. Secchi (Ed.), *Partiti, amministratori e tecnici nella costruzione della politica urbanistica in italia*. Milano: F. Angeli.
Christensen, K. S. (1985). Coping with uncertainty in planning. *Journal of the American Planning Association*, 1, 63–73.
Graziosi, S., & Viganò, A. (1970). *Milano Vendesi*. Milano: Relazioni Sociali.
Healey, P. (2007). *Urban Complexity and Spatial Strategies: Towards a Relational Planning for Our Times*. London: Routledge.
Hillier, J. (2007). *Stretching Beyond the Horizon: A Multiplanar Theory of Spatial Planning and Governance*. Ashgate: Aldershot.

Innes, J., Landis, J. D., & Bradshaw, T. K. (1993). *Issues in Growth Control Management.* IURD Reprint 248.

Kunzmann, K. (1995). Developing the Regional Potential for Creative Response to Structural Change. In J. Brotchie, M. Batty, E. Blakely, P. Hall & P. Newton (Eds.), *Cities in Competition: Productive and Sustainable Cities for the 21st Century.* Melbourne: Longman.

Lindblom, C. E. (1975). *The Sociology of Planning: Thought and Social Interaction.* In Bornstein, M. (Ed.), *Economic Planning East and West.* Cambridge, MA: Ballinger.

Pasqui, G., & Bolocan, M. (1998). *Accompagnare lo sviluppo. Guida alle politiche di sviluppo locale nell'area milanese.* Milano: F. Angeli.

Rittel, H., & Webber, M. M. (1973). Dilemmas in a general theory of planning. *Policy Sciences,* 4, 155–169.

Sernini, M. (1979). *Il governo del territorio.* Milano: F. Angeli.

Webber, M. (1969). Planning in an environment of change, part II: Permissive planning. *The Town Planning Review,* 39(4), 277–295.

Webber, M. M. (1983). The myth of rationality: Development planning reconsidered. *Environment and Planning B: Planning and Design,* 10, 88–99.

21
PARADOXES OF THE INTERVENTION POLICY IN FAVELAS IN SÃO PAULO
How the Practice Turned Out the Policy

Suzana Pasternak & Camila D'Ottaviano

Preamble

Focused on favelas and the recent intervention policies in favela areas, this chapter aims at analyzing how the extremely precarious housing reality of a significant part of the Brazilian low-income population ended up consolidating public policies initiated and conducted "outside of the law." Such as outlined in Chapter 1 by Salet, this volume addresses the dynamic between institutional conditions and the pragmatic development in cities. We will argue that the experiences of housing policies for low-income groups in metropolitan Brazil take a particular position in this field of tension. The prevailing practices of "illegal" housing of low-income groups have become so dominant in the last four decades that institutionalized policies and legislation have turned completely to the prevailing informal practices.

"Favelas" is the Brazilian word for irregular settlements located in invaded land, such as slums, squatter settlements and even shanty towns. Historically, the access to housing for the low-income population in Brazil was obtained, in general, in a precarious way and consisted of three basic types of houses: tenements, favelas and land subdivision in the outskirts of the city, including homeownership and self-building. Since the beginning of twentieth century, favelas have been the landmark of the city of Rio de Janeiro. However, since the mid-century, a house in a shanty town has been an important option for the low-income population not only in metropolitan areas, but also in almost all the Brazilian medium-sized and big cities (Pasternak & D'Ottaviano, 2015). The growth of the Brazilian cities throughout the second half of the twentieth century was characterized by the configuration of two distinct cities: a *legal city*, consolidated by the implementation of official land parceling (regularized), usually located in central areas, and designed for housing the middle and upper classes; and an *illegal city*, designed for housing the low-income class, characterized by the implementation of illegal (or irregular) land subdivision in the peripheral regions of cities, by the consolidation of favelas in diverse areas and by the provision of rooms in tenements in central historical districts.

In 1960, the urbanization rate in Brazil was 44.7%; since then, the concentration of the population in urban zones had gradually grown, changing from 55.9% in 1970 to 67.6% in 1980, and reaching 75.6% in 1991. The 2010 Census indicated that 84.36% of the Brazilian population lived in urban areas.

The demand for housing, urban services and infrastructure has followed the similar process.

> Brazil, like other countries of Latin America, has presented an intense process of urbanization, mainly in the second half of the 20th century. In 1940, the urban population represented 26.3% of the total. In 2000, it was 81.2%. Such growth seems to be more impressive if we consider the absolute numbers: in 1940, the population living in cities was 18.8 million of inhabitants, and in 2000 it was approximately 138 million. Therefore, it was verified that in sixty years the urban settlements were increased in order to house more than 120 million people ... It is a gigantic movement of building a city, necessary for residential settlement of such population as well as their needs for work, supply, transportation, health, electric power, water, etc. Although the path taken by the urban growth has not responded satisfactorily to all these needs, the territory was occupied and the conditions to live in this space were established. In any case, offhanded or not, all of the 138 million inhabitants live in cities.
>
> *(Maricato, 2002, p. 16)*

The urban growth of the population has concentrated, mainly, in the peripheral regions of the Brazilian cities. In absolute numbers, during the last 40 years the urban areas incorporated virtually 108 million new dwellers. The final results are cities with extensive peripheral areas, with a big concentration of inadequate housing located in favelas and illegal land subdivisions. Due to the lack of an efficient housing policy for the low-income population, the informal housing market has been conclusive in the configuration of our cities (D'Ottaviano & Quaglia-Silva, 2010; Pasternak & D'Ottaviano, 2015).

Until the middle of the 1980s, the local government and even the federal government strictly followed the legislation when dealing with such phenomena: according to the regulation, a city should not deal with this use of land. Favelas, for example, were seen as provisional housing and as an illegal solution and, for this reason, were ignored by the government.

According to public policies, innovative experiences, such as the intervention in favela areas of Rio de Janeiro, in the 1950s and, then, in São Paulo, in the 1980s, have paved the way for a new understanding of the ways in which the government could act in the vast irregular areas of the Brazilian cities. Under legal basis, the new Constitution of 1988 advanced by defining the need for an urban policy, as indicated in its articles 182 and 183 (Chapter II of the Urban Policy).

The closing of *Banco Nacional de Habitação* (National Housing Bank), responsible for the construction of big peripheral housing developments and the new Federal Constitution, marked a period of bigger participation of the cities, including in relation to the housing policy.

The approval of the Statute of the City (Federal Law 10.257), in 2001, defines the right to a city, the right to a respectable house and the social function of property as some of the paradigms of the national urban policy. The purpose of this chapter is to show how heterodox practices, even against the strict law, were increasingly used by the government, thus creating new precedents, and, how in some moments, the law was molded by the practice.

Favela in Brazil

Favela is defined and measured in Brazil as a settlement composed of dwellings, inadequate in general, in an area with deficient public infrastructure and improvements, and where the constructions are made without license in a third party land or unknown property. Until the middle of the last century, favelas represented a phenomenon almost exclusively situated in the city of Rio de Janeiro. Therefore, the first survey about favelas was conducted only in 1948, and only in Rio de Janeiro, the federal capital at that time. In 1950, the Brazilian Institute of Geography and Statistics (IBGE) decided, for the first time, to include favelas in the calculation of the population and the Federal District as the specific case study. In 1953, the IBGE, itself, released the first study document on the reality of the favelas of Rio de Janeiro: the census document was entitled "The Favelas of the Federal District" (IBGE, 1953). At that time, however, the quantitative surveys were very disparate from a geographic viewpoint. As such, publications about São Paulo, for example, and specific data about favelas were reported only in 1980.

At first, the concept of favela referred to a group of dwellings with at least two of the following characteristics:

- minimum proportions – building and residential groupings in a number generally above 50;
- housing type – predominantly *casebres* (hovels) or *barracões* (shacks of rustic aspect), constructed mainly with tin plates, zinc plates or similar materials;
- legal occupation condition – construction with no licensing and inspection, in third party lands or unknown property;
- public improvements – absence, in whole or in part, of sewerage, electric power, telephone and piped water;
- urbanization – non-urban area, with no streets, numbering or signal plates.

(Guimarães, 2000, p. 353)

Since the Census of 1991, the IBGE started using the concept of *subnormal agglomeration*.[1] The concept, though generic, was intended to encompass the diversity of irregular settlements existing in the country. Subnormal agglomeration encompasses favelas, invasions, *grotas* (humid land hollows), lowlands, communities, villages, *ressacas* (puddles in the process of drying up), *mocambos* (huts), *palafitas* (houses built on stilts), among others. In that demographic census, the data relating to favelas was collected in a homogeneous way throughout the country.

The last national census, of 2010, provided a great quantity of advances in relation to the identification and collection of data of subnormal agglomerations, based on a specific morphological research, with the geo-referenced identification and preparatory field visit to the agglomerations. Due to the former sub-numbering and advance in 2010, the quantification of favelas by the 2010 Census turned out to be more reliable, thus providing a significant numeric growth of favelas, mainly in the north region of the country.

According to the Sector Delimitation Guide, the 2010 Census ranked as subnormal agglomeration each complex comprising, at least, 51 housing units deficient of, in its majority, essential public services, occupying or having occupied, until recently, third party land (public or private) and arranged, in general, in a dense and disordered way.

Although this chapter uses census data, reliable and available throughout the national territory, we must keep in mind that it was underestimated, since it does not include small agglomerations. Such underestimation varies according to the city. In Rio de Janeiro, the feasibility of invasion

Table 21.1 Households and population residing in favelas, per capital city, 2010

Capitals (selection)	Number of private households in favelas	Population residing in private households in favelas
Brasil	3 224 529	11 425 644
Belém – PA	193 557	758 524
Fortaleza – CE	109 122	396 370
Recife – PE	102 392	349 920
Salvador – BA	275 593	882 204
Belo Horizonte – MG	87 763	307 038
Rio de Janeiro – RJ	426 965	1 393 314
São Paulo – SP	355 756	1 280 400
Porto Alegre – RS	56 024	192 843
Brasília – DF	36 504	133 556

Source: IBGE, Demographic Census (2010)

to *morros* (hills) facilitated the emergence of big favelas. Therefore, the underestimation is likely small. In São Paulo, some field researches indicated that 20% of the favelas have less than 50 houses; however, that data was collected in the 1990s when the favelas were small in size.

The several economic crises, the disparity in income, the land and housing price, in addition to significant urban growth contributed to the substantial increase in the favela population in Brazilian cities: between 1980 and 2000, Brazilian favela dwellings increased by 1,169,953 housing units, from 1.16% of total dwellings to 3.04% in 2000, reaching 5.61% in 2010 (3.22 million dwellings, with 11.4 million dwellers according to the census data). In the city of São Paulo, the percentage of the favela population increased from 7.40% of the total in 1991 to 11.38% in 2010, encompassing 1,280,400 inhabitants. The growth rates of the favela population in the city were significantly above the growth rates of the total population since the 1980s: between 1980 and 2010, 8.18% per year for the favela population and 3.08% for the total population; from 1991 to 2000, 4.18% and 3.07% respectively, and 6.93% and 0.57% for the first decade of the twenty-first century.

Table 21.1 shows the number of households and the population residing in favelas in some of the biggest capital cities of the country, in 2010. At that time, the favela population, even though under-numbered, totaled 11,425,644 people. In the city of Rio de Janeiro alone, 1.4 million of people lived in favelas; in São Paulo, 1.3 million. In the city of Belém, although the absolute number is smaller (758,000 living in favelas), 54% of the households are located in favelas.

The condition of housing and access to urban infrastructure vary considerably among the diverse favelas, cities and regions; however, the numbers show why, during the last four decades, the local, state and federal government idealized and implemented diverse intervention policies for such areas.

The City of São Paulo and the Favelas

The urban fabric of the city of São Paulo is marked by inadequate housing and irregular settlements not provided with ownership documents: tenements, irregular land subdivisions, favelas and even popular housing developments in poor condition. Until the middle of the 1980s, the government of São Paulo applied the strict law when dealing with such phenomena: a city should not, according to the regulation, allow such land use. Favelas, for example, were considered as temporary housing and an illegal solution and, for this reason, they were ignored by the authorities. Tenements, though recognized as multiple housing in 1916 (Municipal Law 2.333), were deleted from the Building Code in 1934, thus wrongly showing that they did not exist for the government. The solution was to root out those tenements and substitute them for respectable housing. But the income profile of the Brazilian population and the significant population growth in urban centers such as the city of São Paulo (in 1940, the city had 1,326,261 inhabitants and in 1991, 9,610,659; in 2010 São Paulo reached more than 11 million residents), in addition to the price of land and construction materials, cause the deficit in housing to increase as well as the irregular alternatives to spread over the urban fabric.

These numbers show how heterodox practices, even against the strict law, have been increasingly used by the authorities, thus creating new precedents. This section demonstrates the evolution of the favela population in the city of São Paulo and its characteristics; the following section deals with the first interventions and their logics, the recent policy of urbanization and maintenance of favelas, whenever possible. The law versus practice is the next item, covering diverse problems. A full collection of knowledge of favela settlement urbanization problems has been formed, thus informing the intervention policy. Finally, new problems, which have resulted from such practice, are reported. The paradigm of intervention has changed especially because of the social acceptance of some types of housing that was previously excluded by the government policies. If expulsion was frequent before, today the inclusion of favela residents is a respectable item. But, on the other hand, two types of urban standard were created: one of the "formal city," with much of the distinct urban fabric excluded and another of the "legalized city," which maintains many of its previous irregular urban characteristics.

The area of the urban fabric of the city occupied by favelas in 2010 was 4,304.6 hectares (10,632.86 acres), less than 3% of the city area. Such small pieces of the urban land house more than 11% of the city's population. The demographic density of favelas of the city of São Paulo is high: an average of 297.4 inhabitants per hectare (1 hectare=2.47 acres, 120.4 habitants per acre). The average density of the city is around 80 inhabitants per hectare. Such high density in favelas causes a series of problems: the proximity between the housing units obstructs insulation and ventilation of the houses, reduces privacy and compromises some of the public services such as garbage collection and mobility. And the space remaining for invasion within the urban fabric is reduced day by day, therefore making vertical growth the sole possibility of increasing such an area, or even constructing new units: in 2010, only 30.48% of the favela households were on the ground floor. More than 61% had two or more stories, built with no structural calculation at all and no space between units. In some favelas of the city the demographic density reaches more than 900 inhabitants per hectare, thus showing the lack of free space.

The intervention policies significantly changed with the offer to provide proper infrastructure in the favelas of the city of São Paulo. In 1980, only 22.6% of the favelas households were provided with a public water distribution system. In 2010, this figure had reached 97.8%. By 2010 electric energy, which in the 1980s was distributed to only 65.4% of the favelas households, was virtually universal (in 99.9% of the favela households). Garbage collection, always a serious problem due to the physical structure of the favela fabric itself, with narrow streets that make difficult the passage of the garbage truck, also increased from 42.8% of the houses having a regular garbage collection in 1980 to 98.9% in 2010. The collection is made with the help of containers; the families have to carry the garbage on foot to the containers if their houses cannot be reached by the trucks. However, at any rate, the garbage may be collected. Sewage is by far the biggest sanitary problem in favelas: in 1980 virtually no favela house was served with the sewage system, and in 2010 only 67.4% of the households were served with the public sewage system.

Slums in the city of São Paulo of the twenty-first century are not how they once were: a place with wood, *barracos* (shack), with no infrastructure at all. It is clear that wood *barraco* remains, mainly in new poorly structured favelas. But it is not the predominant model, as it used to be in 1980, when only 2.40% of the housing units had external masonry walls. In 2010, 96.31% of the favela houses were masonry made. Today, the favela landscape is grey from the concrete blocks on the lower levels and red from the bricks on the upper levels. Such change in the profile is also associated with practices of intervention: since the decade of the 1980s, electric energy and water services have been provided. These were prohibited before given that a state company could not make investments in an illegal area. Such practice has permitted the favela residents to feel safer with respect to the permanence of the site. Therefore, bigger investments in housing have become possible, transforming the *barraco* into a house, and ensuring better structural stability and comfort. In the 1980s, in São Paulo, the increase in the number of favelas and favela residents caused the government authorities to worry about public health and to conclude that the removal of so many people would be complicated. Therefore, they started the installation of infrastructure. In 1980, the external walls of 93% of the *barracos* were made of used wood, 46% of them had no flooring and 36% of the coverage was made of inadequate material.

In relation to occupation conditions, a continuous improvement has been observed over the years; if in 1973 a one-room house was predominant, in 2010 such proportion was less than 1%. Over-population indicators are improving with the number of people per room reducing 3.5 times from 1973 to 2010, and a reduction of 25% in the average number of people per bedroom. The percentage of houses with no individual toilet has virtually disappeared.

The practice of providing electric energy and a water system in the favelas of São Paulo, initiated in the 1980s, and the further practice of introducing periodic garbage collection and a public sewage system has changed the concept of living in a favela. Once the infrastructure was installed by the government, the dwellers observed that they had a consented ownership. After all, after the investment, what would be the logic of expulsion? And the certainty of permanence made possible the investment in improvements to the houses, thus changing the landscape of the favela forever. However, the favela space is distinct from the formal one, even after the urbanization: the streets are narrow, the fabric is heavily dense, the houses have continued to have deficient space and precarious ventilation and insulation conditions. However, the ownership of consumer goods stands out. The households were invaded by industrialized assets: color and flat screen TV sets, sound devices, washing machines, microwaves and even computers are frequently seen in favela households. In 2013, 46% of favela housing units had LCD, LED or plasma TV, such percentage grew to 67% in 2015 (Meirelles, 2015). In 2000, 18% of the households had vehicles, such percentage grew to 24% in 2010, and 15% have motorcycles. In bigger and better structured favelas the commerce is present, as well as the real property and land market.

The best housing conditions also brought a certain change in the profile of the population of São Paulo. Bigger and better structured favelas presented a socio-spatial differentiation, showing distinct sectors that house different social levels.

> The real favela is shown in diversity, full of defects and virtues ... the formula of stigmatization considers it as a set of 3 "p's": preto (black), pobre (poor) and proletário (proletarian) deprived of property.
>
> *(Meirelles, 2014, p. 134)*

The same author, director of Data Popular, showed that the percentage of dwellers of Brazil coming from A and B classes increased from 3% in 2013 to 7% in 2015 (Meirelles, 2015).

According to him, this includes families with income above R$ 5,000.00 (USD 1,600). In some cases, such income may reach up to R$20,000.00 (USD 6,250). The expansion of the formal work that occurred in Brazil between 2002 and 2014 resulted in a social improvement among favela residents.

> De facto, we can see that the entrepreneurial intention causes the emergence of a new elite in the favela, which is not the elite of drug traffic, violence, criminality – it is the elite of entrepreneurship. It is the owner of a bakery, of the grocery store, the guy who distributes water. The one who chooses to be the richest among the poor rather than the poorest among the rich.
>
> *(Meirelles, 2015)*

Flexible intervention programs, whether of urbanization or land regularization, made the favela an option less traumatic and with better life conditions. They are the result either of pressures by social movements associated with the defense of rights of the favela residents or the authorities' awareness that the favelas are the solution for the deficit of housing, less likely to be solved within the Brazilian economic scenario. In a city like São Paulo, how would it be possible to construct 350 thousand houses; where would they place them? Pragmatic solutions such as the improvement in the housing conditions of this population segment are used as a possible alternative. Such practice has been applied in the last decades of the twentieth century, as it is shown in the following item.

Interventions in a Favela: Evolution of the Paradigm.
The First Stage: Attempts to Remove and Replace the Favela

The first intervention in favelas in the city of São Paulo was the removal and the resettlement of the agglomeration in another place. The idea guiding this intervention was associated with the conception that the favela was a center of disease, crime, social disorganization and marginality. This pathology would be extinguished upon extirpation of the settlement and the removal of favela dwellers to adequate units. It must be remembered that the favela population of the city of São Paulo was small, around 100,000 people, thus making the removal possible. Although there was no disagreement between the practice of removal and the legislation applicable protecting the private property, the results were not encouraging. The housing nucleus where the favela residents were removed to was usually located in peripheral land with difficult access. As a result, the increase in transportation costs burdened the favela family's budget. And, the long distance between the service centers and the households prevented the female contribution to the family income. Their purchasing power was reduced, thus making it difficult to pay installments or rents, and so often resulted in a return to the favela.

In the 1970s, it was clear that the removal was justified only in emergency situations or for areas under risk. As a modal form of intervention in favelas, a more efficient and less traumatic policy was needed. So, instead of moving the favela residents to a definitive unit, they were taken to a so called Provisional Housing Villages (VHP). The VHP were constituted of a non-definitive lodging, constructed in the favela land, where an intense social service was rendered, aimed at providing the population with professional education, lettering and documentation and providing them with conditions to integrate into the city and the real property market. Even the physical project of lodging emphasized its temporary character, since non-definitive construction material was used: the VHP were built of wood; masonry was not used and bathrooms were collective. It was expected that after one year a family would be able to integrate into the formal market of housing and employment.

The theoretical applications that measured this form of intervention were inspired in formulations of social integration of the school of thought of functionalist sociology. They emphasized the idea that the favela would be the first housing alternative for a rural migrant, a springboard for the city, a necessary step for the integration to the urban life. At the VHP, the basic concern was to reduce the "necessary time" the migrant would stay in the favela, by providing some basic infrastructure, professional guidance and formal education. Therefore, in some invaded settlements, although the land was not a public property (in that, according to the law, any intervention could only be made with the owner's consent), the socially consented practice was that of allowing temporary housing, associated with social service. It has already been observed to be a more pragmatic and instrumental logic.

Criticism of this project was abundant. Besides the supposition of implicit social integration – and that has not been shown as true – empirical data, based on the favela census, the systematic collection thereof being initiated in the middle of the 1970s, showed that the favela residents were not recent migrants at all and the favela was not their first place of residence. The favelas were increasing inhabited due to poverty more than to direct migration. "At the beginning, the favela residents have not settled in *barracos* where they lived. They moved in the urban space, in a route of 'descendent filtration,' within the process of valuation of the urban land and the impoverishment of the labor class, from central areas to peripheral areas, from masonry houses to favela *barracos*" (Pasternak Taschner, 1997, p. 54, emphasis added).

At the end of the 1970s, the perception that the favela has come to stay and that the favela residents were workers, mostly employees registered in the industry of São Paulo, has showed the need of pursuing new solutions. The presupposition of social integration in a society like the Brazilian society has serious limits: the capacity of the economy of the city of São Paulo to incorporate the labor force into the dynamic poles of the economy is limited, in addition to the pre-requirements of professional competence and schooling. The numerical increase in the favela population in the city of São Paulo, which in 1980 totaled more than 335,000 people and 71,200 households, made difficult the construction of new units in complexes, even in peripheral regions, and the solution of integration into the urban fabric showed to be unfeasible. That fact led to an operational impasse: How should the problem of intervention be addressed? What type of methodology of action will avoid a total rupture of the system?

Some technical sectors believed that large-scale construction, prefabrication, industrialization and rationalization of the construction process would result in lower house costs, thus making it feasible for all. So, complexes such as Itaquera were constructed in the east region of the city, where some lower-cost models were introduced (light prefabrication systems with "Outinord" metallic formworks, structural masonry, etc.), with the support of the Metropolitan Housing Company of São Paulo (COHAB-SP) for the building of around 80 thousand housing units between 1980 and 1985. But the construction costs of the complexes for so many people were still unaffordable. The urbanization of favelas was seen as a possible alternative, and a pragmatic paradigm was considered in an effort to solve certain problems, such as the creation of alternatives for the improvement of infrastructure conditions of settlements and maintaining the population where they were, whenever possible. By doing this, the housing problem would have some type of cheaper solution and the public health problems caused by informal settlements would be minimized.

A basic problem in the favelas of São Paulo was the deficient electric energy supply, which made families resort to using candles or oil lamps. Fire was frequent and power failure either affected the childrens' studies or the possibility of a family to increase their income from night work that could be done at home. Moreover, clandestine connections, in general, would overload the electric system. To solve such problems, Eletropaulo (an electric energy supplier in São Paulo) was permitted to develop efficient ways to supply energy with minimum charges. Pró-Luz, a program for energy supply to favelas units, was established in 1979 and by 1987 it had already installed the system in almost all of the favela dwellings. Also in 1979, the Pró-Água program was established, proposing the extension of the drinking water system to the favelas, with connections to the households wherever possible. This was more expensive and complicated than the Pró-Luz program, due to the fact that the water pipeline is more difficult to instal than external electrical wiring. The objective of this program was to provide the favela residents with drinking water distribution, thus improving the sanitary conditions and reducing the infant mortality rate. Again, it was made an exception to the regulation applicable, which did not authorize state companies to render services in invaded areas. The exception was justified, given that it was not possible to leave so many people living with no sanitation system; not least because the informal urban fabric was local and prone to the propagation of various types of diseases. Even in a conservative government like that of Reinaldo de Barros, in the 1980s, the mass of favela residents (more than 400,000 people, around 5% of the municipal population) made the solution of removal unfeasible. Pró-Luz and Pró-Água were state programs. The same year, the city launched a local program of urban improvement and infrastructure provision, the Profavela, which had less significant quantitative expression. One of its model experiences was carried out in a favela of Jardim Educandário, the west zone of São Paulo, where all the housing units were demolished, and the population were temporarily lodged on land nearby. The former favela was provided with streets, sanitary infrastructure and electricity, and the households were reconstructed. The experience was highly interesting, with the guarantee of permanence in the same place, as well the guarantee of ownership of their houses. But it was expensive work and not replicable.

In any case, a new paradigm of action was observed: the permanence of residents in the favela and interventions that guaranteed the improvement of the whole urban fabric. The removal was first substituted for temporary permanence and then for consented permanence, and the favela territory was integrated into the urban fabric. However, the regulations applicable permitting the urbanization hindered a bigger advance in the land regularization. The proposal of the *Concessão de Direito Real de Uso da Terra* (Concession of Property Rights of Use of Land) allowing favela residents to own the land could not be implemented. In the 1990s, the favela uprading was supported by the Inter-American Development Bank and the World Bank. Also at an international level, the paradigm of intervention in favelas had already been changed: a wide program of land regularization occurred in Peru, with the support of the World Bank and under the inspiration of ideas from the Peruvian economist and author, Hernando de Soto (2000).

These achievements of the favela residents had a short life span. Upon inauguration of the new mayor of conservative profile (1986–1988), the removal actions were recovered mainly in upper class areas. The removal was made under the *Lei das Operações Interligadas* (Interconnected Operation Law) that allowed the exchange of the increase in the constructive potential of land plots due to the construction of popular houses according to a previous partnership between the government and the private sectors.

The Second Stage: Urbanization of the Favela

At that time in Brazil, the emergence of democracy and the end of the military dictatorship were on the march. With the end of the military government, the preparation of a new Federal

Constitution was initiated, which included a specific chapter establishing the principles of social function of property, formerly deemed absolute in Brazil. With the democratization, however, there was a draining of the housing policy at a national level (BNH – the National Housing Bank was closed in 1986). By creating the institution of *usucapião* (adverse possession) within the city, the Constitution provided legal support for the permanence of the population in occupied areas, which was absent before. The constitutional text is a landmark in the change of the paradigm with relation to favelas. However, at the same time, the popular mobilization and the political pressure for housing were increasing. The decentralization – democratic reaction against the excessive centrality of the housing policy applicable until then – made the city the main player of the housing intervention. But the legal mark had already been changed, making way for land regularization.

During the administration of Mayor Luiza Erundina (1989–1992), the urbanization of favelas in the city was one of main items of the housing policy. A government committed to popular movements and union struggles defined the lines of action that showed such commitment. The portrait of the city, drawn up by the government's technicians, showed the existence of a huge illegal city that housed the popular strata. The urban segregation was as an item to be avoided. The urbanization projects of the favelas were encouraged, this time with the participation of the population. Since 1990, in the city of São Paulo "26,000 families in 50 favelas have been assisted, provided with infrastructure: paving, land reparceling, water, sewage, drainage, access opening" (Município de São Paulo, 1992, p. 12). It is observed that favela urbanization practices in the 1990s went beyond the fixing of infrastructure: they included the construction of stairs and pavements. During the urbanization of favelas, the concept of environmental risk was introduced by establishing the intervention priorities. It was about the geomorphological risk for the residents: collapse, flood or undermining. The priority was to urbanize settlements with high geomorphological risk.

It is observed that – within ten years – the interventions in favelas have radically been changed, from the removal and lodging of favela residents in public complexes to the permanence of the residents in invaded land and improvement of sanitary and road infrastructure, maintaining the population in their own living places and maintaining the investment already made in housing.

In 1993, another government assumed the prefecture of the city of São Paulo, representing a political line distinct from the previous government. In the same year, research coordinated by the Economic Research Institute Foundation (FIPE) indicated the increasing percentage of masonry units in favelas – about 75% (FIPE, 1994). The profile of favelas has changed in relation to constructive and economic aspects. The FIPE research also showed a slight increase in the household income in favelas (ibid.).

The new municipal administration had, unlike at the time of Mayor Erundina, no commitment to popular movements. On the other hand, the concept that favela residents were very low-income workers, with a right to the city and to be integrated into the urban life had already been consolidated. The housing policy of the city became focused on a new social housing program, the Urbanization Project of Favelas with Vertical Construction (PROVER), more commonly known as *Projeto Cingapura* (the Singapore Project).

Projeto Cingapura maintains the favela residents on the same land, but in vertical housing units constructed by builders. It differs, then, from the favela urbanization of the previous government since it does not use the urban fabric already defined by the favela residents but provides them with finished and non-extendable units. However, it maintains the residents in the same occupied land.

It must be observed that in two decades the normative paradigm – expulsion of invaders of illegally occupied land and their removal to housing complexes in the periphery of the city – has been modified, applying a practice that has been improving, creating a new culture of intervention with the support of society and also of international organizations. Such practice was ratified by new laws, providing a legal framework (Prezeis[2]). Although left-wing political parties associate urbanization practices with the pressure of popular movements, it is worth mentioning that even conservative governments, probably moved by the conviction that the size of the favela population was huge and the resources available were few, understood that it would be more appropriate to integrate, in any manner, the favela into the urban fabric and guarantee a minimum of healthful conditions to its residents. It changed from a purely operating logic to institutional rules that ultimately ratified the previous pragmatic paradigm, providing legal reason. In relation to ethics, life conditions of a big population segment have been improved, investments already made in their households were maintained, respecting the culture and without imposing standards, and social inclusion has been increased.

The Third Stage: Legally Regulating the Illegal City

In the following administration, of Mayor Marta Suplicy, of the PT Party (2001–2004), programs of urbanization and regularization of the favela were restored. The Strategic Master Plan of the city of São Paulo (2004–2012) was enacted, and anticipated urban instruments such as Special Zones of Social Interest (SZSI), areas intended for social housing, where more flexible rules of organization of territory and units, permitted the regularization of urban areas, separated from the formal areas of the city. As opposed to the PT administration, when the urbanization experiences were mainly geared toward basic sanitation, the program implemented the Legal District, which aimed for a more comprehensive intervention that would consider in an integrated manner the urban qualification, the land regularization, the access to services and public equipment and green areas, in conjunction with social programs. At the same time, the PROVER program, inherited from the previous administration, continued with the construction of low-cost housing in previously occupied areas for the population that needed re-lodging either due to the urbanization works that required a more extensive area and, therefore, required the demolition of constructed housing units, or due to their houses occupying areas of environmental risk.

It must be remembered that the intervention paradigms in favelas had already been changed also at the federal level. In the middle of the 1990s, the federal Habitar Brasil program (1994) was introduced, which was based on the Constitution of 1988, which already emphasized issues such as the right to housing, the recognition of the illegal city, and the urbanization and regularization of land ownership in order to guarantee the permanence of the family in invaded areas. The program, though of small coverage, had the merit of re-opening the national agenda for the urbanization of the favelas and intended to assist the low-income population. The purpose of this was to aid the municipalities to implement the housing policy. In 2000, housing was recognized in Brazil as a social right. In 2001, the adoption of the Statute of the City marks the regulation of articles 182 and 183 of the Federal Constitution, related to urban policy and the social functions of property. The Statute of the City introduced, at federal level, urban instruments of regularization of illegal areas (SZSI, already existing in some Brazilian cities) and recognized the city as the main conductor of urban policy. The urban instruments of federal level provide the favela settlements with a perspective of full urbanization, that is, not only urban regularization but also of land regularization, with usufruct on possession and property.

Upon election of the mayor, again of another political party in 2005–2009, the housing policy was modified with partial abandonment of the projects of moving the low-income population to the center – *Morar no Centro* (Living in the Center), *Locação Social* (Social Rent),

Bolsa Aluguel (Rent Assistance), and PAR-Residential Lease Program – in favor of continuing the emphasis on favela urbanization. Cymbalista (2007) comments that the Marta administration mobilized resources to move the population to an area already served with infrastructure, whereas the Serra/Kassab administration mobilized resources to implement infrastructure for the population in areas deficient thereof. The municipal administration between 2005 and 2012 (Serra and Kassab) emphasized the action in favela urbanization. However, its way of action was different from that of the previous administration, when more structured interventions were predominant, and where in addition to the provision of sanitary infrastructure, public spaces (such as sport courts, plazas, etc.) were opened, thus requiring more removals, but leaving the urban fabric less precarious. The intervention standard of the 2005–2012 administrations anticipated the minimum number of removals possible and the maximum maintenance possible of the previous urban structure, reducing costs and meeting the needs of a bigger part of the population. As a result, the favela would continue with a denser urban fabric, with less equipment, without projects of parks or sport courts. Only basic sanitation equipment, access paving and stairs were considered as priority. The streets of the project were narrower than those of the Marta administration and land for the community and commerce use has not been provided. In relation to the land regularization, the process was continued, with the regularization of 115,000 units (of which 63,000 housing units were located in irregular public developments). The practice continued, but now with institutional support. The favela is now integrated, socially and legally, into the urban fabric. The precarious settlements, ignored before by the public policies, are now contained in maps and registers.

More and more governments at different levels – local and federal – have agreed to the possibility of urban and land regularization of the favelas. In 2007, the federal government launched the Growth Acceleration Program (PAC) that, in addition to works like roads and ports, implemented works of sanitation and urban mobility, divided in four big areas:

1. logistics
2. energy
3. social and urban matters
4. housing and sanitation

Since the beginning, the intervention in favelas has been indicated as a Priority Investment Project. Two main measures were defined:

> Support to enterprises of Integrated Sanitation in Precarious Settlements in Cities of Metropolitan Regions, of Integrated Regions of Economic Development or cities with more than 150,000 inhabitants; … and support to urbanization of precarious settlements.
>
> *(Ministério das Cidades, 2007, p. 3)*

This is the first time the federal government has allocated a high volume of resources for the urbanization of the favelas. The urbanization of the favelas will include basic works of sanitation and infrastructure, complementary works in areas that have already had previous interventions and also interventions in areas of risk or with environmental restrictions, such as watershed areas.

The first phase of PAC (known as PAC 1) was responsible for carrying out 621 operations that benefited 1.24 million families, at a cost of R$ 16.8 billion, about USD 5.4 billion (Comitê Gestor do PAC, 2010). Works such as the integrated urbanization of favelas in the Billings and Guarapiranga Dams, which included the environmental recovery of watersheds; the urban ordering of the *Complexo do Alemão* (a group of favelas in the north zone of Rio de Janeiro), which included works of mobility and the construction of new houses; and the integrated urbanization of the basin of the Beberibe River, with the removal of *palafitas* (stilt houses) and the construction of 5,070 housing units, are some of the interventions financed by the PAC–UAP (Urbanization of Precarious Settlements) program (Comitê Gestor do PAC, 2010). With PAC, the intervention policies in the favelas were not the responsibility of the municipalities alone, and turned out to be feasible only through partnerships between the local governments and the federal government, with significant financial support by the federal government (D'Ottaviano & Pasternak, 2015).

Concomitantly to PAC, the federal government, striving to mitigate the internal effects of the economic crisis of 2008, launched an ambitious house construction program (to be eligible, families must have a combined income lower than ten times the minimum wage). The intention was to encourage the construction sector, the traditional supplier of employment and invigorate the housing sector. The *Minha Casa, Minha Vida* (My House, My Life) program was published in the Federal Official Gazette on March 26, 2009, with the Provisional Decree No. 459, coming in effect on April 14, 2009. In June, 2009, it was substituted by Law 11.977. This law, apart from instituting rules for the financing of construction of housing units (see Chapter III of the Urban Policy), deals with measures on land regularization of urban settlements. It defines what is called:

eligibility of possession: title of recognition of possession of a real property object of the urban demarcation (definition of limits and area of the real property);
irregular settlements: occupation enrolled in informal or irregular land parceling, located in public or private areas, predominantly for housing;
land regularization of social interest: land regularization of irregular settlements occupied predominantly by low-income population, in cases of compliance with the requirements for usucapion or concession of special use for housing purposes, of real property located in SZSI or in areas deemed of public interest.

Again, practice and law are on opposite sides: Law 11.977 recognizes the authority of the city to regularize settlements in permanent preservation areas, occupied up to December 31, 2007, and include them in consolidated urban areas, provided that the study proves that such intervention improves the environmental conditions in relation to the previous occupation. There is a conflict between the "preservationist" and "environmentalist" viewpoint and the regularization of favelas. What is more important, preserving water courses and parks or guaranteeing the right to housing? What does "intervention to improve the environmental conditions" mean? Improve for whom? For a specific group or for the city as a whole? Until then, the favelas located in preservation areas (streamsides, regions of protection such as riparian zones, for example) could not be regularized under the environmental legislation. However, perhaps now they will find a way to make it possible. The Haddad administration (2012–2016), of the PT Workers' Party, followed the previous policy of the urbanization of the favelas with the aim to assist 70,000 families. At the end of the administration, in December 2016, it had assisted 49,000 families. And 200,000 families had their real property regularized.

From Practice to Policy

The favela case is paradigmatic because the favela areas are irregular areas either from the viewpoint of land or the construction of houses there. Due to their total irregularity, such areas constituted spaces where the authorities could not, at first, act under official terms. However, the increasing growth of the Brazilian favelas throughout the second half of the twentieth century caused the authorities to act in such areas, either on account of precarious housing conditions or also on account of problems related to sanitary conditions and public health issues. Specific intervention projects in the favelas, with the construction of infrastructure systems and access works, have become the rule, at first at the local level and, then, at the federal level. Since the end of the 1980s and throughout the 1990s, interventions in the favelas and even in infrastructure systems depended on the entrepreneurship of the local administration which had received partial support or federal resources.

Some cities such as Recife (Prezeis of 1987), Rio de Janeiro (Favela Bairro, starting in 1993), and São Paulo (Luiza Erundina administration, 1989–1993) implemented local intervention policies in favela areas and irregular settlements. But, many of the projects were interrupted due to lack of resources or legal restrictions, such as land regularization.

In the 1990s, urbanization programs started to be incorporated under official terms as an object of public policy in the various government spheres. At that time, specific interventions and gradual urbanization projects were predominant.

The 2000s saw two important changes to the Brazilian urban administration: the approval of the Statute of the City, in 2001, and the creation of the Ministry of Cities, in 2003. With the Statute of the City, normative issues aimed at ensuring the permanence of the favela population in their households were regularized. Instruments such as the concession of special use for purposes of housing (CUEM) and the urban or collective usucapion represented important advances for the population living in irregular settlements. The Statute of the City was approved in 2001, almost 50 years after the first favela interventions in Rio de Janeiro and 20 years after the first favela urbanization programs in São Paulo. It consolidated, under the applicable legislation, the right of the resident population to continue in the favelas, even though such areas have no legal land parceling or officially recognized possession. For the first time, the PAC–UAP program allocated a considerable volume of resources for intervention in favela areas regardless of the legal regularization of such areas or households.

The evolution of thought and action in the Brazilian favelas and in particular of the favelas of the city of São Paulo illustrate the change of paradigm: how a practice has been accepted and recognized to become a law. Today, the practice continues to be the focus of discussion: environmentalists criticize the permanence of precarious settlements in preservation areas, even though this was generally the case before 2007 and even though with urbanization the environmental conditions eventually were improved. At any rate, it must be remembered that the increasingly density observed in existing settlements, in general associated with vertical construction, affected the sanitation conditions.

Samora (2009, p. 28) observes that the area occupied by the favelas in São Paulo in 2003 and 2008 was virtually the same, but with an increase of population. The improvements in infrastructure and the certainty of permanence resulted in high density. In addition to this, the favela households were, in general, self-built, in a precarious way. Despite the "romantic" vision of the favela as a creative environment, the techniques and materials were traditional and often unsafe. And, because they were permanently under construction, the housing units, with unprotected slabs and non-coated walls, suffered from seepage problems and problems of thermal and acoustic comfort. Whatever the parameters for an adequate house, the favela household rarely follows them. According to Coelho (2017), an insulation study was conducted in the *Heliópolis* favela (in São Paulo) to ensure that each dweller could receive at least one hour of sunlight during winter solstice. It was observed that 35% of the units researched did not observe this requirement. In order that the dweller would be able to follow this requirement, it would be necessary to reduce the density from 1,207.5 inhabitants to 772.50 inhabitants per hectare, which would imply a significant removal. The excessive density causes, among other problems, humidity, fungus and mites. Safety problems are also common in favela households: in a hospital of the south zone of São Paulo, it was registered that a collapse of the slab commonly used in the construction of houses (due to a lack of contention grid) was responsible for 23% of hospital cases of spinal cord trauma.

Critics of recent processes of urbanization and regularization commented that urban fabrics and housing units have been legalized totally out of sanitary norms. Coelho (2017, p. 174) exemplifies the case of the *Nações* favela, in Diadema, in the metropolitan region of São Paulo: it is a favela already urbanized, with an incidence of 26.8 dengue fever cases per 1,000 inhabitants, when in the city of Diadema, as a whole, the incidence between 2007 and 2012 was 1.73 cases per 1,000 inhabitants. In the case of leptospirosis, in the city, the incidence for the same period was 0.16, whereas in the favela it reached 7.97 cases per 1,000 inhabitants. Even the urbanization did not provide the expected sanitary improvement. There is still a lot to do.

There are illegal things (such as favelas) that make sense in a country like Brazil. There are legal things (such as removal) that make no sense at all. But illegal things such as the absence of the guarantee of the minimum level of sanitation and survival conditions must not be tolerated: The permanence of favela dwellers in the invasion land and the title of the property, whenever possible, have now been regularized. The favelas, with their urban fabric distinct from the "formal city," now appear integrated on the maps of Brazilian cities and the official public statistics.

Notes

1 For purposes of this chapter, subnormal agglomeration is sometimes used as substitute for "favela."
2 The experience of the Regularization Plan of Special Zones of Interest (Prezeis) in Recife, in the 1980s, can be seen as the pioneer of the process of land regularization in Brazil and also as the instigator of a specific regularization to subsidize the project.

References

Coelho, C. B. (2017). *Melhorias habitacionais em favelas urbanizadas. Impasses e perspectivas*. Dissertação de mestrado apresentada à FAU-USP, abril de 2017.
Comitê Gestor do PAC. (2010). *Programa de Aceleração do Crescimento. Balanço 4 Anos 2007–2010*. Brasília: Comitê Gestor do PAC. Retrieved from: www.planejamento.gov.br/secretarias/upload/Arquivos/noticias/pac/Pac_1_4.pdf (acessado em 06/dezembro2014).
Cymbalista, R., & Samora, P. (2007). *Habitação e o contrlo social da politica publica*. São Paulo: Observatório dos Direitos da Cidadão, Polis, PUC-SP.
De Soto, H. (2000). *El mistério del capital*. Lima: Editora El Comercio.
D'Ottaviano, C., & Quaglia-Silva, S. L. (2010). Regularização Fundiária No Brasil: velhas e novas questões. *Revista Planejamento e Políticas Públicas – PPP IPEA*, 34, 57–84.
Fundação Instituto de Pesquisas Econômicas (FIPE)/Secretaria Da Habitação Do Município de São Paulo. (1994). *Favelas na cidade de São Paulo. Relatório gerencial*. Xerox: Março.
Guimarães, B. M. (2000). As vilas favelas em Belo Horizonte: O desafio dos números. In L. C. Q. Ribeiro (Ed.), *O futuro das metrópoles: desigualdade e governabilidade* (pp. 351–374). Rio de Janeiro: Revan/FASE.
IBGE (Instituto Brasileiro de Geografia e Estatística). (1953). *As Favelas do Distrito Federal*. Rio de Janeiro: IBGE.
IBGE (Instituto Brasileiro de Geografia e Estatística). (2010). *Demographic Census*. Rio de Janeiro: IBGE.
Maricato, E. (2002). *Brasil, cidades. Alternativas para a crise urbana*. Petrópolis: Vozes.
Meirelles, R. (2014). *Um pais chamado favela: a maior pesquisa já feita sobre a favela Brasileira*. São Paulo: Editora Gente.
Meirelles, R. (2015). Radio Interview, *BBC* Brasil (May 3, 2015).
Ministério das Cidades. (2007). *Programa de Aceleração do Crescimento – PAC – Manual de Instruções. Projetos Prioritários de Investimentos – PPI, Intervenções em Favelas. Período 2007–2010*. Brasília: Ministério das

Cidades. Retrieved from: http://downloads.caixa.gov.br/_arquivos/assitencia_tecnica/doc_basic_25/PPI_Favela.pdf (acessado em 06/dezembro2014).

Pasternak, S., & D'Ottaviano, C. (2015). Favelas: Intervention Policies and Practices Regarding Precarious Dwelling in Brazil. In B. Aldrich & R. Sandhu (Eds.), *Low-Income Households in the Urbanizing World: Retrospect and Prospects*. Jaipur: Rawat Publications.

Pasternak Taschner, S. (1997). Favelas e cortiços no Brasil: 20 anos de pesquisas e politicas. *Cadernos de Pesquisa do LAP 18*. São Paulo: FAU-USP (Revista de Estudos sobre Urbanismo, Arquitetura e Preservação, 18).

Samora, P. (2009). *Projeto de habitação em favelas: especificidades e parâmetros de qualidade*. Tese de doutoramento apresentada à FAU-USP. São Paulo: FAU-USP.

Município de São Paulo. (1992). Secretaria da Habitação e do Desenvolvimento Urbano. *Urbanização de Favelas em São Paulo: Uma Experiência de Recuperação Ambiental*. São Paulo: Município do São Paulo.

22
AMBIGUITY AS AN OPPORTUNITY
Coping With Change in Urban Megaprojects

Stan Majoor

Institutional Reflection and Pragmatic Action in Urban Megaproject Delivery

Urban megaprojects that combine investments in real estate, public spaces and infrastructures are a key element of competitive urban policies (e.g. Carmona, 2009; Grabher & Thiel, 2015; Majoor, 2011; Oosterlynck et al., 2011; Orueta & Fainstein, 2008; Salet & Gualini, 2007). Powerful networks of public and private elites stimulate them with narratives about economic growth, improved urban services and the realization of lively urban spaces. Due to their complexity and size, time spans for design, decision making and delivery habitually exceed 20 years. It is therefore not a question *if* projects need to handle changing circumstances, but *how* they can cope with them. As growth oriented mostly speculative plans, turbulence in global real estate markets and economic cycles, such as the 2007–2009 Global Financial Crisis, are a major source of such a changing condition (Enright, 2014; Holgersen, 2014). Next to these, complex *political* environments are an important contingency factor, as electoral dynamics and resulting changes in different levels of government often impact political priorities and public financing (Altshuler & Luberoff, 2003). At the same time, continuous technological and societal developments change the way people use cities, spent leisure time and organize workspaces. These contingencies all have potential, but mostly unforeseen, impacts on the conditions in which urban megaprojects are realized and how their built spaces perform.

Existing studies on urban megaproject planning and delivery show that projects often evolve quite haphazardly and with great difficulty in response to external turbulence (Del Cerro Santamaría, 2013; Fainstein, 2001). As Mintzberg and Waters (1985) have argued in the past, organizational strategies over longer time frames are always characterized by combinations of deliberate interventions and emergent approaches. What is underexplored in the field of urban megaproject studies, however, is the question of to what extent this turbulence can work to improve the results of projects. In other words, how can projects benefit from the changing 'landscapes' in which they are implemented? (Teisman, 2008) The term *evolutionary resilience* has been introduced recently in planning theory to study the ability of such complex socio-ecological systems to change, adapt and, crucially, transform in response to external stresses and strains (Davoudi, 2012, p. 302; Folke, 2006, pp. 259–260).

Salet et al. (2013), in an analysis of urban megaprojects focused on infrastructure connections, suggest that a form of *institutional ambiguity* can be helpful in this regard. Central in this thought is that to intelligently cope with changes, projects should not create simple straightforward missions, but complex, possibly contradicting missions that enable variety in their repertoire of pragmatic actions over time. Projects that are purely focused on narrow strategic missions, such as the realization of a one-sided real estate program, have less capacity to strategically shift in a situation of economic or political turbulence. The concept of institutional ambiguity does not intend to keep things 'vague' but attempts to sustain a field of tension between different norms over the course of the planning and delivery of projects. When missions are created around potentially conflicting economic, social and ecological goals, more resilient capacity is expected since new forms of operational concretization over time can be facilitated.

To realize such an open strategic mission, the relationship between institutional reflection and pragmatic action is key. Both organizational studies and planning literature have shown a peculiar interest in approaches that, in the face of complexity and uncertainty, combine flexibility and adaptability on the one hand with parsimony of decision making and delivery on the other (Giezen, 2013; Hillier & Healey, 2010; Koppenjan et al., 2011, Raisch & Birkinshaw, 2008; Savini et al., 2015; Savini & Salet, 2017). It is exactly this challenge that requires a sensitive interaction between institutional reflection and pragmatic action in the strategic planning and delivery of urban megaprojects. They can therefore be seen as critical cases to find out to what extent it is (im)possible to balance practices geared towards more adaptable planning approaches, which have been popular in recent theoretic and applied debates in planning (Boelens & De Roo, 2016; Lydon & Garcia, 2015), with more traditional practices of creating reliable investment objects for public and private actors.

To foster such a capacity, not only should the strategic mission of an urban megaproject be framed in an ambiguous way, but the organizational features of its project management should complement such an approach. This is a complex requirement, because one of the distinguishing features of complex urban megaprojects lies in their multitude of involved actors, both public and private, that are partly dependent on each other. Organizations coordinating these projects should therefore combine capacities to explore *and* exploit existing knowledge (Majoor, 2015a). While exploration requires activities to enhance search and variety, exploitation requires the capacity to make decisions and be task-oriented. While the former activity requires forms of redundancy or organizational slack, and a cushion of excess resources (Bourgeois, 1981), the latter requires efficiency. These two distinct types of activities fulfil complementary functions; finding an optimal interaction between the two over a longer time frame is seen as crucial for organizations to cope with turbulent contexts (Farjoun, 2010; Lewis, 2000).

This chapter analyses the relationship between institutional reflection and pragmatic action in urban megaprojects that had to cope with external contingencies. The main research question is: *To what extent have urban megaprojects been able to create a form of strategic ambiguity to guide them through changing times?*

We have indicated that the two important indicators for such a capacity are:

1. The presence of a normative ambiguous mission;
2. The presence of an organizational capacity able to combine institutional reflection and pragmatic action.

To study this question, we selected three urban megaprojects because they were comparable in a couple of key aspects. The first criterion was that the cases would need to quantitatively and qualitatively meet the requirements of a megaproject: a minimum size of 100 hectares, a building program of over one million square meters, and a planned development trajectory of at least two decades to represent a certain size and impact. Next to these, a qualitative indicator of 'complexity' was used: cases would need to have a certain programmatic complexity in a combination of interdependent investments in real estate, infrastructures and public spaces. The second criterion was that only cases that faced – during their development and implementation period – substantive turbulence in their economic, financial, political, social or technological conditions would apply. And finally, to optimize comparability, cases were sought that were developed since the 1990s in Western democratic contexts and gave the researcher adequate entrance to primary and secondary sources of data.

Eventually three cases were selected: Amsterdam Zuidas (the Netherlands), Copenhagen Ørestad (Denmark) and Melbourne Docklands (Australia). Zuidas and Ørestad were studied in earlier research projects. All cases have been studied in depth over a long period of time (minimum of three months). A variety of research methods were used: site-visits, semi-structured expert interviews with professionals and academics and literature reviews. The analysis follows a systematic order. First the projects are briefly introduced to set out their strategic mission and their organizational set-up. Then, their response to recent external turbulence is assessed. Finally, the conclusion compares the cases and answers the main research question.

Retrofitting Amsterdam Zuidas

Background of the Project: Strategic Mission and Organization

From the 1990s, Amsterdam's urban policies entered a time frame of more entrepreneurial urban policies (Healey, 2007). The Dutch capital city developed in a monocentric way during most of the twentieth century under strong municipal leadership. Emphasis in planning was on the provision of social housing and services. Under the impression of growing national and international competition for economic functions, interest from the municipality grew to prepare the city for this new era via different bold spatial–economic development schemes (Savini et al., 2016). Initially, the degrading banks of the river IJ were targeted for a major overhaul. However, investors were more interested in the south side of the city, in the emerging corridor of infrastructure between the city and the quickly expanding airport (Salet & Majoor, 2005). From the mid-1990s onwards, the municipality aimed to coordinate some haphazard economic investments there in a more coherent area development project, named *Zuidas* ('South Axis' in Dutch) (Gemeente Amsterdam, 1998). The strategic mission of the project was to develop the area into a 2.5 million square meters 'second city centre', with a combination of high-density office and housing developments centred around the enlarged Amsterdam South station for (high-speed) train and metro (Gemeente Amsterdam, 2009).

The most important actors were the local government, the municipality of Amsterdam, that owned most of the land, and several large financial institutions that operated both as investor and user of the area, most prominently in the first phase two major Dutch (internationally operating) financial institutions: ABN/AMRO and ING. The central infrastructure corridor of the motorway, station and train was under the control of the national government. This created a complex negotiation and bargaining trajectory between the actors, since the municipality preferred to develop a better integration of the two parts of the area via a tunnelling of all the infrastructures with air-rights development (Majoor, 2006). The municipality created a Zuidas project organization to optimize the relations with market actors and work more efficiently (Gualini & Majoor, 2007).

On the waves of economic growth, the project began with mostly office-oriented investments. Quickly Zuidas developed into the most prestigious and expensive Dutch site for financial and legal sectors, with also some presence of international companies. Although Zuidas established itself as a prominent office location, its strategic mission to become a new lively urban district was not fulfilled in its first decade (Majoor, 2009). One of the reasons for this was that the infrastructure tunnelling option – needed to create the conditions for an extensive housing program – stalled in complex negotiations with the national government (Majoor, 2008a). The Global Financial Crisis and an overproduction of office space in the early 2000s coincided at Zuidas with a well-publicized real estate fraud (Van der Boon & Van der Marel, 2009). Altogether, from 2008 onwards, for almost four years, hardly any plot of new land was developed and the image of the project was severely weakened. The major investors, ABN/AMRO and ING, had to be financially saved by the national government. On top of that, the municipality implemented strict budget cuts. The project entered a phase of reconsideration.

Reacting to Turbulence

Our analysis shows that there was not one overarching 'new' strategy in Zuidas in response to its crisis. Its response was a combination of a few programmatic and symbolic changes. Different building plots that became suddenly vacant, because planned real estate investments were delayed or cancelled, were opened up for temporary community usage. This created an interesting disruption in the, until then, business-oriented area, as community gardens and places for temporary sports, arts manifestations and culture popped up. From a programmatic point of view, most interesting was the launch of the '15-by-15' programme, which proactively aimed to repair some of the perceived problems of the project. The ambition was to improve public spaces, create more ground-floor uses, attract events to the area, realize facilities that catered to a wider public and inspire a more open perspective towards change (Gemeente Amsterdam, 2010). Regarding the foreseen building program, gradually a change was made towards the less crisis-prone housing market, in which, next to expensive apartments, new opportunities were created for the addition of middle-income segments and (expensive) student studios. Currently more than 2,000 units have been realized, with plans to create about 5,000 more units in the next 15 years. This is slowly helping to materialize Zuidas's desire to become a mixed urban location.

Next to these ambitions and concrete actions, a new consensus was created for the central dock zone plan. The original plan for a complete tunnel for road and rail with real estate on top turned out to be unfeasible in light of technical difficulties and huge market uncertainties (Van Eekelen et al., 2014). Due to the Global Financial Crisis, private investors became even more reluctant to commit to such long-term schemes. The national government, the municipality and the infrastructure operators slowly came to a more modest proposal: a (shorter) tunnel for the motorway, the train and metro systems would stay above ground, and there would be no integration with real estate development. A deal between public partners was struck in 2012 to develop this new 'dock model' in a public-public partnership (Ministerie Infrastructuur en Milieu, 2012). After a long design and financial engineering process, a development consortium was awarded a building contract at the beginning of 2017. In the years before the Global Financial Crisis, opportunities were explored to develop the area by a completely integrated public-private partnership, a novelty in size and magnitude for the Netherlands. In light of the quickly changing financial parameters, however, this plan was cancelled, and the Zuidas Project Office was re-integrated in the municipal organization as a Zuidas Department (Majoor, 2015a).

Coping With Change in Urban Megaprojects

Figure 22.1 Zuidas's emerging urban programme around het Gustav Mahlerlaan
Source: Picture by Guilhem Vellut is licensed under CC BY 2.0

From 2014–2015, real estate development at Zuidas picked up strongly. Several new housing projects were developed, while masterplans for the last two big development areas have been prepared (Majoor, 2018). In many cases, temporary uses have been replaced by traditional building projects. Moreover, the area has now become livelier due to the new housing program in combination with improved public spaces, particularly around the central public transport station. Under pressure from left-wing political parties in the Amsterdam city council, a decision was made in 2016 to allocate 33% of future housing plans for the area to affordable social housing, and 15% to middle-income apartments. A quite intensive public participation trajectory was made in 2015–2016 to create input for an updated masterplan for Zuidas's development. This new plan emphasizes the quality of public spaces to be constructed and the the temporary use of space during the construction of the central dock zone. It also highlights the desire to enhance the area's international character, the importance of connectivity to green and water infrastructures, and more attention for bike routes and public transport (Gemeente Amsterdam, 2016).

Retrofitting Copenhagen Ørestad

Background of the Project: Strategic Mission and Organization

The Ørestad project was conceived by the Danish state and the municipality of Copenhagen at the beginning of the 1990s as an attempt to solve different political and economic problems (Andersen, 2003). Due to a planned major infrastructure investment in an Øresund railway and motorway bridge between Copenhagen and the Swedish city of Malmö (opened in 2000), the state and city foresaw strategic development potential in a strip of land on the island of Amager, south of Copenhagen's city centre, next to the connecting infrastructure to the bridge (Majoor & Salet, 2008). The development concept was to realize a compact, relatively high-density mixed-use area, serviced by a new public transport system. Internationally oriented offices would be the major (60%) share of the program (Ørestadsselskabet, 1995). New for Denmark, and contested by different left-wing political parties and critical observers, was that the whole development was purely market-oriented.

To organize the development, the Ørestad Development Corporation was established, with the City of Copenhagen (55%) and the Danish state (45%) as stakeholders. This corporation obtained a cheap government-backed loan to develop land and infrastructures and would, over the course of time, pay off its debts by the proceeds of the land sales (Christensen, 2003). The initial urban design structure of Ørestad was completely geared towards the metro and its stations: it was a linear city with high-density urbanization in walking distance of the metro stops (Majoor & Jørgensen, 2007).

The project had a rocky start, with delays in the realization of the metro and disappointing land sales for office construction in its first years (Majoor, 2008b). The forced relocation of state institutions to the area and the development of its prime parcel into an indoor shopping mall that circumvented Danish shopping regulations, did not contribute to its popular image. However, with an uptake in demand for housing, the mid-2000s saw a surge in construction in the area.

Reacting to Turbulence

Denmark was hit hard by the Global Financial Crisis. Just like the Netherlands, the inflated real estate sector became a major source of economic turmoil (Carstensen, 2013). Housing prices in central Copenhagen fell by approximately 40% from 2007 to 2009. The development of apartment blocks in the Ørestad South area came to an abrupt standstill. Plans for a large office complex, Ørestad City, designed by Daniel Libeskind were abandoned. Project developers and financers faced bankruptcies. The crisis forced the development corporation to devaluate their still unsold land and extend their debt repayment periods (By & Havn, 2013). Financial hardship coincided with a deeper general concern about the project's future, regarding its economic and urban ambitions: for the office market and higher segments of housing, the emerging development of Copenhagen's harbour (first in the south, and then from 2009 also in the north) became a successful competitor (Majoor, 2015c). In these difficult circumstances, two major types of planned adaptations were observed: (1) a change in governance and financial structures of the project, and (2) a change in program and urban design ambitions.

Under pressure from financial difficulties, the Ørestad Development Corporation was abolished in 2007 and the development of Ørestad was integrated into a new Copenhagen City & Port Development authority that was also responsible for public-owned development parcels in the port area. At the same time, a new public company, Metroselskabet, was founded that would become responsible for the construction of a much-wanted extension to the new metro system with a city ringline. This company was funded by a new large government-backed loan based on the portfolio value of the undeveloped publicly owned plots in Ørestad and the harbour area. This construction kept the basic premise of the financial model of Ørestad intact – creating land profit to fund public infrastructure – but partly reorganized its risk and extended the payback time horizon (Majoor, 2014).

Figure 22.2 Ørestad's post-crisis housing row development complementing its pre-crisis apartment blocks
Source: Photo by Majoor

With plot development almost at a standstill for four years, the new development authority started to slowly reconsider a change in building program and design ambitions. Different than the governance and financial changes, which were quite strong and quickly implemented, programmatic and urban design adaptations progressed slowly, however. There has not been a specific program to rethink or adapt the project. Rather, we observed a pragmatic set of changes to respond in certain parts of the project to both citizens' demands and the changing positions of the developers and financers of the new real estate projects. Although the main layout principle of a linear city clustered around the different metro stations remained, within the 'development fields' changes were visible. Smaller plot sizes were introduced. That was both a reaction to the reduced capacity of large developers to take on big plots at once, and to an emerging belief by the project's planners that they could enhance the urban character of the area. Another change was to create more single family housing units instead of the original concept of (iconic) large apartment blocks. Connected to this, some of the large green wedges that were originally planned to create proximity to parks throughout the area were reconsidered. The lack of liveliness of the first ones created in the centre of the project, in combination with a demand for more private green spaces (gardens) helped developers convince the development authority to make changes. This is most visible in the Arena quarter, a new 'post-crisis' development that is based on small blocks with private green areas, and a more complex road structure. The densities of blocks of this new development area have been lowered, but by abandoning large collective green spaces the overall building program – and land proceeds – stayed within the original financial framework.

Due to these developments Ørestad slowly re-emerged, not as a major business hub, but as a partly suburban housing location in close proximity to the centre of the city. With a growing population of families, the program had to be adapted to cater for their needs. Schools and a library were added to the program. Due to the crisis, and fuelled by an emerging community of residents, several empty development plots were used for temporal activities. Community gardens and (adventure) playgrounds are examples of a slowly emerging "second layer" in the urban spaces of Ørestad, complementing its extremely planned "first layer" (Ifversen & Lindhe, 2013).

Retrofitting Melbourne Docklands
Background of the Project: Strategic Mission and Organization

The Melbourne Docklands project was initiated at the beginning of the 1990s. Just like in many other harbour cities at that time, transforming (partly) obsolete industrial waterfronts into mixed-use office space, residential and entertainment districts was a popular initiative (Lehrer & Laidley, 2008; Oakley, 2011). The project also fitted well with an overall Australian focus on neo-liberal urbanization strategies (Freestone, 2014). Oakley (2011) emphasizes the importance of the successfully constructed narrative at its time of initiation, that Melbourne would become an international 'backwater' if it would not change its urban development policies. This perceived importance of global competitive pressures helped to create the political capital to pursue a rather bold statement: Docklands would become a prime private sector investment opportunity to complement Melbourne's existing central business district (CBD) and Yarra river developments with a new vibrant area for high-quality office space and housing developments (Wood, 2009).

While the revival of the adjacent inner city into a more 24-hours place was pursued by the City of Melbourne via an incremental strategy called 'Postcode 3000', Docklands was transformed under the leadership of its single landowner, the State of Victoria. The 1991 Docklands Act functioned as the basis for the development of the area, providing general guidelines for the development of the area. To supervise the project a Docklands Authority was created with special powers. By law it had to deliver a profit for the state government in developing the area (Dovey, 2005).

Initially this was seen as a difficult task. Large upfront investments were needed to create linking infrastructures and remove soil contamination. Potential investors saw the redevelopment of Docklands as a risky project as it was an area generally unknown by Melbournians. The Docklands governance was set up to comfort private investors by focusing on speed and removing several planning permission hurdles (Keeney, 2005). Because of the large size of the area, the development organization decided to work with seven separate precincts on which large developers would get a development agreement. The Melbourne municipal council was excluded from the planning approval process, while public participation and options to appeal building proposals were minimized (Oakley, 2011). These ideas also fitted in a timeframe in which planning as a regulatory activity was perceived as an obstacle to economic activity rather than a way to ensure that urban development proceeded in a manner in keeping with strategic community economic, social and environmental goals (Kroen & Goodman, 2012, p. 305).

A coherent overall plan for the area was absent, but in the separate precincts the developers were asked to come up with a – for Australian standards – quite new 'urban product' at that time: offices complemented with inner-city high-rise apartment living (Searle & Bunker, 2010). This policy aim connected well to a longer-term reorientation of the city back towards its historic core to contain urban sprawl (Woodcock et al., 2011).

Reacting to Turbulence

Although real estate projects and infrastructures were realized in its first century, Docklands was heavily criticized by academics and the press for its generic architecture, its oversized building blocks, its lack of social mix and facilities and its underused windswept public spaces (Dovey, 2005; Millar, 2006). In a city with a growing housing-affordability problem, Docklands only offered expensive housing. The state subsidized a big stadium to create a new destination, but its prominent position on the waterfront and the surrounding dead public spaces have done Docklands more harm than good (Dovey, 2005). As Shaw (2013) analyses, policies to improve Docklands have picked up several planning conceptions that were in vogue at the time: from 'environmental and social sustainability' (2000–2005) as a main goal, to a 'creative city' discourse (2005–2009) to a contemporary era of 'social and cultural sustainability'. Nevertheless, although narratives and aspirations for the project have changed remarkably, due to changing governments, economic conditions and public commentaries, little has changed in the form of what was actually built on the ground (Shaw, 2013, p. 2159).

The most concrete response to the project's difficulties was the 'Second Decade' process, announced in 2010 by VicUrban, the Victorian State urban development agency, which took the responsibility of developing Docklands from the Docklands Authority (VicUrban, 2010). The Second Decade process not only promised new public consultations, but also "a scheme of affordable housing, incubators for start-up businesses, creative spaces, recognition of Indigenous heritage, community facilities and diverse, comfortable and active public spaces" (Shaw, 2013, p. 2172). There would be a new community hub, a local library and a community garden, while

Figure 22.3 Dockland's Victoria Harbour development and underused Harbour Esplanade
Source: Photo by Majoor

access to the waterfront would be improved. A study by the Danish consultant Jan Gehl was issued to get a better understanding of its lacklustre public spaces.

Most of the respondents from public and private sectors that have been interviewed have been critical about the Second Decade process and outcome. It eventually focused mostly on public spaces and pop-up 'tactical urbanism' adaptations. An example was that empty storefronts in and around the underused Harbour Town shopping mall became part of a citywide 'Creative Spaces program', which mission was to "identify, secure, develop and manage affordable space for creative use in both the private and public sectors" (Shaw, 2014, p. 143). Artists were put into the role of 'activators' who were forced to leave when market interest for certain locations picked up again. The problem was that these and other temporary interventions had no chance to become part of the more permanent schemes (Majoor, 2015b). At the same time more fundamental problems of the area, such as the lack of affordable housing options, or the massive speculation with apartments were not addressed. Based on an analysis of water use data, about 25% of the housing properties in Docklands were suspected of being sold but unused (Dow, 2014). VicUrban – later renamed Places Victoria – kept on managing the project to maximize land sales. This made proposals to reduce building heights for future development plots, or the creation of more parklands or schemes for affordable housing difficult to realize. Meanwhile, the finished parts of Docklands were transferred to the City of Melbourne, in an attempt to create better governance integration with the adjacent CBD.

Conclusion: Assessing the Resilient Capacity of the Cases

The study hypothesized that urban megaprojects need an intelligent combination of institutional reflection and pragmatic action to create the resilient capacity to cope with external turbulence in a positive way. We have specified that the two important indicators for such a capacity are:

1. The presence of a normative ambiguous mission;
2. The presence of an organizational capacity able to combine institutional reflection and pragmatic action.

Presence of a Normative Ambiguous Mission

In their original planning, all three cases had aspects of an ambiguous mission. The initial concepts for Zuidas, Ørestad and Docklands proposed the creation of a mixed-use, high-density, lively new urban area in a location not previously associated as an urban centre. In their first decade the three projects were comparable in that they faced difficulties realizing these combined missions. Zuidas and Docklands saw a rally in office construction at the expense of housing and facilities, leading to quite one-sided business-oriented locations with uninviting public spaces. Ørestad had an overall difficult start and was saved by different questionable real estate deals that were far from contributing to a lively mixed-use new urban centre for Copenhagen. But to what extent has their mission been helpful to create a recombination of strategies in the face of turbulence?

Table 22.1 summarizes and compares our empirical findings. In all cases the economic and political turbulence created some opportunities to experiment with other urbanization strategies. Although the direction in all three cases is quite similar, with emphasis on temporary uses, events and improvements in public spaces and infrastructures, their strategic significance is different.

Zuidas was able, due to pragmatic choices, to slowly benefit from its ambiguous mission to recombine its economic, social and sustainable goals in the light of its economic turbulence.

Table 22.1 Summary of tactics to adapt Zuidas, Ørestad and Docklands in the face of turbulence

	Amsterdam Zuidas	Copenhagen Ørestad	Melbourne Docklands
Programmatic changes	Delaying development A more varied programme: new emphasis on (student) housing More temporary land uses and events ('15-by-15' programme)	More emphasis on housing and facilities Cancelling large office complexes	Small initiatives to bring life into underused shops, street levels Small new facilities ('Second Decade' project)
Financial changes	Infrastructure project now as pure public investment Financial mechanisms continued	Disconnect budgets from infrastructure investment and urban development New Town formula intact	Hardly any – fixed contracts
Governance changes	Zuidas Department: from public-private partnership back to public sphere New networks Some public participation around new vision 2016	Integration of Ørestad Development Company in City and Port Development Company No fundamental changes in governance model New networks (no public participation)	Responsibility partly transferred back from state development agency to Melbourne municipality Small public participation programme
Urban design changes	Some smaller blocks More emphasis on street-level design	Smaller plots, smaller streets More individual typologies (row houses, private gardens). Second layer tactics Attempts to integrate better with existing built-up environments	More emphasis on public space investments Attempts to integrate better with existing built-up environments

Source: Majoor

Within a quite compact high-density area, new housing projects in different segments of the market were started, public spaces were improved and a new public-public partnership finally created a breakthrough in the long-stalled central infrastructure corridor controversy. At the south side of the project the Free University campus became integrated into the project. Zuidas is still far from being a genuinely mixed, second city centre for Amsterdam, but its crisis-program (particularly its '15-by-15' project) stimulated its development in a more encompassing way and created the opportunities to shift attention to other components of its program, particularly in its social and public space goals, when office construction suddenly halted.

Ørestad's ambition to become a mixed-use internationally oriented office location in a strategic corridor close to the airport never took off as expected. In the years before the Global Financial Crisis the emphasis had already shifted to eco-sensitive large-scale housing development, particularly in the northern and southern segments of the plan. Rather than creating new ways to still realize a mixed urban district with a variety of uses, Ørestad's strategic response to the crisis was to optimize its function as a housing area. Schools, a library and playgrounds were added, and new plans for lower density suburban style housing were implemented. In this way, the crisis contributed to a further process of simplification and disintegration of its mission. The slow farewell to its original much more ambiguous mission to create a dense new urban district, epitomized by its advanced mini-metro system, was made on pragmatic grounds. Other locations, particularly in the harbour area, turned out to be more advantageous for high-end offices and high-density housing construction.

Melbourne Docklands saw subsequent new governments making announcements to 'fix' its problems. However, from the three cases it has shown the least change. This could be partly contributed to the fact that Docklands, in comparison to Zuidas and Ørestad, was not affected directly by the Global Financial Crisis. Its external turbulence was in government changes and a general impression by politicians, investors and the wider public that the first decade of its development had not lived up to expectations. Temporary uses on still empty plots have added some liveliness and change to its very planned layout, but they have to make way when traditional real estate developments are proposed. Docklands has continuously been organized around large precincts in which private investors maximize real estate values at the expense of a more varied and integrated urban development. A peculiar problem for the area is its lack of inhabitants, due to housing speculation. Over time its integration with the rest of Melbourne has improved with new bridges covering railroad tracks and a connection to the tram system, while the new library has finally created a community oriented space. However, its catalogue of pragmatic responses has had little strategic significance till now as the project was not able to recombine its one-sided economic development pathway with genuine social and ecological goals.

Organizational Capacity to Combine Institutional Reflection and Pragmatic Action

The differences in outcomes of the three cases correspond with their organizational capacity to combine institutional reflection and pragmatic action. Zuidas was managed by a public department, Ørestad by a public-public development corporation and Docklands by a development authority at arm's length of the state government. Particularly in their first phases, these massive urban transformations were framed as relatively controlled projects within strict contours of geography, timing and financial arrangements. Obviously, the project initiators understood that over decade-long time frames changes would occur. However, the expectation was that within a general framework of infrastructures, public spaces and public buildings, the projects would concentrate on the 'delivery' of expected privately developed real estate programmes. The project-oriented structures of Ørestad and Docklands were clearly set up to guide these projects through major political uncertainties that were seen, in both places, as harmful to such strategic long-term investment projects. In this way, our findings resemble earlier studies which show that although these projects were highly impacted by these contextual changes, most governance and planning formats introduced have attempted to 'protect' them from such contextual factors by a strategy of "depoliticisation" (Moulaert et al., 2003).

The three cases reveal two major reasons why an organizational capacity to combine institutional reflection and pragmatic action has been difficult. Firstly, the cases are strongly based upon the principles of a market-oriented development model. All three projects aim to develop public lands into profitable cityscapes. Expensive upfront public investments in infrastructure, public spaces and the removal of land contamination (Docklands) were seen as necessary public investments to trigger (much bigger) private real estate investments. From the outset, the three projects were geared towards optimizing land values. Zuidas was able to capitalize on this promise from the beginning. Ørestad and Docklands, however, faced difficulties persuading private investors to finance newly crafted urban spaces that were not naturally associated with high land values. This resulted in a weak bargaining position of the development agencies vis-à-vis private investors. The financial hardship of the Global Financial Crisis has underlined the dependency of Ørestad and Zuidas on creating high land values and the vulnerability of such a model. Lower land proceeds were unacceptable and a period of 'sitting out' the crisis continued in both projects for almost four years. In Melbourne, there was hardly any major economic crisis. However, radical policies to implement other urbanization strategies were as problematic as in the other two cases due to a strict obligation by law for the development authority to keep maximizing land values. Only recently, Zuidas saw a modest change in which a policy decision was made to accept lower land prices for some plots to facilitate social housing and middle-income apartments.

Secondly, and connected, although all cases faced official political consultation in their early phases, the governance and planning formats implemented were set up to facilitate a business-oriented implementation trajectory, rather than an enduring public consultation. Deliberation on their strategic mission at specific intervals in time was hardly organized. In a situation of changing external conditions, these deeper institutional features turned out to be a handicap. Although both Zuidas ('15-by-15') and Docklands ('Second Decade') introduced programs with some new concepts, it was very difficult to change a dominant repertoire of actions and financial deals. As typical project-oriented endeavours geared towards efficiency of implementation, there was a lack of redundancy, organizational slack or explorative capacity to make the development of different options an organizational capacity. When the pressure to change increased, mostly haphazardly, pragmatic changes were made.

We can conclude therefore that these projects faced the classic dilemma to facilitate both interaction and control (Brady & Davies, 2014). It is disappointing that although these projects are located on strategic urban parcels and involve massive public and private investment, they have hardly convinced as engines of change, experiment and innovation in the field of planning. This is also visible in the cityscapes they have realized until now: the plans had little space for contradictions, for more extreme varieties in land use or for conflicts that would make the cityscapes more exciting and more genuinely urban. Change of external context was not seen as an opportunity or an inevitability to reflect on via an ambiguous mission, but rather as a handicap, as something that had to be survived. Based on dominant principles of control and execution, it is questionable if such projects have a future in a world that slowly gets more knowledgeable about the uncontrolled effects of different sources of turbulence that influence planning and city development.

References

Altshuler, A., & Luberoff, D. (2003). *Mega-Projects. The Changing Politcs of Urban Public Investment*. Washington, DC: The Brookings Institution.

Andersen, J. (2003). Gambling Politics or Successful Entrepreneurship? The Ørestad Project in Copenhagen. In F. Moulaert, A. Rodriguez & E. Swyngedouw (Eds.), *The Globalized City: Economic Restructuring and Social Polarization in European cities* (pp. 91–106). Oxford: Oxford University Press.

Boelens, L., & De Roo, G. (2016). Planning of undefined becoming: First encounters of planners beyond the plan. *Planning Theory*, 15(1), 42–67.
Bourgeois, L. J. (1981). On the measurement of organizational slack. *Academy of Management Review*, 6(1), 29–39.
Brady, T., & Davies, A. (2014). Managing structural and dynamic complexity: A tale of two projects. *Project Management Journal*, 45(4), 21–38.
By & Havn. (2013). *2012 Annual Report*. Copenhagen: By & Havn.
Carmona, M. (Ed.). (2009). *Planning through Projects: Moving from Master Planning to Strategic Planning – 30 Cities*. Amsterdam: Techne Press.
Carstensen, M. B. (2013). Projecting from a fiction: The case of Denmark and the financial crisis. *New Political Economy*, 18(4), 555–578.
Christensen, D. (2003). *Ørestad, Historic Perspective, Planning, Implementation, Documentation*. Copenhagen: City of Copenhagen.
Davoudi, S. (2012). Resilience: A bridging concept or a dead end? *Planning Theory & Practice*, 13(2), 299–307.
Del Cerro Santamaría, G. (Ed.). (2013). *Urban Megaprojects: A Worldwide View*. Bingley: Emerald Group Publishing.
Diaz Orueta, F., & Fainstein, S. S. (2008). The new mega-projects: Genesis and impacts. *International Journal of Urban and Regional Research*, 32(4), 759–767.
Dovey, K. (2005). *Fluid City: Transforming Melbourne's Urban Waterfront*. Sydney: University of New South Wales Press.
Dow, A. (2014). 'Ghost tower' warning for Docklands after data reveals high Melbourne home vacancies. Melbourne: The Age (11 November 2014).
Enright, T. (2014). The great wager: Crisis and mega-project reform in 21st-century Paris. *Cambridge Journal of Regions, Economy and Society*, 7(1), 155–170.
Fainstein, S. S. (2001). *The City Builders: Property Development in New York and London, 1980–2000*. Lawrence, KS: University Press of Kansas.
Farjoun, M. (2010). Beyond dualism: Stability and change as a duality. *Academy of Management Review*, 35(2), 202–225.
Folke, C. (2006). Resilience: The emergence of a perspective for social-ecological systems analyses. *Global Environmental Change*, 16(3), 253–267.
Freestone, R. (2014). Progress in Australian planning history: Traditions, themes and transformations. *Progress in Planning*, 91, 1–29.
Gemeente Amsterdam. (1998). *Masterplan Zuidas*. Amsterdam: Dienst Ruimtelijke Ordening.
Gemeente Amsterdam. (2009). *Visie Zuidas 2009*. Amsterdam: Dienst Ruimtelijke Ordening.
Gemeente Amsterdam. (2010). *15-by-15*. Amsterdam: Dienst Zuidas.
Gemeente Amsterdam. (2016). *Visie Zuidas 2016*. Amsterdam: Dienst Zuidas.
Giezen, M. (2013). Adaptive and strategic capacity: Navigating megaprojects through uncertainty and complexity. *Environment and Planning B*, 40(4), 723–741.
Grabher, G., & Thiel, J. (Eds.). (2015). *Self-Induced Shocks: Mega-Projects and Urban Development*. Berlin: Jovis.
Gualini, E., & Majoor, S. J. H. (2007). Innovative practices in large urban development projects: Conflicting frames in the quest for 'new urbanity'. *Planning Theory & Practice*, 8(3), 297–318.
Healey, P. (2007). *Urban Complexity and Spatial Strategies: Towards a Relational Planning for Our Times*. London: Routledge.
Hillier, J., & Healey, P. (Eds.). (2010). *The Ashgate Research Companion to Planning Theory: Conceptual Challenges for Spatial Planning*. Farnham: Ashgate.
Holgersen, S. (2014). Urban responses to the economic crisis: Confirmation of urban policies as crisis management in Malmö. *International Journal of Urban and Regional Research*, 38(1), 285–301.
Ifversen, K. R. S., & Lindhe, J. M. (2013). *Generøs by–Københans nye arkitektur*. Copenhagen: Gyldendal.
Koppenjan, J., Veeneman, W., Voort, H. v. d., Heuvelhof, E. ten., & Leijten, M. (2011). Competing management approaches in large engineering projects: The Dutch RandstadRail project. *International Journal of Project Management*, 29(6), 740–750.
Keeney, J. (Ed.). (2005). *Waterfront Spectacular: Creating Melbourne Docklands, the People's Waterfront*. Roseville: Design Masters Press.
Kroen, A., & Goodman, R. (2012). Implementing metropolitan strategies: Lessons from Melbourne. *International Planning Studies*, 17(3), 303–321.

Lehrer, U., & Laidley, J. (2008). Old mega-projects newly packaged? Waterfront redevelopment in Toronto. *International Journal of Urban and Regional Research*, 32(4), 786–803.

Lewis, M. W. (2000). Exploring paradox: Toward a more comprehensive guide. *Academy of Management Review*, 25(4), 760–776.

Lydon, M., & Garcia, A. (2015). *Tactical Urbanism: Short-Term Action for Long-Term Change*. Washington, DC: Island Press.

Majoor, S. J. H. (2006). Conditions for multiple land use in large-scale urban projects. *Journal of Housing and Built Environment*, 21(1), 15–32.

Majoor, S. J. H. (2007). Amsterdam Zuidas: The Dream of a New Urbanity. In W. G. M. Salet & E. Gualini (Eds.), *Framing Strategic Urban Projects: Learning from Current Experiences in European Urban Regions* (pp. 53–80). London: Routledge.

Majoor, S. J. H. (2008a). *Disconnected Innovations: New Urbanity in Large-Scale Development Projects: Zuidas Amsterdam, Ørestad Copenhagen and Forum Barcelona*. Delft: Eburon.

Majoor, S. J. H. (2008b). Progressive planning ideals in a neo-liberal context, the case of Ørestad Copenhagen. *International Planning Studies*, 13(2), 101–117.

Majoor, S. J. H. (2009). The disconnected innovation of new urbanity in Zuidas Amsterdam, Ørestad Copenhagen and Forum Barcelona. *European Planning Studies*, 17(9), 1379–1403.

Majoor, S. J. H. (2011). Framing large-scale projects: Barcelona Forum and the challenge of balancing local and global needs. *Journal of Planning Education and Research*, 31(2), 143–156.

Majoor, S. J. H. (2014). Ørestad: Copenhagen's radical new town project in transition. *Planning Theory & Practice*, 15(3), 432–438.

Majoor, S. J. H. (2015a). Resilient practices: A paradox oriented approach for large-scale development projects. *Town Planning Review*, 86(3), 257–277.

Majoor, S. J. H. (2015b). Retrofitting Melbourne Docklands. Opportunities and constraints. *Planning News*, 41(2), 12–13.

Majoor, S. J. H. (2015c). Urban megaprojects in crisis? Ørestad Copenhagen revisited. *European Planning Studies*, 23(12), 1–19.

Majoor, S. J. H. (2018). Coping with ambiguity: An urban megaproject ethnography. *Progress in Planning*, 120, 1–28.

Majoor, S. J. H., & Jørgensen, J. (2007). Copenhagen Ørestad: Public Partnership in Search of the Market. In W. G. M. Salet & E. Gualini (Eds.), *Framing Strategic Urban Projects: Learning from Current Experiences in European Urban Regions* (pp. 172–198). Abingdon: Routledge.

Majoor, S. J. H., & Salet, W. G. M. (2008). The enlargement of local power in trans-scalar strategies of planning: Recent tendencies in two European cases. *Geojournal*, 72(1–2), 91–103.

Millar, R. (2006). Docklands a wasted opportunity? Melbourne: The Age (17 June 2006).

Ministerie Infrastructuur en Milieu. (2012). *Structuurvisie Zuidas-Dok*. Den Haag: Ministerie Infrastructuur en Milieu.

Mintzberg, H., & Waters, J. A. (1985). Of strategies, deliberate and emergent. *Strategic Management Journal*, 6, 257–272.

Moulaert, F., Rodriguez, A., & Swyngedouw, E. (Eds.). (2003). *The Globalized City: Economic Restructuring and Social Polarization in European Cities*. Oxford: Oxford University Press.

Oakley, S. (2011). Re-imagining city waterfronts: A comparative analysis of governing renewal in Adelaide, Darwin and Melbourne. *Urban Policy and Research*, 29(3), 221–238.

Oosterlynck, S., Van den Broeck, J., Albrechts, L., Moulaert, F., & Verhetsel, A. (Eds.). (2011). *Strategic Spatial Projects: Catalysts for Change*. Abingdon: Routledge.

Ørestadsselskabet. (1995). *Ørestaden. Master Plan*. Copenhagen: Ørestadsselskabet.

Raisch, S., & Birkinshaw, J. (2008). Organizational ambidexterity: Antecedents, outcomes, and moderators. *Journal of Management*, 34(3), 375–409.

Savini, F., & Salet, W. G. M. (Eds.). (2017). *Planning Projects in Transition: Interventions, Regulations and Investments*. Berlin: Jovis.

Salet, W. G. M., & Gualini, E. (Eds.). (2007). *Framing Strategic Urban Projects: Learning from Current Experiences in European Urban Regions*. New York: Routledge.

Salet, W. G. M., Bertolini, L., & Giezen, M. (2013). Complexity and uncertainty: Problem or asset in decision making of mega infrastructure projects? *International Journal of Urban and Regional Research*, 37(6), 1984–2000.

Salet, W. G. M., & Majoor, S. J. H. (2005). *Zuidas Amsterdam European Space*. Rotterdam: 010 Publishers.

Savini, F., Boterman, W. R., van Gent, W. P., & Majoor, S. J. H. (2016). Amsterdam in the 21st century: Geography, housing, spatial development and politics. *Cities*, 52, 103–113.

Savini, F., Majoor, S. J. H., & Salet, W. G. M. (2015). Dilemmas of planning: Intervention, regulation, and investment. *Planning Theory*, 14(3), 296–315.

Searle, G., & Bunker, R. (2010). Metropolitan strategic planning: An Australian paradigm? *Planning Theory*, 9(3), 163–180.

Shaw, K. (2013). Docklands dreamings: Illusions of sustainability in the Melbourne docks redevelopment. *Urban Studies*, 50(11), 2158–2177.

Shaw, K. (2014). Melbourne's Creative Spaces program: Reclaiming the 'creative city' (if not quite the rest of it). *City, Culture and Society*, 5(3), 139–147.

Teisman, G. R. (2008). Complexity and management of improvement programmes. *Public Management Review*, 10(3), 341–359.

Van der Boon, V., & Van der Marel, G. (2009). *De vastgoedfraude – Miljoenenzwendel aan de top van het Nederlandse bedrijfsleven*. Amsterdam: Nieuw Amsterdam.

Van Eekelen, B., Schnieders, R., & De Wilde, S. (2014). *De dokwerkers. Reconstructie van planontwikkeling en bestuurlijke besluitvorming bij Zuidas en Zuidasdok*. Amsterdam: Neerlands Diep,

VicUrban. (2010). *Docklands. The Second Decade*. Draft shared vision. Melbourne: VicUrban.

Wood, S. (2009). Desiring Docklands: Deleuze and urban planning discourse. *Planning Theory*, 8(2), 191–216.

Woodcock, I, Dovey, K., Wollan, S., & Robertson, I. (2011). Speculation and resistance: Constraints on compact city policy implementation in Melbourne. *Urban Policy and Research*, 29(4), 343–362.

23
INSTITUTING RESILIENCE IN THE MAKING OF THE ISTANBUL METROPOLIS

Ayda Eraydin & Tuna Taşan-Kok

Introduction

Contemporary cities are facing increasing vulnerabilities that are not only ecological and economic in nature, but also increasingly political and social, and planning processes and practices have been unable to fully address such complex changes through the regulation, organisation and implementation of a more resilient urban agenda. There is near consensus on the need to change not only the focus of planning, but also the way of thinking (Hoch, 1996; Taylor, 1998). We have argued previously (Eraydin & Taşan-Kok, 2013) that *resilience thinking* can form the basis of an alternative planning approach, necessitating a reconsideration of the substance of planning within a process that will focus on norms, value systems and the power relations in decision making. However, the institution of resilience thinking into planning is yet to be discussed and elaborated on, and it is the main aim of this chapter to contribute to this discussion.

In complex metropolitan systems like Turkish cities, the installation of resilience is hindered by such hurdles as increasing political pressures, anti-democratic actions and authoritarian state interventions into urban development, on top of the ongoing environmental, economic and social problems. Over the last three decades, market-based urban policies have led to concerns that the implemented 'competitiveness agenda' of the central government, was in direct opposition to the local urban planning agenda. Economic power relations, privatisation and speculation have been prioritised over public interest. These are accompanied by symbolic transformations in the built environment in the form of emblematic mega-projects, large-scale infrastructure, renewal and regeneration schemes, the construction of commercial high-rise buildings, etc. While the economic competitiveness agenda continues to be effective, despite the global economic crisis of 2008, urban development decisions are gradually coming under the influence of political mechanisms and dynamics. This occurs especially in countries where continuous political crises and changes in the models of urban governance are common, a consequence of which is further conflicts and unrest in urban areas. When democratic decision-making mechanisms are overshadowed by political ideologies and their symbols in the built environment, little room is left for democratic processes in planning. In many instances, planning is restricted to the legitimisation of decisions related to urban areas that are defined by national political programs.

In this chapter, we reflect upon the question of whether and how it would be possible to institute resilience in planning in an increasingly politically guided urban agenda, and to this end, we discuss why we need a resilient turn in planning. In the first part of the chapter, we define our understanding of resilience in planning, and then discuss the conditions under which resilience thinking exists in planning, and how it can be instituted. In the second part of the chapter we will focus on the Istanbul case, and will attempt to clarify why there is a need for instituting resilience in the management of this vast metropolis. Finally, we will conclude with a discussion of how it could be possible to institute resilience into the planning and governance of Istanbul.

Why Do We Need a Resilience Turn in Planning?

The last three decades have been marked by neo-liberalisation processes that led to transformations in urban development policies, discourses and institutions. The shift from social to entrepreneurial forms of governance brought with it vulnerabilities that were amplified by the structural problems experienced by cities and eroded their capacity to cope, adapt and react to changing conditions – in short, it eroded their resilience (Hudson, 2010).

Today, there are four types of vulnerabilities that can be defined in cities. First, while the deregulation in the flow of goods, capital and people decreased the level of protection to the external effects of local economies, the volatility of the global economy intensified the defencelessness of urban systems. Today, major cities all around the world face pressures that have forced them to rethink the impacts of policies for competitiveness and integration into global economy on their socio-spatial structures (Boddy & Parkinson, 2004; Fainstein, 2001). Second, cities face increasing environmental and spatial vulnerabilities due to the increasing pressures on urban land created by property markets. The entrepreneurial logic in urban policies and new forms of spatial interventions (project- or property-led development) as policy instruments (Salet & Guallini, 2006; Salet & Majoor, 2005; Swyngedouw et al., 2002; Taşan-Kok, 2008) decrease opportunities to reflect public concerns and long-term strategies related to the sustainable use of resources, and no doubt degrades the resilience of cities. Thirdly, the democratic deficits and vulnerability in governance regarding the transfer of power from democratic citizens to corporations and the privatisation of the state are widely disputed (Albrechts, 2010). Participatory practices and new quasi-public bodies have been as lauded as important agents in increasing levels of democracy since the 1980s, but the practice of participation is limited to certain parts of society (business or political elites, informed or active citizens, discontented residents, etc.). Fourth, the increasing vulnerability of urban ecosystems has become a major threat to the sustainable use of urban land. Recently, discussions of sustainability and their link to increased energy consumption and carbon emissions, leading to climate change, have become a debated issue in urban environmental literature. The new urban forms that are shaped according to market dynamics have been considered inefficient, while increasing built-up areas in water basins, urban growth towards environmentally sensitive areas and the loss of areas with rich biodiversity have been defined as the most critical problems faced by urban areas.

One cannot say that existing urban planning systems have responded competently to these problems, nor were they prepared to deal with such complexities and externalities. Since the 1980s, instrumentalism has lost ground in planning, as although it is pragmatic, it is not dynamic, and it lacks the ability to respond to the ongoing changes in urban governance. Moreover, communicative rationality, which has been the theoretical basis of planning processes over the last three decades, has also faced a number of problems. Huxley (2000), for instance, points out the need for a greater acknowledgement of the relations of power and inequality in planning theory, criticising communicative planning theory for obscuring planning's problematic relationship with the state. There is also increasing criticism of the communicative planning approach, which is rooted in the Habermasian ideal of communicative action (Albrechts, 2010; Fainstein, 2000, 2005; Harris, 2002; Healey, 1999; Mouffe, 2000; Purcell, 2009; Young, 1996, 1999). These criticisms are focused first of all on the priority given to processes and institutions, ignoring power relations and the underlying causes of inequalities, based on the assumption that reason will prevail in a communicative planning approach.[1] Secondly, the criticisms suggest that communicative action tends, in the long term, to reinforce the current status quo, and is "more likely to support the neoliberal agenda than to resist it" (Purcell, 2009, p. 141). Moreover, it suppresses any radical and transformative edge in practice (Harris, 2002), in that it seeks to resolve conflict, eliminate exclusion and neutralise power relations rather than to embrace them as the very terrain of social mobilisation (ibid, p. 155), and favours some social groups over others (Albrechts, 2010; Fainstein, 2000; Young, 1996, 1999). Flyvbjerg (1998, p. 209) spoke also of his "scepticism about the non-politicized processes of mediation and building consensus" underlined in a communicative approach.

In practice, communicative planning faced certain problems related to participation and the reflection of the concerns of different groups. The failures of communicative planning, which underlines the consensus generation among groups with different norms, values and interests, led to an accumulation of planning approaches in urban areas that were based on the dominant economic policies. The forces of neo-liberalisation have slowly taken over each planning subfield. Since the 1980s, there has been an apparent growth of uncoordinated and even chaotic actions driven by fragmented public policies, programs and projects, as well as plans. The existing planning systems of many countries have an eclectic character, following an instrumental planning and technical problem-solving approach, and featuring consultancy processes to obtain the reactions of the public, but with top-down decision making related to critical projects. Moreover, existing spatial planning practices have come to employ a discourse that is full of such terms and buzzwords as 'social justice', 'just city', 'environmental sustainability', 'public interest' or 'community engagement', 'rationality', 'the good', etc. Gunder and Hillier (2009) argue that these terms are mere 'empty signifiers' that mean everything and nothing, and suggest that spatial and urban planning is based largely on the construction and deployment of economic and ideological knowledge claims.

In reality, as part of the processes of beautification, privatisation and commercialisation of the cityscape through mega-projects, skyscrapers, waterfront regeneration projects, etc., these dynamics lead to deepening segregation and exclusion processes in the city, splintering society into opposing social groups. In this era, state interventions through coercive policies intensified dramatically to cope with the effects of the commodification of urban land and its consequences (Eraydin & Taşan-Kok, 2013; Peck et al., 2009; Taşan-Kok, 2011). One way of doing this is to sponsor entrepreneurial interventions, whereby the state acts as a 'speculative investor' in a coalition of private-sector stakeholders (Davidson & McNeill, 2011). City-branding and investments into large-scale infrastructure, waterfront redevelopments and other large-scale urban development projects are well-known elements of the entrepreneurial ethos (Jou et al., 2011), and this process, which can be referred to as political entrepreneurialism, has triggered dynamics that go beyond economic symbolism by enforcing symbols that represent the ideology behind them.

In this period there is a need for a new perspective to enhance the adaptive capacity and sustained development of city regions to cope with the crises of political entrepreneurialism. To this end, resilience thinking has been introduced as a heterodox approach in both the theory and practice of planning. Though conceptually not unproblematic, a resilience turn in planning may allow us to highlight the existing vulnerabilities and assets of urban systems that can allow them to increase their transformative capacities against internal and external disturbances, one of which is coercive policies (Eraydin & Taşan-Kok, 2013).

How Do We Describe Resilience Thinking in Planning?

The resilience concept has attracted considerable interest in recent years, although the lack of consensus in its definition has led to it being praised and criticised by those referring to the different meanings attached to it[2] (Pendall et al., 2010; Davoudi, 2012). Resilience is regarded by those involved in engineering and ecological sciences to be a measure of how fast a system returns to a state of equilibrium after a disturbance (Holling, 1992), in which the main characteristics of resilient systems are defined as follows (Berkes et al., 2003, p. 6): the ability of a system to absorb or buffer disturbances and still maintain its core attributes; the ability of the system self-organise; and the capacity for learning and adaptation in the context of change. There have been various attempts to translate and operationalise the resilience concept for use in regional and urban analyses. According to Christopherson (2010), a resilient region is not just economically successful, but one that can maintain economic success over a long time in the face of the necessary adaptations required as a result of changes in external conditions. Similarly, Wilkinson (2011) suggests the application of social-ecological resilience conceptualisations to deal with unpredictable development in cities. That said, these attempts have been criticised as monitoring exercises of 'immunological practices', which means to "vaccinate people and environments alike so that they are able to take larger doses of inequality and environmental degradation in the future" (Kaika, 2017). Although these critiques may be true for the creation of institutional mechanisms to bypass the real needs of communities, the pure form of the concept of resilience may still provide a frame of thinking for the functioning of planning systems.

The attributes above present a possible choice in the building of a planning framework – whether to follow conservative or radical constructs of resilience (Raco & Street, 2012). The conservative view of resilience defines a return to the steady state of the urban system that existed before the external shock threatened to bring about a fundamental change; while in contrast, the radical perspective sees resilience as a dynamic process that involves the rejection of the status quo (Shaw & Theobald, 2011, p. 7). In this chapter, we define a resilient system according to its two main features: its ability to absorb change and disturbance, and the persistence of the system while retaining its basic functions and structure together with the capacity to survive, adapt and transform itself (Ludwig et al., 1997; Walker et al., 2006).

This definition addresses the major concerns of resilience thinking in planning, underlining the importance of the ability of an urban system to protect its *vital/critical elements/resources and values* for sustained development, as well as its level of preparedness for innovative transformation. What is needed is to ensure the critical resources that would lead the collapse of the urban systems once depleted are retained. These features *(adaptive capacity, self-organisation and learning capacity)* can be enhanced in urban systems by making a critical analysis of the existing weak and strong elements in an urban system, and reflecting on the internal and external dynamics that may affect their sustainable transition. This can be achieved by focusing on three issues (see Figure 23.1).

Priority Setting in Vulnerabilities: What Do We Not Want to Lose?

The use of the resilience concept demands that the concern of planning should not be problem-solving or controlling development, as was the focus of classical planning approaches, or reaching a collective agreement in decision making, as is the case in communicative planning. There is

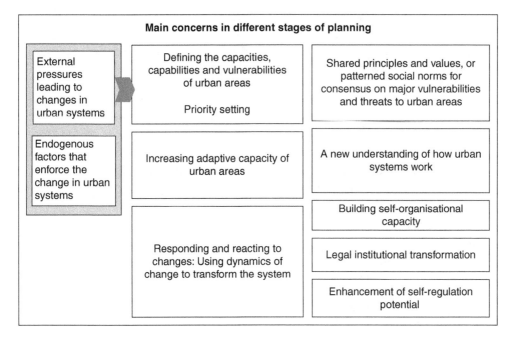

Figure 23.1 Instituting resilience within the urban planning system
Source: Eraydin & Taşan-Kok

a need to define the *no-regret conditions* related to critical issues in planning by considering the vulnerabilities of urban systems, and for this reason, understanding the dynamics of urban systems to identify the vulnerabilities and adaptive capacities of urban areas is essential when deciding upon the priorities for planning and practice. Defining the priority issues and the main principles to be followed when dealing with vulnerabilities, and preparing the system for not only slow changes (mostly defined by endogenous dynamics), but also major expected and unexpected disturbances, becomes the core of resilience thinking in planning. This can only be achieved by thinking about *how cross-scale impacts reverberate across urban systems*. In this vein, resilience thinking in planning practice underlines the need to ensure an urban system can protect its *vital, critical elements, resources and values* for sustained development, but also to be prepared for innovative transformation.

Adaptation to Changes to Achieve Sustainable Development

Adaptive capacity, which is at the core of resilience in planning practice, aims explicitly at equipping urban systems with the means of dealing effectively with both slow and radical changes, although its application to date has been limited. The reason for this is based on its need to respond to a broad range of issues that vary from ongoing changes in the environmental, ecological urban built environment, the movements of people, evolving socioeconomic regimes and the interplay of political ideologies and collective imaginaries. The enhancement of adaptive capacity is a necessary condition for the reduction of vulnerability and the sustaining of ecosystems services, which can be affected significantly by unforeseen ecological and economic problems and political interventions. It necessitates a critical analysis of the primary processes and structural constraints that shape urban areas, which demands a problem-solving approach and methods of instrumental rationality. Moreover, as argued earlier by the authors of this chapter (Eraydin & Taşan-Kok, 2013), planning also needs to shift its aim from controlling change to increasing the *adaptive capacity* of the urban system to cope with, adapt or transform itself. In this regard, *bringing back systemic thinking, substance and context* based upon the vulnerabilities and adaptive capacities of urban areas, as the core focus of planning, is an important feature of resilience thinking. To this end, the substance of the urban system must be defined taking into account three of its dynamic assets, namely *adaptive capacity, self-organisation and transformability*, rather than focusing on the characteristics of the steady state condition.

Responding and Reacting to Changes: Using Dynamics of Change to Transform the System

Transformability, which is a critical requirement under the current conditions, is defined as the capacity to create a fundamentally new system when ecological, economic, social and political conditions make the existing system untenable (Walker et al., 2004). Planning may play a vital role in this process, and the priority issues defined in analytical steps can serve the enhancement of local creativity, innovation and risk-taking, by taking into consideration both proactive as well as transformative assets. In building resilient cities, proactive issues are important, and according to Hudson (2010, p. 17), emphasis should be on moving towards a proactive approach, and learning how to anticipate and cope with a range of externally generated shocks and disturbances. That said, transformative and self-organisational capacities are also needed to reach the envisaged end product/state, which should include "the way resources are used, (re)distributed and allocated, and the way regulatory powers are exercised" (Albrechts, 2010, p. 1117). However, political-economic neoliberalism, which is pretty much based on opportunity-led development, entrepreneurialism and financialisation, brings with it unprecedented and unpredictable situations that are difficult to both foresee and control. Under these circumstances, planning should utilise mechanisms that allow it to adjust to be both innovative and flexible, taking into consideration the norms and values of different groups. As a further step, planning should introduce normalisation processes that can be achieved under all sorts of influences.

How to Institute Resilience in Planning

There are surprisingly few publications addressing how a resilience approach to planning may be pursued in practice (Davoudi, 2012; Eraydin & Taşan-Kok, 2013; Wilkinson, 2011). As elaborated above, the new (resilience) thinking in planning requires an approach that takes into account system dynamics; a moral dimension that will lead practice; recognition of the human dimension; and the transformation of legal institutions. It must institute creative resistance, and should respond to the priorities defined in the planning process and in forums to aid consensus generation on the main principles of urban policies and planning.

Need for a New Understanding

Managing resilience requires an understanding of how path-dependent historical system dynamics have shaped the current system. Since social-ecological systems are dynamic and provide a broad overview of system change over time, they can reveal system drivers, the effects of interventions and past disturbances, and the responses necessary for the building of their future. A system overview also permits the determination of how 'maladaptive cycles' can be broken through intervention. In this respect, resilience assessment is a key step in the analysis and managing of the dynamics of social-ecological systems, and helps in the identification thresholds, drivers, dynamics, and any actions that either contribute to or erode resilience in social-ecological systems (Resilience Alliance, 2010). Following the deciphering stage, complex and non-linear developments in cities need new ways of approaching the unpredictable. This is more or less the opposite of what planning wants to achieve in the end, which is, namely, to control developments, foresee the future and prevent problems. A new planning practice should be flexible enough to allow immediate interventions into the 'maladaptive cycles' when they occur, while following the overall shared values that are set in advance through deliberative processes of dialogue and persuasion. In other words, planning should shift from trying to control what is estimated to happen, to setting principles and values of the system on the one hand, and coming up with rapid pragmatic solutions to problems on the other.

Need for New Shared Principles and Values

As Watson (2002, p. 31) argues, the current sources of moral philosophy in planning lack the depth to provide guidance on issues of ethical judgement in a context of increasing social inequality and market-based rationality. Planning necessitates new ethics (values and rules) that go beyond the current discourses on the common good and public interest. Watson, following Rawls's 'theory of social justice', suggests that a single, universal conception of the good may not be possible, but by shifting emphasis from 'ends to means', it can be argued that the 'right' has 'priority' over the good. Besides advocating equity, empowerment and environmentally sensitive economic development, there is a further need to encourage principles that will define situational ethics. Building shared values and principles is critical in reducing the antagonism and hegemony of power, because if no value systems exist that can define the expectations for the future, then every agreement will silence some and not others, and every decision will favour some over others (Hillier, 2002; McGuirk, 2001; Tewdwr-Jones & Allmendinger, 1998; Purcell, 2009). Therefore, without shared value systems, attempts to reach consensus or agreement may be manipulated by the hegemony of power (Mouffe, 2000, p. 104).

Building the Self-Organisation Capacity of People Who Are Excluded from Urban Decision Making

Whatever the wider institutional or strategic implications of applying the resilience framework to planning theory and practice, perhaps it is ultimately the human dimension that remains the crucial challenge in an era of profound uncertainty. As Folke et al. (2010) suggest, the human dimension is usually seen as the 'external intervener in ecosystem resilience' or as the 'driver of ecosystem dynamics', pinpointing humans as the cause of the changing ecosystem dynamics. From a socioeconomic and political point of view, the human dimension gains a different emphasis, in that politically powerful forces of entrepreneurial governance define new spatial forms and institutional practices in cities, overriding the interests and choices of other social groups. While these exclusive groups that have access to capital investments lead the main capital accumulation channels and investments in cities, there are other groups that take an active part in the self-organisation of spaces through bottom-up initiatives and other forms of social involvement. These groups do not necessarily have access to capital accumulation channels, nor are they able to benefit from the investment decisions of global capital formations or political power through entrepreneurial intentions, but what they do have is the capacity for self-organisation, usually through fragmented channels of bottom-up involvement and active citizenship. Self-organising civil societies and self-organisation are claimed to be instrumental in dealing with slow and sudden changes of different forms (Eraydin, 2013). As Ostrom (1990) argues, "building a self-organization capacity" means a shift in the value system, and can be the basis of a governance model.

Need for Legal Institutional Transformation

Existing institutional structures are often well established and rigid, which hinders their transformation into more flexible systems aimed at increasing the self-organisation capacity of cities. According to Maru (2010), while the capacity to self-organise and adapt is a shared property of social (and ecological) systems, learning is an essential human (and thus individual) capability. According to Gupta et al. (2010), 'adaptive institutions' can encourage learning among actors by questioning the socially embedded ideologies, frames, assumptions, roles, rules and procedures that dominate problem-solving efforts. Olsson et al. (2004), on this issue, speaks about the development of 'adaptive co-management systems'. All of these argue that it could be possible to connect institutions and organisations across levels and scales to facilitate information flows with the help of local groups and their self-organisation, learning and adapting capacities, as well as their social networks. In line with Gunderson's (1999) argument, the adaptive management of a system during and after unexpected events requires a certain level of institutional flexibility and capacity for adaptation if institutional learning and social networking actions are to be encouraged.

Instituting Creative Protests into the Planning Process

Resistance movements, especially those voicing discontent with the existing urban change, become crucial when considering their potential role in developing adaptive capacity. The communication of demands through creative protests requires new forms of communication between organisations and citizens, based on self-organised actions. However, today populardemocratic mobilisations are being articulated 'in fragments', leading to problems in gaining support from wider social groups, and they still maintain an inchoate character. Moreover, the response of the wider political authority – the state – to these movements may not always be accommodating and welcoming (Eraydin & Taşan-Kok, 2014). Accordingly, in political systems in which authoritarian acts overrule local democracy in particular, there is a need for new manoeuvres among these detached sites of protest to forge an institutional transformation that can lead to an enhancement of the resilience of urban and metropolitan systems. As we elaborated elsewhere (Eraydin & Taşan-Kok, 2014), this can be very challenging when any opposition is suppressed by the political forces of power through physical action, although this form of suppression may create new potential for learning how to reorganise social actions and mobilise opposition through different channels.

Instituting Resilience in the Making of the Istanbul Metropolis

The existing urban regulation system in Turkey can be defined as political entrepreneurialism, featuring top-down interference by state agencies in urban development practices (Eraydin & Taşan-Kok, 2013). In this system, the state provides special care and benefits to certain groups to control the social response while using the regulations and practices of state agencies as a means of suppressing dissatisfaction. Mega-infrastructure projects initiated by state organs are used to popularise and legitimise their policies, by either disregarding or completely bypassing local planning decisions through different channels of power. In efforts to legitimise the ideology, the transformation of urban areas through large-scale infrastructure and housing projects has been essential. The neoliberal ideology is used widely in this respect, although in an increasingly mutated form that can be described as authoritarian neoliberalism, which is rooted in the reconfiguring of the state into a less democratic entity through constitutional and legal changes that seek to insulate it from social and political conflict (Buff, 2012). The main features of the recent changes in urban governance and planning are summarised below.

Devolution of Governance Systems but Not Planning Rights: Amendments to Previous Planning Legislation

Since the 1980s, the institutional set up of urban governance has changed substantially, and from 1984 up to 2005, the central government followed a policy of sharing its rights and responsibilities with the municipalities, beginning with local government reform. From the 1990s onwards, several significant changes were introduced in Turkey. First, the decentralisation of public administration became a government priority, and three laws were passed creating new mechanisms to facilitate the transfer of major spending powers to special provincial administrations, metropolitan municipalities and other municipalities. Second, the new regulations redefined the roles of metropolitan governments in the provision of services, which led to a greater role for metropolitan municipalities against central government institutions. Third, new financial regulations were introduced giving local governments additional funds to allow them to carry out their new responsibilities. Fourth, in order to accelerate the privatisation of services and existing state enterprises, several measures were adopted. These attempts at territorialisation were considered progressive by the actors in metropolitan governance and planning.

Along with territorialisation, the planning system at a metropolitan level has undergone substantial changes. The expansion of metropolitan boundaries after 2004 enabled the transfer of high-level planning rights to certain metropolitan municipalities, which included the preparation and monitoring of the regional and strategic plans – a task that was previously the responsibility of the State Planning Organization and the Ministry of Public Works. While the new legislation provided increased planning rights for local governments, the amendments to the article (No. 6785) defining 'special exemptions' to the planning code, show the interest of the central government to control the planning process and decisions. The amendments distributed planning rights to different central government organisations in certain parts of the metropolitan area, named as critical areas, resulting in a loss of control of local governments in metropolitan areas. In particular, the rights provided to the Turkish Mass Housing Authority (TOKI) to prepare plans for housing estates and to implement these plans were critical, not to mention the rights granted to this authority in the transformation of historical sites.

Increasing Central Government Interventions

Over the last decade, the standing government became increasingly concerned with the low political returns from its urban policies and projects, and not only started to intervene in the decision-making processes, but also initiated a number of projects directly. Privileges given to different institutions facilitated the implementation of 'urban projects' and allowed different central and local government departments to benefit from the increasing economic value of urban land. Within this model, the main roles of central and local governments are defined as supporting the competitive power of the existing economic actors, and assisting the market-based operations of both public institutions and private enterprises. As can be seen from debates around the plausibility of government interventions in the neoliberal understanding, this is not very surprising. As underlined by Foucault, one group of liberals suggested that the "state and market economy are not juxtaposed, but that the one mutually presumes the existence of the other" (Lemke, 2001). In fact, what has happened in Turkey has gone one step further over the last three decades – central governments have sought to legitimise themselves by intervening in the urban economy and redistributing building rights to entrepreneurs and public institutions, as well as different social groups.

The Implications of Legal Institutions and Governance on Planning

The amendments to the previous planning legislation brought about a fragmentation of the existing planning system, and in recent years a considerable reduction has been witnessed in the role of the planning code, which had targeted a progressive planning system. The introduction of a communicative or participatory approach in planning, which it was hoped would lead to a consensus generation and participatory action, was not successfully experimented. Different coalitions emerged between real estate developers and local and central government departments with the aim of initiating new real estate projects, some of which were implemented with the help of exceptional amendments to the planning legislation. The main role of NGOs and professional associations, such as the Chambers of Architects and the Chambers of City Planners, in these newly introduced processes was limited to their voicing of concerns and doubts about the projects and policies of local and central governments.

The 'use' of the city as an economic tool for growth, and as a populist political tool for the transfer of income among different social groups, had very deep impacts on both the planning and implementation stages. An examination of planning legislation reveals the different ways in which the revaluation of urban land becomes possible, with each serving for the benefit of a different interest and social group. Changes in building rights and efforts to transform low quality or informal housing into the projects led by Housing Development Agency (HDA)[3] have been exercised as a mechanism for the transfer of income to different groups, including the urban poor. It can be noted further that the new fragmented system is used by local decision-makers to obtain both material and non-material benefits, such as political support, and to stabilise the reactions of different groups, especially those whose interests are not being fully met.

Declining Adaptive Capacity and Rise in Ecological Vulnerabilities

Changes in regulatory institutions and rules, the keen interest of political leaders in creating new large-scale projects while disregarding the need for urban systems, and the ignoring countervailing interests, pressures and visions have all emerged as significant threats to the resilience of urban systems in Turkey. Istanbul, in particular, which is defined as a flagship city and a symbol of the standing government's political legacy, has become more vulnerable in terms of socio-ecological and economic issues.

The city's population increased dramatically after the 1990s, attracting more than 400,000 people from 2007 to 2013 (net migration) from different parts of the country. Furthermore, in recent years, increasing numbers of migrants have been coming from abroad, with figures from the 1995–2000 period indicating the arrival of 54,644 people to the city from overseas. During the same period, Istanbul's economy grew much faster than the rest of the country, with the city's real GDP forecast for the 2012–2017 period being 6.6 per cent, compared to 3.6 per cent in the rest of the country, according to Euromonitor International (2017). Reflecting the rapid population and economic growth, Istanbul decentralised rapidly towards the periphery, while the inner city areas were increasingly intensified as a result of different factors, including renewal projects clearing informal housing areas and luxurious redevelopment projects from the 1980s onwards. Furthermore, the inner city came under additional pressure to intensify as a result of the internationalisation of services and the attractiveness of the city among foreign producers.

These two processes brought with them increasing vulnerabilities for the Istanbul metropolis. Firstly, the sprawl of the city created demand for land at the periphery in the watershed areas of the drinking water reserves, as well as in the forested areas to the north, which are critical to the sustainability of the ecosystem. Second, the intensification and transformation of the inner zones has led to gentrification and deeper socio-spatial segregation, exacerbated by the rapid population growth and migration to the city, while also increasing traffic and pollution, among other problems. Political entrepreneurialism added further vulnerabilities to the already complex urban system of Istanbul through mega-projects, which went against the real needs of the city. According to an Expert Opinion Survey that aimed to define the main vulnerabilities of the Istanbul metropolitan area (Yaman, 2016), the polled public and private stakeholders cited earthquake risk, the lack of infrastructure, the high percentage of unplanned areas, the low share of well-educated and skilled manpower, and the high population density as the major vulnerabilities of the Istanbul metropolis.

The Response of Planning to Increasing Vulnerabilities

To what extent are the existing vulnerabilities of the metropolitan area taken into consideration *in planning* Istanbul? In seeking an answer to this question, a review of three main plans prepared for the Istanbul metropolitan area provides some indications. The first plan, prepared by the Istanbul Metropolitan Planning Bureau that was drawn up in 1966 and approved by the Ministry of Reconstruction and Resettlement in 1980, aimed to define an urban form for the Istanbul metropolitan area. The plan proposed a mixture of compact and linear forms, the revitalisation of the central business district and the expansion of the urban core functions towards the immediate surroundings. The plan aimed to protect the city's environmental resources and applied limits to prevent the spread of the city; however, the construction of the second Bosporus Bridge (1988) and the Trans-European Motorway encouraged urban sprawl by making high-speed commuting by motor vehicle possible, thus changing the geography of the city. In 1984, the Istanbul Metropolitan Municipality formed a new city planning directorate, which prepared a new master plan at 1/50 000 scale that was approved by the council of the Istanbul Metropolitan Municipality in 1995. Still following a pragmatic approach, the plan aimed to provide technical solutions to the emerging problems, targeting a relocation of industry from central locations to the fringe, particularly those causing pollution, and the refunctioning of the former industrial areas for offices and other commercial uses. The plan also designated new housing areas at the fringe to serve the increasing population and to relieve the pressure on land and housing prices in the inner city, along with regularisation schemes for most of the former unauthorised housing areas. In short, the plan sought to adapt the metropolitan area to the changing global economic conditions.

The third plan, at 1/100 000 scale, was prepared by the Istanbul Metropolitan Planning Office (IMP) of the Istanbul Metropolitan Municipality, following the enlargement of the municipal boundaries. Several experts, working under the direction of the IMP, spent more than a year developing the new master plan, which was approved by the Istanbul Metropolitan Municipal Council (IMMC) in July 2006, and circulated subsequently to a wide range of stakeholders. Partly as a result of criticisms of both substance and the planning process, the IMMC were compelled to make another version of the plan, this time making greater use of inputs from district municipalities, university professors, civil engineers and non-governmental organisations. This plan reflected some concerns of planners on the sustained urban development and placed more emphasis on balancing environmental and economic priorities. During the preparation of the plan it was calculated that Istanbul could accommodate a maximum of 16 million inhabitants based on its ecological thresholds – as dictated by its existing preservation zones, water catchment areas and forestry lands, and the plan was prepared taking this figure into consideration, while also trying to promote economic development and Istanbul's status as a global city.

This master plan marked an important turning point in the city's attempt to balance land use development and environmental protection. The implementation, however, has been incomplete, and over time the gap between the plan and actual land use policy and practice has grown increasingly wide. Its emphasis on the protection of water basins and forests in the north can be appreciated as attempts to reflect ecological concerns, but what happened after it was approved is worthy of note. Although the plan was prepared and approved by the Justice and Development Party (AKP), it was the AKP government that first violated the plan. In 2011, the AKP announced the launch of several mega-projects, some of which were aimed at solving long-standing infrastructure problems, while others were more symbolic, and aimed to reflect their ideology. To offer insight into some of these:

- Mega-infrastructure projects that were not proposed in the plan, and even some that are defined as ecologically destructive, have been initiated. The largest and most environmentally significant projects[4] are the third bridge and motorway ring (completed), the third airport (underway), and the 'crazy' Canal Istanbul Project (the location of the project has been recently announced). These projects will negatively affect large forest areas and water reserves that are imperative for the ecological resilience of the Istanbul metropolitan area and will have a tremendous impact on nature and the direction of the residential development, commuting patterns and urban sustainability of Istanbul (Gürçay, 2016). These projects are located in the northern part of the city designated as *preservation areas* in the plan.
- A tremendous amount of construction is underway in the inner city, most of which is being constructed under special planning provisions provided by central government organisations. On the whole, they are aimed at increasing residential and commercial density within the urban core, and include Maslak 1453, the Zorlu Center and the Istanbul Financial Center Project.
- The urban renewal and redevelopment projects and new housing projects that have been initiated by the HDA go against the aim of the plan to control population increase. In direct contrast to these aims, the HDA is becoming increasingly involved in the construction of high-density/high-rise building estates and condominiums.
- The iconic projects have been passed, and some of them are already underway, such as Çamlıca Mosque (which will become the city's largest mosque, and will change the skyline of Istanbul) and the Taksim project (recreating an old Ottoman Barrack in Taksim Square).

All of these projects, which have been made possible through planning decisions and/or amendments to existing planning decisions, point to over-politicised decision making by the central government in urban governance and planning. This form of fragmented decision making does not reflect a problem-solving and pragmatic approach (since the aim is not to resolve problems, but leads instead to the creation of problems, such as urban congestion), nor does it reflect the norms and values of different groups.

Considering resilience thinking in planning, one question remains unanswered. When facing increasingly authoritarian decision making that ignores the local networks of governance, local urban policy-making mechanisms and the preferences of most residents (more than half of the population), would it be possible to launch new policies and decision-making models that institutionalise resilience thinking?

Conclusions: How Is It Possible to Institute Resilience in Complex Metropolitan Cities?

In the previous sections we have underlined three important drawbacks when considering the future of planning in Istanbul. First, urban governance is becoming increasingly authoritarian, and planning decisions that reflect political aspirations are putting great pressure on planning practice. Second, Turkish society is becoming increasingly divided in terms of ideologies, values and norms, which is having significant repercussions on the perception of urban issues. Third, the political leaders know well their followers' demands and the context in which they respond and interact, while disregarding the norms and values of those in opposition. Moreover, the increasing commodification of land and the need to attract larger and larger sums of foreign direct investment make the politics of growth extremely attractive and the appeal of megaprojects almost impossible for some groups to resist.

At the beginning of 2002, the standing government magnified and used the discontent of a part of the population through the manipulation of public desires for economic stability, economic growth and better living conditions. The middle- to low-income groups with strong religious traits, who believed that they had not benefitted sufficiently from the secular republican ideology, became the major supporters of the new ideology. Over the last decade, with the help of the state apparatus, many increased their welfare and emerged as a new affluent group, and under the new conditions, it became increasingly difficult to speak about shared norms, values and principles. With the crackdown on existing institutions in the increasingly polarised society, social intercourse became impossible in urban governance and planning. Under these conditions, in which power relations are dominated by top-down political interventions and value systems and divided through the indoctrination of new norms, instituting a new approach to urban planning can be evaluated as an idealised agenda. Still, it is necessary to discuss possible means of dealing with the above issues, while also thinking about how to resolve existing and emerging problems by paying the necessary attention to the vulnerabilities of the metropolis. At this point, we can refer to our original arguments on the institution of resilience thinking in planning.

First, *priority setting in vulnerabilities is critical*, which demands the definition of no-regret conditions by gaining an understanding of the systemic characteristics. Different forms of resistance can be applied to address the priority issues preventing resilient urban transformation and development. As Foucault suggests (1991), there are some ways in which the exercise of power can be resisted. As he argues, as soon as a power relation emerges, there is the possibility of resistance. Several types of resistance dominate the discussions in resistance studies, including confrontations and public challenges to power; everyday resistance that is hidden; circumventing forms of disguised resistance; and non-violent resistance, which has attracted increasing attention as a form of everyday resistance. In Turkey, Gezi Park can be held up as a good example of non-violent resistance, and this had important impacts on policy makers, being more successful than the other forms of demonstration that were seen.

Second, *defining adaptation strategies to changes to achieve sustainable development is vital* – for example, the creation of platforms for discussion within the planning process can be useful. Active participation and discussion, although not easy to achieve, can be a way of avoiding the top-down decisions that impose different projects upon the metropolis. With limited participation and inclusiveness in planning, as we see in the Istanbul case, it is difficult to build a forum among residents to discuss both the problems and solutions that will enhance urban adaptive capacity. In most cases, like elsewhere, participatory forums bring together selected interest groups, while other groups with limited representative power or those belonging to opposition groups are excluded. The Istanbul case also shows that losing values and resources in built environments have become an entrenched syndrome among the urban elite, which is not shared by the people who are getting material benefit from the change in urban environment.

In earlier decades, obtaining the views of the different groups on issues related to their city was difficult, but today, communication technologies are offering new opportunities in this regard. As experienced within the Gezi movements in Turkey, social media and other forms of digital communication changed the dynamics of participation and inclusion. That said, as Hall (2011) states, excluded social groups whose consent has not been sought, or whose interests have not been taken into account, form the basis of counter-movements, resistance, alternative strategies and visions. Existing organisations, including professional associations, environmental advocates, NGOs, and other citizen and neighbourhood groups, can be useful in increasing public awareness regarding mega-projects by disseminating information through social media, and organising press conferences, public discussion panels, academic lectures and street protests, besides explaining their concerns on urban issues. In the Istanbul case, there are a number of important websites (like www.kuzeyormanlari.org and mulksuzlestirme.org) that give information on the new projects in Istanbul and their possible impacts.

Instituting self-regulation potential is also important. Even a hierarchical regime cannot completely neglect and deny the functional needs of housing and liveability. There have been a number of attempts at self-regulation in Istanbul in different periods, for example, in the Gülsuyu and Gülensu neighbourhoods, which resulted in the local and central government institutions having to take into account the concerns of the local residents. This cooperative behaviour and efforts to build self-organisational capacity were rather successful in this case (Özdemir & Eraydin, 2017).

Finally, while resistance and social intercourse are important, *planning still necessitates new democratic mechanisms and new models of governance*. One of the aims of democratic platforms can be to show people not only what they are gaining from changes to the metropolis and their living environment, but also what they are losing. Several studies show that households that were attracted by rent when seeking new housing projects are not satisfied with their new living conditions (Erman, 2016; Türkün, 2014). Revitalising the institutions of local representative democracy is essential in this respect, and there could be opportunities at the local and community level for urbanites to be more active in issues of urban change and new developments. It is time for a radical rethink of the relationship between the general public and the government, and planners should understand their options in affirmative action when seeking to bridge the deep divisions.

Notes

1 Healey (2003) responded to some of the criticisms, pointing out that substance and process are not separate spheres, but are rather co-constituted. Forester (1999, p. 263) also indicated that the inclusiveness of the process may balance the power differences.
2 Despite its attractiveness, the resilience concept, which has a variety of origins, is yet to be attributed with a universally acknowledged definition (Brand & Jax, 2007).
3 The Turkish Mass Housing Authority (TOKI), which had been created to supply new housing units for low- and medium-income groups, became increasingly active in putting into operation the projects of the central government in urban areas. In such urban redevelopment schemes the HDA acts as a private

enterprise, assigning apartment units (defined according to the size of the land) to land owners (some of which were *gecekondu* or 'slum' owners) in return for their land/property. The remaining apartment units are sold at market value, giving some privileges to those who do not own a housing unit in the same city.

4 According to the extensive data compiled by the Independent Architects' Association (SMD), the third airport (located on the Black Sea) will cover an area of 76,500,000 square meters, while the third motorway ring (Kuzey Marmara Otoyolu) will constitute 421 kilometers of roadway. Compared to these two mega-projects, Canal Istanbul, which will create a second waterway connecting the Black and Marmara Seas, looks quite modest at 42 kilometers.

References

Albrechts, L. (2010). More of the same is not enough! How could strategic spatial planning be instrumental in dealing with the challenges ahead? *Environment and Planning B: Planning and Design*, 37(6), 1115–1127.
Berkes, F., Folke, C., & Colding, C. (2003). *Navigating Social-Ecological Systems: Building Resilience for Complexity and Change*. Cambridge: Cambridge University Press.
Boddy, M., & Parkinson, M., (Eds.). (2004). *City Matters: Competitiveness, Cohesion and Urban Governance*. Bristol: Policy Press.
Brand, F. S., & Jax, K. (2007). Focusing the meaning(s) of resilience: Resilience as a descriptive concept and a boundary object. *Ecology and Society*, 12(1), 23–38. Retrieved from: www.ecologyandsociety.org/vol12/iss1/art23.
Buff, I. (2012). Authoritarian Neoliberalism, the Occupy Movements, and IPE. *Journal of Critical Globalisation Studies*, 5, 114–116.
Christopherson, S., Michie, J., & Tyler, P. (2010). Regional resilience: Theoretical and empirical perspectives. *Cambridge Journal of Regions, Economy and Society*, 3(1), 3–10.
Davidson, M., & McNeill, D. (2011). The redevelopment of Olympic sites: Examining the legacy of Sydney Olympic Park. *Urban Studies*, 49(8), 1625–1641.
Davoudi, S. (2012). Resilience: A bridging concept or a dead end? *Planning Theory & Practice*, 13(2), 299–307.
Eraydin, A., & Taşan-Kok, T. (2013). *Resilience Thinking in Urban Planning*. Dordrecht: Springer.
Eraydin, A. (2013). 'Resilience Thinking' for Planning. In *Resilience Thinking in Urban Planning* (pp. 17–37). Dordrecht: Springer.
Eraydin, A., & Taşan-Kok, T. (2014). State response to contemporary urban movements in Turkey: A critical overview of state entrepreneurialism and authoritarian interventions. *Antipode*, 46(1), 110–129.
Erman, T. (2016). *Mış Gibi Site: Ankara'da Bir TOKİ-Gecekondu Dönüşüm Sitesi*. Istanbul: İletişim.
Euromonitor International. (2017). Istanbul City Review. Retrieved from: www.euromonitor.com/istanbul-city-review/report.
Fainstein, S. S. (2000). New directions in planning theory. *Urban Affairs Review*, 35(4), 451–478.
Fainstein, S. S. (2001). *Competitiveness, Cohesion and Governance: A Review of the Literature*. New Brunswick, NJ: Rutgers University. Retrieved from: http://cwis.livjm.ac.uk/cities/conference/sf.pdf (12 April 2006).
Fainstein, S. S. (2005). Planning theory and the city. *Journal of Planning Education and Research*, 25(2), 121–130.
Flyvbjerg, B. (1998). *Rationality and Power: Democracy in Practice*. Chicago, IL: University of Chicago Press.
Folke, C., Carpenter, S., Walker, B., Scheffer, M., Chapin, T., & Rockstrom, J. (2010). Resilience thinking: Integrating resilience, adaptability and transformability. *Ecology and Society*, 15(4), 1–20.
Forester, J. (1999). Dealing with Deep Value Differences. In L. Susskind, S. McKearnan & J. Thomas-Larmer (Eds.), *The Consensus Building Handbook* (pp. 463–493). Thousand Oaks, CA: Sage.
Foucault, M. (1991). *Discipline And Punish: The Birth of a Prison*. London: Penguin.
Gunder, M., & Hillier, J. (2009). *Planning in Ten Words or Less: A Lacanian Entanglement with Spatial Planning*. Abingdon: Routledge.
Gunderson, L. (1999). Resilience, flexibility and adaptive management: Antidotes for spurious certitude? *Conservation Ecology*, 3(1), 7. Retrieved from: www.consecol.org/ vol3/iss1/art7.
Gupta, J., Termeer, C., Klostermann, J., Meijerink, S., Brink, M. van den, Jong, P., ... Bergsma, E. (2010). The adaptive capacity wheel: A method to assess the inherent characteristics of institutions to enable the adaptive capacity of society. *Environmental Science and Policy*, 13(6), 459–471.
Gürçay, M. (2016). *The Impact of Third Bridge on the Resilience of Istanbul* (PhD Thesis). Ankara: Follow-Up Document, METU.

Healey, P. (1999). Institutionalist Analysis, Communicative Planning, and Shaping Places. *Journal of Planning Education and Research*, 19, 111–121.

Hall, S. (2011). The neo-liberal revolution. *Cultural Studies*, 25(6), 705–728.

Healey P. (2003). Collaborative Planning in Perspective. *Acoustics, Speech, and Signal Processing Newsletter, IEEE*, 2(2), 101–123.

Huxley, M. (2000). The limits to communicative planning. *Journal of Planning Education and Research*, 19, 369–377.

Harris, N. (2002). Collaborative Planning. In P. Allmendinger & M. Tewdwr-Jones (Eds.), *Planning Futures: New Directions for Planning Theory* (pp. 21–43). London: Routledge.

Hillier, J. (2002). Direct Action and Agonism in Democratic Planning Practice. In P. Allmendinger & M. Tewdwr-Jones (Eds.), *Planning Futures: New Directions for Planning Theory* (pp. 110–135). New York: Routledge.

Holling, C. S. (1992). Cross-scale morphology, geometry and dynamics of ecosystems. *Ecological Monographs*, 62(4), 447–502.

Hudson, R. (2010). Resilient regions in an uncertain world: Wishful thinking or a practical reality? *Cambridge Journal of Regions, Economy and Society*, 3(1), 11–25.

Hoch, C. (1996). A Pragmatic Inquiry about Planning and Power. In S. Mandelbaum, L. Mazza & R. Burchell (Eds.), *Explorations in Planning Theory*. Clifton: CUPR.

Jou, S. J., Hansen, A. L., & Wu, H. L. (2011). Accumulation by dispossession and neoliberal urban planning: 'Landing' the mega-projects in Taipei. In T. Taşan-Kok & G. Baeten (Eds.), *Contradictions of Neoliberal Planning: Cities, Policies, and Politics* (pp. 151–173). Dordrecht: Springer.

Kaika, M. (2017). Don't call me resilient again! The new urban agenda as immunology... or what happens when communities refuse to be vaccinated with 'smart cities' and indicators. *Environment and Urbanization*, 29(1), 89–102. Retrieved from: http://dx.doi.org/10.1177/0956247816684763.

Lemke, T. (2001). *Foucault, Governmentality, and Critique*. Paper Presented at the Rethinking Marxism Conference, University of Amherst (MA), 21–24 September 2000.

Ludwig, D., Walker, B., & Holling, C. S. (1997). Sustainability, stability, and resilience. *Conservation Ecology*. Retrieved from: www.consecol.org/vol1/iss1/art7.

Maru, Y. (2010). *Resilient Regions: Clarity of Concepts and Challenges to Systemic Measurement*. No 2010–04, Socio-Economics and the Environment in Discussion (SEED). Working Paper Series from CSIRO Sustainable Ecosystems.

McGuirk, P. (2001). Situating communicative planning theory: Context, power, and knowledge. *Environment and Planning A*, 33(2), 195–217.

Mouffe, C. (1999). Deliberative democracy or agonistic pluralism? *Social Research*, 66(3), 745–758.

Mouffe, C. (2000). *The Democratic Paradox*. London: Verso.

Olsson, P., Folke, C., & Berkes, F. (2004). Adaptive comanagement for building resilience in social-ecological systems. *Environmental Management*, 34(1), 75–90.

Ostrom, E. (1990). *Governing the Commons: The Evolution of Institutions for Collective Action*. Cambridge: Cambridge University Press.

Özdemir, E., & Eraydin, A. (2017). Fragmentation in urban movements: The role of urban planning processes. *International Journal of Urban and Regional Research*, 41(5), 727–748.

Peck, J., Theodore, N., & Brenner, N. (2009). Neoliberal urbanism: Models, moments, mutations. *SAIS Review*, XXIX(1), 49–66.

Pendall, R., Foster, K. A., & Cowell, M. (2010). Resilience and regions: Building understanding of the metaphor. *Cambridge Journal of Regions, Economy and Society*, 3(1), 71–84.

Purcell, M. (2009). Resisting neoliberalization: Communicative planning or counter-hegemonic movements? *Planning Theory*, 8(2), 140–165.

Raco, M., & Street, E. (2012). Resilience planning, economic change and the politics of post-recession development in London and Hong Kong. *Urban Studies*, 49(5), 1065–1087.

Resilience Alliance. (2010). Assessing resilience in social-ecological systems: A workbook for practitioners. Version 2.0. Retrieved from: www.resalliance.org/3871.php (27 February 2012).

Salet, W. G. M, & Guallini, E. (2006). *Framing Strategic Urban Projects: Learning from Current Experiences in European Urban Regions*. Oxon: Routledge.

Salet, W. G. M, & Majoor, S. (2005). Reshaping the urbanity in Amsterdam region. In W. G. M. Salet & S. Majoor (Eds.), *Amsterdam Zuidas: European Space* (pp. 19–24). Rotterdam: 010 Publishers.

Shaw, K., & Theobald, K. (2011). Resilient local government and climate change interventions in the UK. *Local Environment*, 16(1), 1–15.

Swyngedouw, E., Moulaert, F., & Rodriguez, A. (2002). Neoliberal urbanization in Europe: Large-scale urban development projects and the new urban policy. *Antipode*, 34(3), 542–575.

Taşan-Kok, T. (2008). Changing interpretations of 'flexibility' in the planning literature: From opportunism to creativity? *International Planning Studies*, 13(3), 183–195.

Taşan-Kok, T. (2011). Introduction. In T. Taşan-Kok & G. Baeten (Eds.), *Contradictions of Neoliberal Planning: Cities, Policies, and Politics* (pp. 1–20). Dordrecht: Springer.

Taylor, N. (1998). Mistaken interests and the discourse model of planning. *Journal of the American Planning Association*, 64(1), 64–75.

Tewdwr-Jones, M., & Allmendinger, P. (1998). Deconstructing communicative rationality: A critique of Habermasian collaborative planning. *Environment and Planning A*, 30(11), 1975–1989.

Türkün, A. (2014). *Mülk, Mahal, İnsan: İstanbul'da Kentsel Dönüşüm*. Istanbul: İstanbul Bilgi Üniversitesi Yayınları.

Walker, B., Holling, C. S., Carpenter, S. R., & Kinzig, A. P. (2004). Resilience, adaptability and transformability in social-ecological systems. *Ecology and Society*, 9(2), 5. Retrieved from: www.ecologyandsociety.org/vol9/iss2/art5.

Walker, B., Salt, D., & Reid, W. (2006). *Resilience Thinking: Sustaining Ecosystems and People in a Changing World*. Washington, DC: Island Press.

Watson, V. (2002). Do we learn from planning practice? The contribution of the practice movement to planning theory. *Journal of Planning Education and Research*, 22(2), 178–187.

Wilkinson, C. (2011). Urban resilience: What does it mean in planning practice. *Planning Theory & Practice*, 13(2), 319–324.

Wilkinson, C. (2011). Social-ecological resilience: Insights and issues for planning theory. *Planning Theory*, 11(2), 148–169. Retrieved from: http:dx.doi.org/10.1177/1473095211426274.

Yaman, Z. (2016). *Urban Resilience as a New Policy Paradigm for Spatial Planning to Achieve Sustainable Urban Development: The Case of Istanbul* (PhD Thesis). Istanbul: Follow-Up Document, Istanbul Technical University.

Young, I. (1996). Communication and the Other: Beyond Deliberative Democracy. In S. Benhabib (Ed.), *Democracy and difference* (pp. 120–136). Princeton, NJ: Princeton University Press.

Young, I. (1999). Difference as a Resource for Democratic Communication. In J. Bohman & W. Rehg (Eds.), *Deliberative democracy* (pp. 383–406). Boston, MA: MIT Press.

24
URBAN TRANSFORMATION IN THE NORTHERN RANDSTAD
How Institutions Structure Planning Practice

Jochem de Vries & Wil Zonneveld

Introduction

The opening chapter in this volume clarifies the tension between the time-honoured dominance of pragmatism in the field of planning and the need for institutional reflection. Its argument is based on the recognition that planning is a multi-faceted and complex social phenomenon, which requires a sound triangulation of perspectives in order to be understood completely. The acknowledgement that both pragmatism and institutionalism are equally important in shaping and evaluating planning interventions poses a challenge to both planning professionals and academic researchers. The main challenge is to strike a balance between the goal-oriented problem solving of pragmatism and the need for reflection on societal norms. Chapter 1 also provides an overview of the existing institutional approaches relevant for planning and the frictions between these approaches and pragmatism. It comprehensively lays out the way institutions 'work' and describes the frictions between institutional and pragmatic reasoning, but the analysis is predominantly theoretical. In this chapter, we aim to establish the empirical value of looking at planning practice through the institution/pragmatism lenses. Our main objective is to show the added value of putting planning in its institutional context, without losing sight of its problem-solving ambitions.

The concept of institutions – or 'normative patterns' – is very broad: it ranges from fundamental values and norms to widely accepted beliefs about 'how things are done'. This chapter focuses on a specific set of institutions: the law and, more precisely, the legal rules aimed at securing sustainable urban development. The case of environmental regulation and urban development highlights the abovementioned tension between institutional demands and the search for pragmatic problem solving. On the one hand, a broad array of European and national environmental legislation has been put into effect over the past few decades. Much of national legislation directly emanates from regulation made by the European Union as it sets frameworks and goals that national legislators need to meet, which results in a complex multilevel institutional context (Van Tatenhove et al., 2000). Importantly, European and national legislation consists of both specific rules (e.g. air quality standards) as well as general rules such as the 'polluter-pays principle'.

Environmental regulations possess many properties generally associated with institutions. They create a certain degree of predictability, create legitimacy, engender and reinforce certain practices, create meaning, impose constraints that are difficult to negotiate or are even non-negotiable and facilitate interaction between stakeholders. Meanwhile, the planning and management of urban development has become a different ball game in the Netherlands altogether. The post-war greenfield urban extensions based on generic cookie-cutter blueprints has given way to brownfield redevelopments exploiting unique local characteristics. The strict modernist separation of functions has given way to mixed land-use planning. Heavily regulated and subsidised government programmes have been replaced by public-private partnerships and more reliance on market mechanisms. Masterplans are out, public participation is in. While these tendencies have not completely supplanted traditional Dutch planning practice, it has led to more complex planning processes, more variety between projects and more local and regional customisation. In other words, contemporary urban development increasingly resembles the pragmatist approach. Pragmatism is adept at dealing with non-standard or even unique situations where many conflicts have to be resolved simultaneously, where the interests of stakeholders are taken seriously and knowledge and values have become completely intertwined (Campbell et al., 2014; Flyvbjerg, 2005; Hajer & Wagenaar, 2003; Healey, 1993, 1997; Innes & Booher, 1999).

With the above in mind, we pose the main question of this chapter as follows: *how do environmental rules, as institutional conditions, structure the pragmatic search for solutions in communicative planning processes?* By rules as institutional conditions we mean environmental legislation and its associated rules – referred to as legal norms in the remainder of this chapter – and their properties from an institutional perspective. The 'pragmatic search for solutions' refers to the characteristics of planning as a pragmatist endeavour. This is as much about the substantive dimension – what physical interventions are proposed – as the procedural dimension – how are these interventions organised – of planning. Below we will elaborate on the properties of environmental legislation as institutions and the characteristics of planning as a pragmatist endeavour. The emphasis on structuring (Giddens, 1984) implies that we consider institutions both limiting as enabling conditions for practices like planning. As a limiting factor, they may create tensions between the demands of institutions and the ambitions of a planning project. Furthermore, we assume that institutions obtain and maintain their meaning and influence as part of social processes (Dembski & Salet, 2010). In other words, institutions are interpreted in particular instances in social interactions between actors (Van Rijswick & Salet, 2012). Therefore our search to better understand the relationship between institutional conditions and urban planning and development is focussed on enablement, limitations/tensions and dynamics between actors.

The remainder of this chapter is structured as follows. In the following two sections, we will explore and elaborate on the concepts of institutionalism and pragmatism in more detail. Next, we present some of the highlights of a number of case studies undertaken in a large international research project on the contextualisation of environmental norms in planning projects.[1] This is followed by a section that discusses the empirical findings in light of the theoretical discussion. We round off with a short concluding section. The cases we discuss are all located in the Netherlands – the northern part of the Randstad which includes the Amsterdam and Utrecht regions – as we do not seek to compare between countries. Our main interest is to bring forward particular issues about the relationship between institutionalism and pragmatism in 'real life' which hopefully inspires others to study other cases from a similar perspective.

An Institutional Perspective on Environmental Regulation

What does it mean to take an institutional perspective? The concept of institutions is notoriously abstract, multi-interpretable and wide-ranging (Hall & Taylor, 1996). To guide our exploration, we will focus on the properties that are particularly relevant for our view of environmental rules as institutions.

Institutions provide actors with a logic of appropriateness as opposed to a logic of consequence.

> The logic of appropriateness is a perspective on how human action is to be interpreted. Action, policy making included, is seen as driven by rules of appropriate or exemplary behavior, organized into institutions. The appropriateness of rules includes both cognitive and normative components. Rules are followed because they are seen as natural, rightful, expected, and legitimate. Actors seek to fulfill the obligations encapsulated in a role, an identity, a membership in a political community or group, and the ethos, practices, and expectations of its institutions. Embedded in a social collectivity, they do what they see as appropriate for themselves in a specific type of situation.
> (March & Olsen, 2013, p. 1)

March and Olsen's notion of the logic of appropriateness is quoted at length here because it eloquently and concisely outlines the various properties associated with institutions. It should be emphasised that this abstraction and classification is done purely for analytical purposes; in reality, these properties are closely intertwined. Norms and meaning are often two sides of the same coin. Similarly, it is also often impossible to determine whether actors deem particular behaviour as 'appropriate' for reasons of legitimacy or out of fear of sanctions (Giddens, 1984).

As stated in the quote above, institutions have a *behavioural* component. The 'logic of appropriateness' offers a perspective in which policy actors are not solely driven by calculated self-interest. Legal norms are institutions that, at their best, posit that certain rules will and must be followed irrespective of the particular interest actors may have within a specific situation. An obvious and necessary precondition is that these norms are known and, preferably, internalised. Given the proliferation of environmental legislation, such knowledge and internalisation cannot simply be taken for granted; over the past 30 years, the number of legal rules in the Netherlands has grown steadily by about 2% per year (De Jong & Zijlstra, 2009). This is, at least in part, a logical consequence of the legitimate desire to control risks within an increasingly complex society (Van Tatenhove et al., 2000). However, it has also produced a labyrinthine legal framework, which can frustrate the ambitions and aspirations of actors engaged in societal problem solving. To explore this, Van Rijswick and Salet argue that a distinction should be made between instrumental and institutional uses of legislation (Van Rijswick & Salet, 2012). The latter is usually expressed as general principles, rules and material and procedural norms (see also Buijze et al., Chapter 13, in this volume; Evers, 2015).

Contextualisation is crucial in this regard: it should be possible to adapt institutional norms to very different local situations to grant actors the leeway to achieve their objectives as they see fit. It does not require openness but generalisation and abstraction of the institutional conditions. Institutional norms may be articulated in precise ways, but they always act at a general level of abstraction: they set standards under which social interaction occurs rather than dictating individual behaviour. A case in point is the use of general principles such as the precautionary principle or the non-shift principle within the sustainability principle: these two norms indicate *what* should be achieved but not *how* it should be done. Consequently, they allow actors to devise solutions that fit their particular context. The same applies to substantive norms and procedural norms (Van Rijswick & Salet, 2012; Buijze et al., Chapter 13, this volume). More generally, it has been suggested that the present era of late-modernity requires a fundamental rethinking of the relationship between centralised governing through, for example, national and supra-national environmental regulations, and decentralised decision-making in areas such as urban planning. In essence, globalisation and individualisation have led to a situation of 'extreme pluralism', which, among other things, have made nation states increasingly incapable of controlling the behaviour of their subjects. An alternative to micromanaging the behaviour of actors in order to solve environmental problems is to set up institutions that require the same actors to engage in 'self-confrontation' with the environmental risks stemming from their actions (without prescribing how they should be addressed) (Van Tatenhove et al., 2000).

As a second property, institutions provide legitimation. They ascribe legitimacy, and define what is expected of individuals within a particular community. With regard to environmental norms, this function manifests itself in different ways. Of course, abiding to the appropriate legal standards grants an actor the legitimacy to develop. Respecting established safety distances to hazardous materials or observing the principle of good neighbourliness (Van Rijswick & Salet, 2012) contributes to the societal acceptance of a development. However, the legitimating property of environmental norms goes beyond this behaviour-influencing characteristic as institutions define "the role, the identity, a membership in a political community or group" (March & Olsen, 2013; Scharpf, 1997). Environmental norms therefore are also about who is allowed to participate, in what form and in what stage of decision-making. The Environmental Impact Assessment procedure, for example, defines who should take the initiative and who should be consulted. The idea of self-confrontation could be promoted by the formation of ad hoc coalitions of opposing interests where environmental interests are well represented (Van Tatenhove et al., 2000). Hence, legal institutions have a role to play in constructing such 'coalitions of opposites'. A complicating factor is that role-defining institutions bestow different identities on actors at the same time.

A third property of institutions is their cognitive component. Cognitive templates such as symbols, paradigms and assumptions about causal relationships provide actors with meaning and introduce – systemic – biases (see Healey, Chapter 2, in this volume). These frames are used both consciously and unconsciously (Giddens, 1984). They structure the policy belief systems of actors on fundamental issues such as climate change and more instrumental issues such as promoting dense urban development to reduce environmental footprints (Sabatier, 1988). In accordance with the logic of appropriateness, cognitive templates are often taken for granted and unquestioned. Norms obtain their precise meaning through actions in particular contexts. With regard to environmental norms, one can consider how the compensation principle works in practice. As a cognitive frame, it assumes that the loss of a certain environmental quality (e.g. the loss of surface water as a result of housing development) in one place can be offset by developing the same quality (e.g. a new pond) somewhere else. The forms compensation may take in a particular case depends highly on geographical characteristics such as scale and terrain features. Furthermore, because the physical world plays a key role in environmental problems, the cognitive frames within the natural sciences are strongly reproduced by institutions in this field. The ontological and epistemological features of the natural sciences frequently clash with the prevailing cognitive frames within political processes such as planning.

Giddens (1984) adds two important characteristics of institutions that were not explicitly treated so far. First, he emphasises that institutional conditions do not solely constrain action but also shape conditions for action, collective action in particular. If a logic of appropriateness is shared among actors, expectations are stabilised (Healey, 1997; Scharpf, 1997). Furthermore, institutions as patterns of actions should not only be studied in light of the intended consequences but also with regard to unintended consequences (Giddens, 1984). If policy is evaluated solely on the basis of goal-achievement, many relevant effects would be neglected. The Natura 2000 policy, for example, intended to protect endangered species, inadvertently caused some landowners to take measures – such as ploughing and removing surface water – in order to make their land uninhabitable for protected species and, in this way, evaded regulation (Van Dijk & Beunen, 2009).

Using the idea of a logic of appropriateness to identify relevant properties of environmental norms as institutions leads us to the following premises and questions.

1. Environmental norms are at the heart of the tension between, on the one hand, the practice of developing national and supra-national institutions to control risks in an increasingly complex society and on the other hand an increasing pluralism in which local actors demand and require the freedom to come up with tailor-made solutions. Norms that provide a way to force actors to actively consider the environmental consequences of their actions without prescribing how they should act could alleviate this tension.
2. Environmental norms provide legitimation to decisions in at least two ways. As behaviour-influencing rules, they provide a framework for spatial interventions. In addition, environmental norms provide actors with roles, duties and rights.
3. Environmental norms reinforce certain cognitive templates. Institutional rules obtain their specific meaning in practice, which takes place in very different contexts, with, for example, very different scalar and physical characteristics. How do these cognitive templates play out in concrete instances of spatial development?
4. Environmental norms provide constraints for actors and enable them at the same time. How do these norms shape the solution space, or "the conceptual space in which possible solutions might be found" (Forester, 1989, 123)?
5. Environmental norms have both intended and unintended consequences. How do they affect urban development projects?

The Pragmatic Face of Planning

Acknowledging that institutionalism and pragmatism are both important in shaping and evaluating planning interventions creates challenges. Some characteristics of planning as a pragmatic endeavour may be at odds with the logic of appropriateness as structured by institutions. For example, pragmatic-oriented planning implies experimenting with possible local solutions whereas the logic of appropriateness wishes to impose universal norms. Contemporary approaches to planning find inspiration in the conceptual roots of pragmatism. Under banners such as communicative planning (Healey, 1993), collaborative planning (Healey, 1997), deliberative planning (Hajer & Wagenaar, 2003), consensus building (Innes & Booher, 1999) and network governance (Hajer, 2009), planning and policy theory has developed an impressive body of knowledge and theory (hereafter referred to as communicative planning theory), which despite different accents and internal debates shows a remarkable coherence (Campbell et al., 2014). A key characteristic is that it focuses on solving identifiable and often unique – 'wicked' – problems. These problems should be solved through interactive commitment building that takes into account the specific power imbalances and interests of different stakeholders (Healey, 1997). This also implies that the framing of problems and solutions is an interactive process (Schön & Rein, 1995). This process of constructing and re-constructing problems and solutions has been aptly described as a "drifting cloud that continuously changes its shape during the planning process" (Friend & Hickling, 2005). Stakeholders come together and, sometimes by means of trial-and-error, find pragmatic solutions to complex collective action problems (Klijn & Koppenjan, 2000). What Hajer (2009) calls the loss of territorial synchrony – namely the mismatch between scale of territorial government and the scale of societal problems resulting in an 'institutional void' – is overcome by taking the geographical scope of the problem at hand as the point of departure. Since the acceptance of a solution by the stakeholders is the main criterion for success (Teisman, 2000), this adheres to the logic of consequence.

In the Netherlands these views on planning found – explicitly and implicitly – fertile ground. The Dutch practice of consensus building with its 'politics of accommodation' to appease social conflicts (Lijphart, 1975) fits within communicative planning theory. With regard to urban planning in the Netherlands, the practice of urban development or *gebiedsontwikkeling* (literally 'area development') closely resembles many of the characteristics that communicative planning theory expects from planning. Within an urban development project, public and private actors plan and develop an area together on the basis of an integrated vision and in doing so they cross territorial borders and sector boundaries (Needham, 2014). Scope for negotiation and barter is central to this process.

From an institutional perspective, communicative planning theory in general and the Dutch practice of urban development in particular, are not unproblematic. The question of which actors should be involved (and which excluded), the emphasis on equality, particularly between public and private actors, and the ease with which territorial borders are made auxiliary to problem solving, all make it difficult for institutions to perform their legitimising function. For example, environmental norms are meant to connect interests residing at different scales, while interactive planning projects have a tendency to limit themselves to a particular planning site. Not only is there a tendency to downplay or even ignore the institutional conditions in promoting communicative planning, in planning practice environmental norms are not infrequently blamed for producing red tape and thereby obstructing collaborative planning (OECD, 2007). According to Jones (2013) interactive governance,

> constrained by an underlying commitment to Habermasian ideals, according to which, for instance, the state and other external actors should facilitate and support deliberations amongst local actors and assist in enforcing decisions, but they should not instrumentally interfere with or undermine such deliberations.
>
> *(Jones, 2013, p. 47)*

Furthermore, communicative planning emphasises the importance of negotiated agreements and thereby puts into perspective the role of science in societal decision-making. Science should not have the upper hand in decision-making and, in the case of social science, should provide "input for public deliberation and decision-making, i.e. democratic due diligence" through "reflexive analysis of values and interests and how they affect different groups in society" (Flyvbjerg, 2005, p. 39). This may obviously create tensions due to the importance that environmental norms attach to scientific knowledge as a basis for interventions (spatial or otherwise), especially with regard to health and safety. The cognitive frames that are reinforced by environmental norms clearly set scientific knowledge apart from other sorts of knowledge such as the local experiences of inhabitants. One of the reasons to give science a privileged position is to counteract the problem of 'negotiated non-sense' (De Bruijn & Ten Heuvelhof, 2004). This problem arises when negotiations between stakeholders lead to an agreement that serves the interests of the stakeholders directly involved, but makes little sense for society at large.

What expectations are raised by this discussion of communicative planning theory and the practice of *gebiedsontwikkeling* ('area development')? Contemporary institutions, such as environmental norms, experience difficulties in performing their legitimating function in contemporary planning practices. On the other hand, these same institutions frustrate the ambitions

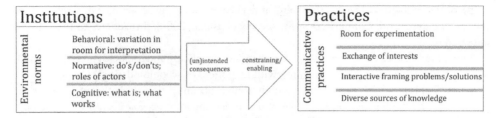

Figure 24.1 Conceptual framework of how environmental norms as institutions structure communicative planning practices
Source: authors' own

of current planning practices because they limit room for experimentation and the exchange of interests. Figure 24.1 lists a number of preliminary findings which may help us to better understand the way environmental norms as institutions structure practices of communicative planning. As stated, institutions have different – partially overlapping – characteristics. As behavioural rules, they vary in the extent to which they structure behaviour. While institutions-as-rules never exercise full control over actors, some form of interpretation and acceptance always exists (cf. Giddens, 1984). Obviously the room for interpretation and to manoeuvre varies considerably. When actors behave according to roles and rules indicated by institutional norms, they gain legitimacy for their actions. As cognitive frames, institutions provide information both about 'what is' and 'what works'. In structuring the behaviour of actors, they generate intended as well as unintended consequences and constrain and enable certain practices. With regard to the tension between environmental norms and communicative planning as a pragmatic practice, it is particularly interesting to look at the effect of institutions on the room for experimentation and give-and-take, the way problems and solutions are framed and which sources of knowledge are deemed acceptable in the process.

Findings: Three Dutch Cases

Amsterdam-Flevoland-North Holland: Markermeer-IJmeer[2]

The Markermeer-IJmeer is a large lake of about 700 km² in the centre of the Netherlands bordering an urban area known as the northern wing of the Randstad. From an ecological point of view the lake is in bad shape. According to European law – specifically Natura 2000 and the Water Framework Directive – the situation needs to be improved until 'a good status' is reached. This has become all the more urgent as there are plans for development at several locations on the edge of the lake (e.g. marinas). There are even plans of late for the construction of 40,000 houses (approximately 100,000 inhabitants) outside the dykes near the new town of Almere. This massive urban development would mean that a new bridge or tunnel would be needed to cross the lake.

An intricate strategy has been drawn up to enable this urban and infrastructural development while still complying with the legal requirement of maintaining 'a good ecological status'. It took nearly ten years before this strategy was laid down in a statutory planning document: the 2013 Structure Vision (*Structuurvisie*) Amsterdam-Almere-Markermeer. This strategy contains a number of ecological projects intended to clean the water – and will hopefully lead to 'good status' as demanded by the Water Framework Directive – as well as offering foraging sites for several protected bird species as stipulated in the Birds and Habitat Directives (which together comprise Natura 2000). The plan even seeks to create a so-called 'ecological surplus' to offset the anticipated negative effects of future development plans in and around the lake.

A strategy called the 'programmatic approach' was employed to overcome tensions between spatial planning practice and environmental legislation. It is set at the level of the entire Markermeer-IJmeer and treats the lake as a single integrated ecosystem. The prevailing cognitive frame used to address ecological issues such as the loss of ecological values due to urban or infrastructural development is to compensate for losses in the vicinity of the development project. The large-scale approach for the Markermeer-IJmeer can be regarded as an innovation in multiple ways. First, it underscores the realisation that the ecological status of a lake like this could not be adequately addressed through stand-alone projects. For this reason, a package of interrelated projects based on the principle 'building with nature' are being realised, including a system of islands with foliage intended to filter silt. The approach is monitored through what is called ecological bookkeeping which synthesizes all kinds of data on the ecological quality of the water. As this approach is unprecedented, it is highly experimental. It was for this reason that the province of Flevoland, as the most involved public stakeholder (almost the entire lake is located within its borders), sent a letter to the European Commission explaining the essence of the ecosystem strategy. The letter asked for an opinion as to whether this strategy adheres to Natura 2000. April 2009, the Commission responded positively but also made clear that this answer in no way bears any legal status as the Commission cannot bind Dutch courts.

The second innovation lies in the process architecture leading to the programmatic approach. This was not designed beforehand but came about in the form of an ad hoc coalition over a period of almost ten years, culminating in the 2013 Structure Vision mentioned above. All in all about 80 different actors were involved, including a number of crucial non-governmental actors, particularly Natuurmonumenten (the Dutch Society for Nature Conservation). The Markermeer-IJmeer case shows that a 'good' process – 'good' in the sense of inclusive based on a willingness on the side of government to include non-governmental actors – can turn potential opponents, who could challenge the project in court, into allies. The approach had been developed a few years earlier on a smaller scale. In the 1990s, the municipality of Amsterdam drew up plans for a major new housing development in the southeast corner of the IJmeer known as IJburg. The project led to massive opposition from environmental groups including Natuurmonumenten. A referendum (in 1997) to stop the plans was unsuccessful, and Natuurmonumenten switched sides and began to lobby for a highly ambitious approach for nature conservation (for an account, see Kinder, 2011).

An important condition for such an outcome was that the project goes beyond minimum requirements (and since the enforcement of minimum requirements can be decided by a simple court decision, more needs to be offered to ensure cooperation).

Amsterdam: Buiksloterham[3]

Buiksloterham is an area of about 100 hectares on the northern bank of the IJ, the waterway that separates Amsterdam's city centre from the northern district. Part of the area consists of vacant land and part is still in use by various types of industry. Because it is so close to the city centre – just a few hundred meters over water – the municipality opted for redevelopment and transformation into a mixed-use urban neighbourhood. The zoning strategy allows for residential development without removing all industrial functions. This was done as follows: sites were first selected for noisy companies that needed a location on an industrial estate. The remainder (and largest part of Buiksloterham) was zoned as mixed-use, but excluding functions that required an environmental (i.e. nuisance) permit since this would enable housing to be built in high densities. The strategy thus enabled new residential development while protecting existing 'pollution' rights and gained the support of industrial interests in the area. It is currently being applied at other locations in Amsterdam. In this sense, it can be called innovative: both in terms of land-use and in terms of governance. At the outset, the companies were wary of residential development because they expected complaints from future residents. The municipality successfully convinced them that the zoning would be designed to avoid this, and even paid for of a second-opinion study from an acoustic consultancy and a legal advisor to double-check the effects. In the end, only one company took legal action but withdrew its complaint after negotiations proved successful (Dembski, 2013, p. 8).

We can identify at least two fundamental issues in relation to how Amsterdam dealt with environmental norms and its 'pragmatic' choice to enable new housing. Buiksloterham demonstrates how environmental 'space' can be created through intricate zoning. It allows for compact and dense development while minimising the risk of residents taking legal action against companies renewing their environmental permit. Nevertheless the approach basically means that the minimum standards, which in this case are set by noise regulations, become maximum standards. This is obviously stimulated by the desire to realise a large housing development in the area.

This brings us to a second issue: the different roles played by the municipality. During the making of the Buiksloterham zoning plan, the municipality was also in charge of enforcing relevant environmental regulations (this is now carried out by a regional environmental agency). The municipality obviously also defined the spatial strategy for the area. The third role played by the municipality, and arguably the most problematic, is that of a property developer: the municipality owns land in Buiksloterham and has a financial stake in the lease of land. Following Dembski (2013), we feel these roles have not been sufficiently disentangled in the Buiksloterham case.

Utrecht Central Station Area[4]

The third case deals with a project known as Utrecht Central Station Area. This project seeks to redevelop 90 hectares in the city centre, including the rail station and an adjacent shopping mall. The project is being led by the municipality of Utrecht in close cooperation with private partners who own the bulk of property in the area. The development includes new shopping and leisure facilities, housing, parking as well as a canal, and is expected to be completed in 2030. We can only highlight a few of the challenges which this project faced (and still has) to face.

The first one regards the desire of the municipality to maintain flexibility with respect to the content of the development over time. However, this also made it rather difficult to draft a zoning plan for the area. The reason for this is that the Administrative Court of the Council of State, which rules on objections to land-use and zoning plans, places great value on legal certainty and therefore often demands detailed planning (this also was an issue in Buiksloterham). Obviously, this requirement is very difficult to deal with when redeveloping or transforming large urban areas over the course of many years. This is a clear example where pragmatism (especially the pragmatic redevelopment of a complex area) is at odds with a legal norm.

The Utrecht case was complicated further by the presence of soil contamination. Normally this would require expensive studies and massive decontamination. The problem was ameliorated by the introduction of an innovative area-oriented approach. The first innovation was technical, namely the installation of a 'bio-washing machine' which uses geothermal pumps to accelerate the natural breakdown of liquid hydrocarbon in the soil on site. However, the law at that particular moment of time – around roughly 2010 – did not allow for this. This is where the second innovation was introduced (a nice example of a synthesis between institutionalism and pragmatism): the bio-washing machine was redubbed a 'pilot project' for a new law dealing with soil contamination and thus was allowed to go forward under these auspices.

Another issue the Utrecht project faced is the fact that many legal norms are defined in relation to the status quo. Many regulations stipulate that the existing situation may not deteriorate – a direct consequence of the stand-still principle – but do not require improvements either. One of the many ambitions of the Utrecht Central Station project was to realise at least 10% surface water on the site, but this ambition initially fell on deaf ears as it was not encouraged by law. Obviously this situation is far from ideal. In fact, it actually encourages environmental concerns to be viewed as an obstacle rather than a goal. In this case, it produced some unexpected consequences. For example, an underground car park was designed close to the restoration of a canal, which had been drained in the 1960s. When the zoning plan for the car park was drafted, the canal was not included because, legally speaking, it was irrelevant as the new canal did not yet exist. However, from a common sense point of view, it would be wise to take the future canal into account when designing the garage in order to prevent potential water damage in the future. The issue was resolved through the water test procedure, which requires developers to consult the water board – in the Netherlands the authority with statutory competences related to water quantity and quality – and seriously consider its advice. As a result, the developer adapted the plans to include the canal. So, in the end, a procedural requirement resolved a rather odd conflict between environmental norms and pragmatism in planning.

Discussion: Dialogue Bridges the Divide

From the above we can draw some tentative conclusions about how environmental norms as institutions structure (i.e. enable and constrain) the pragmatic search for solutions in communicative planning processes. The conceptual difference between the enabling and constraining effects of institutions enables us to observe a clear difference between two kinds of impacts environmental norms can have. On the one hand, environmental norms clearly set boundaries – literally and figuratively – to development and therefore can constrain actors in their search for solutions. In many cases, environmental norms become a precondition to be met at the lowest cost and with minimal consequences for other ambitions in the project. On the other hand, we see instances where norms encourage innovative and creative solutions for environmental problems. In such instances, resolving environmental concerns can become an important goal in itself instead of just an obligation.

Several effects can be observed with respect to environmental norms-as-constraints on ambitions of urban development. First, they can block development (often after a legal ruling), as illustrated by the first plans for housing in the Markermeer-IJmeer. One explanation for this effect is that the emphasis on informality during communicative planning processes, in combination with a particular set of stakeholders, can result in a situation where legal conditions are ignored in the early stages of the process. In the later stages, when the room for developing alternative courses of action has vanished, opponents resort to the courts to protect their interests (see Glasbergen, 2005). If they are successful, the development must be abandoned or started anew.

Another effect is that environmental norms that were meant to function as minimum norms can become maximum norms. The development in Buiksloterham is a case in point: the noise pollution threshold provided a bottom-line for maximising the number of homes; the actual nuisance suffered by future residents was not duly considered. This can be seen as an unintended consequence; the law was never meant to suggest that everything is fine with regard to desirable environmental quality as long as the minimum standards were observed. In this particular case, the triple role played by the municipality seemed to be a driving force behind the transformation of minimums into maximums. As a public authority, it should enforce noise regulations. As a critical planning actor it adopted ambitious goals on housing development. As a landowner, it will benefit from the revenues generated by this housing development.

Another effect of norms-as-constraints results from a principle that is often applied in environmental law, the so-called stand-still principle, which entails that interventions may not lead to a worsening of environmental conditions (Macrory, 2004). As a result, in areas where environmental quality is poor and environmental norms are viewed as constraints, no incentive exists to improve quality. In the case of Utrecht, in order to avoid a reduction in the water storage capacity of the area, the plan should not lead to a reduction in surface water and impervious cover. In the existing situation the water storage capacity was rather poor, and it took an energetic private initiative to restore old waterways to make the area more climate proof. The latter relates to a similar phenomenon with regard to the application of generic norms in a specific case with its own time-space dynamics. In the Utrecht case, we highlighted the situation where a developer wanted to build an underground parking garage next to a proposed new waterway. Only when the procedure of the so-called 'water test'[5] was followed, which requires developers to consult the water authority, was the developer motivated to adapt the design. This water test is in fact an example of an environmental standard that actively, and in an early stage, brings together the actors in a planning project and the agency that is supposed to uphold environmental norms. In so doing, it creates a setting in which environmental norms can be interactively integrated into projects. Therefore procedural norms – which are distinct from the debate on open versus detailed norms – could be seen as a way to overcome tensions between institutionalism and pragmatism.

In addition to examples of norms as restrictions, the case studies also provide examples of how norms enable innovative approaches to environmental problems and sustainable development. In Markermeer-IJmeer, an antagonistic process which led to legal battles between the local authority and environmental groups was transformed into a collaborative process containing a very innovative approach that combined development with environmental quality improvement. Two key factors played a role in turning the process towards larger ambitions. First, the existing norms gave environmental interest groups a foothold because they could frustrate development by going to court. In this way, the norms contributed to the formation of an 'ad hoc coalition of opposites'. The municipality of Amsterdam took an important environmental interest group on board when making the IJburg plans and convinced them to constructively participate by promising to promote a more ambitious environmental agenda. Second, the innovative approach put in practice after consultation with the European Commission convinced the stakeholders that this approach would probably be held up in court. This was particularly important to resolve two issues. The scientific evidence required by environmental regulations to ensure that the environmental effects will not be negative in the long term is difficult to deliver in such a complex area with so much development going on. The system of monitoring – environmental bookkeeping – bridged the gap between the demand for future legal certainty and the uncertainty of the situation. In addition, the innovative approach required a longer timeframe and geographical scope for compensation of environmental impacts than European guidelines seemed to grant. These doubts disappeared after the consultation with the European Commission. In Utrecht, the idea of a 'bio-washing machine' was an innovation triggered by environmental norms but at the same time also required a renegotiation. After intense debate, the national government allowed actors in the Utrecht case to deviate from existing norms and apply norms in a law under development.

If we consider that situations in which norms contribute to innovation and ambitious environmental goals are more successful than situations in which these norms function only as constraints, then the cases also indicate an important success factor. Our cases clearly show that where the relationship between institutions and communicative planning projects is mediated by interaction between actors that are responsible for upholding norms and stakeholders within the project, this increases the chance of constructively integrating norms into pragmatic problem solving. This process has been aptly described as 'negotiated compliance' (Jones, 2013). This concept also posits that environmental norms are a necessary precondition for safeguarding environmental objectives. Our cases of course provide clear examples of behaviour-influencing rules and, in particular, examples of how the definitions of roles contribute to creating coalitions of opposites. However, the existence of norms is not a sufficient condition for the successful use of these norms in practice. In other words, the goals of environmental norms are better served when, in addition to the existence of a norm, a dialogue can take place between the standard-setting or enforcing authority – often the European Commission or the national government – and the regional or local authorities promoting an urban development project. Such dialogue is needed to overcome the tensions between the properties of institutions and the characteristics of communicative planning processes. However, one should be wary of unintended consequences when planning a new project and adapt the norms to a particular timeframe and geographical scope to bridge the gap between scientific evidence and the uncertainty of complex communicative planning projects.

Conclusions

The main objective of this chapter was to show the added value of institutional reflection with regard to the practice of communicative planning projects and, in so doing, engage a theoretical debate with empirical evidence. This must be seen as a first empirical exploration into the frictions between communicative planning practices and institutional demands and how these can be overcome. Tentatively, the following conclusions can be drawn. Environmental norms are powerful institutions: they clearly ensure that environmental interests are taken seriously in planning processes, either as behavioural norms or by providing actors with a role in the process. Both stand at the basis of constructing coalitions of opposites, where they emerge. It is doubtful that pure bottom-up communicative processes would take environmental concerns as seriously if no environmental norms existed. This might sound a truism, but it is important to note for at least two reasons: It provides a counterweight against the discourse that norms unnecessarily frustrate societal progress. Furthermore, it also shows that communicative planning processes do not take place in a complete institutional void and that norms can still perform their legitimating function.

Our analysis also indicates that under certain conditions a better fit can be achieved between the objectives behind environmental norms and the ambitions of urban development projects. Fitting norms to the specific time-space characteristics of the project provides a powerful example. The possibility of a dialogue between the standard-setting or enforcing authority and the project is important in this respect. In addition, one could argue that environmental norms that encourage such a dialogue might provide a way to overcome tensions between norms as institutions on the one hand and pragmatic problem solving in communicative planning projects on the other.

Acknowledgements

The authors have greatly benefitted from comments made by Willem Salet, David Evers and Sebastian Dembski.

Notes

1 The 'Context project' was funded by the Netherlands Organisation for Scientific Research (NWO) and carried out by an international research consortium led by Willem Salet and Jochem de Vries. The study examined the Randstad, Paris and Manchester regions. This chapter draws from the Dutch case.
2 This sub-section is based on: Waterhout, B., Zonneveld, W., Louw, E., (2013) and (2014).
3 This sub-section is based on Dembski (2013).
4 This section is based on Buijze (2013).
5 The water test has a legal basis in a Dutch national government decree and is a protocol that has to be followed when a development might have an impact on the water system. It is a procedural norm that indicates who should be consulted and how decisions affecting the water system should be accounted for. It doesn't contain substantive norms. In terms of our paper, actors are forces in an act of 'self-confrontation' with regard to the water-related consequences of their plans.

References

Buijze, A. (2013). *Case Study Utrecht Station Area, the Netherlands: How PPPs Restructured a Station, a Shopping Mall and the Law* (CONTEXT Report 4). Amsterdam: AISSR Programme Group Urban Planning. Retrieved from: http://urd.verdus.nl/upload/documents/URD-CONTEXT-Report-4_Utrecht-Station-Area.pdf.

Campbell, H., Tait, M., & Watkins, C. (2014). Is there space for *better* planning in a neoliberal world? Implications for planning practice and theory. *Journal of Planning Education and Research*, 34(1), 45–59.

De Bruijn, H., & Ten Heuvelhof, E. (2004). Process arrangements for variety, retention and selection. *Knowledge, Technology & Policy*, 16(4), 91–108.

De Jong, P. O., & Zijlstra, S. E. (2009). *Wikken, wegen en (toch) wetgeven* [About Weighing(up) the Pros and Cons and (still) Making Law]. Series 'Onderzoek en beleid' No. 290. Meppel: Boom Juridische uitgevers.

Dembski, S. (2013). *Case Study Amsterdam Buiksloterham, The Netherlands: The Challenge of Planning Organic Transformation* (CONTEXT Report 2). Amsterdam: AISSR programme group Urban Planning. Retrieved from: http://urd.verdus.nl/upload/documents/URD-CONTEXT-Report-2_Amsterdam-Buiksloterham.pdf.

Dembski, S., Louw, E., & Waterhout, B. (2014). Multi-level Governance and the Contextualisation of Legal and Policy Norms: Amsterdam IJburg and Haarlemmermeer Westflank, the Netherlands. In *Planning, Law and Property Rights Conference: Book of Abstracts* (p. 25). Haifa, Israel: Technion, Israel Institute of Technology.

Dembski, S., & Salet, W. (2010). The transformative potential of institutions: How symbolic markers can institute new social meaning in changing cities. *Environment and Planning A*, 42, 611–625.

De Zeeuw, F., Puylaert, H., & Werksma, H. (2009). *Doorbreek de impasse tussen milieu en gebiedsontwikkeling* [Breakthrough the Stalemate between Environment and Area Development]. Delft: Delft University of Technology. Retrieved from: www.h2ruimte.nl/user_files/file/projecten_gebiedsontwikkeling/280551_rapport_impasse.pdf.

Evers, D. (2015). Formal institutional change and informal institutional persistence: The case of Dutch provinces implementing the Spatial Planning Act. *Environment and Planning C: Government and Policy*, 33, 428–444.

Flyvbjerg, B. (2005). Social science that matters. *Foresight Europe* (October, 38–42). Retrieved from: http://flyvbjerg.plan.aau.dk/Publications2006/ForesightNo2PRINT.pdf.

Forester, J. (1989). *Planning in the Face of Power*. Berkeley, CA: University of California Press.

Friend, J., & Hickling, A. (2005). *Planning under Pressure: The Strategic Choice Approach*. Oxon/New York: Routledge.

Giddens, A. (1984). *The Constitution of Society*. Berkeley, CA: University of California Press.

Glasbergen, P. (2005). Decentralized reflexive environmental regulation: Opportunities and risks based on an evaluation of Dutch experiments. *Environmental Sciences*, 2, 427–442.

Hajer, M. A. (2009). *Authoritative Governance: Policy Making in the Age of Mediatization*. Oxford: Oxford University Press.

Hajer, M. A., & Wagenaar, H. (Eds.). (2003). *Deliberative Policy Analysis: Understanding Governance in the Network Society*. Cambridge: Cambridge University Press.

Hall, P. A., & Taylor, R. C. R. (1996). Political science and the three new institutionalisms. *Political Studies*, 44(4), 936–957.

Healey, P. (1993). Planning through Debate: The Communicative Turn in Planning Theory. In F. Fischer & J. Forester (Eds.), *The Argumentative Turn in Policy Analysis and Planning* (pp. 233–253). Durham, NC: Duke University Press.

Healey, P. (1997). *Collaborative Planning: Shaping Places in Fragmented Societies*. London: Macmillan.

Innes, J., & Booher, D. (1999). Consensus building and complex adaptive systems. *Journal of the American Planning Association*, 65(4), 412–423.

Jones, P. (2013). Governing protected areas to fulfil biodiversity conservation obligations: From Habermasian ideals to a more instrumental reality. *Environment, Development and Sustainability*, 15(1), 39–50.

Kinder, K. (2011). Planning by intermediaries: Making cities make nature in Amsterdam. *Environment and Planning A*, 43(10), 2435–2451.

Klijn, E. H., & Koppenjan, J. (2000). Public management and policy networks: Foundations of a network approach to governance. *Public Management*, 2(2), 135–158.

Lijphart, A. (1975). *The Politics of Accommodation: Pluralism and Democracy in the Netherlands*. Berkeley, CA: University of California Press.

Macrory, R. (Ed.). (2004). *Principles of European Environmental Law*. The Avosetta Series (4). Proceedings of the Avosetta Group of European Environmental Lawyers. Groningen: Europa Law Publishing.

March, J. C., & Olsen, J. P. (2013). The Logic of Appropriateness. In R. E. Goodin (Ed.), *The Oxford Handbook of Political Science*. Oxford: Oxford Handbooks Online.

Needham, B. (2014). *Dutch Land-Use Planning: Planning and Managing Land Use in the Netherlands, the Principles and the Practice*. Oxon: Routledge.

OECD. (2007). *Cutting Red Tape: Administrative Simplification in the Netherlands*. Paris: Organisation for Economic Cooperation and Development.

Rhodes, R. A. W. (1996). The new governance: Governing without government. *Political Studies*, 64(3), 652–667.

Sabatier, P. (1988). An advocacy coalition framework of policy change and the role of policy-oriented learning therein. *Policy Sciences*, 21, 129–168.

Scharpf, F. (1997). *Games Real Actors Play: Actor Centred Institutionalism in Policy Research*. Boulder, CO: Westview Press.

Schön, D. A., & Rein, M. (1995). *Frame Reflection: Towards the Resolution of Intractable Policy Controversies*. New York: Basic Books.

Teisman, G. R. (2000). Models for research into decision-making processes: On phases, streams and decision-making rounds. *Public Administration*, 78(4), 937–956.

Van Dijk, T., & Beunen, R. (2009). Laws, people and land use: A sociological perspective on the relation between laws and land use. *European Planning Studies*, 17(12), 1797–1815.

Van Rijswick, M., & Salet, W. (2012). Enabling the contextualization of legal rules in responsive strategies to climate change. *Ecology and Society*, 17(2), 18.

Van Tatenhove, J., Arts, B., & Leroy, P. (2000). *Political Modernisation and the Environment: The Renewal of Environmental Policy Arrangements*. Dordrecht: Springer.

Waterhout, B., Zonneveld, W., & Louw, E. (2013). *Case Study Markermeer-IJmeer, The Netherlands: Emerging Contextualisation and Governance Complexity* (Context Report 5). Amsterdam: AISSR Programme Group Urban Planning. Retrieved from: http://urd.verdus.nl/upload/documents/URD-CONTEXT-Report-5_Markermeer-IJmeer.pdf.

Waterhout, B., Zonneveld, W., & Louw, E. (2014). *The Innovative Potential of Central Regulation: The Case of Urban Development in the Markermeer-IJmeer Natura 2000 Area*. Paper Presented at the EURA Conference City Futures III: Cities as Strategic Places and Players in a Globalized World (18–20 June 2014). Paris: Special Session 'Contextualization of Legal Norms'.

Reflection

25
WEAVING THE THREADS OF INSTITUTIONS AND PLANNING IN ACTION

Mickey Lauria

In Chapter 1 in this volume, Willem Salet argues that a relational perspective of social interaction is the cornerstone of planning practice and research and that institutional thought and pragmatic philosophy emphasize this relational approach in a complementary fashion. For Salet, institutions (patterned sets of social norms) condition processes and initiatives of social action that are the situated practices and consequences of planning that pragmatic philosophers argue are all we can know and thus all we can evaluate. Pragmatic scholars focus on the resolving specific problems in their rich empirical contexts while institutional researchers strive to recognize the constraints and structuring processes of the specific patterned sets of social norms within a particular context and provide critical feedback for that planning practice. While Salet sees the two approaches as complementary and necessary, he recognizes that the assumptions/premises of each tend to delegitimize the other, thus an integration is problematic because of their deep ontological and epistemological rift. In addition, institutional frameworks are diverse and emphasize different theories of causality (sociological/cultural through historical path dependency to political economy) that would likely require different co-evolutionary paths. Given this simultaneous potential synergy and incongruence, the aim of the volume is to explicitly define productive avenues for conceptualizing "the dialectic between institutional and pragmatic approaches." Regardless, Salet has brought together an impressive array of scholars from around the world that have been developing the literature concerning both institutional and pragmatic approaches to planning in order to initiate a process of probing the potential of such integrated approaches.

While there are many threads to weave (or as some might do, pull) running through the chapters of this volume, I will discuss four that seemed strongly embedded in many of the research frameworks provided: Which institutional lenses offer the most promise in integrating pragmatic analysis? From where do institutional norms and pragmatic action emerge? Is there a dialogical relationship between institutions and action? What is the role of the researcher in institutions in action? Finally, I will bring it back full circle by responding to Salet's introductory chapter and his challenging and perhaps provoking questions.

Mickey Lauria

Which Institutional Lenses Offer the Most Promise in Integrating Pragmatic Analysis?

One evident thread identified by Salet, in Chapter 1 in this volume, is that the institutional lens one uses greatly influences how easily a pragmatic approach can be integrated or, for that matter, whether the scholar perceives the need for a pragmatic approach for their concrete analysis, at all. But which institutional lenses offer the most promise in integrating pragmatic analysis? Or is it necessary to graph pragmatic action within an institutional analysis in order to bring planning practice (or agency and its transformative potentiality) into view? Some authors herein argue that a neo-institutionalist framework allows concrete analysis with its action-centered analysis focused on institutional constraints, unintended consequences and potential innovations, and potential transformations. Healey argues (Chapter 2 in this volume) for a sociological institutional approach to analyzing institutional change in relation to planning, urban regeneration, and place governance. Gualini (Chapter 3 in this volume) introduces a political economy approach to institutions: regulation theory; although, he puts an emphasis on the "symbolic-cognitive and discursive dimension of social orders, and lends ontological and epistemological primacy to these dimensions over formal or structural institutional properties" in order to focus on actors and agency in planning. Interestingly, both Healey and Gualini argue that each of their approaches can bring the acting subjects into view suggesting that graphing a pragmatic analysis on to a sociological institutional approach may not be necessary to answer the pragmatic criticism that institutional concepts become reified when used to understand and prescribe social action.

Most authors in this volume assert a common, although slightly differentiated, conceptualization of institutions emerging from the sociological origins of Anthony Giddens (1984) and later March and Olsen (1989): a patterned set of social norms which impose conditions on social action. While accepting this conceptualization, Davoudi (Chapter 4 in this volume) brings our attention to the influence of ideas on the institutional norms that condition social action. After situating discursive/constructivist institutionalism in the context of the other forms of institutional theory, she calls for "a line of inquiry that focuses on influential ideas in planning, explores their substantive contents, excavates the interactive processes through which they have been conveyed, and identifies the rhetorical appeals employed to produce, communicate and legitimate them" as she believes that this "will undoubtedly advance our understanding of how planning reforms happen and what purpose they serve." De Frantz (Chapter 14 in this volume) uses a discursive institutional (a la Davoudi) approach to understand planning practice and the institutional framework in contingent, relational, and open-ended cases of Vienna and Berlin development projects. She compares these two cases demonstrating how public discourse mediates, reinforces, and reconstructs institutions and interpretively frames the agency of specific actors but not necessarily in a coherent and collaborative fashion. Sorensen (Chapter 5 in this volume) develops a conceptual framework using a historical institutionalist approach that focuses on the particular institutions that surround urban property and development. Here he focuses on the historical co-evolution of the relationships between urban space, the state, and urban infrastructure networks. He emphasizes that these relationships are path dependent (e.g., the evolution of T_2 urban space is enabled and constrained by the prior T_1 spatial patterns), but that the degree of dependence cannot be theoretically predicted and thus is a matter of empirical investigation. Sorensen's path-dependent analysis also suggests that situated pragmatic problem solving will be very different and more transformative at critical junctures (crises) than during times of incremental sedimentary change. Janssen-Jansen and Lloyd (Chapter 15 in this volume) define provenance as a historical institutional analysis of planning practice and planning theory. They argue that the failure to keep land use planning provenance in mind has led to a failure of planning practice to evolve in a fashion that allows it to operate in our radically changed ideological, economic, and socio-political environment. Their chapter implicitly argues for the need to add a historical institutional reflection on traditional pragmatic planning practice. They end with a clarion call to re-engage the promise of planning in the public interest. Boelens (Chapter 6 in this volume) argues, at least in relation to Dutch and Belgian water management laws, that the realization of these institutions is less hierarchical (in contrast to Moroni, Chapter 12, in this volume) and have become realized through the actors' interpretations and actions as flat, with each set of actors recreating differentiated institutional relations. It is through the plural interactions of these institutional actors that innovation through experimentation becomes more pronounced. Regardless of these differences, all of these authors conceive of the relationship between action and institutional norms as recursive, or as a dialectical relationship such that institutions are not conceived as static but rather as being either reinforced or recreated through the actions of those actors they simultaneously enable and constrain. They also indicate that detailed historical analysis is necessary to unpack the dynamics of the actors in action and the institutional innovation.

Metzger (Chapter 7 in this volume) adds the nuance of the Scandinavian institutional tradition and all but explicitly argues that this tradition integrates the new institutional approach with a pragmatic sensibility to both context and action, implicitly challenging the need for integration with a pragmatic approach. Within this tradition, he focuses on how the politics of hope can shape action in both oppressive and progressive directions and argues that planners in action need to think very carefully to critically evaluate whether the "organization of hope" in any particular case is being used to stabilize oppression or instigate positive progressive change. Metzger forewarns that we need to be sure to assess the negative politics of hope that shape action. Following Metzger's implicit challenge, and facing the environmental threats and opportunities, Bertolini (Chapter 10 in this volume) identifies potential dynamics to accelerate evolution. He argues that cities appear to be the most sensible places in the environmental transition. In evaluating new concepts of biological evolution, he finds that the main challenge is to move from blind mutation to directed variation (in terms of timing, rate, location, and scope). In this way, he defines a space for experimentation. Like the pragmatists, he is searching this purposive direction in a process of joint enquiry: co-evolution. Institutions and artefacts shape the conditions that facilitate or hamper the performance of social practices. Mäntysalo, Schmidt-Thomé, and Syrman (Chapter 11 in this volume) explicitly challenge the project of this book (the hybridization of new institutionalist theory and pragmatic action) and propose an alternative approach based on Engeström's (1987) Cultural-Historical Activity Theory (CHAT). CHAT incorporates Bateson's (1987) learning theory: single loop, double loop, and double-bind situations, where the institutions' cultural pathologies lead to a consistent strategy but constant failure (a la Metzger's description of planning's pathological pursuit of the "organization of hope"). At the same time, Mäntysalo et al.'s discussion leads one to wonder if the application of CHAT is different from an iterative use of historical and discursive institutionalism with a pragmatic focus on the actual dynamics of planning in action. Ironically, their case analysis of the Otaniemi process and the City of Espoo, Finland, may be the clearest integration of pragmatic and institutional approaches in this volume.

Another way to think about this thread is to focus on the direction from which an author starts their analysis, institutionalism or pragmatism. By far most authors in this volume start their analysis from an institutional perspective and then conduct or describe a concrete analysis, sometimes with an explicit pragmatic methodology, to illustrate the institutional insights that they wish pragmatic practice would use to move planning forward in an innovative fashion. Only Hoch, Forester, Boudreau, and Pasternak and D'Ottaviano, in this volume, start from a pragmatic approach and discuss the institutional insights that subsequently emerge. Forester (Chapter 9 in this volume) provides a pragmatic and institutional interpretation of a micro political negotiation.

In doing so, he discusses how the institutional roles of the negotiators constrained and enabled their negotiation while focusing on how each actor pragmatically pushed the boundaries of those roles. His exegesis is satisfying for pragmatic-oriented scholars, but I fear it would likely fall short of satisfying institutional scholars because he does not evaluate the interactions and effects of the system of institutions in which these actors are embedded, which would be of primary interest to them (see Sorensen, Chapter 5, this volume). Boudreau (Chapter 16 in this volume) uses a French pragmatist, situated, and ethnographic approach to view institutions in action in Saint-Michel, a disadvantaged neighborhood in Montreal. She demonstrates that institutional norms are revealed in moments of transgression that may or may not precipitate institutional innovation. In order to see these moments, she argues that we need to pay attention to actors' visceral reactions, what they do, as well as what they say. She contends that institutional analysis tends to ignore this aesthetic level of bodily/visceral responses to everyday situations. She values institutional analysis of social regulation, but prefers to empirically use ethnographic methods to unveil transgressive behaviors that challenge, and thus reveal and potentially transform, institutional norms and their underlying power relations. Pasternak and D'Ottaviano (Chapter 21 in this volume) describe the history of Brazil's, and more specifically São Paulo's, attempts to accommodate, and ultimately include, informal settlements (favelas) into the city. After much resistance to their first strategy of removal, Brazilian cities, and São Paulo in particular, realized it would be better to absorb and accommodate the rapidly growing and densifying favelas. This local level pragmatic problem solving led to a learning process that began with realizing that removal, demolition, and resettlement in public housing on the outskirts of the metropolitan area was no longer acceptable. Urban inclusion and accommodation meant that lower levels of administration (the cities) needed to provide basic infrastructure, services (first drinking water, then electricity, and garbage pickup, but sewage is still an unresolved problem), professional guidance, and formal education. The increased service costs created demands for support from the national level to provide resources so that local municipalities (large cities) could improve housing conditions and area services in the favelas. These pragmatic solutions and demands led to national laws to incorporate the new norms, a "right to the city," and a "right to housing." Hoch (Chapter 8 in this volume) argues that pragmatism does not offer a philosophical foundation for planning practice. Instead, pragmatism argues against abstracting from planning practice, preferring to focus on "searching for the practical significance that different planning theories offer for making and using spatial plans." In many ways, Hoch's pragmatic take on institutions is very much in line with the new institutionalism embodied in this book.

> They invent new institutions in the face of disruptive situations where routines continue to fail after repair [unlike Metzger's rehearsal of Brunsson's (2006) Mechanisms of Hope]. Pragmatists alter both means and ends, but rarely start from scratch [Sorensen's path dependency]. Testing options in the context of specific historical and spatial contexts enables pragmatists to assess effects, revise expectations and improve learning. New habits improve responses to earlier trouble and offer an understanding of ourselves and the world. In this way institutions adapt and so may progress.
>
> (Hoch, Chapter 8, in this volume)

From Where Do Institutional Norms and Pragmatic Action Emerge?

Another interesting theme asks at what institutional level do the patterned social norms that constrain and enable planning emanate from, and at what level concrete action analysis must be focused on in order to unveil the constraints and opportunities for innovative and creative planning practice. Moroni's hierarchical/layered approach to institutions, planning, and practice helps here. He distinguishes between five "decisional" levels: the pre-constitutional, the constitutional, the legislative, the administrative, and the civil society (see Moroni, Chapter 12, in this volume). Assuming we are working within a constitutional democracy, our institutions operate at the pre-constitutional and constitutional levels. Theories of justice concern this basic structure of society, not the legislative, let alone the administrative level. The legislative level is constrained by the principles embedded at the constitutional level, and the principles for institutions need to be distinguished from principles for individuals. Individuals' political obligations and duties, while specified at the legislative and administrative levels, assume *just* institutions. Thus, the ethics of planning concerns the principles of institutions, usually at the constitutional level, while the ethics of planners relates to the legislative and administrative levels of non-elected public servants. These individual obligations and duties are necessary for the development of trust. It is here that the pragmatic scholar (see Forester, Chapter 9, in this volume) focuses their description and interpretation. It is important to note that this hierarchical/layered approach is recursive in that individuals through their interpretation of their obligations and duties can at critical junctures restructure institutions at the constitutional level via legislation. Thus, it should not be surprising that all of the empirical and illustrative cases discussed in this volume have focused on the legislative, the administrative (internalized) social norms, and the civil society levels due either to these normal social practices and/or to the legal rules emanating from Moroni's legislative levels. It is at these (legislative and administrative) levels that Buijze, Salet, and van Rijswick focus their chapter. They develop (in Chapter 13, in this volume) an argument for a recursive relationship between central regulation and self-organized regulation (at the level of civil society); in other words, the relationship between government and adaptive governance. The key is how well legal norms are contextualized (defined as legal norms built on substantive principles that can be used as a guide for the interpretation and application of the law in concrete situations). According to Buijze, Salet, and van Rijswick, principle-based contextualization is easier under a common law legal system because it is based on the accumulation of historical interpretations of concrete cases. While principles play a modest role in Dutch legal adjudication, they do play a stronger role in policy documents and plans at the administrative level through rules based on sustainable development principles. Thus, it is at the administrative level that institutional and pragmatic analysis can be fused in the Netherlands. In Chapter 24, de Vries and Zonneveld are concerned with a balance between pragmatic problem solving and reflection on societal norms. They focus on the specific institutions of laws and legal rules aimed at securing sustainable urban development, particularly environmental rules. Their general question is: "how do environmental rules, as institutional conditions, structure the pragmatic search for solutions in communicative planning processes?" They follow a sociological institutional approach and view institutions as both constraining and enabling the conditions for planning practice. In three Dutch cases, they find that environmental norms clearly set boundaries, and therefore constrain actors, in their search for solutions, but at the same time these constraints can encourage innovative and creative solutions. But while the norms were meant to function as minimum norms, their concrete implementation transforms them into maximum norms, to the chagrin of their creators. The environmental stand-still principle, particularly in the case of places with poor environmental conditions, means that there is no incentive to improve that environmental quality. They also found that norms enabled the production of innovative approaches. Most importantly, they found that cases in which the norms created the need for interaction between the actors responsible for upholding the norms and the stakeholders increased the chance of constructively integrating those norms into pragmatic problem solving.

Is There a Dialogical Relationship between Institutions and Action?

Balducci (Chapter 20 in this volume) details the turbulent history of metropolitan governance and planning in Italy with a closer look at the Milan metropolitan area. He focuses on the concrete manifestation of institutionalization through the bottom-up pragmatic but informal (voluntary) cooperative responses to failures and top-down political legislative attempts to deal with the problems of metropolitan growth/sprawl. Interestingly, the pragmatic problem solving that led to informal agreements proved fragile because of higher-level political transitions (thus, they did not lead to concrete institutional change and did not receive higher-level support); while top-down political legislative attempts were considered too rigid and were foiled by lower-level provincial and/or municipal resistance (they were not instituted through local level accepted norms), and were not flexible enough to fit Italy's varying metropolitan contexts. Balducci argues that informal, voluntary bottom-up experiments need to be supported while top-down approaches need to be more flexible, and thus permissive of these bottom-up experiments. Kloosterman (Chapter 19 in this volume) uses an institutional economics approach to examine the agglomeration economies involved in the "urban commons" of cultural/knowledge based economic development. Following Ostrom's (2011) and Scott's (2000, 2004) theory on the commons and cultural economy respectively, he discusses the concentration of internationally oriented architectural design firms in Amsterdam and Rotterdam. These firms rely on a large labor pool of highly educated and creative individuals, and in the case of the architectural design industry, an apprentice system for face-to-face intensive on the job training. He argues that this particular "urban commons" (for generating localization economies) requires an institutional "hybrid of state-led regulation [certification], informal arrangements among firms," "informal institutions [and spaces] enabling the exchange of knowledge," and a "dedicated local institutional infrastructure" (for funding education, grants, and competitions). Kaika's contribution (Chapter 17 in this volume) describes and interprets the transformation of the City of London (Square Mile), in terms of the new starchitect office buildings dominating the skyline, as part of the Corporation's strategy to regain its authority of the Square Mile and its eminence in world finance. Unfortunately, these new signifiers of supremacy ultimately ring hollow because these new urban elites are of the "Transnational Capitalist Class" and are footloose in terms of their commitment to London. Finally, Majoor (Chapter 22 in this volume) uses three megaprojects (Amsterdam Zuidas, Copenhagen Ørestad, and Melbourne Docklands) to evaluate whether or not normative ambiguities, and the organizational capacity to combine institutional reflection and pragmatic action, allows them to innovative during changing times over the long duration of the project. He posits, along with Salet, that megaprojects with a normatively ambiguous mission (containing potentially conflicting goals) and the presence of an organizational capacity to combine institutional reflection with pragmatic action, will manage to innovate effectively. He finds that all three cases had aspects of an ambiguous mission and that their economic and political turbulence created opportunities to experiment. He also finds that the outcomes of the three cases corresponded with their organizational capacity to combine reflection and pragmatic action, but were hindered by their market-oriented development model (they had to optimize land values) and their efforts to depoliticize the projects, which turned out the be a hindrance to innovation during turbulent times.

What Is the Role of the Researcher in Institutions in Action?

De Frantz understands "the political aspects of doing knowledge" as the reflective agency of the researcher (who no longer is viewed as solely observing and describing) in interpreting "between different institutional dimensions," and "between different expert knowledge, policy fields and perspectives of social actors" for practicing planners. Her argument culminates in the normative assertion that planning researchers also have an ethical obligation to "mobilize civic society and empower the less advantaged to participate." Janssen-Jansen and Lloyd (Chapter 15 in this volume) argue for planning educators to pay attention to the history of planning norms and to re-engage the promise of planning in the (I assume, unitary) public interest in a fashion unconstrained by the prevailing neoliberal social norms. Finally, Eraydin and Tuna (Chapter 23 in this volume) propose a redefinition of resilience that should help highlight the existing vulnerabilities of urban systems and increase democratic decision-making in our time of market-based urban policies. They argue for a resilience-thinking that values the ability of the urban system to protect its "vital, critical elements, resources and values for sustained development," as well as its capacity for innovation (adaptive, self-organizing, and learning capacity). Thus, they argue that planning needs to set priorities and main principles, to shift its aim from controlling change to increasing its capacity to adapt, innovate, and become proactive. At the same time, like De Frantz, they imply that planning researchers need to encourage resistance movements concerning urban planning issues, in situations where authoritative politics and institutions overrule local democracy.

Salet's Challenging Questions

Do Institutional Conceptions Necessarily Lead to Reification?

As mentioned above, both Healey (sociological institutionalism) and Gualini (institutional political economy) argue that their approach can bring the acting subjects into view, suggesting that graphing a pragmatic analysis on to a sociological institutional approach may not be necessary to answer the pragmatic criticism that institutional concepts become reified when used to understand and prescribe social action. Both the De Frantz (discussed above) and the Savini and Dembski chapters provide excellent analyzes of how institutional meaning is validated in real, ongoing practices and, in fact, in very different contexts. Savini and Dembski (Chapter 18 in this volume) argue that political coalitions (a la regime theory) mobilize symbolic markers in spatial interventions as a process of institutional change. They illustrate their argument with the recent transformation/gentrification of Amsterdam-North. They utilize a sociological/historical institutional approach (following Giddens, 1984 and Healey, Chapter 2, in this volume), combined with a regime coalition analysis, focusing on coalition transition and the symbols used to pave the way for the spatial and socio-economic transformation of the Northern IJ Bank area of the Amsterdam-North district. They use this case to argue that the role of political coalitions in reconstructing meaning through the political use of symbols is an important explanatory variable of institutional change: in fact, they view political coalition building as part of the process of institutionalization. They demonstrate how planning and planners were important agents (in consort with political elites) in the socio-economic and spatial changes in Amsterdam-North. In this project, planners developed plans, held community meetings, and ultimately linked past understandings of place with a transformed future. Thus, their analysis is a strong concrete analysis utilizing historical political coalition transition and symbolic politics to explain the transformation of the economically moribund Amsterdam-North into a new hipster hot spot of the City of Amsterdam.

Is Pragmatic Action too Instrumental?

The pragmatically propelled chapters mentioned above (Forester, Boudreau, Pasternak & D'Ottaviano, and Hoch) clearly demonstrate critical reflection and institutional deliberation in the pragmatic settings they describe and, in so doing, demonstrate that pragmatic action need not be too instrumental. Boudreau and Pasternak and D'Ottaviano both address dilemmas concerning planning practice and laws in transition. Boudreau does so in the form of institutional reflections on the embodiment of social norms and transgressions, while Pasternak and D'Ottaviano do so in a historical layering of planning practices that overwhelm (via a social imbrication of experiments) and subsequently transform institutional norms and their concrete manifestation into constitutional amendments, laws, and administrative rules and practices.

Do Social and Political Institutional Parameters Constrain the Actual Changes to a City?

A number of the chapters demonstrate that our neoliberal social formation market-based policies both constrain and propel innovative practice. Janssen-Jansen and Lloyd (Chapter 15 in this volume) describe how the normalization of neoliberal norms have led to new norms of contractual relations in planning under private property regimes. De Frantz (Chapter 14 in this volume) discusses the complex/messy results of institutional changes in Berlin and Vienna that demonstrate both the rigid or calcified nature of past institutional forms and the innovative practices that can dissolve and reconstruct new social formations. Kaika (Chapter 17 in this volume) follows suit with a different, but similarly revealing, analysis of the strategies of the Corporation of London used in transforming the Square Mile in London. Balducci (Chapter 20 in this volume) details how politically instigated top-down institutional changes were resisted at local and provincial levels in Italy and, how at the local and provincial level, political and planning practitioners can develop informal collaborative processes and planning practices that innovatively have the potential (however fragile) to transform larger institutional structures. Kloosterman (Chapter 19 in this volume) uses the growth and dominance of the international architectural industry in the Netherlands to create localized agglomeration economies that have rejuvenated Amsterdam and Rotterdam. He argues that this involved a "hybrid of state-led regulation, informal arrangements among firms and a widely spread understanding of the long-term benefits of the apprenticeship system" to create what he calls (after Ostrom, 2011) an "urban commons." Majoor (Chapter 22 in this volume) demonstrates how resistant institutional forms allow the opportunities for potentially transforming experiments in his analysis of three megaprojects. Finally, deVries and Zonneveld (Chapter 24 in this volume) also demonstrate how these institutions, particularly environmental norms emanating from higher legislative levels (the EU and Dutch environment regulations), both constrain and enable innovative and transformative practices.

How Can Political Articulation in Changing Cities and Peripheries Escape the Margins of Hegemony and the Power of Settled Political Institutions?

Because many of the cases in this volume involve different historical and political contexts, the authors suggest different conditions that are viewed as favorable for innovation (critical junctures unveiled via historical institutionalism's path dependencies and the turbulent times of political and technical innovation over long-duration megaprojects) and different innovative strategies (symbolic presage in Amsterdam-North and London, informal/voluntary practices in unstable political institutions, and innovative resistance that has the potential to precipitate previously unrealized options) used to transform the political institutions. Many of the same chapters (as mentioned just above) also indicate the contextual conditions necessary to escape from the hegemony of existing political institutional norms.

How Can Sustainability and Resilience Be Institutionalized in Processes of Sustainable Transition?

Again, the chapters by Buijze, Salet, and van Rijswick (Chapter 13 in this volume) and de Vries and Zonneveld (Chapter 24 in this volume) stand out as focusing on sustainability. Interestingly, both sets of authors focus on the legislative level and how top-down environmental regulations (laws and legal rules of administration) can create the context for innovative collaborative practices being institutionalized as new norms of planning practice. On the other hand, Pasternak and D'Ottaviano (Chapter 21 in this volume) provide an example of how bottom-up local social and political practices become sustainably institutionalized at the legislative and administrative level via national level principals and laws.

Postscript

Astute readers will have noticed that I do not try to answer all the questions posed by the threads that run through the papers in this volume. Any such attempt would suffer from two failings: it would be open to various criticisms from other interpretations, and would, at best, merely reiterate the valuable contributions of the authors in this volume while minimizing the value of the individual chapters. Thus, I must leave it to you, the reader, to work through and develop your own assessment as to the appropriate answers to Salet's challenges and to the most fruitful approach to take. Regardless of this assessment, I am sure you will have found your efforts worthwhile for each essay in this volume independently defines very important and insightful research projects and sometimes entire bodies of work.

References

Bateson, G. (1987). *Steps to an Ecology of Mind*. Northvale, NJ: Jason Aronson.
Brunsson, N. (2006). *Mechanisms of Hope: Maintaining the Dream of the Rational Organization*. Malmö: Liber.
Engeström, Y. (1987). *Learning by Expanding*. Helsinki: Orienta-konsultit.
Giddens, A. (1984). *The Constitution of Society: Outline of a Theory of Structuration*. Oxford: Polity Press.
March, J. G., & Olsen, P. (1989). *Rediscovering Institutions: The Organizational Basis of Politics*. New York: Free Press.
Ostrom, E. (2011). *Governing the Commons: The Evolution of Institutions for Collective Action*. Cambridge, MA: Cambridge University Press.
Scott, A. J. (2000). *The Cultural Economy of Cities: Essays on the Geography of Image-Producing Industries*. Thousand Oaks, CA: Sage Publications.
Scott, A. J. (2004). Cultural-products industries and urban economic development prospects for growth and market contestation in global context. *Urban Affairs Review*, 39(4), 461–490.

INDEX

Note: Page numbers in *italics* refer to figures and in **bold** refer to tables.

Aalto, A. 168
Aalto University 169, 171, 174
Aarhus Convention 205
academic-ideational realm 224
Actor-Network Theory 29, 94
actor-relational approach 92–105; flat ontology 93–97; water management project 97–105
adaptive capacity 349–352, 354, 356–7, 360
administrative level decision-making 185, 187
aesthetic relations: institutional crisis 266; interpretive approach 219; police 248–250; pragmatic approach 245–255; racialization 250–252
agency: agent-based modelling 63; conditional 44; governance and 50; and ideational approaches 65; interpretive approach 31, 224; new forms and public policy 47; non-human 129; power of 28, 36; and resistance 32; in strategic-relational approach 53; transformative agency 276, 352
agglomeration economies 292–295, 297
Albrechts, L. 352
allocative relations 29, 31–33
altruism 191
ambiguity 166, 172, 174–176, 230, 332; institutional 175–176, 331–343
Amsterdam: Buiksloterham development 371–372, 373, 374; Dutch architectural design 293, 295; Northern Bank transformation 275, 280–284, 374; Zuidas project 333–335, 340–343
Anderson, B. 108
antagonism 49, 50, 54, 55, 353
anti-interventionism 236
Appadurai, A. 111
apprenticeships 293, 294

Argyris, C. 12n, 165, 167, 166–168
artisanal courts 100, 101
'aspect change' 30, 37
austerity 230, 296
authoritarianism 354, 355, 358, 359
authoritative power 31–32
authoritative relations 29, 31–33

Banfield, E. 27
Bang, H. 175, 177
Bank Junction, London 260
Bank of England 261
Barnett, R. 192n2
Bateson, G. 166, 167, 168, 180
Baudrillard, J. 269
Beauregard, B. 127–131, 133–136, 137n1
behaviorlist approach 62, 64
Béland, D. 62, 64, 65, 66, 69
Berger, P. L. 45, 278
Berlin, *Schlossplatz* regeneration 213, 214, 215–216, 220, 221–224
Berlusconi, S. 306
Bernstein, R. J. 8, 9
Beunen, R. 94
Bevir, M. 48, 50, 51
blackness 247–250, 253–254
Bleischwitz, R. 233
Bloch, E. 117, 118, 119; *The Principle of Hope* 112
Blomley, N. K. 75
Blyth, M. 68
Bolan, R. 28
Bollier, D. 297
Borch, C. 94
Borgers, H. C. 200
Bourdieu, P. 4, 69, 197, 295

Bourse Consult 261, 262, 271
Boyfield, K. 236
Braithwaite, V. 117, 118, 119
Brazil: *Banco Nacional de Habitação* (National Housing Bank) 316; census 317; end of military dictatorship 323; federal Constitution 324; Growth Acceleration Program (PAC) 326–327; Habitar Brasil program 325; *legal* and *illegal cities* 315; *Minha Casa, Minha Vida* (My House, My Life) program 327; Ministry of Cities 328; PAC–UAP program 327, 328; Statute of the City 316, 325, 328; urban administration 328; urbanization 316, 319, 328; *see also* Rio de Janeiro; São Paulo
Brazilian Institute of Geography and Statistics *see* IBGE
Brennan, G. 187
Brenner, N. 15, 47, 50
Breviglieri, M. 252
British Empire 259, 260
Broadbent, T. A. 233
Brugse Vrije 100, 101, *102*
Brunsson, Nils 109, 116, 117; *Mechanisms of Hope* 112–113
Bryson, J. 28, 29
Buchanan, J. 187, 191
Burdett, R. 257
Business Improvement Districts 236
buzzwords 349

calculus approach 63
Callon, M. 52
Campbell, H. 189
Campbell, H. et al. (2014) 39n33
Canada 83; *see also* Montreal
Canary Wharf, London 265, 270
capital investment, regulation of 74, 75, 76, 80
capitalism 15, 114–117, 274, 291, 297
Capoccia, G. 78
Cassidy, M. 264, 265
Castells, M. 175; *Networks of Outrage and Hope* 111
Castoriadis, C. 266, 278
CHAT (Cultural-Historical Activity Theory) 168, 180
Chicago 126, 131–136
Christensen, T. 109
Christopherson, S. et al. (2010) 350
City Action for Community Development 263
The City Bridge Trust 263
city corporations 75
City of London 259–271; end of isolationism 262–265
The City of London Volunteering Employee Programme 263
civil society: collaboration and 217, 221; and governance 37; level of decision-making 185, 187; political movements 176; resilience 92

civil sphere 33–34
classical-modernist political institutions 175–176
coalitions of opposites 367, 375
Coelho, C. B. 328, 329
Cohen-Portheim, P. 259
collaborative approaches 29, 212–214, 217, 219–225, 229, 231, 369, 374
collective action: calculus approach 63; 'democracy in action' 223–225; institutional conditions and 367; institutional theory and 12, 14, 17; new institutionalism and 214, 217, 218; path dependence and 77; and politics 276; pragmatic approach 368; public discourse 221; sociological institutionalism and 24; urban commons 290–292
colonization 75, 103
common law approach 200–201, 206
communication technologies 360
communicative planning theory 11, 188–189, 349, 350, 368–370, 373, 375
communicative rationality 213, 222, 348–349
community organizations 139–149; democratic inter-subjectivity and 139–140, 144–149
compensation theory 204
complexity science 30
conditional norms 11, 14
condominium property 81, 84, 88
conformism 157, 162, 269
Congleton, R. 191
Connolly, W. E. 29, 252
consequentialism 6, 9
constitutional level of decision-making 185, 186, 189
constitutional design 186
constitutional framework 186–187
constructivist approach 25, 28, 34, 51, 61, 68, 72
contingency 78, 129, 141
Cooke, E. 117, 118
Copenhagen, Ørestad project 335–338, 340, **341**, 342–343
Corporation of London 257–271; defence strategy 262–265; electoral reform Act 2002 264–265; establishment of 259; and foreign companies 260–262; literature on 257–258; new spatial strategy 265–266; strategic response to crisis 266–267, 279
counter-hegemonic movements 50, 54, 55
Cox, R. H. 62, 65, 66, 69
Courville, S. 118
Crace, J. 228
Critchley, S. 71
critical-interpretive policy analysis 12, 47, 48, 50–51, 54
critical normative feedback 7, 11
Crosby, B. 29
Cruise, S. 271
cultural approach 45, 63–64
cultural heritage 171, 215, 217

391

Index

Cultural-Historical Activity Theory *see* CHAT
cultural industries 217, 292–294
Cymbalista, R. 326

Dante 118, 119
Davoudi, S. 67
Day, R. 233
De Carlo, G. 305
De Frantz, M. 214, 220
de-personalization 10
de Soto, H. 323
decisional levels 185–187
"dedicated local institutional infrastructure" 295–296
Deleuze, G. 26
deliberation 11, 12, 16, 19, 219, 221, 296, 343
democratic systems: collaboration and 212–214, 220–226; constitutional framework 186, 276; decision-making mechanisms 347, 360; governmentality and 54–55; justice and 189; legitimacy and 175; local 101, 133–134; neo-liberalism and 50; path dependence 237; pragmatism and 127–130, 139–149; urban 290; and vulnerabilities 348
Dendeen, P. 111
deutero-learning 167
deviance approach 253
Dewey, J. xxi, 5, 8, 8–10, 109, 110–111, 118, 128, 167, 220
difference principle 188, 189
dis-articulation 49, 54–55
discourse coalition 219
discourse institutionalization 219
discretionary powers 202–204; *classic discretion* 202; *jurisdictional discretion* 202–203
discursive institutionalism 61–72, 218–220; calculus approach 63; cultural approach 63–64; governance and 51; ideas 65–71; ideational approaches 64–65; New Institutionalism 62–63
Donaghy, K. 126
double-bind situations 167–168, 177, 180
double-loop learning 166–168, 172–174
Dühr, S. 279
Duineveld, M. 94
Dutch design ('Superdutch') 293
Dutch Society for Nature Conservation *see* Natuurmonumenten
Dworkin, R. 199, 200
Dworkinian court 201
dyke-earls (*dyke-sheriffs*) 100

Eagleton, T. 120n6
ECB (European Central Bank) 262
Economic Research Institute Foundation (FIPE) 324
Eigenlogik 218
Elcock, H. 192n7

Elder-Vass, D. xx
Eley, P. 266
Elkin, S. L. 15
emergent policing order 50
empirical learning 167
endogenist approach 45, 47
Engeström, Y. 168
English Heritage 257, 260
Environmental Impact Assessments 204, 367
environmental regulation 364–375; institutional perspective 365–368; norms 373–375
epistemic consequentialism 16
Erundina, L. 324
Esmark, A. 175, 177
ethics and justice 185–192
ethos 8, 62, 71
EU (European Union): Habitats Directive 202; integration 217; law 201, 203; local circumstances 204; regulation 176, 364; Water Framework Directive 201, 204, 370
Eurodelta, water management project 97–105
European Central Bank *see* ECB
European Court of Justice 201
evidence-based policy 70
evolutionary resilience 331, 332
evolutionary approach 151–163; animal behavioral processes 153–154; determination and transmission of characteristics 153–154, 158; developmental 153; evolutionary dynamics 155–158; new social practices 160–161; selection environment 155, 158; symbols 154; variation 154–155, 158
experimental learning 167
experimentation 17, 25, 30, 152, 158, 163, 312, 370

facework 178–179
fact-object construction 51–52
Faludi, A. 276
favelas 315–329; characteristics of 317; *Projeto Cingapura* (PROVER/ Singapore Project) 324, 325; Provisional Housing Villages (VHPs) 321–323; and urbanization 322–327
The Financial Times 260, 268
Fine, B. 235
Finlayson, A. 71
FIPE *see* Economic Research Institute Foundation
Fishman, S. M. 118
Flyvbjerg, B. 168, 349, 369
Folke, C. et al. (2010) 353
foreground discursive ability 69
Forester, J. 11, 28, 108, 118, 128, 174, 192n4, 368
Foster, N. 269
Foucault, M. 25, 29, 31, 32, 39n24, 62, 68, 70, 95, 104, 356, 359
'frame reflection' 30
framing 53, 54, 95, 97, 114, 275

France 204
French pragmatism 252
Friedmann, J. 27; *Planning in the Public Domain* 125
Friend, J. 368
Fuller, C. 39n30
Fuller, L. L. 13, 14

Gaia hypothesis 155
Game Theory 63
Gaus, G. F. 186, 192n2
GDR (German Democratic Repubic) 215–216
Geertz, C. 278
Gehl, J. 340
Gehry, F. 279
Gezi Park, Istanbul 359
Ghent 161–162
Gibb, P. 233–234
Giddens, A. 26, 28, 31–32, 39n23, 39n24, 44, 45, 65, 128, 156, 213, 277, 285, 367
Global Financial Crisis 334, 336, 342, 343
globalization 104, 175, 214–215, 217–218, 221, 225, 260
Goldstein, J. 68
Gordon, I. et al. (2005) 257
Gottdiener, M. 278, 279
governance: as emergent institutional orders 45–48; *governance institutions* 76; hybridization of 176, 178–179; initiatives in governance change **33**; innovation 33–34, 49–51; interactive 369; as moments of institutionalization 51; multiplicity of work groups 32; neo-institutionalism 46; and power relations 30; practices as inscription devices 51–53; pragmatic approach 37–38; 'problem-solving bias' 47; reform attempts 29–30; sociological institutionalist approach 24–38; as strategic-relational claims 53–54; transformation initiatives *34*; unregulated 204; urban spaces 18; *see also* learning and governance culture
governmentality 29, 32, 48, 51, 54, 67, 70
Gramscian approach 47, 50
Green Heart, Netherlands 279
Greenberg, D. 236
'ground zero' NYC 220
Guattari, F. 26
Guggenheim Museum, Bilbao 268, 269, 279
Guimarães, B. M. 317
Gunder, M. 349
Gunderson, L. 354
Gupta, J. et al. (2010) 354

Habermas, J. 4, 8, 69, 128, 188–189, 192n4, 349
habitus 63, 69, 294, 295
Hacker, J. S. 64
Hadidian, M. 257
Hajer, M. 29, 175–176, 219, 220, 222, 368
Hall, P. 62–64, 67, 70, 71, 234

Hall, S. 360
Halsall, F. 94
Hansard Debates 259, 262, 263, 264
Hardin, R. 190
Hardy, S. A. 228
Harper, T. L. 191
Harvey, D. 15, 117; 'Planning–The Ideology of Planning' 114–116; *Spaces of Hope* 111
Hay, C. 53, 65, 68, 72
Hayek, F. A. 13–14
HAD (Housing Development Agency) 356, 358, 360n3
Healey, P. 3, 13, 74, 88, 119, 125, 212, 213, 220, 221–223, 225, 360n1
The Heart of the City (charity) 263
Heath, D. 264
Heath government, UK 260
Heclo, H. 61
hegemony 32, 49, 53, 71, 117, 231, 353; hegemonic practices 48–51, 54–5
heme law 100, 101, 103
Hendriks, F. 140, 142, 146
Hickling, A. 368
Hidalgo, C. 292
Hillier, J. 25, 125, 349
Hirschman, A. 296
historic materialism 15
historical institutionalism 38n3, 62, 64, 65, 74–75, 79–87; core concepts 77–79
Höffe, O. 192n2
homo economicus 13
hope 108–119; as concept 110–113; function in planning work 113–117
Hopkins, L. 126–127, 129–131, 133, 134, 135
Housing Development Agency *see* HDA
Howe, E. 190
human rights 199, 203
Huxley, M. 348

IBGE (Brazilian Institute of Geography and Statistics), "The Favelas of the Federal District" 317
iconic architecture 257–271, 279
ideal speech situation 188–189
ideational approaches 64–71, 79
The Independent 261
The Independent on Sunday 264
individualism 27, 197
infrastructure institutions 76, 82–83, 85, 86, 87
Innes, J. 28, 29
input legitimacy 175
institutional actor theory 12, 14
institutional ambiguity 175–176, 331–343
institutional change: discursive institutionalist approach 69, 218; endogenist approach 47, 78; inter-subjectivity and 149; political pluralism and 220, 221, 224–226; provenance and 239;

sociological institutionalist approach 25, 30–36; symbolism and 274–279, 282–285
institutional inertia 275–277
institutional innovation 13, 92–105; flat ontology 93–97
institutional mediation 9
institutional paradigms: critical normative feedback 11; critical political analysis 9; cultural and sociological institutions 12; institutional actor theory 9; path dependence analysis 9; philosophy of state and law 12; urban regime analysis 9
institutional thought 9–17; function of 7; logic of 11–15; social norms 7, 10, 11, 16–17; symbols 277
institutional trust 177–178
institutionalism 9, 10, 13, 16, 43, 178
institutionalization 44
institutions: definition of 77; 'institutions in action' 11, 43–55, 223–226; innovation 14, 17, 30; normative feedback 6, 7; and urban space 79–87
Inter-American Development Bank 323
inter-subjectivity 4, 5, 6, 10, 45, 139–140, 144–149
interpersonal trust 177–178
interpretive approach 130, 213, 219–220
Istanbul 347–360; ecological vulnerabilities 357–359; population increase 356–357
Italy 303–313; Christian Democratic Party 305; *Città Metropolitane* 304; *Comprensori* 304, 307; Constitution 303; Law 56, 310; Law 142, 307–308; projects 306; reform law 1990 304; Territorial Coordination Plan 308

Jablonka, E. 153
Jacobs, J. M. 257, 260
James, W. 5, 9, 9–10
Japan 81, 84
Jencks, C. 269; *Iconic Buildings* 270
Jessop, B. 29, 38n5, 39n32, 46–47, 53–54, 95, 104, 105
Jones, P. 369
JP Morgan (investment bank) 270
Judt, T. 235

Kaika, M. 278, 279, 350
Kelemen, R. D. 78
Keynes, J. M. 61, 70
Kiernan, M. J. 192n3
Kingdon, J. W. 67, 70
Klein, N. 235
Kleiner, M. M. 296
Kloosterman, R. C. 294, 295
Klosterman, R. E. 125
Knaap, G. 127
knowledge, exchange of 294–295
'knowledge society' 223
Kolb, D. A. 180n2
Kynaston, D. 257, 259, 260, 261

Lab van Troje (civic organization) 161
labor pool, shared 293–294
Laclau, E. 49, 71
Lægreid, P. 109
Lamb, M. J. 153
land: characteristics of 80; critiques of planning 231–234; as market commodity 237; and neoliberalism 234–235; path dependence 237–238; provenance 230–231; purpose of planning 228–230; social reconstruction of planning 236–237
Lascoumes, P. 51
Latour, B. 52, 128, 136n1, 177–178; *Pandora's Hope* 111
Laurian, L. 177–178
Law, J. 113–114
Le Galès, P. 51
learning and governance culture 165–180; communication 174–176; interpersonal and institutional trust 177–178; learning systems 166–168; Learning III 167, 168, 176–177, 179
legal norms 196–208; area-based approach 206–207; contextualization as principle-based adjudication 199–201; contextualization of legal rules 205–207; open norms 202–204; procedural justice as alternative 204–205; social self-regulation 197–199
legislative level decision-making 185, 187
legitimation: and collaboration 213–214; democratic 128, 133, 174–177; discursive institutionalism 218–220; institutional 6–10, 16–18, 36, 47–48, 95, 166, 221, 225, 277, 366–370; justice system 204, 204, 206; legal norms 196, 198, 223; neoliberalism 50; new institutionalism 218
Lemke, T. 356
Leontyev, A N 168
Libeskind, D. 336
LIFFE (London International Financial Futures and Options Exchange) 261
Lindblom, C. 136
Lipsky, M. 249
Living Street Initiative, Ghent 161–162
Lloyd's building, London 268
local government 75–76, 84
Local Procurement Project 263
lock-in 14, 93, 152, 237, 239
logic of appropriateness 366, 367–368
logos 71
London 257–71; City Plan 265; contemporary iconic buildings 258, 268; contemporary urban signifiers 269–270; end of isolationism 262–265; neo-classical architecture 268; quality of life indicators 268; as residence 267–270; traditional design 260; Unitary Development Plan 265; urban elites 258, 268
London Clearing House 261

London Development Agency 263
London Government Act 1963 259
London International Financial Futures and Options Exchange *see* LIFFE
'loops of learning' 12
Lowndes, V. 78
LSE (London Stock Exchange) 261, 262
Luckmann, T. 45, 278
Luhmann, N. 94, 95, 105
Lukes, S. 39n29, 68

'maladaptive cycles' 352, 353
Mandelbaum, S. 130
March, J. 45, 62, 64, 276, 366, 367
Maricato, E. 316
market commodification 233
Marquand, D. 235
Marris, P. 130
Marshall, A. 293
Martin, I. 265
Maru, Y. 354
Marx, K. 39n15
Marxism 28, 66; Marxist materialism 68, 217
Massey, D. 28
material-symbolic realm 224
materialities and meaning 25, 31
Mattila, H. 189
Mayntz, R. 46, 47
Mazower, M. 296
McCarthy, L. 118
McCarthy, T. 189
McDonnell, J. 262–263, 264
McGuirk, P. 188–189
McManus, S. 117, 118
McNeill, D. 258
mega-infrastructure projects 354–355
Mehta, J. 66, 67, 70
Meirelles, R. 320, 321
Melbourne, Docklands project 338–343
meliorism 110, 111, 112
Merrick, J. 266
Metropolitan Water Reclamation District, Illinois *see* MWRD
Meyerson, M. 27
Miers, T. 236
Milan 303–313; institutional reform 309–311; municipal activism and strategic plan for 'City of Cities' 308–309; *Piano Intercomunale Milanese* (PIM) ('general urban plan') 304–308; territorial districts and metropolitan authorities 306–308
Milano 3 new town 306
Milonakis, D. 235
Ministério das Cidades 326
Mintzberg, H. 331
Mirowski, P. 235, 236
modernist approach 3, 4, 5, 7, 258, 260, 365
Monbiot, G. 289

Montreal, Saint-Michel area 245–254
Moroni, S. 187
Mouffe, C. 29, 49, 50
Moulaert, F. et al. (2016) 29
Municipal Corporations Act 1835, UK 264
MWRD (Metropolitan Water Reclamation District) Illinois, 131–136
Myers, D. 152

nation-state 75, 176, 218, 367
Natura 2000 policy 367, 370, 371
natural monopoly services 82
naturalist tradition 68
Natuurmonumenten (Dutch Society for Nature Conservation) 371
NatWest Tower, London 268
neoclassical economics 229, 234
neo-Darwinism 153–155
neo-institutionalism *see* new institutionalism
neo-liberalism 30, 39n27, 50, 113–117, 217, 230, 234–238, 348–349
neo-pragmatism 111
Netherlands: cases 370–373; certification of architects 295, 296; communicative planning theory 369; contextualization 208; flexibility 205; legislation 200, 201, 206, 366; Natura 2000 367, 370, 371; procedural review of Council of State 207; Soil Protection Act 203, 206; urban development 365; Water Framework Directive 201, 204, 370
network governance 30, 175, 221–222, 224
new institutionalism 44–48, 62–64, 217–218; aim of 25; fact-object construction 52; on ideas 66; and organizational theory 109; and path dependence 69
new public management 27, 30
Newcastle, UK 33–34
NIMBY ('not in my backyard') 81
no-regret conditions 351, 359
nomocracy 14
Nonaka, I. 165
non-conformism 157, 158, 162
North, D. 63, 79, 233
North America, suburban development 87
Norval, A. 30, 37, 139

Offe, K. 177
Ogilvie, W. 228, 233
Olsen, J. 45, 62, 64, 276, 366, 367
Olsson, P. et al. (2004) 354
Ørestad Development Corporation 336
Organization Development 165, 179
Ostrom, E. 14, 292, 354
Ostrom, E. et al. (1993) 197
Ostrom, E. et al. (1999) 198
Otaniemi, Espoo, Finland 166, 168–174, 176–177, 178–180

output legitimacy 166, 175
Oxford Economics Ltd. 270

Paine, T., 'Declaration of the Rights of Man' 4
Panagia, D. 247
Pandora 109
Partnerships Programme 263
Pasternak Taschner, S. 322
Paternoster Square, London 257
path dependence 237–238; and innovation 104–105; legislation 175; new institutionalism and 69; and provenance 230; and urban space 76–78, 80–88, 217
path dependence analysis 9, 12–14
pathos 71
Peck, J. 15
Pedersen, J. 189
Peirce, C. S. 117
Pennington, M. 236
Peters, B. G. 64
Peters, G. 26
Pierre, J. et al. (2008) 39n32
Pierson, P. 77
Pihlström, S. 117
Piper, N. 118
place qualities 26, 29, 31, 85, 213
pluralism 49, 226
Polanyi, K. 89
polderen 97–105
policing and *policing effects* 48–49
Politecnico di Milano (Polytechnic University of Milan) 308
political activism 176
'political ecology' 15
political entrepreneurialism 349, 354, 357
political plurality 213
'polluter-pays' principle 201
population, global 74
positive feedback effects 14, 77, 78, 82, 86, 87, 237
post-empiricist approach 219
post-structuralist approach 25, 29, 37
postcolonialism 214
postivism 9, 25, 27, 187, 229, 231
post-political theories 5, 44, 48, 54, 275, 285
post-positivism 29, 32, 239
Poulantzas, N. 95
Powell, K. 257
power: asymmetrical 64; authoritative 31–32; Foucault on 359; governance and 30; as interaction 94, 95; power coalitions 279; power relations 253; radical power theory 68; structural 31
Power, D. 257
practical judgement, criteria for 128
'practice turn' 25, 28
pragmatist approach 4–6, 9–11, 368–370; American 27; and challenges of public action 10; co-evolution with institutional approaches *13*; democratic and communicative dimension 7, 8; *direct reciprocity* 11; examples 30; experimentation 8–9, 25, 27; French 252; focus on lived experience 29; and governance 37–38; and hope 108, 109–119; and institutional actions 245–255, 303–313; institutional trust 178; interactions 146–149; moral dimension 8, 9; planning theory 125–136; philosophical 4, 7–10, *13*, 15, 18, 55; solution-oriented 15–16
pre-constitutional decision-making 185–186
Pred, A. 87
Prior, A. 233
property rights 84, 93, 231–235, 290, 291
property taxation 84, 86–87
property values 86
proto-learning 167
provenance 230–231, 235, 236–239
public action 6, 8, 10
public health 304, 320, 322, 328–329
public norms 5–7, 10, 11, 13
public of the indirectly affected 5
Purcell, M. 139, 349
purposive relationships 5, 6, 7

Quitzau, M.-B. 82

racial profiling 250
racialization 250–252
racism 251, 260
radical pluralism 29
radical power theory 68
Rancière, J. 29, 32, 39n33, 49, 50
rational actor theories 14
rational choice institutionalism 62, 63, 65, 66, 68
rationalist tradition 27, 28
rationalization of action 197–198
Rawls, J. 186, 188–190, 191, 192n2, 353
re-articulation 46, 49, 50–52, 52, 54–55
reciprocity 11, 45, 94, 177, 191, 229
Reckwitz, A. 156
reflective institutional thought 11–12
reflective practice 220, 224
regime theory 277
regionalism 214, 285
regulation theory 12, *13*, 15, 28, 46
Rein, M. 30
relational approach 3–5, 25, 28, 30, 34–35, 95
Renzi, M. 310
resilience 92, 230, 290–291, 347–354, 358–360
resilience thinking 347, 350
revisionist approaches 61
rhetorical thinking 71
Rhodes, R. 50
Riggs v. Palmer 1889 200
Rio de Janeiro 315, 317–318, 327, 328
Rittel, H. W. 108

Roberts, R. 257
Rorty, R. 109, 111, 117, 118, 119
Rose, N. 31
Rotterdam 293, 295
Roy, A. 118, 119n2
Royal Exchange London 260
rule of law 4, 13, 143, 290, 296
Ryan, B. 130
Rydin, Y. 220

São Paulo 316–329; *Concessão de Direito Real de Uso da Terra* (Concession of Property Rights of Use of Land) 323; consumer goods 320; infrastructure 319–320, 323, 324, 326, 328–329; interventions in favelas 321–327; *Lei das Operações Interligadas* (Interconnected Operation Law) 323; public health 320; social classes 320–321; Special Zones of Social Interest (SZSI) 325; Strategic Master Plan 325
Sager, T. 174
Salet, W. 25, 166, 366
Salet, W. et al. (2013) 332
Samora, P. 326, 328
Sandel, M. 235
Scandinavian institutionalism 109–110
Schagen, A. 140–146
Schama, S. 97, 103
Scharpf, P. 367
Schmidt, V. 39n17, 65, 67, 69
Schön, D. 11, 30, 39n33, 68, 116, 165, 166–168, 220
Schwenkel, C. 255n2
Scientific Management (organization) 165
Scott, A. 289, 295, 297
Searle, J. xx, 69
self-organisation 284, 285, *351*, 352–354
self-regulation 8, 9, 12, 14, 197–198, 208, *351*, 360
self-reinforcing mechanisms 14, 65, 77, 84, 85, 86, 155, 158, 159
Senge, P. 165
Sennett, R. 268
Shaw, K. 339, 340
Shutt, H. 235
signification 71, 278
Simon, H., *Administrative Behavior* 27
Simone, A. 247, 248–249
single-loop learning 166–168
Skinner, Q. 70
Sklair, L. 268
skyscrapers 260
Snyder, M. 270
social and cultural institutions 12–13
social capital 85
social constructivist approach 45, 74, 214, 225
social mobilization 13
social norms 4, 6, 11, 12, 16–17, 219, 274, 279–280
social patterning 28, 45

socio-political realm 224
sociograms 52
sociological institutionalist approach 24–38, 62, 64, 65, 74
Sorensen, A. 14, 26, 39n35, 38n3, 233
'spaces of resistance' 50
spatial displacement 15
spatially differentiated patterns 85, 87
Square Mile *see* City of London
St Paul's Cathedral, London 260, 265, 266
stand-still principle 374
stare decisis 200
state-centred model 46
state and government, Dewey on 9–10
Stein, S. M. 191
Stone, C. N. 29
Storper, M. et al. (2015) 291, 293
strategic-relational approach 38n5, 53–54
Streeck, W. 77
structuration theory 28, 31–32, 65, 92, 156
subject–subject relationships 4
subjectivism 3, 197, 223
'sunk costs' 80
Suplicy, M. 325, 326
sustainable development 115, 197–198, 200, 201, 351–352, 359–360
Swan, P. 260, 261
Swiss Re Tower, London 268, 269
symbolic-cognitive processes 44–45, 51, 52, 53, 55
symbolic communication 274–278

taken-for-grantedness 45
Takeuchi, H. 165
Talamona, M. 313n5
Tannenwald, N. 66
Taussig, M. 254
Taylor, R. 62–64
technograms 52
teleocracy 14
think tanks 236–237
Thatcher government, UK 260
Thelen, K. 77
Theodore, N. 50
Thompson, E. P. 4
The Times 261
TOKI *see* Turkish Mass Housing Authority
Tops, P. 140, 142, 146
Torfing, J. 39n35
trade 101, 103, 259
Trans-European Motorway 357
transformative agency 276, 352
transformative learning 36
transgression 253–254
translation 52–53, 223
Trom, D. 252
trust 177–178

Turkey: central government interventions 355–356; devolution of governance 355; Housing Development Agency (HDA) 356; Justice and Development Party (AKP) 358; planning 356–359; *see also* Istanbul
Turkish Mass Housing Authority (TOKI) 355, 360n3

UK (United Kingdom) 234, 235, 237, 260; *see also* London
uncertainty 174–175
unequal distributional effects 78
urban commons 290–292, 295
urban development: culture-led 213–216; land and property institutions 76, 80; mobility 159–162; political dimension 43–55; property institutions 80–82; property parcels 76–77; property values 80–81; restructuring 274; transportation systems 82–83; vulnerabilities 348
urban infrastructure institutions 80, 82–87
urban regime analysis 12, 14–15
urbanization 17–18, 74, 322–327
US (United States) 83; *see also* Chicago
utopias 25, 30, 37, 105, 119
Utrecht 206, 372–374

Van Assche, K. 94
Van Assche, K. et al. (2015) 79
Van de Wijdeven, T. 140
Van Rijswick, M. 366

veil of ignorance (*veil of uncertainty*) 185–186
VicUrban 339, 340
Vienna, 'Museumsquartier' regeneration 213, 214–216, 220, 221, 222, 223
virtues 191
visualisation 279
vulnerabilities 3, 95, 144, 145, 347–352, 356–359
Vriesendorp, M. 270
Vygotsky, L. 168

Warner, J. 268
Warren, M. E. 178
Water Framework Directive (EU) 201, 204, 370
water management 97–104
Waters, J. A. 331
Watson, V. 353
Webber, M. M. 3, 108
Weber, M. 217
Wendt, A. 65
Wilkinson, C. 350
Williams, K. 113–114
Williamson, O. 92
Wirth, L. 290
World Bank 323
Wynne Rees, P. 265, 268, 268–269

Yanow, D. 279

Žižek, S. 116